The Origins of the Peloponnesian War

Farewell of a warrior, by the Kleophon Painter, on an Attic
stamnos of *c.* 430 B.C. (Photo: Museum Antiker Kleinkunst,
Munich)

The
Origins
of the
Peloponnesian
War

G. E. M. de Ste. Croix

CORNELL UNIVERSITY PRESS

ITHACA, NEW YORK

First published 1972 in the United Kingdom by
Gerald Duckworth & Co. Ltd. and in the
United States by Cornell University Press.

This edition is not for sale in the United Kingdom and
British Commonwealth.

International Standard Book Number 0-8014-0719-2
Library of Congress Catalog Card Number 72-627

Library of Congress Cataloging in Publication Data
(For library cataloging purposes only)

de Ste. Croix, G   E   M
  The Origins of the Peloponnesian War.

  Includes bibliographical references.
    1. Greece—History—Peloponnesian War, 431–404
B.C.   2. Greece—Historiography.   I. Title.
DF229.2.D46 1972   938'.05   72–627
ISBN 0-8014-0719-2

PRINTED IN GREAT BRITAIN

To the memory of
A. H. M. Jones
this book is dedicated
with gratitude and affection

Contents

Preface

This book is intended not only for the professional historian and Classical scholar but also for the intelligent undergraduate and the 'general reader'. In the hope that it will be read by some who know little or no Greek, I have as far as possible excluded quotations in Greek from the main text, reserving them for footnotes and appendices. Where the use of Greek words or phrases has been necessary, I have nearly always (at the risk of irritating the specialist) given the Greek in transliterated form, and as far as possible I have tried to relegate complicated discussions of the ancient evidence to the appendices. I realise that I have not been able at certain points to avoid detailed arguments, sometimes of a technical character; and of course the whole book is far from being a narrative— it is above all (see the Introduction) a discussion of the main problems. But most of my main text should be intelligible even to those whose knowledge of the fifth century B.C. comes mainly from a reading of Thucydides in translation, or from a standard textbook such as 'Bury-Meiggs' (J. B. Bury's *History of Greece*, in its third edition, revised in 1951 by Russell Meiggs—a further revision by the same hand is expected shortly). Anyone who is not able to read Greek should have no difficulty in following most of my main text, at least if he has by him a translation of Thucydides, and if possible of Aristophanes' *Acharnians* and Plutarch's fifth-century *Lives*. (These last are all included in a very useful volume by Ian Scott-Kilvert, published in the Penguin Classics series under the title, *The Rise and Fall of Athens. Nine Greek Lives by Plutarch*, 1960.)

I wish to record my gratitude to numerous colleagues, friends and pupils, at Oxford and elsewhere, who have read some of my many successive drafts or discussed problems with me. Although many have welcomed the radical reinterpretation I am offering here, others have been un-sympathetic in varying degrees, and if I mention a few to whom I feel particularly indebted, they must not necessarily be assumed to approve of my conclusions, in general or in detail.

I can never sufficiently express my deep sense of gratitude to the late A. H. M. Jones, who was primarily responsible for teaching me Ancient History when I was an undergraduate at University College London, in 1946–9 (in my late thirties), and to whom this book is dedicated. Professor P. A. Brunt has perhaps done more than anyone else since I came to Oxford in 1953 to clarify my understanding of Thucydides; and his detailed and frank criticisms of some of my early drafts have helped me greatly. Professor A. Andrewes has also read and criticised some drafts and has been characteristically kind and patient in expressing his disagreements on certain issues on which (as the following pages will show) he and I take very different views. Correspondence with Professor K. J. Dover has been very profitable to me. Among other friends with whom I have been able to discuss some of the topics dealt with here are Mr. John Boardman, Professor D. Geoffrey Evans, Mr. W. G. Forrest, the late Mr. A. R. W. Harrison (Warden of Merton College), Mr. Russell Meiggs, Professor Martin Ostwald, Mr. Donald Russell, Mr. E. C. Yorke, and Miss Susan Sherwin-White. And I must not omit to mention my many able Greats pupils, in New College and Magdalen College, who have read some of my drafts and discussed them with me: the list of those who have in one way or another contributed something to this book is much too long to give here, but I may single out Messrs. Alan Cameron, P. A. Cartledge, William Charlton, Peter Garnsey, C. H. Grayson, Edward Hussey, J. H. McDowell, M. B. Mosse, R. W. Nowell-Smith, R. C. T. Parker and M. B. Wallace of New College, and Malcolm R. Green, T. H. Irwin and R. J. Lane Fox of Magdalen College.

I count myself fortunate to be a Fellow of New College, which contains among its former undergraduates an unparalleled number of distinguished ancient historians and archaeologists, including A. Andrewes, N. H. Baynes, Sir Maurice Bowra, Peter Brown, V. R. Desborough, W. G. Forrest, C. F. C. Hawkes, A. H. M. Jones, F. A. Lepper, Sir John Myres, J. N. L. Myres, C. E. Stevens, H. T. Wade-Gery, W. P. Wallace and Sir Leonard Woolley; also G. L. Cheesman and L. W. Hunter, who were killed in the First World War. I was able to do much of the work for this book during two sabbatical years, 1962/3 and 1969/70, for which I have to thank the Warden and Fellows of the College.

I also owe a great debt of gratitude to my wife, who has been extraordinarily patient, understanding and helpful throughout the long period during which this book gradually took on its present form.

And to Mr. Colin Haycraft, who is responsible for the publication of this book, I wish to record my warmest thanks for his expert skill and efficiency and his sympathetic assistance at every stage.

I

Introduction

(i)
Introductory

The Peloponnesian war is a central topic in Greek history, and it is the
subject of by far the best historical work that has come down to us from
antiquity: that of Thucydides. A very great deal has of course been written
about the war and its antecedents in modern times, both in the standard
histories and in individual books and articles on various matters connected
with it, especially the work and outlook of its great historian, that enig-
matic figure about whom controversy continues to rage, with little more
prospect of general agreement today than a hundred years ago.

On the subject of the origins of the war, I believe that the modern
literature is disappointing in the extreme and that a thorough-going
revaluation is necessary. Indeed, some important pieces of evidence have
not merely been misused and made to lead to false conclusions: they have
commonly been misunderstood from the outset and misrepresented in
such a way that their real significance has been obscured. How often are
we not told, for instance, even by reputable scholars, that Thucydides,
in his famous statement about the origins of the war in I 23.6, is distinguishing between a 'superficial' or 'immediate' or 'proximate' cause
and a 'profound' or 'more remote' or 'underlying' cause; that in the same
passage, by using of the Athenians the word *anankasai* ('compel'), he is
placing upon Athens the responsibility for the Spartan declaration of war
in 432; that the Athenians, as shown by the Melian Dialogue, preached
the doctrine that 'Might is Right'; or that by the Megarian decree (for
the contents of which Thucydides is by far our most important witness)
'Megara' was excluded 'from all markets and harbours of Attica and the
Athenian empire', or 'from all trade with Athens and her empire'?
Yet in none of these cases is there any justification for so misrepresenting
what Thucydides actually says—not to mention the fact that such a
description of the Megarian decree also reveals a gross misunderstanding
of the mechanism of Greek trade.

And that is by no means the end of the indictment. Many scholars have
held views on the Megarian decree, and other subjects, which ought to
have led them to be sharply critical of Thucydides' reconstruction of the
origins of the war, as at best incomplete, and perhaps even distorted and
dishonest. But too many of them have pulled their punches. A few have
said outright that Thucydides just did not properly understand the forces

at work in the second half of the fifth century: the extreme example of this is a book with a title that arouses unhappy expectations, more than fulfilled by its text, Cornford's *Thucydides Mythistoricus*. Others, like Schwartz and Andrewes, have detected what they believe to be inconsistencies in Thucydides' narrative, due to a late and incomplete rewriting of an earlier version. Others again have seen reason to assume an unjustified playing down (whether unconscious or deliberate) of the Megarian decree by Thucydides, in order to exculpate his hero Pericles (who moved the decree and did most to prevent its repeal) from the charge of either purposely or recklessly bringing on the war. Now this opinion surely ought to lead to a general questioning of Thucydides' whole account of the origins of the war, which, if it contains at least one culpable distortion, can hardly be assumed to be accurate in all other respects. However, so strong is the general instinct in favour of accepting Thucydides that this necessary step has not been taken, even by those who, like Beloch, have held the view just mentioned in an extreme form.[1]

In my opinion, modern historians have not sufficiently faced the difficulties involved in what I may call the 'standard view' of the origins of the war—for most recent accounts have followed a very similar line, taking Athens to be the real aggressor (or 'morally the aggressor') and the Megarian decree as a deliberate provocation and one of the main exciting causes of the conflict, if not, indeed, the 'real cause' or at least the 'generally accepted cause' of the war. One leading German scholar, Joseph Vogt, has faced some of these difficulties more honestly than most historians and is willing to admit that the standard interpretation of the origins of the war (in particular of the Megarian decree), which he simply takes for granted, leads to a serious dilemma ('Aporie', BPT 261–2). How could Thucydides have given such wholehearted approval to the policy of Pericles? We ourselves may well hesitate, says Vogt in his last sentence, to allot the highest rank as a statesman to Pericles, who was neither able *nor willing* to avoid war. Another prominent German historian, Strasburger (TPSDA), has been so impressed by arguments such as Vogt's (the basic fallacy in which has escaped him) that he has retreated ultimately into the position adopted by Grundy sixty years ago (*THA* 1^2 207–10), that Thucydides had no personal sympathy with Athenian policy, even as embodied in Pericles. (This is not at all the view taken by most recent historians, many of whom would agree with Wade-Gery's remark, in *OCD*² 1069, that Thucydides 'had for Pericles a regard comparable to Plato's for Socrates and an equal regard for Pericles' Athens'. And Strasburger's conclusions are firmly rejected by de Romilly, 'L'optimisme de Thucydide et le jugement de l'historien sur Périclès', in *REG* 78 [1965] 557–75, at p. 574.)

[1] See Beloch, *APP* 19–28; *GG* II² i.292–8 (emphasising particularly the Megarian decree). Beloch had his own curious way of escaping from the dilemma I have described: he thought (see esp. *GG* II² i.298 n. 2) that Pericles deliberately provoked the war for selfish personal reasons, but that Thucydides saw nothing wrong in this at all (and so, presumably, did not try to conceal it)!

As I shall demonstrate, the standard view of the origins of the war is in reality based largely upon uncritical acceptance of the brilliant fantasy presented by Aristophanes in the *Acharnians*. The consequences of accepting this view can indeed be unfortunate. And if we do accept it, have we not cut the ground from beneath our own feet? If Thucydides is held to be seriously misleading (whether consciously or not) on one central issue, how can we continue to feel absolute confidence in the rest of his narrative? The great bulk of our information comes from him. On many vital questions, for example the reasons for the bitter Corinthian hostility towards Athens which reached a climax in the late 430s, we have virtually no other evidence: we are entirely dependent on Thucydides for the elementary facts. And if we have good cause to distrust Thucydides as a partial witness, what chance have we of making a satisfactory alternative reconstruction, our other possible sources of information being so scanty?

I believe that we can trust Thucydides to a very high degree for the events of his own day,[2] and that if we study his narrative carefully and attend to what he says rather than what modern scholars assume he said (often two very different things), we shall find his account consistent, penetrating and very satisfying. I have only one serious complaint to make about Thucydides' treatment of the origins of the Peloponnesian war: that *his* war began only in 431, and not (as it should have done) some thirty years earlier. As I shall explain in Chapter II, Part i below, he has fastened upon us for ever the conception of a 'Peloponnesian war' which lasted for twenty-seven years, from 431 to 404, and has told us almost nothing about how the war really began, in *c.* 460—for it was essentially the same war, merely interrupted for less than fifteen years by the Peace of 446/5 (for the terms of which, see Appendix I). Although Thucydides himself never used the expression 'the Peloponnesian war' (for which see Appendix II), he has made it impossible for anyone to employ the term for anything except the twenty-seven years war; and I am obliged, under protest, to submit to his authority. When I refer to the war of *c.* 460–446/5, therefore, I shall follow current usage and speak of 'the First Peloponnesian war', reserving the expression 'the Peloponnesian war' for the war, or rather series of wars, between 431 and 404, which Thucydides saw as a single whole.

Proceeding step by step on the basis of Thucydides' account, supplemented by a certain amount of other contemporary evidence, we shall soon find ourselves obliged to reject a whole series of suppositions which have generally prevailed in modern times. But if these suppositions are, as I believe, in conflict with reliable ancient evidence, the sooner they are discarded the better. I hope I have at least made a fresh start, clearing

---

[2] He is of course very much less reliable as a source for earlier history—even for the 470s, the years shortly before he was born. His sketch of the activities of Pausanias and Themistocles in that decade (I 128.3–139.6) has come under sharp and justifiable criticism: see most recently Cawkwell, FT; Rhodes, TPT.

away a great deal of dead wood. Others will build better than I have done in the clearing.

I realise that I have used the first person singular in many parts of this book far more than is usually acceptable; but I am anxious not to present statements which are often highly disputable as if they represented generally received opinion. My hope is to open a new debate.

In this book I shall not attempt to give a complete narrative of all the events leading up to the war (although I shall discuss some of them in detail), but concentrate on certain problems, upon the solution of which our opinions about the origins of the Peloponnesian war must mainly depend. If I have devoted a disproportionate amount of space to Sparta and her alliance, it is because so little has been written about Sparta and the Peloponnesian League that is worth reading, and I know of no modern work that is of much use in helping one to understand how policy was made at Sparta. In several ways, above all in relation to the Peloponnesian League, I have gone into greater detail than may appear necessary on some of the events of the Peloponnesian war itself and the years that followed, well into the fourth century. In my opinion this is necessary to enable us to see fifth-century Sparta in perspective.

There are plenty of books which provide a narrative of the events that led up to the war, with or without discussion of their significance. Scholars will not need bibliographical guidance here, but those who are not specialists in Greek history may wish to read a more complete and general account of fifth-century history.

Still supreme in many ways is the great *History of Greece* written over a century ago by George Grote, whose judgment on many historical and philosophical matters is superior to that of most subsequent writers. Grote's *History* should be read in the standard 'New edition' of 1888 (of its ten volumes, nos. IV-VII are relevant), rather than in the condensed version in one volume by J. M. Mitchell and M. O. B. Caspari (M. Cary), published in 1907, which is probably much more used nowadays than the original, by undergraduates in this country at any rate. The latter work not only omits and abbreviates; as it ends with chapter lxv (in vol. VI of the original), it does not contain the splendid chapter lxvii (in vol. VII), which is still the best treatment of 'the Sophists' and makes an essential contribution to the 'intellectual history' of the second half of the fifth century. Modern epigraphic, numismatic and archaeological discoveries have not made Grote's work nearly as 'out of date' as is generally supposed,[3] even if a glance at a modern collection of Greek inscrip-

---

[3] Grote's most recent—and best—biographer, M. L. Clarke, *George Grote. A Biography* (London, 1962) 128, could say that 'his *History* has been superseded in the sense that it is no longer used'! The best introduction to Grote as an historian is A. Momigliano's admirable Inaugural Lecture at University College London, entitled *George Grote and the Study of Greek History* (London, 1952), reprinted in his *Contributo alla storia degli studi classici* (Rome, 1955) 213–31, and again in his *Studies in Historiography* (London, 1966) 112–26.

tions of the period (e.g. M/L or Tod I²) will show that a great deal of epigraphic information is now available which was unknown in Grote's day.

The most recent work in English on the subject of this book is by Donald Kagan, *The Outbreak of the Peloponnesian War* (1969, pp. xvi + 420). Although it does not deal satisfactorily, to my mind, with many of the major problems, it devotes over 200 pages of text and appendices to the earlier history of the Athenian and Spartan alliances and the events down to 435, and then treats the developments of 435–1 in detail, taking account of course of the new epigraphic and other evidence not available to Grote.

For the serious historian, the three 'standard' general histories of the period are still Busolt's indispensable *Griechische Geschichte* (III i and ii, 1897 and 1904), with its very full references; Beloch's briefer and less reliable, but far more lively, *Griechische Geschichte* (II² i and ii, 1927 and 1931); and Eduard Meyer's *Geschichte des Altertums* (III³, IV i⁵ and ii⁴, edited posthumously in 1954–6).

(ii)
Thucydides

A very large part of the evidence for the Peloponnesian war and its origins is provided by Thucydides. A modern historian who makes considerable use, as we all must, of the History of Thucydides ought to begin by explaining to his readers (having first cleared his own mind on the subject, as scholars too often fail to do) in what light he sees the History. In particular he should discuss his attitude to the speeches, so that it will be clear what criteria he has employed when utilising the evidence they provide, and how these criteria differ from those he has applied when using the narrative passages. This I now propose to do, more briefly than I could have wished, concentrating upon a few essential aspects of Thucydides' outlook and technique which seem to me to have been insufficiently understood.

We must begin, of course, with what Thucydides himself says about his methods in I 22.1–4. We may accept what he says in §§2–3 (cf. v 26.5), on the narrative of events, as both true of his intention and justified in his performance: that he took the greatest possible care to get his facts right, checking one report against another and making allowances for the prejudice and the defective memory of his informants. It is very strange that some modern writers have believed Thucydides to have been primarily interested not in historical events but in 'laws' or 'principles' lying behind the events: for this view there is no valid basis at all. Collingwood in particular, in a brilliantly written but perverse attack on Thucydides (*IH* 28–31), compared him very unfavourably with Herodotus. 'Herodotus', he says, 'may be the father of history, but Thucydides is the father of psychological history. Now what is psychological history? It is not history at all, but natural science of a special kind. It does not narrate facts for the sake of narrating facts. *Its chief purpose is to affirm laws, psychological laws* [my italics]. . . What chiefly interests Herodotus is the events themselves; what chiefly interests Thucydides is the laws according to which they happen. But these laws are precisely such eternal and unchanging forms as, according to the main trend of Greek thought, are the only knowable things. Thucydides is not the successor of Herodotus in historical thought but the man in whom the historical thought of Herodotus was overlaid and smothered beneath anti-historical motives'. Similar views have been expressed recently by W. P. Wallace,[4] who speaks of Thucydides as being led, by his determination 'to win his way through the tangle of events to the ultimate and intelligible reality which he feels must lie behind them', into 'the bog of pseudo-explanation, the kind of explanation which has made some see in history gold, silver, bronze, and iron age cycles, or preparation for the return of the Messiah, or the patterned rise and fall of civilisations'. Realising no doubt that there is not the least sign of any such type of explanation in Thucydides, Wallace hastily adds, 'It is to Thucydides' credit that he never made explicit the explanation towards which he obviously felt that he was making his way'. (That 'obviously' takes one's breath away.)

To dispel such speculations one has only to ask what these 'psychological laws' are which it was Thucydides' 'chief purpose to affirm'. The answer is that there are none. Clearly Thucydides believed in a number of what might be called 'general laws' of human behaviour: that human nature is very constant and not likely to change in the foreseeable future; that men (at any rate when acting in organised States or in politics generally: see below) always do what they believe to be in their own best interests, and in particular 'rule wherever they can'.[5] But it was never his *purpose* to *affirm* any of these 'laws': far from feeling that he was making his way towards them, he seems to take it for granted—perhaps with inadequate justification!—that all his readers will accept them as completely as he does. He has drawn certain conclusions about human behaviour from his study of the events he is writing about and other events; and when he comments, as he does quite often, upon the actions or the mentality of his characters, he tends to do so in the light of those conclusions,[6] sometimes with profound insight, sometimes (one may feel) mistakenly. But, for him, *getting the facts right* was all-important, and I can only record the deepest disagreement when I read that 'the investigation of particular events, the discovery of what actually did occur, probably

---

[4] 'Thucydides', in *Phoenix* 18 (1964) 251–61, at pp. 260–1. Collingwood's views have also left their mark elsewhere, e.g. in M. I. Finley's Introduction to his *The Greek Historians* (1959), esp. 10, 13; contrast the essay in Finley's *Aspects of Antiquity* (London, 1968) 44–57, with the title, 'Thucydides the Moralist'.

[5] I do not myself believe that Thucydides was as exclusively obsessed by the idea of *power* as is argued by Woodhead, *TNP*.

[6] I have in mind such a series as II 65.4; IV 28.3; VI 63.2; VIII 1.4, on the sort of thing a ὅμιλος or ὄχλος or δῆμος φιλεῖ ποιεῖν, or the long string of assertions of the constancy of human nature, mentioned below.

seemed to Thucydides, as it must have seemed to Plato, to be a matter of little importance, an unintellectual pursuit'.[7] That may be all too true of Plato; it is totally untrue of Thucydides. His narrative can rarely be checked; but when it can, it usually stands up very well, and when it cannot, there is seldom reason to doubt it. However, we need not accept the comments and opinions which Thucydides intersperses with the facts. And very often, of course, the very selection of the facts, and the way they are presented, may impose upon us a particular interpretation (not always the best interpretation), unless we are on our guard against it.

Thucydides scarcely ever gives us any clue about the nature of his sources. He (as it were) slaps his book down on the table in front of us, with a 'Here is what you need to know about the Peloponnesian war. It's the definitive account, and you won't be able to better it'. The fact that he appears to lavish extraordinary care on certain incidents, some of them rather unimportant ones, while giving us all too little information about other matters which may seem to us more important, can doubtless be explained sometimes by variations in the quality of the evidence he was able to obtain. If he felt particularly well informed on some minor topic, but was dissatisfied with what he had been able to discover about some major one, he would have some excuse for saying more about the former than the latter.

Thucydides I 22.1, dealing with the speeches, has evoked an enormous amount of discussion, which is still going on, with little sign of general agreement. (The bibliography can easily be discovered from the standard works; cf. Appendix III. I shall mention only a few writings which I have found particularly helpful.) In a paper published in 1954 (CAE 2) I expressed the rather superficial opinion that some of the speeches, above all that of the Athenians at Sparta in 432 (I 73–8), 'represent what the speakers would have said if they had expressed *with perfect frankness* the sentiments which the historian himself attributed to them, and hence may sometimes depart very far from what was actually said, above all because political and diplomatic speeches are seldom entirely candid'. I still think that is broadly true, but it represents only a small and unimportant part of the truth.

The famous sentence about the speeches (I 22.1) ends with a statement in two essential parts.[8] In the main clause Thucydides says he has made

---

[7] Wallace, *op. cit.* (in n. 4) 260. Many complaints about Thucydides' 'silences' do not allow sufficiently for the different assumptions of fifth–century historiography. For example, I am sure it never occurred to Thucydides that any of his readers would suppose that the Peloponnesian invasion of Attica in 431 went otherwise than by land across the Isthmus; contrast Wallace, *op. cit.* 255 (with his paper in *Stud. in Honour of G. Norwood = Phoenix*, Suppl. I [1952] 80–4); and against him see Gomme, *HCT* II 68; Hammond, MRBP 112.

[8] I give here the text of the second half of I 22.1 (after the colon): ὡς δ' ἂν ἐδόκουν ἐμοὶ ἕκαστοι περὶ τῶν αἰεὶ παρόντων τὰ δέοντα μάλιστ' εἰπεῖν, ἐχομένῳ ὅτι ἐγγύτατα τῆς ξυμπάσης γνώμης τῶν ἀληθῶς λεχθέντων, οὕτως εἴρηται. It would have been interesting to know what opinion Polybius had of Thucydides' method in composing

his speakers say 'for the most part what was in my opinion demanded of them by the various occasions' (Crawley's translation), 'what in my opinion the situation called for', 'what in my opinion was most appropriate in the situation'—the vital words are *ta deonta*. In the participial clause he qualifies that: he has 'kept as close as possible[9] to the *xympasa gnōmē* of what was actually said'.(I am leaving the Greek untranslated for the moment: the precise meaning of those two words is the nub of our enquiry.) Fairly general agreement seems to have been reached about the meaning of *ta deonta* in the main clause, and I do not feel that I need argue in favour of the translations I have given.[10] Thucydides uses *ta deonta* on only four other occasions, and on each of these the expression can only mean something like 'what was necessary in the circumstances': I 70.8; 138.3; II 43.1; 60.5; cf. the singular, *to deon*, in IV 17.2; v 66.3. Particularly apposite here is I 138.3, where Themistocles is said to have been supremely good at 'improvising what the situation required' (*ta deonta*).[11]

We can now turn to the participial clause. There is still some dispute about the precise meaning of *gnōmē*. As von Fritz has wisely remarked,[12] it is a mistake to think we can always render a Greek word by the same

---

speeches, as stated in this passage. I cannot think he would have approved in principle. For some admirably succinct remarks on Polybius' views on the use of speeches in a history, see Walbank, *HCP* I 13–14, 261–2; II 397–8.

[9] This qualification, ὅτι ἐγγύτατα, surely means 'as close as possible *having regard to the reliability of my sources of information*'. Cf. VII 86.5 (where the same words reflect the doubts expressed by ὡς ἐλέγετο in §4); v 74.1 (on which see Gomme, *HCT* IV 125). Sometimes, even what I am calling the 'main thesis' of a speech might not be simple, but might consist of a number of separate points, which Thucydides could have some difficulty in verifying and reporting with complete confidence: a good example is the γνώμη of Nicias in VI 47. Thuc. shows some uncertainty about the facts he relates (even those of the fifth century) more often, perhaps, than is generally realised. See I 13.2; 24.4; 93.7; 118.3 (contrast 123.1–2; II 54.4); 132.5; 134.1; 138.1,6; II 5.6; 18.5 and 20.1; 48.1; 77.6; 93.4; 98.3; 102.5,6; III 79.3; 87.3; 89.5; 94.5; 116.2; IV 104.2; v 68.2 and 74.1,3; VI 2.1,2,4; 27–8 and 60 (esp. 60.2,5); VII 44.1; 86.4; 87.4; VIII 46.5; 50.3; 56.3; 64.5; 87.1,2,3,4,5,6; cf. also I 1.3; 3.1,2; 9.1,3; 10.1,4; II 17.2; 54.5; III 96.1; IV 24.5. Incidentally, Thuc. never uses ὡς εἰκός in the sense of 'probably' (to indicate a lack of confidence in the statement): see Westlake, *EGHGH* 153–60, esp. 156.

[10] I cannot accept Gomme's 'roughly as I thought the several individuals or groups *would have said what they had to say*' (*HCT* I 140; cf. *EGHL* 160), because Gomme shows in what follows that by 'what they *had to say*' he really means 'what they *actually said*' (cf. Walbank, *SGH* 3, who does not reject this interpretation) or at least 'what they were *trying to express*'; and even if this were a permissible alternative translation of the Greek in other contexts, I feel sure Thuc. would not have used τὰ δέοντα in that sense here, as it is not how his readers would naturally take it. And I agree with A. R. W. Harrison, in *CR* 51 (1937) 6–7, that Thucydides must be making a deliberate contrast between the ὡς δ' ἂν ἐδόκουν ἐμοί, said of his speakers in I 22.1, lines 20–1 *OCT*, and οὐδ' ὡς ἐμοὶ ἐδόκει, said of his narrative of events just afterwards, in §2, line 25 *OCT*.

[11] Very similar is the meaning of τὸν πρέποντα in II 34.6, and πρόσφορα in II 46.1.

[12] *GGS* I [Text] 621–2; [Anm.] 283–4 n. 5, discussing the use of *Gesamtsinn, Gesamtintention*. (Against 'aim', 'intention', 'purpose', advocated by various scholars, see Gomme *EGHL* 156–89, at pp. 156–60.) For other German alternatives (*gesamt Planung, Gesamttendenz, praktischer Erkenntnisgehalt, Hauptinhalt, Gesamthaltung, politische Gesamtwillensrichtung*, etc.) see Schmid *GGL* I v.164 and n. I; F. Egermann, 'Zum historiographischen Ziel des Thuk.', in *Historia* 10 (1961) 435–47, at p. 442 n. 5 (with references to his two earlier articles).

modern one; but here I think most people would accept 'purport', 'sense', 'meaning' (*Sinn* in German), as I do. The crucial question is: what precisely is the force of *xympasa*? Above all, does it guarantee that Thucydides will give the *arguments* actually used?

If one examines all the uses of *xympas* in Thucydides, who employs the word on more than 90 occasions, one finds a large group of cases in which it signifies the whole *as distinct from its parts*.[13] There are eight passages in particular where *xympas* is used as part of a phrase meaning 'to sum up': *to xympan eipein*, I 138.3 and VII 49.3; or *to xympan gnōmen* or *gnōte*, IV 63.2 and VII 77.7; or just *to xympan*, I 145; III 92.4; IV 64.3; VI 37.2. Each of these relates to a very brief summary of the matter in question, sometimes of only a couple of lines and never more than five or six lines, and there is little enough in the way of 'arguments'. Take VI 37.2, from the speech of Athenagoras: 'To sum up, I do not believe they could conquer our land, so much greater do I think our resources'.[14] I have cited here every passage I can find in which Thucydides employs *xympas* in a context that is particularly relevant for establishing its meaning in I 22.1: every one without exception refers to something that can be expressed *in a single sentence*. Unless other passages can be quoted (as I do not think they can) in which Thucydides uses the word in the same sort of context in a distinctly broader sense, that should be allowed to settle the question of its meaning in I 22.1.

In one of the most penetrating and important papers yet published on the subject of the speeches (MD, esp. 64–71), Andrewes begins with an analysis of I 22.1 in which, translating our phrase 'the general sense of what was actually said', he shows that the *xympasa gnōmē*, for him as for so many other scholars, includes the *arguments* used by the speakers.[15] It seems to me that this is to extend the meaning of *xympasa gnōmē* beyond the minimum which is all we have a right to demand of it; and it is no surprise to find Andrewes concluding, with Pohlenz, that 'Thucydides laid down this principle comparatively early in his writing life, but diverged from it later'. I on the other hand would give a very restricted meaning to

---

[13] A different classification from that which follows in the text may be useful here. Thuc. IV 63.2, 64.3, VI 37.2, VII 77.7 and 49.3 all occur in actual speeches (the first four in direct speech) at points where the speakers are summing up; I 145 reports an Athenian decision, made ('both in individual points and in general') in accordance with a speech by Pericles which has just been given; and in I 138.3 and III 92.4 Thuc. is summing up his own personal opinion. In addition to the passages mentioned in the text, see (in the singular) II 60.2 and 65.4, IV 87.6, VI 41.2, and VIII 96.4, in each of which there is a contrast (express in every case except one) between the ξύμπασα πόλις and its individual citizens; and (in the plural) I 36.3; II 64.3; IV 64.4; V 68.2; VI 32.1; 67.3; VII 28.2; 64.2.

[14] Thuc. also uses kindred expressions in the same sense, e.g. Cleon's ἕν τε ξυνελών in III 40.4, followed by a brief summary, giving in the next three lines (or is it the next seven?) just what I think Thuc. would have called the ξύμπασα γνώμη of the speech.

[15] See MD 67, line 8 ('the general line of the speaker's argument'); 68, lines 9–10 ('The question is whether what he [Thuc.] set down is preponderantly based on arguments actually used'). Cf. Brauer, *KSFGU* 9, who goes from 'der wesentlich Inhalt' to 'alle Hauptgedanken'.

xympasa gnōmē:[16] one that fits the eight passages cited in the last paragraph. 'Overall purport' (preferred e.g. by Walbank, *SGH* 4) or 'general gist' or 'upshot' probably conveys well enough what I mean; but I think the best translation is perhaps 'main thesis'. If I may offer examples of a *xympasa gnōmē* which Thucydides records without actually calling it that, I would cite two passages which appear in close succession in VIII 53. In the first (53.1) Peisander and his associates, addressing the Athenian Assembly in about December 412, are made to say above all 'that it would be possible for them, if they brought back Alcibiades and did not continue with the democracy in the same fashion, to have the King as an ally and to get the better of the Peloponnesians'. In the second (53.3) Peisander is made to enlarge upon this in the first person: 'There is no possibility of our saving the State unless we have a more moderate form of government and entrust the offices to a few, so that the King may have confidence in us. We should consult now about the safety of the State rather than its form of government (for later on we can always change anything we do not like), and we should bring back Alcibiades, the only person alive who can accomplish this'. Those, the bare bones of speeches, are what I take to be the *xympasai gnōmai* of the speakers concerned.[17] Either might have been written up into a full-length speech, had Thucydides lived to finish his work. If I may offer my own conception of a *xympasa gnōmē* for what is undoubtedly the set of speeches most often accused of having no basis in fact, namely the Melian Dialogue (v 84–113), I would suggest that it is the Athenians' assertion that the Melians are far too weak to be able to resist Athens on their own and can hope for no assistance from outside, and therefore would be wise to surrender without further ado, and the Melians' denial of this assertion.

I would add, against the interpretation adopted by e.g. Polhenz and Andrewes, a point well made by A. R. W. Harrison in a very brief article published in 1937: 'An unbiased reading of I 22 suggests that it is describing a method which *has been* followed' ('Thucydides I 22', in *CR* 51 [1937] 6–7). Surely this is true. The opening of 22.1 refers both to speeches dating from before the war and to those delivered while it was in progress; both to those Thucydides heard himself and to those reported to him by others. All the main verbs in 22.1–3 are in the past tense. It is hard to believe that all this was written before the History began, or even while it was in its earlier stages. Surely it represents Thucydides' assessment

---

[16] The view has been expressed to me that had Thuc. meant something like 'the γνώμη taken as a whole', including the arguments, it would have been more natural for him to use the words ξυμπάσης τῆς γνώμης.

[17] I must ignore minor questions of interpretation, except to reply to one criticism of a draft of this chapter, based on taking the word ἀκρίβειαν in I 22.1—too narrowly, as it seems to me—in the sense of the 'exact words' used. 'I could not memorise the *actual words* and so will keep as close as I can to the *actual proposal*' would indeed not be meaningful; but Thuc. would hardly have found it necessary to say anything as obvious as that he could not remember the exact words, and he must be using ἀκρίβεια in a less narrow sense. Cf. the use of ἀκρίβεια in I 22.2; τὸ ἀκριβές in v 90; ἀκριβῶς in I 97.2; VII 49.1; ἀκριβής in IV 47.2; and esp. v 26.5; VI 54.1.

of at least a good part of what he had actually written, in the form in which we have it today.

If we understand 1 22.1 in the way I have advocated we need not convict Thucydides of having been false to his own principles. In no case do we have the right to expect anything closely resembling a speech actually delivered, except in its main thesis. This will be true whether Thucydides heard it himself or not. Although in the first part of 1 22.1 (before the colon) he happens to distinguish between speeches he heard himself and those reported to him by others, he does not carry this distinction over into the vital second half of the sentence. There he says of all the speeches in his work, without exception, that he has in general made the speakers say what in his opinion the circumstances demanded, although he has kept as close as possible to the main thesis of each speaker. In 1 22.1 Thucydides makes it clear that he has taken out a licence to supply his own arguments whenever he wishes to do so. We can never be sure that any particular argument used in a speech, or any particular statement made in it, can be attributed to the actual speaker, or was necessarily true (cf. e.g. IV 85.7 with 108.5, and note the contradictions in opposed pairs of speeches). Some commentators have been worried by the curious character of the arguments in many of the speeches and the fact that arguments of the same type (couched above all in terms of expediency) appear in speech after speech; but this of course is precisely what we must expect if the interpretation I have offered of 1 22.1 is correct. I cannot agree with Walbank (*SGH* 4) that there is a 'contradiction' between the participial clause and the main clause in the latter part of 1 22.1 because (as he puts it) 'the criterion of the one is quite simply the truth, the criterion of the other is suitability'. Outside the central core of a speech, its *xympasa gnōmē*, the 'criterion of suitability' alone rules, and no 'criterion of truth' (in the sense of what was actually said) can be applied at all; whereas in regard to that central core it is the criterion of suitability which is entirely absent, and the criterion of truth only which prevails. It is certainly true, however, that Thucydides (in Walbank's phrase) left 'an unfortunate legacy' to his successors, none of whom possessed his passion for truth and accuracy or could bring out the essentials of a situation as he did. And however much we may admire the speeches as vehicles for the acute reflective judgments of a man of extraordinary perceptiveness and insight, there is one criticism against which they can hardly be defended: we can seldom be sure that we know how extensive the *xympasa gnōmē* is, and therefore we may often not be able to decide how much of a speech represents what was actually said, and how much is Thucydides' own formulation of the issues. This can give rise to disastrous misjudgments.

I come now to what we might call the main distorting factor in the speeches: the reason why some of the speeches may give a very misleading impression of what was actually said on the occasion in question. This is that the outlook of Thucydides was not at all typical of the men of his day: he was an intellectual through and through, and in a world where illusions about international affairs (patriotic illusions in particular) were as prevalent as they are today, he was a complete and ruthless realist. Hence what seemed to Thucydides the most appropriate sentiments on a given occasion (*ta deonta*) might be very different from those which would have seemed appropriate to most people—including the actual speaker and his audience. What seemed *ta deonta* to Thucydides may often not seem so to us, unless we could suppose the speech to have been delivered to an audience of Thucydideses. I will illustrate this briefly from three speeches (or debates).

First, the Athenians at Sparta in 432 (1 73–8). This speech has troubled many commentators, and those who have not felt able to dismiss it as a pure invention have always found it puzzling. Their dilemma is stated by Gomme (*HCT* 1 252–4), who says that 'taken by itself it would seem to have been purposely provocative. . . . What other purpose can this have had than to provoke the honest Spartans to a hasty declaration of war? What other effect did it have? The simple Sthenelaïdas falls straight into the trap. . . . There would be nothing surprising if the Athenian aim had really been to provoke a declaration of war. . . . They thought, and rightly, that, if war was to come, the sooner the better for them'. But Gomme then remembers that it was Thucydides, after all, who wrote the speech as we have it, and that *he* 'quite clearly . . . did not think that it was the Athenian aim to be provocative, but the contrary (72.1)'! Thucydides does indeed say most specifically in 72.1 that the Athenians were trying to prevent an immediate declaration of war. The explanation is that we have here a series of arguments of a peculiarly Thucydidean character, with a number of generalisations of which Thucydides is particularly fond:[18] men are moved by fear, honour and self-interest (75.3; 76.2); a State cannot be blamed for judging great issues in terms of expediency (75.5); people in reality think in terms of expediency, even when they talk in terms of justice, 'a consideration no one ever brought forward to hinder his own aggrandisement when he could get what he wanted by force' (76.2); it has always been the rule that the weaker should be subject to the stronger (76.2; cf. 77.3 *fin.*);[19] it is human nature[20] to accept empire (76.2,3), and those who nevertheless respect justice more than they are obliged to, having regard to their power, deserve praise (76.3);[21] men are more indignant if unjustly treated in a law court than if subjected to outright

---

[18] Against e.g. Strasburger, TPSDA, who thinks that such generalisations represent not Thucydides' own views but opinions of which he actually disapproved, see the last paragraph of this Part of Chapter I, with Chapter IV, Part vi below.

[19] Cf. the famous fragment of Democritus, 68 B 267, in Diels-Kranz, *FVS* II⁵⁻⁸ 200.

[20] For the role of human nature in Thuc., see below. In Greek authors of the sixth to the fourth centuries, φύσις is nearly always something unchanging and unchangeable. But see the very remarkable fragment of Democritus, 68 B 33 (διδαχή can remake φύσις): cf. the φύσις/διδαχή opposition in Thuc. 1 121.4; and note Hippocr., *Airs Waters Places* 14 (νόμος becoming φύσις). For Thuc., was human nature 'unchangeable'? I suggest that all we have a right to infer (see esp. III 82.2) is that he felt it would not change much in the foreseeable future.

[21] It is this sort of behaviour the Spartans are asking the Athenians to display in IV 19.2–4. And cf. v 111.4 *fin.*

violence (77.4; cf. IV 86.6); in war, the unexpected is only too likely to happen (78.1–2). All these general statements are paralleled elsewhere in Thucydides. Indeed, it is precisely the characteristically Thucydidean nature of such generalisations that should make us beware of this and any other such speech. It is the very fact that the generalisations in some of the speeches constantly echo each other and follow a few standard patterns that makes them suspect as the contributions of Thucydides himself. And this speech has another feature that makes it highly implausible as a whole: its consistently intellectual and even sophistic character, making it peculiarly unsuitable for delivery to an audience of Spartans, most of whom would have been likely to scratch their heads and wonder what on earth these over-educated highbrows were trying to put over on them.[22]

Secondly, the speech of Diodotus in the Mytilenaean Debate (III 41–8). For reasons that have often been noticed,[23] it is at first sight very strange that in the circumstances Thucydides entirely omits all arguments based on mercy and pity, or protesting against cruelty, and makes Diodotus argue, as Cleon had, entirely in terms of the self-interest of Athens. Diodotus, of course, may conceivably have delivered such a speech as Thucydides gives him, but some of the other speakers will surely have argued very differently. Are the arguments reported by Thucydides limited within such a curiously narrow scope because Thucydides believed that this was in principle the *best way to argue* such a case, or because he thought this type of argument was *successful in practice* in convincing the Athenians and inducing them to change their minds? After wavering between these alternatives, I am now inclined to accept both; but the first of the two explanations is the basic one and the second follows from it. I believe Thucydides thought that public and political argument should always be conducted on purely rational lines, and that emotion should be excluded altogether, on the ground that although emotions such as pity may be useful, or at least harmless, yet once emotion is allowed in at all it is the more violent ones, such as hatred and the desire for revenge, which are likely to swamp the rest and lead to dangerous behaviour.[24]

Thirdly, the Athenians in the Melian Dialogue (V 84–113),[25] a debate which 'rises above the particular incident of Melos in the same way as the speech of the Athenians rises above the debate at Sparta' (de Romilly, *TAI* 274). This is a text about which some extraordinary misconceptions

[22] I am almost tempted to say that I would accept this speech as a fair indication of the one actually delivered only if we could suppose that Thucydides himself was the ambassador who delivered it!

[23] See e.g. my CAE 15–16; Andrewes, MD 71 ff. (who has many interesting things to say about this speech and that of Cleon).

[24] Cf. esp. Arist. *EN* x 9, 1179^{b}26–9 (passion yields only to force, not to argument); *Rhet.* I 1, 1354^{a} 16 ff.

[25] Here I have found most helpful Andrewes, MDPLS 1–6, 9–10, by no means entirely superseded by his commentary in Gomme, *HCT* IV 182–8. On the historical background, see my remarks in CAE 12–14; Andrewes, MDPLS 1–2, and in Gomme, *HCT* IV 156–9.

have prevailed, from at least the time of Dionysius of Halicarnassus to our own day. The first thing I wish to say about the Dialogue is something that is too often forgotten: it has nothing whatever to do with the massacre of the Melians, which we know is going to follow, and the whole purpose of the Athenians is to persuade the Melians that they would be well advised to surrender, because resistance would be futile.[26] It would be a bad mistake to say that Thucydides is 'on the side of the Melians' in any sense. The fact that they are being foolishly over-optimistic is made very clear by the Athenians (see esp. 103; 111.2; 113). Their confidence in the divine benevolence that the justice of their case deserves (104; 112.2) is given short shrift (105.1,2,3; 113); and when they express their confidence that the Spartans will help them (104; 106; 108; 110; 112.2), the Athenians reply with a correct and excoriating analysis of Spartan behaviour (105.3-4; 107; 109; 113), which was certainly justified by the event. Thucydides has made the Athenians speak here, as at Sparta in Book I, in his own peculiar terms, with much generalisation. We hear again that the strong do what they can and the weak suffer what they must, with the addition that justice is only in question between those who have equal power (89; cf. 1 76.2), and that the best course to follow (v 111.4) is not to give way to equals, and to behave politely to superiors and with moderation to inferiors. (The terms used are severely practical and do not constitute a series of moral judgments.)[27] But the passage which has evoked most comment is 105.2, where the Athenians say, 'Of the gods we believe, and of men we know for certain, that by a necessary law of their nature they always rule wherever they can'. (For the attitude shown here towards the gods, see the illuminating remarks of de Romilly, *TAI* 298 = *TIA*[2] 250.) This statement, which merely repeats, in rather more vivid language, what Thucydides had made the Athenians say at Sparta (1 76.2,3), was thought shocking nearly two thousand years ago by Dionysius of Halicarnassus,[28] who saw in it an angry desire on Thucydides' part to be revenged upon the fellow citizens who had exiled him, by blackguarding them in the eyes of the Greek world. Until recently most of Thucydides' modern readers have taken it for granted that he meant this statement of the Athenians to be shocking (as Dionysius believed) and intended it as a

---

[26] W. Liebeschuetz, 'The Structure and Function of the Melian Dialogue', in *JHS* 88 (1968) 73–7, builds heavily on the false premise that the Dialogue is 'at the same time a *debate about* the expediency of *destroying* an independent city that refuses to become a subject' (p. 73, my italics). The argument (all contained in the second paragraph) designed to establish this premise is simply irrelevant, as anyone will discover who goes right through the Dialogue. What Liebeschuetz should have said here is that the Dialogue, though *not at all* 'about' the *destruction* of Melos, suggests to him various reflections upon that topic and makes him feel that Thuc. must surely be condemning the Athenians. On this question, contrast Andrewes in Gomme, *HCT* iv 183–5.

[27] Just as καλῶς here is entirely non-ethical, so are μέτριοι and πλεῖστ' ἂν ὀρθοῖντο (cf. ὀρθῶς βουλεύεται in II 64.5).

[28] Dion. Hal., *De Thuc.* 37–41, esp. 39 (*init.*), 40 (*med.* and *fin.*). Cf. *Epist. ad Cn. Pomp.* 3.9, where Dion. says that Thuc., although he had no need to do so, described the origins of the Peloponnesian war in such a way as to put the blame on Athens.

denunciation of Athenian imperialism.[29] It has even been customary to speak of the Athenians as proclaiming at this point the doctrine that Might is Right;[30] but there is no justification for this whatever. As Brunt has recently put it, the Athenians 'exclude *all* considerations of justice (v 89), and in v 105 they do *not* say that the stronger ought to rule, but that "we believe of the gods and know of men" that they actually do; if Callicles or Thrasymachus had argued thus,[31] Socrates could have refuted them only by appeal to historic facts and not by the tricks of dialectic'.[32] Andrewes too has stated the position admirably: Thucydides' assertion here is 'that empire is a fact of nature, impervious to moral considerations: not that might is right, but that might is an inescapable fact, however little we like it or approve of it . . . For empire itself there can, morally speaking, be neither blame nor praise' (MDPLS 6; cf. Andrewes in Gomme, *HCT* IV 164).

This is true, and we must be careful, if we ever speak of Thucydides as a believer in *Realpolitik* or *Machtpolitik*, to make it clear that it was something he accepted as a fact of life, which even the best intentioned men are obliged to take account of because all States practise it, without exception. There can be no doubt that this was his view: he presents it as invariably observed in practice, and he attributes it not only to the Athenians but to Hermocrates the Syracusan, one of his characters whom

[29] M. F. McGregor, 'The Politics of the Historian Thuc.', in *Phoenix* 10 (1956), at p. 100, makes it a denunciation of Athenian democracy too: 'Thucydides' indictment of popular government . . . reaches a climax in the shameful words of the Athenian in the Melian Dialogue'.

[30] In such contexts English-speakers perhaps have an advantage over some others, in that English shares with Greek the lack of a concept of *ius = Recht = droit = diritto*. Anyone thinking in English or Greek will have no linguistic reason to confuse the *statement of fact* that men by their very nature (ὑπὸ φύσεως ἀναγκαίας, Thuc. v 105.2; cf. πέφυκε γὰρ τὸ ἀνθρώπειον, IV 61.5) *do in practice* 'rule wherever they can' with the *moral judgment* that it is *right* they should do so, that they 'have a right' to do so. Those accustomed to think in terms of *Recht* etc. may find it much harder to keep the two concepts distinct, for *Recht* imports the idea of 'right' in the sense of a claim that is *legally or morally justified*. It is interesting to see how Kiechle (UWMPT 302) can shift within a single paragraph from 'Naturrecht' to 'Naturnotwendigkeit' to 'Naturgesetz', without deciding which of these terms, if any, is the real equivalent of what Thucydides' Athenians are saying in v 105.2. (I am very grateful to Martin Ostwald for his invaluable assistance with the foregoing.) Cf. also von Fritz, *GGS* I [Text] 719 ('einer brutale Verkündigung des Rechts des Stärkeren'); G. De Sanctis, *Studi di storia della storiografia greca* (1951) 81–2; W. Jaeger, *Paideia* (Eng. trans., Oxford, 1939) I 399; and many others. I cannot even accept the view that the Dialogue is 'a sophistical treatise on might and right', as believed by e.g. M. I. Finley ('Myth, Memory and History', in *Hist. and Theory* 4 [1965] 281 ff., at p. 302). And it is not legitimate to translate δικαιοῦμεν (at the end of 105.1) by 'what we *deem just*', as W. K. C. Guthrie does (*Hist. of Greek Philosophy* III [Cambridge, 1969] 92), taking it with 105.2. In fact Thucydides normally uses the words δικαιόω, δικαίωσις, δικαίωμα not for people's judgments of right and wrong but for their claims/professions or decisions/verdicts, irrespective of 'justice' or other moral considerations: see e.g. I 141.1; II 61.4; 71.4; III 40.4; 82.4; IV 86.6; v 17.2; 26.2; VI 79.2; 80.2; 89.6.

[31] The reference is to Plato, *Gorg.* 482e ff. (esp. 483 b–e); *Rep.* I 338c ff. On Callicles, note the wise words of Grote, *HG* VII 65–7 (ch. lxvii).

[32] P. A. Brunt, in *CR* 83 = n.s. 19 (1969), at p. 200. Cf. my CAE 36–7; Andrewes, MDPLS 6, and in Gomme, *HCT* IV 164; also Woodhead, *TNP* 37 ff., on Thuc.'s conception of δύναμις. And cf. Ps.–Lys. II 19, repudiating the 'Law of the Jungle'.

he evidently most admired.[33] Although Hermocrates is the bitter enemy
of Athens, he is made to say at the Congress of Gela in 424 that Athens
has every excuse for her behaviour, and that he blames not those who want
to rule, but those who are too ready to become subjects, for it is just as
much a part of the nature of man to rule those who submit as to resist those
who attack (IV 61.5). In each case, with the Athenians and with Hermocrates, the sentiments are Thucydidean.

Although I do not see in the Melian Dialogue the 'repulsiveness' which
Andrewes (MDPLS 9) and so many others find there, I admit that it is
at first sight a strange document. But I suggest that we need no longer find
it nearly so strange if we force ourselves to see the Athenian case as what
it was intended to be: essentially an attempt to convince the Melians that
they have no hope of successful resistance and ought to surrender without
fighting—but with the Athenians adopting the kind of argument (including
appeal to general principles) which would have been necessary to convince
Thucydides had he been in charge of the policy of Melos or any other small
state threatened by a much greater power. I am sure Thucydides simply
did not realise that most of his readers would be unable to forget the
massacre that was to come and would therefore feel strongly prejudiced
against the Athenian speakers—any more than he realised that the speech
he gave to the Athenians at Sparta, intended as an eirenicon, would seem
anything but that to many people. If he had been confronted with
Andrewes' criticism (MDPLS 5) that 'the Athenians seem throughout
to be represented as much more brutal than the abstract argument
demands', I suspect that he would have been astonished. (I shall return
below to the question of Thucydides' attitude to the Athenians' cruel
treatment of the Melians when they took the city.)

There is another major point I want to make about Thucydides. I believe
that in practice he drew a fundamental distinction—though he never
frames it explicitly, in general terms—between, on the one hand, the
relations of *individuals inside the State*, where there are laws, enforced by
sanctions, which may enable the weak to stand up to the strong from a
position of approximate equality and where ordinary ethical considerations can apply, and on the other, the relations *between States*, where it is
the strong who decide how they will treat the weak, and moral judgments
are virtually inapplicable. The passage in fifth/fourth-century Greek
literature where this distinction is made most explicit occurs in Demosthenes' speech, *On the Liberty of the Rhodians* (xv 28–9), where the reasoning
on which it is based can be seen more clearly than it ever can be in
Thucydides, and where it can be considered more dispassionately, free
from the horror that tends to cloud it in the minds of many modern

---

[33] See VI 72.2, where Hermocrates is second to none in ξύνεσις (a quality also attributed
to Themistocles, I 74.1; 138.3; Brasidas, IV 81.2; the Peisistratids, VI 54.5; and cf.
Archidamus in I 79.2, and Phrynichus in VIII 27.5), is also well endowed with ἐμπειρία
and moreover is conspicuous for ἀνδρεία, a virtue attributed to no one else in the History.

readers when it appears in the Melian Dialogue. What Demosthenes says (if I may give a close paraphrase) is that within States there are *nomoi* (laws and customs), which *put the weak on an equality with the strong* and enable them to deal with each other on equal terms; but that in international disputes (inter-State disputes, *en tois Hellēnikois dikaiois*) the strong simply coerce the weak. Although Demosthenes does not say it in so many words, he clearly implies that it is the impossibility of enforcing law by effective sanctions (for these exist only within the State) which makes force the sole ultimate arbiter in international affairs. From the way he speaks, I am not sure how far one can infer that the idea was already familiar to a mid-fourth-century Athenian audience. Of course Demosthenes himself, even in the same speech (§§8, 21, 25, 28, 30), and often in other speeches, advocates above all a course he describes as 'just' or 'right' (*dikaion*); but that does not detract from the value of his statement of international fact in §§28–9. (It is interesting to remember that Demosthenes was credited in antiquity with having made a particularly close study of Thucydides: we need not doubt the fact, even if some of the details are fictitious.) Similarly, Aristotle in the *Politics* (VII 2, 1324^b 22–36, esp. 33–36) laments the fact that 'most people seem to think sheer domination is what is appropriate in the political sphere; and they are not ashamed to practise in regard to outsiders what they deny to be just or even expedient in their dealings with each other as individuals. For their own affairs, among themselves, they demand an authority based on justice; but in regard to outsiders justice is no concern of theirs'. (Cf. Isocr. VIII 69, where the same situation is implied for the time at which Isocrates is writing, *c.* 355, even if it is contrasted with an idealised picture of the Athenian attitude during the Corinthian war.)

Thucydides never lays down the general principle as explicitly as Demosthenes or Aristotle, but he shows over and over again that he accepted it in practice. An example is III 44.4. Diodotus, in the Mytilenaean Debate, has just proclaimed his intention of speaking strictly in terms of what is expedient for Athens (44.1–3). He now makes the interesting admission that Cleon's speech may be the more persuasive because in the present passionate state of Athenian feeling it seems 'more just'. (We may compare 40.3,4: for Cleon, justice requires vengeance.) And then he rounds upon his audience with the words, 'But we are not litigating in court among ourselves, in a case where justice is appropriate: the subject of our discussion is the Mytilenaeans, and how we can make them useful to us'. There is an even better example in V 105.4, just after Thucydides has put into the mouths of the Athenians at Melos the most outright of all his statements about men 'ruling wherever they can' (105.2)—a formulation which is certainly in quite general terms but is prompted by the Melians' mistaken assumption that they could rely upon help coming to them from Sparta. Immediately after establishing the general principle, the Athenians turn back to the particular case of the Spartans. 'In dealings among themselves', they say (105.4), 'and in matters that involve their own country's institutions, the Spartans practise what is honourable[34] in the highest degree. One could say plenty about the way they conduct themselves towards outsiders; but, to sum up, it could be demonstrated that they, most of all the men we know, consider what is agreeable to themselves honourable, and what is expedient just'.

It is indeed not the Athenians alone whose foreign policy Thucydides sees as founded purely upon self-interest and expediency: that is how all States behave. In IV 81.2 he first speaks of an individual Spartan general, Brasidas, as showing himself 'just and moderate' (*dikaion kai metrion*) towards certain towns which he either persuaded to revolt from Athens or gained over with the aid of traitors within. And then *in the very same sentence* Thucydides goes on to attribute to the Spartan State an entirely selfish and indeed cynical attitude towards these same towns. Their adhesion was very useful to Sparta, he remarks, because it shifted the burden of war away from the Peloponnese, and when the Spartans were ready to negotiate for peace, as in due course they were, they had *antapodosin kai apodochēn*: 'places to offer in exchange' to Athens! Brasidas, a man possessing *aretē kai xynesis* ('virtue and ability', perhaps), was doubtless sincere enough in the promises he made, confirming by his personal oath the oaths already sworn officially by his city (see Thuc. IV 86.1; 87.1; 88.1). But to Sparta the cities that came over or were betrayed to her, on the faith of these oaths, were mere bargaining counters, to be used to extract from the Athenians concessions that Sparta herself really valued.

I was once much impressed by a reading of Paul Shorey's penetrating article (which seems unfortunately to be ignored nowadays), 'On the Implicit Ethics and Psychology of Thucydides',[35] where the 'ethical positivism' of Thucydides, as Shorey calls it—his 'amoralism', as others might put it—is amply documented and subjected to hostile criticism. Shorey does not distinguish, however, between the few passages dealing with individual morality within the State and the main body of the History which treats almost entirely of affairs of State and inter-city dealings. The amorality of Thucydides, which is very thorough-going in almost everything that pertains to what we call 'international affairs', has certainly shocked most of those people (Shorey, for instance) who have been honest enough to recognise it for what it is and have not tried to ignore its presence as far as possible. Few of these have found it anything but distasteful. The attitude of this group, who at least do not try to palliate something they deplore, is nicely expressed in a phrase I have come across somewhere: 'the moral bleakness of Thucydides'. This quality, however, is so much in

---

[34] The word used is ἀρετή, which Thuc. employs in a variety of senses, but sometimes in a moral one—as here, and in I 37.2 (opposed to κακουργία); II 40.4 (twice, 'generosity'); III 10.1 (twice, perhaps 'honesty'); IV 19.2,3 ('generosity'?); 86.5 ('honesty'?); VII 86.5 (see below); also perhaps III 53.4; 56.7; IV 81.2 (perhaps 'valour', but note δίκαιον καὶ μέτριον in §2 and ἀγαθός in §3); some (including Classen-Steup, *Thuk.* I⁵⁻⁷ lxvii) would even add VI 54.5 and VIII 68.1.

[35] In *TAPA* 24 (1893) 66–88. It is not always fair. I would not admit, for example, that Thuc. is 'cynical', even though he can give vent to some nasty sneers.

view because Thucydides is writing almost entirely of international and public affairs. When he deals with the relations of individuals inside the State he is quite prepared to make moral judgments, of a sensible if conventional kind, in his own person, as in II 53; III 82.2–83;[36] the words he puts into Pericles' mouth in II 37 (esp. §3); and the judgment on Nicias in VII 86.5, which Dover (in Gomme, *HCT* IV 463) translates, 'because he had ordered his whole life by high moral standards'; cf. V 105.4 (cited above), on the behaviour of the Spartans at home among themselves. Thucydides' 'amoralism' does not extend to dealings between individuals inside the State.

When he is dealing with relations between States, and matters of public policy involving such relations, Thucydides makes no such moral judgments. His characters, of course, frequently do; but when he records appeals to 'justice' he usually makes them come—surely by design—from men on the losing side, whether in diplomatic exchanges (the Athenians in 420)[37] or in war (the Corinthians in 435)[38] or in debate (Cleon against Diodotus; for it is Cleon, not Diodotus, who appeals to justice!)[39] or in war and debate (the Corinthians in 433,[40] the Plataeans on two different occasions,[41] and the Melians[42]). In II 63.2 Pericles is made to say that the rule of the Athenians over their empire is 'like that of a tyrant': he add that according to the consensus of Greek opinion (this, I think, is the force of the *dokei*) to acquire such a tyranny is wrong, but he goes on to say that to give it up would be dangerous. As for appeals to the gods, they are apt to make us expect the very worst. It is true that King Archidamus calls the gods and heroes of Plataea to witness that the Spartans are not committing unjust aggression in invading Plataean territory,[43] and Sthenelaïdas[44] and Pagondas the Boeotarch[45] make passing references to the divine help they feel they have a right to expect, and yet come out on the winning side; but there are special circumstances in each case. Three of Thucydides' speakers make more specific and serious appeal

[36] Esp. 82.4,6,8; 83.1, where expressions like εὐσέβεια, τὸ γενναῖον etc. are used with approval in a normal way.

[37] Thuc. V 42.2; 46.5 (cf. 39.3).

[38] I 25.3, where we have hatred of Corcyra to reinforce τὸ δίκαιον.

[39] III 40.3,4; cf. 44.4. For Cleon, justice takes the form of vengeance. Again we have something to reinforce τὰ δίκαια: this time it is τὰ ξύμφορα.

[40] I 38.4–5; 39.2–3; 40.1–2,4; 42. The Corcyraeans have much less to say about Corinthian ἀδικία: see only 33.1; 34.1–2; cf. 37.1.

[41] II 71.2,4; III 56.1,3,5; and note the references to Greek custom in 58.3; 59.1.

[42] V 86; 89; 90; 98; 104. De Romilly claims that Thucydides 'takes care to secure the reader's sympathy for the Melians' by (inter alia) recalling 'the fact [sic] that they have right on their side' (*TAI* 290); but this is not justified: see above.

[43] II 74.2. But Archidamus is making a necessary reply to the appeal of the Plataeans to the same gods and others, in 71.2.

[44] I 86.5. Doubtless Sthenelaïdas already knew that Apollo would give a favourable response to an enquiry about a declaration of war (cf. I 118.3); and since the Spartans were famous for their religiosity, some phrase like 'with the gods' help' was almost *de rigueur* in such a situation. And see I 123.1–2 (Corinthian speech).

[45] IV 92.7. In this case the Athenians were alleged to have committed a form of sacrilege (90.1–2; 97.2–98.7).

to the gods: the Plataeans (II 71.4; III 58.1; 59.2) and the Melians (V 104; 112.2), who are going to be overwhelmed and massacred, and Nicias (VII 77.2–4). When poor Nicias, well known as a religious man, makes a speech to the army at Syracuse before the retreat, and dwells upon the kindness he thinks the Athenians may now hope to receive from the gods, whom he has always devoutly served, our worst apprehensions are aroused about what is likely to happen to him and his men.[46] Thucydides, I am sure, would have seen nothing shocking or even strange in the remark made by an unknown speaker in a fragment of one of Euripides' lost plays, the *Bellerophontēs*: 'I know small States which have honoured the gods and yet have to obey larger States that are ungodly, because they are overwhelmed by a greater number of spearmen' (Nauck, *TGF*², Eur. fr. 286.10–12).

For Thucydides, there was evidently no such thing as 'international law', in anything like the same sense as that in which there can be laws within the State. But he did, I believe, condemn the breaking of sworn treaties,[47] understandably enough—against this, one could advance reasons of expediency as well as religion and morality. (A State in a dangerous position which is suing for terms, but has acquired a reputation for treaty-breaking, may find the other side demanding exceptionally stringent conditions, to guarantee that this time there will be no breach.) And I dare say Thucydides would have agreed with the standard Greek view expressed by Diodorus xxx 18.2 (from Polybius) about the 'quasi-laws' of warfare. How much further he was prepared to go we can only guess. He makes only the very briefest possible mention (V 116.4) of the most notorious of the war-crimes the Athenians committed, by massacring the men and enslaving the women and children of Melos at the end of the siege—just as he refrains from commenting upon the other cruelties he recounts of a similar nature, such as the Athenian actions in regard to the Aeginetans from Thyrea in 424 (IV 57.3–4), the Toronaean women and children in 422 (V 3.4) and the Scionaeans in 421 (V 32.1), and the Spartan treatment of the merchants they captured at sea (II 67.4), of the prisoners they took during the expedition of Alcidas in 427 (III 32.1–2), of the Plataeans later in the same year (III 68.1–4), of the 2,000 Helots in 424 (IV 80.2–4), and of the Argives captured at Hysiae in 417 (V 83.2). Consistently faithful to his own principles, Thucydides refused to be drawn into passing moral judgments in matters of this kind, involving inter-State relations—contrast his outright condemnation of revolutionary excesses inside cities, in III 82.2–8, replete with terms of moral disapproval: *hyperbolēn, . . . tōn timōriōn atopiāi, . . . pleonexiāi, . . . paranomēsai, . . . apatēi, . . . kakourgoi, . . . hē dia pleonexian kai philotimian, . . . ta deinotata epexēisan, . . . meta psēphou adikou katagnōseōs, . . . tēn autika philonikian ekpimplanai,*

---

[46] For a brief discussion of the passages in Thuc. which shed light on his religious outlook, see Classen-Steup, *Thuk.* I⁵⁻⁷ lx-lxiv.

[47] Among several relevant passages are I 85.2; III 68.1; IV 23.1 (with 16); V 39.3 (with 23.2); 42.1–2 and 46.2–5; and of course VII 18.2–3. Cf. III 82.7; 83.2.

* *

and the like. I may add that I can only express astonishment at Strasburger's conclusion, from his list of atrocities committed during the war on both sides ('Kriegsgreuel', TPSDA 36 n. 1 = 524–5 n. 66), that the Spartans were 'more humane' than the Athenians towards the defeated. The point is surely that before the Ionian war (which Strasburger for some reason ignores; but cf. my CAE 38 & n. 2) Sparta was less often in a position where she might be tempted to commit *Kriegsgreuel*. How can we profitably compare the actions of the two sides, in their very different circumstances, especially if we are to take into account also (as of course we must) more moderate actions, such as those recorded in Thuc. IV 54.3; 130.7; even III 49–50?

We may wish to know whether Thucydides disapproved of all atrocities committed by States against each other, or whether—like most people today, in practice—he was willing to make an exception for what those who commit such acts are apt to call 'necessary (even 'wholesome') severities'—that is to say, cruelties which are expedient, as opposed to 'unnecessary' ones, going beyond what is likely to serve a 'useful' purpose. If, as I believe, Diodotus is voicing Thucydides' own sentiments in III 45, then we may surely infer that he believed the effect of all alleged 'deterrents' to be too uncertain to justify resorting to them, at least to any extreme degree. But those who are inclined to think that he 'must have' condemned (or, if he did not, ought to have condemned) all cruelties committed by States against each other should at least ask themselves what their own judgment is of some of the wholesale acts of destruction committed in their own time: not merely those perpetrated by the Germans under Hitler and by the Japanese, but also the indiscriminate bombing of enemy cities by the Western allies, and the obliteration of Hiroshima and Nagasaki, and especially of Dresden, an act involving an even greater mass killing, which served no essential military purpose. These were all 'unfortunate necessities' in the eyes of those responsible for them, and easily forgotten by the victors when they arraigned the vanquished for 'war crimes' at Nuremberg and elsewhere. Such things may indeed pose moral problems, about which disputes will long continue. Thucydides may have felt unhappy and uncertain about such problems, as many of us do today. His solution was to avoid pronouncing *judgment* in such matters and to content himself with *analysis*, bringing out the essential factors involved. In regard to Melos, in particular, it must be evident to anyone who reads Thucydides without preconceived ideas that there is no reference whatever *in the Dialogue*, direct or indirect, to the appalling sequel—even *ta deinotata pathein* in V 93 need imply no more than the horrors that would anyway be likely to attend a desperate but hopeless resistance. Indeed, Thucydides' Athenians are evidently anxious to persuade the Melians to surrender quietly rather than resist: this, they emphasise (91.2; 93), would be to the advantage of both parties. We may *speculate* about Thucydides' intentions in writing that extraordinary Dialogue. My own guess is that he was trying to state some of the basic and brutal *facts* about the position of imperial States and of those threatened by them, but to *state* those facts only, in the most general way possible, and not to pretend that he had any *solution* to the *problems* that arise out of them.

One's judgments about such a difficult and elusive writer as Thucydides are bound to be highly subjective,[48] but my own feeling is that if one had been able to corner Thucydides and press him to give an explicit summary of his views about the behaviour of States, he would have answered roughly as follows:

All States ('yours' and 'mine' included, just as much as others) always do what they believe, rightly or wrongly, to be in their own best interests, and in particular they rule wherever they can. They provide above all for their own security, and they seek to extend their power as far as possible. In doing so, they often collide with other States. If it is they who are stronger, they will if necessary apply coercion, and the other States, just because they are weaker, will be forced back on appeals to a notional 'justice'. But how is what is 'just' decided in such cases, and whose decision prevails, if not that of the stronger State? Have independent States a 'natural right' to remain 'free and independent'? But how is such a right acquired? I recognise no such right. Any State may claim it for itself, or for the subjects of its enemies, but it will seldom hesitate to coerce a weaker State when that is what its own interest requires. Of course, proclaiming the necessity for 'justice' and 'freedom' and so forth can sometimes be very useful as a propaganda weapon. But look at the Spartans, who began the war with the promise to 'free the Hellenes', while in practice keeping their own allies carefully under control, by maintaining friendly oligarchies among them as far as possible, and ended up by selling many of Athens' former subjects to Persia, and putting others, including Athens herself, under small oppressive oligarchies, entirely subservient to Sparta's interests.

That is the way States do in fact behave, and you had better begin by taking full account of it. Take 'your own' State. If you are weak, you should be properly deferential to great powers and try to convince them that they would not really profit by conquering you—that is the argument that is most likely to appeal to them. If they do attack you, calculate your chances as coolly as possible, and if you have no reasonable chance of successfully resisting, submit. Take warning from the Melians, who would not have had to suffer Athenian rule for much more than a decade if they had had the sense to give in when the Athenians had obviously determined to subject them. Don't, of course, give way unnecessarily to equals. If you are strong enough to be an imperial

---

[48] To M. I. Finley, *Aspects of Antiquity* (1968) 56, Thuc. was 'not an original thinker'. I disagree entirely. But how can such a question be settled, when we know so little of the political thought of the fifth century? On the absence of any provable close connections between Thuc. and any contemporary or earlier thinker, see Classen-Steup, *Thuk.* 1⁵⁻⁷ lxiii–viii.

power yourselves, then, human nature being what it is, you are bound to become one anyway. In that case, your rule (except when some very special circumstances apply) will be resented by all your subjects, and you may find yourselves driven to do some rather unpleasant things to them, in the effort to keep them down. But don't be a Cleon, and resort unnecessarily to terror, a weapon whose deterrent effect (like that of all deterrents) cannot anyway be relied on. Be rather more moderate with your subjects and with other weaker States than you need be, having regard to your power, as the Athenians generally were. Restrain yourselves as far as you can from always grasping at more, as the Athenians eventually did not. You may sometimes be able to risk a generous gesture, such as the Athenians refused to the Spartans during the Pylos affair;[49] but it would be foolish to go too far in that direction, because it is exceedingly unlikely that other States will behave equally quixotically to you.

You ask me whether I don't deplore all this, and advocate moral behaviour in dealings between States, as between individuals inside the State. Of course the situation is deplorable; but I seldom waste time on such useless reflections. I see the world as it is, and you would be well advised to do so too.[50] Morality is an admirable thing inside a State, which can have both a code of behaviour acknowledged by all and sanctions for maintaining it, so that conflicts of interest can be resolved by the arbitration of courts of justice and not by the strong coercing the weak. No one could doubt that Right is preferable to Might—when Right is both accepted as such by all parties and can be enforced. But neither condition obtains in international affairs: what is conceived as 'right' or 'wrong' in any given instance depends almost entirely on whose interests are in question, and the issue is settled ultimately by force, except in the rare cases in which strength is nicely balanced and both sides are sensible enough to realise that war can be an extraordinarily hazardous business. Learn all this from me, and you will be the better able to make the most of whatever chances you have.

It is precisely this 'moral bleakness' of Thucydides *in regard to international affairs* which is for me his unique virtue, shared with no other historian of antiquity and with few of any age. It is his wholesale application of the principle that 'moral' considerations of the kind that can and should be regarded inside the State are simply not transferable in their existing

[49] Gomme (*HCT* III 454 ff., esp. 458-60) makes quite a good case for the view that we need not necessarily think Thuc. believed Athens ought to have accepted the Spartan proposals (IV 17-20). But on seven of the nine other occasions on which, as in IV 21.2, Thuc. uses some form of the verb ὀρέγεσθαι, it has a strongly pejorative force; only in VI 16.6; 83.1 is it colourless. I feel that in IV 21.2 and 41.4 Thuc. is condemning the Athenians, if with no great acerbity; and cf. V 14.2; 15.2.

[50] As Woodhead (*TNP* 20) has well said, 'It is the confounding of morally and emotionally evocative words with the realities of the situation which is morally reprehensible, and that is in fact, as Thucydides is well aware, what people do'.

form to international affairs, *even to the actions of one's own State*, that gives him his unparalleled realism. He sees men as they are and not as he or we might wish them to be. And he ruthlessly applies to his own city, Athens, to which he was deeply devoted, the same analysis in terms of power politics as that which he applies to other cities—perhaps in an even more merciless way, because it is usually the Athenians who are in the foreground, and he views them with the same dispassionate eye as everyone else. (Even Polybius shows up poorly in contrast. In XVI xiv.6 he makes a 'concession to patriotism' in principle, and he shows patriotic bias frequently in practice: see Walbank, *HCP* I 12–13.) It is this realism and honesty in Thucydides which has made so many moderns unhappy in his company: it invites the *universal* application of criteria from which the patriot is bound to ask for his own State an exemption Thucydides would never be willing to grant.

This attitude of Thucydides is quite foreign to most of us today. In a world of competing States, almost every one of us obediently identifies with his own State and sees foreign affairs through its eyes; and if he criticises its behaviour, what he is usually criticising is the behaviour of a political faction different from the one to which he himself belongs. Speaking of Greek history, Andrewes has said (in Gomme, *HCT* IV 164), 'Evidence enough remains to show that the ordinary citizen, even of a great power acting arbitrarily, preferred to think that his city's action was morally justified'. That is very true. In what way has the situation changed in the modern world? We ourselves often condemn the narrow 'city particularism' of the Greeks and their limited brand of patriotism, hardly ever extending beyond a man's own *polis*. (Aristotle, *Pol.* VII 7, 1327^{b}29–33, said that the Greek race could have ruled the world if it could only have achieved a single *politeia*—though precisely what he meant by that must remain a problem!) But we conveniently forget the narrow nationalism which is the curse of the modern world, causing 'national security' to be exalted everywhere as the paramount and overriding consideration in State policy. What makes matters even worse now is that much of the world is divided into two basically hostile camps, between which a simple morality holds: broadly speaking, what 'We' are and do is good and right, what 'They' are and do is bad and wrong. ('We' may sometimes adopt a wrong policy, but this is due to mere misjudgment and not any moral deficiency.) The morality of the Cold War has imposed itself to an extent which scarcely anyone has altogether escaped, however much he may fancy himself to be unaffected. This makes the study of Thucydides more relevant than ever today, for 'Thucydides the Athenian', as he calls himself at the very opening of his History, looks at the Peloponnesian war not *as* an Athenian but as a man and a Greek, for whom (among Greeks at least) there was no 'we' and 'they', and who applied the same devastating analysis to the behaviour of both sides. His aim was not to teach moral lessons, but to make men better equipped to deal with life, by understanding it more profoundly. This has shocked some of those who have only partially understood him. Dionysius of Halicarnassus (*Epist. ad Cn. Pomp.* 3.9), criticising his account of the origins of the Peloponnesian war, condemns him for not putting the actions of his own city in a better light, as befits a patriot (an *anēr philopolis*).

The Greeks, who spent so much of their time fighting each other, admitted in theory that war was an evil. 'No one is so foolish as to choose war instead of peace', says Herodotus' Croesus (1 87.4), 'for in peace time sons bury their fathers, but in war, fathers bury their sons'. Thucydides was more realistic: he knew that in practice men indulge in war freely when they think they can gain something by it (IV 59.2; 62.2–3). He understood the consequences of war, that 'teacher by constraint', as he calls it,[51] and he never glorifies it. Above all he stresses, and he makes his characters stress, that to enter upon war, as men do, from a calculation that it will provide some advantage is dangerous in the extreme, because it is precisely in war that the unforeseen, the incalculable, the unexpected, is most likely to happen, and hence even informed calculation beforehand about its probable outcome is hazardous.[52] It is not a negligible contribution to the arguments that may deter a prospective aggressor, even in the twentieth century.

The reader may perhaps have been expecting a comparison to be drawn between Thucydides and two leading political theorists of more modern times: Machiavelli and Hobbes.[53] Thucydides and Machiavelli are certainly alike in their uncompromising realism; but as far as I can see at present the similarity does not otherwise go very deep. In at least one way the Florentine and the Athenian are poles apart: the former was above all a political theorist who constantly used historical examples (often bad ones, derived from misleading sources) to prove his many generalisations; the latter was a historian pure and simple, who mostly (as we have

---

[51] III 82.2, βίαιος διδάσκαλος. Gomme translates in one place 'teacher of violence', in another 'violent taskmaster' (*HCT* II 373, 384).

[52] See e.g. IV 62.4 on the part played by τὸ ἀστάθμητον (cf. III 59.1); note also II 11.4 (ἄδηλα); and I 78.1 ff., II 85.2, III 16.2, VII 28.3, 55.1, 61.3, 71.7, VIII 24.5 (all παράλογος). On the part played in war by τύχη, see most of the passages cited in n. 57 below.

[53] The one recent work I know which has much to say about these two writers in their relationship to Thucydides is Woodhead, *TNP* (see his Index, *s.vv.*). But our respective approaches and conclusions are different. Woodhead seems to have used, of Machiavelli, only *Il principe* and not the *Discorsi*, and of Hobbes, mainly those parts of *Leviathan* which emphasise striving for power. And a reader who does not already know his Hobbes may not realise that in Hobbes the ceaseless strife of man against man, described in the quotation from §11 of *Leviathan* given at the beginning of the book (*TNP* 2), is conceived by Hobbes as occurring in the 'state of nature' and as abandoned by common consent within a 'commonwealth'. I may add that I have not been able to obtain any illumination from Karl Reinhardt's essay, 'Thuk. und Machiavelli', in his *Vermächtnis der Antike* (Göttingen, 1960) 184–218. But see H. Strasburger, 'Die Entdeckung der polit. Gesch. durch Thuk.', in *Saeculum* 5 (1954) 395–428, at pp. 427–8 = *Thukydides* (*Wege der Forschung* 98, ed. Hans Herter, Darmstadt, 1968) 473–6. It was only after this book was in proof that there appeared the most illuminating analysis of Machiavelli that I have seen: Sir Isaiah Berlin's 'The Question of Machiavelli', in *New York Review of Books* XVII 7 (4 Nov. 1971) 20–32.

seen) took his generalisations for granted, as truths too obvious to require demonstration, and made no attempt at all to prove them by means of carefully selected historical examples. The one prescribed, the other described. Nor do we find in Machiavelli—so far as I have been able to discover from reading *The Prince* and the *Discourses on the First Decad of Livy*—the distinction drawn (as I have argued) by Thucydides between the moral behaviour which can properly be expected of individuals within the State and the entirely amoral actions of States in their dealings with each other. Machiavelli too recognised a fundamental dualism (which, like Thucydides, he did not explicitly formulate), but it was of a very different kind: between the canons of behaviour demanded by ordinary ethics and upheld by Christian principles, and those imposed by political expediency, not only upon States in their mutual dealings, but also, and more centrally, upon individuals who seek the welfare of their States, *even in their dealings with one another*. For Machiavelli, as Bernard Crick has put it in his recent English edition of *The Discourses* (Pelican Classics, 1970, pp. 65–7), 'Two standards are at work simultaneously. . . . He sees all the time two moralities side-by-side each making conflicting demands: the morality of the soul and the morality of the city'. Machiavelli ended with 'an uncomfortable and at times almost unbearable dilemma: two sets of traditional standards, often leading in completely opposite directions, but neither of them to be abandoned. There are times when it is necessary to do admittedly evil things for the preservation and the welfare of the political community—and if one is not so willing, one is simply stepping outside politics and, incidentally, abandoning it to those who have no scruples. But if one is willing, then, he seems to say, for God and man's sake, recognise that what for the moment you are doing is evil, and do not fall into calling it good'.

If any such painful moral conflict perplexed Thucydides, I for one can see no sign of it, although I dare say that others may. He would, I think, have been puzzled, and perhaps a little shocked, at Machiavelli's view that a wholehearted commitment to the welfare of one's State is likely to involve one in behaviour to one's fellow-citizens which is flat contrary to the useful ethical rules normally regarded as binding upon men in their relationships with each other. For Thucydides, within the individual community (the *polis* **or** whatever) the morality of that community could reign unquestioned, and only outside this sphere of recognised Right was Might the ultimate authority. The rule of Might there was a bitter fact, but it was one which men disregarded at their peril. Ethics had its own proper sphere, that of the community; but if one tried to use it to regulate the relations between sovereign States, it was all too likely to turn in one's hands into something very like mere self-justification—so Thucydides believed; and can he be refuted, even by those who most dearly wish that the facts were otherwise?

Much nearer to Thucydides in one single respect, his conception of inter-State relations, is another great 'realist', Thomas Hobbes, the author of what has been described as 'the greatest, perhaps the sole, masterpiece of political philosophy written in the English language' (Michael Oakeshott, in the Introduction to his edition of Hobbes' *Leviathan* [Oxford, 1955], p. viii). It is a material fact that the earliest published work of Hobbes was a translation of Thucydides (1628)—the first English translation to be made direct from the Greek. 'Sed mihi prae reliquis Thucydides placuit', wrote Hobbes in his old age, in the autobiography he composed in Latin elegiac couplets in 1672 (*LWTH* i lxxxviii). Hobbes, much more clearly than Thucydides, lays it down as a general principle that sovereign States, not being restrained by any external force, are as between themselves in 'the state of nature': his *Philosophical Rudiments concerning Government and Society* (the English translation, 1651, of the *De Cive*, of 1642), x §17 (= *EWTH* ii 141), is most explicit on this point. For Hobbes, of course, the 'state of nature' was anything but an ideal condition: in it the life of man was 'solitary, poor, nasty, brutish, and short' (*Leviathan*, §13). In the 'state of nature', for Hobbes, 'nothing can be unjust. The notions of right and wrong, justice and injustice have there no place. Where there is no common power, there is no law: where no law, no injustice' (*Leviathan*, §13). 'In the state of nature, profit is the measure of right' (*Philosophical Rudiments*, i §10). And so, 'in states, and commonwealths not dependent on one another, every commonwealth (not every man) has an absolute liberty, to do what it shall judge, that is to say, what that man, or assembly that representeth it, shall judge most conducing to their benefit. But withal, they live in the condition of a perpetual war, and upon the confines of battle, with their frontiers armed, and cannons planted against their neighbours round about' (*Leviathan*, §21). 'Covenants, without the sword, are but words' (*Leviathan*, §17).

Hobbes had a great admiration for Thucydides (see R. Schlatter, 'Thomas Hobbes and Thucydides', in *JHI* 6 [1945] 350–62), and in some ways he understood him thoroughly. 'But Thucydides is one, who, though he never digress to read a lecture, moral or political, upon his own text, *nor enter into men's hearts further than the acts themselves evidently guide him*: is yet accounted the most politic historiographer that ever writ'—thus Hobbes, in the Preface to his translation (*EWTH* viii viii): the words I have italicised seem to me marvellously perceptive. But the main body of his thought lies far from that of Thucydides; and, like most of us, he could grievously misunderstand the historian when it suited his political position to do so, as when he insisted that Thucydides 'least of all liked the democracy' and 'best approved of the regal government' (*Ibid.* xvi–xvii)— merely on the strength of the historian's favourable verdict on the Peisistratids (vi 54.5–6), and the famous passage on the ascendancy of Pericles (ii 65.9), in which Periclean Athens is described as 'in name a democracy, but in fact on the way to becoming rule by the first citizen'. Failing, like nearly all other translators, to grasp the significance of the imperfect tense of the verb (*egigneto*) in this much-quoted sentence, Hobbes, himself a believer in monarchy, read more into the passage than

Thucydides intended: under Pericles, Athens 'was in name, a state demo-cratical; but in fact, a government of the principal man'. (Cf. Chapter III, Part ii below.) Hobbes imagined that Thucydides had shared his own view of democracy: 'Is Democratia ostendit mihi quam sit inepta, et quantum coetu plus sapit unus homo' (*LWTH* i lxxxviii).

The History of Thucydides, as we have it, is unfinished: probably it never was finished. It may be that Thucydides would have ended with some grand generalisations, revealing those beliefs about society and government which we are mainly obliged to infer from a series of state-ments in his work dealing with specific facts and occasions. I do not myself believe for one moment that Thucydides would have done this; I think he would have agreed with Hobbes' verdict on him: 'Digressions for instruction's cause, and other such open conveyances of precepts, (which is the philosopher's part), he never useth; as having so clearly set before men's eyes the ways and events of good and evil counsels, that the narration itself doth secretly instruct the reader, and more effectually than can possibly be done by precept' (*EWTH* viii xxii). But Hobbes evidently felt that he himself had grasped Thucydides' 'message'; and in one respect at least I believe he had—better, perhaps, than anyone else has done. Since Hobbes' admiration for Thucydides was so unqualified, I think we must allow for the possibility that one of the strands which went to make up the complicated system of thought developed by Hobbes was provided partly by the History of Thucydides. The translation of Thucy-dides (1628) was published twelve years before Hobbes produced (in manuscript form, for the edification of his own circle) the work in which his political ideas can first be seen fairly complete: *The Elements of Law* (1640, published 1650: see the edition by F. Tönnies, Cambridge, 1928). What Hobbes made of the 'instruction' he believed he had found in Thucydides is another matter. Many of us may dislike much of the general philosophical theory of government which Hobbes devised, partly on the basis of his experience of the contemporary world and his reading of Thucydides, and we certainly have no reason to father it upon the his-torian; but is there not one thing the two men have unmistakably in common: the belief that a system of ethics applicable inside a political community can have no relevance in dealings between sovereign States?[54]

Again and again Thucydides concentrates his narrative upon climactic moments at which men had to make *important collective decisions* (see Appendix IV); and he tries—often with the aid of speeches—to put us in possession of the essential circumstances and show us what *caused* those decisions to be made. (The speeches actually delivered will frequently

---

[54] Of numerous recent books on Hobbes that I have consulted, none considers the poss-ibility of a direct influence of Thucydides upon Hobbes, of the kind I have suggested above; most hardly mention Thucydides except to record the fact that Hobbes' translation of the History was his first published work; the only one that has much to say about Thucydides is Leo Strauss, *The Political Philosophy of Hobbes* (Oxford, 1936): see his pp. 44, 59–60, 64–8, 79–80, 86 and n.2, and esp. 108–12.

have been among the most powerful determinants of the decisions in question.) It is this feature of Thucydides' method above all, I suggest, that gives his History the 'usefulness' he himself said he wished it to have (I 22.4).

Many recent writers have felt able to deny that Thucydides intended his History to have any particular usefulness, except in the realm of pure understanding. Thus de Romilly (UHT 42) can say that when Thucydides proclaims his work to be 'useful' (*ōphelima*, I 22.4) he is referring only to 'utilité dans le domaine de la seule connaissance'. The same point of view is to be found in Gomme (*HCT* I 149–50), H. P. Stahl (*Thuk.*, esp. 15–19) and others. I cannot see that a good case has been made for limiting Thucydides' claim that he wants his work to be found 'useful' to the sphere of knowledge alone. Thucydides used the word on some twenty-two other occasions, but never with the kind of meaning which this interpretation of I 22.4 requires: even in IV 59.3, for instance, the *advice* can be called useful because if taken it will result in the right *action*.

Now it is true that during the past forty years or so several scholars, notably Cochrane,[55] have made too much of similarities in outlook and method (real or imaginary) between Thucydides and some of the early Hippocratic writers who were his contemporaries, and have sometimes attributed to him a very practical purpose almost like that of the doctor. But the reaction against such views has gone too far. We need not suppose that Thucydides' approach to history was determined, or even greatly influenced, by the Hippocratic attitude to medicine. Nevertheless, as J. H. Finley has well said (*Thuc.* 70), 'in the latter half of the fifth century, similar tendencies appeared at the same time in different fields of investigation and the ideas proper to one subject proved fruitful in another'. The idea that most unites Thucydides and the best of the early Hippocratics is that human nature is constant in many ways, and that if you have observed precisely how it works in detail in a large number of actual cases, you can sometimes makes an accurate *prognōsis* of what is about to happen. A good brief explanation of this will be found in an article by D. L. Page, published in 1953.[56]

Thucydides refers to human nature or behaviour as a constant in a series of important passages: I 76.2,3; II 50.1; III 39.5; 45.7; 82.2; [84.2;] IV 19.4; 61.5; 108.4; V 68.2; 105.1,2; cf. I 121.4, etc.; he uses such expressions as *to anthrōpeion, anthrōpeia physis, physis anankaia, hē physis tōn anthrōpōn, pephyke anthrōpos, eiōthotes hoi anthrōpoi*, and the like. His employment of the 'compulsion'-words *anankē, anankazein* and their cognates is closely connected with his belief in the tendency of men to react to

[55] *TSH*, criticised by e.g. Schuller, TUAII (an able contribution); and Stahl, *Thuk.* (*passim*). Weidauer, *THS*, certainly went too far in assimilating Thuc. and certain Hippocratic works, but there is nevertheless much of value in his monograph.

[56] TDGPA 98–110. The fact that Page's identification of the Great Plague as measles has not been well received should not be allowed to obscure the usefulness of the passage I have cited. It is surprising not to find the article cited in Stahl's 8-page bibliography (*Thuk.* 172–9).

situations in a constant and sometimes predictable manner (see Chapter
II, Part ii below, on *anankasai* in 1 23.6). It is futile to object that he
never steps aside to point out what 'lesson' may be learnt from a particular sequence of events, or offers *advice* on the basis of the actions he has
described. The remarkable case-histories in the Hippocratic *Epidemics
I & III* also contain no therapeutic advice and record scarcely anything
in the way of 'treatment', yet it will hardly be maintained that they
were not compiled in order above all to be of practical use to the physician
in treating the sick. To clinch the matter beyond doubt, it is only necessary
to recall the terms in which Thucydides commends the two men on
whom he lavishes most praise: Themistocles and Pericles (cf. Chapter V,
Part ii below). Themistocles, he says, had exceptional foresight (*proheōra
malista*, 1 138.3); he was able to infer, on the basis of past experience,
what was going to happen in the future (*tōn mellontōn aristos eikastēs*).
Pericles also had foreknowledge of the future (*prognous*, II 65.5, cf.
proegnō, §13) and the ability to plan wisely in advance (*pronoia*, II 65.6;
cf. 62.5).

Very relevant here is the passage (II 48.3) in which Thucydides explains
why he is giving a detailed account of the Plague of Athens: it is to enable
men, if it should break out again, 'above all *to have some knowledge in advance*
and not be ignorant about it (*ti proeidōs mē agnoein*)'. Too often all attention
is concentrated on *mē agnoein* alone (Stahl, *Thuk.* 15 n. 19, quotes only
those two words!), and Thucydides is taken to be expressing the hope
that men will merely 'recognise' the disease—we are to suppose that he
would have been satisfied for people to nod their heads and say, 'Oh yes,
of course, this is the Plague they had at Athens during the Peloponnesian
war'! This is nonsense, and it ignores *proeidōs*. It is true that on four other
occasions Thucydides used *agnoein* to mean 'fail to recognise' (friend from
foe in a battle, for instance): but in v 68.2 he uses the word when he is
saying that the number of Spartans fighting at the battle of Mantinea
'*was not known* (*ēgnoeito*) on account of the secrecy of their political system'.
In II 48.3 he is saying that he wants people to have all available facts about
the Plague, so that they will *know in advance* what course the disease is
likely to take, including no doubt its disastrous effects in the moral
sphere. Whether they can actually *do* anything about it is up to them:
Thucydides warns that at Athens no treatment was found which would
work in all cases; what helped one sufferer harmed another. But the mere
knowledge of what is likely to happen, based on past experience (your
own, or what is communicated by others), is itself important, and will give
you the best possible chance of making use of what ability you have.

Now it has been ably argued by Stahl (*Thuk.*) that Thucydides did not
at all see men as consistently acting in a rational, calculating manner,
and always making logical and sensible choices—far from it: the historian
realised very well that human nature is subject to gusts of passion and
irrationality, resulting in entirely unpredictable behaviour. Moreover, he
knew that all kinds of unexpected things might happen at any time—

random, fortuitous events, to which he applies in particular the terms *tychē*[57] ('fortune' is the standard translation) and *ho paralogos* ('the incalculable': see n.52 above; add II 61.3). Of course this is true. It is worth citing in particular a passage in which Thucydides records how even the Chians, a people he has just praised warmly for their combination of good fortune and prudence (in which they were surpassed, he thinks, only by the Spartans!), came to grief to some extent *en tois anthrōpeiois tou biou paralogois*, 'by those incalculable factors which beset the life of man' (VIII 24.5). Of course these factors make long-term prediction a hazardous business.[58] But the passages praising Themistocles and Pericles which we have noticed already are conclusive proof, against Stahl (who does not even cite them),[59] that Thucydides did think the very wise and experienced man could plan for the future, and might be justified by the event, provided his plans were not upset by too many unforeseeable circumstances. Although in time of war it is very hard to behave prudently, in peace time men's judgment is better, and they are not constantly subjected to 'constraints which allow them no choice' (Thuc. III 82.2).

Thucydides surely wanted his History to be of practical use to the citizen (not just the politician, of course, if particularly to him), in very much the same way as the author of *Epidemics I & III* designed his work to be used by the practising physician. The History of Thucydides would provide the citizen with a series of political case-histories, complete with all the relevant facts—above all, the motives from which the men concerned had acted—brought out as fully and accurately as possible. Government in Greek cities was direct rather than representative: instead of electing men every few years, as we do, to make all the major decisions for them, those Greek citizens who had political rights constantly had to take decisions in person, on small matters and great. So I believe that Thucydides, like the author of the Hippocratic *Epidemics*, intended the *knowledge* gained from his case-histories to issue in informed and intelligent *action*. His readers would have to make their own decisions, based on knowledge of which he could supply only a part. A less didactic writer than Polybius ('le faux Thucydide', as he has been called!),[60] he did not feel the need to labour the usefulness of his work in the way Polybius does from his first chapter onwards (I i.2; cf. esp. xxxv.9).

Thucydides says in I 22.4, 'It will be sufficient if my work is judged useful by those who wish to examine the clear truth both about what has been (*tōn genomenōn*) and about what is to be at some time in the future and will, *kata to anthrōpinon*, be the same or similar (*toioutōn kai*

---

[57] The most important passages are I 78.2; 84.3 (with 140.1; IV 55.3; VII 61.3); II 62.5, with 87.2; III 49.4 (with IV 3.1); 97.2; IV 18.3–5; 64.1 (with VI 78.2); V 75.3; 102; 104 with 112.2; VI 23.3.

[58] Though Thuc. sometimes refers to 'unexpected' events which were by no means unforeseeable, e.g. in II 85.2; III 16.2; VII 28.3; 55.1.

[59] Stahl similarly omits most of the passages about human nature that I have quoted above. Cf. Brunt's review of Stahl, in *CR* 81 = n.s. 17 (1967), at pp. 279–80.

[60] De Romilly, UHT 57.

paraplēsiōn)'. Now the meaning of *kata to anthrōpinon* has been disputed. Some would translate 'human nature being what it is', 'according to the laws of human nature'—with the implication that it is because of the constancy of human nature that succeeding events will be 'the same or similar'. Stahl (*Thuk.*, esp. 33–5), insisting that 'to anthrōpinon' is not merely human *nature* but the human *situation*, with all its uncertain factors, both internal and external, would translate 'in the conditions of human existence' ('die Bedingungen menschlicher Existenz'). But if that is what Thucydides meant, why did he put *kata to anthrōpinon* in the middle of his phrase *kai tōn mellontōn pote authis . . . toioutōn kai paraplēsiōn esesthai*? I see no escape from the conclusion that in this sentence the things that happen at some time in the future will be 'the same as or similar to' those that have happened in the past *because* they will be *kata to anthrōpinon*; and *kata to anthrōpinon* must then be a factor making for constancy. Stahl, rightly stressing that the inconsistent factors can sometimes play a very important role, minimises the enduring ones, and ignores Thucydides' emphasis on the possibility of intelligent foreknowledge.

We can also now reply effectively to those who, like Gomme (*HCT* 1 149), wish to make the events which in 1 22.4 are still about to occur 'future to Thucydides, but past or contemporary to the reader'. We can say that if, human nature being what it is, there will be much in common between what Thucydides describes and what happens between his day and ours, then the same process will continue, however much it may be disturbed by external factors, into the indefinite future—'as long as the nature of man remains the same' (III 82.2; cf. n. 20 above). If you, the reader of Thucydides, really understand your own particular situation properly, in the light of all you know of men's behaviour in similar situations in the past (including of course the information provided by Thucydides), you will know how events are likely to develop; and then—and only then—you will be able to make effective use of whatever judgment and ability you possess, and perhaps alter the course of events. Sometimes, as in the case of the Plague at Athens, there may be nothing you can effectively do. Sometimes you may be overwhelmed by random events of which you could not be expected to take account. But on many occasions you may be able to influence events, or at any rate shape your own behaviour wisely. Thucydides, of course, was not such a fool as to think that 'history repeats itself'—although this has been said of him by people who ought to know better. It is above all *patterns of behaviour* which are likely to be repeated, although even then there will always be different factors involved. Thucydides, as we have noticed, does not try to give practical advice: he knew very well that in every situation in the future there will be new elements, features different from those of the situations he himself has described. But because of the constancy of human nature there will also be features you will recognise as being 'the same as, or similar to' those described in the History, and the recognition of these will help you to make your own decisions wisely. That is surely why

Thucydides conceived his History as 'useful', and 'a possession for all time' —as indeed it is.

I believe that Lucian, in his excellent little satire, *How to Write History* (composed in A.D. 166), very well understood what Thucydides is saying in I 22.4. 'He introduces the concept of usefulness', says Lucian, 'and the purpose (*telos*) which a sensible man would attribute to history: according to him, it is that if men ever again encounter similar circumstances, they should be able, by paying attention to what has been recorded of the past, to deal properly with the situation that confronts them'.[61] Men certainly realised in Thucydides' time that historical knowledge of the past could be used as an indication of what was likely to happen in the future, and hence as a guide to prudent action in the present. Even Andocides (III 2), hardly a profound thinker, could advise the Athenians in 392/1 to treat the events of the past (which he relates with considerable distortion) as indications of what was about to happen, and to act accordingly.

We may once more go back to Hobbes, who declares in the Preface to his translation of Thucydides (*EWTH* VIII vii) that 'the principal and proper work of history [is] to instruct and enable men, by the knowledge of actions past, to bear themselves prudently in the present and providently towards the future', and who defines 'prudence' in *Leviathan* §3—in terms that remind us of Thucydides' appreciation of Themistocles, cited above—as 'a *presumption* of the *future*, contracted from the *experience* of time *past*'.

It has not been possible, in this brief analysis, to deal adequately with several rival interpretations of Thucydides. Most of them, however, rest upon beliefs about the actual historical events of the late fifth century which I hope to have disproved in this book. For example, the position adopted by Vogt (BPT: see Part i of this Chapter) is derived from assumptions about the nature and effects of the Megarian decree which I shall show in Chapter VII below to be untenable. And Strasburger's view (in TPSDA: see Part i again) that Thucydides was deeply critical, upon what one can only call moral grounds, of the imperial policy of Pericles can also be seen to be fallacious when we have understood the equally self-centred and selfish nature of Spartan policy—for it is an essential part of Strasburger's case (see TPSDA 35 ff. = 523–4 ff.) that the self-interested characteristics attributed by the historian to the Athenians are presented not (as I of course believe) as natural and almost inevitable in any powerful State, but as peculiar to Athens, and that the Spartans are depicted by Thucydides in a very different light, as being morally superior! That Thucydides was not such a simpleton as this, and that there is not the least reason to think that he accepted Strasburger's idealised picture of Sparta, will emerge clearly at a later stage in our investigation (Chapter IV, Part vi below). As Gomme has pointed out (*HCT* I 245), 'we

---

[61] Lucian, *Quomodo sit historia conscribenda* 42 (reading ἐν ποσί). There is a translation of this work in the Loeb edition of Lucian (vol. VI 3–73), by K. Kilburn (1959).

always judge Athens by the highest moral standard. We seldom speak of the "aggression" or the "selfish purposes" and "narrow outlook" of the Persians, of Philip and Alexander, of the early Romans, not to mention later empires.' If only we can rid ourselves of the almost universal tendency to expect Athens to behave better than other great powers and to condemn her more harshly than other States when she fails to come up to our expectations, we shall have less difficulty in understanding Thucydides.

(iii)
Athens

I intend to say very little of a general nature about Athens. Russell Meiggs' book on the Athenian Empire should be published at about the same time as this book, and there is every reason to think that it will admirably fill the large gap in the modern literature caused by the absence of any proper treatment of this subject which takes account of all the new evidence that has been accumulating during the past generation, above all through the inscriptions revealed by the excavations conducted by the American School at Athens.

Athens, hegemon of the anti-Persian Delian League[62] since its foundation in 478/7, became by degrees the mistress of an empire, in the sense that Athens could and did control the allied cities to almost any extent she wished, although in practice they continued to govern themselves much as before, enjoying a precarious *autonomia* in theory, and to a considerable extent (though in varying degrees) also in practice.[63] I believe the process of transformation from *hēgemonia* to *archē* was virtually complete by the time of the Thirty Years Peace between Athens and Sparta and their respective allies in 446/5. In an article published in 1954[64] I expressed certain views about the nature of the Athenian empire and the attitude of the allies towards it which have since been referred to by many other historians, with varying degrees of approval and disapproval. I was then mainly concerned to correct widespread misconceptions about the empire, and I expressly disclaimed any attempt to give a 'balanced judgment' upon it (CAE 40; cf. NJAE II 279). I do not propose to undertake that task now either, as it seems to me unprofitable to do so without placing

---

[62] On various problems of the nature and constitution of the Delian League, see Appendix V.

[63] For the meaning of αὐτονομία (and ἐλευθερία), see the very acute analysis of Bickerman, APT; cf. my CAE 20–1. Against the very popular view that the allies were officially divided into two groups, 'autonomous' and 'subject', see CAE 16–21.

[64] CAE; cf. NJAE, esp. II 277–9. Those who have expressed agreement include Pleket, TPAE (specifically on Thasos); Forrest, *EGD*, esp. 243 (cf. 38–42); Andrewes, MDPLS 6; and MD 78–9 and nn. 33–4; Bickerman, APT 318 & n. 20; D. Gillis, 'Collusion at Mantineia', in *Istituto Lombardo, Rend. Lett.*, 97 (1963) 199–226; and 'The Revolt at Mytilene', in *AJP* 92 (1971) 38–47; contrast e.g. D. W. Bradeen, in *Historia* 9 (1960) 257–69; T. J. Quinn, in *Historia* 13 (1964) 257–66; and 18 (1969) 22–30; H. Popp, in *Historia* 17 (1968) 425–43. See also J. de Romilly, 'Thuc. and the Cities of the Athenian Empire', in *BICS* 13 (1966) 1–12.

the whole subject in a much wider context: the class struggle in Greece, from the earliest episode in which we are able sufficiently to identify the forces involved (the Solonian crisis in Attica at the beginning of the sixth century), through the sixth, fifth and fourth centuries, and into the Hellenistic and Roman periods. I propose to deal with that subject in the 'J. H. Gray Lectures' which I shall be delivering at Cambridge University early in 1973 and which I hope to publish in the same year. Seen against that background, the social conflicts which are revealed by Thucydides and our other sources in the second half of the fifth century can be much better understood. However, in view of the controversy which is still going on about the character of the Athenian empire, I feel obliged to give a brief summary of what seem to me the main elements in the situation.

We must start from the fact that by the fifth century, when rule by hereditary aristocracies had become rare in the Greek world, the members of the governing class who alone possessed full political rights in a Greek oligarchy would be defined by a property qualification. (If the richest third of the citizens enjoyed political rights, a late-fifth-century oligarchy might be considered relatively broad-based, to judge by the one surviving contemporary work which has anything relevant to say on the matter.)[65] The fifth- and fourth-century sources, including of course Plato and Aristotle, always treat oligarchy as the rule of the men of property, the rich;[66] and it is recognised that oligarchy exists to promote the interest of those who are well off,[67] and tends to produce extremes of wealth and poverty (with most of those who do not enjoy political rights becoming paupers, *ptōchoi*), and out of one city to create two, one of the rich and the other of the poor, each combining to oppose the other.[68]

---

[65] Ps.-Herodes, *Peri Politeias* 30–1. Speaking of the oligarchies maintained or installed by the Spartans in his day, the orator asks, 'Where is there so small a city in which a third [of the citizens] does not share in the control of affairs?', and he adds, 'For he who has no arms or any other means to participate in public affairs is deprived—and has been for as long as precedents can be cited—not by the Spartans but by Fortune'. (According to the conventions of Greek oratory, the 'third' need hardly be considered a minimum.) On this speech, see esp. Wade-Gery, KH (= *EGH* 271–92), who gives a full bibliography; cf. A. Fuks, 'Kritias, Ps.-Herodes, and Thessaly', in *Eos* 48 (= *Symb. R. Taubenschlag dedic.* II, 1957) 47–50. For editions, esp. by Drerup and Meyer, see Wade-Gery, KH 19 n. 1 (= *EGH* 271 n. 1); add now U. Albini (Florence, 1968), whose edition I have not seen. The date of the speech is almost certainly mid-404, as demonstrated by J. S. Morrison and Wade-Gery.

[66] Aristotle is by far the most important witness: see e.g. *Pol.* III 8, 1279^{b}17–18 (οἱ τὰς οὐσίας ἔχοντες); IV 4, 1290^{b}1–2 (οἱ πλούσιοι); and many other passages, e.g. III 8, 1279^{b}20–80^{a}6 (esp. 79^{b}39–80^{a}1); 5, 1278^{a}21–5; IV 4, 1290^{b}17–20. For Plato, see esp. *Rep.* VIII 550c (οἱ πλούσιοι), 551ab (ὅρος πολιτείας ... πλῆθος χρημάτων), 553a (ἐκ τιμημάτων); *Polit.* 301a. It would be very wrong to suppose that the picture presented by Plato and Arist. is true only of the fourth century and not of the fifth: see my CAE 21 ff., esp. 24–8. Even a fifth-century poet like Euripides takes for granted a political classification according to property: see e.g. *Suppl.* 238–45, 406–8, 433–41 etc.

[67] See esp. Arist., *Pol.* III 7, 1279^{b}7–10 (οἱ εὔποροι). Cf. Cicero, who (anticipating Marx, but from an opposite point of view) declared that States exist above all in order to preserve the right of private property: *De Offic.* II 73, cf. 78, 85; I 21.

[68] See esp. Plato, *Rep.* VIII 552b, d and 551d.

In the late fifth century, political subjection, whether total or partial, and whether of one class within a Greek state to another or of one state to another (or to an outside power such as Persia), was often described by words which in their strict sense referred to actual slavery: the verb *douleuein* (to enslave), and the nouns *doulōsis* (the act or process of enslavement: see Thuc. I 141.1; III 10.4) and *douleia* (the condition of slavery).⁶⁹ These words could be applied not only to cases where a considerable degree of subjection was involved, but to any restriction of complete liberty of action (see Thuc. I 141.1). Thucydides can make the Mantinean generals in 418 refer to their earlier membership of the Peloponnesian League as *douleia* (v 69.1). Too often modern historians use the words 'slavery' and 'enslavement' of the condition of the allies of Athens in the Delian League, without even placing them in inverted commas;⁷⁰ and in particular they fail to realise that for large numbers of poor citizens in allied states, who could not hope to qualify for political rights in an oligarchy, the prospect of enjoying a very considerable degree of political freedom in a democracy upheld by Athens would involve a far smaller degree of *douleia* than the total, or almost total, subjection to their own propertied class which would necessarily occur under an oligarchy, dependent upon Sparta or Persia or even completely free from outside control.

The point of view of the determined would-be oligarch of the late fifth century is admirably expressed by the author of the pseudo-Xenophontic *Athēnaiōn Politeia*, who is usually known in the English-speaking world as 'the Old Oligarch'.⁷¹ With a really good constitution, he says, under which the ablest men make the laws in their own interests, and the 'good' discipline the 'bad' and refuse to allow 'madmen' to do any of the talking, the lower classes (the demos) would quickly fall into *douleia* (Ps.-Xen., *Ath. Pol.* I 9, cf. 4, 6); but as things were, the Athenian demos to some extent took measures to prevent this from happening in the allied cities (I 14, 16, 18; III 10; cf. esp. Thuc. VIII 48.6). The lower classes, he realised, did not want to be in subjection under what seemed to him a

⁶⁹ See *ATL* III 155–7 for a useful collection of the evidence in Thucydides. But it is a mistake, in my opinion, to treat παρὰ ȷτὸ καθεστηκός in Thuc. I 98.4 as meaning 'in breach of the constitution' of the Delian League (*Id.* 156–7). The phrase means 'contrary to custom' on the only other occasion on which it is used by Thuc. (VII 67.2; cf. I 130.1; IV 97.3 etc.), and it surely has that meaning in I 98.4.

⁷⁰ A recent example is provided by C. W. Fornara, *Herodotus* (Oxford, 1971) 80–1, who can speak of the Peloponnesian war as 'begun for the sake of freedom' (p. 81), and of the Athenian empire as threatening 'enslavement—limitation of autonomy like that effected by Cyrus for the Ionian Greeks, like that Xerxes would have effected for Athens by installing his partisans' (p. 80). This nicely illustrates how scholars can confuse themselves by using words like 'freedom' and 'enslavement' in a mechanical and abstract way, without asking the vital question, 'Freedom (or enslavement) for whom, and of what sort?' To pretend that the subjection of the Ionians to Persian-backed despots was subjection in anything like the same sense, or for the same people, as that involved in membership of the Athenian empire, is to obscure the vital issues beyond hope of clarification.

⁷¹ Ps.-Xen., *Ath. Pol.*: see CAE 24–5. On the date and purpose of this work see Appendix VI.

good form of government, but to be free and to rule (Ps.-Xen., *Ath. Pol.* 1 8).

Only one reference has survived from antiquity, as far as I know, to an artistic personification of Oligarchy in which a man like Pseudo-Xenophon might have taken pleasure. On a memorial to the Athenian oligarch Critias (in what city, we do not know) was a sculptured lady, doubtless labelled 'Oligarchia': she was shown 'carrying a torch and setting fire to Dēmokratia' (another lady, perhaps of meaner bearing), and she was accompanied by a spirited hexameter couplet, commemorating the 'good men who for a brief while held the accursed Athenian demos in contempt' (Schol. Aeschin. 1 39, reproduced as Critias, 88 A 13, in Diels-Kranz, *FVS* II⁵⁻⁸ 374.

In those cases in which an allied city could be reasonably sure of securing its independence outside the Athenian empire *and* in which a democracy could maintain itself without interference from beyond its borders, I can see no reason why the lower classes should have any desire to remain within the empire. But with the exception of Amphipolis and perhaps Olynthus and a few other cities (especially islands in the western Aegean), how many of the allies were in this category? In the first place, a large number of the cities in the empire were in serious danger of falling under Persian or native control as soon as the Athenian alliance collapsed —not merely the mainland cities of Asia, for there is a good deal of evidence, from the late sixth century down to the time of Alexander, showing island states as well as mainland ones suffering interference from Persian satraps and nobles, if not actual Persian rule. (As far as I know, this evidence has never been fully collected and analysed.) The main cause of the Ionian Revolt of 499–3 was the desire of the Greeks to be free not merely from Persian domination but from the rule of the 'tyrants' who were maintained in power in their cities by the Great King and his satraps (see esp. Hdts IV 137.2 ff.; V 37–38). After the crushing of the Revolt, Darius ordered the installation of 'democracies' throughout Ionia (Hdts VI 43.3; cf. Diod. X 25.4); but tyrants turn up several times thereafter in Greek and Carian cities of Asia and the neighbouring islands (see How and Wells, *CH* II 80). In the 450s the revolt of Erythrae from Athens was very probably effected by tyrants backed by Persia (see M/L 40 = Tod I² 29 = D 10 in *ATL* II 54–7, lines 27, 33, with M/L's notes; and cf. *ATL* III 252–7). In 440 Pissuthnes, satrap of Lydia, helped the Samian oligarchs in their revolt (Thuc. 1 115.4–5 etc.); and in 427 there were expectations that he might similarly join in the revolt of Lesbos (III 31.1). Between 430 and 427 Itamanes and Pissuthnes interfered in more than one episode of a *stasis* at Colophon and Notium, doubtless on the side of oligarchs (III 34). Many Athenians in 412–11 believed that if a more oligarchical form of government were introduced at Athens the Great King would be prepared to trust them and give them financial help in their war against Sparta (Thuc. VIII 48.2; 53.1, 3; 54.1 etc.). In the fourth century the influence of Persian satraps—often men of enormous wealth[72]—and local dynasts like the Hecatomnids of Caria was by no means limited to the mainland Greek cities (which in theory were fully under Persian rule from at least 387/6 to the time of Alexander), but extended also to some of the islands, which were supposed to be independent.[73] And except in very special circumstances (for instance, when leading Persians were themselves at odds, as in *c.* 404–1, when Cyrus was in Asia, planning to capture the throne),[74] a Persian nabob or a native dynast who found reason to interest himself in a Greek city was unlikely in the extreme to favour democracy: he would naturally back oligarchs or tyrants. Even if he were partly hellenised, he might simply take over Greek cities as his own personal possession—as when in the so-called 'Xanthian stele' (M/L 93 = Tod I² 93) of the late fifth century we find a Lycian dynast boasting, in Greek hexameters, that he had 'sacked many acropoleis' and bestowed them upon his relatives as part of their dominion.

Xenophon, when writing about north-west Asia Minor in *c.* 400 B.C., several times mentions Greek dynasts who, under Persian patronage, ruled over extensive areas of land and even Greek cities. Zenis and his talented widow Mania, both of Dardanus, acted as under-satraps for Pharnabazus of a very large district in the Troad; their son-in-law Meidias of Scepsis aspired to succeed to Mania's position but was thwarted by the Spartan general Dercyllidas (*HG* III i.10–28), who was able to free from his control the cities of Scepsis and Gergis (on the hills above the Scamander valley), where much of the vast movable wealth of this family was stored—enough, according to Dercyllidas, to provide pay for an army of eight thousand men for nearly a year (§28)! Doubtless they owned extensive areas of land as well. All three of the Achaemenid kings who ruled the Persian empire in the first half of the fifth century had made valuable grants of lands (or of the Persian revenues therefrom) to leading Greeks who settled in Asia Minor. Thucydides (I 138.5) records the gift by Artaxerxes I to Themistocles of the revenues of three Greek cities: Magnesia on the Maeander, and also (but see Gomme, *HCT* I 292, 445) Lampsacus and Myus. Two other Greek families were still ruling in *c.* 400 B.C. over lands in southern Aeolis which their ancestors had received from the Great King. Eurysthenes and Procles had inherited a large tract, including Teuthrania and

---

[72] See M. Dandamayev, 'Achaemenid Babylonia', in *Ancient Mesopotamia: Socio-Economic History. A Collection of Studies by Soviet Scholars*, ed. I. M. Diakonoff (Moscow, 1969), 296–311, at pp. 299–303. Some native princes of Asia Minor were also reputed to be vastly rich: see e.g. Hdts VII 28.2 for Pythius the Lydian.

[73] See e.g. Dem. xv 9 (Samos); Tod II 192 = *SIG*³ 283 (Chios: see Tod's notes), with Alexander's other letter to Chios, recently re-edited by W. G. Forrest, in *Klio* 51 (1969) 201–6; and other evidence relating to these islands and Rhodes, Cos, Lesbos, etc. Among some interesting inscriptions, the most obvious and easily available are perhaps Tod II 191 (Eresus on Lesbos), and—in relation to cities on the mainland—Tod II 138 (Mylasa) and 155 (Erythrae), also 165, a treaty between Erythrae and Hermias, the ruler (in succession to Eubulus) of Atarneus and Assos (see the refs. in Tod II, p. 190). For the Hecatomnid dynasty, see esp. Glotz-Roussel-Cohen, *HG* IV i.21–9.

[74] See Diod. XIII 104.6 (where for 'Pharnabazus' we must read 'Tissaphernes'); Xen., *Anab.* I i.7; cf. ix.9.

Halisarna, granted by Darius I to their ancestor, King Damaratus of Sparta (*HG* III i.6; *Anab.* II i.3; VII viii. 17; cf. Hdts VI 70.2). And Gorgion and Gongylus were ruling a wide area containing the Greek cities of Myrina and Gryneion on the Gulf of Elaea and Gambreion and Palaegambreion up the valley of the Caicus, donated to their ancestor, Gongylus of Eretria, by Xerxes, for services rendered (Xen., *HG* III i.6; cf. *Anab.* VII viii.8, 17; Thuc. I 128.6); their mother Hellas was living at Pergamon (*Anab.* VII viii.8), and perhaps the family ruled that city too. Of the Greek towns known to have been subject to the families of Damaratus and Gongylus, only Myrina and Gryneion are recorded among the tribute-paying members of the Delian League; the others no doubt remained under Persian rule throughout the fifth century, as did a number of other Greek cities in Asia, some of them of appreciable size, like Smyrna and Magnesia.

We may be sure that the three great Greek families we happen to know about from Xenophon were by no means the only ones which exercised something like despotic power under Persian patronage. We know of others later, in the fourth century. Shortly before the middle of that century the satrap Ariobarzanes is said to have given possession of various Greek cities to his *protégé* Philiscus of Abydus (Dem. XXIII 141–2; cf. Xen., *HG* VII i.27; Diod. XV 70.2). Other Greeks (and doubtless hellenised native dynasts) received similar favours. Memnon the Rhodian *condottiere*, for example, seems to have owned a wide extent of land in the Troad, which was known in Alexander's time as 'Memnon's country' (Arr., *Anab.* I xvii.8; Polyaen. IV iii.15; cf. Dem. XXIII 154, 157; Ps.-Arist., *Oecon.* II ii.29; 1351^{b}1 ff.; perhaps Strabo XIII i.11, p. 587; and see Beloch, *GG* III^2 i.148 and n.1). It is hard to believe that Greeks of this sort would tolerate democracy if they could help it, although some of them may have been citizens of states with democratic constitutions, and may have owned property in the area controlled by their city, in addition to 'King's land' upon the revenues of which they would be liable (unless specifically exempted) to Persian taxation.[75] Of course there will have been exceptional men who preferred to work with democratic Athens rather than with Persia, like Heracleides of Clazomenae, nicknamed 'King' (Arist., *Ath. Pol.* 41.3), who received Athenian citizenship and is even said to have been elected Strategos (see M/L 70 = *IG* II^2 8, with M/L's notes; and the literary references given by Kirchner, *PA* I, no. 6489). But such men are likely to have been very rare. Xenophon (*HG* III i.20–8) implies that it would be a humiliation for Meidias to have to live as an ordinary private citizen in his native Scepsis. No doubt it was Greeks of this stamp among whom Lysander found his most ardent supporters in the last years of the Peloponnesian war (see Chapter IV, Part vi below). These people were very likely to be better off under Persian rule. And their cities as a whole might sometimes benefit economically (as in the Hellenistic period) from their

---

[75] J. M. Cook (PCI 16–17; *GIE* 122–3) believes that Hdts VI 42.2 refers to the taxation of such individual landowners; but see Appendix VII.

'conspicuous consumption' and their occasional benefactions—but equally the political consequences to the lower classes would be serious: oligarchy or even tyranny would surely be an almost inevitable consequence.

The Greek cities in Asia, therefore, had potential Greek tyrants or oligarchs of great substance to worry about, as well as Persian and native grandees who might try to interfere in their affairs. But even if individual tyrants or groups of oligarchs were successful in holding on to power in some of the cities, with Persian support, the Greeks of Asia in general evidently wanted to be entirely free of Persian domination. (For the late fifth and early fourth centuries, see e.g. Thuc. VIII 84.4–5; Xen., *HG* III i.3, 16 ff.) When Alexander in 334 proclaimed that democracy was to be universal in the Greek cities of Asia which he had 'liberated'[76] he surely did so because he realised that it was precisely the democrats in those cities who were most anti-Persian. In the area ruled or threatened by Persia, therefore, democrats in the fifth century would have particular reason to desire the continuance of the Delian League, even after it had turned into an Athenian empire. And even apart from the considerable area of possible Persian interference, how many Greek cities could be sure of satisfying a desire to be both independent and democratic? Surely not many.

It would be a mistake to exaggerate. Apart from a few leading politicians who might expect great gain from being the recipients of Athenian trust and goodwill, I doubt if many of the ordinary citizens of the subject states felt any real enthusiasm towards Athens: they may rather have seen Athenian domination simply as a 'lesser evil' than being subjected to their own oligarchs. And in some cities ruling groups might be able to stamp out all overt opposition, or keep it to a minimum by curbing the natural oppressiveness of oligarchy. Especially in some backward areas, peasants accustomed to an age-old system of government by their 'betters' might have come to accept their lot with resignation (cf. Arist., *Pol.* IV 13, 1297[b]6–8; VI 4, 1318[b]16–20). But political freedom was a matter of the highest importance to very many Greeks, and the cardinal fact that under an oligarchy only the propertied classes enjoyed real freedom was bound to drive many of the lower orders in many cities into reliance, however reluctant, upon Athens, as the evidence shows that in fact it did.

Even where there is no proof of any positive attachment to Athens on the part of the lower classes we can at least see on several occasions, not least at Mytilene in 427 (Thuc. III 27–8),[77] a marked difference of attitude towards the imperial city between the ruling Few and the mass of lower-class citizens. The Mytilenaean governing class ardently desired their own

[76] Arr., *Anab.* I xviii. 1–2; cf. xvii.10; II v.8; Tod II 192.3–4, etc. See E. Badian, 'Alexander the Great and the Greeks of Asia', in *ASI* (Ehrenberg) 37–69, at pp. 43–6.

[77] After more than one unsuccessful attempt by critics of my CAE to get rid of the evidence provided by Thuc. III 27–8 (see CAE 4), it is a relief to turn to Gillis' recent article in *AJP* (see n. 64 above), where full references will be found to recent works on the subject, and a very sensible analysis of the whole incident. For the lack of enthusiasm for revolt in Lesbos during the Ionian war, see my CAE 8 (with nn. 4–7).

particular brand of 'freedom'—limited of course to their own circle,
for the continued subjection to themselves of the demos in their own city
was just as much an essential element in that 'freedom' as their own
liberation from Athenian control. The lower classes, when at last they were
given arms (for a sortie), at once mutinied. It would be very simple-
minded to interpret their one immediate demand (for a general distribution of the little remaining food) as the sum total of what they wanted.
The fact that the Mytilenaean oligarchs did not see fit to comply with
their very reasonable request but incontinently surrendered at discretion
to the Athenian general is a sufficient indication that they took the first
demand of the demos at more than its face value, and realised that the
lower classes could not be relied upon to fight, even if that first demand
were met. But whatever conclusion may be drawn about the probable
attitude of the demos, the inescapable fact is that there were two distinct
groups, with two very different attitudes to revolt: one was determinedly
hostile to Athens, the other uninterested in fighting for a 'freedom' which
would benefit not themselves but their rulers, and indeed would be likely
to result in increased domination by the Few.

The demos (in the sense of the lower classes) had leaders who were very
rarely men of humble origin and might well be rich and even blue-
blooded. (It was hardly possible for a Greek to play an important role in
politics unless he was well off.) If such leaders were not available in
sufficient numbers, the lower classes by themselves would probably have
little chance of either setting up or maintaining a democracy. Sometimes
we find the expression 'the demos' applied to their leaders alone (for an
extreme example, see Xen., *HG* v iv.46), although as a rule these leaders
are called by some such name as 'the *prostatai* of the demos' (see e.g. Thuc.
iv 66.3, carefully distinguishing between the *prostatai* of the demos and their
followers). Now some of the leaders of the demos in cities within the
Athenian empire might well be acting entirely in their own selfish
interests. The temptation to pretend to a democratic outlook might be
greatly increased by the political and economic advantages to be derived
from acting as a leader of the pro-democratic faction in such a city (see my
NJAE ii 270–9). But even if we allow for the existence of many such people,
the fact remains that a man would normally gain his position as a 'leader of
the demos' because the mass of the people believed, rightly or wrongly,
that they could rely on his being *on their side*—a *dēmotikos*,[78] who could be
expected to promote their interests, whatever his inner motives might be.
And there will have been a certain number of men among the upper
classes who preferred democracy for its own sake—men who agreed with
Democritus that 'Poverty in a democracy is as much to be preferred to

---

[78] See my CAE 22–4 on the meaning of this word. Cf. the *populares* of the Roman Republic: *popularis* is the Latin equivalent of δημοτικός. Many of the leading *populares* were
anything but 'democratic', but they were believed to be 'on the side of the common
people'.

what is called prosperity under the control of potentates (*para tois dynasteisi*) as is freedom to slavery' (68 B 251, in Diels-Kranz, *FVS* II⁵⁻⁸ 195).

Of great interest in this connection is the text in which Thucydides (VIII 73.2) shows most clearly just what he means by the word 'demos' when he wants to be precise. In VIII 21 he had mentioned a revolution at Samos in 412 in which the 'demos' had risen against their men of power (*dynatoi, dynatōtatoi*), executing 200 and exiling another 400, and appropriating their land and houses. This 'demos' now administered the State, entirely excluding the *geōmoroi* (the old ruling class of landowners) from public affairs, and making it illegal for them to intermarry with members of the demos. Shortly afterwards, in the spring of 411, we find this 'demos' in its turn trying to set itself up as an oligarchy, numbering as few as 300. But as soon as the demos which had led[79] the revolution of 412 ceased to be the leading section of the lower classes and aspired to oligarchic rule, Thucydides felt unable to call it the 'demos', a term which had been perfectly appropriate during the 412 revolution: he now transferred that term to the lower classes, whom the 300 intended to dominate. 'Those of the Samians', he says (73.2), 'who, as the demos (*kai ontes dēmos*), had risen against the *dynatoi*, now changed their role, . . . entered into a conspiracy to the number of 300, and were going to make an attack on the other Samians, as being the demos' (*hōs dēmōi onti*). The conspiracy was crushed, with Athenian help, and the real Samian demos, now referred to twice by Thucydides as 'the majority' (*hoi pleiones*, 73.3, 6), after executing about thirty and exiling three of the 300, effected a reconciliation with the others and lived with them under a democracy (73.6).

Quite apart from any desire to establish or preserve democracy with Athenian help, a small city may sometimes have been glad to secure Athenian protection against powerful neighbours who were oppressing or exploiting it, even at the price of incorporation in the empire. A well-known series of Athenian decrees passed early in the Peloponnesian war shows Athens concerned to assist Methone against King Perdiccas II of Macedon: M/L 65 (= Tod I² 61 = *IG* I² 57 = D 3–6 in *ATL* II 48–9), lines 16–27, 47–51 (see Forrest *EGD* 42). Another obvious example is Neapolis, on the coast of Thrace, a former colony of Thasos which, during the Ionian war at any rate, was bitterly hostile to its mother-city, repudiating it as its founder and fighting with Athens against it when it revolted in 411–07: see M/L 89 = Tod I² 84 = *IG* I² 108.(Hostility to Thasos on the part of her colonies may also be indicated by M/L 83 II 1–2.) Neapolis, which had long been a member of the Delian League, paying the very small annual tribute of 2,000 drachmae (⅓ talent), may well have been liberated by Athens from Thasian control in 463/2, when Thasos surrendered to Athens at the end of her first revolt and lost control of her Peraea on the mainland of Thrace (Thuc. I 101.3), of which Neapolis must have formed part. It is always taken for granted that

[79] The 300 must have had a large popular following, to overcome a dominant and experienced ruling faction twice their own size.

Athens was the aggressor in her quarrel with Thasos in 465 'about the *emporia* on the coast of Thrace opposite and the mine which the Thasians possessed' (100.2; cf. 101.3, and Plut., *Cim.* 14.2). But there is evidence, from a Thasian law regulating the wine trade,[80] of control exercised by Thasos over her Peraea. One wonders whether Athenian intervention in 465 may not have been invited by one or more of the *emporia* in question, including Neapolis, which perhaps regarded Athenian control as less burdensome than Thasian. At any rate, half a century later Neapolis clearly preferred Athens to Thasos.

Although Athens certainly exploited her allies to some extent, I see no evidence that she did so in any extensive way. Although the total amount of tribute she received was very large, by Greek standards, few individual allies paid very much. Anyone who uses the convenient 'Index to Amounts of Tribute' in *ATL* II 122–4, with the quota lists and assessment decrees, will easily discover that before the great reassessment of 425, during the Peloponnesian war, only 13 or 14 cities are known to have paid more than 10 talents in any year, and only 5 of these more than 15 talents.[81] The tribute, of course, was far from being the only way in which the Athenians benefited from their empire. The very fact that it made Athens a 'Great Power' brought her additional prosperity in various ways, for instance by making the Peiraeus a magnet which attracted commerce from all over the Aegean world, and beyond (see e.g. Thuc. II 38.2; Ps.-Xen., *Ath. Pol.* I 16–17; II 7, 11; Hermippus fr. 63, *ap.* Athen. I 27ef, etc.). Some thousands of individual Athenians, doubtless mainly poor ones, profited from colonies and cleruchies, in which they received parcels of land, or from which (like the Lesbian cleruchs in 427, Thuc. III 50.2) they drew regular rents. Some rich Athenians may have made money by acquiring land in the territory of the allies (see D. M. Lewis in *ASI* [Ehrenberg] 182 and 190 n. 29)—I would suppose that the Athenian State claimed the right to dispose of lands confiscated from the allies, or from individual allied citizens convicted in the Athenian courts, not only through colonies and cleruchies but also by making grants *viritim* to individual Athenians,

[80] *IG* XII Suppl. 347. II (late fifth century), first published by G. Daux, in *BCH* 50 (1926) 214–26, and reprinted by H. W. Pleket, *Epigraphica* I (Leiden, 1964), no. 2. Among other provisions, this law forbids the import of foreign wines into the Thasian Peraea in Thasian ships (II 8–10). The purpose of this clause could hardly have been anything but the simple desire of the Thasian landowners to ensure the sale of their own produce in the area on the mainland which they controlled, free from all except local competition, while reserving to themselves the right to import into their island such foreign wine as they wanted. There may have been many other regulations detrimental to the inhabitants of the Peraea. I must add that the elaborate reconstruction of the background of this inscription, and of Thasian-Athenian relations, by J. Pouilloux, *Recherches sur l'histoire et les cultes de Thasos* I (= École française d'Athènes, *Études thasiennes* III, Paris, 1954), ch. ii–iii, is highly speculative and implausible: I agree with the criticisms of M. I. Finley, *TPAW*: CG 28–32.

[81] The five paying over 15 talents are Aegina, Byzantium, Chersonese, Paros and Thasos. The others are Abdera, Aenus, Cyme, Erythrae, Lampsacus, Mende, Potidaea and Torone—and possibly Scione in 435/4, but see *ATL* III 64–5, with which I agree.

who would presumably purchase at public auction.[82] And leading Athenians might sometimes have greater opportunities, which they would never have enjoyed but for the empire, of making profits for themselves by acting as *archontes* of allied cities, *episkopoi*, phrourarchs (garrison commanders) and the like.[83] Thucydides makes the realistically-minded oligarch Phrynichus recognise that it was the top layer of Athenians, their *kaloi kagathoi*, who 'devised the measures injurious to the allies, introduced them to the demos, and themselves gained most of the benefit from them' —but were repressed ('chastened') by the Athenian demos, 'the refuge of the allies' (VIII 48.6). Unlike those who would sit in judgment on a Roman Republican proconsul, the bulk of Athenians sitting in the jury-courts would have no feeling of class solidarity with an Athenian magistrate accused of ill-treating allies, and might indeed feel that a man who was allowed to escape punishment for misbehaviour in an allied state might be only too likely to misbehave in a similar manner against them at home.

The evidence is insufficient to enable us to decide how much exploitation and oppression took place in the Athenian empire. No doubt there was a good deal—imperialism is not a pleasant thing. But I suggest that many humble men among the allies had good reason to fear their own oligarchs—men of the stamp of the Pseudo-Xenophon—far more than the Athenians, whose deeply rooted belief in democracy and equality before the law made them concerned in principle to protect the mass of the people, however much they might on occasion sacrifice their principles to their own greed or desire for power or security. When an Athenian orator in the early fourth century claimed that the fifth-century Athenians had 'kept their allies free from civil strife, not allowing the many to be in political subjection to the few, but obliging them all to observe the principle of equality' (Ps.-Lys. II 55–6), it was not entirely an empty boast.

Athens was not only an imperialist state: it was also internally a 'slave society', in the sense that slave labour was an essential part of the economic system, and furthermore that without it the political democracy would have been unworkable.[84] We, who rely mainly upon hired labour rather than that of slaves, are entitled to regard slavery as an indelible stain upon Classical civilisation. We must certainly not forget that even the Athenian democracy, more highly developed and more firmly rooted

---

[82] I see no reason to explain Tod II 123 (= *IG* II² 43). 35–46 by supposing that the Athenians in the fifth century had given themselves *en bloc* the right of owning land in allied territories, as some have believed. Specific grants *by the Athenian State*, in the way I have suggested above, would account for individual owners as well as colonists and cleruchs.

[83] Tod II 152 (= *SIG³* 193), of 357–6, may give some indication of how an unscrupulous phrourarch might make a profit for himself if he were so inclined. Cf. Aeschin. I 107–8.

[84] See my review, in *CR* 71 = n.s. 7 (1957) 54–9, of W. L. Westermann, *The Slave Systems of Greek and Roman Antiquity* (1955), esp. the last two paragraphs, criticising also the views of the role of slavery at Athens expressed in 1952 by A. H. M. Jones and now available in his *AD* (1957), chapters i and iv. For a useful collection of articles on various aspects of Greek and Roman slavery, see M. I. Finley (ed.), *SCA*.

than any other known to us from the ancient world, was a dictatorship by a minority of the population (though not a small minority, as sometimes alleged), and that at the outbreak of the Peloponnesian war there may well have been more than a hundred thousand slaves in Attica.[85] Nevertheless, when we are thinking about the ancient world we must judge it not from one point of view only, that of the twentieth century, but also, and *simultaneously*, by the most advanced standards which *then* existed— and by those standards our judgment may be very different. It is a fact that down to the end of the ancient world, and beyond, there was virtually no criticism of the institution of slavery as such, and we know of no demand for its abolition. (In these respects the introduction of Christianity made no difference.) The only serious objection to slavery in principle that we ever hear of in the ancient world is the one mentioned in a couple of isolated passages in Aristotle's *Politics* (1 3, 1253^{b}20-3; 6, 1255^{a}5-12), where we are told that there were those who declared that slavery, being founded on force, was contrary to nature and wrong—not merely 'not according to nature' (*ou kata physin*), but '*contrary* to nature' (*para physin*). And there is no indication that these bold unnamed thinkers—whom we cannot identify—had advocated the abolition of slavery, any more than those Roman lawyers who acknowledged that slavery was *contra naturam*, *contra ius naturale*, while maintaining it as firmly as ever in practice.[86] Some Utopian Greek writers liked to imagine societies in which slavery did not exist. Otherwise, slavery was universally accepted without question. We cannot, therefore, condemn the Athenians by the standards prevailing in their day: by those standards, no one did any better. And slavery, whatever its cost in human suffering and degradation, did play a role in the Greek economy which was beneficial, from the strictly economic point of view. Indeed, if I had to choose the three fundamental advances in social institutions which enabled the Greeks to develop beyond anything mankind had known before, I think I would emphasise above all the more efficient and intensive exploitation of the techniques of slave production (mainly by imported 'barbarian' slaves), with the rapid growth, from the seventh/sixth centuries onwards, of responsible self-government, leading ultimately to full citizen democracy, and perhaps the introduction of a 'free market' to a much higher degree than in previous societies.[87]

In the fifth century Athens certainly pursued a policy of naval imperialism, but for this there were very special reasons. It was not, as so often represented, just naked aggressiveness and greediness (what the Greeks

[85] On the much-disputed question of the number of slaves in Attica, see esp. W. L. Westermann, 'Athenaeus and the Slaves of Athens', in *Athenian Stud. Pres. to W. S. Ferguson = HSCP*, Suppl. 1 (1940) 451-70, repr. in Finley (ed.), *SCA* 73-92.

[86] See *Dig.* 1 v.4.1 (Florentinus); i.4 (Ulpian); xii vi.64 (Tryphoninus); *Inst. J.* 1 ii.2. The lawyers concerned were, of course, all pagans. Probably the ideas referred to by Arist. had been transmitted through some of the Stoics.

[87] Cf. the end of my review, in *Econ. Hist. Rev.*, 2nd Series, 12 (1959-60) 510-11, of Karl Polanyi, C. M. Arensberg and H. W. Pearson (eds.), *Trade and Market in the Early Empires* (Glencoe, Illinois, 1957).

called *pleonexia*)—although doubtless that was present too—but was
bound up with the whole Athenian way of life, which in one essential
respect was different from that of all other major Greek states: the very
large Athenian population of citizens, metics and slaves was fed by imported corn to a far greater extent than that of any other important Greek
city. This was fully realised by the Athenians (see e.g. Dem. xviii 87; xx
31). I hope to deal elsewhere with some of the problems of the Athenian
corn supply,[88] and I wish to avoid facts and figures here as far as possible.
I think it would be universally agreed that Athens, unlike any other Greek
city we know about, imported by far the greater part of her corn supply;
and, as I shall explain, this led almost inevitably to naval imperialism.

Corn, preferably wheat, was the staple food of the Greeks.[89] Almost
any Greek city might need to import corn sometimes, either because of
a crop failure in its own territory or because its land had been ravaged in
war; but most Greek cities, unlike Athens, produced within their own
territory most of the corn they consumed. It was indeed the almost
universal reliance upon home-grown corn which dictated the general
pattern of Greek land warfare: the destruction of the enemy's crops and
the protection of one's own were the prime factors involved everywhere,
until Athens made herself into the one great exception to the rule.[90]

It is sometimes said that from the time of Solon onwards the Athenians
began to change over from cereal production to the cultivation of fruit
trees: above all the olive, also the vine and fig. There must certainly have
been a strong tendency in that direction, for such cultivation is better
suited to the soil of the greater part of Attica. The majority of Athenian
farmers, if they could, would surely always try to produce, if not enough
wheat for their own families, at least enough barley to feed their slaves
and domestic animals. (Many modern writers have underestimated the
suitability of Attic soil for growing barley, emphasised by Theophrastus,
HP viii viii.2, a passage which is rarely quoted.) But even the farmers
might often need to buy imported corn, when their crops were poor or
failed altogether,[91] and during the fifth century the large and growing
urban population must have become increasingly dependent upon foreign
corn. The only figure we have in an ancient source for Athenian annual
corn imports[92] relates to the mid-350s and works out at about 800,000
medimnoi (say about 1,200,000 bushels); but for reasons I cannot go into

---

[88] I cannot accept the figures or the arguments of Jones, *AD* 77–8. I prefer Gomme,
PAFFC 28–33. Gernet, *AAB* (1909), is still the standard work on the Athenian corn
supply; but his figures for the population of Attica (500,000–600,000), and hence for
the quantity of corn required, seem to me much too large: they should perhaps be roughly
halved.

[89] The standard work is still A. Jardé, *Les céréales dans l'antiquité grecque, I. La production*
(Paris, 1925).

[90] An excellent brief summary of the position is given by Gomme, *HCT* i 10–12 (based
on Grundy, *THA* i², ch. ix–x).

[91] See e.g. Ps.-Dem. l 61 for the severe drought of 361, in which even the wells in Attica
dried up.

[92] Dem. xx 30–3, esp. 31–2.

now I suspect this of being an underestimate.[93] And in the 430s, before the Peloponnesian war and the Plague, the population of Athens may have been a good deal larger, with more citizens and metics and probably more slaves; and an annual import of at least $1\frac{1}{2}$ million bushels is likely, and probably a good deal more.

In regard to the supply of corn, *autarkeia* (self-sufficiency) was generally regarded as an important asset. Thucydides (VI 20.4) makes Nicias say that the Syracusans have a great advantage over Athens in growing their own corn instead of importing it. For a city to rely to any great extent upon imported corn was dangerous, because it placed that city at the mercy of any other power which was able to interrupt its supply. In war time, needless to say, this was particularly likely to happen, if the enemy state controlled even a small part of one's corn route. But I believe that even in peace time any city which was itself suffering from a corn shortage enjoyed a tacitly recognised right to *katagein* ('bring to land') corn ships passing near by:[94] that is, to compel them to come into its own port and discharge their cargoes there. (The merchants concerned would doubtless be paid for what was taken, though I would guess that the State might fix prices below their natural high level.) Although I cannot prove this, I believe that such an action would not necessarily be regarded as an act of war against the city to which the ships were sailing, and that the only remedy that city would have would be to send out warships in future to convoy the corn ships past the danger point, as we find Athens doing in the autumn of 362 and 361, when corn ships sailing to the Peiraeus were intercepted off Byzantium, Chalcedon and Cyzicus (Ps.-Dem. L 4–6, 17–19).

Athens, then, became during the fifth century, as her population grew, increasingly dependent upon imported corn, in exchange for which she could send abroad her silver, her olive oil and other natural products, her painted pottery, and other manufactured goods. But this necessarily involved her developing a policy of naval imperialism, because her corn routes were now becoming lifelines which must be protected at all costs, and this meant that she must have 'bases' (in a very rudimentary sense, to be defined in a moment) all along these routes, for the Greek trireme had only a very restricted range of operation and had strict limitations as an escort vessel for merchant ships.[95] Broadly speaking, we can say that the Greek merchantman, normally propelled by sails, could make quite long voyages of several days' duration (even across the open sea) without coming to land, while the trireme could not. Although it had sails of a sort and could use them in favourable conditions, the Greek warship was normally rowed, and it had to come to land, if possible, every few hours, because the crew could not cook a meal on board or sleep there—it

---

[93] See n. 88 above.

[94] See Appendix VIII for the evidence I have collected.

[95] For what follows, see the fundamental article of Gomme, FFGNS, which gives sufficient references (note esp. Xen., *HG* VI ii.27–30; Ps.-Dem. L 22).

was regarded as a hardship to have to spend a night at the oars, or several nights anyway. The trireme was little more than 'a glorified racing eight', as Tarn put it; and it had to keep fairly close to the shore, if possible a friendly or neutral shore—that is the essential point. If it was being used for convoying (or for commerce raiding), it must be able to come to land at least every night, as a general rule. Opinions have differed about the distance a trireme could ordinarily cover in a day's rowing, but I myself do not believe it could operate efficiently over a radius of more than about 20–30 miles from its base. If it was to operate usefully, therefore, over more than a very small area, it needed to have *a series of bases*. (When I use the expression 'base' in this connection, I mean no more than a friendly or at least neutral port, or even shore.)

When Demosthenes, looking back in 330 on the struggle with Philip II of Macedon, was listing the duties of a 'right-minded citizen' during that period, he included 'providing for the corn supply, and making sure that it should pass along a continuously friendly coast all the way to Peiraeus' (XVIII 301). A large part of Athens' corn came from the Black Sea area, especially the Pontic kingdom centred at Panticapaeum at the eastern end of the Crimea. The sea route along which this corn travelled was Athens' principal lifeline, and throughout most of the fifth and fourth centuries she made certain that the passage across the Aegean would be secure, by holding Imbros, Lemnos and Scyros. But the route also included two narrow 'bottle-necks', where it could most easily be cut: the Bosphorus and the Hellespont. Demosthenes, imagining what would have been the result if he had not been successful (as he claimed he was) in stirring up the Athenians to take the necessary measures, said that Philip would then have got control of Byzantium and thence of the Hellespont and 'would have become master of the corn supply of Greece' (XVIII 241, cf. 87). For him, the two places in the whole world of the greatest value to Athens were 'Thermopylae, as far as the land was concerned, and the Hellespont for the sea route' (XIX 180). Aristotle, in the *Rhetoric* (III 10, 1411ᵃ14), records the Athenian Peitholaus as applying a rather striking expression to Sestos, the town right in the middle of the northern shore of the Hellespont (the 'Thracian Chersonese'): he called it 'the meal-table (*tēlia*) of the Peiraeus'. Sestos was indeed the perfect base for convoying ships through the narrows. It is described by Herodotus as a place of great natural strength (IX 115; cf. Xen., *HG* IV viii.5), and in Thucydides we find the Athenians early in 411 using it as the kingpin of their defence of the whole Hellespont (VIII 62.3). When Lysander in 405 got complete control of the sea, after the battle of Aegospotami (in the Hellespont), Athens was soon starved out and had to surrender to Sparta; and when again in 387 a Spartan fleet under Antalcidas cut the corn route at the Hellespont (Xen., *HG* V i.28–9), Athens was once more brought to her knees and was compelled to subscribe to the King's Peace. The same thing might have happened again in 376, but was averted by the Athenian victory in the battle of Naxos (Xen., *HG* V iv.60–1; Diod. XV 34.3 etc.).

The last phase of the struggle with Philip of Macedon began when Philip seized a large fleet of merchantmen sailing out of the Black Sea into the Propontis in the autumn of 340.[96]

Most of the specific examples I have quoted come from the fourth century; but it is very necessary to look at this evidence (too often ignored by those whose eyes are fixed on the earlier period), for in the fifth century Athens' dependence upon corn imports from the Pontus and elsewhere was quite as great, but is (so to speak) masked by the overwhelming predominance of Athens at sea, so that Athens, right down to 405/4, does not appear to have to take military measures to preserve her supplies—and we tend to take them for granted, and to forget that Athens was in this happy position because of her naval power and her empire, which made it possible for her to control all the bases she needed. In the fourth century, when Athens was much weaker at sea, and more dependent upon allies whom she could not dominate as in the great days of the fifth century, we can see the forces at work more clearly and reach a better understanding of the causes of Athenian imperialism, in the fifth century as well as the fourth.[97]

Athens made peace with Persia about 449 B.C.: the much discussed Peace of Callias. As I believe that the implications of this peace have been very wrongly interpreted by most scholars in recent times, I have dealt with the subject in Appendix VII.

[96] Philoch., *FGrH* 328 F 162 (230 ships); Theopomp., *FGrH* 115 F 292 (180 ships); Justin IX i.6.

[97] The fifth-century evidence for the Athenians' concern for their corn supply is scanty, for reasons which will be clear from the foregoing; but see esp. Plut., *Per.* 37.4, with Philoch., *FGrH* 328 F 119, *ap.* Schol. Ar. *Wasps* 718; *IG* I² 31 (= *SEG* X 22 = Hill, *S²*, *B* 47).6. There is much fourth-century evidence, particularly for corn shortages, above all that of *c.* 331–25 B.C. In addition to the passages cited above it is worth drawing attention to Tod II 167 (= *IG* II² 212 = *SIG³* 206).11–16; 196 (= *SEG* IX 2).2–5; 200 (= *IG* II² 1629; cf. *SEG* XV 125).217 ff.; *SIG³* 304 (= *IG* II² 360), esp. lines 8–12, 28–31, 54–6, 66–8, 70–1; *IG* II² 283.2; 342.3–6; 363.8–12; 398.11–13; 400.3–11; 401.10–12; 407.4–8; 408.8–14; 409.8–15; 416.10–14; 499.14–20; 1628.37–42; perhaps 423.13–14. The literary references include Dem. XVIII 248; XX 31–4; XXXIV 38–9; LVI 7–9 (cf. Ps.-Arist., *Oecon.* II ii.33, 1352^{b}14 ff.); Arist., *Ath. Pol.* 51.3 (evidence for price control of this kind in the Greek world is very rare); Ps-Plut., *Mor.* 851b.

II

Thucydides' judgment on the origins of the war

Thucydides is so much the most important witness for the causes of the war that we must first consider carefully what he has to say. Whatever opinion we may ultimately form on the correctness of his judgments, we must begin by making sure that we understand precisely what those judgments are. They have often been seriously misunderstood, and I know of no modern account which seems to me satisfactory.

(i)
432/1 and *c.* 460

First, we may try to answer a question which, curiously enough, has received no attention at all from historians. Why does Thucydides confine his explanation of the causes of the war to the outbreak of the Twenty-seven Years war, of 431–404?—the Peloponnesian war proper, as we must call it, because Thucydides' treatment of its various episodes as one war has ensured that that is what 'the Peloponnesian war' shall mean, for all time. (See Appendix II on 'the Peloponnesian war' and kindred expressions.) Surely, in so far as the different phases of the Twenty-seven Years war deserve to be considered as a single war, what is often called (and will be called here) the 'First Peloponnesian war', of *c.* 460 to 446/5, ought to be regarded as part of the same war: it was merely suspended by the Thirty Years Peace of 446/5, which was no more final than the Peace of Nicias and, like that peace, recognised a division of a large part of the Greek world into two rival hegemonies, headed by Sparta and by Athens respectively. (For the terms of the Thirty Years Peace, see Appendix I.) Thucydides gives us a detailed account of the events that provoked the Peloponnesian war proper; of the outbreak of the First Peloponnesian war he tells us virtually nothing. Why does he give that war only the most cursory treatment and fail to explain how it began? He does indeed use the expression 'the first war', as in v 20.3; 24.2; 26.3 (cf. 'the former war' in vii 18.2), but he applies it to the Ten Years war (see v 25.1) of 431–21, thereby emphasising his choice of 431 as the very beginning of his great war. For him, the Twenty-seven Years war filled the whole picture: it was a long war (i 23.1) by Greek standards, and it brought unparalleled suffering upon the Greeks (i 23.2–3).

To my mind, Thucydides is much at fault in saying so little about the outbreak of the war that began in *c.* 460 (a subject that will be dealt with in Chapter V, Parts iii–vii below). But I think we can at least understand the reasons for his attitude. In the first place, this war occurred entirely during his infancy and youth, and any notes he may have made about it and any cross-examining of participants he may have conducted (cf. 1 22.2–3) will not have been close in time to the events, and not trustworthy enough, therefore, to bear the weight of a detailed narrative. And there is an even more important factor. For Thucydides, the Peloponnesian war was essentially a war between Athens and Sparta; but in the First Peloponnesian war nearly all the fighting that took place was between Athens and Sparta's *allies*. (There were very good reasons for this, which will emerge in due course: see Chapter V, Part vi below.) But a war in which Sparta played very little part and the brunt of which was borne by her allies was not, in Thucydides' eyes, entitled to be ranked with the Twenty-seven Years war; it was a mere prelude, to be treated simply as part of the whole series of events during the Pentecontaetia (the period of roughly fifty years between the Persian and Peloponnesian wars), to which Thucydides devoted a brief excursus (1 89–118.2), with the express aim of explaining how the hegemony of Athens had grown into an empire: see 1 89.1, and especially 96–7, beginning with *hēgemonia* and ending with *archē*. The outbreak and the consequences of the First Peloponnesian war can best be treated when we come to consider the relations between Sparta and Athens (Chapter V below). We can now turn to Thucydides' account of the reasons for the outbreak of the Twenty-seven Years war, the Peloponnesian war proper.

(ii)
Thucydides 1 23.5–6; 88; 118.2

Ideally, we should first treat the much discussed problem of the time and order of composition of the various parts of Thucydides' work—'*the* Thucydides problem', as it has come to be known (cf. Appendix III). This, however, is beyond the scope of the present book, and I can do no more than state my own position, which is not very far, I think, from those of Gomme and de Romilly.[1] I believe that the History as we have it must be treated essentially as a unity,[2] and that even though many of us may have a strong *feeling* that this or that passage is 'early' or 'late', no important changes of opinion or general development of outlook can be *securely identified*. But I would not wish to deny (1) that Thucydides may have revised parts of the work many times and made numbers of additions and deletions; (2) that certain passages (usually brief ones, carrying little or none of the context with them) may be identified, with certainty or probability, as having been written earlier or later than specific datable historical events (see Appendix IX); and (3) that a good case can be made

---

[1] I say this in spite of the fact that de Romilly (*TAI* 371 n. 3) commented on my remark (*CAE* 31) that 'agreement has not been reached on any of the major problems involved' to the effect that 'Perhaps this is altogether a pessimistic view of the situation'.

[2] This must not be taken to imply acceptance of the extreme view of J. H. Finley (*Thuc.*, and *TET*) that the whole work in its present form dates from after 404.

for thinking that certain statements can be distinguished as having been written—or at least, thought—at different times from certain other statements (see Gomme, FPT).

When de Romilly was writing her influential book, *Thucydide et l'impérialisme athénien* (published only in 1947), 'during the first years of the [Second World] war',[3] the problem of the composition of Thucydides' work, as she says, 'dominated all studies, and particularly German studies'. She adds that, as a believer in 'a great unity of thought' in Thucydides' History, she could not be 'either shocked or sorry to see this much vexed problem of composition now cast aside' (*TAI* 370).

It is true that interest in 'die thukydideische Frage' largely died away for thirty years after Schadewalt's monograph in 1929 (*GST*), until the problem was raised again in a closely argued paper by Andrewes in 1959 (TCW), which we shall have occasion to discuss later. The particular theme that concerns us here, developed above all by Eduard Schwartz (*GWT*) and, with new arguments, by Andrewes, is the question whether the three Thucydidean passages we have set out to examine were inserted (as believed by Schwartz, Andrewes and a few others) after the end of the war, or at any rate after 413, into a narrative written much earlier, at a time when Thucydides held a different opinion about the origins of the war, and in particular attributed to Corinth a much more important role in bringing about the war. We shall consider this question a little later. For the present it will be enough to say that if the analysis of Spartan-Athenian relations presented in this book is valid (above all the interpretation of the attitude of Sparta in 465/4, 440 and 433–1), then it is hard to see how a man of Thucydides' acuteness could long have failed to grasp the real nature of the conflict and could have been over-impressed by the part played by Corinth. However, for the present we will leave this question open and look carefully at those three passages in Thucydides.

A. In I 23.5[4] Thucydides says that he has begun by setting out the *aitiai* and *diaphorai*, 'the grounds of complaint (or 'charges') and differences'. (The word *aitia* is the noun of the verb *aitiaomai*, the root meaning of which is 'accuse, blame'.) In §6 Thucydides goes on, 'In my opinion, *the truest explanation*[5] (*alēthestatē prophasis*), although it was least publicised,

---

[3] See de Romilly, *TAI* 369 (the Eng. trans., 1963); cf. the French original, *TIA* 307.

[4] For convenience, I give the Greek of I 23.5–6: (5) διότι δ' ἔλυσαν, τὰς αἰτίας προύγραψα πρῶτον καὶ τὰς διαφοράς, τοῦ μή τινα ζητῆσαί ποτε ἐξ ὅτου τοσοῦτος πόλεμος τοῖς ῞Ελλησι κατέστη. (6) τὴν μὲν γὰρ ἀληθεστάτην πρόφασιν, ἀφανεστάτην δὲ λόγῳ, τοὺς ᾿Αθηναίους ἡγοῦμαι μεγάλους γιγνομένους καὶ φόβον παρέχοντας τοῖς Λακεδαιμονίοις ἀναγκάσαι ἐς τὸ πολεμεῖν. αἱ δ' ἐς τὸ φανερὸν λεγόμεναι αἰτίαι αἵδ' ἦσαν ἑκατέρων, ἀφ' ὧν λύσαντες τὰς σπονδὰς ἐς τὸν πόλεμον κατέστησαν.

[5] 'Motive' would be a possible alternative translation for anyone who wants to insist, as Kirkwood does (TWC 47), that both *prophasis* and *aitia* have regularly in Thucydides 'a *subjective* reference, that is, they are concerned with the emotions of, or the influences on, the persons participating in the events, and do not mean the historian's objective analysis of the situation'. In view of the word ἡγοῦμαι in §6, it is pointless to deny that Thucydides is here giving an 'objective analysis' (in Kirkwood's sense), even if he happens

was that the Athenians becoming great and instilling fear into the Spartans compelled them to go to war. But *the openly expressed grounds of complaint (aitiai)* on each side, on the basis of which they broke the truce and turned to war, were these'. There follows an account of these *aitiai*, which for Thucydides seem to be specifically the two Athenian clashes with Corinth, first over Corcyra (1 48.3 ff.; 55.2) and then over Potidaea (56.1 ff.; 66.1; 67.1), although other complaints are mentioned on the part of Aegina, Megara and others (67.2–4).

What is the contrast Thucydides is drawing, between the explanation which was 'truest although least publicised', and the 'openly expressed grounds of complaint'? This question has been discussed over and over again, with an almost invariable failure to grasp the essential point. Virtually all recent writers have taken it for granted from the very start that the contrast is between an 'immediate cause' (or causes) and a 'more remote' or 'underlying cause', or (to put essentially the same idea a little differently) between a 'superficial cause' and a 'profound cause': the last is the way Momigliano puts it (OCWAH), and Kagan (*OPW* 345) begins his chapter on 'The Causes of the War' with the statement, 'It was Thucydides who invented the distinction between the underlying, remote causes of war and the immediate causes'. There have been many similar formulations.[6] In fact, Thucydides does not try to distinguish, *either here or anywhere else in his work*, between immediate or superficial and underlying or profound causes, and it is extraordinary that such an intention should so often have been foisted upon him,[7] sometimes with a good deal of grumbling about the supposed obscurity of his meaning, and even with accusations of paradox.

We can ignore from the outset the many analyses which assume, wrongly, that there is some inherent opposition between the expressions *prophasis* and *aitia*.[8] In fact the meaning of these two words often partly overlaps, and on one occasion Thucydides himself refers to what he has

---

to present it in the form of an explanation of the Spartans' real motives. Kirkwood (TWC 47 n. 15) is wrong in seeing a *difference* 'between objective analysis by the historian and a presentation of the minds of the participants'.

[6] E.g. Bengtson, *GG*⁴ 223 (Thucydides 'als erster zwischen den *tieferen Gründen* des Krieges und den *äusseren Anlässen* geschieden hat'); Wilcken, *GG*⁹ 159 ('In fundamentaler weise hat er, zum ersten Male in der Menschheitsgeschichte, den Gedanken erfasst und durchgeführt, dass zwischen den tiefliegenden *Gründen* und den äusseren *Anlässen* zu scheiden sei'); Ehrenberg, *SS* 253 ('Thucydides distinguishes the "truest cause of the war" from the more immediate "grievances and conflicts" '); Gomme, *HCT* 1 465 ('his view of the immediate and ultimate causes of the war'; cf. 153–4); Weidauer, *THS* 8 (on Thuc. 1 23.6: 'Mit Recht beruft man sich auf diesen Satz, wenn man dem Thukydides das Verdienst zuschreibt, als Erster zwischen dem zutage liegenden Anlass einer geschichtlichen Entscheidung und deren eigentlicher, tiefer liegenden Ursache unterschieden zu haben'), endorsed by Kiechle, UWMPT 290.

[7] Most recently, von Fritz, *GGS* 1 [Text] 623–9.

[8] Andrewes (TCW 226, 230) is one of the few who have avoided this mistake; but when he concentrates on 'the essential identity of *aitiai* and *prophasis*', and asserts that 'the *prophasis* and the *aitiai* are for 432 merely two aspects of the same thing', he fails to realise the nature of the essential contrast between 'truest' and 'openly expressed' but untrue.

just called a *prophasis* as the *aitia* (v 53, lines 27 and 30 *OCT*).⁹ Often Thucydides, like other Greek authors,¹⁰ uses *prophasis* for a pretext which is *not* true (e.g. III 82.4; 86.4; 111.1; IV 47.2; v 80.3; VI 8.4; 76.2 with 78.1 and 79.2; VIII 87.5), once even making one of his speakers contrast a (false) *prophasis* specifically with what is the truth (VI 33.2).¹¹ The real force of the antithesis in I 23.6 is between 'the *truest* explanation' and 'the *openly expressed* grounds of complaint' (which on the Peloponnesian side were bogus, as we shall see in Chapter III, Parts ii and iii below): it is the adjective and the participial phrase, not the nouns, which provide the essential features of the contrast. Only in one other passage, VI 6.1, does Thucydides use the expression 'the truest explanation' (the same Greek words), and it is very significant that here, exactly as in I 23.6, he is opposing a *real* motive (again, unavowed) to a *publicly proclaimed* intention which was actually specious (note *euprepōs*), a mere cloak for more ambitious designs.

What Thucydides is saying in I 23.6, although misunderstood to a greater or less degree by nearly everyone in modern times, was thoroughly grasped by Dionysius of Halicarnassus two thousand years ago. Dionysius was not a man of intellectual penetration, and the ideas which inspired Thucydides were often beyond his limited power to grasp; but when it comes to explaining in simple words some involved or peculiar passage the meaning of which is not obvious at first sight, Dionysius can sometimes be very useful. (He did not underrate the difficulty of comprehending Thucydides, and those of us who find some of Thucydides' Greek appallingly difficult may take comfort from the fact that Dionysius, a leading literary critic whose native language was Greek, declared that few can understand everything in Thucydides, and for some passages even they need the help of literary exegesis!¹²) It is strange that recent writers have made very little use of Dionysius' lengthy writings on Thucydides, except in the purely literary and stylistic sphere. Dionysius brushes aside any difference between the words *prophasis* and *aitia* in I 23.6. In one work he

⁹ Crawley translates both words 'pretext'. I can find no reference to this passage in Kirkwood's article: it is of course very inconvenient for his view that '*prophasis* was not used synonymously with *aitia* by Thucydides' (TWC 46). Another passage that might be cited against Kirkwood is I 118.1, on which see Gomme, *HCT* I 153, and Kirkwood, TWC 53.

¹⁰ In the only two examples of *prophasis* to be found (according to Diels' Index) in the Presocratics, namely Democr. 68 B 119, 222, it refers to a specious excuse.

¹¹ Cf. VI 76.2. Thucydides certainly endorsed Hermocrates' opinion here: see VI 1.1; 6.1.

¹² Dion. Hal., *De Thuc.* 51 (ed. Usener-Radermacher, v 410.15–17). Dionysius has much of interest to say about Thucydides, not only in *De Thuc.* but also in *Epist. ad Ammaeum II* (*De Thuc. Idiomatis*) and more particularly in *Epist. ad Cn. Pompeium Geminum.* There is a convenient edition of these two letters (and *Epist. ad Ammae. I*), with Eng. trans. and commentary, by W. Rhys Roberts, *Dionysius of Halicarnassus. The Three Literary Letters* (Cambridge, 1901). See also G. M. A. Grube, 'Dionysius of Halicarnassus on Thucydides', in *Phoenix* 4 (1950) 95–110. Dionysius' unfavourable comparison of Thucydides with Herodotus (in the *Epist. ad Pomp.*) aroused the scorn of Thomas Hobbes, forcibly expressed in the Preface, 'On the Life and History of Thucydides', to his English translation of the historian (*EWTH* VIII, at pp. xxiii–xxx): 'I think there was never written so much absurdity in so few lines', was Hobbes' verdict (p. xxvi).

quotes Thucydides as referring here to 'tēn alēthestatēn *aitian*';[13] and in another, giving his main analysis of this text, he speaks of 'twofold *aitiai*', one of which is 'the true one, though not announced to everybody', namely the aggrandisement of the city of Athens, and the other is '*not true, but cooked up by the Spartans*' (*hypo de Lakedaimoniōn plattomenēn*).[14] Again, he speaks in a third work of the Spartans as undertaking the war out of envy and fear but putting forward *prophaseis* of a different character.[15] This is the essential point. I hope to show in Chapter III, Parts ii and iii below, that if Thucydides is correctly understood he makes it very clear that the Spartans had no genuine reason for claiming that Athens had broken the Thirty Years Peace (which still had rather more than half its course to run) and therefore no legitimate excuse for resuming the war. We must not ignore the existence of a sworn peace-treaty which neither side could lawfully break unless perhaps released from its oaths by a clear and open breach by the other side; any alleged but disputed breach had to be referred to arbitration before there was any resort to war. Too often discussions of who was the aggressor in this war have been conducted in general terms, without beginning—as they should—from the terms of the treaty (for which see Appendix I). Curiously enough, the only ancient author known to me who explicitly blames the Spartans for breaking the Peace and invading Attica is one whose account of the fifth century is in general very feeble and full of gross errors: Justin (III vii.1–2: 'His malis fracti Lacedaemonii in annos xxx pepigerunt pacem, sed tam longum otium inimicitiae non tulerunt. Itaque extra xv annos rupto foedere cum contemptu deorum hominumque fines Atticos populantur . . .').

Now in I 23.4–6 Thucydides speaks of 'the Athenians and Peloponnesians' as beginning the war and breaking the Thirty Years Peace, and he adds that in order to explain why they broke the peace he has given by way of prelude (he is referring to I 24–66) an account of the *aitiai* and *diaphorai*, 'the grounds of complaint and differences'. Later (I 55.2; 66) he repeats that these were the *aitiai* the Athenians and Peloponnesians had against each other: the Corinthians complained that Athens had fought against them, as an ally of Corcyra, during the continuance of the Peace (I 55.2), and was now besieging their colony, Potidaea, with Corinthians and Peloponnesians inside it (66), and the Athenians that the Peloponnesians had caused Potidaea, a tributary ally of theirs, to revolt and had openly fought on the side of the Potidaeans (66). But we then have to ask whether one of the two sides took the initiative in breaking the Peace, declaring war and launching the first attacks—because if so, Thucydides

---

[13] *Epist. ad Ammae. II* (*De Thuc. Idiom.*) 6, ed. Usener-Radermacher, v 427.10.

[14] *De Thuc.* 10 (v 338.15–23). I cannot at the moment recall any modern author who has taken the same view (the right view) of Thuc. I 23.6, except Hobbes, who in the Preface to his translation remarks that Thucydides has 'declared the causes, *both real and pretended*, of the war' (*EWTH* VIII, p. xxi, my italics).

[15] *Epist. ad Cn. Pomp.* 3.9 (VI 235.12–13). Dionysius here attacks Thucydides' whole presentation of the causes of the war, as in *De Thuc.* 10–11.

will necessarily be concentrating on that side's actions when he gives his explanation of the outbreak of hostility. As we shall see, there can be no possible doubt about this, if we accept Thucydides' narrative: quite apart from the fact that the Corinthians first broke the Peace, it was the Spartan Assembly which (ignoring Athenian appeals to arbitration) declared, quite falsely, that the Athenians had broken the Peace and that the war should be renewed, the Peloponnesian League Congress which endorsed that decision, the Thebans who thereafter committed the first overt warlike act, and the Peloponnesians who made the first major assault. Pearson, who has given the best analysis known to me of Thucydides I 23.5–6,[16] is therefore right to say, 'Since it was the Peloponnesians who opened hostilities, it is they, not the Athenians, who are on the defensive in the inquiry that Thucydides is conducting. . . . No *prophasis* is offered for the Athenians, as they are not technically the aggressors and have no need to defend themselves.'

This is indeed true. As Pearson puts it (PA 206), '*Prophasis* . . . means in the most general terms something that you show or say, an explanation that you offer for behaviour, giving the reason or the purpose. . . . Your explanation may be true or false, reasonable or unreasonable, convincing or worthless, creditable or discreditable.' The Athenians had their 'grounds of complaint' in the actions of Corinth, but no explanation of their conduct is required, because they neither declared war nor attacked the other side.[17]

There is still one phrase qualifying the *prophasis* in Thuc. I 23.6 which we have not yet examined: the 'truest explanation' was *aphanestatē logōi*, it was 'least publicised', or 'very little spoken about [at the time]'. We must be sure we are taking these words in the sense Thucydides intended. Do they mean that the 'truest explanation' was hardly mentioned *by anyone*, or is the scope of *aphanestatē logōi* less wide than that?

Let us begin by considering the first of these alternatives. In the Peloponnesian councils, if the speeches in the History have any historical value at all, it was discussed freely. The Corinthians, in their two speeches at Sparta, can talk of little else but the danger of Athenian imperialism; they make only passing references to the *aitiai* (I 68–71; 120–4). The Athenians pointedly dismiss the *aitiai* as matters capable of being satisfactorily settled by arbitration (73–8, esp. 73.1; 78.4). Archidamus alludes to Potidaea and the other grievances of the allies only to propose the sending of an embassy to Athens to negotiate for a settlement (80–5, esp. 82.1; 85.2). Sthenelaïdas says nothing directly about the *aitiai*, and in his last sentence, with the words, 'And do not allow the Athenians to become greater', returns to the 'truest explanation' (86, esp. §5). There are even echoes of the 'truest explanation' in the Corcyra-Corinth debate at Athens in 433, when the Corcyraeans tell the Athenians that the Spartans are planning war, because they are afraid of Athens, and the

---

[16] PA (esp. 205–6, 215–23), at p. 221.
[17] Sealey, THCW 8–12, fails to realise this.

Corinthians try to weaken the force of this argument (33.3, with 36.1; 42.2). If, then, we accept our first alternative and take Thucydides to mean that the 'truest explanation' was very little in evidence in *all* discussion or propaganda, we are led into absurdity, for we make Thucydides contradict himself, quite uncharacteristically, in the most flagrant manner. Andrewes, in a recent discussion of Thucydides' treatment of the causes of the war (TCW, esp. 237–8), has not shrunk from such a conclusion. Starting from the view that *aphanestatē logōi* is to be taken in the most general sense of 'not discussed in public', and that we should 'allow *logōi* to refer to *logoi*', in the sense of the speeches in Book I, Andrewes actually finds himself driven to narrow the justified application of *aphanestatē logōi* to a single speech, that of Pericles at the end of Book I! He then proceeds to admit that the expression 'is on this hypothesis obscure', adding 'but it is obscure on any hypothesis'. In fact, if Andrewes were right, there would be no *obscurity* about *aphanestatē logōi*: it would simply be a crude piece of self-contradiction of the most obvious kind, the like of which is hardly to be found elsewhere in Thucydides! Before accepting such a despairing solution, let us try the second of our two possible alternative explanations of *aphanestatē logōi*, which would give it something less than the most general meaning.

In examining any expression the meaning of which is disputed, the first thing to do is to look at it in the light of the whole context. In our sentence the 'truest explanation', which is *aphanestatē logōi*, is set against the 'openly expressed grounds of complaint', the *es to phaneron legomenai aitiai*. The verbal parallelism of the two phrases is as close as it could be: *aphanestatē/es to phaneron*, and *logōi/legomenai*. Clearly we must equate the *logos* in which the 'truest explanation' is *aphanestatē* with that in which the *aitiai* are expressed *es to phaneron*. Now in I 23.6 the *aitiai* are said to be 'the grounds of complaint expressed *on either side*, from which they broke the Peace and turned to war'. But we have already seen that the only complaint Thucydides mentions on the Athenian side is that Corinth had brought about the revolt of Potidaea (I 66); and although this *aitia* was a justifiable one,[18] the Athenians were not proposing to make it an excuse for launching a war: they gave it as a necessary reply to the Corinthian allegation that Athens had attacked Potidaea (66).[19] The only *aitiai* which were brought forward as an excuse for breaking the Peace and initiating a general war were those on the Peloponnesian side, and they were not valid, for Athens had not in fact broken the treaty in any way of which the Peloponnesians were entitled to complain, and if she had, they should have responded to her appeal to arbitration. For all

---

[18] See Chapter III, Part iii below.

[19] Athens is always on the defensive in the negotiations of 432/1. To the first Spartan demand in Thuc. I 126.2 she retorts with a similar demand, 128.1. To the further Spartan demands in 139.1,3 (withdraw from Potidaea and leave Aegina autonomous, repeal the Megarian decree, leave the Greeks autonomous), she replies appropriately (145, with 144.2). The Megarian decree had been a response to provocation, real or imaginary (139.2): see Chapter VII below.

practical purposes, then, just as the *prophasis* in 23.6 is the explanation of the *Peloponnesian* decision to go to war, the *aitiai* are 'the grounds of complaint openly expressed' *by the Peloponnesians* in their official decisions and propaganda—their formal decision that the Peace had been broken by Athens, their embassies to Athens in which this view was expressed (126 ff., esp. 139.1), and their justification of their action to the outside world. In all this official Peloponnesian propaganda the *aitiai* would of course be 'openly expressed' ('so that the Spartans might provide themselves with the best possible pretext for going to war', 126.1), and it is precisely in this context that the 'truest explanation' was *aphanestatē*. The Spartans could never afford to admit publicly that their 'grounds of complaint' were bogus and that their real reason for declaring war was fear of Athens' growing power: had they done so, they would have convicted themselves of breaking the oaths by which they had sworn to keep the Peace for thirty years. This solves a problem Andrewes has created for himself, when he says, 'It is not clear why Thucydides should be at pains to tell us, somewhat obscurely, that this was a conception which lay just below the diplomatic surface, an idea which could be freely expressed at Sparta but not by a Spartan at Athens'. The reality *did* lie 'below the diplomatic surface' and the fear of the growth of Athenian power as a reason for breaking the Peace *was* 'an idea which could be freely expressed at Sparta but not by a Spartan at Athens'—because it gave Sparta no valid pretext for her war: only the *aitiai*, had they been justified (as they were not), could have done that. When Andrewes says, 'There is one place only, Athens itself, where no one could usefully assert in public that Athenian expansion justified war,' he overlooks the fact that the Peloponnesians could never afford to advance that argument in public *anywhere*, for it provided no legal justification for a renewal of the war, in breach of the treaty!

We have now found a perfectly natural interpretation of Thucydides' words, in the light of which all that he says is consistent and reasonable. To take the passage in any other way leads to quite unnecessary difficulties. The meaning and implications of the vital word *anankasai* ('compel') in 23.6 remain to be clarified, but it is better to postpone discussion of this until we have considered the two parallel passages: 88 and 118.2.

B. In 1 88 Thucydides tells us that in 432 the Spartans decided to go to war 'not so much because they were won over by the speeches (*logois*) of their allies as because they saw most of Greece already subject to Athens and feared she might grow still more powerful'.[20] The allies, too, were mostly anxious to declare war: Corinth was the most insistent and was strongly supported by Megara; but there were other states, an actual majority of the members of the Peloponnesian League (67.4; 119; 125.1), which also desired war; and outside the League itself Aegina[21] (a former

---

[20] On the meaning of this and similar oὐ τοσοῦτον clauses in Thucydides, see Westlake, in *CQ* 52 = n.s. 8 (1958) 102–10 = *EGHGH* 161–73.

[21] Thuc. 1 67.2; II 27.1.

ally of Sparta, but now within the Athenian empire) and King Perdiccas of Macedon (56.2 to 57.5; 58.2) were prominent in urging an immediate attack on Athens. We shall return later to consider the attitude of some of these powers. At this stage we need only make sure that we understand precisely what Thucydides means by the passage under consideration (88). Nearly always *logois* is translated 'arguments'—a permissible rendering of the word in many contexts, but here rather misleading. To take *tōn xymmachōn tois logois* as referring to the *arguments* advanced by the allies is to convict Thucydides, unnecessarily, of a confusion, for we must surely accept the first Corinthian speech at Sparta, with its concentration on the general menace of Athenian imperialism, as representative of the allied speeches referred to in I 88; and if we then interpret *logois* as 'arguments' we shall be driven to conclude that in I 88 Thucydides is in effect saying that Sparta was moved not so much by fear of Athens as by fear of Athens. Surely what Thucydides means in this passage is that the Spartans made up their minds on their own account, taking essentially their own interests into consideration, and did not simply respond to allied pressure. He is saying that they were not primarily 'persuaded by the speeches of their allies'—by the fact, that is to say, that their allies made speeches in favour of war. He is not necessarily saying anything about the arguments used by the allies. Again, we need not convict Thucydides of confusion or inconsistency: there is a simple explanation, which we can easily accept.

We now have on our hands a definite statement by Thucydides, attributing the main motive force in the declaration of war to Sparta rather than her allies. We shall later find reasons for thinking that in this Thucydides was right. Sparta was not nearly as reluctant to go to war in 432 as most modern historians have supposed.

C. In I 118.2 Thucydides adds something to what he has already told us in 23.6 and 88: he now reveals that the fear which the growth of Athenian power inspired in the Spartans was above all fear for their symmachy, for the Peloponnesian League. Earlier, he says, the Spartans had not been quick to go to war 'unless compelled to do so', and they were hampered by wars at home, until the power of Athens clearly rose to a height and began to encroach on their own symmachy.[22] Thucydides has earlier provided the explanation of this: at the end of their speech to the Spartan Assembly (I 71.4–6) the Corinthians had made an open threat to secede from the Spartan alliance if Sparta refused to protect them. If Sparta failed to act now, they had said, she would be breaking her oaths

[22] καὶ τῆς ξυμμαχίας αὐτῶν ἥπτοντο. It has been represented to me that we cannot give meaning to these words without at least including 'the Corinthian grievance', and that therefore my interpretation of I 88 is in effect that 'Sparta was moved by her allies' grievances but not by the fact that they expressed them'. I believe (and I think Thucydides' essential point is) that Sparta was not really *concerned* about her allies' interests (she never was: compare her disregard of them in settling the terms of the Peace of Nicias), and that the fact that Corinth had a *grievance* left her cold—until that grievance issued in a *threat to secede*: this put the symmachy in peril and thus *affected Sparta herself*. (Cf., however, Chapter V, Part ix below, *ad init.*)

to them (cf. Xen., *HG* IV vi. 1–3), and Corinth (and the other allies) could legitimately turn 'to some other alliance'. 'To Argos', comments the scholiast. Perhaps. Corinth did ally herself with Argos for a time in 421 (v 31.6), in a purely defensive alliance, which Thucydides calls an 'epimachy' (v 48.2; cf. 27.2, and see I 44.1). But in 432 the Thirty Years Peace which Argos had made with Sparta in 451/50 still had more than ten years to run (see Thuc. v 14.4; 22. 2; 28.2; 40.3), and events were to show that Argos did not intend to break that Peace. Sthenelaïdas later urges the Spartans not to give up good allies 'to the Athenians' (86.3); and if a threat of 'turning to some other alliance' was really used, it might well have been purposefully vague, leaving open the possibility that Corinth would seek an arrangement with Athens, which might have been willing to receive her into a separate alliance not involving subjection. If Corinth deserted Sparta, Megara would be isolated and might find it hard to remain in the Peloponnesian League. With Corinth and Megara alienated, and Argos at best neutral, Sparta might have to think twice before trying to march out of the Peloponnese, and Athens (as we shall see in Chapter V, Part vi below) might be able to block the Megarid against her. Athens would therefore have had every reason to offer Corinth an alliance on exceptionally favourable terms, involving special concessions to Corinth and a cessation of anti-Corinthian activities.[23]

It has often been remarked that the power of Athens was hardly as great in 432 as it had been in some earlier years before the Thirty Years Peace, above all in 457–4, after the conquest of Boeotia and before the disaster in Egypt. I believe that for Thucydides, a Periclean through and through in foreign policy, the 'land empire' that Athens had acquired for a time in the 450s, including as it did Boeotia, was not really an asset to Athens. (See Appendix X on the question whether Pericles was connected with the 'land empire'.) And whatever we may think about the comparative strength of Athens in the mid-450s and in 432, she was certainly stronger in 432 than she had been at any time since the Thirty Years Peace. Her vital reserves of money were growing steadily once more; she had demonstrated her power to control her allies by crushing the revolt of Samos, the greatest naval power of them all (cf. Thuc. VIII 76.4); she was no longer the precarious mistress of Boeotia, an area she could never hope to dominate except temporarily, when internal divisions happened to be rife;[24] and she now had a defensive alliance with Corcyra, the next strongest naval power in Greece after herself.

We must now ask ourselves what Thucydides means when he says in I 23.6 that fear of the growth of Athenian power 'compelled' (*anankasai*)

---

[23] Compare the alliance with Corcyra (Chapter III, Part ii below), which evidently involved no subordination of Corcyra and of course no payment of tribute.
[24] Cf. Thuc. III 62.5; IV 92.6; Arist., *Rhet.* III 4, 1407ª1–5.

the Spartans to go to war—a famous statement which, being generally misinterpreted, has probably done more than any other single passage to create the current misconception of the Athenians as the aggressors in 432–1. The compulsion-words in Thucydides (usually *anankē, anankazein, katanankazein, anankaios*) can often, of course, refer to actual compulsion, where the person compelled has no real liberty of action. Often, on the other hand, as in other writers,[25] they imply no more than strong pressure and do not by any means exclude a large measure of choice by the person under constraint—and so it is here. Whenever people are placed, as they so often are, in situations where their only possible choice is between two or more evils, and they choose the least unpleasant alternative, Thucydides is prepared to speak of *anankē*.[26] This is too often ignored: Sealey,[27] for instance, simply takes it for granted that *anankasai* in 1 23.6 must have the strict meaning of 'compel'; for support, the best he can do is to appeal to the translation of Henry Dale—hardly a powerful argument, and there is no other. The Spartans were not in any literal sense 'compelled' to declare war, certainly not without resorting to arbitration first, as Thucydides makes their own king point out (85.2).

It is important to realise too that Thucydides is not making any kind of moral judgment, on the Spartans or the Athenians. Modern scholars sometimes speak as if Thucydides were here declaring Athens to be the 'real aggressor'; but to draw such a conclusion would be to read into Thucydides conceptions quite alien to his habits of thought (cf. Chapter I, Part ii above). We ourselves may ask who was the 'real aggressor', but this is not the sort of question Thucydides set himself. Pearson (PA 220) has acutely observed that if Thucydides had wanted to *blame* the Athenians he could easily have done so by using slightly different language.[28] 'He does not *blame* the Athenians here', Pearson continues, 'because he is not concerned with praise or blame, like some later Greek historians, but with explaining the Spartan point of view. He wants to give their *prophasis* for going to war, their motive, excuse, or occasion, and, as he tells us again later, this was really *fear*—the fear of a worse alternative to war. . . . There is compulsion upon them only in so far as they are compelled

[25] Pearson, PA 220, refers to Hdts 1 11.3–4, where Gyges is 'compelled' to kill Candaules. Large numbers of other instances might be quoted, e.g. Hdts VII 144.2, where the Athenian-Aeginetan war in the 480s 'compelled' the Athenians to become proper sailors. See also Arist., *Magn. Mor.* 1 15, 1188ᵇ15–24.

[26] Here are some examples. (*a*) ἀναγκάζειν: 1 28.3; III 53.3; IV 25.1; V 7.1; 25.3; VI 87.2; 92.3; VIII 41.3. (*b*) καταναγκάζειν: 1 75.3; V 61.1. (*c*) ἀναγκή: 1 32.5; 73.2; 124.2; 144.3; II 17.2; III 2.1; 40.3; 45.4; IV 20.1; 87.3; 98.5; VI 10.2; 18.3; 82.1. (*d*) ἀναγκαῖος: IV 60.1; V 105.2; VI 89.1.

[27] THCW, at pp. 9 ff. Sealey's statement about the consequences to be drawn from the use of the aorist infinitive is sufficiently refuted by von Fritz, *GGS* 1 [Noten] 284–5 n. 13; and Sealey himself has admitted that he has lost faith in his interpretation of 1 23.6 (see *Proc. of the African Class. Assocns.* 7 [1964], at p. 57 n. 2).

[28] E.g. by writing αἰτίους ἡγοῦμαι τοὺς Ἀθηναίους ἀναγκάσαντας, as Socrates in Plato's *Gorgias* (447a) blames Chaerophon for delaying him: τούτων . . . αἴτιος Χαιρεφῶν ὅδε, ἐν ἀγορᾷ ἀναγκάσας ἡμᾶς διατρῖψαι.

to choose between two disagreeable alternatives'. Nor does Thucydides attribute to the Athenians (or Pericles) an imperialistic motive driving towards war. As de Romilly has said, 'The war is the result of an imperialistic development of Athenian power, not the expression of an actual imperialistic ambition' (*TAI* 18 n. 3).

What Thucydides is saying, then, is in effect that the growth of Athenian power had placed Sparta in such a position that it was only natural, it was only to be expected, that being what she was (this qualification is essential; cf. Chapter IV, Part i below) she would act as she did. Thucydides realised that human beings, especially when acting collectively (cf. Chapter I, Part ii above), tend to react to certain situations in certain ways, which are more or less predictable. He would not have denied that they have a real power of choice: a large part of his History is centred upon climactic moments at which great decisions have to be made and the issue sometimes remains in doubt until the end (for a list, see Appendix IV). But he evidently believed that in some cases one can be reasonably certain, human nature being what it is, what choice will be made; and in such cases he is quite ready to speak of 'compulsion'.[29] (In one passage, v 25.3, he can even speak of both sides in the war as being 'compelled' to break the Peace of Nicias!) Thucydides was far from being a determinist, in the strict sense of the word. The root of the matter is that for him the chain of causation did not consist of only three links: (1) the declaration of war, caused by (2) Sparta's fear, caused by (3) the growing power of Athens. The primary link in the chain, the natural cause of the growing power of Athens, was 'human nature', driving men (at least when organised in States) to pursue their own interest, above all to 'rule wherever they can' (cf. Chapter I, Part ii above).

One other Greek writer, Polybius, shows special interest in historical causation.[30] In his opinion (vi 2.8) it is the study of causes (*aitiai*) which is the most attractive and beneficial feature of historical study. Polybius' conceptual apparatus and terminology, however, are very different from those of Thucydides. As Walbank has said,[31] Polybius 'uses *aitia* to describe such events as lead the individual to conceive a will to war; the pretext for war then given (which may or may not be genuine) is the *prophasis*. The first action of the war itself . . . is the *archē*'. Among the more interesting passages in Polybius on this subject are III 6.1–7, 9–14;

---

[29] Thucydides' attitude to compulsion is at the opposite extreme from that taken by the predominant section of Spanish theologians in the fifteenth and sixteenth centuries, when the question arose whether the baptism of Jews and Moriscos who had been compulsorily converted to Christianity could be considered valid. According to the prevailing view, the mere fact that they had '*chosen* baptism as an alternative to death or exile meant that they had exercised the right of free choice: there was therefore no compulsion, and the sacrament was valid' (H. Kamen, *The Spanish Inquisition*, 1965, paperback 1968, pp. 60, 111). In the words of Paulus (*Dig.* IV ii.21.5), 'tamen coactus volui'.

[30] See esp. P. Pédech, *La méthode historique de Polybe* (Paris, 1964) 75–98 ('Théorie de la cause chez Polybe'), 99–203 ('Les causes historiques: L'origine des guerres').

[31] Walbank, *HCP* I 305, cf. 461.

7.4–7; 12.7; 31.11–13; IV 3.1–4; 13.6 (where *aphormē* stands for *prophasis*; cf. II 52.3; 59.9); 56.1; and (in strongest contrast with Thuc. I 23.6) III 15.9, where Hannibal, 'altogether full of irrational and violent anger, did not adduce the true reasons (*aitiai*) but took refuge in unreasonable pretexts (*prophaseis alogous*)'—here the *prophaseis* given by Hannibal are false, and are contrasted with the real *aitiai*.

III

The immediate background, c. 435–1

(i)
The attitudes of the parties in 432–1

At this stage I wish only to take a general look at the attitudes of the parties in 432–1, leaving most of the detailed consideration of the attitudes of Sparta and Athens to a later Chapter (V, Part ix).

In 432 Corinth and Megara and the majority of Sparta's other allies, not to mention Aegina and King Perdiccas of Macedon, were eager for war against Athens.[1] A qualification is necessary here: all we have a right to say is that war was desired by what we may call for convenience the 'governments' of these states[2]—those who possessed the political franchise and could hope to influence the decisions of their city. This qualification is essential, because Corinth and the great majority of the other Spartan allies were under more or less oligarchical governments, in which effective political rights were confined to the upper classes—strictly, the propertied classes (cf. Chapter I, Part iii above). In most cases, however, it is only the actions of the 'governments' concerned about which we have any information at all; and when I speak of a Greek city as (for example) 'Corinth', or 'the Corinthians', I must be understood to mean those of its citizens who exercised effective control over its policy. Neglect to consider precisely who were involved in a State decision can lead to gross confusion, as when a recent writer[3] remarks, 'The Samians deified Lysander, not Pericles', oblivious of the fact that it was the Samian decarchy set up by Lysander in 404,[4] after the bulk of the citizens had been expelled or deprived of political rights, which paid him quasi-divine honours![5] (In spite of the war of 440–39, the mass of Samians during the Ionian war, as is well known, were perhaps the most enthusiastically pro-Athenian of all the allied states, and Samos resisted the victorious Lysander longer than any other city.)

At Sparta the great majority of citizens were in favour of war, at least by the time of the Assembly in the second half of 432 at which the Spartan

[1] Thuc. 1 66–7 (allies and Aegina). For Perdiccas, see 1 56.2; 57.2–5; 58.2; 61.3 with 62.2–3 etc.; and Appendix XI.

[2] Of course no Greek city ever had a 'government' in the modern sense. For the bearing of this on the making of treaties, see my ASPAP 115–16.

[3] P. J. Bicknell, in *JHS* 89 (1969) 175.

[4] Xen., *HG* II iii.6–7; Diod. xiv 3.4–5; Plut., *Lys.* 13 (general), 14.2.

[5] Plut., *Lys.* 18.5–6 (Duris, *FGrH* 76 F 71); cf. Duris F 26; Paus. VI iii.14–15 (contrast 16). See Christian Habicht, *Gottmenschtum und griechische Städte*[2] (*Zetemata* 14, Munich, 1970, 2nd edn.) 3–6, 243–4.

decision to go to war was taken (Thuc. 1 79.2; 87.3). The Thirty Years Peace had forbidden resort to war by either side if the other appealed to arbitration (see Appendix I, §3), and the Athenians appealed at once to this clause; but the Spartans, evidently realising that their own case was a very bad one, ignored the appeal. Thucydides makes a whole series of references to this:[6] he actually goes so far as to say (in VII 18.2–3) that the Spartans later on had a bad conscience about their behaviour and felt that it had deservedly brought misfortune upon them. This surely goes well beyond the question who was *technically* the aggressor. The Spartans felt that they rather than the Athenians had been guilty of transgression (*paranomēma*, twice over) in beginning the war, not only because of the Theban attack on Plataea in time of peace but also because of their own refusal to arbitrate in accordance with the terms of the treaty. 'For this reason', Thucydides says, 'they thought they deserved their misfortunes': they were thinking of Pylos and other setbacks. I for one cannot believe that Thucydides is not implicitly endorsing the Spartans' judgment upon themselves here—though not, of course, their superstitious beliefs. Why otherwise should he mention their guilty feelings? Against the theory, so popular nowadays, that Athens was the aggressive party in 433–1, I myself have no doubt that the real aggressors were Sparta and her allies, and that Thucydides fully realised this: not only this passage but his whole narrative in Book I and early in Book II proves it. It is often noticed that Thucydides says Pericles 'urged the Athenians on to war'.[7] But the historian says this of a late stage in the proceedings, when both the Spartan Assembly and the Peloponnesian League Congress had taken formal decisions in favour of war. It is less often noticed that Thucydides has used much the same phrase earlier (1 87.2) of the behaviour of the presiding ephor Sthenelaïdas at the crucial meeting of the Spartan Assembly, when Sthenelaïdas 'wanted to make the Spartans declare their decision manifestly and to urge them on the more to go to war'. Here there is a significant difference: we have *es to polemein*, 'to *go to* war', and not, as in Pericles' case, *es ton polemon*, to a war that had already been declared by the other side. The Spartan embassies sent to Athens in the winter of 432/1 do not significantly alter this picture (cf. Appendix XII).

The attitude of Athens is to be judged, of course, not only by her appeals to arbitration, but by her whole conduct in these years. If the only evidence for the anxiety of Athens to avert war were her offer of arbitration, we might brush that aside as a mere manoeuvre, designed to put the Peloponnesians in the wrong and oblige them to assume the role of aggressors. Is there not, some will say, ample evidence of Athenian aggressiveness, to offset the facts we have established about the arbitration appeal? For an unguarded statement of the extreme view we may turn to a recent article on the causes of war as they appeared to Herodotus and Thucydides.[8]

---

[6] Thuc. 1 78.4; 140.2; 144.2; 145; and esp. VII 18.2–3; cf. 1 85.2; 86.3.
[7] Thuc. 1 127.3: ἐς τὸν πόλεμον ὥρμα τοὺς ᾿Αθηναίους.
[8] Sealey, THCW 8–12.

'In the years 433–2 the Athenians were spoiling for a fight. They tried to provoke the Peloponnesian League to war by sending help to Corcyra, by Phormion's attack on the Ampraciotes, by making exorbitant demands on the Potidaeans, by the Megara-decree, and perhaps by some action in Aegina. By these incidents they sought to precipitate war'. Here are five accusations against Athens. The Megarian decree is a major question, but it is convenient to leave it to the end of our investigation (Chapter VII). We shall not find in it a provocation to war. The affair of Aegina can be quickly dismissed. We have no way of discovering whether Aegina's complaints in 432 were justified: we have no information about the terms of capitulation of Aegina to Athens in *c.* 457; we do not know what, if any, provisions concerning her were contained in the Thirty Years Peace; and we cannot tell whether Athens had recently changed her policy in regard to Aegina.[9] There remain the Athenian decision to help Corcyra, the affair of Potidaea, and Phormio's campaign in the Gulf of Ampracia, which we can now deal with in succession.

(ii)
Epidamnus and the Athenian-Corcyraean alliance

It is extraordinary how harshly many modern scholars have judged the action of Athens in entering into a defensive alliance with Corcyra in 433. Thus the authors of *The Athenian Tribute Lists* (*ATL* III 320) have spoken of 'the crisis over Kerkyra' as 'virtually offering a choice between peace and war'; and their opinion is that 'Athens, by accepting Kerkyra's alliance, chose war'. According to Hignett (*HAC* 260), why Pericles 'decided in 433 and 432 to take steps which inevitably precipitated war with the Peloponnesian League was a riddle to his contemporaries and still is to us'. (This attitude, treating the decisions made by the Athenian Assembly as if they were made purely by Pericles or some other statesman alone, is a frequent cause of serious misunderstanding.) Again, Hammond has spoken of '*the balance of naval power* between Athens and the Peloponnesians, which formed a realistic basis of the Thirty Years Treaty': he thinks that this supposed 'balance of naval power' would have been 'decisively overthrown' by a major Athenian naval expedition in support of Corcyra, and that if Athens merely 'sent nominal help and watched the fleets of Corcyra and Corinth wear each other down, the *balance of naval power* would incline in favour of Athens'; later he adds that by her actions Athens did 'upset *the balance of naval power* and threatened the cohesion of the Spartan Alliance" (*HG²* 319, 322, cf. 311–12: my italics).

The notion of a '*balance* of *naval* power' between the two sides is fanciful.

[9] See the very sensible remarks of Gomme, *HCT* I 225–6, and of Brunt, MD 272. Cf. *ATL* III 303–4, 320. Athens may have taken some punitive action against Aegina in 432, on the ground that she had paid only part of her tribute for 433/2 (see List 22 I 88, in *ATL* II 27: only 9 or 14 talents paid, instead of 30). A tantalising scrap of evidence, *IG* I² 18 (= *SEG* III 5 = XIV 2), is discussed by D. M. Lewis, in *BSA* 49 (1954), at pp. 21–5. I do not accept the views of Mattingly, in *Historia* 16 (1967) 1–5.

Athens, rarely even troubling to ask for Corcyraean contingents to assist her,[10] was completely dominant at sea,[11] as the Peloponnesians were by land, and she was never seriously challenged until Persian silver, the price of the surrender of the Greeks of Asia to the Great King, enabled Sparta at last to match her. Sparta might in theory be able to ask her allies for naval assistance, but the numbers of ships supplied in practice were not impressive,[12] perhaps mainly because of the great financial expense of keeping triremes in service (cf. Thuc. 1 80.4; 81.3–4; 82.1–2; 83.2–3). The fighting quality of the Peloponnesian warships was also vastly below that of the Athenian fleet, their tactics being still old-fashioned and inefficient: see Thuc. 1 49.1–3 (with some scathing comments). In 429, Phormio with a mere 20 Athenian ships severely defeated Peloponnesian fleets of 47 and 77 (Thuc. II 83–92).

But is it true to say that Athens, by receiving Corcyra into a defensive alliance in 433, 'chose war' with the Peloponnesians? In order to answer this question it is necessary to look carefully at the whole course of the dispute between Corinth and Corcyra, which led to Corcyra's appeal to Athens. As soon as we do that, we can see that Corinth was being quite extraordinarily aggressive towards Corcyra and must bear virtually the whole of the responsibility for the consequences which ensued. This has not been sufficiently realised by modern scholars. It is a merit of Kagan's recent book[13] to have emphasised the insane aggressiveness of Corinth in the Epidamnus affair, although as regards Potidaea even Kagan, owing to his misunderstanding of one vital text (the last few words of

[10] We hear of 50 Corcyraean ships co-operating in the Athenian expedition around Peloponnese in 431 (Thuc. II 25.1), and of up to 60 (of which 13 were lost) in service off Corcyra in 427 (III 77.1–80.1); 15 helped for a time in the attack on Leucas in 426 (III 94.1; 95.2); and 15 sailed with Demosthenes' expedition to Sicily in 413 (VII 31.5; cf. 44.6; 57.7). But we never hear of any Corcyraean ships in the Aegean. There is a disparaging reference to Corcyraean shilly-shallying in the comic poet Hermippus, fr. 63.10–11, from the *Phormophoroi*, *ap.* Athen. 1 27f. I may add that the full symmachy planned in 427 (Thuc. III 70.6; 75.1) must have become a fact, in view of VII 57.7, which seems to refer to a treaty obligation (see Dover in Gomme, *HCT* IV 411, 433–4).

[11] See the striking passage in Thuc. v 56.1–2, where the Argives actually complain because the Athenians had not prevented a Peloponnesian garrison of 300 men from getting into Epidaurus by sea: they pretended this was a breach of the treaty obligation of Athens not to allow enemies to pass διὰ τῆς ἑαυτῶν—which of course meant Athenian *territory*!

[12] Except for the obviously wrong number of 500 in Thuc. II 7.2 (on which see Gomme, *HCT* II 7), it is hard to see any basis for Hammond's statement (*HG*[2] 311–12), 'So long as her colonies were loyal to her, Corinth and the other naval states in the Spartan Alliance were soon able to muster a combined fleet of some 300 triremes, quite apart from the fleet of Syracuse, for the conduct of operations in the west'. The actual figures are very different: in 433 (Thuc. 1 31.1; 46.1), 150 ships were mustered, with a great effort on Corinth's part, from 'nearly every state that could provide ships for the Peloponnesian League' (Gomme, *loc. cit.*); and the only other Peloponnesian fleets of any size that we hear of in action in the Ten Years war consisted of 100 ships (430: Thuc. II 66.1), 77 (429: II 86.4), and 40 (428: III 16.3; 29.1). In 413, only 100 were ordered (VIII 3.2). In view of Hammond's statement (*HG*[2] 345) that 'the naval strength of the Spartan Alliance had been severely damaged by the defection of Corcyra', is it uncharitable to suggest that Hammond must be including Corcyra's 120 in his 300 triremes?–when in fact Corcyra was entirely independent of Corinth and Sparta, and not controlled by either.

[13] *OPW* 205 ff.—much better in this respect than e.g. Brauer, *KSFGU*.

Thuc. 1 66: see Part iii of this Chapter), has let Corinth off too lightly and failed to see that she was also the first city to break the Thirty Years Peace.

Corinth and Corcyra, instead of enjoying the friendly relations that were normal between mother-city and colony, had always been hostile[14] and had gone to war again in 435[15] over Epidamnus (Dyrrhachium, the modern Durazzo), originally a colony of Corcyra under a Corinthian founder (*oikistēs*). The demos of Epidamnus had expelled the 'men of influence' (*dynatoi*), who thereupon joined the local non-Greek population and plundered the Epidamnians by sea and land. The demos of Epidamnus asked the Corcyraeans to reconcile them with the exiles and put an end to the hostile activity of the non-Greeks. The Corcyraeans refusing to intervene, the Epidamnian demos consulted the Delphic Oracle. In accordance with common practice, they gave a strong hint of the advice they would like to receive, and they duly received it: they were to 'hand themselves over to Corinth and accept her leadership'. This they did. The Corinthians, feeling the Epidamnians to be their own colonists as much as Corcyra's, gladly undertook the suggested task, both as a kind of duty *and because of their hatred for the Corcyraeans*, who, although their colonists, slighted them (Thuc. 1 25.3; 26.1). Already we find an unpleasant motive attributed to the Corinthians; and their resentment against Corcyra and desire to humble her play a large part in what follows.

The first phase of direct conflict between Corinth and Corcyra over Epidamnus began with the Corinthians sending some volunteer settlers to Epidamnus, with a garrison to protect them. They knew very well that Corcyra was likely to take their action as a provocative one and intercept the settlers if they went by sea; they therefore sent them at least part of the way by land (see Gomme, *HCT* 1 160, on Thuc. 1 26.2). The Corcyraeans reacted at once, peremptorily ordering the Epidamnians to expel the garrison and settlers and to receive back the exiles—who also (like the demos, but with more success) had appealed for help to Corcyra. They made an announcement that those inside the city might depart, with safe conduct, or be treated as enemies; and when this had no success, they began a siege of Epidamnus.

On hearing of this the Corinthians made plans for a military expedition and proclaimed a colony to Epidamnus. Anyone not wishing to go out immediately was to be allowed to secure his share by putting down a deposit of 50 Corinthian drachmae: many did so, and many sailed out. The colonists were to be convoyed by a fleet of 75 ships, of which 30 were from Corinth herself, the other major contributors being Leucas (10 ships), Megara and Ampracia (8 each), and Epidaurus (5); and there were to be two or three thousand Corinthian hoplites on board (Thuc. 1 27.2; 29.1).

Thucydides now tells us (1 28.1; cf. 34.2) that when the Corcyraeans

---

[14] Hdts III 49.1 ff.; Thuc. 1 13.4; 25.3–4; 38; and see Graham, *CMCAG* 146 ff., with 128–33 (and see his Index, *s.v.* 'Corinth, Corinthian . . . and Corcyra').

[15] For the whole story, see Thuc. 1 24 ff.; for the chronology, Gomme, *HCT* 1 196–9.

heard of these preparations they sent an embassy to Corinth to make counter proposals, 'in company with ambassadors from Sparta and Sicyon'. Their proposals were eminently reasonable, and it is very significant that they received the support of Sparta and her ally Sicyon (Corinth's nearest neighbour on the west), both of whom had good reason to be nervous about the unforeseeable consequences of Corinth's headstrong behaviour.[16] Epidamnus, said the Corcyraeans, was not Corinth's affair, and Corinth must remove the garrison and settlers. If she objected, the Corcyraeans were prepared to refer the dispute either to the arbitration of such Peloponnesian states as they and Corinth should agree upon, or to the Delphic Oracle.[17] They warned Corinth that if she persisted, and war resulted, they would be 'compelled by Corinthian violence, in their need for assistance, to acquire friends they would rather not have, different from their present ones' (Thuc. 1 28.3)—a very plain warning that they would be driven to appeal to Athens, the only power capable of giving effective help against such a large naval expedition. The Corinthians refused to negotiate at all, or submit to arbitration, unless the Corcyraeans withdrew their fleet and barbarian auxiliaries from Epidamnus, whereupon the Corcyraeans made the very reasonable rejoinder that they would do so if Corinth too withdrew her forces from Epidamnus, or alternatively that a truce should be made pending a settlement by arbitration. In all this, the Corcyraeans went as far as any state in their position could have been expected to do in their attempt to effect a settlement. Their proposal for arbitration by *Peloponnesian* states (most of which were fellow-allies of Corinth in the Peloponnesian League) was one conciliatory gesture to Corinth, and the suggested reference to the Delphic Oracle was another, for it was Delphi which had authorised the appeal of the Epidamnians to Corinth in the first place (Thuc. 1 25.1).

Turning a deaf ear to all the Corcyraean proposals, the Corinthians completed their preparations, made a formal declaration of war against Corcyra, and sailed out with their formidable armament in the summer of 435, disregarding a last warning by a Corcyraean herald (Thuc. 1 29.1–4). Of the Corcyraean fleet of 120 triremes, 40 remained to continue the siege of Epidamnus, but the remaining 80 were enough to inflict upon Corinth a decisive defeat, at the battle of Leucimme (a headland of Corcyra), 15 Corinthian ships being sunk. On the very same day Epidamnus capitulated. The Corinthians inside the town were kept as prisoners for the time being, and presumably in due course were ransomed. As for the other prisoners, in the sea-battle and from the town, Thucydides' narrative is not perfectly clear, but probably the citizens of other states who surrendered in the town, including the Epidamnians themselves, were

---

[16] Gomme (*HCT* 1 162) rightly points out, against Forbes, that the envoys of Sparta and Sicyon are called πρέσβεις and must therefore have been official ambassadors, not just private persons.

[17] See the useful comment of Graham, *CMCAG* 134–5, on the meaning of τούτους κρατεῖν in Thuc. 1 28.2.

sold as slaves, and the non-Corinthian prisoners taken in the naval battle were treated as privateers and killed.[18]

So ended the first phase of the Corinthian-Corcyraean struggle. The Corcyraeans made some retaliation by ravaging Leucas, which had furnished ships for the Corinthian expedition, and besieging Cyllene, the harbour of Elis, because Elis had provided Corinth with ships and money. They also made attacks on the shipping of Corinth's allies. Early in the summer of 434 the Corinthians sent out an expedition of unknown size to protect their allies: Corinthians and Corcyraeans set up military stations opposite each other, but no further naval engagements occurred before both sides went home, at the approach of winter (Thuc. 1 30.3–4).

The whole matter could and should have ended there, but the Corinthians still felt passionately about the war, and from 435 to 433 they did their utmost to prepare another expedition (1 31.1), building ships and hiring mercenary rowers from the Peloponnese and the rest of Greece, many of them (1 35.3–4) from states allied to Athens. Only later (46.1), after recounting the successful Corcyraean appeal to Athens, does Thucydides tell us what a vast armament they were planning: when they sailed against Corcyra in the late summer of 433 they had no less than 150 ships, twice the size of the fleet which had been defeated at Leucimme two years earlier. Ninety of these ships were their own and sixty were provided by their allies: 27 by Ampracia, 12 by Megara, 10 each by Elis and Leucas, and one by Anactorium. The Corcyraeans had always pursued a deliberate policy of refraining from foreign alliances, as Thucydides makes them say to the Athenians; and they now found themselves with no allies at all, in a desperate situation (Thuc. 1 31.2; 32.4–5; cf. 37.2–5). They therefore turned to Athens.

The acceptance of the Corcyraean appeal by Athens is often taken as the moment at which the Peloponnesian war became inevitable; and, as we have seen, the Athenians in general and Pericles in particular are often blamed for the decision then taken. It will be well, therefore, to analyse the situation carefully. Most scholars have admitted that Athens was not precluded by the terms of the Thirty Years Peace from making the alliance, but many have nevertheless tended to see it as a provocative action, leading inescapably to war with the Peloponnesians.

In reality Corinth was now an unashamed aggressor. She had begun her intervention at Epidamnus partly out of hatred of Corcyra. At quite an early stage Corcyra, supported by Sparta and Sicyon, had vainly urged her to go to arbitration, and had issued a warning containing the clear implication that if Corinth persisted, Corcyra might be forced unwillingly into the arms of Athens. Yet Corinth had declared war and launched a direct attack on Corcyra. When this failed, at Leucimme, Corinth should have cut her losses and accepted the *fait accompli*, even with the serious loss of face which this might have entailed. Corcyra, after making some

---

[18] See Gomme, *HCT* 1 164–5, on Thuc. 1 29.5; 30.1. Cf. the Corinthian slaughter of their prisoners after Sybota, Thuc. 1 50.1.

attempt in 435–4 to retaliate against Corinth and her allies, evidently did not want to continue the conflict, and if Corinth had not been highly aggressive the whole unhappy affair could have ended in 434. But Corinth was determined on revenge and the subjection of Corcyra, and the expedition she was planning was of very great size. Corinth was taking the calculated risk that Corcyra would ally herself with Athens, a combination which would certainly prove too strong for Corinth—unless of course she could induce Sparta and the Peloponnesian League to take part in the struggle.

Athens was certainly entitled to ally herself with Corcyra under the terms of the Thirty Years Peace, which had explicitly provided (see Appendix I, § 6) that any city among the *agraphoi poleis*—that is to say, those not included in the two lists of allies appended to the Peace—could join either side. The Corcyraeans appealed to this provision (Thuc. 1 35.2); in reply, the Corinthians admitted its existence but lamely tried to argue it away, with specious provisos. Thucydides, in a tortuous and almost untranslatable sentence (40.2), makes them claim that (this provision of) the treaty was 'not intended for those who are out to damage others, but for those who seek security *without defecting from another State*, and who will not bring war to those who receive them, instead of the peace accompanying sensible behaviour—as will happen to you if you are not persuaded by us now'. Here, in a very Thucydidean way, the Corinthians are saying that the provision about 'cities not listed' (*agraphoi poleis*) was not intended to apply to a State such as Corcyra which is (1) out to damage others, (2) defecting from another State, and (3) about to bring war on Athens if received into alliance with her. The force of the curious phrase about 'defecting from another State'[19] emerges a little later, when the Corinthians have the audacity to urge the Athenians not to 'receive those who revolt from other states',[20] meaning that the Corcyraeans are subordinate allies of their own who have revolted, a notion they proceed to illustrate immediately (40.5; cf. 41.2; 43.1) by pluming themselves on the fact that they stopped the Peloponnesians from intervening in favour of Samos during her revolt from Athens (in 440), insisting that each state should be allowed to chastise (*kolazein*) its own allies. In this picture Corcyra stands to Corinth in the same relationship as Samos to Athens: that of a subject ally. In fact Corcyra was, and had been for centuries, entirely independent of her mother-city. One wonders whether the Corinthians did actually advance such a ludicrous argument, or whether Thucydides put these words into their mouth by way of demonstrating how weak their case was. If the latter, he has certainly failed to convey his meaning to most modern scholars!

Thucydides says (1 44.1) that at the end of the first of the two days of the debate the Athenians were rather inclined to accept the Corinthian position, but that on the second day they changed their minds; however,

---

[19] Thuc. 1 40.2: ἄλλου ἑαυτὸν ἀποστερῶν.
[20] Thuc. 1 40.4; τοὺς ἑτέρων ἀφισταμένους δέχεσθαι.

what they decided to conclude was 'not a symmachy, on the terms that each side should have the same friends and enemies (for then, if Corcyra required them to join in a naval expedition against Corinth, they would be breaking their treaty with the Peloponnesians), but an epimachy (*epimachia*),[21] on the terms that each side was to help the other if there were an attack on Corcyra or Athens or their respective allies'—in other words, a purely defensive alliance. How many Athenians remained hostile to any alliance with Corcyra, and how many would have preferred an all-out symmachy, we have of course no means of telling. It is tempting to suggest that on the first day the issue was between accepting or rejecting a full symmachy with Corcyra, but that on the second day an epimachy was proposed as an acceptable compromise. It seems rarely to be noticed that what the Corcyraeans ask for in Thucydides,[22] and what the Corinthians argue against,[23] is a symmachy without qualification: a full offensive and defensive alliance. Although the Thirty Years Peace, in allowing 'cities not listed' to '*join* whichever side they please', is represented as using an imprecise phrase (35.2; cf. 40.2), a full symmachy was obviously not excluded—after all, each of the two grand alliances *was* a symmachy, and any state joining either side would naturally join in the symmachy. But as we have seen, what Corcyra got was an epimachy, a purely defensive alliance, which did no more than bind the parties to assist each other against outside attack. And anyone who reads Thucydides' version of the debate carefully and without preconceived ideas can see that much of the Corinthian argument, even if it has some validity against a full symmachy between Athens and Corcyra, has none whatever against an epimachy—for it now lay entirely with Corinth herself whether the war with Corcyra was to be renewed: only if she herself launched an attack would there be any question of Athens entering the struggle against her.

I find it incomprehensible that anyone who has read the preceding narrative in Thucydides should find the Corinthian speech plausible. Yet many have done so. Recently, for example, it has been said that the reader of the two speeches 'receives the strong impression that the Corinthians have the better case, and that the Athenians, in accepting the Corcyraean alliance, precipitated the war. . . . Arguments based on justice were the strongest that the Corinthians had . . . and such arguments *ought* to have convinced the Athenians, if they had been in a normal frame of mind' (S. Usher, *The Historians of Greece and Rome* [1969] 48–9). Kagan too (*OPW* 231–2) is willing to accept part of the Corinthian argument. 'Surely no one in 446/5', he says, 'envisaged a situation in which a signatory would accept into alliance a neutral state already at war with the other signatory'. But this ignores three facts: that Athens made a purely defensive alliance with Corcyra; that at that time military operations were not actually being carried on by either state against the other; and that

---

[21] On symmachy and epimachy, see Appendix XIII.
[22] Thuc. I 32.2,4; 33.2,4; 35.3,5; cf. 31.2; 44.1.
[23] Thuc. I 39.2; 42.4; 43.3.

Corcyra was apparently contemplating no action against Corinth, from which alone the aggression was about to come. The result of the Athenian-Corcyraean alliance should have been to warn the Corinthians off the war they had been threatening, for they would obviously have no chance against the combined navies of Corcyra and Athens. Their persistence in their aggressive plans proves one of two things: either they calculated, recklessly and falsely, that Athens would not dare to send effective help to Corcyra and thus bring on herself the danger of a general war with the Peloponnesians,[24] or, less probably, they actually wished already (as they undoubtedly did a little later) to provoke such a general war.

The Athenian-Corcyraean alliance is probably to be dated in early July 433: see Appendix XII §2 below.

The two-day debate is particularly interesting as a corrective to the popular view of Pericles as the uncrowned king of Athens, whom the people at this period meekly followed. The famous passage in Thucydides (II 65.9) which one so often hears quoted in justification of this view is commonly understood in a more extreme sense than Thucydides intended: he is not quite saying that 'what was in name a democracy *became* a rule by the first citizen', but rather that it was '*tending to become*' such a rule—the verb, *egigneto*, is in the imperfect tense, not the aorist. Some very exaggerated views have been propounded about the position of Pericles and the way Herodotus and others conceived it, but these have been sufficiently refuted by Gomme.[25] We find a long and hard-fought debate taking place in the Assembly on both the occasions just before the outbreak of the war on which the Athenians had to make vital decisions in matters of foreign policy; now, and on the reception of the final Spartan embassy in the winter of 432/1. On the latter occasion there were many speakers on each side, and the advice of Pericles prevailed (Thuc. I 139.4; 145). It seems very likely that the epimachy with Corcyra was his choice also. Was it a wise choice?

There are four factors in the situation which need to be examined. Thucydides (I 44.2–3) mentions the first three immediately after recording the Athenian decision to make the alliance with Corcyra.

1. The Athenians believed that a war with the Peloponnesians was coming anyway (44.2). Thucydides makes the Corcyraeans say as much in their speech, alluding to the war as 'imminent and all but in being' (36.1). The Spartans, they say, are afraid of Athens and want war, and Athens' enemy Corinth has influence at Sparta and is trying to conquer

---

[24] Cf. Kagan, *OPW* 235–6, for some sensible reflections on how the Corinthians came to make 'the most serious of errors in judging that the Athenians would refuse the alliance with Corcyra'. But their persistence in attacking Corcyra after the alliance had been made was an even more extraordinary miscalculation—if that is all it was.

[25] E.g. J. S. Morrison, 'The Place of Protagoras in Athenian Public Life', in *CQ* 35 (1941) 1–16; and 'Pericles Monarchos', in *JHS* 70 (1950) 76–7; contrast Gomme's reply, *Id.* 77; also his *MEGHL* 137–8.

Corcyra as a prelude to attacking Athens herself (33.3). Although Thucydides allows the Corinthians a riposte on this question, it is hardly an effective one: they merely say that the coming of the war is still uncertain and the Athenians should not allow the Corcyraeans to use it as a bugbear to drive them into 'doing wrong' and incurring the immediate and manifest hostility of Corinth (42.2). It may conceivably have been on this occasion that Pericles said he could already 'see war bearing down from the Peloponnese'.[26] We have independent contemporary evidence that at least as early as autumn, winter or spring of the year 434/3 (well before the appeal of Corcyra) the Athenians were apprehensive about a possible major war, which could only be with the Peloponnesian League. This evidence is provided by the 'Callias decrees'.[27] Here we see a change in financial policy: the treasures of the gods other than Athena, known collectively as 'the Other Gods' (treasures which presumably until now were scattered in their temples and shrines all over Attica), are to be concentrated on the Acropolis, in the care of a new board of magistrates, the 'Treasurers of the Other Gods', and are to be recorded in official accounts and inventories; money borrowed from the Other Gods is to be repaid to them (and thus accumulated, with their existing treasures, as a further reserve, additional to Athena's); surplus revenues are to be used for the dockyards and walls; and, apart from certain specified expenditure, not more than 10,000 drachmae are to be taken out of Athena's funds without a previous vote of indemnity (*adeia*). As the authors of *ATL* say,[28] 'The instruction to collect the treasures of the temples of Attica into the Akropolis of Athens, and the general tone of economy, probably imply that Athens was facing the likelihood of war and making provision against a possible invasion'. The bringing of the treasures from the countryside to the Acropolis is certainly a most significant move; and when taken in conjunction with the financial measures outlined above, it surely points to an expectation of war in the near future. We cannot yet decide whether these Athenian apprehensions were justified by threatening behaviour on the part of the Peloponnesians, or whether they are simply an indication that Athens herself was preparing for aggression, and 'projecting' her own aggressive designs into the minds of her potential adversaries. We shall return to this question after we have looked at all the circumstances, and in particular the attitude of Sparta. Meanwhile we can keep an open mind.

---

[26] Plut., *Per.* 8.7; cf. (on Pericles' own attitude) 23.2; 29.1; Thuc. 1 127.1–3; 140–4; 11 61.1. Another possible occasion for Pericles' remark quoted in the text is 440 (see Chapter V, Part viii below) or 435–4 (Meyer, *FAG* 11 324).

[27] M/L 58 = D 1 and 2 in *ATL* 11 46–7 = Tod 1² 51 = *IG* 1² 91–2. The best approach is through the admirable commentary in M/L.

[28] *ATL* 111 320 (cf. 326 ff.). That the Callias decrees signify a deliberate preparation for war was seen clearly long ago by Ed. Meyer (*FAG* 11 88 ff., esp. 105–18), who believed, probably rightly, that Pericles must have foreseen in 435–4 the appeal of Corcyra and the dangerous consequences that might follow.

2. Thucydides' second point is that the Athenians did not want Corcyra, with her great navy (the largest in Greece after the Athenian),[29] to be abandoned to the Corinthians. Surely this was by far the most important consideration, although it was essentially a negative one. It was not a question of Athens' wanting to add the Corcyraean fleet to her own, which was already more than capable of dealing with the whole naval forces of the Peloponnesians. But if Athens refused to intervene, there was a very real danger that Corinth would defeat Corcyra and then take her over as a subject ally—as we have already seen, the Corinthians already pretended that that was her proper relationship to themselves. The Corinthians would then have at their disposal the Corcyraean fleet, which would greatly increase the strength of the Peloponnesian naval forces and would at least put them in a position to make a serious challenge to Athens at sea. The importance of the Corcyraean fleet to the Peloponnesians is emphasised by Thucydides not only here (1 36.3; 44.2) but also in the first debate at Sparta in 432, when he makes the Corinthians express annoyance that Athens had prevented them from taking over Corcyra, 'which would have contributed a very great navy to the Peloponnesians' (68.4). Thucydides also remarks (44.2) that the Athenians, rather than let the Corcyraean fleet be handed over to Corinth, wanted them to wear each other down and become weaker, against the day when Athens might be at war with Corinth and the other naval powers.

3. Thucydides makes a third point (44.3; cf. 36.2): Corcyra 'seemed to lie conveniently on the coastal voyage (the *paraplous*) to Italy and Sicily'. The Corcyraeans, using this as an argument in favour of their plea for an alliance, are made to assert that their island (among its other advantages) can 'both prevent the passage of a war fleet (*nautikon*) from Italy and Sicily to the Peloponnesians, and assist the voyage of one westwards'. Thucydides does not repeat this statement when he is giving the reasons for the Athenian decision, and it is quite possible that he regarded a Corcyraean claim actually to be able to *stop* a fleet coming from (for instance) Syracuse to join the Peloponnesians as an exaggeration. However that may be, we must not fail to notice that the Corcyraean statement refers specifically to the strategic position of the island in regard to *war fleets*, not merchant vessels. The adherence of Corcyra to Athens would have very little effect upon *trade* between Athens and Italy or Sicily, as we shall see more clearly when we come to deal at a later stage with the development of Athenian policy towards the West (Chapter VI, Part iii). To conceive of Corcyra as '*the* one critical point on the western trade route', as Grundy did (*THA* I[2] 409), is a serious error. We cannot hope to decide how much influence the strategic position of Corcyra had upon the Athenian decision, but it is surely safe to conclude that it was merely an additional recommendation of an alliance, and that the decisive argument was the necessity of not letting Corcyra's fleet fall into Peloponnesian hands.

[29] Thuc. 1 33.1; cf. 25.4 (120 triremes at the beginning of the war); 29.4; 36.3; Hdts VII 168.3.

4. Before we finally pass judgment on the Athenians' decision to accept Corcyra into alliance, we ought to look at their subsequent behaviour, in particular towards Corinth, for this may help to illuminate their intentions in making the alliance. Here there are three episodes to consider: (*a*) the choice of generals to command the expeditions that were sent to help Corcyra, and the instructions given to them; (*b*) the conduct of the Athenian squadrons in the battle of Sybota; and (*c*) the attitude of the Athenians at the parley after the battle. We may look at these briefly in turn.

(*a*) The first expedition, consisting of ten ships, was commanded by Lacedaemonius, Diotimus and Proteas, and the second, of twenty ships, by Glaucon, Metagenes and (very probably) Dracontides.[30] That as many as three Strategoi should have been sent out with each squadron, making six in all out of the whole body of ten Athenian generals, to command only thirty ships, is itself remarkable, suggesting that 'the occasion was politically important' (as Gomme says, *HCT* 1 188). And there is something even more significant: the personality of the first-named general, who was Lacedaemonius *the son of Cimon*. As is very well known, and as we shall have occasion to notice in Chapter V below, Cimon had been the most prominent upholder of that 'dual hegemony' of Sparta and Athens which had allowed Athens to build up the Delian League and turn it into an Athenian empire. Cimon had been dead for nearly twenty years, but his son, who would have automatically inherited his father's position as a Spartan proxenos, would certainly have inherited also his father's policy of friendship with Sparta, to which his very name (*Lakedaimonios*, Spartan) was an eloquent testimony. We know nothing of his earlier career, except that he had been a hipparch *c.* 446 B.C. and as such had dedicated an equestrian statue on the Acropolis from enemy spoil (*IG* 1² 400 = *DAA* 135). The significance of his appointment to this command is that, as 'Lacedaemonius' and as the son of Cimon, he if anyone could be trusted to ensure that no armed conflict took place with Corinth or the other Peloponnesians unless it became absolutely necessary. Plutarch, in his *Life of Pericles* (29.1–3), speaks of Pericles as sending Lacedaemonius out against his will and with only ten ships, 'as if to insult him', adding that Cimon's family was on terms of special goodwill and friendship with Sparta, and that Pericles was trying to make sure that if Lacedaemonius achieved no great success he would be discredited as a Laconiser. This is characteristic of the attitude to Pericles of most of our sources, other than Thucydides,[31]

---

[30] M/L 61 (= Tod 1² 55 = *IG* 1² 295), lines 7–9, 18–21; cf. Thuc. 1 45.1–2; 50.5, with 51.4. See M/L p. 168 on Thucydides' errors (esp. the reference to Gomme, *HCT* 1 31, 85, 188–90). For Lacedaemonius, see below. On Diotimus, see the entries in Kirchner, *PA* no. 4,386; Proteas, no. 12,298; Glaucon, no. 3,027; Metagenes, no. 10,088; Dracontides, no. 4, 551. Davies, *APF* (with the same numbers), adds information about Diotimus, Glaucon and Dracontides.

[31] It may well come from the very unreliable Stesimbrotus (*FGrH* 107), because of the similarity between Plut., *Per.* 29.2 and *Cim.* 16.1, the latter specifically mentioning Stesimbrotus. Kagan, although he rejects the motive suggested by Plutarch (*OPW* 244),

and we need do no more than note the propaganda. The instructions given to the generals of the first squadron were 'not to have a naval engagement with the Corinthians, unless they sailed to Corcyra or one of her possessions and were about to land. These instructions were given *with a view to avoiding a breach of the treaty*' (the Thirty Years Peace: Thuc. 1 45.3). From the Athenian attitude at the parley to be described presently, we can infer that the generals of the second squadron received exactly the same instructions (53.4).

(*b*) During the battle of Sybota, in August 433, the Athenians, on the right wing of the Corcyraeans (48.3), avoided any actual fighting as long as they could; but the part played by the Athenians seems to have been the decisive factor which prevented the Corinthians from pressing home their initial advantage on the left of their line (49.4,7; 50.4,5; 51.1,4).

(*c*) Particularly interesting is the attitude of the Corinthians, the Corcyraeans and the Athenians the day after the battle (52–3). The Corinthians had retreated, on the arrival of the second Athenian squadron, to a 'deserted place' on the mainland, where they were under various difficulties, such as the necessity of guarding their many prisoners[32] and the lack of all means of refitting their ships. They were much concerned as to how they would be able to get home (evidently there was no thought of renewing the attack): they were afraid that the Athenians might consider the Thirty Years Peace to have been broken by the preceding day's fighting, and might not allow them to sail away. Putting a bold face on it, they sent some men in a small boat to parley with the Athenians, not furnishing them with the herald's wand which would have been an admission that the peace had been broken. Their envoys reproached the Athenians for initiating war and breaking the treaty. 'If you intend to stop our sailing to Corcyra or wherever else we wish, and to break the treaty', they added, 'begin by taking those of us who are here and treating us as enemies'. Those of the Corcyraeans who were within earshot immediately shouted out advice to take them and kill them (53.3). Had the Athenians wished to break the treaty, they could not only have taken the men prisoner; they could probably have effected, with the Corcyraeans, the destruction or capture of the whole Corinthian fleet. The Corinthians dared not risk a renewal of the battle, even though they may have had more ships still in fighting trim than the Corcyraeans and Athenians combined—unfortunately, the figures are uncertain (see Gomme, *HCT* 1 190–5).

At any rate, the Corinthians now returned home, manifestly the losers in their war with Corcyra. They had not gained control of Epidamnus. (Did the prospective settlers who had paid their 50-drachmae deposits get

---

proposes another which is hardly more plausible (*Id.* 243): for him, as for so many modern scholars, everything has to be explained in terms of the wishes of *Pericles*. But what if the third general of the second squadron is the Dracontides of Plut., *Per.* 32.3 ff.?—as seems very likely, although of course it is far from certain (see M/L, p. 168).

[32] Over 1,000 (Thuc. 1 54.2), or about 1,050, of whom 800 were slaves and most of the remaining 250 were Corcyraeans of some distinction (55.1).

their money back, one wonders.) They had not reduced Corcyra to submission, or even damaged her seriously, except by sinking a good many Corcyraean ships. All in all, they had expended a vast amount of money and effort to no purpose—except the seizure of Anactorium, a small town at the mouth of the Gulf of Ampracia, which they captured on the way home, with the aid of traitors within, leaving settlers there (Thuc. 1 55.1), only to lose the place to Athens in 424 (IV 49).

Such was the first Corinthian grievance (*aitia*) against the Athenians: that they had fought a naval battle against them, with the Corcyraeans, during the continuance of the Thirty Years Peace (Thuc. 1 55.2). Enough has been said to show how groundless was the Corinthian claim that these events amounted to a breach of the Peace by Athens: it was the Corinthians who had initiated the attack, off the coast of Corcyra and hundreds of miles from Corinth, knowing as they did of the existence of the defensive alliance between Corcyra and Athens which, in the circumstances (dictated by Corinth), was bound to bring Athens in on the Corcyraean side. I am sure Thucydides supposed that his readers would realise all this without his having to spell it out for them even more plainly. Yet modern scholars have often failed to grasp the point.[33]

Very considerable aggression on Corinth's part towards Corcyra has been revealed by the events of 435-3. This need not surprise us if we take into account the detailed analysis published in 1964 by A. J. Graham of Corinth's attitude towards her colonies in the fifth century (*CMCAG*, Chap. vii, pp. 118-53). The whole subject is a difficult one and much of the evidence is far from clear, but Graham has made a good case for seeing 'a general Corinthian attempt to gain a stronger hold over her colonies' in the fifth century, and in particular 'a general Corinthian plan to increase her control in the North West at Corcyra's expense' (*CMCAG* 141, 132). Also, in the late 460s Corinth was apparently the aggressor against her north-eastern neighbour Megara in a war about boundary land (Thuc. 1 103.4), which for a time drove Megara into the arms of Athens; and Corinth probably took the initiative in a clash with her south-western neighbour Cleonae, involving an armed invasion of Cleonaean territory.[34]

Thucydides evidently saw 'the affair of Epidamnus and Corcyra' as the prime 'immediate cause' (as we might call it) of the Peloponnesian war, for at the very end of Book I, after bringing his narrative down to the very verge of hostilities, he says (1 146), 'These were the *aitiai* and *diaphorai* on both sides before the war, *beginning directly from the affair of Epidamnus and Corcyra*'.

In furthest opposition to the analysis I have presented of 'the affair of Epidamnus and Corcyra' is a recent work by D. W. Knight (*SSAP* 1-12).

---

[33] E.g. Brauer (*KSFGU* 40), who thinks that in various passages, esp. 1 55.2, Thuc. 'speaks plainly of the guilt of the Athenians in relation to the war with Corinth'!

[34] The only evidence is Cimon's retort to the Corinthian Lachartus in 462, recorded by Plut., *Cim.* 17.2. This may well derive from Ion of Chios, as suggested by Jacoby, in *CQ* 41 (1947), at p. 9.

Its author is one of those who mistakenly see Pericles in virtually sole control of Athenian policy for a long time before the outbreak of the Peloponnesian war, apparently from 461 onwards. He even finds it 'tempting to see the hand of Pericles' behind all the events that caused trouble between Athens and Corinth in 435–1 (*Id.* 9–10). He is obliged to admit that there is no *evidence* of 'Periclean provocation in the dispute that arose between Epidamnus and Corcyra in 435'. Indeed, in Thucydides' account there is simply no place for such 'Periclean provocation' at any point in the whole Corcyraean affair. We are therefore given a series of 'must-have-beens'. 'Is it feasible to think', asks Knight, 'that he [Pericles] did nothing for two whole years [435–3], as the silence of contemporary history suggests . . . ?' To suppose this, he replies, would be 'to disregard the political intellect of Pericles and make all his previous actions aimed at Athenian predominance meaningless'. To such lengths are we driven if we refuse to accept Thucydides' picture, in which Pericles does not try to establish Athenian dominance *over Corinth or any of Sparta's other allies*, for fear of breaking the Thirty Years Peace. Anyone who makes the kind of supposition which we find in Knight's paper ought at least to begin by attacking in detail the credibility of Thucydides.

(iii)
Potidaea

No sooner has Thucydides finished recounting the first Corinthian grievance against Athens than he goes on to explain how there now arose another 'difference leading to war' (*diaphora es to polemein*),[35] this time over Potidaea.[36]

We must begin with the fact that Potidaea, although a Corinthian colony, had long been a tribute-paying member of the Athenian empire, and must certainly have been placed on the Athenian side in the lists of allies appended to the Thirty Years Peace, where it was specifically provided that each side should 'keep what they have' (Thuc. 1 140.2; cf. Appendix I). As far as Corinth, Sparta and the other members of Sparta's alliance were concerned, this provision of the Peace had overridden the fact that Potidaea was a colony of Corinth. Having abandoned Potidaea to Athens by the Peace, the Peloponnesians were not now entitled to intervene militarily on its behalf against Athens, so long as the Peace continued.[37]

Unfortunately, it is very difficult to reconstruct the exact chronological

[35] Thuc. 1 56.1 ff. On the εὐθύς of 56.1 (and 57.1), see Gomme, *HCT* 1 199.

[36] For an up-to-date account of what is known about Potidaea, see J. A. Alexander, *PHR*.

[37] Busolt, *GG* III ii.829–31; Brauer, *KSFGU* 41–3, and others seem to have concluded from Thuc. 1 66 that there were genuine grounds for complaint on both sides over Potidaea, which they see as having a kind of 'Doppelstellung' (Busolt) in both spheres. I can only repeat that *as between Athens and the Peloponnesians* Potidaea was fully in the Athenian sphere.

order of the various events described briefly by Thucydides 1 57–8 (see Appendix XII); but we can at least say that Potidaea revolted in the spring of 432, with 'the Thraceward[38] Chalcidians' and the Bottiaeans, two federations (tributary to themselves) which the Athenians normally preferred to ignore as such, insisting on referring to their individual cities: Olynthus (and sometimes others as well) for the Chalcidians, and Spartolus (sometimes similarly with others) for the Bottiaeans.[39] All these states paid their tribute in March 432 (List 22 II 45, 70, 73 etc., in *ATL* II 27), and must therefore have revolted after that time—or at any rate after they had despatched their tribute, conceivably in a deliberate attempt to gain time and prevent Athens from putting in garrisons or taking some other action against them before their plans for revolt were mature. It is perhaps a material fact that Athens had recently raised the tribute of Potidaea from 6 to 15 talents: see Appendix XIV.

In the background of these revolts stand King Perdiccas II of Macedon and the Corinthians. Perdiccas, who had become king of Macedon in succession to Alexander I at some unknown date before 432 and reigned until some time between 414/13 and 411/10, may seem at first sight one of the most slippery characters known to history: he swung back and forth into and out of friendship and alliance with Athens no less than nine times. (For his relations with Athens, see Appendix XI.) But in his day Athens was the one Greek power from which Macedon might have most to fear, and the extraordinary manoeuvres of Perdiccas may all have been undertaken with the best of patriotic motives, to preserve the freedom and independence of his country. He had at first been a friend and ally of Athens, but he had already, by at least 433, been made into an enemy by Athenian support of his brother Philip and his cousin Derdas.[40] (The rights and wrongs of all this are of course quite beyond our reach.) Perdiccas had sent to Sparta, trying to bring about a war between Athens and the Peloponnesians; he had been trying to win over the Corinthians, in order to procure the revolt of Potidaea from Athens; and he was negotiating with the Thraceward Chalcidians and the Bottiaeans, to induce them to join with Potidaea, hoping that all these cities when in revolt would become his allies (Thuc. 1 57.2–5). These intrigues all became known at Athens by the spring of 432 at the latest (57.6), and some at least in the course of 433 (56.2, *fin.*).

'The Corinthians', says Thucydides (1 57.2), just before recounting the diplomatic activities of Perdiccas, 'were already openly antagonistic to Athens (*phanerōs ēdē diaphoroi ēsan*). A few lines earlier (56.2) he says, 'The Corinthians were taking measures to revenge themselves [on Athens], and the Athenians divined their hostility' (*echthran*)—and he goes on at

---

[38] Chalcidice was not regarded as being *in* Thrace: it was 'by' or 'in the direction of' Thrace, ἐπὶ or ἀπὸ Θρᾴκης. 'Thraceward' is the best translation.

[39] See Gomme, *HCT* I 203–8; *ATL* I 550. In 422 Athens entered into a treaty with the Bottiaeans as such: Tod I² 68 = *IG* I² 90 = *SEG* x 89; and see Gomme, *HCT* I 207.

[40] See Gomme, *HCT* I 202–3; and cf. Appendix XI.

once to describe how the Athenians, 'directly[41] after the naval battle at Corcyra' (57.1; cf. 56.1), ordered Potidaea to pull down its wall facing into Pallene, on its southern side (see Gomme, *HCT* I 200), to give hostages, to dismiss the magistrates (*epidēmiourgoi*) sent to it annually by Corinth, and not to receive them in future (56.2). He then explains the reason for these demands: the fear (thoroughly justified, if his own narrative is accurate) that the Potidaeans might be induced by Perdiccas and the Corinthians to revolt, and might draw the other Thraceward allies into revolt with them. A few lines later, after the explanation of Perdiccas' attitude which we have already noticed, he mentions an expedition which the Athenians were sending off under Archestratus and others, to operate against Macedon, and adds that the Athenians instructed the commanders to take hostages from Potidaea, destroy the wall, and take precautions against the revolt of the neighbouring towns (57.6). This expedition could hardly have sailed before April 432, and the date may have been even later, in May or even at the beginning of June. We learn (59.1) that when it arrived at Potidaea, it found that city 'and the other places'[42] already in revolt, the Potidaeans, Chalcidians and Bottiaeans having exchanged formal oaths of alliance (58.1). For the chronology, see Appendix XII, §3.

In Thucydides I 58 we hear of all sorts of activities which had apparently been going on during the winter of 433/2, between the delivery of the original demands by Athens to Potidaea and the arrival of Archestratus' expedition with orders to enforce them. Perdiccas had given to the Thraceward Chalcidians every encouragement, and even a portion of his own territory, in a successful attempt to make them abandon and destroy their towns on the sea coast and settle in a body at their principal city, Olynthus, 2½ km. inland and more easily defensible (58.2). The Potidaeans had not been idle. They had sent envoys to both Athens and Sparta (separately, it seems: see Gomme, *HCT* I 210). Those who went to Athens failed after long efforts to induce the Athenians to change their minds; but those who went to Sparta, in company with a Corinthian embassy, were more successful, eliciting a promise from 'the authorities at Sparta' (*ta telē tōn Lakedaimoniōn*) to invade Attica if the Athenians took action against Potidaea (58.1). This very significant incident can merely be noted now: we shall come back to it later (Chapter V, Part viii), during an analysis of Spartan attitudes to Athens in the fifth century. The Corinthians, accompanying the Potidaeans to Sparta, of course knew of this promise (see Thuc. I 71.4).

It is impossible for us to say how far the Athenians were 'justified' in making their demands on Potidaea, or Potidaea in 'revolting'. There is much that might be said on these topics, from different points of view. But what we are concerned with here is the origin of the Peloponnesian war,

[41] But see Gomme, *HCT* I 199: εὐθύς 'may mean no more than the next possible event'; and 'μετὰ ταῦτα εὐθύς is a possible expression, even though some months elapse'.
[42] For a list, see Gomme, *HCT* I 211.

and that means that we must concentrate on *the relations between Athens and the Peloponnesians*. In the Potidaean affair we have seen Corinth, a leading ally of Sparta, helping to instigate the revolt of Potidaea, an important and strategically placed ally of Athens, and sending ambassadors to Sparta, in company with Potidaea's, to elicit a promise of military help should Athens take action against Potidaea. Yet, as we have also seen, neither Sparta nor Corinth could have had any right, in view of the terms of the Thirty Years Peace, to intervene militarily against Athens in favour of an Athenian ally, even if that ally was a Corinthian colony, *and even if Athens' action against it was not justified*. There was of course nothing to prevent the Peloponnesians from protesting against such behaviour by Athens and asking for it to be referred to arbitration, under the Peace. But that was as far as they could go without breaking their oaths.

Sparta in fact took no action until the early summer of 431 in fulfilment of her promise to Potidaea. What Corinth—the city of Corinth, 'the Corinthians'—now did is a matter of dispute, turning upon the interpretation of certain passages in Thucydides (1 60.1,2; 66), and above all upon the precise meaning of a single word, *idiāi* (ἰδίᾳ), in 1 66, where Thucydides uses it of the actions of 'the Corinthians'. Did the Corinthians (the State of Corinth) intervene officially, although *separately* (*idiāi*) from the other Peloponnesians? If so, Corinth certainly broke the Thirty Years Peace.[43] Or did the Corinthians not intervene officially at all, and was the intervention merely that of individual Corinthians, acting *in a private capacity* (*idiāi* as the opposite of *dēmosiāi*, in a public capacity), so that 'the Corinthians' as such had not broken the Peace? It has been argued by many scholars, including the two leading Thucydidean commentators, Steup and Gomme,[44] that there was no official action by the Corinthian State. I shall argue that this is wrong and that official action by 'the Corinthians' as such can be proved beyond question.

Let us first look at the scanty evidence. Forty days after the revolt of Potidaea there arrived in Chalcidice a force of 1,600 hoplites and 400

---

[43] I can see no justification for Ed. Meyer's statement (*GdA* iv ii⁴ 15) that Corinth could only break the Peace by an attack on the territory of Athens herself. *Potidaea having been placed in the Athenian sphere by the Thirty Years Peace*, Corinth's armed assistance in her revolt, on her territory, involving fighting against Athenian troops, was a clear breach of the Peace. See above and Appendix I, §4.

[44] Gomme, *HCT* I 224–5 (and see 212); J. Steup, *Thukydideische Studien* II (Freiburg, 1886) 24–9; Classen-Steup, *Thuk.* I⁵⁻⁷, pp. 430–1. Steup's view was accepted by Busolt, *GG* III ii.798–9 n. 3, 829 n. 2, and has been taken for granted by many historians, including e.g. Kagan, who speaks of Corinth as taking 'extreme care to avoid a formal breach of the peace' and believes that 'the fiction that Aristeus led a volunteer army was meant to show that Corinth was not officially involved' (*OPW* 282–3, cf. 285). In fact, although Thucydides often employs the word ἰδίᾳ to mean 'privately' (as opposed to δημοσίᾳ), he does not use it in that sense when he is speaking of the actions *of a State*: οἱ Ἀθηναῖοι, οἱ Λακεδαιμόνιοι etc. The one apparent exception, iv 121.1, is not a real one: οἱ Σκιωναῖοι, when coming up to Brasidas ἰδίᾳ, are not behaving differently from the way they acted δημοσίᾳ, but are greeting him *individually*, 'man by man', as opposed to collectively (cf. III 2.3, where it is individual Mytilenaeans who give information to Athens). Thucydides uses ἰδίᾳ in the same sense as in 1 66 and v 30.2 in III 54.5; v 42.2 (cf. 39.3; 40.1); vI 13.2.

light-armed, led by Aristeus son of Adeimantus, a staunch friend of Potidaea: some were Corinthian volunteers (*ethelontai*), serving out of particular personal regard for Aristeus, and the rest were mercenaries from other Peloponnesian states, serving for pay (Thuc. i 60.1–3). The subsequent fighting with the Athenian forces, reinforced by two further expeditions (61–5), need not concern us. After describing an Athenian victory and their final investment of Potidaea, Thucydides pauses to sum up, before turning to his next main topic, the first meeting at Sparta at which war against Athens was advocated and decided upon. Thucydides remarks (i 66) that the Athenians and the Peloponnesians had the following *aitiai* (grievances or complaints) against each other: the Corinthians, that the Athenians were besieging Potidaea, Corinth's colony, with Corinthians and Peloponnesians within it; while the Athenian complaint against the Peloponnesians was that they had procured the revolt of a tribute-paying city in the Athenian alliance, and had gone there and fought openly with the Potidaeans. 'However', Thucydides adds (66 still), 'war had not yet broken out, but it was still a time of truce, for the Corinthians did these things *idiāi*'.

There are two decisive arguments in favour of taking *idiāi* to mean 'separately from the other Peloponnesian states':

1. It is true that Thucydides speaks of the Corinthians who went with Aristeus as 'volunteers' (*ethelontai*, 60.1). But the use of that term by itself does not tell us whether they were mere freebooters, on a private venture, or men who *volunteered for an official expedition*, proclaimed by their city—for *ethelontai* is also frequently used in that sense: see e.g. Thuc. iii 20.2; *SEG* xii 26 (= *IG* i² 97 = Tod i² 76), lines 15–16; Xen., *HG* v iii.9; Dem. iv 29; xviii 99; xlv 85; Diod. xi 84.4–5; Plut., *Per.* 18.2 etc. (Numerous other examples could be given.) And Thucydides makes it clear that these men were official Corinthian troops, for he speaks of the Corinthian State as sending them (*hoi Korinthioi*, i 60.1);[45] it is the Corinthian State again which sends out and pays the Peloponnesian mercenaries (60.1); and he uses of their leader Aristeus the verb *estratēgei* (60.2), which he employs on nearly forty other occasions, always for an official commander appointed by his city.

2. The second argument puts the matter beyond any possible doubt. In 421 the Corinthians refused to accept the Peace of Nicias, in spite of the fact that it had been accepted by Sparta and a majority of her allies in the Peloponnesian League and was therefore, *prima facie*, binding upon them too. They sought to avail themselves of the one excuse which could legitimately be pleaded in such a case against acceptance of a majority decision of the League states: that 'something to do with gods or heroes

---

[45] Contrast iv 80.5, dealing with the expedition of Brasidas to the 'Thraceward region' in 424: it was certainly an official State mission, for the Spartans sent 700 hoplites; but it was apparently Brasidas himself (helped perhaps by his friends) who paid the 1,000 (78.1) mercenaries, for Thucydides speaks of Brasidas as bringing the mercenaries μισθῷ πείσας.

prevented it' (Thuc. v 30.1: see Chapter IV, Part iv, Section B, §7 below). In this case, they said, there was something of that sort. Without adducing their real reasons for refusing to accept the League decision (such as the fact that they were not to receive back Sollium or Anactorium from the Athenians), they put forward the pretext of not betraying their friends in the Thraceward region. 'For they said they had sworn oaths to them *idiāi*, both when they revolted in the first place with Potidaea [i.e. in 433/2], and others afterwards . . .; and having sworn to them upon the faith of the gods, they would not be keeping their oaths if they betrayed them' (30.2–3). These oaths are referred to in the next sentence as 'their long-standing oaths' (30.4). Pretext it may have been, but evidently it was legally valid, and the Spartans had to accept it.

Now if there is one thing that could not be done 'unofficially' by a Greek city, it was the swearing of oaths; and in any event the oaths in this case had to be oaths sworn by the Corinthian State,[46] or they would not have availed, under what we are pleased to call 'the constitution of the Peloponnesian League', as a legitimate excuse for Corinth's refusing to accept the Peace of Nicias (cf. Chapter IV, Part iv, Section B, esp. §7, below). The nature of the oaths is not stated, but they must have created a military alliance of some sort, probably with a specific promise by each party not to make peace without the consent of the others.[47] Who were the 'Thraceward' states (Thuc. v 30.2) to whom Corinth swore these oaths in 433/2 and subsequently? Presumably at least the Thraceward Chalcidians and Bottiaeans—all of them allies of Athens, who must have been listed as such, city by city, in the Thirty Years Peace. They were worth mentioning in 421, because at least some of them were still unsubdued by Athens, and Corinth's treaties with them would still be valid. Aristeus and his men certainly acted as allies of the Chalcidians and Bottiaeans;[48] but their main objective was of course to help Potidaea (Thuc. i 60.1,2), and twice (63.3; 64.1) Thucydides can refer to the forces opposed to Athens as 'the Potidaeans and their allies'. We cannot doubt that the 'allies' to whom Corinth swore oaths of alliance in 433/2 included three sets of *Athenian* allies listed in the Thirty Years Peace: not only the Thraceward Chalcidians and the Bottiaeans but also the Potidaeans. (By 421, of course, Potidaea had ceased to exist as an independent city, and oaths sworn to it might be considered to have lapsed.) The Athenians, therefore, probably had a right in 432 to claim that Corinth had technically broken the Peace by merely swearing these oaths, even before she

---

[46] I do not know why Hammond (*HG*[2] 321) writes, '*Aristeus* concluded a *secret* alliance *on behalf of Corinth* with the Bottiaean and Chalcidian states' (italics mine). Against such speculative constructions, see my ASPAP.

[47] Cf. Thuc. v 23.1,2; 39.3; 46.2; and 47.3,4 = Tod I[2] 72 (= *IG* I[2] 86), lines 11–12, 17–18; etc.

[48] See Thuc. i 62.3 (note καὶ τοὺς ἔξω ἰσθμοῦ ξυμμάχους); 63.1 (Aristeus hesitates whether to make for Olynthus or Potidaea); 63.3 and 64.1 (the forces opposed to the Athenians are described as 'the Potidaeans and their allies'); and 65.2 (Aristeus 'remains among the Chalcidians' and fights with them).

actually commenced hostilities by sending out the expedition under Aristeus.

Gomme misunderstands the situation when he asserts that 'if Corinth had had a formal alliance with the Chalkidians and sent forces to help them, there would have been war—between her and Athens, if not with the Peloponnesian League' (*HCT* 1 225). Before a war could become a League war, first Sparta and then the League had to meet and vote (see Chapter IV, Part iv, Section B below). As for war between Athens and Corinth, the Corinthians would hardly dare acknowledge its existence on their own initiative, until the League had voted the right way; and the Athenians, in their anxiety to avoid war with Sparta and her League, were prepared to forego taking action against Corinth. Had Athens attacked Corinth in retaliation, she would have brought in the Peloponnesian League at once against her, and that was just what she wanted to avoid. She believed she could crush Potidaea and the other revolting allies whatever Corinth might do, and she eventually did reduce Potidaea, though at much greater cost than she had anticipated. Her behaviour provides further evidence of her pacific intentions towards the Peloponnesians in 432. If she had really wanted to fight them, she would have had a perfectly good excuse for beginning hostilities by claiming that Corinth had been guilty of a manifest breach of the Peace (as indeed she had), and making a punitive expedition against her in the summer of 432.

There is no need at this point to do more than mention the renewal in 433/2 of the Athenian alliances with Rhegium and Leontini,[49] which had been concluded earlier, apparently at some time in the forties. We shall glance at these later (Chapter VI, Part iii), as part of a general examination of Athenian policy in regard to the West.

(iv)
Phormio in the Ampraciot Gulf, and the Athenian alliance with the Acarnanians

One set of events remains to be discussed at this point: Phormio's undated expedition to the Ampraciot Gulf and the Athenian alliance with the Acarnanians which followed. The only source is Thucydides (II 68, esp. §§7–8), who in dealing with the year 430 mentions a campaign by the Ampraciots and some barbarian allies against Amphilochian Argos, and in a brief 'flash-back' explains the origin of the hostility (*echthra*) between these two states.

Ampracia was a Corinthian colony, founded in Cypselid times, and in the 430s it was in friendly relations with Corinth: Ampraciots assisted in Corinth's original attempt on Epidamnus in 435, and they supplied naval contingents for both the Corinthian expeditions against Corcyra

---

[49] M/L 63/64 (= *SVdA* II 162/3 = Tod I² 58/57 = *IG* I² 51/52).

in 435 and 433.[50] In view of some speculations by Kahrstedt and others about the constitutional position of certain Corinthian colonies in west Greece, it will be well to mention that there is no reason to suppose Ampracia was not a fully independent state.[51] At some time before the Peloponnesian war which we cannot fix, Argos, the principal city of Amphilochia, lying at the south east corner of the Gulf of Ampracia (see Hammond, CAAW), came under outside pressure and asked for help from the Ampraciots, her neighbours on the north, who responded by supplying an effective reinforcement of her citizen population—Thucydides (II 68.5) calls these new settlers *xynoikoi*. But after a time[52] the Ampraciot *xynoikoi* at Argos expelled the original Amphilochians and held the city themselves. Thereupon the Amphilochians sought the help of the Acarnanians, and the two peoples together called in the Athenians, who sent an expedition of thirty ships under Phormio. Argos was stormed, the former Ampraciots who now held it were enslaved, and the town was shared between the original Amphilochians and the Acarnanians. It was 'after this', adds Thucydides (68.8), that the alliance between the Athenians and Acarnanians came into existence.

From our present point of view, there are two questions here: when is the Athenian intervention to be dated, and was it likely to have exacerbated Corinthian feelings towards Athens? The first question has often been discussed, notably in recent years by Beaumont, Gomme, Jacoby, Kagan, Wade-Gery and *ATL*;[53] but most scholars have taken an affirmative answer to the second question for granted. The answer to the first question, however, may depend partly on our attitude to the second: those who have argued for a late date, in the spring of 432 (Beaumont, Wade-Gery, *ATL*, Kagan), have done so because they see the affair, quite wrongly, as part of a struggle between Athens and Corinth. According to the authors of *ATL*, 'the strongest argument . . . is that if such a decisive Athenian appearance against Korinth's allies in the west, and especially the selling into slavery of the Ambrakiots, had happened before 433, the Kerkyra crisis loses its critical quality; the careful argumentation of both parties in Thucydides, 1, 32–43 and the circumspect behaviour of Korinthians and Athenians in 1, 53 become meaningless'. I see no force at all in this argument. We have already noticed that both sides in the parley recorded by Thucydides 1 53 had the best of reasons for their 'circumspect behaviour', and that the debate in 32–43 is fully explicable in terms of Thucydides' narrative. We cannot simply take it for granted

---

[50] Thuc. 1 26.1; 27.2 (8 ships in 435); 46.1 (27 ships in 433).

[51] See Graham, *CMCAG* 118 ff., esp. 138–42. The garrison put into Ampracia by Corinth in 426 (Thuc. III 114.4; IV 42.3) was no doubt supplied at the request of Ampracia, then in a very weakened condition (see Thuc. III 109–13, esp. 113.6). Such requests to other cities for garrisons were not uncommon.

[52] Unfortunately Thucydides gives only the vaguest possible indication of time: χρόνῳ.

[53] R. L. Beaumont, 'Corinth, Ambracia, Apollonia', in *JHS* 72 (1952) 62–73, at pp. 62–3; Gomme, *HCT* 1 198–9, 367; II 202, and esp. 416; Jacoby, in *FGrH* III b (Suppl.) i.128–9; ii.122–4 (n. 28); Kagan, *OPW* 233–4, 252–3, 384–5; Wade-Gery, *EGH* 253–4 and n. 5; *ATL* III 320 and n. 84.

that Corinth would have regarded the Athenian intervention at Amphilochian Argos and her alliance with the Acarnanians as a menacing action on the part of Athens towards herself. Thucydides never mentions Corinth at all in connection with these events. *Athens made no attack on Ampracia,* which, as an ally of Corinth and probably of Sparta as well, is likely to have been a party to the Thirty Years Peace. It was not really 'the Ampraciots' who were enslaved on the capture of Argos (although Thucydides for convenience gives them that title, to distinguish them from the original Amphilochian Argives): it was only that section of the Ampraciots who had removed to Argos, as *xynoikoi* of the Amphilochians, and had thereby ceased to be Ampraciots and become Argives! They can hardly have had any justification for driving out the other inhabitants and keeping the city for themselves. Corinth may well have disapproved of their dangerously provocative behaviour and been prudently reluctant to incur unnecessarily the hostility of the Amphilochians. It is easy to overrate Corinth's interest in this rather isolated area, at the far end of a very land-locked gulf and therefore having little or nothing to do with trade between Corinth and the west—an issue which is often dragged in. If Corinth needed a base for triremes convoying merchantmen in Western waters, there were several friendly states (some of them her own colonies) which were far better situated for that purpose.[54] And both Amphilochian Argos and Ampracia were too much hemmed in by mountains to be centres of trade in any great volume.

There is one consideration which may be held to strengthen the view that a date for our expedition in the Athenian archon-years 433/2 or 432/1 is unlikely: there is not a trace of it in the accounts of the Treasurers of Athena which survive from these years (see Appendix XV). All the expeditions of the two years which we know about from Thucydides (those to Corcyra, to Macedonia and Potidaea, and around Peloponnese) do appear in these accounts, and the absence of any reference to Phormio's Ampraciot campaign does perhaps create some presumption that it did not take place in these years. But this argument must not be pressed, for the accounts we have are not complete, and anyway we cannot be quite certain that the expenses of Phormio's squadron of thirty ships would have been paid by Athena's Treasurers: as an alternative, they might have been paid by the Hellenotamiae out of current revenue.

It is not possible to be at all precise, but the arguments of Jacoby, Gomme and other scholars who have preferred an early date for Phormio's expedition have some force. With the removal of any ground for thinking that Corinth would necessarily treat the Athenian participation in the capture of Argos and the Athenian-Acarnanian alliance as developments

---

[54] E.g. Sollium, also Leucas and Anactorium (in both of which Corinth had some interest), Apollonia (between Corcyra and Epidamnus), Astacus (see Thuc. II 30.1; 33.1–2). For Corinth's dependencies in this area, see Beaumont, *op. cit.* (in the last note); Graham, *CMCAG* 118 ff., esp. 128–42. I do not think there is anything in the suggestion (see Graham, *CMCAG* 142) that Corinth was mainly interested in securing 'the route to the silver mines of Illyria': cf. M. I. Finley, *TPAW: CG* 14–18.

seriously dangerous to herself, the exact dating of these events becomes a far less important matter. The early 430s are perhaps the most likely time, but the 440s are equally open, and Gomme thought even the 450s possible.[55]

[55] See Gomme, *HCT* II 416. The argument of Busolt, *GG* III ii.763–4 n. 6 (not 'p. 736', as in Gomme, copied by Kagan, *OPW* 384), in favour of 437–6 has been accepted by many scholars (e.g. Glotz-Cohen, *HG* II 614), but should not be pressed too hard, in view of the considerations set out above.

IV

Spartan foreign policy, and the Peloponnesian League

Before we can begin to consider the position of Sparta vis-à-vis Athens in 432–1, we must make sure that we understand Spartan foreign policy and how it was formed. It is of course the Pentecontaetia with which we are primarily concerned, but we know so little about Sparta during that period that we must be ready to make use of all the evidence we have about Sparta's relations with the outside world in the sixth, fifth and fourth centuries, for although Sparta's policy was anything but consistent (see Part vi of this Chapter), it is possible to discover the considerations which dominated the minds of her leaders. Sparta was the most conservative of Greek states, and evidence drawn from periods before and after the Pentecontaetia can be used, if cautiously, with less danger of anachronism than in the case of other cities.

(i)
The Helots

The cardinal fact about Sparta[1] is her uniquely dangerous position as mistress of the Helots, above all the Messenian Helots. Most of the Helots, according to Thucydides (i 101.2), were descendants of the Messenians of old, conquered by Sparta, and so all the Helots came to be called Messenians. Sparta was the one Greek state which held in total subjection large numbers of fellow Greeks, who never lost their consciousness of being Messenians (we might call it loosely a 'national consciousness'), who might revolt at any time when a good opportunity arrived, and who ultimately did revolt successfully, in 370/69, with outside help, and re-establish the ancient *polis* of Messene (*hoi Messēnioi*), after it had been in abeyance for many generations.[2] The response to a Theban call for Messenian exiles to

---

[1] Books on Sparta are numerous and mostly bad. The best in English is Forrest, *HS*; but this is very brief (only 160 pages). In French, see especially F. Ollier, *Le mirage spartiate* (2 vols., Paris, 1933 and 1943); and P. Roussel, *Sparte*[2] (Paris, 1960). Tigerstedt, *LSCA* i, is useful not so much for any illumination it provides as for the great quantity of bibliographical material in its notes (pp. 310–591). Among the few articles particularly worth reading, apart from those mentioned below, are C. G. Starr, 'The Credibility of Early Spartan History', in *Historia* 14 (1965) 257–72; M. I. Finley, 'Sparta', in *Problèmes de la guerre en Grèce ancienne*, ed. J.-P. Vernant (Paris, 1968) 143–60. Still invaluable is V. Ehrenberg, in *RE*, 2te Reihe, iii (1929) col. 1373–1453, *s.v.* 'Sparta (Geschichte)'.

[2] I would date the First Messenian war in the late eighth century and the Second in the mid-seventh. The *polis* of Messene may have ceased officially to exist as such at the end of either the First war or the Second. I doubt if Epaminondas' alleged figure of 230 years from 370/69, i.e. 600 B.C. (Plut., *Mor.* 194b; Ael., *VH* xiii 42, accepted by Jones, *Sp.* 4), has a secure basis, any more than those of e.g. Isocr. vi 27 and Deinarch. i (*c. Dem.*) 73

return and re-found their city was enthusiastic: they came from Italy, Sicily and Cyrenaica, from 'yearning for their fatherland and hatred of the Spartans' (Paus. IV xxvi.5).

The status of the Helots (Laconian as well as Messenian) is best described in modern terminology by calling them 'State serfs'. The Greeks had no regular technical term for serfdom, and the Spartans commonly referred to the Helots as their 'slaves' (*douloi*); but we can best call them *serfs*, because they were attached to the lands they worked (and could therefore enjoy, if precariously, a family life), and *State* serfs, because they belonged to the Spartan *polis* and could not be manumitted by the individual Spartiates to whom they were granted out (see esp. Strabo VIII v.4, p. 365, including Ephorus, *FGrH* 70 F 117; also Paus. III xx.6). Now all other Greek cities owned slaves, sometimes in considerable numbers; but they were a heterogeneous, polyglot mass (cf. Ps.-Arist., *Oecon.* 1 6, 1344^{b}18), who could often communicate with each other only in their masters' language, and who might run away individually or in small batches but would virtually never attempt large-scale revolts. Only the Spartans lived on top of a potentially active human volcano. In Sparta, therefore, more than in any other Greek state, we can see a real and bitter class war, with full Spartiates and Helots at its opposite poles, an inter-mediate position being occupied by the Perioikoi and those Spartans who lacked full political rights—*hypomeiones*, as they may have been called, although the term occurs only once, in Xenophon (*HG* III iii.6). In most other Greek states it is useless to look for manifestations of an active class struggle between citizens and slaves, because the slaves were mainly inert and helpless and in no position to conduct any kind of collective resistance, whereas their masters were always ready to unite against them. 'Citizens', said Xenophon (*Hiero* IV 3), 'act as unpaid bodyguards of each other against their slaves'. The kind of class struggle which does force itself upon our attention again and again throughout Greek history (and much of Roman history) is mainly that between rich and poor *citizens*. Marx, in a letter to Engels of 8 March 1855, gave a general characterisation of the internal history of Republican Rome as 'the struggle of small versus large landed property, specifically modified, of course, by slave conditions'.[3] We may think of the internal history of most Greek cities in a similar way, above all in terms of a struggle between the propertied classes and the poor, precisely as many Greek thinkers did, from Solon to Aristotle (cf. Chapter I, Part iii above). In Sparta, the conflict was much more sharply

---

(400 years) or Lyc., *c. Leocr.* 62 (500 years). If I had to choose between the various alternative dates for the end of the Second Messenian war given by, or deducible from, the ancient sources, I would prefer 657/6, i.e. 287 years before 370/69, given by Paus. IV xxvii.9 (against xxiii.4).

[3] *Karl Marx & Friedrich Engels. Correspondence 1846–1895*, a selection translated by Dona Torr (London, 1934, 1936) 127. For the German original, see K. Marx & F. Engels, *Briefwechsel* (Berlin, 1949) II 105, no. 349; also E. Ch. Welskopf, *Die Produktionsverhältnisse im alten Orient und in der griechisch-römischen Antike* (Berlin, 1957) 197 ff.

polarised between Spartiates and Helots: it was both more open and more intense and bitter than elsewhere.

The conquest of Messenia gave Sparta some of the most fertile land in Greece and an ample supply of State serfs to till it. But because of the refusal of the Messenians to submit quietly, the Spartans were driven to organise themselves as a community of professional soldiers, dedicated not (like many militaristic peoples) to foreign conquest—which might prove highly dangerous if it extended Spartan commitments too far—but above all to maintaining strict internal discipline and harmony, so that a united body of Spartiates could ruthlessly dominate their numerous Helots and Perioikoi. The Greeks realised the simple fact (stated as such by Plato's Socrates) that changes in a State begin from dissension among the ruling class, and that the constitution cannot be upset as long as that class is united, small though it may be (Plato, *Rep.* VIII 545d). As long as the rulers are not at variance among themselves, the rest will not be at odds with them or with each other (v 465b). Aristotle speaks in much the same vein: an oligarchy which preserves harmony inside itself will not easily be overthrown from within (*Pol.* v 6, 1306ᵃ9–10). The famous *eunomia* of Sparta was carefully constructed to maintain unity among Spartiates.[4] But Spartan life, which until well into the seventh century resembled that of any other progressive Greek state, and in some artistic fields was outstandingly creative, was now miserably impoverished. In the apt words put into the mouth of King Archidamus III by Isocrates (VI 81), doing his poor best to produce a panegyric of Sparta, the government of that city was 'like that of a military camp, well administered and willingly obeying its commanders'. Like Fafner, who after appropriating the Rhinemaidens' treasure was obliged to turn himself into a dragon and live a nasty life in a cave, the Spartans could never again relax and enjoy the cultural and intellectual life which was the birthright of so many other Greeks of the propertied classes. Aristotle, of all surviving ancient writers, expresses this most clearly: the Spartans, he says, by imposing on their young men exercises designed solely to impart courage, have made them 'beast-like' (*thēriōdeis, Pol.* VIII 4, 1338ᵇ9–38, esp. 11–19; cf. II 9, 1271ᵇ2–6; VII 14, 1333ᵇ11–21; 15, 1334ᵃ40–ᵇ3); and 'now that the Spartans no longer rule over others, it is clear that they are not a happy people and that their legislator was not a good one' (VII 14, 1333ᵇ21–5).

It is unnecessary to dwell at length upon the mutual detestation of Spartiates and Helots, which is well known and amply documented. Sometimes Helots (mainly Laconian ones, no doubt, rather than Messenians) might give loyal service to Sparta, in response to a promise of freedom: we hear

---

[4] I agree with Wade-Gery, *EGH* 37–85, and Toynbee, *SPGH* 221–6, 250–60, 413–16, that the 'Lycurgan' reorganisation is to be dated shortly after the Second Messenian war (and not before it, as by Forrest, Jones etc.: for this view, which seems to me to have little to recommend it, see esp. Forrest, *HS* 55–8, and 'The Date of the Lykourgan Reforms in Sparta', in *Phoenix* 17 [1963] 157–79). The much earlier dates advocated by e.g. N. G. L. Hammond, 'The Lycurgean Reform at Sparta', in *JHS* 70 (1950) 42–64; and Chrimes, *AS* 305–47 etc., seem to me entirely indefensible.

of some during the Pylos affair in 424 (Thuc. IV 26.5–7); 700 went out as hoplites with Brasidas in the same year (IV 80.5; V 34.1); 'the best of the Helots and of the Neodamodeis',[5] 600 altogether, sailed as hoplites to Sicily in 413 (VII 19.3; 58.3); in the fourth century, Helots served as rowers in the Spartan fleet (Xen., *HG* VII i.12); and over 6,000 are said by Xenophon, perhaps with some exaggeration, to have joined in the defence of Sparta against the invading army of Epaminondas in 370–69.[6] We also hear, between 421–18 and 370–69, of Neodamodeis serving as hoplites in the Spartan army, sometimes in considerable numbers: in view of the definitions in Pollux (III 83) and Hesychius (*s.v.*), we must presumably conclude that these were emancipated Helots, freed on enrolment in the Spartan army. The basic relationship between the Spartiates and at any rate the Messenian Helots, however, was one of fear and hatred on both sides. Of the evidence, it will be sufficient to cite four passages.[7]

1. Arist., fr. 538, *ap.* Plut., *Lyc.* 28.7 (just after a reference to the *krypteia*): the ephors, immediately after entering upon office each year, made a formal declaration of war upon the Helots, so that killing them might be 'lawful'—*euages*, not 'unholy', not incurring the religious pollution (*agos*) that came from killing anyone inside one's own borders without 'due process of law', except an enemy of the State. The careful religiosity for which the Spartans were famous allowed them to cut the throats of their Helots at will, provided only they had gone through the legal formality of declaring them 'enemies of the State'. (This kind of religious scruple reminds one of the Roman way of getting round their own rule forbidding the execution of a virgin—by having the executioner rape her first: Tac., *Ann.* v 9.3; Dio Cass. LVIII 11.5; cf. Suet., *Tib.* 61.5.)

2. Arist., *Pol.* II 9, 1269^{a}38–9: the Helots, who often revolt, lie in wait, as it were, to take advantage of the Spartans' misfortunes.

3. Thuc. IV 80.3: Spartan policy is always mainly governed by the necessity of taking precautions against the Helots.[8]

4. Thuc. IV 80.3–4: in 424, after the occupation of Pylos by the Athenians, the Spartans were alarmed by the prospect of a Helot revolt (cf. IV

---

[5] For the Neodamodeis, see Andrewes, in Gomme, *HCT* IV 35–6; Busolt-Swoboda, *GSK* II 668; Kahrstedt, *GSISS* 46–8. Against the view of the Neodamodeis taken by R. F. Willetts, in *CP* 49 (1954) 27–32, see Toynbee, *SPGH* 201 n. 2. About 1,000 Neodamodeis went to Asia with Thibron in 400 (Xen., *HG* III i.4), and about 2,000 with Agesilaus in 396 (iv.2). And see I iii.15; v ii.24; vi i.14; v.24. The Neodamodeis are distinguished by Thucydides both from the 'Brasideioi' (the Helots who had been freed *after* fighting with Brasidas: v 34.1 and 67.1, with 71.3 and 72.3) and from Helots serving as hoplites while still Helots (VII 19.3; 58.3).

[6] Xen., *HG* VI v.28–9. But Diod. XV 65.6 gives the number of 1,000, and Xen. himself (VII ii.2) speaks of '*all* the Helots' as well as 'many Perioikoi' as revolting from Sparta after Leuctra. Perhaps all the Messenian Helots revolted, while many Laconian ones remained faithful to their masters.

[7] I omit various texts from later authors, such as Athen. XIV 657cd (= Myron, *FGrH* 106 F 2).

[8] According to Gomme, *HCT* III 547–8, the word-order demands some such translation as 'most of the relations between the Lacedaemonians and the Helots were of an eminently precautionary character'. That may be right.

41.2–3; 55.1; V 14.3). In fear of the obstinacy of the Helots and their great numbers, they made a proclamation, promising freedom to those Helots who claimed to have done most service to Sparta in her wars—for the Spartans thought that those Helots who came forward first to claim their freedom would be the most self-confident and also the most likely to revolt. Some 2,000 were chosen: they were crowned with garlands and went the round of the temples, as if now free. But soon afterwards they were all done away with, and no one knew how each of them perished.

It was not only the Helots who hated the Spartiates. Cinadon, the leader of an abortive revolt in the first year of the reign of King Agesilaus II (Xen., *HG* III iii.4–11), probably 400–399, said that any Helot, Neodamodes, *hypomeiōn* or Perioikos—anyone, in fact, below the class of *homoioi*, the Spartiates who alone had full political rights—would be delighted to eat the Spartiates raw. This no doubt exaggerates the extent of the resentment against the Spartiates, for even the Perioikoi, the class next lowest in the scale after the Helots, are rarely recorded to have given way to disaffection:[9] Xenophon (*HG* V iii.9) can apply to some of them a term (*kaloi kagathoi*) only used for gentlemen of good social position (see the Additional Note at the end of Appendix XXIX below); and on occasion we find a Perioikos employed by the State on a confidential mission (Thuc. VIII 6.4) and even in command of a detachment of the fleet (22.1). But Xenophon, a lifelong Spartophile, was hardly likely to record (or invent) such a remark unless it had a certain element of real truth.

The Spartan, then, was 'ever on the strain, holding, as it were, a wolf by the throat'.[10] Sparta's uniquely insecure position demanded that she isolate herself completely from outside attack, which might encourage the Helots to rise. It is a striking fact that the very first time a large hostile army of good hoplites penetrated deeply into the Peloponnese, in 370/69 under Epaminondas, Sparta lost Messenia and lost the firm control she had had for much of the last two hundred years over Arcadia, and she sank to the position of a second-rate power. Her defeat by the Boeotians at Leuctra in 371 had been a serious blow to her, especially in the loss of precious Spartiates it entailed (cf. Appendix XVI); but the loss of Messenia was an even greater disaster, and from now on Sparta was no longer the leading power in Greece.[11] Her attempts to regain control of

---

[9] The main examples are those mentioned by Thuc. I 101.2 (*c.* 464); and Xen., *HG* VI v.25, 32 and VII ii.2 (370–69). Cf. also VII iv.21 (Sciritis had apparently revolted). Perioikoi were increasingly used as hoplites. Cf. Isocr. XII 177–81, also exaggerated, but partly true.

[10] Grundy, *THA* I² 219. Grundy has some good things to say about Spartan foreign policy, but he is sometimes very unreliable, e.g. on the question of the numbers of Spartiates, Perioikoi and Helots.

[11] Contrast the very different view of Jones, *Sp.* 134, 137, that the Spartans' 'effective strength had not been greatly reduced [by the loss of Messenia]. The Messenian Helots had always been more of a liability than an asset, and the independent state of Messene proved to be less of a threat than the discontented Helots had been. . . . The reduction of

Arcadia in the 360s were unsuccessful, and for over a century after the battle of Mantinea in 362 Sparta made little impression on the historical record, except during the ill-timed and disastrous, if heroic, revolt against Alexander the Great, led by Agis III in 331 or 330 (see the end of Part vi of this Chapter). Only with Agis IV (244–1) did a real revival begin, reaching a climax under Cleomenes III (236–22) and again under Nabis (206–192). Now at last, long after Sparta had lost Messenia and the greater part of her Helots for ever, we find a social conflict erupting at Sparta among the citizens, of a type with which we are familiar in other Greek states. Had King Cleomenes III lived a century or two earlier, Aristotle might well have said of him, as of Pheidon of Argos (*Pol.* v 10, 1310ᵇ26–8), that he turned himself from a king into a tyrant. Changes then took place at Sparta which might have had some effect if they had been made in, say, the reign of the first Cleomenes (*c.* 520–490). But in the age of Macedonian overlordship (soon to be succeeded by Roman rule) it was too late for even a tyrant to reform Sparta successfully. Of Cleomenes' new citizen army, 6,000 fought at the great battle of Sellasia in 222, and it was said that all but two hundred of them perished (Plut., *Cleom.* 28.8). It was nearly the end of Spartan greatness. After one more remarkable upsurge under Nabis, Sparta slid away into insignificance.

(ii)

'Not quick to enter upon wars unless ...' (Thuc. 1 118.2)

Historians in general have not drawn the right conclusions from the statement of Thucydides (1 118.2) that the Spartans even before 432 were 'not quick to enter upon wars unless compelled to do so'. That is doubtless true of Sparta, at any rate after the time of King Cleomenes I—but only if the qualifying words are interpreted in much the same way as the word 'compelled' in 1 23.6, where it is used, as we saw (Chapter II, Part ii above), in a very broad Thucydidean sense. Most scholars have paid little or no attention to the vital qualifying clause: even Gomme actually ignores it entirely in his Commentary (*HCT* 1 360) and later quotes the passage ('the Spartans were ever slow to go to war', *HCT* III 511) with the qualifying words omitted! (Once more we see how easy it is to be misled by neglecting Thucydidean usage.)

Now according to Thucydides in this passage (1 118.2) 'wars at home' had contributed to prevent Sparta from going to war with Athens earlier; and elsewhere (18.3) he speaks of wars during the Pentecontaetia by both Athens and Sparta 'against their own revolting allies'. (Cf. 80.1, where he

---

Helot numbers by the refoundation of Messene might be regarded as a gain, since it reduced the gross disproportion between rulers and subjects'. I cannot accept this: it would leave unexplained the marked decline of Sparta from the 360s on—for Jones himself, in a chapter dealing with 'Sparta in Eclipse' (after 362), admits (*Sp.* 148) that Sparta was 'now a second-rate power'. The loss of the rich and fertile Messenian plain, with its Helots, was the worst disaster Sparta ever suffered.

makes King Archidamus II open his speech in 432 by saying that he is a man 'experienced in many wars'.) The only relevant wars that we know of, as far as Sparta is concerned, are the Messenian revolt which began in 465–4 and the mysterious campaigns of Tegea and Dipaea (Dipaieis).[12] Are these sufficient to account for the statements of Thucydides, or should we infer that there were further Spartan campaigns no record of which has survived? At any rate, no one will suppose that in these wars Sparta was the victim of outside aggression: she was obviously reducing unwilling allies who had 'revolted', as indeed Thucydides (I 8.3) specifically states. The Spartans, Thucydides would have said, were of course 'compelled' to suppress revolts inside their confederacy, just as they were 'compelled' to make war on Athens in order to hold their confederacy together when the growth of Athens' power threatened it. All Thucydides means by the statement that Sparta was 'not quick to enter upon wars unless compelled to do so' is that Sparta, unlike some other Greek states, did not lightly undertake wars of aggression. We must not take Thucydides to be implying that in 432–1 most Spartans were reluctant to go to war with Athens. The case is within the qualifying words: as we know from I 23.6, the Spartans *were* (in the Thucydidean sense) 'compelled' to fight in 432–1. *And in such a situation they had never been slow to do so.*

Immediately before the words we have been discussing (in I 118.2) Thucydides says that during most of the Pentecontaetia the Spartans *hēsychazon*. Strasburger treats this as a 'definitive and explicit statement that most of the time they preserved peace' (TPSDA 36 n. 1 = 524 n. 66), and elsewhere he can speak without irony of 'Spartas Friedensliebe' (38 n. 1 = 527 n. 74). In proof of this Spartan 'love of peace' he is content to cite just three passages: Thuc. I 71.1; 118.2; IV 108.7. But in I 118.1 the context shows clearly that (as usual, when Thucydides employs the verb *hēsychazein*) the emphasis is on Sparta's *inactivity* in face of the growth of Athenian power; and Crawley is right to translate by the colourless 'remained inactive'. (This is partly explained by Sparta's having to fight 'wars at home', as we have seen; but of course she must have been formally at war with Athens from *c.* 460 to 446/5: see Parts iii and vi of Chapter V.) As for the other two passages cited by Strasburger as evidence of Sparta's alleged 'love of peace', I 71.1 is a curious piece of special pleading by Thucydides' Corinthians, addressing the Spartan Assembly in 432; and IV 108.7 is merely a statement that the Spartans failed to reinforce Brasidas in the 'Thraceward' region in 424, partly because of 'jealousy on the part of their principal men', and partly because they wished to recover the Spartan prisoners taken on Sphacteria and to put an end to the war—which of course had been distinctly unprofitable to them!

[12] The meagre sources for Tegea and Dipaea are in Hill, *S*² 358 (Index IV 2.6–7). For the chronology and general interpretation, see the two masterly articles by Andrewes, SAEFC, and Forrest, TA.

(iii)
Sparta's 'natural' foreign policy, and the Peloponnesian League

Sparta's precarious position as the mistress of the Helots forced her to take special precautions to prevent any hostile power from invading her territory and inducing the Helots to rise, as the Messenian ones anyway were always ready to do. We have already noticed that on the very first occasion on which a large hostile army did penetrate deeply into Laconia and Messenia, in 370/69, the Messenians threw off the Spartan yoke for ever. Once they had revolted, and consolidated their position, a reconquest was out of the question, even when outside help was no longer available to the Messenians: the main reason for this was the great mountain barrier between the two countries, as anyone who has crossed the formidable Taygetus range will easily realise. (The foundation of the great fortified city of Megalopolis, close to the turning-point of the easiest route from Sparta into the upper Messenian plain, created an additional hazard.) That Sparta had ever been able to conquer Messenia in the first place, and crush the first revolt in the seventh century, is remarkable enough. The feat could not now be repeated.

After their conquest of Messenia the Spartans seem at first to have thought they could extend their conquests, with annexation on the Messenian pattern, and acquire further Helots; but about the middle of the sixth century they decided to be content with a much more modest programme, and they began instead to build up the system of military alliances which we know as 'the Peloponnesian League'.[13] We have very little information about the growth of the League, after what was perhaps the first episode, involving Tegea. This was associated with the bringing to Sparta of the bones of Orestes, a talisman the significance of which has often been noticed:[14] Sparta was now ceasing to regard herself as a purely Dorian power[15] and was claiming to be heir to the 'Achaean' hegemony of Agamemnon, whose tomb was now conveniently located at Amyclae, a little south of Sparta, and whose son Orestes was said to have

[13] Many problems remain which are not sufficiently relevant to be discussed here. Hdts 1 82–3 seems to date the war with Argos for the possession of Thyreatis at the time of the fall of Sardis (*c.* 547); some believe that Cythera and other (possibly Argive) territory was acquired by Sparta at the same time (see e.g. G. L. Huxley, *Early Sparta* 70–1). The Sciritis may also have been acquired about now, as believed by Moretti (*RLG* 45); others would give a much earlier date, well inside the eighth century (e.g. Huxley, *op. cit.* 22). Cf. also T. Kelly, in *Amer. Hist. Rev.* 75 (1970), at pp. 976–84.

[14] The main source is Hdts 1 65–8. (Cf. Paus. vii i.8: the bones of Orestes' son Teisamenus, brought from Achaean Helike, probably not much later. See D. M. Leahy, 'The Bones of Tisamenus', in *Historia* 4 [1955] 26–38.) There is a very stimulating account of this period in Forrest, *HS* 73–6, 79–83; but the minor Arcadian hero Oresthes (p. 74) is a red herring which should not be dragged in.

[15] Note esp. the reply of King Cleomenes I to the priestess of Athena at Athens: 'I am not a Dorian but an Achaean' (Hdts v 72.3). On the significance of his brother's name, Dorieus, see Forrest, *HS* 82–3.

succeeded his uncle Menelaus as Sparta's king. With the co-operation of the Delphic Oracle (Hdts I 66–7) and the poet Stesichorus[16] (not to mention Pindar in the fifth century),[17] the new policy was an unqualified success. What is very probably a fragment of the treaty now[18] concluded between Sparta and Tegea, recorded on a stele standing on the bank of the River Alpheius (which is likely to have been the frontier between the two States), has survived in a quotation by Plutarch from Aristotle. This fragment reveals how much the suppression of the Messenians was still uppermost in the minds of the Spartans, for in it the Tegeates swore 'to expel the Messenians from their country and not to make them citizens'.[19] Later treaties between Sparta and her allies probably contained some such clause as the one we find in the Spartan-Athenian alliance of 421, where the Athenians promise to help Sparta put down 'slave' revolts (Thuc. v 23.3).

Although the growth of Sparta's alliance cannot be traced stage by stage, we know that by the early 540s at the latest it included a large part of the Peloponnese (virtually all of it, indeed, apart from Argos and the Achaean cities[20] along the southern shore of the Corinthian Gulf), and made Sparta already the strongest power in Greece. The evidence for this is provided by Herodotus, who explains that Croesus sent to Sparta to make an alliance because she was the most powerful of the Greek states (I 56.1–2; 59.1; 65.1; 69.1–2), and speaks of 'most of the Peloponnese' as having been '*made subject (katestrammenē)* by the Spartans' (68.6). In the fifth and fourth centuries, in theory, Sparta's allies were 'free and autonomous'. We shall see in Part iv of this Chapter, dealing with the structure of the Peloponnesian League, why Herodotus spoke of the allies as having been 'subjected' to Sparta in the sixth century.

This Spartan alliance, evolving into 'the Peloponnesian League',[21] was the strongest force in Greek politics for two centuries, until it finally disintegrated in the mid-360s.[22] Thucydides (I 141.6) makes Pericles pay it a striking tribute in 432: although he depreciates its organisation (rather unfairly), he admits that 'in a single battle the Peloponnesians and their allies are capable of holding their own against all the Greeks'. The League

---

[16] See C. M. Bowra, in *CQ* 28 (1934) 115–19; M. L. West, in *ZPE* 4 (1969), at p. 148.

[17] See Pind., *Pyth.* xi 16, 31–2; *Nem.* xi 33–4.

[18] Other dates have been proposed: e.g about the middle of the fifth century, by Busolt-Swoboda, *GSK* ii 1320 and n. 3; and 464 or a little later, by Moretti, *RLG* 46–9. But the mid-sixth century seems most likely. And see Wade-Gery, in *ASI* (Ehrenberg) 297–8, 302.

[19] Arist., fr. 592, *ap.* Plut., *Q.Gr.* 5 = Mor. 292b; cf. *Q.Rom.* 52 = Mor. 277bc; see *SVdA* ii 112. Aristotle seems to have misunderstood the archaic language, the right interpretation of which is surely that given by Jacoby, in *CQ* 38 (1944) 15–16 = *AGGS* 342–3.

[20] These were as yet unimportant: this and their isolated geographical position made them not worth subduing.

[21] See Part iv of this Chapter for an answer to the question why it is necessary to distinguish, within the 'Spartan alliance' as a whole, an inner circle of allies which, from *c.* 505–1 or rather later, may be given the name, 'the Peloponnesian League'.

[22] The reluctant defection of the Corinthians and others in 366/5 (Xen., *HG* vii iv. 7–9; cf. Isocr. vi 11–13) marks the real end of the League. Cf. the totally different situation in 362: Xen., *HG* vii v.1–3.

gave Sparta the security she needed. As long as it held together, Sparta had no need to fear Helot revolts, for she would be able to call upon her allies to help crush them.

In order to hold her alliance together, Sparta on her side had to defend her allies from outside attack, whether from Argos or from beyond the Peloponnese, give them 'freedom and autonomy' (in a very special sense, as we shall see in a moment), and attach them to herself by making them acquiesce in their submission to her hegemony. If she broke her treaty obligations, the allies concerned, in theory, would automatically be released from theirs, although of course in practice they might not dare to repudiate their treaties and thus 'revolt' from Sparta: this would depend on their strength relative to Sparta's and the external situation at the time. In general, Sparta's allies (or rather, their 'governments')[23] did acquiesce in the existence of the Peloponnesian League, which, unlike the Delian League of which Athens was hegemon, placed no financial or military obligations upon the allies at all except when a League war was actually in progress. One can see why Megara or Aegina or even Corinth, exposed to attack from outside, or the small towns of the Argolid, in fear of Argive domination, might find League membership a useful protection. But why should the Arcadian towns, for example, submit indefinitely to Spartan hegemony?

Sparta found the right answer, from her own point of view: in a world where democracy was slowly gaining ground, she would support 'ancestral' oligarchies, and thus enlist the enthusiastic co-operation of the propertied classes in whose hands power would in this way be permanently retained. Only at Mantinea[24] and probably Elis[25] did democracies exist in the fifth century in the area controlled by Sparta, as far as we know. In general oligarchies 'suited to Sparta's interests' were the rule: Thucydides is most explicit about this.[26] In the fifth century they may not have needed a great deal of propping up by Sparta, and many of them were probably not very narrowly based: they may have extended at their widest to the whole hoplite class.[27] But in the fourth they seem to have become more of an anachronism than ever, and after the battle of Leuctra in 371 there was a widespread expulsion of Laconisers.[28]

This policy involved interference with 'freedom and autonomy' on a large scale,[29] but it was a type of interference which was much less visible

[23] Cf. Chapter III, Part i, *ad init.*

[24] Thuc. v 29.1; and see Hdts ix 77.1–2; Strabo viii iii.2, p. 337; Arist., *Pol.* vi 4, 1318ᵇ25–7; Xen., *HG* v ii.1–7.

[25] See the Eleian decrees, probably of the fifth century, in Hill, *S*² 325 (b 124); and see Hdts ix 77.3; Strabo, *loc. cit.* in n. 24; Diod. xi 54.1; cf. Paus. x ix.5; Arist., *Pol.* v 6, 1306ᵃ12–19.

[26] See Thuc. i 19 and 144.2 (ἐπιτηδείως); 76.1 (ὠφέλιμον); and cf. the use of ἐπιτήδειος in such passages as v 76.2; 81.2; 82.1.

[27] See Chapter I, Part iii, n. 65.

[28] Diod. xv 40 (misdated to 375/4); cf. 5.1–3; Dem. xviii 18; Polyb. iv 27.5–7, etc.

[29] See my CAE 20–1 (with its n. 5, giving references to Sparta's main interventions in favour of oligarchs in the fifth and fourth centuries). On the meaning of *autonomia*, see esp. Bickerman, APT.

than, for example, the Athenian kind. Gomme,[30] in a useful brief discussion of the meaning of *autonomia*, defines it as 'the freedom of a state
to conduct its own internal affairs, that is, to choose and control its own
magistrates, and to try its own citizens', and he adds that 'if the state was
a member of a league (or of a federation), its freedom in foreign relations
was necessarily limited by that membership; if it was not free to leave the
league, and if a garrison or an expeditionary force from another state
would forcibly prevent its leaving, that limited still further its *eleutheria*
['freedom'], but not, properly speaking, its *autonomia*'. Certainly Athens
frequently interfered with her allies' freedom and autonomy in all these
ways, Sparta on few specific occasions (as far as we know) until she began
sending out harmosts to be more than purely military commanders (from
423 onwards),[31] although Sparta's allies were not free to leave her League,
any more than Athens' allies were allowed to do so: to abandon the
alliance of Sparta or of Athens was to 'revolt'.

Athens did far more than Sparta in the way of visible, day-to-day
interference with her allies' freedom and autonomy: the installation of
supervisory magistrates and of garrisons, limitation of independent jurisdiction, and so on. But, as I have already pointed out elsewhere,[32] a
definition of *autonomia* such as Gomme's omits an essential element: the
right of a city to choose, alter and administer its own laws, above all its
own political constitution. I would suggest that this was really by far the
most important ingredient, and that Sparta infringed the autonomy of
most of her allies at least as seriously as Athens did, by maintaining in
them oligarchies which would otherwise have tended to disappear. Experience of modern satellite States in both the great camps has taught us that
if a Great Power can maintain a sufficiently complaisant government in a
satellite State (however dissatisfied many of its population may be with
their subservient position), open coercion of that State may never be
necessary unless there is a full-scale revolution. Two out of many examples
of Spartan 'satellite' rulers zealously serving their protectors must suffice.
When Sparta in 385 had destroyed the walls of Mantinea and broken the
city up into its four original constituent villages, the propertied class of
landowners were delighted, as they were now under an 'aristocracy' and
no longer troubled by 'burdensome demagogues'; and they 'came for
military service with the Spartans from their villages far more enthusiastically than when they were under a democracy' (Xen., *HG* v ii.7). So too
Leontiadas the Theban and his party, when they betrayed the Cadmeia
to the Spartans in 382 and were set up as a small governing oligarchy,
'gave the Spartans even more service than was demanded of them'
(ii.36).

The heading of this Part of the present Chapter includes the words

---

[30] *HCT* i 384–5; cf. Bickerman, APT.
[31] Thuc. iv 132.3. On the harmosts, see G. Bockisch, ''Αρμοσταί (431–387)', in *Klio* 46
(1965) 129–239; Parke, DSSE; Kahrstedt, *GSiSS* 112, 115–16, 229–31.
[32] CAE 20–1; cf. Bickerman, APT.

'Sparta's "natural" foreign policy'. The policy which she mainly pursued until the last years of the fifth century was indeed natural and almost inevitable: to concentrate on keeping her League together, and to avoid foreign adventures and above all the sending of any large armies of Spartiates outside the Peloponnese. The Spartans' reluctance to send a large force into central Greece is shown most strikingly by Herodotus' account (IX 6–11.3) of their long delay in 479. There were, however, some factors which did not make for the stability Sparta so urgently needed. To ensure that the Peloponnese was sealed off from foreign invasion, and at the same time provided with a secure exit for the invincible hoplite army of her own League, Sparta had to keep not only Arcadia but also Corinth and Megara friendly. This, however, meant that she had to consider their interests and protect them against outside attack; and Corinth in particular, as we saw earlier (Chapter III, Parts ii–iii above), was capable of undertaking an entirely independent and on occasion very aggressive foreign policy of her own. Sparta herself had no particular reason to take an interest in affairs outside the Peloponnese (except of course when she was aspiring to an extra-Peloponnesian hegemony), and anyway she had cleverly helped to create a long-lasting hostility between the two principal states north of the Isthmus, Athens and Thebes (see Chapter V, Part i below), and had attached Thebes firmly to her alliance. But Corinth and Megara remained a possible source of trouble, especially as they were not always on good terms, and in *c.* 460 Corinth's territorial designs on her weaker neighbour drove Megara for some fourteen years into the arms of Athens and provided one of the main immediate causes of the First Peloponnesian war.

Now if Corinth and Megara were to be defended by Sparta against Athens, it could only be done effectively in one way: by full-scale Peloponnesian League invasions of Attica If these were not decisive, Sparta might be drawn into a naval war, to which she was very ill-suited in every way; and even when she was victorious, she might find herself virtually obliged to administer extra-Peloponnesian territory, a task which was alien to the Lycurgan regime. The more successful foreign adventures were, one might say, the worse they were likely to be for the cherished Spartan 'way of life'. There is a very interesting passage in Polybius (VI 49.3–10), pointing out how unsuited the Lycurgan constitution was to extra-Peloponnesian operations, which would involve expeditions by sea as well as land and would therefore prove expensive and involve the employment of some currency in general use and supplies drawn from foreign parts. 'And for these reasons they were compelled to go and wait at the doors of the Persians, impose tribute on the islanders, and exact money from all the Greeks'. A reference a little earlier to the Spartan 'betrayal of the Greek cities by the Peace of Antalcidas in order to procure money with a view to their dominance (*dynasteian*) over the Greeks' shows that Polybius has particularly in mind the events of 387/6, which he refers to elsewhere more than once; but the remarks I have quoted apply even better to what happened in 412–403 (see Part vi of this Chapter).

As we shall see, there was a strong current of opinion at Sparta, dominant or nearly so on several occasions in the Pentecontaetia, which was very unwilling to tolerate the rise of Athens to a position equalling Sparta's. The evidence which demonstrates this will be discussed in detail below (Chapter V, Parts ii–ix). In the late sixth century Sparta had liberated Athens from her tyrant Hippias and had subsequently, under King Cleomenes I, tried to control her internal affairs. And Sparta had been the hegemon of all the Greeks who fought against Persia in 480–78. It is easy to understand why so many Spartans found it galling to see Athens achieving a hegemony equal in strength to her own, and including states which, during the Persian war, had been under Spartan hegemony.

(iv)
The Peloponnesian League

Very different views have been taken about the nature of Sparta's relationship with the main body of her allies, the members of 'the Peloponnesian League', as it is generally called nowadays. The most detailed account is Kahrstedt's,[33] but I do not find it at all satisfactory[34] and much prefer that of Busolt.[35] In English there is hardly anything worth reading apart from Larsen's important articles published in 1932–4:[36] these are certainly on the right lines but do not seem to me to give a wholly correct or complete picture. I cannot attempt here to give a comprehensive account, and what follows is mainly confined to those aspects of the subject which are relevant, directly or indirectly, to the Peloponnesian war (including the First Peloponnesian war). If I sometimes go into greater detail than may appear necessary about the constitution and procedure of the Peloponnesian League, it is partly because of the surprising inadequacy and inaccuracy of most of the literature on the subject.

The most recent treatment, the first chapter of Kagan's book (*OPW* 9–30), is seriously confused and misleading. Beginning with a praiseworthy determination to avoid the over-legalistic attitude of many of his predecessors, Kagan ends by failing to realise that however much treaty obligations might be broken and their performance often determined partly by considerations of expediency, there were nevertheless such obligations, backed by solemn oaths, and one must begin by discovering precisely what these obligations were. For Kagan, 'constitutional analysis

[33] *GSiSS* 26–39, 81–118, 267–73, 277, 280–2, 286–94, 311–18, 321–2, 327–31, 336–42. Cf. Wickert, *PB*, esp. 26–33; Moretti, *RLG* 5–95, esp. 76–81.

[34] See the review by H. T. Wade-Gery, in *JHS* 46 (1926) 293–7 (esp. 294: 'its conclusions are, I think, worthless, though as a collection of material it has great value'); and Ehrenberg, *GS*[1] 246: Kahrstedt 'operates with Roman and modern conceptions and is often capricious in his interpretations'.

[35] Busolt-Swoboda, *GSK* II 1320 ff. (esp. 1330–7); cf. Busolt, *Die Lakedämonier und ihre Bundesgenossen* I (Leipzig, 1878).

[36] Larsen, SIR and CPL I and II, rightly praised by Hampl, *GSV* 117 n. 2.

is beside the point' (*OPW* 18). He fails even to notice the most important single provision governing the relations of the allies within what I call 'the Peloponnesian League' (and indeed treat as its distinguishing feature): that a majority decision at a League Congress bound all the allies, even those who had voted against it, 'unless something to do with gods or heroes prevented it'.[37] And when pressing into the service of his argument the passage in Xenophon (*HG* v iv.36–7) which mentions Agesilaus' order to Orchomenus and Cleitor to desist from fighting while his campaign lasted, he denies (*OPW* 19) that there is 'any evidence that anyone raised a constitutional issue', oblivious of the fact that Agesilaus specifically said he was acting 'in accordance with the decision of the allies', and was evidently obeyed. Kagan is wrong, too, in refusing (*OPW* 17–18) to treat as 'typical' or 'characteristic' the very precise details Thucydides gives of the operation of the League before and during the Peloponnesian war. Just because of the importance and the magnitude of the war they were about to undertake, the Spartans had to be very careful in 432 to observe the essential formalities, so that no ally might have an excuse for not playing its full part; and in 421 and the years following Thucydides gives us some particularly good opportunities of seeing the working of the regular League machinery, such as it was.

Sparta was undoubtedly more inclined to take a dictatorial line with her allies on occasion after the Peloponnesian war was over, and more especially after the King's Peace. Xenophon puts into the mouth of the Athenian Autocles a very critical speech to the Spartans in 371, before Leuctra, including the accusation, 'You make enemies for yourselves without sharing the decision with your allies, and against these enemies you lead them, so that often those who are said to be autonomous are obliged to campaign against their best friends' (*HG* vi iii.8). As far as possible I shall ignore changes in Sparta's treatment of her allies after the Peloponnesian war.[38]

A. '*The Spartan alliance*' and '*the Peloponnesian League*'

Just as the official designation of the Athenian alliance was 'the Athenians and their allies', so that of the Spartan alliance was 'the Spartans and their allies'. Within the Spartan alliance I propose to recognise an inner circle of allies which, like most people, I shall call 'the Peloponnesian League'. No ancient source, as far as I am aware, draws any distinction of this nature. It can nevertheless be demonstrated beyond doubt that such an 'inner circle' did exist, and I submit that 'the Peloponnesian League', as something not quite as extensive as the whole Spartan alliance,

---

[37] Thuc. v 30.1; cf. 32.6. Neither text even appears in Kagan's index of sources (*OPW* 417).

[38] These changes are dealt with at length by Kahrstedt, *GSiSS* 92 ff., 291 ff., many of whose opinions I cannot accept.

is a useful concept, provided it is strictly defined. We also encounter the untechnical expression 'the Peloponnesians', which is used very frequently: it may refer to the Spartan alliance in general or the Peloponnesian League in the narrow sense, or its denotation may be purely geographical. I should add that I do not regard the Peloponnesian League as having any direct connection with the Hellenic League of 481 ff.: on this question I entirely agree with Brunt (HLP, esp. 141 ff.).

Analogy with the Athenian alliance is helpful. Again, no ancient source distinguishes an inner circle of Athenian allies, but in modern times it has become customary to apply the term 'the Delian League' (or 'the Con-federacy of Delos') to the anti-Persian alliance founded under the hege-mony of Athens in 478/7 B.C., which grew by degrees into the Athenian empire.[39] It is clear that several states which were allied with Athens at one time or another in the fifth century were outside that League: Plataea, allied with Athens from 519/18 onwards; the other cities of Boeotia in the years 458–7 to 446; the Thessalians, who had an 'ancient alliance' with Athens (Thuc. II 22.2–3); Sicilian and south Italian cities such as Egesta (M/L 37) and Rhegium and Leontini (M/L 63, 64); Corcyra, from 433 onwards; the four cities of Cephallenia, from 433 onwards (Thuc. II 30.2); most of the Acarnanians (II 9.4; 68.8); 'the Messenians in Naupactus' (II 9.4; cf. I 103.3); and several other powers, including at various times Perdiccas of Macedon. As everyone knows, Athens' allies in the Delian League originally either furnished ships with their crews or paid tribute (Thuc. I 96.1), although we later find the tributary allies also providing land troops.[40] No one will suppose that the other allies (outside the Delian League) had to pay tribute: their obliga-tions would depend upon their individual treaties with Athens. Yet Thucydides, in his brief and very unsatisfactory[41] description of the allies on both sides in 431 (II 9), draws no distinctions, either (among allies with navies) between Corcyra on the one hand and Chios and Lesbos on the other, or between those of the other allies who belonged to the Delian League (now the Athenian empire) and those who did not. There was nevertheless a very real difference. Chios and the Lesbian towns had to provide whatever naval contingents were demanded of them, perhaps in theory still by Athens and the League synods, but in practice by Athens alone, whereas Corcyra must have been allied on a much more inde-pendent basis; and I see no reason to suppose that Athens either had a

[39] Of course in a sense 'Delian League' is 'a modern misnomer unrelated to the Greek name' (Hammond, ONAA 43 n. 9); but why should we not continue to use that con-venient expression, provided we define it properly?

[40] Thuc. II 9.5. The supply of land troops by tributary allies is recorded from at least the 450s: see Hill, S² 354–5 (Index III 3.4); cf. ATL III 60–1, n. 61. The obligation may have existed from the very beginning of the League, as maintained by Hammond, ONAA 55.

[41] 'A meagre and beggarly description. . . . This chapter in fact looks like a short note (made at the time?), which was never properly worked into the main narrative', says Gomme, HCT II 12. I agree—though I am less happy about Gomme's note on II 9.5.

right to demand, or did demand, tribute from Plataea, the Messenians, the Acarnanians or the Cephallenians.[42]

In his description of the Spartan alliance, in II 9.2–3, the one distinction Thucydides draws between the allies is a geographical one, between 'Peloponnesians within the Isthmus' (if the text is sound: see Gomme, *HCT* II 10) and 'those outside the Isthmus', the latter including the Megarians, who were certainly members of the Peloponnesian League. Similarly, in II 10.1 Thucydides speaks of the Spartans as sending for troops 'around the Peloponnese and her allies outside'. He also distinguishes in V 57.2 between 'allies from the rest of the Peloponnese' and 'those from outside', in order to emphasise that both sets of allies assembled at Phlius. The short-lived treaty of 418/17 between Sparta and Argos also spoke of allies of Sparta within and outside the Peloponnese (Thuc. V 79.1,2; cf. 77.5,7).

In place of a pointless geographical classification I wish to establish one on quite a different basis, singling out within the whole Spartan alliance an important group of allies who could, and in certain cases must, be asked by Sparta to *vote* on a particular issue, with the consequence that *the decision of the majority bound them all, 'unless something to do with gods or heroes prevented it'.*[43] These states were, so to speak, the hard core of the Spartan alliance, and only in respect of them is it permissible to speak of a 'league' without straining the use of that word far beyond its normal limits. (For convenience, I may sometimes refer to these allies as members of 'the Peloponnesian League' before a proper 'league' came into existence, at the end of the sixth century or a little later—see Section B, §6 below.) In German, which is richer than English in technical terms for this sort of thing, the Peloponnesian League can be described as something less than a 'Bundesstaat' (a Federal State) but more than a mere 'Waffenbündnis' (such as the Spartan alliance as a whole): in fact as a 'Staatenbund',[44] or at any rate a 'Bündnissystem'.[45] The distinction between the two senses of the expression 'the Spartans and their allies' is relevant in one context only: members of the Peloponnesian League were bound by majority decisions of the League Congress (subject to the proviso already mentioned) even if they had voted against them; the other members of the

---

[42] The ingenious formula, found e.g. in *SEG* x 35 (= D 16 in *ATL* II 69–70 = *IG* I² 17). 11–12, and in M/L 52 (= Tod I² 42 = D 17 in *ATL* II 70–2 = *IG* I² 39).26–7, 'I will pay the tribute which I may persuade the Athenians [to fix]', well represents the reality: it would merely give the allies the right to be heard when the Athenians fixed their assessments. But we should remember that the original assessments had been made by an Athenian, Aristeides, and (more remarkable) that it was the Athenians who had decided in the first place which cities should furnish ships and which should pay tribute (Thuc. I 96.1).

[43] See Section B, §§6–7 below. The most important text is Thuc. V 30.1–4.

[44] Thus Busolt-Swoboda, *GSK* II 1330.

[45] Thus Wickert, *PB* 32–3. Contrast Kahrstedt, *GSISS* 81–2 etc., who (in spite of what he has to admit on p. 277) will not even allow the existence of a proper *Bund*; also Hans Schaefer, *Staatsform u. Politik. Untersuch. zur griech. Gesch. des sechsten u. fünften Jahrh.* (Leipzig, 1932), who is sufficiently refuted by L. I. Highby, *The Erythrae Decree* (= *Klio*, Beiheft 36 = n. F. 23, 1936) 58–74.

Spartan alliance were not, although of course they sometimes might be indirectly affected by such decisions, if only because Sparta's own course of action could be influenced by them. For the present we need not consider precisely which allies belonged to which category (see Section c below, and Appendix XVII).

In case anyone not well acquainted with Greek diplomatic procedures is sceptical about the legitimacy of drawing fine distinctions between different senses of the words 'and their allies', he will find a useful illustration in the way the 'Peace of Philocrates' was concluded at Athens in 346, with Philip II of Macedon. At the Assembly on the 19th of Elaphebolion, a vote was finally taken that 'the Athenians and the allies of the Athenians' should enter into the Peace (see Dem. xix 159, 278). But these words were capable of more than one interpretation, and on this occasion they were deliberately left undefined. They might be held to include all those states which had treaties of alliance with Athens, including the Phocians, Halus, and King Cersobleptes of Thrace: attempts were made to exclude these three specifically, but without effect (see Dem. xix 159, 174). Or they might be held to include only those allies who were members of what we usually call 'the Second Athenian Confederacy', and as such had official representatives (*synedroi*) at Athens. The question was left undecided until the vital Assembly held a few days later, preparatory to the administering of the oaths. Everything now depended on who was actually allowed to swear. The decree then proposed was that 'the *synedroi* of the allies' should swear: this of course excluded all allies except the members of the Confederacy, to whose representatives alone the term *synedroi* applied. An attempt was made to amend the resolution so as to allow Cersobleptes' representative to swear in his name, but this was defeated.[46] Up to the last moment, however, the issue remained legally in doubt.[47] I may add that we never hear of any similar ambiguity about the meaning of the expression 'and their allies' in the fifth century. I have mentioned the events of 346 only to show that in principle there might be occasions on which that expression could be interpreted in more than one sense.

B. *The 'constitution of the Peloponnesian League*

It is essential to begin a consideration of 'the constitution of the Peloponnesian League' by reminding ourselves that this convenient phrase has no direct Greek equivalent and can only be translated into Greek by a periphrasis. I suggest 'the oaths and treaties sworn by the Spartans and their allies, and the decisions (*dogmata*) of [the Spartans and] the allies': *hoi horkoi kai hai synthēkai has ōmosan Lakedaimonioi kai hoi symmachoi, kai ta*

[46] See Aeschin. ii 82–4; iii 73–4. (Aeschin. ii 84 has misled some people: he is not claiming that the motion of Aleximachus was passed, but only that it was put to the vote. It was certainly not passed: see Aeschin. ii 86; iii 74; cf. Ps.-Dem. xii 8.)

[47] A book shortly to be published by M. M. Markle makes a valuable and original contribution to our understanding of the Peace of Philocrates.

dogmata tōn symmachōn.[48] This brings out the fact that the League 'constitution', in so far as such an expression is permissible at all, came about solely
through treaties, sworn to by Sparta and her allies, with the addition only
of specific decisions (*dogmata*) of League Congresses, passed at the suggestion and with the approval of Sparta. It is the first part of the definition
which is the essential one: it could be phrased in any form of words that
concentrated upon *sworn treaties*. A Greek alliance was what the oaths of
alliance had made it. Nowadays treaties are 'signed'; in antiquity they
were sworn. The 'decisions (*dogmata*) of the allies' are very secondary, and
some might prefer to omit them from the definition. Certainly some of
them,[49] like the *dogma* proclaiming a League war against Olynthus in 382
(Xen., *HG* v ii.37, cf. 20), were simply individual decisions taken once
for all and having no further constitutional consequences; but in 378 King
Agesilaus invoked against Orchomenus an allied *dogma* (Xen., *HG* v
iv.37) which had evidently forbidden (or had allowed the hegemon at
its discretion to stop) any war between allied states during the continuance
of any League expedition outside the Peloponnese, or perhaps only during
a particular campaign or series of campaigns against Thebes (see §8
below). Although the actual term *dogma* is not used elsewhere of resolutions
creating general rules affecting the behaviour of the allies, clear examples
may be found in Thuc. v 31.5[50] (where the term used is actually *xynthēkē*,
'covenant'), also in Xen., *HG* v ii. 21–3 (certainly establishing a general
rule, in view of vi ii.16; and cf. v iv.37), and in Diod. xv 31.2. (I believe
that in this last case only members of the Peloponnesian League were
concerned: see Appendix XVII, *C*, §8.)

Ignoring various minor matters, I shall merely discuss what seem to
me the essential features of the League constitution that are relevant for
the purposes of this book. The subject is a difficult and complicated one
and will involve a number of technicalities and detailed arguments. I have
therefore given, in Appendix XVIII, a brief and simple summary of the
views expressed in the remainder of this Section.

§1. The League, of 'the Spartans and their allies', was purely and simply
a symmachy: a series of offensive and defensive alliances, contained
in treaties between each individual ally and Sparta, in which each ally
swore 'to have the same friends and enemies as the Spartans, and to follow
the Spartans whithersoever they may lead' (see Xen., *HG* ii ii.20; v
iii.26),[51] and received in return an undertaking by Sparta to defend her
against attack in certain specified circumstances. I do not think we can be
absolutely sure that each ally did not swear to (and receive oaths from)

---

[48] See e.g. Tod ii 118 (= *SVdA* ii 248 = *SIG*³ 142 = *IG* ii² 34).9–12; 142 (= *SVdA*
ii 289 = *SIG*³ 173 = *IG* ii² 111).17–19, 69 ff.
[49] Cf. the *dogmata* of the Second Athenian Confederacy, of which some made general
rules and others dealt with specific cases.
[50] Against the exegesis of this passage given by Andrewes, in Gomme, *HCT* iv 28–9, see
§8 below.
[51] Cf. §3(*a*) below, and Appendix V.

'the Spartans *and their allies*'; but most scholars have believed—rightly, I think—that the alliances were all with Sparta alone, so that no mutual obligations existed between the allies, except in so far as they were all bound to Sparta. (For one or two texts which may seem to give a contrary impression, see §§4 and 5 below.) The statement in Thucydides III 15.1 that 'the Spartans *and their allies*' made allies of the Lesbians in 428 is not relevant, in my opinion, since I believe that the Lesbian cities were not becoming members of the Peloponnesian League but merely of the Spartan alliance in the broad sense (see Section A above, and Appendix XIX).

An important argument against Sparta's allies being automatically bound to each other as well as to her is the fact that they were evidently free as a general rule to fight each other: see §8 below. And in 389–8, when the Acarnanians submitted to Sparta and entered into a symmachy with her, we are specifically told by Xenophon (*HG* IV vii.1; cf. *Ages.* II 20) that they merely made peace with the Achaeans, the allies of Sparta who had called her in against the Acarnanians in the first place (*HG* IV vi). My own belief is that the Acarnanians were now joining the Peloponnesian League, of which the Achaeans were already members (see Section C below and Appendix XVII); and if this is so, then the fact that the Acarnanians merely made peace with the Achaeans should be conclusive against Peloponnesian League alliances being made with all the other allies.

As far as I can see, there is only one text, Thuc. V 54.3–4, which could possibly furnish evidence that Peloponnesian League allies had the right to appeal for military assistance from each other even if Sparta made no move, and I do not think it does in fact provide that evidence: see §5 below.

§2. The alliances were permanent, or at least of indefinite duration. At any rate, secession was not allowed, unless of course one side proved false to its engagements and thereby in effect nullified its treaty and released the other side from its obligations. This is not always realised, but it seems to me certain, in view of Thuc. I 71.4–5 and Xen. *HG* IV vi.1–3, where a breach of treaty by Sparta is seen as a necessary excuse for secession, and also Thuc. V 30.1, where the Spartans tell the Corinthians that they will be breaking their oaths if they revolt from Sparta and become allies of Argos. It used to be said (see *e.g.* Tod II, pp. 14–15) that there is no evidence for a Greek military alliance specifically designed to last for ever until the early fourth century (Tod II 101 = *SVdA* II 223 = *SIG*³ 122); but we can now point to M/L 10 (= *SVdA* II 120), a treaty between Sybaris and the Serdaioi, probably of the third quarter of the sixth century, which is explicit made eternal (*aeidion*, lines 4–5), and is commemorated on a bronze plate deposited at Olympia. The ceremony associated with the swearing of the oaths at the formation of the Delian League (see Appendix V) proves that that alliance also was deliberately designed to last for ever, and there are other examples of fifth-century treaties intended to be permanent: the so-called 'Peace of Epilycus' between Athens and Persia, of 424 or a little later (Andoc. III 29; and see Appendix VII), and probably the mid-fifth-century Athenian alliances with Rhegium and Leontini, renewed in 433-2 (M/L 63 and 64 = *SVdA* II 162/3 = Tod I² 58/57 etc.). Cf. also Aesch., *Eumen.* 291, 670, 763-4, discussed in Chapter V, Part iv below.

§3. All members were in theory autonomous (cf. Thuc. v 77.5; 79.1) and in the League Congress each had an equal vote (1 141.6); but Sparta, as hegemon, was in a superior position, above all in five ways:

(*a*) First, each ally was always under an obligation 'to have the same friends and enemies as the Spartans and to follow the Spartans whithersoever they may lead' (*hepesthai Lakedaimoniois hopoi an hēgōntai*). It is nearly always said that at least the latter part of this oath ('to follow the Spartans whithersoever they may lead'), if not the whole of it, first appeared in the oaths of alliance in the late fifth century only: either *c.* 418-17 or earlier, or when the whole of the oath is first explicitly attested, in the case of Athens in 404 (Xen., *HG* II ii.20; cf. *Anab.* VI i.27; Diod. XIII 107.4).[52] Certainly the oath as a whole was then common form: see Xen., *HG* iv vi.2 (Achaeans, 389); v iii.26 (Olynthus, 379); VI iii.7 (371, general); cf. v ii.8; VII i.24.[53] I believe it was *always* a standard oath, applying to all states which entered the Peloponnesian League; members of the Spartan alliance who remained outside the League would probably not have to swear to such a provision. It seems not to be generally appreciated that the oath of a symmachy, 'to have the same friends and enemies', either might be a mutual one, in which the obligation was reciprocal, each side binding itself to have the same friends and enemies as the other or others, or, as in this case, might create a subordinate relationship in which an ally bound itself in effect to have those friends and enemies which the hegemon chose for it. Examples of each kind are known: see Appendix V. It was precisely the imposition of the oath I have just described, subjecting the foreign policy of each ally to Sparta's dictation and thus depriving the ally of an essential part of its freedom (*eleutheria*),[54] which led to the adoption of that feature of the League constitution which I regard as the hallmark of League membership in the fifth and fourth centuries: the provision (mentioned below) for participation in certain circumstances in a League Congress, deciding by majority vote. I suggest that the two go

[52] See e.g. Kahrstedt, *GSiSS* 92-4, 291; Larsen, *CPL* II 9-10; *RGGRH* 67-8; *EAL* 812-13; Forrest, *HS* 88. Contrast Bengtson, *GG*⁴ 135-6. Busolt's attitude is not clear to me: contrast *GG* I² 710 and n. 2; II² 388; with *GSK* II 1325; and note 1340 n. 6 (on p. 1341) and *GG* III i.72 n. 2.

[53] All these passages mention the oath to follow the Spartans wherever they lead; *HG* v iii.26 also gives the part about having the same friends and enemies.

[54] But not of its *autonomia*, as claimed by Kahrstedt, *GSiSS* 85, who can point to no evidence except a deliberately tendentious speech (Xen., *HG* VI iii.7), where the Athenian Autocles, who is really speaking of *eleutheria*, is invoking the King's Peace, which spoke only of *autonomia*, and is therefore obliged to follow its terminology (v i.31)!

together: having the same friends and enemies as Sparta and following wherever she leads, with the severe limitation of external freedom which that involves, soon necessitates some limitation of Sparta's right to exercise her hegemony irresponsibly and against the wishes of most of her allies. The proof that even in the sixth century the League treaties contained a provision that the ally would 'follow the Spartans whithersoever they may lead' is as follows:

(i) First, there is the statement of Herodotus (i 68.6) that most of the Peloponnese had been *subjected* (*katestrammenē*) by Sparta by the mid-sixth century. Sparta's allies were always in theory autonomous so far as their internal affairs were concerned, but the use of the very strong word 'subjected' would be fully justified if they were obliged to follow Sparta into war at her bidding. I do not see what other justification it could possibly have.

(ii) Secondly, the allies could be called out for an attack on Athens in *c.* 506 without being told the reason for the expedition.[55] The fact that was not disclosed to the allies was not, surely, that the expedition was to be against Athens, but that its object was (according to Herodotus) to install Isagoras as tyrant—probably in fact to set up a close oligarchy (a *dynasteia*) with Isagoras at its head. It was evidently when the allies discovered that King Cleomenes was proposing to interfere drastically with the form of government of another state, and thus create a precedent dangerous to themselves, that they refused to take part: 'the Corinthians first, telling each other that they would not be acting justly, changed their minds and deserted', as did the others, after Cleomenes' co-king Damaratus had also gone home (Hdts v 75.1,3). But the fact that the allies deserted after joining the expedition must not be allowed to obscure the significance of the fact that they did come at Sparta's call, evidently because they were obliged to do so—this is often overlooked. It is interesting to find Herodotus saying specifically (v 74.2) that Sparta's Boeotian allies joined in Cleomenes' expedition 'by agreement' (*apo synthēmatos*; cf. vi 121.1): this otherwise unnecessary detail confirms the indication that the Peloponnesian allies were bound to come when summoned.[56]

(iii) Three other interesting texts are not without relevance. First, the Arcadians, whom Sparta had never been willing to recognise as such (for she always insisted, as Athens did, on dealing only with individual cities—*divide et impera*!), swore, or were invited to swear,[57] oaths to King Cleomenes, when he was in exile in 491–90, that they would follow him

---

[55] Hdts v 74.1: οὐ φράζων ἐς τὸ συλλέγει.

[56] I would suppose that the Chalcidians too, who are also mentioned separately, joined the expedition voluntarily. We do not know how Cleomenes persuaded them and the Boeotians to participate, but both may have been tempted by the promise of booty, and the Boeotians in addition by the hope of annexing part of Attica, e.g. Oenoe and Hysiae: see Hdts v 74.2.

[57] Hdts vi 74.1. The main verb, ἔπρησσε, is in the imperfect tense, and it is not clear whether the oaths were actually sworn or not.

'whithersoever he might lead them'. The formula is exactly the same, with the oath merely sworn to the king instead of the city: it proves that the formula was already current in the Peloponnese before the Persian wars. Secondly, when the Athenians made their desperate appeal to the Spartans in 479 to march out of the Peloponnese and fight the Persians north of the Isthmus, they threatened that they themselves, if left any longer in the lurch, would become allies of the King and make military expeditions jointly to any land against which the Persians might lead them (Hdts IX 11.2). And thirdly, the occurrence of a similar formula in Hdts I 151.3 also shows that, for Herodotus, subordination to a hegemon was expressed by an undertaking to follow whithersoever the hegemon might lead. (The fact that the same form of words is found in Hdts IX 66.2 is irrelevant for our present purposes, as the reference there is to a commander's control over his own troops.)

Sparta was thus able, from the very beginning of the League, to oblige her allies to follow her into war on demand. And this always remained the rule, subject to the proviso, introduced not earlier than the last years of the sixth century, that no ally need follow Sparta into a war (or at any rate an aggressive war, as defined in §5 below) unless a majority of the allies at a League Congress had first voted to that effect: see §6 below. But Sparta's hegemonic role remained otherwise unimpaired: Thucydides (II 7.1) speaks of Athens and Sparta as appealing for allies in 431 'outside the areas of their power' (*dynamis*). For him, the allies of Sparta, as well as of Athens, were within her 'power'. Once a war was declared, Sparta had complete management of it, under the provision I have been discussing whereby the allies were obliged to follow her whithersoever she led them. This accounts for the fact that the Spartans could answer the appeal of the Achaeans in *c.* 389 by sending out an expeditionary force including allies, to attack the Acarnanians, without summoning a League Congress: Sparta and her allies were already at war with a number of states, led by the quadruple alliance of Athens, Boeotia, Argos and Corinth, and the Arcananians were among the enemy states (Xen., *HG* IV vi.1–3 and ff.). But after the Peloponnesian war, when Sparta was relatively far stronger than she had been earlier, she may sometimes have neglected to summon a League Congress on occasions when she ought to have done so (cf. Xen., *HG* VI iii.8, cited above, just before Section A).

(*b*) Secondly, Sparta had a constitutional power of decision equal to that of all the allies put together: she exercised this by taking her own decision first (cf. §6, and Chapter V, Part viii below), in her own Assembly (as we see her doing in Thuc. I 67 ff., esp. 79.1; 87.1–3, 4), before summoning a League Congress in which the allies made their decision. I need waste no time on the theory of Hampl (*GSV* 117–34) that Sparta—like Athens in the Delian League and her Second Confederacy, as Hampl wrongly supposed (cf. Appendix V)—had nothing

but one vote in the League Congress and had to submit to majority decisions of the Congress, positive as well as negative. The arguments of
Hampl have already been sufficiently refuted.[58] It is simply inconceivable
that Sparta should have consented to be committed to positive action by
majority decisions of her allies, nor is there any evidence that she ever did
so consent. To the arguments advanced by others I would add a powerful
one derived from the careful wording of Thucydides I 120.1, giving the
opening of the Corinthian speech at the League Congress in 432. The
Corinthians address themselves not to 'Spartans and allies' but purely to
'Fellow allies' (*ō andres xymmachoi*, cf. 124.2); and they begin by drawing a
clear distinction between the vote of the Spartans, which *has already been
given* for war, and the vote of the allies, which *is about to be given*. (See also
the detailed argument in Chapter V, Part viii below.)

(*c*) Thirdly, only Sparta could summon a League Congress: this is
highly probable *a priori* and is proved by the complaint of the Corinthians
at Sparta in 432, that in spite of 'frequent' warnings from themselves about
the danger of Athenian aggression, the Spartans have delayed to call the
allies together until, as now, the harm has actually been done.[59] (Against
a recent assertion by Andrewes [TCW 235 n. 4] that a League Congress
'might be called by some other member, to judge from Thuc. I 67.1',
see Chapter V, Part viii below, in relation to the events of the year 440.)

(*d*) Fourthly, as Sparta convened the League Congress, so she naturally
provided the chairman who presided: see Thuc. I 125.1 (cf. 120.1), where
it is 'the Spartans' who 'took the vote of all the allies who were present,
one after another'. This chairman was probably always an ephor. Whether
Sparta herself had a vote in the League Congress we cannot be sure, but
it seems to me highly probable that she had not. Sparta's attitude, of
course, would always be known in advance, because she would have
summoned the Congress to put a specific proposal accepted by herself
(cf. §6 below); and since the vote of her own Assembly was equipollent
with that of the League Congress as a whole (see para. [b] above), the
question whether she *also* had a vote *among the allies* is of very small importance. Apart from general probability, I know of only one argument which
is relevant here: the forms of address used by Thucydides' speakers.
When addressing themselves to a Spartan Assembly, they always say
'Spartans' (*ō Lakedaimonioi*, I 68.1; 69.4; 71.1; 75.1; 76.1; VI 92.1, 5; cf.
I 80.1; 85.3; 87.2). The Mytilenaeans, when not as yet members of even
the Spartan alliance in the broad sense (see Section A above and Appendix
XIX below), address themselves to 'Spartans and allies' (*ō Lakedaimonioi
kai xymmachoi*, III 9.1; 13.1). But the Corinthians, already members of the

---

[58] See esp. Larsen, COPDL 194–6 n. 2 (esp. the middle para. of the note on p. 195).

[59] Thuc. I 68.2; cf. 120.1. Apparently the Spartans had earlier accused the Corinthians
of being inspired by purely selfish motives: see I 68.2, with 82.6. In view of the Corinthian
claim to have *prevented* the League from taking action against Athens in 440 (see Chapter
V, Part viii below), their claim to have 'often' warned the Spartans about Athenian
aggression must be confined within eight years at the most, and probably goes back only
to 433!

Peloponnesian League, address the League Congress in 432 not as 'Spartans and allies' but as 'Fellow allies' (*ō andres xymmachoi*, I 120.1; 124.2); and since Thucydides[60] is always most precise and consistent in the forms of address he gives to his speakers, this may be taken as an indication that Sparta, though presiding at the League Congress, did not even have a vote there. (The expression 'Fellow allies' would not, of course, exclude the Spartans; but if they were among those who had votes one would expect them to be specifically mentioned.) As we had occasion to notice in paragraph (*b*) above, Thucydides (I 120.1) speaks of the Spartan vote in favour of war in 432 as having been given already, before the League Congress in which the vote of the allies is about to be given.

(*e*) Fifthly, Sparta supplied all commanders of League forces, and from at least *c*. 431 onwards even placed *xenagoi* in charge of individual allied contingents (Thuc. II 75.3; Xen., *HG* III v.7; IV ii.19; v.7; V i.33; ii.7; VII ii.3). The League armies were normally commanded in the field by a Spartan king, to whom complete obedience was due during the campaign (Thuc. v 66.3). When King Agis II astonished and displeased his army in 418 by ordering a return home, the Spartans and their allies followed him (60.2) *dia ton nomon* ('because of the rule', or 'out of respect for the law').

§4. We cannot say for certain what rules there were, if any, about the introduction of new members. I would myself suppose that Sparta could in theory make what new allies she wished, within the League framework or outside it. It is just possible that the introduction of new members could only take place with the approval of a League Congress, but the examples sometimes quoted in support of this position prove nothing: see Appendix XIX.

§5. It is convenient for us to draw a distinction (which is never made explicitly in the sources) between the obligations of League members in regard to 'offensive' and 'defensive' wars. We may call those wars 'defensive' which occurred as a result of manifest and unjustified aggression against Sparta or an ally, either *ex nihilo* or in breach of a peace treaty (like the Thirty Years Peace or the Peace of Nicias) entered into by 'the Spartans and their allies'. If the alleged aggression were not perfectly clear and indisputable, then a League Congress would have to be called. In 432 it was alleged at Sparta that Athens had broken the Thirty Years Peace; but (as we have seen) the boot was very much on the other leg and, the rights and wrongs being not immediately obvious, Sparta had first to decide for herself the question whether Athens had broken the Peace, and then, when she herself had given an affirmative answer, to summon a League Congress and take a vote of the allies. In each case the motion put was 'that the treaty [the Thirty Years Peace] has been broken (by the Athenians)';[61] but from this there followed the corollary 'that there must

---

[60] Unlike Xenophon, who is characteristically imprecise in such matters: cf. (in one and the same speech) *HG* v ii.14 with 12 and 18.

[61] Thuc. I 67.1,3,4; 79.2; 87.2,3,4; 88; 119; cf. VII 18.2.

be war':[62] the decision, therefore, was tantamount to a declaration of war, and that is how it is sometimes described. In 413, on the other hand, we do not hear of a League Congress being summoned before Sparta called out her allies for an invasion of Attica (Thuc. VII 18.1–4; 19.1; with VI 105.1–2). It may be that a clear majority of the allies were now glad to resume the war (as the Corinthians certainly were, VII 18.1), while Athens was heavily engaged in Sicily, and a Congress may therefore have been considered unnecessary; but it is also possible that Sparta was not bound to call one, as she could now claim that Athens had manifestly broken the Peace. (Cf. Dover, in Gomme, *HCT* IV 488, addendum to p. 395.)

At this point we may confine ourselves for the time being to *defensive wars*, in the sense defined above.

(*a*) We never hear of Sparta herself being directly attacked by an outside power in time of peace; but had this happened, the Spartans would surely have had the right to call out their allies at once, without having to delay to summon a League Congress. They very probably had the same right in the event of a Helot revolt.[63]

(*b*) Probably any ally equally had the right to call for Spartan help if clearly the victim of an outside attack, by a state not a member of the League; and of course, if Sparta responded, she might well wish to call out her other allies, except in trivial cases which she could easily deal with on her own. If the aggression complained of had been manifest and indisputable, there would presumably be no need for an allied Congress before allied contingents were summoned by Sparta (cf. Busolt–Swoboda, *GSK* II 1333–4, with 1334 n. 1). Thus in 418 we see the Spartans launching a full League expedition against Argos (Thuc. V 57.1 ff.), in defence of Epidaurus, which the Argives had attacked repeatedly in 419–18. The Argives claimed to have a legitimate excuse for their aggression (V 53), and at this time, although the Thirty Years Peace between Sparta and Argos concluded in 451/50 had expired and the negotiations for a new peace treaty had proved abortive (V 36–41; 44.1), a state of war did not exist between Sparta and Argos. This may have had some effect in preventing a League expedition from taking place earlier, for if Sparta's allies were disinclined to help Epidaurus they might be unwilling to march, and Sparta might even be obliged to summon a League Congress before declaring a League expedition. By the early summer of 418 the situation was becoming serious (57.1), and the Spartans delayed no longer.

(*c*) An earlier stage of the attack of Argos upon Epidaurus raises a

---

[62] Thuc. I 67.2; 79.2; 86.5; 87.2,4; 88; 119 (thrice); 120.1; 124.2,3; 125.1.

[63] See Part iii of this Chapter. Two League states which are recorded as helping Sparta in the great Helot revolt of 465/4 ff. are Aegina (Thuc. II 27.2; IV 56.2) and Mantinea (Xen., *HG* V ii.3); but we also hear of assistance being given by two states which were not members of the League: Plataea (Thuc. III 54.5) and Athens (Thuc. I 102.1–2; Ar., *Lysistr.* 1137–44; etc.).

problem of a different kind, to which I have alluded in §1 above: namely, whether the allies of Sparta were bound to each other in such a way that they could invoke each other's assistance independently of any action by Sparta. In Thuc. v 54.3–4 we read that in 419 the Argives attacked Epidaurus and ravaged its territory and that the Epidaurians 'appealed for assistance to their allies'. Some complied (55.1); others either refused, on the excuse of a 'sacred month',[64] or merely advanced to the Epidaurian frontier and remained inactive there (54.4). Andrewes, (in Gomme, *HCT* IV 75) thinks that 'in the absence of any other indication, we must take these to be the other members of the Peloponnesian League, who could be called out directly since an attack on a member was already in progress'. But what 'other indication' could we expect? Thucydides uses the expression *tous xymmachous*, the natural meaning of which is 'their [the Epidaurians'] allies', and it is quite possible that he is referring simply to Sparta and certain other states with which Epidaurus had individual alliances—the other cities of the Argolic peninsula, perhaps, which may well have felt the need of close-knit alliances among themselves, as a security against Argive aggression, in addition to their association in the Peloponnesian League. (When Mantinea and Tegea fought each other in the winter of 423/2, each had its own allies: Thuc. IV 134.1; cf. v 47.1, 2.) We cannot take it as a fact that the other members of the Peloponnesian League could be called out directly *by a member other than Sparta*, even in a case of manifest aggression from outside, since this would be (as far as I can see) the only known example. The question is best left open,[65] but for my own part I am not prepared to take this one incident as a proof that members of the Peloponnesian League who were the victims of aggression by a state outside the League had an automatic right to call out all the other members of the League in their defence. On general grounds it seems to me unlikely that Sparta would have accepted such a principle.

(*d*) It is convenient at this point to consider what the legal situation was if an ally 'revolted' from Sparta—a term which would include refusal to supply a contingent when legally obliged to do so, as well as acting in a hostile manner or allying with a hostile power. It seems unlikely to me that 'the constitution of the Peloponnesian League' contained any definite rule regarding 'revolts' by allies.[66] It would be generally understood, no doubt, that Sparta, when suppressing a revolt which clearly prejudiced the security of the League, could summon the allies to march with her (cf. Appendix XX). But if the fact of 'revolt' was not perfectly evident and indisputable, allies might well refuse to march, if they dared risk the resentment this would arouse at Sparta. Or they might conceivably —although I know of no evidence for this—refuse to march unless Sparta's call was endorsed by a League Congress. Everything would then depend

[64] See 54.2: 'it was the month of Carneius, a sacred month to Dorians'.

[65] Kahrstedt (*GStSS* 87 ff., 287) of course has no doubt that the allies could not call automatically for each other's assistance.

[66] But see e.g. Busolt-Swoboda, *GSK* II 1334 and n. 1; Larsen, *CPL* I 268–70.

on the general situation, on Sparta's own strength in relation to that of the recusant allies, and on whether the other allies would help to bring them to heel. Sparta waited until *c.* 402 to begin the reduction of the Eleians,[67] with whom she had had bad relations for a long time. After the King's Peace of 387/6 she began to address herself to the problem of chastising refractory allies in general, beginning with Mantinea.[68]

The fact (if it is a fact) that there were no explicit rules regarding the liability of Sparta's allies to join in suppressing 'revolts' is not at all surprising: it is precisely what we ought to expect from a Greek symmachy. It must not be taken, as by Kagan (*OPW* 15–19), as an indication that the Peloponnesian League did not have anything that we can call a 'constitution'.

§6. We now come to the League Congress, which provided an essential part of the machinery for initiating and ending League wars. To be rather more precise, we could perhaps say that a League Congress was necessary in order to declare an offensive war, or for a decision that—in breach of treaty or otherwise—an outside State had committed open aggression against a member of the League (whereupon a League war would automatically ensue), or for the making of a peace at the end of a League war. There is no clear evidence (cf. §4 above) that a League Congress had to be called for any other purpose. *The creation of the League Congress should be seen as a modification of the fundamental right of Sparta to make her allies follow her 'whithersoever she might lead'.* The Congress expressed the will of the allies, which could be in principle, and was sometimes in practice, opposed to that of Sparta.

It is only in relation to the year 421 that we find in Thucydides (v 30.1–3) the formula providing for the general acceptance by the allies of majority decisions at a League Congress: 'It had been agreed', he says, 'that whatever the majority of allies decided by vote should be binding, unless something to do with gods or heroes prevented it'.[69] On this occasion Corinth was determined not to accept the Peace of Nicias, against which she had voted, with the Boeotians, Eleians and Megarians (v 17.2), and, in the presence of envoys from the other dissident states,[70] she was making a formal defence of her attitude to a Spartan embassy sent to remonstrate with her and accuse her of a breach of treaty in refusing to accede to the Peace and being about to enter into alliance with Argos. Her real reasons, which were selfish ones (especially the retention by Athens of Sollium and Anactorium: Thuc. v 30.2), would have provided

[67] See Xen., *HG* III ii.21–3; Diod. XIV 17.4–7.

[68] See Xen., *HG* v ii.1; cf. ii.8–9; III v.5.

[69] The vital words are εἰρημένον κύριον εἶναι ὅτι ἂν τὸ πλῆθος τῶν ξυμμάχων ψηφίσηται, ἢν μή τι θεῶν ἢ ἡρώων κώλυμα ᾖ (30.1). This looks like a verbal quotation of a typically 'Laconic' formula. The 'unless' clause appears in almost exactly the same form in 30.3.

[70] I assume that τῶν ξυμμάχων ὅσοι οὐδ' αὐτοὶ ἐδέξαντο τὰς σπονδάς refers to the other three states named. If some of Corinth's own allies are referred to, Thuc. v 17.2 is misleading.

no legal justification for a refusal to accept the Peace, now that it had been endorsed by a majority of the allies, and so she produced an excuse which, specious as it was, enabled her to take a possibly legitimate advantage of the proviso about 'gods and heroes'. (We shall look at the scope of this proviso in §7.)

We cannot tell precisely when the formula for acceptance of majority decisions at a League Congress was generally endorsed. It is obvious from what was said in §3(*a*)(ii) above about the League expedition against Athens in *c.* 506 that up to that time there had been no restriction of Sparta's right to summon her allies to follow her on any expedition against an outside power: the essential fact (as I have already pointed out) is that *all the allies in the Peloponnese*[71] *came* (even the Corinthians), and must therefore have been *obliged* to come at Sparta's call.

The miserable failure of this expedition, and the severe defeat of the Boeotians and Chalcidians which resulted (Hdts v 77), must have been a great blow to Sparta's prestige. Evidently the Spartans now realised that if they wanted the League to remain strong and united, they must make one essential concession to their allies. To drag them into a war which most of them had no heart for, and thus risk their deserting on the battlefield, was seen to be unwise. The allies must be consulted before Sparta led them out on a campaign the justice or desirability of which might be in doubt. If Sparta allowed the allies to vote in a League Congress on her own proposal to take some particular action, and agreed in advance to accept a veto by the majority, it could at the same time be made binding upon the minority to accept the majority decision, and if necessary Sparta could then call upon the majority to help coerce any states among the minority who refused to comply. Precisely how and when this concession was implemented we do not know: it may have taken some time before the position was reached that we first have a chance to see in operation in the second half of the fifth century. All we know can be briefly stated.

(*a*) At some time between 505 and 501 the Spartans[72] decided to reverse the policy they had adopted towards Athens in 510, and restore the tyrant Hippias, whom they themselves had driven out. Before beginning any military operations, however, they consulted their allies; and, when the allies (led by Corinth) unanimously refused to accept this policy, they abandoned it without further ado (Hdts v 91–3).

(*b*) It is in Thucydides' account (I 67 ff., 119 ff.) of the events of 432 that we first see the new procedure working clearly: Sparta, after allowing

---

[71] The fact that the purpose of the expedition was not announced is said only in relation to those allies who came from Peloponnese, not the Boeotians and Chalcidians.

[72] Whether King Cleomenes was behind this policy is not known, and it must not be confidently attributed to him, as it too often is. This is about the only piece of Spartan policy during his reign (*c.* 520–*c.* 490) that Herodotus (v 91.1) does *not* associate with him by name; and my guess is that it was not his doing, but was the work of his political opponents, taking advantage of the serious setback he must have suffered in *c.* 506.

some of her allies (not to mention an Athenian embassy) to address her Assembly, first votes for war herself; and subsequently she summons a League Congress and takes a vote of the allies, the majority of whom follow her lead (see esp. Thuc. 1 87.4; 125.1). All the allies are said to have an equal vote (141.6).

(*c*) This situation can be carried back to 440, when we can be certain that Sparta herself first decided to attack Athens in support of Samos but accepted a majority decision of her allies (led by Corinth once more) against a war. This incident is of great significance in Spartan-Athenian relations in the years preceding the Peloponnesian war. It is convenient to defer detailed consideration of it until a later Chapter (V, Part viii).

In view of the reference to 'the *oaths* of the allies' in Thuc. v 30.3, we can be sure that at some stage the allies took an oath to Sparta to abide by a majority vote at a League Congress, with the proviso already mentioned concerning 'gods or heroes'. Sparta herself, of course, could not be bound by such votes to take any positive action, and cannot have sworn to abide by them. She had a secure protection against being manoeuvred by her allies into a war or a peace which she did not want: she would not summon a League Congress except to vote on some course of action which she herself had already decided upon. This general principle was well understood by Grote[73] more than a century ago. Describing the decision to declare war in 432, he says that it was necessary for the Spartans alone to decide first whether they wanted war. 'If the determination of Sparta herself were in the negative', he remarks, 'the case would never even be submitted to the vote of the allies. But if it were in the affirmative, then the latter would be convoked to deliver their opinion also. . . The only question ever submitted to the allies was whether they would or would not go along with [Sparta's] previous decision.' That is perfectly correct. And subject to the one qualification that Sparta could not commit her allies to an aggressive war, or to peace terms, without first obtaining the approval of a majority of them at a League Congress, she retained her original right to make them 'follow her whithersoever she might lead' (see §3(*a*) above). Once war was declared, Sparta alone decided—unless for some reason she *wished* formally to consult her allies—what campaigns to conduct, and she provided all the commanders, who took complete charge of individual campaigns.

I think we should consider the moment (if there was a single moment) at which the allies took the oath mentioned at the beginning of the last paragraph as the real inauguration of a Peloponnesian *League*, a *Staatenbund*, with a 'constitutional' structure, if a rudimentary one. The earliest

[73] *HG* v 4-5 (ch. xlviii). Cf. Busolt-Swoboda, *GSK* II 1330-3; Kahrstedt, *GStSS* 271, 286-7, neither of whom, however, realised, as Grote did, that Sparta would always consider the question first (cf. Chapter V, Part viii below, on the events of 440). I can see no force whatever in the arguments of Hampl, *GSV* 119-23, in favour of the view that Sparta herself voted merely as one of the allies and was bound by a majority vote; cf. Appendix V, Section *C*, §3 n. 18.

possible date will be 505-1,[74] when the Spartans consulted their allies about their proposal to restore Hippias to Athens before attempting to carry out that policy, and upon receiving a unanimous rebuff abandoned the project. That event may well mark the beginning of the Peloponnesian League proper, as believed, for example, by Larsen and Hampl.[75] But it is by no means certain that the rules summarised above concerning League Congresses were already in force. In the form in which we know them, from 432 (or 440) onwards, they may have evolved gradually over a long period; and conceivably it was not until some date towards the middle of the fifth century that the oaths to accept a majority decision were sworn by the allies, and the Peloponnesian League, in the strict sense, came fully into existence. It is a mistake to force the slender evidence, and the best we can do is to give the date of the foundation of the Peloponnesian League proper as '*c.* 505-1 or rather later', but within at most the next half-century.

In some cases, undoubtedly, a Congress might be summoned to decide some specific point of which the allies had had prior notice (as in Thuc. 1 87.4), and to which they could presumably, if they wished, mandate their representatives in advance: see in particular Thuc. 1 119, where the Corinthians canvass the other *cities*, not their delegates. Kahrstedt was certain that allied representatives were always so mandated, but the evidence against him is virtually conclusive.[76]

After the meeting in 404 at which the terms of peace with Athens were decided we rarely hear of any more League Congresses, but this is partly because our main sources (Xenophon, Diodorus and Plutarch) betray the usual Greek unconcern—not shared by Thucydides—with technical constitutional details, and often we cannot be sure from their narratives what procedure was being followed.

§7. The formula which allowed a member of the Peloponnesian League to avoid obeying a majority decision of the League Congress 'if something

---

[74] I see no cause to follow Moretti, *RLG* 76–81, who decides for 535–25 on grounds that seem to me capricious. There is not the least reason to regard the expedition against Samos in 525–4 (Hdts III 44.1–48.1; 54–6) as a League enterprise, or to think it was undertaken mainly at the instigation of Corinth, as believed by Moretti and others (e.g. E. Will, *Korinthiaka* [Paris, 1955] 634–8, who does not treat it as a League expedition). According to our evidence the enterprise was a Spartan one, in which Corinth voluntarily participated. I myself believe it was probably inspired mainly by an influential group at Sparta which was concerned about the sudden medising of the Samian tyrant Polycrates (Hdts III 44); cf. Busolt, *GG* II² 512.

[75] Larsen, SIR and CPL I; Hampl, *GSV* 117–19.

[76] Kahrstedt, *GSLSS* 267–70; contrast Wickert, *PB* 66–7. The evidence against Kahrstedt includes in particular (*a*) Xen., *HG* III v.8, which Kahrstedt felt he could ignore because he believed the Boeotians were not members of the League (p. 269, cf. 30 and n. 1), as in fact they were (see Section c below, and Appendix XVII); and (*b*) the fact that the Corinthians and other allies made speeches at the Congress in 432 (Thuc. 1 119; 120–24; 125.1: Kahrstedt, pp. 270–1, has no effective answer to this) and also in 440—for the Corinthian claim to have influenced the result of the vote concerning Samos surely does not refer merely to the casting of a vote which gave a majority of one against intervention (Thuc. 1 40.5; 43.1: the word δίχα in 40.5 need not mean *equally* divided).

to do with gods or heroes prevented it' is a very interesting one. Its precise scope is difficult to delimit, and there may well have been arguments in ancient times about particular cases that were claimed to fall within it; but some examples are clear:

(*a*) The principal one is that acceptance of a majority decision by a member of the League in a particular case would involve it in a breach of a treaty made by it with some other State. Greek treaties were backed by oaths sworn by gods and sometimes heroes too. It was precisely this type of exemption which Corinth claimed in 421, when she refused to accept the Peace of Nicias (Thuc. v 30.1–4) : she had entered into binding treaties with 'her Thraceward allies', to whom she had sworn oaths by the gods, separately from the rest of the Peloponnesian League cities (*idiāi*: cf. Chapter III, Part iii above), 'when they revolted [from Athens] in the first place with Potidaea, and others subsequently'; and she would 'not be keeping her oaths if she betrayed them'. Now it is hardly possible to say for certain whether this claim was legitimate or not: much depends on the terms of the treaties between Corinth and the 'Thraceward' cities, and the attitude of the cities concerned, of whom the most important now (after the collapse of Potidaea) were probably those who called themselves 'the Chalcidians', but who are referred to in the Peace of Nicias, doubtless on Athenian insistence, as 'the Olynthians' (Thuc. v 18.5). If, for example, Corinth was bound by a provision which is often found in Greek treaties of alliance, not to make peace without her allies' consent (see e.g. Thuc. v 23.1 *ad fin.*, 2; cf. 39.3; 46.2), and if any of them objected to the Peace, she was surely in the right—and 'the Chalcidians' (Olynthians) had almost certainly objected, since, like the Boeotians, they had a special form of temporary truce with Athens (Thuc. vi 7.4; cf. 10.3). Athens professed to regard the Corinthians as bound by the Peace (Thuc. v 32.6: cf. Appendix XVII), and perhaps that implies that Sparta had not accepted the Corinthian excuse; but of course we cannot be certain.

The Corinthians in the case just quoted were appealing, under the 'gods or heroes' proviso, to a prior treaty they had entered into by themselves separately from the other League members. In 403 and *c.* 401 (and subsequently) the Corinthians, acting with the Boeotians, refused to obey Spartan orders to join Peloponnesian League expeditions; and when describing the Boeotian and Corinthian refusal to follow King Pausanias to Athens in 403 Xenophon gives the official excuse made by these states: that they would be 'violating their oaths if they went on a military expedition against the Athenians, who were doing nothing contrary to the treaty' (*HG* II iv.30). This was not an appeal to the 'gods or heroes' proviso we have been considering, for we hear nothing of a League Congress. It was a point-blank refusal to follow the Spartans 'whithersoever they led', on the ground that Athens had not infringed the peace treaty of 404 and that the Peloponnesians would thus be breaking that treaty if they marched against her. (This series of incidents involving Boeotia and

Corinth in the years immediately following the Peloponnesian war is of great interest and will be discussed in Appendix XXI.)

(*b*) Another type of exemption depending upon 'gods or heroes' would be the celebration of a festival, involving a 'sacred truce' (*ekecheiria*). This would not, of course, excuse an ally from entering upon a war or accepting a peace treaty, but it would, for example, give exemption from participating in a particular campaign until the truce expired. In the fourth century the Phliasians and the Mantineans put forward such claims. The Phliasians managed to avoid fighting in the Nemea campaign of 394 (Xen., *HG* IV ii.16): their excuse seems to have been accepted, although they were probably disaffected anyway and using the sacred truce as a mere pretext (see iv.15). The Mantineans were also allowed to get away with it on the same ground, apparently more than once; but the Spartans remembered it against them (v ii.2). If the expression 'their allies' in Thuc. v 54.4 refers to other members of the Peloponnesian League, then we would have another example of the type of excuse we have been considering: this is not entirely clear, however (see §5(*c*) above). One can easily imagine that the Spartans themselves might on occasion want to plead such an excuse: see Hdts VI 106.3; VII 206.1; Thuc. v 82.2–3.

Claiming a sacred truce, sometimes with obviously crooked intent, was a well known piece of Greek strategy, resorted to in particular by Argos against Sparta (see Thuc. v 54.2–3; Xen., *HG* IV vii.2–3). Xenophon's account of how King Agesipolis I dealt most appropriately with one such Argive ruse is one of the most delightful stories in the *Hellenica* (IV vii.2–3; cf. Arist., *Rhet.* II 23, 1398^{b}32–9^{a}1; Ps.-Plut., *Mor.* 191b).

(*c*) A bad omen, such as a temple going up in flames, might conceivably satisfy this proviso: the Corinthians may have pleaded it in 396 (Paus. III ix.2).

(*d*) Yet another possible form of involvement of 'gods or heroes' (though no specific example can be quoted) might perhaps be the kind of unfavourable sacrifices recorded by Thucydides v 54.2; 55.3; 116.1, if any of Sparta's allies conducted these, as she did herself. The Spartans certainly set great store by the *diabatēria* they performed before crossing over their frontiers on a military expedition (cf. Xen., *Lac. Pol.* XIII 2–5).

(*e*) Finally, a claim to exemption might surely be based upon an oracle, although again there is no known example. If the Delphic Oracle in particular had clearly warned a city against doing something, it might have been able to claim that it was 'prevented by a god' from doing it.

§8. In the fifth century and the early fourth we hear of no legal restrictions on the absolute freedom of Sparta's allies to deal with each other as they pleased, even to make war upon each other.[77] But under the year 378 we

[77] See Thuc. I 103.4 (cf. Diod. XI 79.1); IV 134; V 29.1 and 33; 31.2–5; Xen., *HG* v iv.36. Thuc. v 32.2 is another example if the 'Locrians' are the eastern, the Opuntian or Epicnemidian Locrians (who were allies of Sparta), as assumed by Andrewes, in

hear of a resolution of the League Congress (a '*dogma* of the allies') that any state indulging in hostilities against a fellow member while the League forces were on an expedition outside Peloponnese might be coerced by the hegemon (Xen., *HG* v iv.37).[78] We do not know whether this was a mere *ad hoc* resolution, passed in connection with the war against Thebes or even the campaign of that particular year, or whether it had been passed (perhaps some time before 378) as a general 'constitutional' rule, having permanent validity.

It is worth noticing that in the Delian League Athens, as hegemon, certainly had the right to coerce allies which fought each other.[79] Although this has not been generally realised, there can be no doubt about it, because Hermocrates, in Thuc. vi 76.3, is made to speak of the Athenians as reducing their allies to subjection, 'accusing some of military desertion, *others of fighting each other*, others on whatever *fair-sounding charge* (*aitian euprepē*) they could find in each case', the clear implication being that fighting each other (at any rate after being ordered to stop) was, like military desertion, a *legitimate* pretext.[80]

We hear from Thucydides (v 31.5) of a 'covenant' (*xynthēkē*) providing that at the end of the Peloponnesian war (naturally referred to by the Peloponnesians as 'the war with Athens', the *Attikos polemos*) each member of the League should be entitled to keep whatever it had when it entered the war. I see no reason to agree with Andrewes (in Gomme, *HCT* iv 28–9) that this provision 'presupposes a quite extraordinary distrust between the members [of the Peloponnesian League]', and that we should try to find an alternative explanation. The only alternative he can suggest strains the meaning of *xynthēkē* beyond reason. If, as I assume, the covenant in question was entered into when war was declared,[81] or not long afterwards, it was surely an ingenious device to prevent the allies from being tempted to fight each other while the war lasted, without openly placing any restraint on their right to do so. Territorial gains were the main object of Greek wars (cf. Chapter VI, Part ii below), and if each ally knew that at the end of the war it would be called upon to

---

Gomme, *HCT* iv 30. Contrast the *OCT* Index, *s.v.* Λοκροὶ Ὀζόλαι. It is true that Thucydides usually employs the words Locrians and Locris to refer to the Opuntians, but in iii 102.1 διὰ τῶν Λοκρῶν certainly refers to Ozolian Locris. For the problem whether it was the Opuntian or Ozolian Locrians who were first involved against the Phocians in 395, see Tod ii, p. 16 (note on no. 102).

[78] The treatment of this episode by Kagan, *OPW* 19, is most unsatisfactory (see the beginning of this Part).

[79] Perhaps a League Congress had in theory to be summoned to give Athens this right. (Jones, *TSDPL*, maintains that Athens did summon a special Congress in 440 to empower her to coerce Samos. He may be right, but I do not think so.) It is worth drawing attention to the statement by Plut., *Per.* 25.1 (not found in Thucydides), that the Athenians, before coercing Samos, first demanded without success that she submit the affair to arbitration by themselves.

[80] This point has evidently been missed by e.g. *ATL* iii 228–9; cf. Hammond, *ONAA* 56.

[81] As believed by Busolt, *GG* iii ii.857–8, following Grote.

disgorge any such gains it had made at the expense of the other allies, it would have much less inducement to attack them. In the one case in which we hear of specific appeal being made to this resolution, during the dispute between Elis and little Lepreum in 421, the results were unfortunate. Elis had rejected an award in favour of Lepreum given by Sparta as arbitrator, and Sparta had put a garrison into Lepreum. Elis invoked the resolution (with some justice, it seems) against Sparta's action, and when her appeal fell on deaf ears, she made an alliance with Argos, which was tantamount to a 'revolt' from Sparta.[82] In another case, a Mantinean reduction of a slice of Arcadia during the Ten Years war, Thucydides mentions no appeal to the resolution we have been considering and indeed records the Mantinean action before referring to the resolution; but again we can see that its existence led to a revolt, for the Mantineans, evidently realising that their annexation was a breach of the resolution, and expecting that Sparta would make them restore the territory concerned, 'revolted' and made an alliance with Argos.[83]

I see no evidence that members of the Peloponnesian League were ever constitutionally bound to submit disputes among themselves to arbitration. In one recorded case Elis, as we have seen, rejected Sparta's award. The only other case of attempted arbitration known to me occurred in 395: the Phocians, at war with the Locrians and Boeotians, urged Sparta to tell the Boeotians not to invade their territory. Sparta did so, adding that if the Boeotians felt aggrieved, they should submit the dispute to arbitration *en tois symmachois* (*Hell. Oxy.* 18 [13].4–5), which could mean 'within the Spartan alliance' or 'within the Peloponnesian League' or 'to the League Congress'. In the event, the Boeotians disregarded the Spartan demand: the 'Corinthian war' was now imminent. (I believe, as explained in Appendix XVII, that the Phocians were members of the League; but even a member of the Spartan alliance which did not belong to the League proper might not be unwilling to submit a dispute to the League Congress or to an arbitrator nominated by it. And cf. Thuc. 1 28.2.)

There were other League rules, about the supplying of contingents and so forth, which do not concern us here. Sufficient information about most of them is given in the works cited in the first four notes to this Part of Chapter IV. (In Appendix XXII I discuss a technical problem arising out of Thuc. v 54.1.)

Enough has been said to show that there were a few basic 'constitutional' rules governing the behaviour of members of the Peloponnesian League, and that we can clearly identify some of them, even if on occasion they were ignored or overriden either by Sparta herself or by allies whose

---

[82] See Thuc. v 31.5: ἀφίστανται. Cf. 29.2: ἀποστάντων τῶν Μαντινέων, who had similarly allied themselves with Argos.

[83] Thuc. v 29.1–2; cf. 33. Forrest, *HS* 116 is surely unfair to Sparta in referring to the ejection of the Mantineans from Parrhasia as 'brutality' if, as seems very likely (in spite of Thucydides' failure to make any connection between 29.1 and 33), Parrhasia is the area referred to in 29.1.

position at the time was strong enough to make it unwise for Sparta to attempt to coerce them. Examples of such a situation occurred conspicuously in 403, when the Boeotians and Corinthians refused to join in a Spartan expedition against Athens, and in *c*. 401, when the same states again refused to march with Sparta, this time against Elis. The attitude of these two states is often misunderstood. In Appendix XXI I shall explain the circumstances of both cases and show how they fit into the general picture.

c. *Membership of the Peloponnesian League*

In a few cases it is hard to be certain whether a particular member of what I am calling 'the Spartan alliance' ever joined the inner circle of 'the Peloponnesian League' proper. As the arguments in these cases tend to be intricate and fatiguing, I shall relegate them to an Appendix (XVII), and concentrate here on giving what I believe to be the main facts.

We know from Herodotus (i 68.6, discussed in Section B §3(*a*) (i) above) that by the mid-sixth century the Peloponnesian League included 'most of the Peloponnese': it may already have embraced all Peloponnesian states except Argos and her dependencies and the Achaeans. Mycenae and Tiryns at least were presumably added as a result of the campaign of *c*. 494 B.C. in which King Cleomenes I defeated Argos at Sepeia,[84] but they were again reduced by Argos a generation afterwards and ceased to exist as independent cities.[85] The Achaeans joined the League later, Pellene before 431 (Thuc. II 9.2) and the Achaean League as a whole apparently by the spring of 417 at the latest (Thuc. v 82.1).[86] Outside the Peloponnese itself, Megara and Aegina are very likely to have joined the League before the end of the sixth century and were certainly members in the first half of the fifth; but Megara deserted Sparta in *c*. 460, to ally herself with Athens, and only returned to the fold in 446, and Aegina was conquered by Athens and became a member of the Delian League in *c*. 457, rejoining Sparta only in 405/4.

It is hard to define the position of the Boeotians[87] (or of the individual Boeotian cities, Thebes and the rest) until the years after 447/6, when the Boeotian League was reorganised and took on the shape described in

[84] Nauplia (where Cleomenes landed) and Sepeia itself were near Tiryns (Hdts VI 76.2; 77.1), and after the battle Cleomenes went to the Argive Heraeum (VI 81), which is near Mycenae. One objective of Cleomenes' back-door entry into the territory of Argos, I feel sure, was the freeing of Mycenae and Tiryns from Argive control, thereby seriously weakening Argos. In 479 both these two states were independent and sent contingents to Plataea (IX 28.4; 31.3; cf. Diod. XI 65.2; Paus. v xxiii.2; M/L 27, coils 6–7).

[85] Hdts VI 83 (Tiryns); Diod. XI 65 (Mycenae); Strabo VIII vi.19, p. 377. On the chronology, see Andrewes, SAEFC; Forrest, TA.

[86] See Larsen, EAL 804 ff. (including a discussion of the problem how many votes the Achaeans had in the Peloponnesian League Congress); GFS 80–9; J. K. Anderson, 'A Topographical and Historical Study of Achaea', in *BSA* 49 (1954) 72–92, at pp. 80–5.

[87] Hdts v 74.2 seems to prove that in *c*. 506 the Boeotians were not bound to follow the Spartans wherever they might lead (see Section B above, §3 [*a*] ii); but of course this is just before the formal organisation of what I am calling the Peloponnesian League proper.

the *Hellenica Oxyrhynchia*, chap. 16 [11], and in certain passages in Thucydides (esp. II 2.1, with IV 91 and V 37.4 to 38.4, for the Boeotarchs; and, for the four-panel Federal Council, 38.2–4).[88] Certainly by 431 the Boeotians were members of the general Spartan alliance. I am convinced that 'the Boeotians' as a single unit were by then an actual member of the Peloponnesian League proper, and that in the years before 431 the Phocians[89] and the eastern Locrians (Epicnemidian, Hypocnemidian or Opuntian)[90] also joined the League, each as a unit, on the same footing as the Boeotians. It is quite possible that Ampracia, Leucas and Anactorium, mentioned by Thuc. II 9.2 in the same breath as Megara and the Locrians, Boeotians and Phocians, were also in 431 members of the League; but they were unimportant and there is so little evidence either way that I propose to ignore them.

The great majority of the members of the Spartan alliance, then, were within the inner circle of the Peloponnesian League—even, if I am right, the Boeotians, Phocians and Locrians, probably (in 431) Ampracia, Leucas and Anactorium, and certainly in the fourth century the Acarnanians and Olynthus. I myself would accept all the states mentioned in Diodorus XV 31.2 as members of the Peloponnesian League at the time of which Diodorus is writing, 378 (see Appendix XVII, Section *C*, §8). On the other hand, there were a few Spartan allies which could never have been members of the League, in particular those in Italy and Sicily which had declared for Sparta[91] and from which she requested ships in 431, or the various states formerly under Athens which came over to Sparta, such as the four cities of Lesbos other than Methymna (Thuc. III 15.1),[92] Acanthus (IV 88.1; cf. 86.1), Chios and Erythrae (VIII 6.4), and others.[93]

(v)
How Spartan foreign policy was determined

I am going to argue here in favour of the following propositions, which I will first state briefly and then justify in detail:

A. (1) In the fifth and fourth centuries Spartan foreign policy was made, according to constitutional theory, in the Assembly; and the Gerousia as

---

[88] See esp. Larsen, *GFS* 26 ff. (esp. 33–40); *RGGRH* 31–40; Grenfell and Hunt, *Oxyrhynchus Papyri* v (1908), pp. 223–8; I. A. F. Bruce, *An Historical Comm. on the Hell. Oxy.* 102–9, 157–64; cf. Moretti, *RLG* 97–170.

[89] Coerced by Sparta in 458–7 (Thuc. I 107.2), but subjected by Athens afterwards (108.3), the Phocians must have regained their independence when Boeotia did, in 446 (113). In 431 they were allies of Sparta (II 9.2,3).

[90] Thuc. II 9.2,3.

[91] Thuc. II 7.2. Did these states have any formal alliance with Sparta?

[92] Sparta allowed her League allies to participate in the decision to receive the Lesbians, having good reason to do so even if the Lesbians were not joining the Peloponnesian League proper: see Appendix XIX.

[93] See Busolt-Swoboda, *GSK* II 1324 n. 2. On Thuc. V 104 (Melos), see Andrewes, in Gomme, *HCT* IV 172–3.

such could seldom have played much of a part, and perhaps had no constitutional right to play any part, in the making of decisions about future foreign policy. (Nearly all our evidence concerning the Assembly in this period relates to decisions in the sphere of foreign affairs, and we should be prepared to contemplate the possibility that the machinery of decision-making may have been different in this field from what it was in home affairs.)

(2) We do not, however, know anything for certain about how the debates in the Assembly were conducted, or whether the ordinary Spartiate could speak in them without being invited to do so by the presiding ephor; and we need not conclude that policy-making was in the hands of more than a few of the most influential Spartiates as a general rule—what happened in 432 is likely to have been altogether exceptional.

B. The Gerousia as such did play a vital role (which has been unduly neglected in some recent discussions) in foreign affairs, if only by retrospective action: by its control of criminal jurisdiction (even over the kings), a function which, in Greek eyes, was thoroughly political in character.

C. The kings, except when they were men of little ability, could be expected to be very important indeed in deciding policy, not strictly as kings, but as the individuals who could most easily possess the greatest prestige, dignity and influence of all Spartiates—the greatest *auctoritas*, to use the Latin term. Spartan foreign policy can often be seen to be controlled by a king. The ephors in theory had far greater constitutional powers than a king, but they were rarely men of any great consequence, and they could probably often be dominated by a strong king. The *potestas* of the ephors would tend to be exercised with due regard for the *auctoritas* of an influential king.

I will take these three propositions in order. I do not intend to analyse Spartan constitutional machinery more than necessary. It has been discussed again and again, partly because the obscurities and contradictions in the sources give exceptional scope for conjecture to those who have a taste for that kind of thing. A recent paper by Andrewes (GCS)[94] is valuable for its copious citation of evidence and for some of its conclusions; but I hope to show that in some respects (the political role of the Gerousia, the amount of genuine decision-making in the Assembly, and the extent to which the ordinary Spartiate was likely to participate actively in political decisions) the picture it presents is seriously mistaken. I shall stick very closely to the evidence.

At least it is no longer necessary to controvert the once popular theory of a series of struggles between kings and ephors, put forward by Dickins

[94] Esp. 1–8, 14–17. Cf. A. H. M. Jones, 'The Lycurgan Rhetra', in *ASI* (Ehrenberg) 165–75; Brunt, SPSAW 278–80. I must also mention W. G. Forrest, 'Legislation in Sparta', in *Phoenix* 21 (1967) 11–19; but I am very much out of sympathy with the method and conclusions of this paper, and I cannot see that it has made out even a *prima facie* case.

in 1912, which lacks any real evidence in its support and has long been discredited.[95]

A. In foreign affairs, in the broadest sense (see below), it was the Assembly which had the supreme constitutional right of decision. (The Assembly, by the way, was called 'the Ecclesia', not 'the Apella': see Appendix XXIII.) The ephors had considerable powers,[96] mainly to implement decisions of the Assembly, and the kings had great authority over the forces under their command while actually on campaign; but the Gerousia *as such* apparently played no part in the *formulation* of *future* foreign policy. (I have deliberately phrased that sentence in such a way as not to exclude the vital influence on foreign policy which the Gerousia could on occasion exercise through its judicial powers, or the powerful personal influence of individual gerontes.) Provided we restrict ourselves to foreign policy, for which alone our evidence is sufficient, we can agree with Andrewes when he says, 'The fact seems to be that the major decisions of Spartan policy were taken in full assembly, and that the Gerousia[97] played a relatively inconspicuous part' (GCS 7). In particular, as he points out, Thucydides' 'record of the great debate in 432, whether to go to war with Athens, practically excludes the Gerousia from any serious share in the decision', and 'much the same could be argued of other occasions when the assembly took a vote after hearing foreign ambassadors' (GCS 4). Only once is the Gerousia so much as mentioned in relation to the making of foreign policy: this is in Diodorus' account (XI 50, esp. §§2,5,6) of the Hetoimaridas affair, to be dealt with later (Chapter V, Part ii below), where the constitutional details, as one might expect from Diodorus, can hardly be pressed.

Now in the Great Rhetra and its Rider (Plut., *Lyc.* 6.2, 8),[98] as in Plutarch's whole picture of the activity of 'Lycurgus' (*Lyc.* 5.10–6.1), the Gerousia is in the forefront, and it would seem to be given both the sole power of introducing resolutions into the Assembly (*probouleusis*) and a

---

[95] G. Dickins, 'The Growth of Spartan Policy', in *JHS* 32 (1912) 1–42. It is surprising to find countenance given to his views recently by A. Hönle, *Olympia in der Politik der Griechischen Staatenwelt* (Diss., Tübingen, 1968) 148 ff.

[96] I agree in principle with what is said about their role in foreign affairs by Andrewes, GCS (esp. 8–10); and Brunt, SPSAW 278–9. When, as in Xen., *HG* v ii.9; iii.10–13 (Phlius, late 380s), we find the ephors not merely giving orders to another city but even calling up the army for an expedition, apparently on their own initiative, we must suppose either that an unrecorded meeting of the Assembly took place, or that the ephors were confident that their policy would be affirmed by the leading men—as they could certainly have been in the case mentioned, for they were carrying out the policy of King Agesilaus (cf. iii.13 ff.). But the powers of the ephors must not be exaggerated, as they are by Chrimes, *AS* 210 n. 2, who gives them 'the right of concluding peace', on the strength of Xen., *HG* II ii.12,13,17,18: §19 alone should have prevented her from making such a statement. And the ephors of iv.38 are not the two with Pausanias, but the three at home, who were not 'competent to conclude peace' without summoning the Assembly.

[97] Andrewes, in GCS, in fact speaks of the Gerousia as 'the council'.

[98] The literature on the Rhetra is very extensive: see Tigerstedt, *LSCA* I 351 n. 344. The best brief account is still that of A. Andrewes, *The Greek Tyrants* (London, 1956) 66–77, the best detailed analysis that of Wade-Gery, SRPL. See most recently Toynbee, *SPGH* 269–74, with bibliography. On the date, see n. 4 to Part i of this Chapter.

right of subsequent veto on motions passed by the Assembly which it disliked. In the sixth, fifth and fourth centuries there is no evidence at all of the Gerousia's either refusing to 'proboul' a motion desired by a majority of Spartans or vetoing a decision of the Assembly; but the failure of King Agis IV and his Ephor Lysander to pass their reforms in 243/2 affords proof of the survival of one or other of these functions—surely the first.[99] Whatever the scope of the two special powers of the Gerousia may have been in regard to legislation and other internal affairs, I would suggest that they may have had *no application*, in the historical period at any rate, *to questions of foreign policy*—questions of 'war and peace', as the Greeks put it,[100] including not only declaring war and making peace, but entering into treaty relations, and indeed most if not all relations with the outside world. Aristotle, in the *Politics* (IV 14, 1298ᵃ3 ff.), discusses various ways in which the deliberative power in the State may be organised, and in two of his examples (1298ᵃ24–8, 1298ᵇ5–8) questions of 'war and peace', with the appointment and examination of magistrates, are separated from matters such as legislation and the exercise of judicial powers, and are placed in different hands.

The Assembly was above all the organ of the collective warriors and ex-warriors, and it would not be surprising if it had complete control of matters of 'peace and war'. But we are very badly informed about its procedure, and in particular some scholars[101] have been worried by what they take to be contradictions between the Great Rhetra, the *Politics* of Aristotle, and our records of debates in the Assembly in the fifth and

---

[99] What kills the reforms in Plutarch's story (*Agis* 8–11, cf. 12–13) is the refusal of the Gerousia to 'proboul' them (note *Agis* 11.1: οἷς τὸ κράτος ἦν ἐν τῷ προβουλεύειν). We hear of no vote by the general meeting described in *Agis* 9–10, which, with Busolt (*GSK* II 682 n. 1) and Andrewes (GCS 5), I would take to be merely what the Romans called a *contio*, a meeting without power to legislate; cf. Jones, *op. cit.* (in n. 94 above) 169, esp. the last paragraph. I would also suppose that Diod. XI 50.3–4 refers to a mere *contio*.

[100] See esp. Arist., *Pol.* IV 14, 1297ᵇ37–8ᵃ6, 1298ᵇ6, where we find some such phrase as 'about war and peace' four times, twice by itself (1298ᵃ21–2, 1298ᵇ6), once as 'about war . . . and alliance' (1298ᵃ26), and once with the addition of καὶ συμμαχίας καὶ διαλύσεως. All these expressions are virtually equivalents.

[101] E.g. Andrewes, GCS 6–7 (cf. 2–3, 15, 20 n. 24), and Wade-Gery, *EGH* 51–4, both of whom are disinclined to accept Arist., *Pol.* II 11, 1273ᵃ9–13 (cf. 10, 1272ᵃ10–12). Both evidently take the ὅπερ . . . οὐκ ἔστιν clause, applied to Sparta and Crete in 1273ᵃ12–13, as referring back not merely to τῷ βουλομένῳ . . . ἀντειπεῖν ἔξεστιν (to which I would limit it) but also to κύριοι κρινεῖν εἰσί. This is wrong: in 1272ᵃ10–12 we find that in Crete and (note the reference to the *gerontes* in line 12) at Sparta the Assembly *is* κυρία to συνεπιψηφίσαι the proposals put to it (by *cosmoi* or *gerontes*); and the ὅπερ clause in 1273ᵃ12–13 therefore cannot be referring to κύριοι κρινεῖν εἰσί and cannot be denying to the Spartan Assembly (or the Cretan) a sovereign power of decision. To understand this properly, we must realise that the use of the very strong word κύριος with the verbs συνεπιψηφίσαι (1272ᵃ11) and κρινεῖν (1273ᵃ11) proves beyond question that these verbs attribute to the Spartan Assembly the power to ratify *or reject* the proposals of the Gerousia, while the choice of the word συνεπιψηφίσαι shows that it did not have the *further* power to *amend* or make *counter-proposals*. To use the language of *Pol.* IV 14, 1298ᵇ32 ff., esp. 35–7 (and 39–40), the Spartans in Assembly were ἀποψηφιζόμενοι κύριοι (they had the right of *veto*) but were not καταψηφιζόμενοι κύριοι: they had no power to *make decisions initiated by themselves*. It is no wonder that, in Aristotle's eyes, it was its eligibility for the ephorate (II 9, 1270ᵇ21–6) and not the powers of the Assembly which

fourth centuries.[102] I myself see no problem at all and believe that Aristotle's picture in the *Politics* can be accepted as substantially true, provided we make just two assumptions which are eminently reasonable and probable in themselves and are not contradicted by any evidence: first, that the Spartan Assembly could merely ratify, or refuse to ratify, proposals put to it, but could not in theory introduce amendments to them, let alone new resolutions of its own; and secondly, that individual Spartiates had no absolute right to speak, but could do so only if they were kings, ephors or gerontes, or if they were invited to speak by the presiding ephor.[103] (I would suppose that both these features applied in all debates, on home as well as foreign affairs.)

This alone may well lead to our rejecting the suggestion of Andrewes (GCS 1) that 'Sparta had in some ways a more open constitution than most oligarchies', especially when we take into account, as we must, the extreme deference to the magistrates which was expected of the Spartan and is strongly stressed by Xenophon (*Lac. Pol.* II 10; VIII 1–3), and the exaggerated reverence for the old which was also a well-known Spartan characteristic (see e.g. Xen., *Lac. Pol.* VI 1–2; *Mem.* III v.15–16; Plut., *Mor.* 235f; and the amusing story in Plut., *Lyc.* 20.15—perhaps a deliberate satire on Spartan gerontocracy?). Plutarch (*Mor.* 826f), taking Persia as the prime example of 'absolute and uncontrolled monarchy' and Athens of 'self-governing and undiluted democracy', chose Sparta as the chief specimen of 'outright aristocratic oligarchy'; and he was surely right. Sparta was indeed a strongly hierarchical society, in many ways more akin to Republican Rome than to Classical Athens.

Andrewes seeks to show that genuine debates could often take place in open Assembly; but, even if we restrict his statement to the field of foreign affairs (where, as we shall see, his own evidence is strongly against him), I think it would be surprising if more than a handful of senior and influential Spartans actually ventured to speak. Andrewes lists eleven occasions between 432 and 371 (three mentioned by Thucy-

---

kept the Spartan rank-and-file content with the constitution. As Andrewes rightly says (GCS 3), 'If he had thought that the *demos* in its assembly played an important part in formulating policy, he could be expected to have reckoned that among the reasons why it was content'.

[102] I agree with Andrewes (GCS 20 n. 24) in rejecting the silly anecdote which appears in two different forms in Aeschin. I 180 and Plut., *Mor.* 801bc.

[103] Cf. Busolt, *GSK* II 692 and n. 2; and the sensible remarks of G. T. Griffith, 'Isegoria in the Assembly at Athens', in *ASI* (Ehrenberg) 115–38, esp. 118–19, 133–4 nn. 19–20 (but his whole paper is relevant). Contrast Andrewes, GCS 20 n. 24: I cannot understand his statement that Plut., *Lyc.* 6.7 and the Rider to the Rhetra 'are inexplicable unless amendments from the body of the assembly were allowed'. Plut., *Lyc.* 6.6–8 plainly states that under the Rhetra the common people were *not* allowed to give their opinions but only to ratify or reject the proposals put before them, and that when 'by adding or omitting words they distorted and perverted the sense of proposals' (contrary to what had been intended by Lycurgus), the Rider was added to give *specific* power to the Gerousia to refuse to countenance any amendment of which it disapproved and to dismiss the Assembly. (And see n. 101 above.)

dides and eight by Xenophon) on which he thinks it is 'clear that there was considerable debate in the Assembly' (GCS 6). All were on questions of foreign policy. There is in fact no evidence of *any* debate, let alone 'considerable debate', *by Spartans* on any of these occasions except the first and last: at the nine other assemblies, although of course at least one or two Spartans must always have spoken, we hear *only* of speeches by foreigners! The first assembly, that of 432, was altogether unusual in that a king who had more prestige than anyone else at Sparta was voted down (see Section *C* below). As for the last assembly, that in the summer of 371 (Xen., *HG* VI iv.2–3), it is true that Xenophon, uniquely, does happen to mention a worthy contribution to the debate by an individual Spartan, Prothous;[104] but he adds at once that 'the Spartans, after listening to him, thought he was talking nonsense', as if opinion were fairly unanimous against him; and it should come as no surprise to us to find Plutarch (*Ages.* 28.6), who also mentions Prothous, specifically attributing the policy that was in fact adopted to King Agesilaus, then the dominant figure at Sparta. In not one of Andrewes' nine other examples is there a single word in Thucydides or Xenophon (or any other source) about Spartan spokes-men: it is always foreigners alone who are mentioned, and in some cases[105] there are indications against our supposing any important division of opinion in the Assembly. Andrewes has effectually refuted his own case by the very arguments he has sought to use in support of it. It is very significant indeed that our evidence about debates taking place in the Spartan Assembly should be limited almost entirely to occasions on which foreign envoys spoke. I suggest the reason is that the decisions of the sovereign Assembly were largely a foregone conclusion as far as the Spartans themselves were concerned, and that in so far as speeches in the Assembly did have any important effect in influencing Spartan policy, it was precisely when, and as a rule only when, they were made by repre-sentatives of foreign States, who (like Alcibiades in 415–14: Thuc. VI 88–93) might have some new proposals or unfamiliar arguments to put forward.

Andrewes, in choosing his eleven examples from Thucydides and Xenophon, limited himself strictly to cases in which the two authors make explicit reference in one way or another to the Spartan Assembly. If we enlarge his list to include cases in which no one could reasonably doubt that a meeting of the Assembly is in question, even though the word *ekklēsia* (or *ekklētoi*) is not actually used, we find that the situation is exactly the same: we sometimes hear of speeches by foreigners, but never by Spartans (see *e.g.* Xen., *HG* III v.4–6; v ii.1–3; iv.60–1; VI i.2–3, 17; v.10). When Xenophon (*HG* VI i.17) says that 'the Spartans put off their answer' to Polydamas, and spent the next two days calculating their

---

[104] I do not know why he is taken to be ephor by Poralla, *PL* 169, cf. 110.

[105] E.g. in *c.* 402 (when Xen., *HG* III ii.23 speaks of angry feeling at Sparta—perhaps fairly unanimous, then?), and in early 382 [383 Andrewes], when *HG* v ii.20 suggests that the allies spoke as they did because they already knew very well what the Spartans wanted to do.

resources, before eventually deciding they were unable to send the help requested, there is no reason to suppose—as we might have had to do if Athens and not Sparta were in question—that there was a three-day debate in the Assembly: the investigation and final decision must surely have been delegated to a much smaller body, probably the ephors with or without the Gerousia. The impression Xenophon gives here is not that there was any division of opinion or debate on the desirability in principle of sending aid to Polydamas, but that the Spartans would have been only too glad to go to his assistance and check the further growth in the power of Jason (an ally of Thebes), but were obliged to take account of their existing commitments (see *HG* vi i.14–15, with 5, 8–9). Two thirds of their own army (four out of six *morai*) and apparently a corresponding proportion of the forces of their allies, as was usual in such cases, were in Phocis, under King Cleombrotus (vi i.1). Only once, as far as I know, do we hear of a series of assemblies being convened to discuss a particular matter,[106] and then the problem was a 'religious' one: how to atone for the murder of Darius' heralds in 491 (which had resulted in bad omens at State sacrifices) and to find, with the aid of public proclamation, 'if any Lacedaemonian was willing to die for Sparta'—an appeal to which Sperthias and Boulis duly responded, with unfortunate results for their sons half a century later, as it appeared to Herodotus (vii 134–7; Thuc. ii 67).

As a general rule, then, there was probably little doubt, if any, what the Assembly would decide, for the question would have been settled beforehand by the most influential men. I would add that only on a few occasions between the mid-fifth century and the mid-fourth is there any clear evidence of decisions being taken by the Assembly which were not in accordance with *the policy favoured by a prominent king*. One of these occasions may have been in 418, when the Spartans[107] were highly critical—reasonably enough, in the circumstances—of the conduct of King Agis II, and another two were in 440 and 432, involving war with Athens. (For the events of 440, see Chapter V, Part viii below.) In my opinion, the atmosphere of 432, when the entirely sensible policy advocated by the very respected King Archidamus II was rejected, was altogether exceptional—we shall return to this question later (Section C below).

No genuinely democratic spirit or procedure is likely to have developed in the Assembly of a community which deliberately preserved a primitive method of decision 'by shouting and not by vote' (Thuc. 1 87.2), long after proper voting procedures had evolved in other Greek states (see Appendix XXIV); and which elected its gerontes, and very probably its ephors too, in a similarly archaic manner, stigmatised by Aristotle as

---

[106] Hdts vii 134.2: ἁλίης τε πόλλακις συλλεγομένης (in the late 480s).

[107] Andrewes (GCS 3) takes it for granted that the Assembly was at work in this case. That is just possible; but see Section *B* below.

'childish'[108] and known to us from Plutarch's description (*Lyc.* 26.3–5): the candidates came before the Assembly one by one, to be greeted by the shouts of their supporters; a number of judges ('chosen men'), placed so that they could hear but not see the proceedings, 'recorded the loudness of the shouts' (in the Spartan equivalent of decibels?), and eventually announced the winner, designated by his appearance 'first' or 'second' or whatever. Unfortunately we do not know who the judges were or how they were chosen. It is a sobering reflection that our knowledge of the persistence of these extraordinary procedures depends upon an aside of six words in Thucydides, a couple of isolated remarks in Aristotle, and a single passage in Plutarch. There may well have been other unique features of Spartan constitutional procedure which our sources have failed to record. (What was the 'Little Ekklēsia', of Xen., *HG* III iii.8?)

If there was no unanimity among the leading men, the theoretical possibility was always open, of course, that the faction which was not dominant among the leaders would insist on transferring the decision to the Assembly. However, our evidence, such as it is, seems to suggest that this rarely happened—indeed, the decision to declare war in 432 (see Chapter V, Part ix below) is the only clear example. This should not surprise us.

B. Too many scholars have overlooked the great political importance, even in the field of foreign affairs, of one side of the Gerousia's activities: its control of jurisdiction in the most serious criminal cases.

An essential part of the political process in Greek cities (and here Sparta is for once no exception) was the 'political trial', in the broadest sense: accusation before a duly constituted legal tribunal of a public figure, either openly for some act alleged to have been committed 'not in the best interests of the State',[109] or in a disguised form, as when in 427 the pro-Athenian Corcyraean Peithias, after being prosecuted and acquitted on a charge of bringing Corcyra into subjection to Athens, got his own back on five of his accusers by successfully prosecuting them for cutting stakes on sacred ground (Thuc. III 70.3–4), the charge of impiety being a mere cover for a 'political' accusation.[110] Such trials might arise out of general political disagreement or mere personal enmity.

At Athens political trials in this sense were very frequent, especially in the fourth century, when (as is well known) the use of the *graphē paranomōn* became very common, and any decision of the Assembly that aroused opposition might, by this procedure, be in effect reviewed by a court. Indeed, one might go so far as to say that the Athenian democracy was just as dependent upon the composition of its law courts, membership

---

[108] *Pol.* II 9, 1271ᵃ9–10: παιδαριώδης, used of the election of the gerontes. Earlier (1270ᵇ28) Aristotle uses the same term to describe the election of the ephors, and in a heightened form: παιδαριώδης γάρ ἐστι λίαν.

[109] Among numerous Athenian examples, see Hyper. IV or III (*Pro Euxen.*) 29–30, col. 22–3, where οὐ/μὴ τὰ ἄριστα τῷ δήμῳ τῷ ᾿Αθηναίων appears four times.

[110] Cf. my NJAE I 95; II 277–9.

of which was available to all citizens over the age of thirty, as upon the fact that all citizens could attend the Assembly. Aristotle (*Ath. Pol.* 9.1) believed that the Athenian demos, when it acquired control of the courts (under Solon's legislation, as he saw it), became 'master of the constitution'. In discussing, at the beginning of Book III of the *Politics* (1, 1275ᵃ22– 5ᵇ 20), the fundamental rights which make a man a citizen in the full sense of the term, Aristotle treats the ability to take part in judicial decisions as a vital element: it enters into his discussion both under the heading of *krisis* and under that of *archē*, for sitting as a dicast is to him an important form of *archē* ('magistracy', 'office').[111] Again, in his acute, if rather difficult, discussion of the three elements (*moria*) in a constitution, Aristotle (*Pol.* IV 14, 1297ᵇ37 ff.) first distinguishes what we might call the deliberative (*to bouleuomenon*), the executive (*to peri tas archas*), and the judicial (*to dikazon*), and then proceeds to define the 'deliberative' element in such a way as to include not only 'war and peace', legislation, and the appointment and examination of magistrates, but also 'death and exile and confiscation of property'—in short, the trial of important criminal cases. Even his comparatively brief section on the judicial element (IV 16, 1300ᵇ13 ff.), which draws a theoretical distinction between eight different types of court, concentrates on five as being specifically 'political': one is for examining the conduct of magistrates (*euthyntikon*), another for dealing with offences against any public interest, a third for cases involving the constitution, and a fourth for trying disputes about the imposition of penalties; a fifth, concerned with private dealings involving large amounts of property (doubtless cases of disputed inheritance in particular), may be a less obvious source of political conflict to us, but not to Aristotle.[112]

The Gerousia, of twenty-eight members aged over sixty plus the two kings, was by far the most important court at Sparta.[113] The ephors sometimes, perhaps always, formed part of the court when it was trying major cases; but they would supply only one seventh of the total membership of the court (5 out of 35), and would be able to exercise real influence only when the gerontes were equally divided (as at the trial of King Pausanias in 403), or nearly so. It has often been taken for granted, for example by Kahrstedt and Andrewes,[114] that at least some important political trials must have taken place in the Assembly; but in fact there is not a particle of evidence that the Assembly conducted trials of any sort at any time, and it is highly improbable, especially since we know that even the kings, whose position was more exalted than that of other citizens, were tried

---

[111] See esp. 1275ᵃ23–33, on ἀόριστος ἀρχή, 'indeterminate' or 'indefinite' office.

[112] Cf. *Pol.* V 4, 1303ᵇ31–4ᵃ17. (In view of the story about Mytilene in 1304ᵃ4–10, it is just as well we have Thuc. III 2!)

[113] See Xen., *Lac. Pol.* X 2 (capital charges); Arist., *Pol.* II 9, 1270ᵇ38–40 (important cases), 1271ᵃ5–6 (gerontes were ἀνεύθυνοι); III 1, 1275ᵇ9–11 (homicide); IV 9, 1294ᵇ31– 4; Isocr. XII 154; Plut., *Lyc.* 26.2; Ps.-Plut., *Mor.* 217ab; cf. Dem. XX 107; Polyb. VI 45.5.

[114] Kahrstedt, *GStSS* 154–5; Andrewes, *GCS* 3, 19 n. 15.

before the Gerousia and ephors.[115] As Andrewes himself says,[116] 'the Gerousia was the highest lawcourt in Sparta, the only court that could inflict the graver penalties of death or exile or loss of civil rights'. Explicit evidence against political trials being conducted by the Spartan Assembly can be found in Aristotle, *Pol.* III 1, 1275ᵇ9–11, a statement which proves that at Sparta there was nothing corresponding to trial by a popular court such as the Athenian Heliaea, and that the right of deciding legal cases was never enjoyed by the ordinary Spartan citizen as such but only if he were an ephor, a member of the Gerousia, or the holder of some other office.(For a discussion of the passage, see Appendix XXV.) In Xen., *HG* v ii.32–5, the Assembly merely decides what to do about Thebes; nothing is said about its trying Phoebidas (or Ismenias, cf. §§35–6). Among all the major Spartan trials we know of, I would admit only one possible (though not probable) exception to the rule that the tribunal was the Gerousia: the case of King Agis II in 418, about which Thucydides (v 63) is uncharacteristically imprecise (see Appendix XXVI). There is no reason to suppose that a judgment took place in the Assembly merely because we are told that the decision was taken by 'the Spartans' (Thuc. I 128.3; Xen., *HG* v iv.13; Plut., *Lys.* 30.1; *Pelop.* 6.1; 13.3; and similar passages) or 'the citizens' (Diod. XIV 89.1); cf. Xen., *HG* VI iv.5, where 'by the city' must refer to a court consisting of Gerousia and ephors (see n. 115). Verdicts of Athenian courts are regularly referred to as decisions of 'the Athenians', although delivered as a rule by panels of a few hundred dicasts. So it will have been at Sparta and elsewhere.

There was no lack of important 'political' trials at Sparta:[117] in a little over a hundred years, from the 490s to 378, there were not only at least seven (and perhaps more) trials of kings (see Appendix XXVI) but also several of military men, including those of Cleandridas (the adviser of King Pleistoanax) in 446;[118] Aristocles and Hipponoidas in 418 (Thuc. v 72.1); Gylippus in 404 (Diod. XIII 106.8–9; Plut., *Lys.* 16–17.1; Athen. VI 233f–4a); Clearchus, *c.* 403 (Xen., *Anab.* II vi.4); Thibron in 399 (Xen., *HG* III i.8); Herippidas, Arcesus and Lysanoridas in 378 (Plut., *Pelop.* 13.3; *Mor.* 598f: see H. W. Parke in *CQ* 21 [1927] 159–65); and in particular those of Phoebidas (382) and Sphodrias (378), to be examined presently. Any Spartan, even a king, might be influenced in his course of action by the knowledge that he was likely to be prosecuted if he pursued an

---

[115] Paus. III v.2; cf. the references by Herodotus to a δικαστήριον in connection with both the condemnations of Leotychidas (VI 85.1; 72.2). And see Xen., *Anab.* II vi.4, where Clearchus is condemned to death ὑπὸ τῶν ἐν Σπάρτῃ τελῶν—evidently not just the ephors, whom Xenophon has mentioned twice in the last few lines, §§2, 3.

[116] GCS 16—correctly, in view of Xen., *Lac. Pol.* x 2; cf. Arist., *Pol.* II 9, 1270ᵇ38–40.

[117] I leave aside cases of dangerous conspiracy against the State, such as those of Cinadon in *c.* 399, described by Xen., *HG* III iii.4–11; Polyaen. II xiv.1 (the ephors seem to have acted mainly on their own initiative here), or the two in 370–69, mentioned by Plut., *Ages.* 32.6–11, where in the one case King Agesilaus and in the other Agesilaus and the ephors are said to have killed the conspirators (who were citizens) secretly, an act 'without precedent at Sparta'.

[118] See Chapter V, Part vii and its n. 95.

unsuccessful policy, in opposition to the wishes of the faction then dominant in the Gerousia. There is an illustration of this in Xenophon (*HG* vi iv.4–6), when King Cleombrotus was leading the army in Boeotia, and his friends told him that if he let the Thebans escape without a battle, he would be 'in danger of suffering the extreme penalty at the hands of the city'. And his enemies commented that this time Cleombrotus would really show whether the rumour of his partiality for the Thebans was true or not. The result was that Cleombrotus, who would have been only too well aware of the personal influence on many gerontes of the passionately anti-Theban King Agesilaus, was prompted to join battle, perhaps against his better judgment.

The cases of Phoebidas and Sphodrias became *causes célèbres* throughout Greece, and we must look at them carefully, as they are very revealing (that of Sphodrias in particular) about procedure at Sparta and the way in which important decisions could be taken there. We will take Sphodrias first, although his trial took place about four years later than that of Phoebidas.

Sphodrias[119] was the rash and foolish man who, one night in 378, when harmost of Thespiae, made a sudden and unprovoked attack on Athens, with which Sparta was then officially at peace, hoping to get possession of the Peiraeus before daybreak. He failed ignominiously, and his action was a disaster for Sparta: it was one of the direct causes of the Athenian alliance with Thebes and the inauguration of the Second Athenian Confederacy. His exploit was all the more unfortunate in that a Spartan embassy, including at least one friend of King Agesilaus (Etymocles: see Xen., *HG* v iv.22, 32) was at Athens at that very time: the Athenians immediately arrested the ambassadors and only released them when persuaded that Sphodrias would be duly tried and executed. Sphodrias, who was generally considered to have done something grossly improper (*deina*: Xen., *HG* v iv.25), was recalled by the ephors and prosecuted. Feeling certain that he would be convicted, he fled, and was tried in absence—and was actually acquitted, the only person I can recall in the whole of Greek and Roman history who took to flight when put on a capital charge and yet had judgment pronounced in his favour!

We have a detailed account of what happened, in particular from Xenophon, who is obviously very well informed and who says roundly that the decision in this case was 'the most unjust ever given at Sparta' (*HG* v iv.24). I am inclined to say that this is the most valuable account we have in any source of the way in which great issues might be settled at Sparta, behind the scenes. The significance of this story is that it reveals how entirely dependent the verdict was upon the personal decision of King Agesilaus: he obviously 'controlled' an appreciable number of the votes in the court, which can only have been the Gerousia, sitting with or without the ephors. Those of the judges who belonged to the personal following

---

[119] See Xen., *HG* v iv.20–33; Plut., *Ages.* 24–26.1; *Pelop.* 14; Diod. xv 29.5–6; and other sources.

of the other king, Cleombrotus I, were bosom friends (*hetairoi*) of Sphodrias, and he could evidently count on them to vote for his acquittal. (We are not told about Cleombrotus' personal position, but he was a much younger man than Agesilaus and had as yet had no opportunity to acquire renown, and he would have counted for very much less than the great Agesilaus.) Sphodrias, however, was afraid that he would be condemned by Agesilaus and his friends, and also by those whose position was 'intermediate between the two kings' (*tous dia mesou*)—an interesting phrase which shows that not all the gerontes were 'clients' of one or other of the two kings. A homosexual relationship between the sons of Sphodrias and Agesilaus led to Archidamus, the son of Agesilaus, interceding with his own father for the father of his friend. At first Agesilaus was unresponsive, stressing the gravity of the crime, which had indeed done Sparta great harm; but eventually he yielded and procured an acquittal. His reason for doing so is made perfectly clear by Xenophon: it was not the fact of his son's intercession, but his own deep conviction that a good soldier like Sphodrias was indispensable to Sparta.[120] Scarcity of Spartiates, the *oliganthrōpia* of which Aristotle makes so much in the *Politics*,[121] was already a very serious problem (see Appendix XVI). Seven years later we find Sphodrias among the personal following of Cleombrotus, and (with his son) dying with the king at Leuctra (Xen., *HG* VI iv.14).

It is very significant that in Xenophon's account (*HG* V iv.32–3) *the moment Agesilaus decides to vote for acquittal, Sphodrias' son can take it for granted that that will be the court's verdict.*

Some four years earlier Agesilaus had also prevented the punishment of another military commander, Phoebidas,[122] who, with the assistance of an oligarchic party of Thebans led by the Polemarch Leontiadas, had seized the Theban Cadmeia in 382, on his own initiative, without any official instructions from the Spartan State, however much private encouragement he may have received beforehand from Agesilaus and others. There is a conflict of evidence in the sources on what happened to Phoebidas.[123] The truth is almost certainly given by Plutarch's statement in his *Life of Agesilaus* (23.11), that 'Agesilaus saved Phoebidas': he will have done this by using his great prestige and influence, either to settle the result of the trial, exactly as in the case of Sphodrias a little later, or to have it shelved, or conceivably he may have consented to the infliction of

---

[120] Xen., *HG* V iv.32: τὴν γὰρ Σπάρτην τοιούτων δεῖσθαι στρατιωτῶν.

[121] *Pol.* II 9, 1270ᵃ15–34. Cf. Xen., *Lac. Pol.* I 1: ἡ Σπάρτη τῶν ὀλιγανθρωποτάτων πόλεων.

[122] See Xen., *HG* V ii.25 ff., esp. 32; Diod. XV 20 (esp. §2); XVI 29.2–3; Isocr. IV 126; Plut., *Ages.* 23–4; *Pelop.* 5–6; *Mor.* 576a; Polyb. IV xxvii.4; Nepos, *Pelop.* 1.2–3 etc.

[123] He was fined, according to Polyb. IV xxvii.4; Diod. XV 20.2; Nepos, *Pelop.* 1.2–3; Plut., *Mor.* 576a—according to Plut., *Pelop.* 6.1, the enormous sum of 100,000 drachmae (nearly 17 talents)! Cf. Thuc. V 63.2–4, where King Agis II is nearly fined the same sum, again 'ten myriads of drachmae'. (Perhaps this was essentially intended as a ruinous fine calculated to drive the victim from Sparta.) It is impossible to believe that such a fine was actually inflicted on Phoebidas, and I suggest that in *Pelop.* 6.1 (contrast *Ages.* 23.11, cited in the text below) Plutarch may be misrepresenting a source that used much the same language as Thuc. V 63.2.

a fine, and perhaps paid it himself. Phoebidas certainly turns up again only five years later, as harmost of Thespiae (Xen., *HG* v iv.41–5 etc.), in which capacity he, like Sphodrias, justified Agesilaus' faith in him, dying bravely in battle. Xenophon affords some confirmation that his hero Agesilaus did indeed 'save Phoebidas', whether or not some official condemnation was pronounced, for—characteristically, in the circumstances—he says nothing at all about the result of any trial, although he mentions that 'the ephors and most of the citizens were angry with Phoebidas' (*HG* v ii.32), and expresses his own disapproval of the Spartan action in not only seizing but retaining possession of the Cadmeia (iv.1). He also mentions the revealing opinion of Agesilaus, that all a Spartan ought to consider was whether Phoebidas had produced a result which was good or bad for Sparta; and that if it was good, there was an old-established rule that such acts of initiative were permissible (ii.32). For the Spartans, even more (if anything) than for other Greeks, the interest of their own city was an absolutely paramount consideration. They might even be brought to realise that other Greeks too could legitimately act upon similar principles. Plutarch (*Alc.* 31.8) tells how Anaxilaus of Byzantium, put on trial at Sparta (in 405–4) for surrendering his city to the Athenians a few years earlier, proved to his judges that the situation had been hopeless and that he had only been 'following the example of the best of the Spartans, for whom what was expedient for their State was the one single criterion of honour and justice'!—and was acquitted, with his colleagues. (Cf. Xen., *HG* i iii.19, omitting this part of the story.)

The action of Phoebidas, and the Spartan retention of the Cadmeia, shocked the Greek world. Plutarch (*Ages.* 23.6–8) makes some rather severe comments on the prominent part played in this disgraceful affair by Agesilaus, who was always prating about justice. Like Xenophon, he records disapproval of Phoebidas at Sparta (*Ages.* 23.6). But the failure of the Spartans to punish Phoebidas is far more easily understandable than the acquittal of Sphodrias, for Phoebidas might be regarded as having performed a useful task, whereas the action of Sphodrias was an unmitigated blunder.

At Sparta, according to Andrewes (GCS 17), 'when it was necessary to take a decision the question erupted in open assembly, and Xenophon makes it clear that in the cases of both Phoibidas and Sphodrias the general opinion of the citizens was a serious factor'. On the contrary, in so far as any 'general opinion' at Sparta is allowed to appear in Xenophon, or for that matter in Plutarch or elsewhere, it is strongly hostile to the men concerned, and—far from its being a 'serious factor'—the court simply takes no notice of it! We are not very well informed about Phoebidas, but in the case of Sphodrias the court is divided into three groups: one is anyway willing to acquit on purely personal grounds, and Agesilaus is able to bring enough of the other two over to the same position. There could hardly be a greater contrast with the Athenian courts, where everything was done in the open, and even the persons who would make up the dicastery were not known until the last moment. I am not suggesting that things were 'rigged' in this way when matters were settled in the Spartan Assembly. But I do suggest that even there the extreme deference paid to great men, above all to those kings who had proved themselves worthy of their office, could place enormous influence in their hands.

It was a commonplace among writers on political theory[124] that Sparta had a 'mixed constitution', a blend of monarchy, oligarchy (or aristocracy) and democracy. If we neglect the very great importance of the Gerousia in jurisdiction, we shall be likely to underrate the oligarchic element, surely by far the most weighty. I agree with Forrest (*HS* 113): 'When Pindar[125] singled out for praise at Sparta the "counsels of the Elders" he put his finger on what must still have been the mainspring of policy-making, the Gerousia, and, behind the Gerousia, the tight and ever-tightening circle of noble families which could hope to provide its members.' (On the question whether the Gerousia was recruited from a *legally* limited circle of families, see Appendix XXVII.) From these few families will have come the men of greatest wealth and influence, so often mentioned in our sources, from Herodotus and Thucydides to Plutarch and Pausanias. There was marked inequality of wealth at Sparta, not only in 'pre-Lycurgan' times (Plut., *Lyc.* 8–11 etc.) but also in the fifth and fourth centuries (see Arist., *Pol.* II 9, 1270ª15–39, esp. 16–18). Many different expressions are used for the upper crust of the Spartiates: they are the 'prosperous ones' (*olbioi*, Hdts VI 61.3), those who were 'of good family, and in wealth among the first' (VII 134.2), 'those who had great possessions' (Thuc. I 6.4), the 'first men' (IV 108.7; V 15.1; Plut., *Nic.* 10.8), the 'rich' (Xen., *Lac. Pol.* V 3; Arist., *Pol.* IV 9, 1294ᵇ22, 26) or 'very rich' (Xen., *HG* VI iv.10–11), those 'from whom the greatest offices are filled' (Xen., *Lac. Pol.* II 2), the 'gentlemen' (*kaloi kagathoi*, Arist., *Pol.* II 9, 1270ᵇ24; Plut., *Lyc.* 17.2). From these same families, too, will have come the great majority of the numerous men (and even women: *Inschr. von Olympia* 160 = *Anth. Pal.* XIII 16; Xen., *Ages.* IX 6; Plut., *Ages.* 20.1; *Mor.* 212b; Paus. III viii.1–2; xv.1; xvii.6; V xii.5; VI i.6 etc.) who made a conspicuous demonstration of their exceptional wealth by breeding horses and even winning chariot races at Olympia and elsewhere, from the mid-sixth century onwards (see Appendix XXVIII). One of these horse-breeders, Evagoras, was the only man, apart from Cimon of Athens (father of the great Miltiades), to win three successive victories in the four-horse chariot race at Olympia with the same team (Hdts VI 103.4). Among the others were Arcesilaus, who won the Olympic chariot race twice (Paus. VI ii.1–2, etc.), and his son Lichas (Thuc. V 50.4; Xen., *HG* III ii.21; Paus. VI ii.1–3), proxenos of Argos (Thuc. V 76.3) and victor in the same contest when an old man, who became famous all over Greece for his lavish

---

[124] See e.g. Arist., *Pol.* II 6, 1265ᵇ33–66ª1; IV 9, 1294ᵇ14–36; cf. II 9, 1270ᵇ6–26; IV 7, 1293ᵇ14–18; Polyb. VI iii.8; x.6–12, etc., with Walbank, *HCP* I 638–41, 646–8; K. von Fritz, *The Theory of the Mixed Const. in Antiq.* (New York, 1954), Index, *s.v.* 'Sparta'. I have not seen G. J. D. Aalders, *Die Theorie der gemischten Verfassung im Alt.* (1968).

[125] Pind., fr. 199.1 (Snell³), *ap.* Plut., *Lyc.* 21.6.

hospitality to strangers visiting Sparta for the festival of the Gymnopaediae (Xen., *Mem.* I ii.61; Plut., *Cim.* 10.6). Other such Spartans turn up in anecdotes, sometimes of doubtful authenticity: the best attested of these men is the corpulent Naucleidas, who incurred the enmity of Lysander (Agatharch., *FGrH* 86 F 11, *ap.* Athen. XII 550d; cf. Ael., *VH* XIV 7), doubtless by his conduct as an ephor in 404/3, when he supported King Pausanias (Xen., *HG* II iv.36).

The picture of Spartan wealth given in Ps.-Plato, *I Alc.* 122c-3b, is no doubt exaggerated, but the emphasis on the extent and fertility of Laconia and Messenia and the large numbers of Helots and other servants and of horses and other domestic animals (122de) is not misplaced. But Spartan wealth was very unevenly distributed, at least in the fifth century and later, and the Spartan *homoioi* were 'Peers' in little more than name. We may remember Diodorus' comment (II 39.5) on his idealised Indian society: 'It is foolish to make laws on a basis of equality for all, but to make the distribution of property unequal'.[126]

C. We can now look at the evidence which shows prominent kings exercising a dominant effect upon Spartan policy. In spite of Cloché's well-documented article, RRS (1949), the subject has received far less than its due share of attention in recent times. This aspect of Spartan politics happens to be particularly relevant for our purposes, as we shall see that the situation in 432, in which we are specially interested, was exceptional. King Archidamus II, of the Eurypontid house, a man of considerable prestige, was at least opposed to an immediate declaration of war and (as we shall see in a moment) may well have been a believer in the 'dual hegemony' of Sparta and Athens who hoped to avoid war entirely. The Agiad king, Pausanias, was still a boy and too young to have any personal influence; but he was the son of Pleistoanax, who seems to have been anything but an enemy of Athens (see Part VI of this Chapter, and also Chapter V, Part VII), and he himself in 403 was to rescue the Athenian democratic Resistance and effect a remarkably generous settlement which left the restored democracy as free as it could well be in the circumstances (see Part VI of this Chapter). I can think of no other occasion in Spartan history, at any rate down to the end of the fourth century, when the State adopted a policy that we can be fairly sure was favoured by neither royal house.

The very great importance of some of the more prominent kings in Spartan politics is often not sufficiently appreciated. One reason for this may be the way they are presented by Aristotle, during most of whose adult life the Spartan kings happened to be men of no great quality. The Agiad King Cleomenes II (370–309) seems to have been a complete

---

[126] A perfectly clear passage which modern editors and commentators have often obscured by gratuitous emendation of οὐσίας to ἐξουσίας or συνουσίας. See B. Farrington, *Diodorus Siculus* (Inaugural Lect., at Swansea, 1936, published 1937) 18, 37 n. 5 = *Head and Hand in Anc. Greece* (London, 1947) 68–9, 86–7 n. 5.

nonentity. The Eurypontid Archidamus III (*c.* 361/60–338) never distinguished himself; his son Agis III, who reigned from 338 to 331 or 330, is notable only for his unsuccessful revolt against Alexander the Great;[127] and after him the Eurypontids almost disappear from view until Agis IV (244–1) brought the monarchy into the forefront again. Aristotle saw the kings mainly as life generals,[128] and only once does he suggest that they had any political importance, when he describes them as having power in great affairs,[129] and adds that when they are men of low calibre (*euteleis*) they can do great harm to the city and have in fact done so (*Pol.* II 11, 1272ᵇ41–3ᵃ2.) Actually it was not so much their royal powers themselves that made the kings the natural political leaders at Sparta: these powers were strictly limited, and if we think only in terms of them we shall miss the really significant factors. Only a man of ability, especially in war, could make effective use of the royal position, but if he did have ability the king could easily stand out head and shoulders above his fellow countrymen. In the first place, since the Spartan army (and of course that of the Peloponnesian League) was always led if possible by a Spartan king, it was a king, if anyone, who could hope to obtain the highest form of prestige possible in Spartan eyes: that of having led the State to military victory. And even apart from this, the king, who was 'the seed of the demigod son of Zeus' (Thuc. v 16.2) and therefore of all men the most blue-blooded (Isocr., *Epist.* IX 3), was in a very special position. To lay hands forcibly on a king was unthinkable.[130] Except for the ephors, everyone, even the gerontes, had to stand up when a king appeared (Xen., *Lac. Pol.* xv 6). The kings had other privileges also, calculated to increase their dignity (see Hdts VI 56–7, 59; Xen., *Lac. Pol.* xv). When they died, their funerals were conducted with such extraordinary solemnities (recounted in some detail by Hdts VI 58) that Xenophon was moved to describe them as befitting 'heroes rather than men' (*Lac. Pol.* xv 9); and when Xenophon mentions the funeral of King Agis II in *c.* 400 he refers to it as having been 'more solemn than belongs to a man' (*HG* III iii.1). The kings, furthermore, were accounted the wealthiest men at Sparta (Ps.-Plato, *I Alc.* 122c-3a; cf. Plut., *Agis* 4.1). A Spartan king could easily be larger than life—if he was worthy of his role, as not all kings were. Of the individuals whose sayings or alleged sayings are recorded in the Plutarchian *Apophthegmata Laconica* (*Mor.* 208b–232d), a majority are members of the royal houses, and their sayings make up roughly two thirds of the

---

[127] See the end of Part vi of this Chapter. I do not know why E. Badian, 'Agis III', in *Hermes* 95 (1967) 170–92, at p. 182, refers to Agis as 'the greatest soldier Greece had produced for a long time'. Do we know anything about his military career before 332, when he campaigned in Crete (Diod. xvii 48.2)?

[128] στρατηγοὶ ἀΐδιοι, *Pol.* II 9, 1271ᵃ18 ff. (esp. 40); III 14, 1285ᵃ3–10; cf. 15, 1285ᵇ33 ff.; v 11, 1313ᵃ25–33.

[129] The words he uses (μεγάλων κύριοι καθεστῶτες) remind one of his description of the ephors as ἀρχὴ κυρία . . . τῶν μεγίστων, in *Pol.* II 9, 1270ᵇ7–8.

[130] Plut., *Agis* 19.9; cf. 21, and note the revealing story in Hdts VI 85.2–3: the Aeginetans do not care to revenge themselves on Leotychidas, even when he is handed over to them by the Spartans.

text; of the 'commoners', not one is given more than two or three sayings, apart from Antalcidas, Brasidas, Callicratidas and Lysander.

One factor which might on occasion serve to prevent the kings from becoming too influential was the existence of rivalry, differences of opinion or even open hostility between them. It was said in the time of Herodotus (VI 52.8) that the founders of the two royal houses, Eurysthenes and Procles, were always at variance (*diaphoroi*), and that their descendants continued in the same way (cf. Arist., *Pol.* II 9, 1271ª24–6; Plato, *Laws* III 691de); but any tendency towards personal hostility would have been mitigated by the fact that when they were together at Sparta the two kings were *syskēnoi*: they shared the same tent or mess (Xen., *HG* v iii. 20; *Lac. Pol.* xv 4; Plut., *Ages.* 20.8). The most notorious example of hostility between two Spartan kings is that between Cleomenes I and Damaratus (see esp. Hdts VI 50.3; 51.1; 61.1; 64–67.1); and even they are said by Herodotus (v 75.1 *fin.*) never to have been at odds until they clashed— surely on an important question of policy—during the expedition against Athens *c.* 506. We do not actually hear of differences between kings again until the time of Agesipolis I (395/4–380) and Agesilaus II, when Xenophon (*HG* v iii.20) makes the significant comment that Agesilaus, on hearing of the death of Agesipolis, 'did not rejoice over it, as one might have expected, as over the death of an adversary', but wept and mourned. He explains this by adding, 'For the kings share the same tent (or mess) when they are at home', and goes on to say how admirably suited these two kings were to chat together about 'youthful exploits, hunting, horses, and love affairs'— an interesting side-light on the kind of conversation likely to appeal to leading Spartans! Xenophon's comment shows that although personal relations between these two kings may have been good, they had serious differences: we hear enough about these to be sure that the foreign policy preferred by Agesipolis (like that of his father Pausanias and brother Cleombrotus) was very different from that of Agesilaus.[131] But there is reason to suppose that there were also serious differences in regard to foreign policy between Agis II and Pausanias, if not between Agis and Pausanias' father Pleistoanax (see below and Part vi of this Chapter).

Our earliest evidence for a Spartan king playing a dominant role in foreign affairs is for the reign of Cleomenes I (*c.* 520–490). There is scarcely an event of any importance in his reign, apart from the proposal to restore Hippias (on which see Part iv above, n. 72), in connection with which Cleomenes is not named by Herodotus as playing the leading role. Men who came to Sparta to seek its aid, like Maeandrius of Samos (Hdts III 148, *c.* 517–16 B.C.) and Aristagoras of Miletus (v 49–51, 500–499 B.C.), went first to Cleomenes, because he was the most influential personage.[132]

[131] See Smith, OAFP, esp. 279–84. The main texts are Xen., *HG* v iii.10 ff. (esp. 10, 13, 20, 23–5); iv.25; Diod. xv 19.4; Polyb. IX xxiii.7.

[132] Cf. Plut., *Mor.* 774b, where Scedasus, failing to get satisfaction from the ephors, goes next to the kings. His visit to Sparta must have taken place between 404 and 377. (The story may be partly a fiction, but it is fairly well attested: see Plut., *Mor.* 773b–4d; *Pelop.* 20.5–7; Diod. xv 54.2–3; Paus. IX xiii.5–6; cf. Xen. *HG* VI iv.7.)

In relation to Athens from 510 to *c.* 506 (see Chapter V, Part i below), Argos in the whole Sepeia campaign,[133] and the coercion of Aegina in 491 (Hdts VI 49–50; 73), Cleomenes is represented as deciding Spartan policy. And the one and only person who is thought worthy to be mentioned as opposing Cleomenes is his co-king Damaratus, who first helped to foil his attack on Athens *c.* 506, and then did his best to stop him from taking hostages from Aegina in 491, until Cleomenes had him dethroned and replaced by Leotychidas, whereupon Aeginetan resistance to Cleomenes collapsed. When Cleomenes' suborning of the Delphic Oracle in the matter of Damaratus' deposition became known, he thought it best to leave Sparta, but neither then nor on his return and alleged suicide is any individual Spartan mentioned as playing a particularly prominent part. Presumably the ephors took the lead, but they seem to have been men of too little stature for their names to be remembered.

Next comes Pausanias, Regent from 480 onwards for the child Pleistarchus, son of King Leonidas. Although a young man at the time of his great victory over the Persians at Plataea,[134] he immediately achieved a position of great prominence; but it is impossible to discover the truth about him, as we have (to quote Forrest)[135] 'little beyond the official story which justified his extermination'. (Cf. Chapter V, Part ii and its n.23 below.) Of the Eurypontid king during the Persian war, Leotychidas, we know virtually nothing, except that he came to the throne as the henchman of Cleomenes and was eventually sent into exile for allegedly pursuing personal ends in Thessaly.[136] After the death of Leotychidas in 469, the Eurypontid kingship was for over a century in the hands of three men: Archidamus II (469–427/6) and his two sons, Agis II (427/6–*c.* 400) and Agesilaus II (*c.* 400–361/60). There were six Agiad kings in roughly the same period: Pleistarchus (480–58), Pleistoanax (458–446/5 and 427/6–408), Pausanias (446/5–427/6 and 408–395/4), Agesipolis I (395/4–380), Cleombrotus (380–71), and Agesipolis II (371–70).

We have no very good information about Archidamus II[137] before he emerges into the full glare of Thucydides' narrative in 432; but he is always spoken of with respect,[138] and since his co-king Pleistarchus would

[133] The main source is Hdts VI 75.3–82; 92.1–2; VII 148.2. For the other evidence, see Busolt, *GG* II² 561–5.

[134] He was hardly much over 30, and may have been only about 25, as believed by White, *ADPS*. This would have been regarded as excessively young for a Spartan commander. Alcibiades was about 32–33 (see Andrewes, in Gomme, *HCT* IV 48–9; Hatzfeld, *Alc.*² 27–8, 62–6) when Thucydides (V 43.2) speaks of him as still young in years by the standards of any city other than Athens; and cf. VI 12.2 (with 17.1), where Alcibiades is νεώτερος ἔτι ἐς τὸ ἄρχειν, in Nicias' eyes, although he is now at least 36.

[135] *HS* 103. Forrest's whole account of Spartan foreign policy in the years following 479 (*HS* 98–105) is very stimulating; and cf. his *TA*.

[136] The main sources are in Hill, *S*² 358 (Index IV 1.8). Speculation about what Leotychidas was trying to do is futile.

[137] Hdts VI 71.2 reveals that he married his aunt, Lampito.

[138] See e.g. Thuc. I 79.2; Diod. XI 63.5–64.1; Plut., *Cim.* 16.6 (cf. §4); *Ages.* 1.1; Paus. III vii.10–11; Polyaen. I xli.1–3. (It is a pity we know nothing more of the incident described in *Id.* 2!)

have been too young to command in the 460s,[189] Archidamus doubtless led the Spartans to victory at the battles of Tegea and Dipaea.[140] He certainly seems to have played a major part (see esp. Diod. xi 63.4–7; Plut., *Cim.* 16.4–7) in overcoming the dangerous Helot revolt, which began just after the great earthquake of 465/4 and soon became a very serious threat to Sparta, a force of 300 Spartans being destroyed in the plain of Stenyclarus (Hdts ix 64.2). As we saw earlier, Thucydides (i 80.1) makes him begin his speech to the Spartan Assembly in 432 by describing himself as a man of experience in many wars. During the First Peloponnesian war Archidamus was the one experienced general Sparta had, and it is a very surprising fact, at first sight, that he is not recorded as playing any part whatever in that war. The commander of the Peloponnesian army in the Tanagra campaign of 458–7 was the otherwise unknown Nicomedes, acting for Pleistoanax ('still a young man', Thuc. i 107.2); and Pleistoanax himself, although perhaps not more than 25–30, led the invasion of 446 (see Chapter V, Part vii below). It has been suggested[141] that if the Helot revolt was still going on in 458–7 there may have been good reason for the experienced Archidamus to remain at home; but his absence in 446 would still be surprising—until we remember his attitude to the war in 432–1 and the fact that he was a guest-friend (*xenos*) of Pericles (Thuc. ii 13.1; Plut., *Per.* 33.3).

In 432 Thucydides (i 79.2–85.2), introducing Archidamus in the warmest terms, as a man with a reputation for ability and prudence, makes him speak seriously and persuasively against an immediate declaration of war. He does not proclaim himself as being altogether against a war with Athens, and indeed urges that Sparta should prepare for one, over the next two or three years (i 82.1–3; 83.3; 85.2). If he spoke in this vein, it may have been because that was how he genuinely felt, but I think we should also allow for the possibility that he did not really want war with Athens at all but thought it politic not to be entirely frank in public about this, in view of the obvious bellicosity of a large proportion of his audience, whom he could best hope to influence by pretending to share their desire to punish Athens. At any rate, the essential point is that he was strongly against an immediate declaration of war. Later, it must have been at least partly due to his influence that of three embassies which went to Athens in the winter of 432/1 the second at least was apparently ready to effect a compromise, even though war had been formally declared both by Sparta and by the Peloponnesian League Congress (cf. Appendix XII). And when Archidamus led the first Peloponnesian invasion of Attica in the early summer of 431, he first, while still at the Isthmus, sent a personal envoy to Athens to try to obtain its surrender—evidently a man holding views similar to his own, who deeply regretted the war (Thuc. ii 12.1–3)—and even after that advanced so

---

[189] He was born about 485, according to White, ADPS 149, 150–1.
[140] See n. 12 to Part ii of this Chapter.
[141] By White, ADPS 140 n. 3.

slowly as to bring much censure upon himself (II 18, esp. §§3–5; cf. 20). We know almost nothing of internal politics at Sparta in the 430s. We cannot even give a name during this period to any of those who wanted to break the Peace with Athens, except Sthenelaïdas, the ephor who presided at the fateful assembly in 432 and was eager for immediate war. Apart from Thucydides (I 85.3–87.3), no ancient source mentions Sthenelaïdas, except Pausanias (III vii.11), who speaks of him as an influential man who, in his year as ephor, was mainly responsible for the war; and it is quite possible that Pausanias' only source of information was Thucydides. Sthenelaïdas deserves special notice as the first Spartan outside the royal houses who is named by any ancient author as playing an important part in the formation of Spartan foreign policy, apart from Hetoimaridas, and perhaps the Ephor Chilon.[142] But it is an even more significant fact that the vote of the Spartan Assembly for war in 432, by a very large majority, was against the strong opposition of King Archidamus; and as I have said, I know of no parallel to this overruling of a king who was the leading Spartan of his day, except perhaps in 440, when the Spartan Assembly must have voted for war with Athens (see Chapter V, Part viii below), and we can surely infer that this also was against the will of Archidamus. Certainly Pausanias, the Agiad king, could have counted for nothing in 432, when he will hardly have been much more than 14 or 15 (cf. White, ADPS 141, 149, whose dates seem to me a little too low).

Another king who played an important and decisive part in Spartan policy was Pausanias, whose reign was in two separate spells, from 445 to 427/6, during his father's exile, and again after the death of his father, from 408 to 395/4. We scarcely hear of Pausanias at all before 403, but in that year he suddenly moved to the very centre of the stage, at a crucial moment in the affairs not only of Sparta but of Athens (and of Greece). The only notice Pausanias receives from Thucydides is an incidental one: we are told that the Peloponnesian invasion of Attica in 427 was commanded by Cleomenes on behalf of King Pausanias, who was still rather young (*neōteros*, III 26.2)—Pleistoanax was still in exile, although he was to return a few months later and resume the kingship. Only once more before 403 is Pausanias' name so much as mentioned: in the autumn of 405, his co-king Agis being already in command of the garrison at Decelea, Pausanias is said by Xenophon (*HG* II ii.7) to have led the main Peloponnesian army into Attica. But when Athens refused to surrender, Pausanias and the main force must have returned to the Peloponnese,[143]

---

[142] On Hetoimaridas see Chapter V, Part ii below. Chilon, ephor *c.* 556/5 (see T. J. Cadoux in *JHS* 68 [1948], at pp. 108–9), is likely to have had something to do with Sparta's new 'Achaean' policy, initiated at about that time. According to G. L. Huxley, *Early Sparta* 69, this policy was 'certainly due' to Chilon; cf. Forrest, *HS* 76 (an 'easy guess'). There has been much speculation about the role attributed to Chilon in *P. Ryl.* 18 = *FGrH* 105 F 1.

[143] See Busolt, *GG* III ii. 1628 and n. 2. I leave open the question whether Busolt (1627 n. 2) is right in seeing the bringing up of the army by Pausanias as 'a move obviously directed against Agis' (cf. Thuc. VIII 71.1,3).

and we hear no more of any activities on the part of Pausanias until 403, more than a year after the surrender of Athens.

In Part vi of this Chapter, dealing with major changes in the conduct of foreign affairs at Sparta, we shall have occasion to notice how Spartan policy in the Aegean, from early 405 onwards, came to be dominated by Lysander, an outright imperialist. He had a powerful personality and great gifts as a naval commander, and his remarkable success in finally defeating Athens, combined with his skill in organising oligarchies directly dependent upon himself in many Aegean cities, brought him very great personal influence, hitherto unequalled by a Greek, as Plutarch puts it—he was even given divine honours by at least one of the oligarchies he installed in power in 404-3, that at Samos (Plut., *Lys.* 18). Theopompus (*FGrH* 115 F 20, *ap.* Athen. xii 543bc) could describe him as 'master (*kyrios*) of almost all Greece'. In 404, probably some months after the official end of the war,[144] Lysander arranged for power at Athens to be entrusted to the Thirty, a small oligarchy of the type he had already been instrumental in bringing to power elsewhere. In 403, however, the Thirty were defeated by the democratic Resistance led by Thrasybulus,[145] and withdrew to Eleusis, leaving the democrats in control of Peiraeus, and at Athens itself a ruling board of Ten appointed by the Three Thousand who now composed the citizen body enjoying the franchise. Embassies went to Sparta from both Athens and Eleusis to appeal for help. At first there was no full-scale intervention (Lys. xii 58-9), but a loan of 100 talents was granted to the oligarchs by Sparta (doubtless to pay mercenaries), and the two men who were sent out to take charge of operations by land and sea were Lysander himself, who joined his *protégés* at Eleusis, and his brother Libys as navarch, who blockaded Peiraeus.[146] To all appearances, Lysander would continue to dominate Spartan policy, and he would help the Athenian oligarchs to crush the democrats decisively.

It was at this point that King Pausanias, who now 'persuaded three of the ephors' (Xen., *HG* ii iv.29), was able to bring about a sudden and drastic change in Spartan policy. Presumably the Assembly had already taken some decision which the ephors of the day, acting by a majority of three to two, were able to use as a justification for calling out the general levy of 'the Spartans and their allies',[147] and despatching it to Athens under King Pausanias. A king in command of the Spartan army was superior in authority to anyone else, even a harmost and a navarch, and Pausanias (after no more than the necessary minimum of a military victory over

[144] I despair of proving the correctness of any of the alternative chronological schemes, between the surrender of Athens in late April 404 (16 Munychion, Plut., *Lys.* 15.1) and the final restoration of the democracy in Sept./Oct. 403 (12 Boedromion, Plut., *Mor.* 349f = *De glor. Athen.* 7). See Hignett, *HAC* 378-89.

[145] The whole story of the restoration of democracy is told at very great length by Cloché, *RDA* (a book of 493 pp.). See also Hignett, *HAC* 285-98. For the events with which we are primarily concerned, see esp. Cloché, *RDA* 186-244. For the curious statements in Lys. xviii 9-12, 22, see *RDA* 93-4, 214-19.

[146] Xen., *HG* ii iv.28-9; Lys. xii 58-9; Arist., *Ath. Pol.* 38.1; 40.3; Isocr. vii 68.

[147] The Boeotians and Corinthians refused to march: see Appendix XXI.

the democrats) completely overturned the policy inspired by Lysander. After three separate Athenian embassies had gone to Sparta, the Spartan Assembly appointed a commission of fifteen men to bring about a settlement 'in conjunction with Pausanias', whose wise policy was now adopted in its entirety. A reconciliation was effected, with an amnesty which on the whole was faithfully observed, but the effect of the settlement was to give control of Athens to the democrats (Xen., *HG* II iv.38–43). The Spartan garrison was withdrawn, and Athens was allowed full autonomy in her internal affairs. Although in the sphere of foreign relations the treaty Athens had concluded with Sparta in 404 still bound her to 'follow the Spartans whithersoever they might lead' (cf. Part iv of this Chapter, Section B), her internal condition was totally transformed from what it had been under the regime of the Thirty, and the democracy was fully restored. The civil strife at Athens apparently ended in the autumn of 403: the festival which celebrated this event is said to have taken place on the 12th Boedromion, in late September or the first few days of October.[148]

Here we see a Spartan king taking full control of a vital part of Spartan foreign policy and abandoning a line of action which, on the surface, must have seemed brilliantly successful: a new imperialism which had enabled Sparta greatly to extend her power through the support of small oligarchies dependent upon herself. Of that policy Lysander had certainly been both the originator and the supervisor; but I would suggest that he, probably the first Spartan outside the royal houses who had ever played a dominant role in Spartan affairs (with the possible exception of the Ephor Chilon: see n. 142 above), owed his extraordinary influence not merely to his own undoubtedly great ability, but also to the support of the Eurypontid king, Agis II.[149] This cannot perhaps be proved beyond doubt, but there are some pieces of circumstantial evidence which point to such a conclusion. First, when Pausanias was prosecuted by his enemies on his return to Sparta, and acquitted, Agis and half the members of the Gerousia (many of them probably among Agis' personal following) voted for his condemnation (Paus. III v.2). And if Agis was a political opponent of Pausanias, he is very likely to have been in favour of Lysander's policy. (The two kings may have been personal enemies, although we have no information to that effect; but if they were, they might be all the more likely to adopt opposite policies.) Secondly, Lysander had been the lover of Agis' second son Agesilaus, the future king (Plut., *Lys.* 22.6; *Ages.* 2.1). And thirdly, there is the fact that in the winter of 413/12 Agis, entirely on his own authority, appointed (as he was able to do, Thuc. VIII 5.2–3) a Spartan named Alcamenes to a command in Euboea (which failed to materialise) and then as harmost of Lesbos.[150] Now Alcamenes was the son of Sthenelaïdas (5.1), the leading Spartan 'hawk' in 432, and it is not unlikely that he would have inherited his father's policy, although of

---

[148] See n. 144 above.
[149] Cf. Busolt, *GG* III ii.1627: 'König Agis, einen Freund Lysanders'.
[150] Thuc. VIII 5.1,2; 8.2; 10.2–4. He was killed in a minor battle in 412.

course this cannot be regarded as certain. (According to the view I am advocating, Agis had abandoned the conciliatory policy of his father Archidamus.)

It is surely right to place great emphasis on King Pausanias' action. It must have produced a great revulsion of feeling at Athens in favour of Sparta, after a bitter period during the rule of the Thirty, the creatures of Sparta, during which most Athenians must have felt deeply hostile to their conqueror, and with good reason. Not since the Persian wars had Sparta so conspicuously earned the respect of the Greeks as by the admirable settlement of Athenian affairs by King Pausanias, nor would she earn that respect again for a very long time. Jealousy of Lysander is the only motive attributed to Pausanias by Xenophon (*HG* II iv.29), while Justin (v x.7) sees him, with even less plausibility, as moved by pity for the Athenian democratic exiles. Diodorus (XIV 33.6), who also speaks of Pausanias' jealousy of Lysander, does at least have an inkling of the truth when he adds that Pausanias saw Sparta was acquiring a bad reputation among the Greeks (cf. Paus. III v.1).[151] In fact Pausanias was surely acting in what he believed, rightly, to be Sparta's best interests. He was returning to what I have called Sparta's 'natural' foreign policy (see Part iii of this Chapter): concentration on the Peloponnese and the deliberate avoidance of extra-Peloponnesian imperialism. Athens was now too powerful to be left entirely to herself, and she had to be incorporated in Sparta's League, but she was now to be given full internal autonomy.

A fact that needs to be stressed here is that although King Pausanias had to win over a majority of the ephors before he could put his own policy into operation, yet once he had secured the support of that majority it was clearly he, and not the ephors, who was the dominant figure in the settlement with Athens. Xenophon (*HG* II iv.29 ff.), by far our most important source, always speaks of Pausanias as the prime mover in the new policy: he not only takes all necessary military steps, as a Spartan king had to do, but also instructs the democrats how to proceed to obtain the best results (§35), and he is ultimately entrusted by Sparta with the task of effecting a settlement, in conjunction with 15 commissioners despatched for that purpose (§§37–8; cf. Arist., *Ath. Pol.* 38.4). The other sources (Diod. XIV 33.6; Just. v x.7) attribute the whole settlement to Pausanias. Xenophon, after his initial statement about the ephors, makes no further mention of them, except to remark that two of them, Naucleidas[152] and another he does not even name, went with Pausanias and the army to Athens, as Spartan custom required, and that both of them 'adhered to the policy of Pausanias rather than that of Lysander' (*HG* II iv.36). It is Pausanias who takes the lead and directs the course of action, not the ephors.

---

[151] We may ignore the variant provided by Plut., *Lys.* 21 (chronologically confused), according to which both kings (Agis and Pausanias) were jealous of Lysander and worked together against him. This is inconsistent with Paus. III v.2 (cited above), which gives every impression of coming from a well-informed source.

[152] See Section B above, *ad fin.*

The predominance of the kings in Spartan foreign policy continued well into the fourth century. Even in the detailed narratives of Thucydides and Xenophon we still have few names of Spartans, apart from kings, who played any part in foreign affairs except as military commanders carrying out the orders given to them. Only Brasidas, Lysander and Antalcidas are figures of any real significance, as far as our evidence goes, and for our present purposes Antalcidas does not require separate treatment, as he was essentially carrying out King Agesilaus' policy (see Part vi of this Chapter). Brasidas in 424–3 was thwarted by powerful opposition at Sparta at a time when his successes in the 'Thraceward' region gave promise of achieving far-reaching results (see Part vi of this Chapter). Lysander, a man of consummate ability, who had done more than any other single individual to bring Sparta to victory over Athens, enjoyed very great influence for a time—partly, as I have argued, because he must have enjoyed the support of King Agis II. But we have seen that his whole foreign policy was completely overturned by one king, Pausanias, in 403; and although he continued to be very influential (cf. Nepos, *Ages.* 1.5: 'factiosus et iis temporibus potens'), he was easily and thoroughly brought to heel by another king, Agesilaus, in 396–5, when his personal influence with the Greeks of Asia became too apparent (see Xen., *HG* III iv.2 ff., esp. 7–10; Plut., *Lys.* 23–24.1; *Ages.* 6.2–5; 7–8).

Apart from Brasidas, Lysander and Antalcidas, a handful of navarchs and harmosts who may have had a chance to take an independent line on occasion,[153] and the ephors of 421/20 (Xenares and Cleobulus, mentioned only during their year of office: Thuc. v 36; 37.1; 38.3; 46.4), we know of very few prominent Spartan commoners in the late fifth and early fourth centuries: the most notable are Endius the philo-Athenian,[154] an ephor in 413/12, and Lichas the Argive proxenos, who protested in vain against the first two Spartan-Persian treaties recorded by Thucydides in 412/11 but accepted the last one.[155] Although Xenophon names over 120 Spartans in the *Hellenica* (mostly military men of one sort or another), none except those already mentioned are known to have played important political roles of their own. What happened when an individual Spartan dared to oppose the settled policy of an Agesilaus is probably well illustrated by the story of Prothous, mentioned in Section *A* above.

This situation evidently continued down to the end of the 360s.[156] Then, Sparta's power having greatly declined, and Agesilaus being dead, Spartan kings could hardly hope to do great deeds, and for some time most of them were nonentities. Until the advent of the reforming kings,

---

[153] Callicratidas would clearly have liked to, but could not: see Xen., *HG* I vi.1 ff., esp. 4, 5–6 (he had to obey orders given him from Sparta), 7–11.

[154] Thuc. v 44.3; VIII 6.3; 12; 17.2; Diod. XIII 52.2–8.

[155] Thuc. VIII 43.3–4 and 52 (the treaties are in 18 and 37); contrast 84.5 (the treaty is in 58). For Lichas, see also v 22.2; 50.4; 76.3; VIII 39.2; 87.1; and Section *B* above, *ad fin.*

[156] When we find the Spartan Assembly giving *carte blanche* to King Agesilaus, then serving as a mercenary captain in Egypt (at the age of over 80), to decide Spartan policy in relation to that country: Plut., *Ages.* 37.9.

Agis IV and Cleomenes III, in the second half of the third century, Sparta only once figured prominently in Greek affairs, and this was during her futile revolt against Macedonian rule in 331 or 330 (see the end of Part vi of this Chapter). The Spartan general who led the revolt, and indeed the only Spartan who is ever mentioned as playing an important role in it, is King Agis III. The whole episode is commonly known as 'the revolt of Agis'.

As for the ephors, the fact that the names of very few of them are so much as mentioned in the literary sources ought to warn us against over-estimating their influence, important as their constitutional powers were during their year of office. After Chilon, in 556/5 or thereabouts (see n. 142 above), I cannot find the name of a single ephor for over a hundred years. Cleandridas, who accompanied King Pleistoanax on his invasion of Attica in 446 and went into exile with him (see Appendix XXVI), may well have been an ephor of that year, although the only source to say so explicitly seems to be the Souda (*s.v. ephoroi*; contrast the entry *s.v. deon*). Apart from the musical purist Ecprepes (Plut., *Agis* 10.7), and of course Sthenelaïdas, ephor either in 433/2 (eponymous?) or in 432/1, we seem to have no other names in the literary sources until we reach the period of the Peloponnesian war, for which we have a complete list of eponymous ephors for the years 432/1–404/3 in Xen., *HG* II iii.10 (an interpolated passage). A few of these men, and some other ephors of the same period, turn up in Thucydides' narrative or elsewhere (e.g. Sciraphidas or Phlogidas in Plut., *Lys.* 17.3); but with the possible exception of Leon (419/18), who may or may not be identical with one of the Leons of Thucydides (III 92.5; v 44.3; VIII 28.5; 61.2), not one of them seems to have been a man of real importance, apart from Brasidas (eponymous ephor in 431/30) and three or four ephors who were not eponymous but have already been mentioned: Xenares and Cleobulus (421/20), Endius (413/12) and perhaps Naucleidas (404/3). Between 403/2 and the late fourth century I can trace the names of only five ephors in the literary sources,[157] and only two of them are known to have been men of any consequence: Diphridas, ephor in 395/4 (Plut., *Ages.* 17.1) and a military commander in 391 (Xen., *HG* IV viii.21–2; cf. Diod. XIV 97.3), and Antalcidas the diplomat, ephor in 370/69 (Plut., *Ages.* 32.1). Inscriptions, and documents such as the Peace of Nicias (Thuc. v 19.2), enable us to add a few more names, but they are no more than names to us. The ephor's term of office was short, and a man who had once been ephor could not be re-elected. Moreover, there was no *cursus honorum* at Sparta, no other important State office giving political influence to which the ex-ephor could aspire, unless at the age of sixty or over he were elected to the Gerousia. I suggest that the prestige of the royal houses and the few

---

[157] The three not mentioned below are Lacratidas, Antiochus and Eteocles, who are remembered only for isolated utterances: Plut., *Lys.* 30.5; *Mor.* 217f; *Mor.* 235b and Ael., *VH* XI 7. I have not included Epitadeus, named only once, in Plut., *Agis* 5.3. I agree with Forrest, *HS* 137: if he ever existed at all, he must have lived well before the fourth century. But I believe that the story about him is probably a fiction.

families of greatest wealth and noblest birth is likely to have been far too strong for an ordinary Spartan to contend with, and that a young man who was eager for power and influence would have been most likely to attach himself to some royal or noble patron. Perhaps a king could usually bring about the election as ephor of a particular favourite, as Agis IV procured the election of Lysander in 243 (Plut., *Agis* 8.1).

Aristotle is illuminating on the nature of the Ephorate and its occupants: see esp. *Pol.* II 9, 1270ᵇ6–35; 10, 1272ᵃ27–31; 11, 1272ᵇ33–7. He sees the ephors as having power in the greatest affairs (1270ᵇ7–8); they are judges in important cases, deciding at their own discretion (*autognōmones*) and not according to written laws (1270ᵇ28–31; cf. Xen., *Lac. Pol.* VIII 4); the Ephorate is indeed 'too great and akin to a tyranny', and even the kings were compelled to pay court to its holders, thereby harming the constitution (1270ᵇ13–16; cf. 1265ᵇ40; Plato, *Laws* IV 712d). But the ephors are often poor men and therefore liable to be venal (1270ᵇ8–13); the choice of ephors is made 'from everyone' (1272ᵃ31–2); 'just anyone' can hold the office (*hoi tychontes*, 1270ᵇ29; cf. 1272ᵃ27–30, 1272ᵇ34–7). Similarly, in Plato's opinion the Ephorate 'comes close to a power conferred by lot' (*Laws* III 692a). All this points the contrast between the great powers of the office and the often insignificant men who held it. Even a powerful king like Agesilaus might be careful to make a great show of honouring the ephors, just as he made presents to newly elected members of the Gerousia (Plut., *Ages.* 4.5; *Mor.* 482d); but both parties must have well known in whose hands the real, long-term influence lay. An ephor who used his constitutional powers unwisely against an Agesilaus might find himself, after the expiry of his year of office, uncomfortably exposed to the retaliation of a man of far greater influence than himself.

I end this Part of the Chapter with a brief discussion of the puzzling statement in Hdts VI 56 that the Spartans had given to their kings the right 'to make war on whatever land they please', and that any Spartan opposing their exercise of this right was 'to be liable to the curse'. Is this a correct statement of Spartan constitutional law?

Busolt, *GSK* II 675–6, accepts the passage as true down to *c.* 506. On the other hand, Andrewes (in Gomme, *HCT* IV 74) insists that the words 'cannot mean that the king [note the singular] had a right to "declare" war on any land he chose, for Herodotos is speaking of his own time, when such decisions were conspicuously taken by the assembly'; and he adds a reference to his *GCS*, where there is a full collection of the remaining evidence (pp. 10–12), with no mention of Hdts VI 56. But if Herodotus is not to be taken to mean what he says in VI 56, what sense can we possibly give to his words? It is true that Herodotus is not the best of authorities on constitutional matters. But the interesting statement about the 'curse' to which anyone opposing the kings' right to levy war made himself liable strongly suggests that Herodotus is reproducing the Spartan opinion of his day—or at least one current of that opinion, whether or not it was accepted by all Spartiates. Yet there is no certain example to confirm this assertion, even in the late sixth century or the early fifth, let alone his own time, and in the late fifth and fourth centuries the right attributed to the kings, if it ever existed, certainly seems to have lapsed: Xenophon, indeed, says that the kings have the right 'to lead the army whithersoever the city despatches it' (*Lac. Pol.* xv 2), and he shows that the call-up was now the responsibility of the ephors (see the excellent account of Andrewes, GCS 10–11).

The two incidents described by Herodotus at Aegina (vi 50.2; 73.2) and Athens (86.1) may or may not be directly relevant to vi 56. In each case a people from whom a single Spartan king had demanded either the giving of hostages (Aegina) or their return (Athens) refused to comply, while admitting their liability in the case of a joint demand by both kings. In neither case, we can be sure, had there been an official decision by the Spartan Assembly concerning the hostages. (I may add that at the time in question Aegina was a member of the Peloponnesian League, but Athens could not have been: see Appendix XVII, Sections *A* and *B*.) The case can be argued in either of two ways. On the one hand, these incidents could be claimed as evidence that the two kings, *acting together*, had the right to demand the giving or the return of hostages on their own authority, and that this makes it easier to believe in their joint right to make war, as stated by Hdts vi 56. On the other hand, it could be argued that no question of *the kings' constitutional rights* is involved. The Aeginetans seem to be represented as saying that they would be liable to hand over the hostages if there had been a demand *by the Spartan State*, of which a visit by the two kings jointly, though not by one alone, could be *accepted as evidence* (50.2). This argument, however, had been adopted by the Aeginetans on the prompting of King Damaratus (50.3), who may simply have been suggesting *a bluff* that seemed certain to succeed; he could not foresee that it would be called by Cleomenes' taking extreme and unexpected measures. What really happened at Athens is not so clear: all we are told (86.1) is that the Athenians said they had received the hostages from both kings and did not feel obliged to return them to one only—nothing is said about a demand by the Spartan State as the decisive factor. The second of the two positions outlined above seems preferable to me, and I do not think we can be certain that in the early fifth century both kings had a constitutional right to demand hostages, although in view of Hdts vi 56 it would be unwise to deny that such a right can have existed.

I suggest (1) that Herodotus is in fact speaking of an ancient right possessed in constitutional theory (at least according to some Spartiates) *by both kings acting together* (a situation he may be illustrating, or may have believed himself to be illustrating, in *c.* 506);[158] but (2) that the Spartan

---

[158] Hdts v 74–5. It is Cleomenes who calls out the Peloponnesian League army (74.1), while Damaratus leads out the Spartan force (75.1). But of course Herodotus' narrative does not preclude an initial decision by the Spartan Assembly, as in v 63.2 and 64.1, where it is 'the Spartans' who send out first Anchimolius and then Cleomenes to drive out

decision taken as a result of the great fiasco of *c.* 506, that the two kings should no longer go out jointly on a military expedition (reported by Hdts v 75.2), made any further exercise of their ancient right very unlikely in practice, and (3) that henceforth they preferred not to exercise it, and in due course it became obsolete.

(vi)
The instability of Spartan foreign policy

It is seldom realised how unstable Spartan foreign policy was from the middle of the fifth century until the first or second decade of the fourth, when it came to be completely dominated by King Agesilaus II until his death in 361/60, by which time Sparta's League had disintegrated and her power was so much less than it had been in her great days that her actions were very much circumscribed and her capacity to act as she would have wished was severely reduced.

Sparta was far from being the 'monolithic' State she is so often innocently assumed to have been, especially by those whose attention is concentrated on the fifth-century evidence and who may therefore tend to neglect the detailed picture given by the most informative source we possess on Spartan political life: Xenophon, who really knew the Spartan scene from inside, at first hand. Of course Xenophon cannot be trusted to give the whole truth, even as far as it was known to him, in the way Thucydides or Herodotus can. It is well known that he altogether fails to mention—as subjects too painful for him to recall!—the liberation of the State of Messenia and its reconstruction as an independent entity, under Theban auspices, in 370–69; the building of the great fortified city of Megalopolis at about the same time, in a position commanding the main route from Laconia to Elis and unpleasantly close to the best way into the upper Messenian plain; even the formation of the anti-Spartan Second Athenian Confederacy in 378/7. Useful confirmatory evidence of accounts in other sources that show Sparta in a bad light can sometimes be extracted from his very silences, as when he fails to say what happened to Phoebidas in 382 (cf. Part v of this Chapter), or to describe the circumstances in which the oligarchy of the Thirty was set up at Athens in 404 (under the aegis of Lysander: see Lys. xii 71–6).

Spartan policy was subject to violent fluctuations. We shall see that Sparta's attitude to Athens underwent some interesting changes in the 460s and 440s (Chapter V, Parts ii–iii and vii–viii below). At the outbreak

---

Hippias, evidently as a result of a decision of the Assembly. Herodotus can even speak as if Cleomenes was acting solely on his own authority, not only in his attempt to stop the reforms of Cleisthenes in 508/7, when he went to Athens 'with no great force' (72.1) and may well have been acting on his own initiative (in the expectation that any resistance would be easily overcome), but even in the campaign against Argos that led to the great victory at Sepeia (vi 76.1 ff.), where the war must certainly have been voted by the Assembly.

of war in 432/1 no long-term strategy was devised, for the majority of Spartans expected a quick and easy victory.[159] (This was not so foolishly over-optimistic as it may seem to us, for the Spartan view was shared by virtually all Greece: see Chapter V, Part ix below.) But from as early as the spring of 431 they decided to send ambassadors to the Great King;[160] in the summer of 430 we actually hear of some of these being captured on their way to Persia (Thuc. II 67); and in 425/4 the Athenians intercepted a Persian, Artaphernes, on his way to Sparta with despatches from the King, who complained that he did not know what the Spartans wanted, as no two of their many embassies to him told the same story (Thuc. IV 50.1–2). This raises a question which, with hindsight, we can see to have been of the utmost importance, indeed decisive of the war, but on which Thucydides is strangely silent until his last Book: was Sparta prepared to pay the price Persia would demand for helping her to win the war? When, indeed, did Sparta discover what Persia's price was? Before we go into this question, however, we had better glance at the few pieces of evidence which give us some insight into the forces at work in Spartan foreign policy during the war.

When the Athenians tried to negotiate for peace in 430, the Spartans evidently proposed harsher terms than they would accept, and nothing came of it.[161] The next time peace negotiations took place was in 425, during the Pylos affair, and this time things were very different: the Spartans actually offered not only peace but a military alliance (*symmachia*, Thuc. IV 19.1), and may very well have hinted, as Thucydides (20.4) suggests, at a joint domination of Greece—the old 'dual hegemony', at the prospect of which Aristophanes was to lick his lips four years later.[162] I suggest that the remarkable change in the Spartan attitude since 430 was due not only to the unfavourable circumstances of the moment and their own failure in six years of war to get any nearer to the victory which had seemed so certain at the outset, but also to the fact that in 427/6 King Pleistoanax had returned to Sparta after nearly nineteen years of exile.[163] We shall presently find Pleistoanax conspicuously working for peace in 421, and his son Pausanias (as we saw in Part v of this Chapter) behaved in a remarkably generous way to the Athenian democrats in 403. And in the next Chapter (V, Part vii) we shall look back closely at the conduct of Pleistoanax in 446, and find that he *may* have deliberately let Athens off lightly, in order to stop the war and return to a condition of peace in which the 'dual hegemony' could be restored—as in fact it was, in theory, by the Thirty Years Peace.

[159] Brunt, SPSAW, gives an excellent account.
[160] As did Athens: Thuc. II 7.1 (with Gomme, *HCT* II 6–7). Cf. I 82.1.
[161] Thuc. II 59.2; cf. 65.2. The eponymous ephor for this year, 431/30, was Brasidas (Xen., *HG* II iii. 10), a strong opponent of peace in 423–2 (Thuc. V 16.1).
[162] Ar., *Peace* 1080–2 (Trygaeus), ending with the prospect that if Athens and Sparta made peace they could 'rule Greece together' (κοινῇ τῆς Ἑλλάδος ἄρχειν). This is one of the passages showing Aristophanes to have been a 'Cimonian' in attitude, and refuting the curious picture of his outlook presented by Forrest, AA: cf. Appendix XXIX.
[163] Thuc. V 16.1–3. See Gomme, *HCT* III 664.

The first major success Sparta had in the Ten Years war came in the second half of 424, with the achievement of Brasidas in getting through to the 'Thraceward' region and then procuring the secession from Athens of several of the cities there. After winning over Acanthus and Amphipolis, Brasidas made preparations to build triremes on the Strymon (where there was much good timber for shipbuilding), and appealed to Sparta for reinforcements. These were refused, partly, according to Thucydides (IV 108.6–7), because of 'jealousy among the leading men' (the *prōtoi*), and partly because the Spartans were anxious to get back the prisoners taken by the Athenians at Pylos (cf. v 15.1, where we again hear of the *prōtoi*) and put an end to the war. A golden opportunity was thereby lost, for a military force sent immediately could very probably have got through; later, the Spartan government changed its mind and twice tried to send reinforcements to Brasidas, in 423 and 422 (Thuc. IV 132.2; V 13.1), but failed each time, because King Perdiccas of Macedon had by then turned against Sparta (IV 128.5; 132.1), and he used his influence in Thessaly to stop the men getting through that country.

In 422–1 Thucydides (v 16.1–2) names Pleistoanax as the principal figure on the Spartan side working for peace; he is indeed the only person so named. Thucydides saw in this activity of Pleistoanax nothing but personal motives—very much as he allows virtually nothing but selfish objectives to Cleon and Brasidas, who had both wanted war, and Nicias, who like Pleistoanax was eager for peace.[164] Would Thucydides, like Xenophon (*HG* II iv.29) and other sources, have attributed the altogether admirable policy of Pleistoanax' son Pausanias in 403 to 'jealousy of Lysander'? In view of what we know of the rest of Pleistoanax' career and that of Pausanias, we may take leave to question Thucydides' opinion, and to suppose that Pleistoanax *may* also have thought Sparta's interests would be best served by reaching a permanent settlement with Athens.

In the autumn of 421, after Sparta had not only made peace with Athens but had concluded a treaty of defensive alliance with her (Thuc. v 22–4), a new board of ephors took office, 'some of whom', Thucydides says (v 36.1), 'were even opposed to the Peace'. He does not say explicitly that a majority were against the Peace, but he implies this when he speaks of Cleobulus and Xenares as 'those of the ephors who were *most* against it' (36.1), and again when he mentions 'Xenares and his associates' as being successful in inducing the Spartans (clearly the Assembly) to refuse to abandon the recent alliance with the Boeotians, which the Athenians claimed was a breach of Sparta's treaty with themselves (46.4). Certainly all Spartan ephors together were supposed to pursue the policy decided by the majority of them (see Xen., *HG* II iii.34; cf. iv.29).

Spartan policy from 421 until the occupation of Decelea in the spring

---

[164] Only καὶ τοὺς πολίτας παῦσαι, said of Nicias in 16.1 (line 18 *OCT*), suggests that any of the four might have been thinking of anything except his own personal interests. Cf. Gomme, *HCT* III 659–63.

of 413 is sometimes difficult to understand, and I cannot try to elucidate it here. I would only suggest that there seems to have been an uneasy balance between 'doves', among whom King Pleistoanax is likely to have been prominent, and 'hawks', who seem to have had no leader of great ability until the emergence of Lysander in 407.[165] When a king is needed for military operations, it is nearly always Agis II (427/6–c. 400) who is employed. Apart from leading a reinforcement of 'the oldest and young-est' in 418, which saw no action (Thuc. v 75.1), Pleistoanax is mentioned as commanding in only a single campaign: that against Mantinea in 421 (v 33). After that neither he nor his son Pausanias, who succeeded him in 408, is known to have been in charge of a Spartan army until after the final victory over Athens at Aegospotami, when Pausanias with the full Peloponnesian levy in the autumn of 405 marched into Attica, where Agis was already encamped at Decelea (Xen., *HG* ii ii.7).[166]

After two or three years of war, when the annual invasions of Attica failed to make the Athenians either surrender or come out and fight a pitched battle which could only have ended in a major Peloponnesian victory, intelligent Spartans must have begun to realise that the eventual outcome of the war depended above all on whether Sparta could obtain financial aid from Persia, sufficient to help her to win a naval war, success in which depended largely on money for paying crews. The issue was surely simple enough. The Great King must have wanted most of all to recover the territories in Asia Minor (if not the adjoining islands) which his ancestors had once ruled: for those, he might be expected to pay over gladly at least some hundreds of talents, which could be decisive in a naval war, and it was not impossible that he might be persuaded to supply a few score Phoenician triremes.[167] Now the Athenians would clearly never be willing to pay the King's price, at any rate unless they were on the very verge of defeat, as they were in 412/11[168]—although one may feel that they could probably have ensured at least Persian neutrality by surrendering to the King the mainland cities of Asia and those of Cyprus (as they were obliged to do later, in 387/6: see below), while insisting on the independence from Persia of the island states alone. Be that as it may, the Spartans could pay the King's price, as soon as they overcame any scruples they might have about selling the Asian Greeks to the King, after entering upon the war with the proclaimed intention of 'liberating

---

[165] Of the two alternative chronological schemes for the years 410–406, I follow the one advocated by (among others) Grote and Beloch. The whole question is admirably dealt with in a brief note by W. S. Ferguson, in *CAH* v 483–5.

[166] Pausanias and the main army were soon withdrawn: see Busolt, *GG* iii ii.1627–9 (esp. 1628 n. 2).

[167] On these, see Thuc. i 116.3; viii 46.1,5; 59; 78; 87.1–6; 88; 99; 108.1; 109.1. Cf. D. M. Lewis, 'The Phoen. Fleet in 411', in *Historia* 7 (1958) 392–7.

[168] See Thuc. viii 47.2 and 48 ff. (esp. 56.4); contrast 48.4 (Phrynichus' view). In spite of viii 81.2–3, I can only express astonishment that even such an intelligent Athenian as Thrasybulus should seriously suppose that Alcibiades might obtain help for Athens from Tissaphernes (81.1)—unless of course Athens surrendered to the King at least all the Greek cities on the mainland of Asia, if not the neighbouring islands as well.

the Hellenes'.[169] No wonder they wavered and kept changing their minds (cf. Thuc. IV 50.1–2). Evidently for nearly twenty years they were not prepared to pay the King's price; but by 412 their scruples had substantially disappeared, and they entered into a series of treaties with the Persians,[170] the first of which (Thuc. VIII 18) actually gave King Darius II all territory (*chōra*) and cities (*poleis*) which he or his ancestors had possessed —in other words, the whole Greek area of Asia Minor, many of the Aegean islands, Thrace, Macedon, Thessaly and most of Greece north of the Isthmus! The second treaty (VIII 37) was not quite so extreme, and the third (of early 411, VIII 58) was decidedly more reticent: its first clause was that the territory (*chōra*) of the King *in Asia* was to belong to the King. The word 'cities' was tactfully avoided, but in its absence there would be no doubt, in the King's mind at any rate, that the word 'territory' was meant to include the cities, and that the Asian Greeks were being handed over to Persia. That the Spartans accepted this interpretation for the immediate present is proved by the fact that even Lichas, who had strongly objected to the two earlier treaties (Thuc. VIII 43.3–4; 52), said, after the conclusion of the third one, that 'the Milesians and the rest in the King's country[171] ought to show a reasonable submission to Tissaphernes [the satrap at Sardis] and pay him court until the war should be happily settled'—an attitude which bitterly offended the Milesians (84.5). (See the last paragraph of Appendix VII for the possibility—it no more—that the Spartans, or some of them, intended, when the war with Athens was over, to claim that they had never meant to hand over to the King the Greek *cities* [*poleis*] of Asia, and to adduce in support o their claim the omission of any reference to the *poleis* from the definitive treaty of early 411.)

At first, owing to the attitude of Tissaphernes,[172] Persian subsidies to the Peloponnesians were irregular and unsatisfactory, and the Spartans were obliged to levy contributions from their Greek allies—32 talents from Rhodes alone late in 412, according to Thucydides (VIII 44.4). However, the allegation in Diodorus XIV 10.2 that at the end of the war the Spartans were levying tribute on those they conquered, amounting to over 1,000 talents a year, is likely to be a considerable exaggeration. The situation improved when the Peloponnesians could deal mainly with the satrap of north-west Asia Minor, Pharnabazus;[173] but it was only in the spring of 407 that things became entirely satisfactory from the Spartan point of view, on the arrival of Cyrus, the King's younger son,

---

[169] See Thuc. I 139.3; IV 85.1; and other passages cited in my CAE 3 n. 3.

[170] Thuc. VIII 18; 37; 58: see the parallel texts in Bengston, *SVdA* II 200–2 (with bibliography).

[171] The words are ἐν τῇ βασιλέως (χώρᾳ understood). In Thucydides, both here and in VIII 43.3 (see esp. line 19 *OCT*), Lichas certainly uses the expression 'the King's territory' in such a way as to include its Greek cities.

[172] See Thuc. VIII 46; 56.2; 57; 78; 83.2–3; 85.2–3; 87.1, 2–4; 99; Xen., *HG* I v.9.

[173] See Thuc. VIII 80.2; 99; Xen., *HG* I i.23–6; iii.5–7, 8–9 and ff.

with 500 talents and more on which the Spartans could draw and instructions to give them as much help as they needed.[174] It happened that the
very gifted and unscrupulous Lysander had become Spartan navarch
just before this, and he and Cyrus evidently got on very well indeed.
Persian funds now flowed freely through Lysander's hands. The total
amount of these subsidies received by the Spartans during the Ionian war
is put at 5,000 talents or more by Andocides (III 29) and Isocrates (VIII
97); but this may be a pure guess and we have no means of ascertaining
the real total. Lysander also now began to devise an imperialistic strategy
which proved highly successful in the short run, even if it ultimately
brought great discredit on Sparta: he got together small groups of
the most influential citizens in the Greek cities of Asia and the islands,
promising to give them control of their cities, and urging them to organise
themselves politically for the seizure of power and the final defeat of
Athens.[175]

In spring 406 there arrived at the Peloponnesian naval headquarters
at Ephesus Lysander's successor as navarch, Callicratidas, who had very
different ideas about how the political and financial side of the war should
be managed. (His appointment may well have been due to the efforts of
those Spartans who were dismayed by the new imperialism of Lysander.)
There was an open quarrel between the two men, and Lysander, before
he left for home, actually handed back to Cyrus the remainder of the
Persian money he had left, so that Callicratidas, to his disgust, had to go
and dance attendance on Cyrus to obtain pay for his men.[176] He made no
secret of the fact that he disapproved of 'toadying to barbarians to get
money', and he announced his intention of trying to reconcile Athens and
Sparta if he returned home safely[177]—as he never did, being killed at the
battle of Arginusae in the autumn of 406. Callicratidas also evidently
disapproved of Lysander's policy of promising control of the 'liberated'
cities of the Athenian empire to small oligarchic groups. But he did not
succeed in making any significant change in Spartan policy: he had his
orders, and willy-nilly he had to carry them out (Xen., *HG* I vi.5–6). His
navarchy was only a brief interlude, scarcely interrupting the development
of Lysander's plans.

At the urgent request of Lysander's influential friends, the Spartans
now decided to do something they had never done before: to entrust
the superior command of the Peloponnesian fleet (evidently with a very
large measure of personal control over policy and operations) to Lysander,[178] even though he could not legally be appointed navarch again and
served continuously from 406/5 to the end of the war in 404 in theory as
epistoleus—literally 'Secretary', but 'Vice-admiral' would be more appro-

---

[174] See Xen., *HG* I iv.2–3 and ff.; v.1–7; II i.7, 11–12, 14–15; Diod. XIII 70.3; 104.3–4;
Plut., *Lys.* 4; 9.1 ff.
[175] Diod. XIII 70.4; Plut. *Lys.* 5.5–8; 6.1; cf. Xen., *HG* I vi.4. And see below.
[176] Xen., *HG* I vi.1 ff., esp. 2, 4, 7, 10, 11; Plut., *Lys.* 6.
[177] Xen., *HG* I vi.7; Plut., *Lys.* 6.8.
[178] Xen., *HG* II i.6–7; Diod. XIII 100.7–8; Plut., *Lys.* 7.2–3.

priate, as the man who held that office was nominally second-in-command to the navarch. In that capacity Lysander finished the war and ruthlessly carried through the imperialistic policy he had so carefully planned, installing small oligarchies in the cities that had formerly been part of the Athenian empire. These puppet governments, usually known as 'decarchies' (although specific evidence for as few as ten men being appointed to govern any particular State is scanty), were of course dependent upon the provision by Sparta of a garrison under a harmost, and Sparta could therefore rely upon their loyalty.[179] The only example of these narrow oligarchies about which we have detailed information is the 'Thirty' at Athens, created at an Assembly at which Lysander himself was present and threatened the Athenians with punishment for a technical breach of the peace treaty if they did not act as he and his friends desired.[180]

This policy, of which Lysander was the architect, was drastically revised in (I believe) 403, when Sparta withdrew her support for the 'decarchies' and gave the cities more freedom in the choice of their constitutions.[181] The date of the general change is disputed,[182] but there is no doubt at all that in relation to Athens it was 403: the momentous events of that year have already been noticed in Part v of this Chapter. As we saw there, the final restoration of democracy at Athens seems to have taken place in September or October 403. King Pausanias was brought to trial at Sparta for the settlement he had been instrumental in effecting at Athens: this will have been in the Spartan year 403/2, for the ephors changed annually in the autumn (see Appendix XII). It appears that Pausanias and his followers were now temporarily in the ascendant, for all five ephors (of 403/2) are said to have voted for the king's acquittal (Paus. III v.2). Evidently at the election of ephors in 403 Pausanias and his faction had swept the board.

Sparta was now more powerful than she had ever been; and Xenophon, writing some years after, could say that about 400 B.C. she 'ruled over all the Greeks' (*Anab.* VI vi.9)—an exaggeration, but an understandable one.

At this point I wish to step aside for a moment and glance at a recent article (Strasburger, TPSDA) which presents a very sympathetic view of Spartan policy in the late fifth century and even supposes that Thucydides himself accepted it as morally superior to that of Athens (cf. Chapter I,

[179] See on the whole subject Parke, DSSE, esp. 50–63, 76–8; Bockisch, *op. cit.* in n. 31 to Part iii above.

[180] The vital text is Lys. XII 71–6, esp. 74; see also Diod. XIV 3.5–7; Plut., *Lys.* 15.2,6; and cf. Xen., *HG* II iii.13–14; iv.28–9.

[181] Confusion ensued in many places: see Xen., *HG* III iv.2,7, etc.

[182] R. E. Smith, 'Lysander and the Spartan Empire', in *CP* 43 (1948) 145–56, argues for 397; Parke, DSSE 53–4, for 403–2. I have been convinced that the true date is late 403 or early 402 by a paper of Andrewes, to be published shortly in *Phoenix*, which he has been kind enough to show me. He points out, rightly, that in some if not most of the Greek cities of Asia it was Tissaphernes rather than the Spartans who first deposed Lysander's friends. [See now Phoenix 25 (1971) 206–26.]

Part ii above). This thesis, mistaken as it is, deserves attention, if only because of the eminence of its proponent. The most serious fault in Strasburger's paper is his failure to take proper account of what happened from 412 onwards (and especially in 407–4), when Sparta acted in the most blatantly selfish manner towards the cities which she had won over from Athens, and to which she had promised 'freedom': as we have just seen, in return for lavish Persian subsidies she placed all the Asiatic Greeks under the Persian yoke, and Lysander installed small and oppressive oligarchies in many cities, including Athens herself. This alone should be sufficient to show that the Spartan promise to 'liberate' the allies of Athens was mere propaganda, except in so far as it happened to coincide with Sparta's own selfish interests; yet Strasburger can take that promise seriously and even say that Thucydides accepted it as 'predominantly honest' (TPSDA 37–8 = 527)—mainly, it seems, on the strength of the superficially attractive speech of Brasidas to the Acanthians (IV 85–7). But let us look at how Sparta actually treated Acanthus and the other cities (including Amphipolis, Scione and Torone) which came over to her during Brasidas' campaign in the 'Thraceward' region. By the Peace of Nicias Sparta conceded that Acanthus itself, with five other cities, should pay tribute to Athens (Thuc. v 18.5; see Gomme, *HCT* III 669–70); she actually undertook to surrender Amphipolis outright to Athens (Thuc. v 18.5; 21); and concerning Torone (already retaken by Athens, v 3.2–4) and Scione (still under siege, IV 130.7 ff.; cf. v 32.1) she consented to the Athenians' taking 'whatever decisions they pleased' (v 18.8)—a 'base betrayal' of Scione in particular, as Gomme says (*HCT* III 674), adding that 'it is indeed remarkable that Sparta retained in the Thracian district and acquired in Ionia any reputation at all for either sincerity or reliability'. The facts Thucydides carefully narrates speak loudly enough: they needed no underlining by him, although he can sometimes make a sly comment (too subtle, perhaps, for most of his readers), as when he explains in a deceptively casual way in IV 81.2 exactly how Sparta benefited from the 'just and moderate' behaviour of Brasidas in the 'Thraceward' region. The passage has already been discussed (Chapter I, Part ii): it shows Sparta cynically using the cities that had come over to her as pawns to be exchanged with the Athenians for things Sparta herself wanted. And when Thucydides goes on to say (in IV 81.3) that Brasidas, 'having achieved the reputation of being a good man in all respects, left behind him the confident expectation that the others would be just such men as he was', the natural inference is that this expectation was disappointed.

For Strasburger, it is above all through the medium of their speeches that Thucydides depicts the Spartans as 'sympathischer als die Athener' (TPSDA 37 = 526): he mentions in particular their speech at Athens in 424 (IV 17–20: the last sentence of this hardly suits Strasburger's picture!) and, again, the speech of Brasidas to the Acanthians; also, though with less emphasis, the speech of Archidamus in I 80.1–85.2. But Archidamus failed to persuade the Spartans, and the fine sentiments of Brasidas were, as we have seen, falsified by Spartan official policy. And Strasburger ignores the one speech which we are entitled to accept as fully representative of Spartan opinion (because the great majority of Spartans immediately voted in accordance with it): that of Sthenelaïdas (1 86), than whom no one in Thucydides speaks in a more bellicose way or concentrates more exclusively on the selfish interests of his own city, in contempt of all other considerations! Thucydides did not need to spell out any further the selfish motives of Sparta: both the speech of Sthenelaïdas and the facts the historian himself narrates tell us the essential things we need to know about Spartan policy down to 411; and what happened after that, especially under Lysander, needed no comment, and would probably have received none, had Thucydides lived to finish his History.

I cannot deal here except in the briefest outline with the subsequent developments in Spartan foreign policy, but clearly it soon became expansionist and aggressive once more. First, Elis was attacked by a Spartan army under King Agis II, over a period of two or three years (probably 402–400: see Beloch, *GG* 1² ii.185–6; 111² i.19 n.1), and disciplined. Next, the Greek cities of Asia which she had earlier betrayed to Persia implored Sparta for help, and from 400 onwards she began to operate in Asia Minor once more. This was another striking reversal of Spartan policy, but it was natural enough, now that the Athenian empire had collapsed and Sparta no longer needed Persian subsidies. There may have been strong support of this policy at Sparta: it was certainly backed by King Agesilaus II, who had succeeded his half-brother Agis in (I believe) 400/399, and who in 396 commanded in person in Asia, seeing himself in the role of a new Agamemnon.[183] Agesilaus was egged on by Lysander, who had been instrumental in having him appointed king and was eager to re-establish Spartan control of the Greeks of Asia through the oligarchies which had proved so useful earlier but had been overthrown when the ephors withdrew Sparta's support (in 403–2). But although Agesilaus soon discarded Lysander as a personal rival (see Part v of this Chapter), the imperialistic aims that Sparta was now pursuing became more and more evident. There are good reasons for supposing that in the early 390s she was endeavouring to increase her influence in central and northern Greece, and developing the policy of expansion there, which she had begun with the foundation of Heraclea Trachinia in 426.[184]

[183] See Xen., *HG* 111 iv.2–3 and other sources.
[184] Thuc. 111 92–3. Andrewes (see n. 182 above) discusses these developments. He adds much to the account of the origins of the Corinthian war given by S. Perlman in *CQ* 58 = n.s. 14 (1964) 64–81. That there was a Spartan garrison in Pharsalus in 395 (Diod. xiv 82.5–6) is an important fact which is seldom noticed. As Andrewes emphasises, Sparta's natural way of expansion was by land; the pursuit of naval hegemony in the Aegean was an aberration, successful only over short periods when the interests of Sparta and Persia happened to coincide.

The result, in 395, was the so-called Corinthian war, in which a somewhat depleted Peloponnesian League was opposed by a quadruple alliance of Athens, Thebes, Argos and Corinth. In 394 the Spartans were obliged to recall Agesilaus from Asia. He spoke of returning there, and (fired by the example of Xenophon's 'Ten Thousand') did not yet abandon his intention of making vast conquests in Persian territory—a task which would in reality have been well beyond his reach. He mismanaged naval affairs (entrusted, exceptionally, to his control) by appointing as navarch the incompetent Peisander, his wife's brother (Xen., *HG* III iv.27–9; Plut., *Ages.* 10.11); and the command of the sea now passed out of Spartan hands, making any further dreams of conquest in Asia quite out of the question. After the naval battle of Cnidus in August 394, won by the able Athenian Conon at the head of a Persian fleet, the Spartan 'empire' in the Aegean collapsed,[185] Athens rebuilt her walls, and for a time Sparta lost much of her dominance. In 395/4, too, King Pausanias was again put on trial by his enemies: convinced that he had no chance of being acquitted this time, he fled to Tegea and was condemned to death in his absence. It is interesting to note that the charges against him included not only the mismanagement of a campaign at Haliartus in 395, in which Lysander was killed, but also 'letting the Athenian demos escape after he had got it into his power in the Peiraeus' (Xen., *HG* III v.25), in 403!

During much of the 390s, and conspicuously during most of the 380s, 370s and 360s, it was King Agesilaus who clearly dominated Spartan counsels.[186] He was 'the most influential man in the city' (*dynatōtatos*, Xen., *Ages.* VII 2), and could be called 'the greatest and most distinguished man alive' (Theopomp., *FGrH* 115 F 321, *ap.* Plut., *Ages.* 10.9–10). In his imperialism he was the heir of Lysander, but there is little evidence of hostility on his part to Athens, and probably after 394 his concern was almost entirely with mainland Greece, Thebes above all, so that he did not need to regard Athens as an irreconcilable enemy. Even writers who otherwise admired Agesilaus remark on the fact that he had a passion for gratifying and rewarding his friends in other cities (Xen., *Ages.* I 17–19; II 21–2; XI 12; Plut., *Ages.* 5.1–2), and that when they were exiled he caused much trouble by his eagerness to restore them and put them in control of affairs (Isocr. V 86–7; *Epist.* IX 13–14: good examples of this

---

[185] See esp. Xen., *HG* IV viii.1–2. There is an able treatment of this period by R. Seager, 'Thrasybulus, Conon and Athenian Imperialism, 396–386 B.C.', in *JHS* 87 (1967) 95–115.

[186] There is no reason to think he lost this position while he was physically incapacitated from commanding in the field, from late 377 to 371 (Xen., *HG* v iv.58; VI iv.18; Plut., *Ages.* 27.1 ff.). No military activities on his part are known after 377 until 370 (Xen., *HG* VI v.10, cf. 4–5), but he is prominent in 371, before Leuctra (iii.19–20; iv.1–3; with Plut., *Ages.* 28.1 ff.). I believe that Smith, OAFP, somewhat exaggerates the extent of *successful* opposition at Sparta to the foreign policy of Agesilaus. In particular, he is mistaken (OAFP 277–8) about the peace congress at Sparta early in 391; contrast V. Martin, 'Le traitement de l'hist. diplom. dans la trad. litt. du IVe siècle av. J.-C.' in *Mus. Helv.* I (1944) 13–30; 'Sur une interprét. nouv. de la Paix du Roi', in *Mus. Helv.* 6 (1949) 127–39; Seager, *op. cit.* (in n. 185 above) 104–8; Beloch, *GG* III² i.80–4. The terms offered at Sparta represent necessary concessions offered to Athens and Thebes; the Asiatic Greeks were still to be surrendered to the King (see Seager, *op. cit.* 105 and n. 92).

habit can be found in Xen., *HG* v 1.34; ii.8–10 and iii.10–17, 21–5; vi v.10–21; *Ages.* ii 21, 23 etc.).

The Corinthian war dragged on until 387/6, when there was a 'general peace' (*koinē eirēnē*), usually known as 'the King's Peace' (because it was dictated by the Great King), but sometimes as 'the Peace of Antalcidas', after the very able Spartan who negotiated it with the King.[187] This peace marked a stage in Greek history second in importance only to the fall of the Athenian empire in 405/4. Sparta in effect forced her opponents, including Athens, to agree to abandon the Greeks of the Asiatic mainland and Cyprus to the Great King; the other Greek cities were to be autonomous.[188] This gave Sparta everything she really wanted, above all the right to break up the Boeotian League (an act on which Agesilaus had particularly set his heart), and the empire which Athens was just beginning to re-create in the Aegean, and to insist on the reconstitution (under an oligarchy, of course) of Corinth, which (under a democracy) had been absorbed by Argos.[189]

The King's Peace is perfectly summed up in Agesilaus' defence of it, in a remark quoted by Plutarch in three different works:[190] the Spartans were not medising, rather the Medes were laconising! The Peace, in other words, was in Sparta's interests above all, and the King was giving her what she most wanted. It is best seen, indeed, as a 'package deal', in which, in return for Sparta's forcing on the other Greeks, including Athens, the acknowledgment of his supremacy over the Asiatic Greeks which the King desired most of all, the King proclaimed the absolute independence of all individual Greek cities, which was of far greater concern to Sparta than to him, for Sparta's aims, as we have seen, were to break up the powerful Boeotian League, the slowly re-forming Athenian empire, and the union of Argos and Corinth. The terms of the King's *Diktat* on which the Peace was based, carefully drafted so as to prescribe the autonomy of 'the Greek *cities*', enabled Sparta to achieve all three of these aims—quite 'legitimately', once the peace terms had been generally accepted. If the King's Peace really represents, for Greece, 'einen der tiefsten Tiefpunkte aller Zeiten', as Bengtson has put it (*GG*⁴ 271), it is not so much because the Peace was dictated by the Great King as because it was designed by Sparta, which had nothing good to offer to the Greek states. Callicratidas in 406 had made indignant protests at Lysander's policy of co-operation with Persia against Athens (see above, and n. 177). But we hear of no similar objection by any Spartan to the King's Peace— the nearest thing is an isolated remark attributed by Xenophon (*HG* v

---

[187] Antalcidas was the personal friend of at least one Persian satrap, Ariobarzanes (Xen., *HG* v i.28), and he seems to have made a great impression on King Artaxerxes II (Plut., *Artox.* 22.1–2). It was he who negotiated with Tiribazus the abortive peace of 392/1 (Xen., *HG* iv viii.12–16; cf. n. 186 above), and in 371 he was apparently once more involved in negotiations with the King (vi iii.12).

[188] Xen., *HG* v i.28–36 (esp. 31); cf. Diod. xiv 110.2–5 (esp. §3). Lemnos, Imbros and Scyros were to be subject to Athens.

[189] Griffith, UCA, is particularly useful on these events.

[190] Plut., *Ages.* 23.4 = *Artox.* 22.4 = *Mor.* 213b (= *Apophth. Lac., Ages.* 61).

i.17) to the navarch Teleutias, the half-brother of Agesilaus, shortly before the King's Peace, in praise of abstention from 'toadying to Greek or barbarian for the sake of pay'. As early as 392 Sparta had been willing to surrender to the King the Greek cities on the mainland of Asia (Xen., *HG* IV viii.14); but the peace which Antalcidas then negotiated with Tiribazus proved abortive,[191] and it was only in 387/6 that the Spartans, by joining in the oaths of the Peace which Antalcidas now successfully carried through, formally abandoned the Greek cities of Asia to the Great King. This may well have been a blow to the aspirations of Agesilaus in regard to Asia Minor; but the Peace as a whole was so remarkably advantageous to Sparta that we need not be surprised that Agesilaus, who placed the selfish interests of Sparta above every other consideration (see Xen., *HG* V ii.32 etc.), welcomed the Peace and tried to justify it, as we have already seen. Not even his admirer Xenophon can try to pretend that he was opposed to it: Xenophon's treatment of this delicate issue in his panegyric of the king (*Ages.* II 21) is carefully evasive. It would be futile to try to make Agesilaus into a 'Panhellenist',[192] nor is there any good cause for suspecting that he and Antalcidas were not pursuing substantially the same policy, at least between 392 and 383. Only Plutarch (*Ages.* 23.3; *Mor.* 213b) asserts antagonism between the two men, and there is every reason to suppose that he is drawing a false inference from Antalcidas' *later* criticism of Agesilaus' insane aggressiveness towards Thebes (Plut., *Ages.* 26.3; *Mor.* 189f, 213f, 217e).[193] Agesilaus' epigram (quoted at the beginning of this paragraph), stressing that Persia's peace served Sparta's best interests, affords conclusive proof of his acquiescence in the terms arranged by Antalcidas.

After the King's Peace Sparta, her fortunes at the highest level they had ever reached, showed herself at her most aggressive, and her policy, under Agesilaus' leadership, was consistent. The crowning folly was the occupation of the Cadmeia of Thebes and, when that city was liberated at the end of 379, the unrelenting pressure which Sparta exercised upon Thebes, under the influence of Agesilaus, right down to 371, when the battle of Leuctra marked the beginning of Sparta's great decline. The pious Xenophon saw the liberation of Thebes and the battle of Leuctra as divine retribution upon Sparta for her disgraceful seizure of the Cadmeia in time of peace (*HG* V iv.1; cf. Isocr. IV 122–8; Diod. XV 1.2–5; 28.2;

---

[191] For some recent treatments of this peace, see n. 186 above.

[192] Cf. Xen., *Ages.* VII 4 (φιλέλληνα) to 7. Isocr., *Epist.* IX (*ad Archid.*) 11 is, I think, the only text that can be quoted in favour of such a view, and it is surely worthless. Only until *c.* 394 may Agesilaus be said to have had 'Panhellenist' sentiments, of a sort (cf. Plut., *Mor.* 191ab, 211ef). Xenophon, in his panegyric of Agesilaus (*Ages.* II 28–9), says that one of the king's motives for taking mercenary service under the rebel king of Egypt, in extreme old age, was 'to set the Greeks in Asia free once more'; but any such objective, even if professed, could have little direct connection with the Egyptian revolt. More relevant, I suggest, is the end of Xenophon's sentence (II 29): Agesilaus wanted to punish the King of Persia, in particular for telling Sparta to give up her claim to Messenia!

[193] See Smith, OAFP 277 and n. 6; and cf. Grote, *HG* VIII 348–50. (All that can be said in favour of Agesilaus has been said by Grote, *Id.* 347–8.)

and other sources). Actually, even Leuctra need not have spelt the end of Sparta's hegemony *in the Peloponnese*. That could hardly have come about but for a combination of four factors: the eagerness of the Messenians to be free, Spartan *oliganthrōpia* (the decline in the number of Spartan citizens), the implacable aggressiveness of Sparta for more than twenty years towards Thebes, and the repressive policy which Sparta had long conducted (more openly than ever under Agesilaus) towards other Peloponnesian states, the Arcadians in particular. As I shall briefly explain, it took a conjunction of these four factors to bring Sparta down to the level of a second-rate power.

Of the Messenians we have already spoken sufficiently (see Part i of this Chapter). The decline in the number of full Spartan citizens had long been continuing: by the time of Leuctra the total number of Spartiates was not more than 1,000–1,200, a dangerously small body to form the governing class of such a large area as Laconia and Messenia.[194] When 400 Spartiates fell at Leuctra, out of 700 engaged in the battle (Xen., *HG* VI iv.15), something like a third of the whole male citizen population was wiped out at a blow. Even so, it required a combination of our two other factors to bring about the expeditions of Epaminondas in 370/69 and later, which freed Messenia and removed from Sparta's control the bulk of the Arcadians, who formed themselves into a league, centred on Megalopolis, newly built and strongly fortified. Thebes was, so to speak, a very 'land-locked' power, interested mainly in keeping a firm control over the rest of Boeotia. She had thought of launching a counter-attack against Sparta immediately after her victory at Leuctra, but had easily been dissuaded by her ally, Jason of Pherae (Xen., *HG* VI iv.22–5). She had never yet ventured on an expedition deep into the Peloponnese, nor is there any reason to suppose that she would ever have done so had she not received an urgent invitation from certain Peloponnesians: at least the Arcadians, Argives and Eleians,[195] who in 370 went first to Athens, begging for assistance against Sparta, and when they were rebuffed there, went on to Thebes, which duly received them into alliance with Boeotia. Thebes had been exasperated by the constant attempts made by Sparta to break up her Boeotian League, the instrument through which her control over the rest of Boeotia was exercised, and to inflict as much damage upon herself as possible. This made Thebes ready to listen to an appeal for intervention in the Peloponnese. And the appeal came because many of the Peloponnesians were tired of the close control that Sparta had long been exercising over their internal as well as external affairs. The kings of the Agiad house in recent years seem to have realised that this policy was a mistaken one, but Agesilaus was intent upon it, and he was able to carry the majority of the Spartans with him. Even after Leuctra he was up to his

---

[194] See Appendix XVI.

[195] Diod. xv 62.3; cf. Dem. xvi 12, speaking of 'all the Peloponnesians'. Xenophon, characteristically, fails to mention the appeals to Athens and Thebes, and gives no reason for the arrival of the Boeotians (*HG* VI v.19, 22 ff.).

old tricks, interfering in 370 in the internal affairs of Arcadia (Xen., *HG* VI v.3–5, 10 ff; Plut., *Ages.* 30.7)—the last straw, which produced the successful appeal to Thebes. The nemesis that overtook Sparta was of her own making.

The last episode in the fourth century in which Sparta played a prominent role, namely her revolt against Alexander the Great in 331 or 330, is of great interest: it can be seen as a final verdict by the other Greeks on Sparta's evil record as a hegemon in the past.

Sparta had taken no part in the campaign against Philip II led by Athens and Thebes which ended at Chaeroneia in 338. One important reason for her abstention may have been the haughty attitude she is later said to have adopted towards accepting Macedonian hegemony in the League of Corinth: according to the Spartans themselves, it was their ancestral custom not to follow others but to lead them (Arr., *Anab.* 1 i.2). But in 331 (or 330) Sparta rose in revolt against Macedonian rule, under the leadership of King Agis III.[196] It is worth looking carefully at the list of allies who followed Sparta's call, and at such information as we have about the numbers involved on either side. According to Justin (XII i.6 ff.), 'nearly all Greece' fought with Sparta, and Diodorus (XVII 62.7) speaks of 'most of the Peloponnesians and some of the others' as supporting her. In reality, however, the list of Sparta's allies whom there is good reason to accept as such is meagre: it includes only Elis, the Achaean cities (except Pellene, held by a pro-Macedonian tyrant), and some of the Arcadians, including Tegea but not the chief Arcadian city, Megalopolis. There were rumours of support from Thessalians and Perrhaebians and others (see Aeschin. III 165–7; Dein. I, *c. Dem.*, 34; Curt. VI i.20), but there is no reason to think it ever materialised. The army of Agis is said by Diodorus (XVII 62.7) to have amounted to at least 20,000 infantry and about 2,000 cavalry: of these, some 10,000 are likely to have been mercenaries.[197] It seems, then, that Agis' army contained not many more than 12,000 citizen hoplites. Against him, Alexander's general Antipater is said to have mustered not less than 40,000 men (Diod. XVII 63.1).

Now when starting for Asia early in 334 Alexander had left with Antipater a force of 12,000 infantry and 1,500 cavalry (Diod. XVII 17.5): these, it is generally believed, were all Macedonians (see Beloch, *GG* III² ii.325–6). Four sets of reinforcements (three of them large ones) had to be sent to Alexander from Europe between the winter of 334/3 and the end of 331: about 9,800 (or perhaps some 12,000) of these were Mace-

---

[196] Modern writers (e.g. E. Badian, 'Agis III' in *Hermes* 95 [1967] 170-92) often speak of the whole affair as if it were due to a series of personal decisions by Agis. This may not be far from the truth, although there must have been at least one vote of the Spartan Assembly, declaring war. Cf. Part v of this Chapter.

[197] This is the figure given by Dein. I (*c. Dem.*) 34. According to Diod. XVII 48.1, Agis had recruited 8,000 of the Greek mercenaries who had fought for the Persians at Issus in 333, and he had no doubt obtained further mercenaries in Crete in 332; cf. Diod. XVII 48.2.

donians, and another 13,730 or so were allies (Greeks and Thracians) or mercenaries. (See Appendix XXX on these reinforcements and other problems of the revolt of Agis.) Even if we allow these forces to have consisted mainly[198] of Macedonians who had been too young to be called up in 334 (and must therefore be considered as additional to the original 13,500 left behind), they must have been stiffened by drafts from Antipater's troops, and Antipater therefore will surely not have had more than 12,000 Macedonians *at the very most* under his command in the final battle against Sparta and her allies near Megalopolis, even if he left Macedonia itself entirely denuded of effective troops. He must, then, have raised very large additional forces, amounting to 28,000 or more. Where did they come from?

The fullest recent account of the revolt of Agis,[199] which gives Sparta and her king very respectful treatment,[200] makes no attempt to answer this question and indeed fails even to ask it, although the answer is given explicitly by Diodorus and is indeed one of the few facts of major historical importance we know about these events. Antipater, we are told,[201] 'built up an army of over 40,000—far more than the best that Agis *and the Greeks* could now do' [my italics]. The truth, revealed by Diodorus (XVII 63.1), is that Antipater's additional troops—outnumbering by themselves Agis' whole army, including his mercenaries—were raised *from Alexander's Greek 'allies'* of the League of Corinth! Even if we suppose that Diodorus is speaking loosely, and that as many as 5,000 of Antipater's reinforcements of 28,000 or more were Thracians, Illyrians or the like (see Appendix XXX), the fact remains that Sparta's revolt was crushed by an army which is likely to have contained roughly twice as many Greek citizen soldiers as the 12,000 or so who fought for and with Sparta. This puts the revolt of Agis in a very different light.

Although many Greek cities were already chafing under the Macedonian yoke, only a small handful were prepared to rebel against it under Sparta's leadership; far more preferred to curry favour with their new masters by helping them to crush Sparta. The list of those who followed Athens' lead in the final struggle for liberation from Macedon, during the Lamian war of 323–2, is very much longer than that of Agis' allies. Many Greeks had long had good reason to hate or fear Sparta: Philip II had

---

[198] Thus P. A. Brunt, 'Alexander's Macedonian Cavalry', in *JHS* 83 (1963), at p. 37. But even if we accept Brunt's very probable theory of a great increase in the Macedonian population, can we really suppose that anything like 3,300—let alone 5,800—young Macedonians (see Appendix XXX, §2 [*a*]) reached military age *in a single year*, between Alexander's departure early in 334 and the beginning of 333, and another 6,500 (*Id.*, §2 [*d*]) in 333–1? I would guess that several thousand of the 3,300 (or 5,800) and 6,500 came from Antipater's original 13,500.

[199] By Badian, *op. cit.* (in n. 196 above).

[200] As in the statement (*op. cit.* 172), 'An experienced soldier and king of Sparta would judge more rationally than an Athenian politician'—a mere Demosthenes! One remembers that even more 'experienced soldier and king of Sparta', Agesilaus, whose judgment is well exemplified in Xen., *HG* v ii.32; iv.32; and in his famous epigram expressing satisfaction with the King's Peace, quoted above.

[201] By Badian, *op. cit.* 184.

adroitly appealed to these feelings (see e.g. Isocr. v 74–5; Dem. v 18; VI 9, 13–15, 19–27; XVIII 18–19, 64, 295; XIX 10–11, 260–2, 303–6, 310; Paus. IV xxviii.2; v xx.9–10; VIII xxx.6). Two centuries later the great Arcadian historian, Polybius (XVIII xiv.1–7, 15), could warmly defend those whom Demosthenes (see e.g. XVIII 295) had denounced as 'traitors' to Greece, especially leading Arcadians and Messenians, who (says Polybius) 'by bringing Philip into the Peloponnese and humbling the Spartans' brought liberty to the Peloponnesians. Alexander continued Philip's successful policy. When he heard the news of the battle of Megalopolis, he is said to have referred to it as 'a battle of mice' (Plut., *Ages.* 15.6). That was far from true, but it suggests that Alexander thought of the battle as one fought between Greeks—as to a large extent it was. He knew well what he was doing when he made his dedication to Athena of the spoils of the Granicus: 'From Alexander and the Greeks, except the Spartans' (Arr., *Anab.* I xvi.7). In fact, of course, the victory had been won entirely by the Macedonians; but Alexander evidently felt that it paid to emphasise, in his propaganda, the fact that Sparta had remained outside the League of Corinth. What, indeed, had Sparta done for the Greeks since 479, when she led them to victory over the Persian invaders at Plataea?— her one great achievement on behalf of Hellas. Her record ever since then had deprived her of any claim to hold herself out as 'the protector of Greek freedom'.[202] The city which had produced Lysander, Agesilaus, Phoebidas, Sphodrias and Antalcidas had made it certain that the appeals of Agis would fall largely on deaf ears.[203]

---

[202] In Ps.-Plut., *Mor.* 219ab = *Apophth. Lac.*, *Archidamus [III] son of Agesilaus* 9, some unidentified 'Greeks' do not want to break 'the treaty with Antigonus and Craterus' at the behest of Sparta, on the ground that 'the Spartans will prove more burdensome (χαλεπωτέρων) than the Macedonians'. The attribution to Archidamus III (who died in 338) and 'the treaty with Antigonus and Craterus' must be mistakes; but the anecdote could well be attached to the revolt of Agis III if, as has been suggested, we replace 'Antigonus' by 'Antipater'.

[203] I have ignored Frontinus, *Strateg.* II xi.4, the historical basis of which is unfathomable. Unfortunately in the seventeenth century Freinsheim worked this anecdote into the supplement with which he filled the gap at the beginning of Book VI of Curtius and which is printed in some editions of that author (e.g. the Teubner and the Loeb, though not the Budé).

V

Sparta's relations with Athens

(i)
Before 478/7

Although it is the Pentecontaetia with which we are now primarily concerned, we may conveniently make a brief review of Sparta's behaviour towards Athens in earlier times.

During the last years of the sixth century the Spartans made no fewer than four separate expeditions into Attica and would have organised a fifth if they had been able to carry their allies with them.[1] The first expedition, in 511 or 510 under Anchimolius, was unsuccessful; the second, in 510, resulted in the expulsion of the tyrant Hippias; the third, an attempt by King Cleomenes to set up a close oligarchy under Isagoras in 508/7, failed ignominiously after an initial success; the fourth, in *c.* 506, a large-scale attack with much the same object, concerted with Sparta's Peloponnesian allies and also Thebes and Chalcis, disintegrated after reaching Eleusis. And at some time between 505 and 501, at what some people would call the first known Congress of the Peloponnesian League (see Chapter IV, Part iv above), the Spartans proposed the restoration of Hippias to Athens, but were voted down (or dissuaded) by their allies. The interventions, actual or proposed, after 510 must all have seemed to the bulk of the Athenians to be aggressive attempts to gain control over their internal affairs: we should take this into account when trying to understand the attitude of Athenians towards Sparta in the fifth century.

Cleomenes' suggestion to the Plataeans, probably in 519/18,[2] that they ally themselves with Athens, in order to secure their independence from Thebes, very probably had the objective alleged by Herodotus (vi 108.3), of embroiling Athens and Thebes in war. The Plataean-Athenian alliance must certainly have weakened Thebes, by removing from her control a small state only a few miles from her walls. For Athens it represented at first an accession of strength, a thorn in the flesh of her nearest strong neighbour; but in the long run it did Athens no good—or Plataea, for that

---

[1] Much of this paragraph contains material which is too well known to require the citation of evidence, and I have therefore given no references. For a convenient summary of Sparta's relations with Athens during this period, see Larsen, SIR 146 ff. See also Jones, *Sp.* 50–6 (with main source refs.); Forrest, *HS* 86–94. I know of no discussion of Spartan foreign policy in the reign of Cleomenes which seems to me satisfactory.

[2] The date, which depends on our MSS of Thuc. iii 68.5, has often been disputed, without convincing arguments. And if the numeral is rejected, there can be no confidence in any *other* date.

matter. Its effects continued right down to 339, making friendly relations between Athens and Thebes very precarious. If Cleomenes' object was to create a long-lasting bone of contention between Athens and Thebes, the two most powerful states in central Greece, and thus prevent them from uniting against Sparta, he certainly achieved that object with remarkable success.

Cleomenes' coercion (at the request of Athens) in 491 of Aegina, a member of the Peloponnesian League[3] which was about to medise, may have been decisive in saving Athens from Persia at the time of the invasion in 490 under Datis and Artaphernes, for if the Persians had been able to land on Aegina and use the island as a base and its fleet as that of a subject, it is hard to say whether Athens could have resisted successfully. This friendly policy was maintained throughout the great Persian invasion of 480–79, although Sparta showed reluctance to campaign on any scale outside Peloponnese until the expedition of 479 which led to the decisive battle of Plataea—an attitude which caused some indignation at Athens.[4] During this period, however, Spartan-Athenian relations seem otherwise to have been good,[5] and Spartan admiration for the outstanding part played by the Athenians showed itself in the conferring of signal honours on Themistocles, presumably in the winter of 480/79 (Hdts VIII 124.2–3; Thuc. I 74.1; 91.1; Plut., *Them.* 17.3).

Already, however, there was anxiety among Sparta's allies, especially Aegina,[6] about the recent great growth of Athenian naval power, and Thucydides (I 90.1) attributes mainly to the prompting of the allies the Spartan embassy sent to Athens in 479/8 to propose that Athens should not rebuild her own walls and should join Sparta in pulling down the fortifications of all other Greek cities outside the Peloponnese, on the very feeble pretext that if this were done the Persians, should they attack again, would find no ready-made strongholds. The well-known story of Themistocles' ruse by which the rebuilding of the walls of Athens was nevertheless carried out may be somewhat embroidered, even in the form in which it appears in Thucydides (I 90–3); but it does show that the Athenians at least believed they had cause to dread Spartan interference, for unless they actually feared *forcible intervention* by Sparta, to stop them from rebuilding their walls, why did they not simply tell Sparta politely to mind her own business? It cannot have been for nothing that they risked incurring the deep resentment of the Spartans by tricking them. However, despite the Athenian rebuff to Sparta on the question of the walls, there was no overt hostility between the two states for some seventeen years.

[3] See Appendix XVII, Section *B*.
[4] See the discussion by Hignett, *XIG* 272–85.
[5] Even Plut., *Arist.* 20.1, suggests no more than the usual Greek *philotimia*. But this story, in spite of several touches which make it seem plausible at first sight, was not in Herodotus or (to judge by Diod. XI 33.1) Ephorus, and it has been thought to come from the miserable Idomeneus, *FGrH* 338 (see *e.g.* Hignett, *XIG* 19–20), who was much used by Plutarch but is unreliable in the extreme.
[6] See Plut., *Them.* 19.2 (Polyarchus); and cf. Appendix XVII, Section *B*.

It would be interesting to know when the oracles prophesying woe to Sparta and Corinth from Athens began to be circulated. The Spartans were exceptionally superstitious people and might have paid a good deal of attention to such things. According to Herodotus (v 90.2), Cleomenes brought back to Sparta certain oracles which Hippias had possessed, threatening 'many unpleasant things' to Sparta from Athens: among these may have been the sayings referred to elsewhere by Herodotus (VIII 141.1) as being known to the Spartans during the Persian wars, which foretold that the Persians and Athenians would drive the Spartans and the other Dorians out of the Peloponnese. Herodotus (v 93.1–2) also represents Hippias as speaking (at some date between 505 and 501) of the appointed time when the Corinthians would be vexed (*aniasthai*) by Athens: he says Hippias knew this because of his unrivalled knowledge of 'the oracles'. In such cases as this it is only too tempting to fit the facts into a preconceived scheme of interpretation. It is better to admit that we cannot tell what truth there is in these statements of Herodotus. Some of the prophecies he refers to may have been current before the end of the sixth century, but we should allow for the possibility that many of them may be inventions of the Pentecontaetia.

(ii)
The Spartan 'hawks', 478/7 and 465/4, and Themistocles

Although Spartan-Athenian relations remained outwardly friendly until 462, there was evidently at times a large and influential group of Spartans which deeply resented the transference from Sparta to Athens of the leadership of the anti-Persian alliance and the resulting growth of Athenian power, and wished to regain the hegemony by force. This group has sometimes been referred to as 'the war party'; but one may perhaps be forgiven for preferring the current catchword 'hawks', for two reasons. First, there is no reason at all to suppose that the members of this group actually desired at all times to make war upon Athens, although they would tend to do so when circumstances seemed favourable. Secondly, in relation to the politics of ancient Greek cities it is always best to avoid using the word 'party', which for us has inescapable overtones conveying highly misleading associations. In the Greek cities there were of course alliances between politicians, sometimes long-lasting, sometimes not, and leading politicians would have their followers, attached to them either for what would nowadays be called ideological reasons or from personal motives. But such alliances and followings always remained fluid, and the two most essential features of the modern political party were entirely absent: there was *no organisation*, no defined circle of members, with a chairman, secretary and treasurer; and there was *no common programme*, like that of a modern political party, to at least the principal elements of which all members can be expected to adhere—on the contrary, A and B might be allies on some issues against C and D, whereas on other issues A and C were opposed to B and D.

By 'the Spartan hawks' in the fifth century I mean those who were unwilling to accept the 'dual hegemony' of Sparta and Athens, with Sparta as the acknowledged leader in at least the Peloponnese, Megara and Boeotia, and Athens dominant in the naval Confederacy of Delos which by the mid-fifth century had become the Athenian empire. The 'hawks' would not accept Athens as an entirely independent 'Great Power', roughly the equal of Sparta in prestige and with a hegemony of her own.

The first piece of evidence for the existence of this group is to be found in Diodorus (xi 50), who under the year 475/4 describes meetings of the Spartan Gerousia and (allegedly) the Assembly,[7] at which 'the younger men and most of the others' (§3), amounting indeed to 'almost all the citizens' (§5), at first were anxious to resume the hegemony by force, until a Spartiate named Hetoimaridas succeeded in persuading the Gerousia and the people to change their minds, and they 'abandoned their impulse to make war on Athens' (§7). The narrative rings true, and even if the almost complete unanimity of feeling at first in favour of a war against Athens is an exaggeration, the story is most unlikely to be an invention, especially since the hero is the otherwise entirely unknown Hetoimaridas, and this therefore is not one of those fabrications which tend to cluster around famous names. Some modern historians have at least put a question-mark against this story, and Busolt went so far as to dismiss it entirely, as 'obviously' a product of Ephorus' imagination.[8] But Busolt was not at his best here: he asserted, for example, that the 'ancient oracle' (quoted by Diodorus, §4) against 'letting the [dual] hegemony go lame' is a product of the controversy between Agesilaus and Leotychidas, of *c.* 400 B.C., in which the rival interpretations of Diopeithes and Lysander were of an oracle which referred to lameness in the Spartan *kingship*.[9] Busolt overlooked the relevance of the valuable fragment of Ion of Chios preserved by Plutarch,[10] in which Cimon is recorded as saying in 462 that the Athenians should not allow Greece to go lame or Athens' partner to be weakened, a proof that the 'lame hegemony' metaphor—which might well be derived from an oracle—was already current by 462 at the latest. It has been pointed out by D. M. Lewis (IA 414–15) that Diodorus appears surprisingly well informed about Peloponnesian history in the fifth century, and that Ephorus, his main source, may well have used 'a Peloponnesian historical source', showing 'a fairly detailed knowledge of Sparta', possibly Charon of Lampsacus, already suggested by Jacoby.

[7] Probably a mere *contio*: cf. Chapter IV, Part v above, n. 99.

[8] Busolt, *GG* III i.71 n. 2. Ed. Meyer (*GdA* IV 1.³⁻⁵459 n. 1; cf. H. D. Meyer, VGDAS 433–4) at least noticed that the metaphor was as old as Cimon, but rejected the story *a priori*, as a retrojection of the later situation.

[9] See Xen., *HG* III iii.1–3; Plut., *Lys.* 22.10–12; *Ages.* 3.6–8.

[10] Ion, *FGrH* 392 F 14, *ap.* Plut., *Cim.* 16.10; μήτε τὴν Ἑλλάδα χωλὴν μήτε τὴν πόλιν ἑτερόζυγα ('unevenly yoked') περιιδεῖν γεγενημένην.

The year under which Diodorus inserts his account of the debate, namely 475/4, must, as so often with Diodorus, be treated as approximate only, particularly in view of a circumstance which too often passes unnoticed: that Diodorus had nothing else to record under the year 475/4 and so would in any event have had to use some undated material to fill the gap! A very much more likely date is the spring of 477 (or just possibly the autumn of 478), when Dorcis and the Peloponnesian contingent returned home after their rejection by the rest of the Greeks.[11] In the recent past the Spartans had been well disposed towards Athens; their relationship no doubt had been somewhat clouded by the incident of the rebuilding of the walls of Athens, but even on that occasion the Spartans showed no open anger against the Athenians and kept their annoyance to themselves, as Thucydides puts it (1 92). It is precisely upon the return of Dorcis, and not two or three years later, that the Spartans might be expected to give way to a sudden burst of hostility against the upstart city which had deprived them of the hegemony. In the event, as Diodorus tells us, they allowed themselves to be pacified by Hetoimaridas; and since the Spartans accepted the new situation and gave no outward sign of resentment, Thucydides is quite justified in his summing-up (1 95.7): they feared that any other leaders they sent out might follow the bad example of Pausanias, and they were glad to be quit of the war against Persia, believing the Athenians to be both competent to exercise the hegemony and friendly at that time towards themselves.[12] Herodotus (VIII 3.2) seems to have viewed the change rather differently: the Athenians, he says, deprived the Spartans of hegemony, using as a pretext the highhanded behaviour of Pausanias.[13]

There may just possibly be another trace of discontent on the part of a certain section of the Spartiates in the curious expression Thucydides applies to the ostensible purpose of Pausanias' expedition to the Hellespont, in a trireme of Hermione, 'without the [approval of the] Spartans': he went there, says Thucydides (1 128.3), 'ostensibly for the Hellenic war (Hellēnikos polemos), but in reality to carry on his intrigues with the King'.

---

[11] Thuc. 1 95.6–7; cf. Diod. XI 46.5. In ATL III 192, and Hammond, ONAA 49 and n. 20, the sending out of Dorcis is dated to the late summer of 478: this seems to me improbable. And see Cawkwell, FT 46 and 55 n. 14.

[12] There is no 'contradiction' between this passage and Diod. XI 50, as asserted by e.g. Meyer, GdA IV 1.³⁻⁵ 459 n. 1.

[13] We cannot hope to reconstruct what really happened. I am not at all convinced by e.g. H. D. Meyer, VGDAS; Hammond, ONAA. I do not believe we can even be sure what Aristotle meant by the word ἀκόντων in Ath. Pol. 23.2; but I think Gomme (HCT 1 272) and others may be right in taking it to mean 'unwilling to hold the leadership' (Thuc. 1 75.2 is very relevant here, but the later evidence, e.g. Xen., HG VI v.34, is of little value). Wickert's argument (PB 36) against Gomme, based on the sending out of Dorcis as successor to Pausanias, is not valid: when Dorcis was despatched the Spartans could not have known of the transfer of the hegemony to Athens. A possibility which is too often neglected is that in later times the Spartans deliberately exaggerated the personal misbehaviour of Pausanias, in order to cover up allied dissatisfaction with Spartan leadership in general.

It is generally considered that 'the Hellenic war' must be the war of the Greeks against Persia; but Thucydides always calls this by some such name as 'the Median war' (*Mēdikos polemos*, as in I 90.1; 95.7; 97.1,2 etc.), and the expression 'Hellenic war' is not, as far as I know, applied to a war by Greeks against foreigners until the Lamian war against Macedon of 323–2 B.C. One would expect the term 'the Hellenic war', then, to refer to a war between Greeks,[14] as in Thuc. I 112.2 and elsewhere. If that is its meaning here, we must suppose that Pausanias, dissatisfied with the official Spartan decision to countenance the transfer of the hegemony, sailed east, after his first recall, with the declared intention of displacing the Athenians by force and recapturing the hegemony for Sparta. However, it seems to me that the casual way in which Thucydides uses the expression 'for the Hellenic war', and the employment of the definite article, without any elucidation, make this explanation unlikely. Some mysteries about the activities of Pausanias remain: for instance, he is said to have had a *skytalē* (Thuc. I 131.1), 'only granted to a commanding officer sent abroad by the State' (Gomme, *HCT* I 433)—a strange fact which even the usually unhelpful Thucydides scholia notice (ed. Hude, pp. 95–6). It has been conjectured[15] that 'there was sufficient doubt about the first charge of Medism for Sparta to allow Pausanias to return to Byzantium in the hope that he might restore Spartan authority in that area, with the warning that if he failed the consequences would be on his own head. It was a hazardous venture and he failed'. Certainly Pausanias was not at this time acting officially on behalf of Sparta (see Thuc. I 131.1).

During the 470s and 460s the man who emerged as by far the most important and influential figure in Athens was Cimon, son of Miltiades, a staunch believer in the 'dual hegemony' of Sparta and Athens and a devoted friend of Sparta,[16] whose proxenos he was.[17] He even named one of his sons—probably the eldest—Lacedaemonius (*Lakedaimonios*: 'Spartan'), after the city whose goodwill he so valued.[18] As long as he remained the leading figure in his city, the Spartans could be sure that Athens would pursue a policy friendly to themselves. As late as 462 it was Cimon above all who was responsible for the sending of a large Athenian hoplite army (numbering 4,000, if we can accept the figure given by

[14] This is the view taken by Cawkwell, FT 53, 58 n. 33, who has some excellent things to say about Thucydides' account of Pausanias' alleged medism and dealings with the Helots.

[15] By White, ADPS 152. See also Cawkwell, FT, and Rhodes, TPT, with references to some of the other literature. As I indicate below, I feel too sceptical about the details of the tradition to wish to contribute to the controversy about the conclusions that should be drawn.

[16] It will be sufficient to cite Plut., *Cim.* 16 (note esp. ἀπ' ἀρχῆς in §1; also §9 = Critias, B 52; and §10 = Ion, F 14); 14.4; 15.4 (= Eupolis, fr. 208); *Per.* 29.1–2.

[17] Andoc. III 3; Theopomp., *FGrH* 115 F 88; cf. Aeschin. II 172.

[18] Lacedaemonius was a hipparch not later than 446 and perhaps a good deal earlier (see *IG* I² 400, with Meiggs, DFCAI 94–5), and of course general in 433/2; and I suggest he is likely to have been born not later than the 470s.

Aristophanes, *Lysistr.* 1138–44) to the aid of the hard-pressed Spartans, against the revolting Messenians on Mount Ithome.[19]

The Athenians equally showed that the majority of them wished to remain on good terms with Sparta by rejecting Themistocles, who certainly developed a strongly anti-Spartan policy very soon after the end of the Persian invasion (see below). Apart from his victory in the tragic competition early in 476, as choregus for Phrynichus (Plut., *Them.* 5.5), nothing whatever is known of Themistocles' activities[20] from the time of his embassy to Sparta during the rebuilding of the walls of Athens in 479/8 (see Part i of this Chapter) down to his ostracism, which took place in the late 470s, the most probable year being perhaps 472.[21] When Themistocles, after his ostracism, became the object of bitter hatred on the part of the Spartans, who accused him of Medism, the Athenians joined the Spartans in trying to hound him down.[22] The whole chain of events has been discussed again and again in modern times,[23] and there is no need to go into it afresh. I share the deep scepticism expressed by Rhodes, Cawkwell and others about many of the elements in the stories we are given, even by Herodotus and Thucydides, about Pausanias and Themistocles, and as far as possible I shall avoid making use of this material. Certain aspects of the story of Themistocles' 'fall' must be singled out, however, as they are very relevant for our purposes.

It can now surely be taken for granted that immediately after his ostracism Themistocles was conducting anti-Spartan activities in the Peloponnese, and with some success, until the exasperated Spartans turned

[19] The sources are listed in Hill, S^2 341–2 (Index 1 4.2–3). I have no hesitation in rejecting the *two* Athenian expeditions to Ithome, which some historians have accepted on the strength of the doublet in Plut., *Cim.* 16.8–10; 17.3. Against *e.g.* Hammond, HG^2 290–2, and in *Historia* 4 (1955) 398–400, see Reece, DFI 115–17. On Diodorus' misdating to 469/8 (instead of 465/4) of the Laconian earthquake, see Jacoby, *FGrH* III b (Suppl.) i.455–61 (esp. 458–9); ii.365–71 (esp. n. 17); and Gomme, *HCT* 1 401–8. I see no reason to believe that the Helot revolt broke out before the earthquake, to which Thuc. 1 101.2 clearly dates its outbreak. (I have been unable to discover anyone who accepts the arguments of Sealey, in *Historia* 6 [1957] 368–71.)

[20] Timocreon, fr. 1 (Diehl), *ap.* Plut., *Them.* 21.3–4, seems (from the names) to have been composed in 478/7, but refers to earlier events. It is commonly taken for granted nowadays, on no better evidence than this poem of hate by a mediser (cf. Timocr., fr. 3, *ap.* Plut., *Them.* 21.7), that Themistocles made an expedition to Rhodes and extracted 3 talents from Ialysus. If this did happen, it must have been in 480: see Busolt, *GG* III i.14 n. 1; *ATL* III 185 and n.10, 191 n. 26; contrast Beloch, GG II² ii.144–5 and n. 1. But is Timocreon a trustworthy witness? And even if 3 talents were paid to Themistocles by Ialysus or by Timocreon's enemies there (which is far from certain), why need we suppose that Themistocles sailed there with a fleet? Cf. A. Kirchhoff, in *Hermes* 11 (1876) 1 ff., esp. 'Anhang. Die angebliche Expedition des Themistokles nach Rhodos', pp. 38–48.

[21] The time of the production of Aeschylus' *Persae* (see the *Hypoth.*). For the chronology, see White, ADPS 142–9; R. J. Lenardon, 'The Chronology of Themistocles' Ostracism and Exile', in *Historia* 8 (1959) 23–48.

[22] For the sources, see Hill, S^2 349 (Index II 2.2–6). The best modern account is that of Forrest, TA (cf. n. 24 below).

[23] Most recently by Knight, SSAP 33–44; and (much more profitably) by Rhodes, TPT, and Cawkwell, FT, who between them give all necessary references to modern work, by R. Flacelière, C. W. Fornara, A. Lippold, J. Wolski and others.

upon him.[24] (These activities were carried on at great personal risk, and we can surely therefore conclude that they were undertaken from motives that can fairly be described as patriotic rather than selfish—Themistocles must have been acting in what he regarded as the best interests of Athens.) And this allows us to infer with a high degree of probability that Themistocles had been acting against Sparta's interests before his ostracism, and indeed was ostracised mainly on that account. We cannot attribute the absence of any reference to political activity by Themistocles between the rebuilding of the walls of Athens and his ostracism to his having merely retired into private life: such a course of action can hardly be paralleled among prominent Greek statesmen and is incongruous with what we know of Themistocles' behaviour both earlier and later, and it would make his ostracism inexplicable. Themistocles must surely have been politically active in the late 470s, in a way that the majority of his fellow-citizens condemned sufficiently to make them forget his very great services to Athens.

If we can accept the story in Plut., *Them.* 20.3–4 (which some have rejected, for no very good reason, as a fourth-century fiction), about Themistocles' successful opposition to Sparta at an Amphictyonic Congress, presumably that of spring 478,[25] then Themistocles will have become *persona non grata* to the Spartans in the year after the retreat of the Persian army from Greece, if indeed he had not made himself so already in the preceding winter by the role he played in the rebuilding of the walls of Athens. And there is one account, that of Ephorus,[26] which describes an earlier accusation by the Spartans and trial of Themistocles at Athens, dated to the period before his ostracism.[27] Although accepted by Grote (*HG* iv 369–70, ch. xliv), this earlier accusation and trial are generally rejected out of hand nowadays (see e.g. Busolt, *GG* iii i.110 n. 1, 126 n.1), for no better reason than the one given by Plutarch (*Mor.* 855f): that Thucydides does not mention them. But why should he? The story may of course be false; but if it is true, it certainly proves (if proof were needed) that Themistocles had been acting against Sparta's interests before his ostracism.

---

[24] See esp. Andrewes, SAEFC; Forrest, TA, esp. 229–32, 236–8. (The main texts are of course Thuc. 1 135.3; Diod. xi 54.1, with Strabo viii iii.2, pp. 336, 337; and see Hill, *S*² 358, Index iv 2.3–5.) Forrest's brilliant paper deserves close (and critical) study. I myself feel much less confident of the details (esp. of the chronology) than he does. His case concerning Aeschylus' *Supplices*, although basically correct, needs to be completely re-argued, without ignoring the other two plays of the trilogy.

[25] See R. Flacelière, 'Sur quelques points obscurs de la vie de Thémistocle', in *REA* 55 (1953) 5–28, at pp. 19–28; H. Bengtson, 'Themistokles und die delphische Amphiktyonie', in *Eranos* 49 (1951) 85–92, both of whom accept the Congress and date it to the autumn of 479 or the spring of 478. I prefer spring 478, if only because Themistocles' activities at Sparta over the rebuilding of the walls of Athens, in the winter of 479/8, are more easily understandable if he had not already antagonised the Spartans.

[26] *FGrH* 70 F 189, *ap.* Plut., *Mor.* 855f = *De Herod. Malign.* 5. Ephorus' account is best known to us from Diod. xi 54.2–5; 55.4–8.

[27] Contrast Plut., *Them.* 23.2–3, where Pausanias does not reveal his plans to Themistocles until after the latter's ostracism.

In the late 470s Cimon and his associates could claim with great plausibility that Themistocles was endangering the friendship with Sparta which was a vital necessity if Athens were to develop her naval hegemony in the Delian League, now already beginning to turn inevitably into an Athenian empire. (This claim would have had even greater force if the Athenians were by now aware, as they may possibly have been,[28] that the Persians were preparing a large expedition against at any rate the Greeks of Asia and the islands—the one that was eventually crushed at the battle of the Eurymedon in, probably, 469.) And the fact that Themistocles is not known to have played any part whatever in the Delian League is surely significant: it suggests that he did not want to participate, because he did not support the policy of large-scale reprisals against Persia. I believe that he had probably not offered himself for election as a general, to carry out a Delian League policy which was favoured by the great majority of Athenians, but of which he disapproved. Even if the Athenians preferred to entrust Aristeides with the first assessment, and Cimon with the supreme command subsequently, they would surely have been only too glad to avail themselves of Themistocles' experience and expertise as a naval commander had he himself wished to be employed in the operations of the League. Indeed, the League itself must have appeared to many as the natural culmination of the whole Athenian naval policy of which Themistocles had been the great architect.

We cannot hope to reconstruct Themistocles' policy in detail; but if I might hazard a guess I would suggest that he may well have advocated a cessation of hostilities against Persia and an attempt to make peace on the terms that the Greek cities of the mainland of Asia should belong to the King and the island cities remain independent in the Delian League, which Athens of course needed to maintain. This was the policy the King adopted from 387/6 onwards (see esp. Xen., *HG* v i.31), and he might well have been induced to accept it in the 470s, for there was now little chance of his recovering the islands, or even those cities on the mainland of Asia which he had already lost, and there was indeed some likelihood that he would lose still more of the south-western coast of Asia Minor—as he soon did, especially after the battle of the Eurymedon. To those Athenians —still a majority as late as 462 (see esp. Plut., *Cim.* 16.8–10)—who believed the dual hegemony of Sparta and Athens could be maintained indefinitely, the surrender of the mainland Ionians (or even a part of them) to the King would have been a betrayal, an act shameful enough even to make them vote for the ostracism of the man who had done more than anyone to defeat Xerxes' expedition and make the great growth in Athenian power possible.[29] At any rate, the very fact that the Spartan

[28] See Cawkwell, FT 46–8, 52–3, whose argument applies to the condemnation rather than the ostracism of Themistocles, but may perhaps be carried back to the ostracism. Cawkwell shows very well that major Persian expeditions sometimes took several years to prepare and would be known to the Greeks well in advance.

[29] I see no reason to believe, with Cawkwell (FT 44–6, and see the last note), that Themistocles had expected an *immediate* attack on Athens by Sparta after 479, or that any

charges of Medism against Themistocles were accepted at Athens shows that his conduct after 479 had made them seem plausible.

The two main aspects of Themistocles' policy which we have just noticed fit together perfectly: Themistocles was, in some sense which we have yet to define, 'anti-Spartan', and surely it was *because* he was anti-Spartan that he did not approve of an aggressively anti-Persian policy. (The signs of a 'Western policy' on Themistocles' part, which can just be detected from the meagre evidence, may also be used to support the idea that he was averse to committing Athens to a policy of all-out attack in the East: see Appendix XXXI.) The paramount consideration for anyone planning Athenian foreign policy after the Persian invasion was that Athens could not afford to fight both Persia and Sparta simultaneously. (It was large-scale Persian financial aid to Sparta which ultimately brought Athens to defeat in the Peloponnesian war.) Now Persia had been so thoroughly defeated in 480–79 that she was unlikely to mount another invasion of mainland Greece. Persia was no longer, therefore, a positive menace to Athens. But what of Sparta? Could the Athenians rely on her being willing to tolerate indefinitely a great growth in Athenian power?

I believe that a negative answer to that question was the foundation of Themistocles' policy in the years after 479. He cannot, surely, have entertained designs against Sparta which were positively aggressive—for what could Athens hope to gain from an *unnecessary* struggle with the greatest of Greek land-powers, and how could Athens ever hope to *win* such a struggle? The theory of Hammond (*HG*² 264), that Themistocles had a 'policy of opposing Sparta and attacking Persia, which envisaged the possibility of war on both fronts', makes Themistocles into an utter fool, and fails to provide an explanation of his absence from all Delian League operations. I believe that Themistocles *foresaw that sooner or later Sparta would attack Athens*, even if Athens did not directly threaten Sparta herself or the Peloponnesian League. This alone makes his policy not merely explicable but defensible. Themistocles had had opportunities for discovering the real situation at Sparta: he had visited the place at least twice after the Persian war, once when he was received with signal honours for the role he had played in the naval resistance to Persia (Hdts VIII 124.2–3; Thuc. 1 74.1 *fin.*; 91.1; Plut., *Them.* 17.3), and again in connection with the rebuilding of the walls of Athens (see Part i of this Chapter). In judging that the real enemy Athens had to prepare herself against was no longer Persia but Sparta and the powerful League of which she was hegemon, Themistocles, I suggest, was right. What is more, I think there is every reason to believe Thucydides knew he was right. It is interesting that the faculty in him which seems to have most

news of Persian preparations in the late 470s would have made Themistocles' position at Athens *worse*. Indeed, he could have turned any such news to his own advantage, by pointing out that Persian retaliation had been needlessly provoked, against his advice!

impressed the historian (surely not at all an easily impressible person) was his ability to foresee what was likely to happen and take appropriate steps to meet it. Just as Thucydides makes Pericles claim to be second to none in the capacity to grasp, and to expound, what the situation required (II 60.5), so in his extraordinary panegyric on Themistocles (I 138.3, a very difficult passage to translate adequately) what he concentrates on is the man's remarkable power of *judgment*, of *understanding* situations that confronted him and taking the *right action*. He was a man of exceptional genius, Thucydides says, of inborn ability (*oikeia xynesis*); he was both outstandingly qualified to judge a present situation after the briefest deliberation and very well able to infer most extensively what was actually going to happen.[30] He could not merely explain what he himself was used to; he was also not without the capacity to arrive at a sufficiently accurate judgment on things he had no experience of: he had an exceptional gift of foreseeing (*proheōra malista*)[31] the good and evil which still lay hid in the future. And then Thucydides sums up: Themistocles, by his own natural ability,[32] and with little training, was supremely good at using his own initiative to devise whatever a situation required.[33]

The sustained superlatives in this passage[34] and the piling up of some of Thucydides' favourite expressions of approval[35] must be taken very seriously. They go far beyond what is necessary to correct Herodotus' inadequate picture of the great man, at which Thucydides may have felt some justifiable irritation—in Herodotus, Themistocles even has to be given an elementary lesson in naval strategy at the eleventh hour before Salamis by Mnesiphilus,[36] who may be seen as a kind of proto-Sophist. Thucydides is praising to the skies a man who would have been remembered by the Cimonians of the late fifth century as the great opponent of Cimon's 'sensible' policy after the Persian invasion, the man who in effect devised the 'disastrous' anti-Spartan policy which Ephialtes and

[30] The passage ends, τοῦ γενησομένου ἄριστος εἰκαστής. Thucydides does not use εἰκαστής elsewhere, but it must have much the same force as εἰκάζειν in such passages as I 9.4; 10.2; III 20.4; IV 126.3; VI 92.5; VIII 46.5; 87.3. One paints a mental picture in the *likeness* of what one already knows; one uses one's existing knowledge to make intelligent *inferences* about the future.

[31] Cf. II 65.5 (προγνούς), 6 (πρόνοια), and 13 (προέγνω), all of Pericles.

[32] φύσεως ... δυνάμει, recalling βεβαιότατα δὴ φύσεως ἰσχὺν δηλώσας a few lines earlier.

[33] The use of initiative in an unforeseen situation is also the force of αὐτοσχεδιάζειν (not used again by Thuc.) in such passages as Xen., *HG* v ii.32.

[34] In eleven *OCT* lines there are no less than seven (βεβαιότατα, ἐλαχίστης, κράτιστος twice, ἐπὶ πλεῖστον, ἄριστος, μάλιστα), as well as three adverbial expressions of approval (διαφερόντως, μᾶλλον ἑτέρου, ἱκανῶς).

[35] φύσεως ἰσχύν, φύσεως δυνάμει, γνώμων, κρῖναι, προεώρα, τὰ δέοντα.

[36] Hdts VIII 57–8. Of course it is not Mnesiphilus who is made to think of the decisive argument for fighting in the narrows at Salamis (60. α–γ), but Themistocles produces it only at this late hour, having used the absurdly obvious point made by Mnesiphilus to persuade Eurybiades to summon another meeting of the Greek admirals, who had been on the point of sailing off to the Isthmus. There are other slanders against Themistocles which ought not to have taken in Herodotus: see Cawkwell, FT 40–3; How and Wells, *CH* I 42–3; II 236–7, 272.

Pericles[37] and the radical democrats had put into effect. When we remember that Thucydides himself may well have been related to Cimon's family on both sides,[38] and when he returned to Athens in 404 must have found many Athenians depreciating Themistocles and harking back to the 'good old days' of Cimon's supremacy, his total approval of Themistocles appears all the more remarkable. It is astonishing that those who, like Gomme (*HCT* 1 442-4), have been much impressed by Thucydides' heartfelt admiration for Themistocles should have failed to realise that he could never have bestowed such an unqualified eulogy on the man if he had disapproved of the course Themistocles took in his later years. Thucydides' commendation of Themistocles' political acumen is total, without reserve, and cannot have been intended to apply to only the first of the two main phases of his political career. And may it not be significant that the context in which Thucydides—a great literary artist— has chosen to place his panegyric of Themistocles is the outbreak of the very war which there is good reason to believe Themistocles foresaw? When Thucydides returns to his main narrative, in 1 139, we are on the verge of war, and in the midst of peremptory demands made to Athens by Sparta.

It is to my mind extraordinary that so many modern scholars (even Grote, *HG* IV 367-8) should have been willing to accept the stock picture of Themistocles as a politician who was above all self-seeking and entirely unscrupulous in his pursuit of his personal interest. The evidence for such a view comes mainly from stories in Herodotus which obviously contain much fiction (see n. 36 above) and from the medising poet Timocreon, a very unreliable witness (cf. n. 20 above).

Now what matters about Themistocles, for Spartan-Athenian relations at the time with which we are concerned, is the fact that the Athenians of the 470s and 460s totally rejected him. They ostracised him, and when the Spartans complained about his activities they condemned him, assisted the Spartans in pursuing him, and thus eventually drove him to take refuge with the Persian King[39]—the only safe place for a Greek whose head was sought by both Athens and Sparta.[40] Could the Athenians have demonstrated their regard for Sparta in any more effectual way than this?

The Spartan 'hawks' nevertheless make their second appearance in 465/4 during the revolt of Thasos from Athens. According to Thucydides (1 101.1-2) the Thasians, after being defeated at sea and blockaded,

---

[37] Cf. Appendix X.

[38] See Wade-Gery, *EGH* 246-7; but cf. Davies, *APF* 232-6.

[39] For the gift by Artaxerxes I to Themistocles of the revenues of Magnesia on the Maeander, Lampsacus and Myus, see Thuc. 1 138.5; cf. Gomme, *HCT* 1 292, 445. Magnesia still maintained a festival in Themistocles' honour at least as late as *c.* 200 B.C. (see H. G. Lolling, in *Ath. Mitt.* 6 [1881], at pp. 103-5 = Hill, *S*², B 122), and bestowed special privileges upon his descendants down to Plutarch's day (see Plut., *Them.* 32.4,6; cf. Nepos, *Them.* 10.3).

[40] I agree with J. D. Smart (*ap.* Knight, *SSAP* 43 n. 58): 'The Athenian and Spartan establishments agreed to co-operate in the removal of their respective agitators, Themistokles and Pausanias.'

appealed to Sparta to invade Athens. The Spartans, says Thucydides, promised to do so, without the knowledge of the Athenians, and would have fulfilled their promise (*kai emellon*) had they not been prevented by the earthquake, at which time the Helot revolt occurred. This is a definite statement which Thucydides would surely not have made if he had not been convinced of its truth on what he regarded as reliable evidence; and the doubts which have sometimes been cast upon its accuracy seem to me unjustified. It is not difficult to believe that the appeal was kept secret at the time. Thucydides had special interests in the Thracian area opposite Thasos (see IV 105.1) and must have been on familiar terms with prominent Thasians; and his certainty about Spartan intentions strongly suggests that he had had information about this incident from Spartan sources also. It is true that 'the historian should beware of statements about secret undertakings and unfulfilled intentions';[41] but such things do sometimes occur, and in this case the statement is made by Thucydides: that is an entirely different matter from finding it in Diodorus or Plutarch. The incident deserves more emphasis than it is commonly given. It is all the more striking in that outwardly Spartan-Athenian relations, as far as we know, were still entirely friendly, and only two or three years later Cimon was to lead a large Athenian expedition to the help of the Spartans against the Messenians. Clearly at that time Sparta's promise to Thasos cannot yet have become known at Athens.[42]

It was the ignominious dismissal of Cimon's force from Ithome, more than anything else, which led to Cimon's ostracism early in 461 and the coming to power of the radical democrats, with their new foreign policy which soon led to armed conflict with the Peloponnesians. To dismiss an ally which had come to help in time of need was an extraordinary act, unparalleled (as far as I know) in the whole of Greek history. It represents one of those major changes in foreign policy of which Spartan history affords so many examples (cf. Chapter IV, Part vi above). Some modern historians have imagined that the reason for the dismissal of the Athenians was the arrival of the news of the reforms of Ephialtes; but this absurd speculation must be rejected, with the chronology adopted by Plutarch, *Cimon* 15.2–3, on which it mainly depends.[43] Thucydides (1 102.3) gives a perfectly credible explanation of the sending away of the Athenians from Ithome: the Spartans were alarmed by their initiative and their capacity for innovation; they felt them to be aliens (*allophyloi*: this must refer to their non-Dorian descent); and they thought that if they stayed on, the Athenians might fraternise with the Messenians and change sides! The ordinary Athenian hoplite, who had had a rosy picture of Sparta presented to him by Cimon and his philo-Laconian friends, may well have been shocked

---

[41] R. Sealey, in *Historia* 6 (1957), at p. 369, citing Thuc. 1 128.7 as a parallel. But in that case Thucydides was surely deceived by a forged document which seemed plausible to him

[42] For the debate at Athens in 462, see Plut., *Cim.* 16.8–10; cf. Ar., *Lysistr.* 1137–44.

[43] The reforms of Ephialtes must have taken place on Cimon's return, not (as Plut. represents) during his absence. It should be sufficient to refer to Jacoby, *FGrH* III b (Suppl.) i.458–9; ii.369–70 n. 17.

when he arrived in Messenia and found that the revolting 'slaves' of the Spartans were Greeks, the majority of them Messenians, who had never lost consciousness of the fact that their ancestors had been citizens of the *polis* of Messene, and were now fighting for their freedom and the right to be 'the Messenians' once more.

(iii)
The outbreak of the 'First Peloponnesian war', *c.* 460

We are exceedingly ill-informed about the 'First Peloponnesian war', of *c.* 460 to 446/5.[44] As we have seen already (Chapter II, Part i), Thucydides treats this not as a part of his war, the war he was describing in detail, but as something quite distinct, a mere prelude, no more indeed than a series of incidents, which he could shuffle off in seven pages (1 102.4–115.1), or less than six if one discounts chapters 104 and 109–10, dealing with the Egyptian expedition. About the origins of this war he leaves us in serious perplexity. (The few indications he gives will be examined presently.) Yet surely we ought to treat this as part of 'the Peloponnesian war'. It ended, very much as did the Ten Years war of 431–21, with a Peace that settled nothing finally, and was only intended to last for thirty years—even the Peace of Nicias in 421 was designed to last for fifty. Why should the First Peloponnesian war be treated as something quite different from the various stages of the Twenty-seven Years war, which were not themselves continuous but were separated by an interval, or rather intervals, between 421 and 415/14 during which there were few armed clashes and only one important one (the battle of Mantinea in 418), and for a time Sparta and Athens were not merely at peace but actually in alliance?

I have suggested (in Chapter II, Part i) that there were two reasons why Thucydides, so to speak, 'swept the First Peloponnesian war under the carpet': only in the late 430s did he begin that rigorous collection of information and enquiry of contemporaries which in his mind was a prerequisite for a proper History; and in the First Peloponnesian war there was little direct conflict between Athens and Sparta, for the fighting on the Peloponnesian side was nearly all done by Sparta's allies, whereas Thucydides' great war was essentially a confrontation between the two great powers.

We may now look at the way in which the First Peloponnesian war broke out. Thucydides' brief survey (1 102.4–103.4) enables us to isolate three items before we hear of the first armed clash (in 1 105.1). Let us first list these items individually and then discuss them together.

1. First, the alliance with Argos and Thessaly. The dismissal from Ithome had gravely offended and bewildered the Athenians, who could

---

[44] All the sources are listed in Hill, *S²* 342–3, 344–5 (Index 1, 5 and 7). For a chronological outline, see the end of Part vi of this Chapter.

see no justification for the affront put upon them (1 102.4) and lost no time in breaking off their alliance with the Spartans[45] and contracting alliances instead with two other powers: the Argives, described by Thucydides as the enemies (*polemioi*) of the Spartans (and so presumably in a state of war with them), and the Thessalians.

2. Secondly, the settlement of the Messenians at Naupactus. When the rebels on Ithome surrendered to Sparta, on condition that they left the Peloponnese and never entered it again, they were received by Athens, 'in accordance with the hatred she now felt for Sparta', and settled by her at Naupactus, a colony founded in the first quarter of the fifth century in Western (Ozolian) Locris by the East Locrians,[46] and strategically situated on the north shore of the narrow entrance to the Gulf of Corinth. One of the major chronological problems of the Pentecontaetia is whether we should accept 'in the tenth year' (*dekatōi etei*) [after the beginning of the Helot revolt] in Thucydides 1 103.1 (giving 456–5), or emend to the 'fourth', 'fifth' or 'sixth' year (giving a date between 462 and 459). I am ashamed to say that I have never been able to make up my mind on this question. There is a whole string of arguments on each side, but none is anywhere near decisive. For a judicious preliminary survey see R. A. McNeal, 'Historical Methods and Thucydides 1 103.1', in *Historia* 19 (1970) 306–25. I have nothing new to say, and I propose to leave the question open, with a reference to a few recent works which persuasively state the case in favour of[47] or against[48] accepting the date given in all the manuscripts of Thucydides. I do not myself think that the chronological question is in itself very important. My own views about the First Peloponnesian war would be little affected if I came down completely on one side of the fence or the other.

3. Thirdly, the alliance with Megara. As a result of a war with Corinth 'about boundary land',[49] in which Corinth (to judge by the way Thucydides expresses himself in 103.4) was apparently the aggressor, Megara abandoned her connection with Sparta and allied herself with Athens, which now controlled Megara and Pagae (Megara's port on the Corinthian Gulf), built Long Walls from Megara to Nisaea (Megara's port on the Saronic Gulf), and installed a garrison. At this point Thucydides delivers a personal opinion about the effect of these Athenian actions upon Corinth: 'It was particularly from this affair that the intense hatred (*sphodron misos*) of Corinth for Athens first began to exist'.[50] Here the word *prōton* must mean (as I have translated it) 'first' and not 'especially': it

---

[45] See Appendix XXXII.

[46] See M/L 20, with the commentary.

[47] Reece, DFI, makes the best case for this view, not vitiated (as are most other defences of δεκάτῳ) by dating the beginning of the Helot revolt *c.* 469 (cf. n. 19 to Part ii of this Chapter).

[48] *ATL* III 162–8; Gomme, *HCT* I 302–4, 401–11.

[49] For earlier wars of this nature between Corinth and Megara, see N. G. L. Hammond, 'The Heraeum at Perachora and Corinthian Encroachment', in *BSA* 49 (1954) 93–102.

[50] καὶ Κορινθίοις μὲν οὐχ ἥκιστα ἀπὸ τοῦδε τὸ σφοδρὸν μῖσος ἤρξατο πρῶτον ἐς Ἀθηναίους γενέσθαι.

goes with *ērxato*, 'began', and if it meant 'especially' it would be pleonastic, duplicating *ouch hēkista* ('particularly'). Translations such as Crawley's, 'This was the principal cause of the Corinthians conceiving such a deadly hatred against Athens' fail to bring out the force of *prōton* and are sometimes founded on erroneous ideas about the causes of the 'intense hatred'—a question to which we shall return when we consider the history of Corinthian-Athenian relations (Chapter VI below).

The alliance with Argos and Thessaly must fall in 462–1, and that with Megara, although mentioned rather later by Thucydides, must come very soon afterwards, for Athens' reception of Megara would have involved her in war with Corinth, and in Thucydides I 105.1 we hear of an Athenian landing at Halieis and a battle with the Corinthians and Epidaurians, and a subsequent naval battle with a Peloponnesian fleet at Cecryphaleia (in the channel between Epidaurus and Aegina): no one will wish to place these events later than 458, and most people would probably choose, like Meiggs and Lewis,[51] either 460 or 459.

The alliances with Argos, Thessaly and Megara are all easily understandable, once we have grasped the fact that the Athenians must have been not only annoyed but thoroughly alarmed by the hostility the Spartans revealed towards them in 462. When the Spartan Pericleidas made his appeal for Athenian help against the Messenians, and Cimon urged that an expedition be sent, to preserve Athens' partner and prevent Greece from going lame, Ephialtes opposed him on the ground that Sparta was 'a city antagonistic (*antipalon*) to Athens'.[52] When the Athenians were dismissed from Ithome, it became clear that the Cimonian 'dual hegemony' could no longer be regarded, as it had been ever since 478/7, as a secure foundation for Athenian foreign policy. Perhaps at this time the news of the Spartan promise to Thasos also became known at Athens. Now Athens was exceedingly powerful at sea, but by land she was very vulnerable to a Peloponnesian invasion, the Long Walls being still in the future (see Thuc. I 107.1,4; 108.3) and Athens' hoplite army obviously no match for the combined armies of Sparta, her Peloponnesian allies and the Boeotians. What she needed, and quickly (in case of a sudden Peloponnesian attack), was two things: allies who could provide hoplites and cavalry, and a barrier against a Peloponnesian invasion across the Isthmus. So Athens turned to Argos, the one State outside Sparta's alliance which might be able to supply large hoplite reinforcements; to Thessaly,[53] which had the best cavalry in Greece (and had sent them to

---

[51] See M/L 33 = Tod I² 26 = *IG* I² 929. *ATL* III 174 n. 53 gives rival views on the date. Some valuable remarks on the early campaigns of the First Peloponnesian war down to the mid-450s will be found in Jeffery, BOSP 52–7.

[52] See Plut., *Cim.* 16.8–10. For Pericleidas, see also Ar., *Lysistr.* 1137–44. Pericleidas, who had a son named Athenaios (Thuc. IV 119.2; 122.1), is likely to have been Athenian proxenos at Sparta.

[53] See Jeffery, BOSP 52 n. 49, for a useful note. Cf. Thuc. I 107.7; 111.1; also II 22.2–3 (with Gomme, *HCT* II 77–9), on the events of 431; and IV 78 (esp. §§2–3); V 13.1.

Athens' help before);[54] and to Megara, whose territory might supply means of preventing a Peloponnesian entry into Attica. In the past Athens had not needed the help of any of these States, but now she would be in real danger, should the latent hostility revealed by Sparta be translated into military action. To ally herself with Argos, Sparta's traditional rival, was a desperate step, for it would confirm Sparta's suspicions and might accelerate a Peloponnesian League attack, especially if Argos was already (as Thucydides implies: see above) in a state of war with Sparta. Some may regard it as a mistaken and provocative step. Others may be content to give Athens the benefit of the doubt and to suppose that she would not have allied herself, for the first time in the history of the democracy, with a State which had even stood aloof from the Greek alliance in the Persian war, if she had not been driven to do so by a very real fear of Sparta.

For the attitude of Pericles, see Appendix X.

(iv)
Aeschylus

One Athenian of the day whose outlook is known to us, and who will hardly be regarded as either irresponsible or an alarmist who was too easily frightened, had no doubt at all that Athens' future lay not with Sparta but with Argos: this is none other than the poet Aeschylus. In the *Eumenides*, produced early in 458 (see *Hypoth. ad Agam.*), Aeschylus goes right out of his way, and far beyond the demands of the plot, to stress the necessity of *a military alliance for ever* between Athens and Argos[55]—which could only involve perpetual hostility to Sparta. It is seldom noticed how emphatic, even extreme, the language is. It is not only Orestes who speaks

[54] In 511–10: see Hdts v 63.2–4; 64.2; Arist., *Ath. Pol.* 19.5; and cf. Thuc. II 22.3 ('the ancient alliance'). According to Dem. xxIII 199, Menon of Pharsalus had contributed 12 talents of silver and 300 horsemen (from his own *penestai*) at the time of the Athenian campaign against Eïon (in the early days of the Delian League, under Cimon). Another testimony to cordial relations between Cimon and at least some Thessalians is the fact that Cimon named one of his sons Thessalus (see Plut., *Cim.*, 16.1; *Per.* 29.2; *Alc.* 22.4). Apparently Cimon was not a Thessalian proxenos at Athens (see Plut., *Cim.* 14.4). But the Thessalian cavalry deserted the Athenians on the battlefield of Tanagra in 458 or 457: see Part v below and its n. 66.

[55] Cf. J. H. Quincey, 'Orestes and the Argive Alliance', in *CQ* 58 = n.s. 14 (1964) 190–206; A. J. Podlecki, *The Political Background of Aeschylean Tragedy* (Michigan, 1966) 82 ff. The most valuable treatment of the problem of Aeschylus' political attitude is still K. J. Dover, 'The Political Aspect of Aeschylus' *Eumenides*', in *JHS* 77 (1957) 230–7. E. R. Dodds, 'Notes on the *Oresteia*', in *CQ* 47 = n.s. 3 (1953) 11–21; and 'Morals and Politics in the *Oresteia*', in *PCPS* 186 (1960) 19–31, at p. 22, is certainly wrong about *Eumen.* 693–5: it is unthinkable that Aeschylus could intend such contemptuous expressions as κακαῖς ἐπιρροαῖσι and βορβόρῳ ... ὕδωρ λαμπρὸν μιαίνων to refer to the great Athenian hoplite class, of which he himself was a member. Cf. Jacoby, in *FGrH* III b (Suppl.) ii.528. It is interesting to compare the fervent *Eumenides* passages cited below with the more negative tone of the oath Athena imposes upon Adrastus (on behalf of Argos) in Eur., *Suppl.* 1185–1209, where only line 1193 contemplates military help to Athens, and purely defensively at that. On Euripides' attitude to Argos, see Andrewes, in Gomme, *HCT* IV 50; and on the date of his *Suppl.*, see Appendix XXIX n.1 below.

in this vein, soon after his first entry (lines 287–91) and in his speech of farewell (762–74); Apollo too is made to stress the necessity for perpetual military alliance between the two States in a solemn passage (667–73) at the end of his speech in defence of Orestes. Mere advocacy of Athenian-Argive friendship, *philia*, would have been quite sufficient, dramatically, as a consequence of the acquittal of Orestes by the Athenian Areopagus: coming some three years after the breach with Sparta and the alliance with Argos, it would have been a tactful indication of Aeschylus' political attitude. But the poet had no intention of being tactful about this burning political issue, and he went far beyond what was dramatically necessary. Deliberately using technical terms of Greek diplomatic language, he stressed in each of the three passages the need for *a full military alliance* (*symmachia*) between Athens and Argos, which should *last for ever*. Orestes speaks of Athens as having the Argive people as its *symmachos* (291); Argos will always honour the city of Pallas with its *symmachon dory* (its allied spear, 773); and Apollo echoes the vital word *symmachon* (671). Orestes proclaims that Argos will be Athens' ally 'for ever' (*es to pan*, 291), and he hammers home this point again when he speaks of oaths 'sworn to the land and the army of Athens for all the whole length of time'.[56] Apollo too stresses that Argos will be 'faithful for the whole of time' (*pistos es to pan chronou*, 670). This is all the more remarkable when we remember that at least some months (and perhaps two years) before the *Oresteia* was produced war had broken out between Athens and the Peloponnesian League (see Part vi of this Chapter). Yet Aeschylus, who had himself fought as a hoplite at Marathon and Salamis, was not dismayed at the consequences of the breach with Sparta: he was anxious that that breach should be confirmed and made permanent by a perpetual alliance with Sparta's enemy, Argos.

Nor are the passages we have noticed the only demonstration of Aeschylus' wholehearted approval of the Argive alliance. Sparta, it will be remembered (see Chapter IV, Part iii above), had since the middle of the sixth century been claiming for herself 'the heritage of Agamemnon' and making that hero and his son Orestes into the ruling house of Sparta. Aeschylus in the *Oresteia* goes right in the opposite direction, associating Agamemnon and Orestes not with Mycenae, where they had ruled in Homer, but with Argos, which had captured and officially 'destroyed' Mycenae a few years earlier[57]—another indication of his approval of the new turn in Athenian foreign policy.

Aeschylus also provides a useful link between Themistocles and the radical democrats.[58] In the Athens of the late 470s, Cimon's Athens, there

---

[56] Lines 763–4: εἰς ἅπαντα πλειστήρη χρόνον ὁρκωμοτήσας. It can no longer be said that Greek alliances were not made 'for ever' until the fourth century: see Chapter IV, Part iv, Section B, §2 above.

[57] Diod. xi 65—under 468/7 B.C., but see Andrewes, SAEFC; Forrest, TA 229–32.

[58] Cf. Jacoby, *FGrH* iii b (Suppl.) ii.532: 'It does not seem doubtful to me that his [Themistocles'] ideas in foreign policy (which envisage what amounts to a break with the leading power of Sparta) entail a position in home policy which brought him into close

was a tendency to glorify Marathon rather than Salamis,[59] partly, no doubt, because Athens alone (with a little help from Plataea) had won the battle of Marathon, whereas Salamis was a Greek victory in which Athens merely had the leading role, but also because the man who could be regarded as the architect of victory at Marathon was Cimon's father Miltiades, and because Marathon was a purely hoplite victory which the Athenian upper classes could claim as theirs alone. There is some very interesting evidence from a later period, showing the existence of such class feelings: it is to be found not only in the aristocratic orator Andocides[60]—whose descent from the god Hermes, through a rather surprising pair, Telemachus and Nausicaa, is recorded by Hellanicus (*FGrH* 323a F 24a,c)—but also in a revealing passage in Plato's *Laws* (IV 706b–7c), where the battles of Salamis and Artemisium are disparaged in favour of Marathon and Plataea, and the Athenian speaker inveighs strongly against relying on sailors (always drawn mainly from the lower classes) rather than hoplites.

Now Aeschylus' *Persae*, produced early in 472, comes as near as a tragedy could to mentioning a living individual, in its reference to the message of Sicinnus, the slave of Themistocles, in lines 353–63 (cf. Hdts VIII 75). And the very fact that the play celebrates the victory of Salamis, at that particular time, makes one inclined to regard it as a deliberate attempt to remind the Athenians of the debt they owed to Themistocles—who was probably at that very moment a likely 'candidate' for the ostracism to which he fell a victim. If one wished to support Themistocles, and prevent his ostracism, could one do so more effectively than by tactfully reminding the Athenians of his finest hour?

The link with the radical democrats is provided by the fact that the choregus for the trilogy of which the *Persae* formed part was Pericles.[61] And the group of radical democrats, of which Pericles became the leading figure at some time (whether immediately or not) after the death of Ephialtes in 461, certainly took over Themistocles' policy,[62] probably in all three of its major aspects (see Appendix XXXI).

---

connexion with what later became the democratic party'. Although I do not see how this statement could be proved, my instinct is to agree with it—except that I would prefer to speak of Ephialtes, Pericles and their political associates as 'the radical democrats' rather than 'the democratic party': there is no reason to think that Cimon and his followers were not 'democrats', if of a more conservative kind. As regards foreign policy, the link between Themistocles and the radicals is perfectly clear: see below, and Appendix XXXI.

[59] See esp. P. Amandry, 'Sur les "épigrammes de Marathon"', in Θεωρία. *Festschr. für W. H. Schuchhardt* (1960) 1–8. I am not convinced by B. D. Meritt, 'The Marathon Epigrams Again', in *AJP* 83 (1962) 294–8, that the first as well as the second epigram refers to Marathon. See M/L 26, with the very useful notes. For an attempt to invent for the Athenian hoplites a special role at Salamis, see C. W. Fornara, 'The Hoplite Achievement at Psyttaleia', in *JHS* 86 (1966) 51–4.

[60] Andoc. 1 107–8, where the circumstances are all those of Xerxes' invasion, but the only battle mentioned, anachronistically, is Marathon.

[61] *IG* II² 2318.9–11 (= Hill, *S*², B 7), with *Hypoth. ad Pers.*

[62] Cf. Jacoby, *FGrH* III b (Suppl.) ii.123 (Pericles 'the heir of so many of Themistocles' ideas'), 387 ('Themistokles, whom Perikles did not love [?], but whose heir he was').

(v)
Argos and Megara

Argos is not recorded as giving Athens much help in the First Peloponnesian war. The Athenians and Argives together claimed a victory over the Spartans at Oenoe, in Argive territory;[63] a thousand Argives fought at the battle of Tanagra in 458 or 457;[64] and early in the war Argos dedicated at Olympia spoils taken from the Corinthians.[65] The Thessalians are not known to have done anything at all except send cavalry for the Tanagra campaign, which deserted to the Spartan side during the battle.[66]

The adhesion of Megara was very much more valuable to Athens, bringing her two quite distinct advantages of the greatest importance. First, while Athens held Pagae, the Megarian port on the Corinthian Gulf, and could secure her land communications with it, a large Athenian fleet could easily operate at very short notice in the Gulf, especially at its eastern end, close to Lechaeum, the main port of Corinth. Naupactus, at the other end of the Gulf, was in Athenian hands during the whole of the First Peloponnesian war, but Naupactus was well over 300 miles from the Peiraeus by sea: the voyage would take a fleet several days and might often be impracticable or dangerous for long periods—the journey around Cape Malea is notoriously unpleasant. As Gomme says (*HCT* I 305), 'the crews should sleep on land on several successive nights. In war-time, only Argos (the first stage) and Zakynthos (the last) were neutral or friendly, to afford this help; until the capture of Kythera and Pylos the crews had no safe and certain place of rest between them.[67] This hindered considerably the proper use of Naupaktos to control the Gulf.' At Naupactus, not only would the actual ships be confined to this particular sphere of operations for perhaps months on end; their crews too, two hundred men to a ship, would be tied down there—and Athens could certainly spare, say, fifty triremes very much more easily than their complement of 10,000 men, who would have to be fed and paid into the bargain. During the Peloponnesian war proper, when Pagae was back in Peloponnesian hands, Athens put little effort into operations in the Corinthian Gulf. It was impossible to spare large naval forces for this isolated theatre of war, and a small squadron could be effectively neutralised by the Corinthian navy, as happened in 414/13.[68] As for a fleet based on Pagae, the ships would be even farther removed from operations in the Aegean, but their crews

[63] See Jeffery, BOSP, esp. 52–7; Bengtson, *GG* [4] 210.
[64] Thuc. I 107.5 and other sources listed in Hill, *S*[2] 360 (Index IV 4.2). See now M/L 35.
[65] Hill, *S*[2], B 110 (p. 322) = DGE 80.
[66] Thuc. I 107.7; Diod. XI 80.1–6; Paus. I xxix.9; and cf. Thuc. I 111.1.
[67] Gomme here presupposes knowledge of his fundamental paper, FFGNS, often mentioned in this book. One might add that much of the coast of the Peloponnese is rocky and dangerous, and very inhospitable to triremes seeking shelter from a storm.
[68] See the most illuminating story (prompting comparison with 'fighter cover' for bombers in the Second World War!) in Thuc. VII 17.2–4; 19.3–5; cf. 31.4; 34. And see II 80.4, where Cnemus evades the Athenian fleet.

could be marched across the Megarid and put aboard, or brought back, in a matter of days, even in winter. Through Pagae, too, a fleet at Naupactus could be much more quickly and safely supplied or reinforced. And at Pagae an Athenian fleet would be a mere twenty miles or so from the entrance of the bay in which lie the ports of Corinth and Sicyon, and if large enough could be a serious nuisance to shipping entering or leaving those ports—not merely, like a fleet at Naupactus, to ships passing through the entrance to the Gulf.

Athens did station a considerable fleet at Pagae during at any rate part of the First Peloponnesian war. The fifty ships mentioned by Diodorus[69] under the year 458/7 may have been those stationed at Pagae; and Pericles, in his expedition in the Corinthian Gulf in *c.* 454 (Thuc. I 111.2–3), certainly used the fleet then at Pagae, consisting according to Plutarch (*Per.* 19.2–3) of a hundred triremes and according to Diodorus (XI 85.1) of fifty. Plutarch's figure is not necessarily wrong, as Pericles is said by both Thucydides and Diodorus to have had 1,000 marines, and by the time of the Ten Years war, if not before, there were usually ten marines (*epibatai*) to each Athenian trireme.[70]

The Nisaea-Megara-Pagae route may perhaps have been used sometimes by merchants trading between Athens and the West if and when the way across the Isthmus of Corinth was closed to them, during a war between Corinth and Athens. The difficulty and expense of transport between Nisaea and Pagae, however, would make this route unsuitable except for articles of great value in relation to their bulk and weight. Corn and timber (the most important commodities Athens might expect to receive from the West), and pottery and oil exported from Attica, would not be among these exceptions. It would be wrong to conceive the Athenian interest in Pagae as commercial[71] rather than strategic and naval.

The other reason why a Megarian-Athenian alliance was so valuable, from the Athenian point of view, was the protection which possession of the Megarid might under certain conditions afford to Athens against Peloponnesian invasions. It is this above all which explains the very different part played by Sparta herself in the two phases of the long conflict with Athens: the First Peloponnesian war and the Peloponnesian war proper. This subject will be dealt with in Part vi of this Chapter.

(vi)
Sparta in the First Peloponnesian war, and the importance of Athenian control of the Megarid

We cannot doubt that Sparta regarded herself as being at war with Athens from the time that Megara deserted the Peloponnesian League and

---

[69] Diod. XI 80.1. Cf. Part vi of this Chapter, *ad fin.*,

[70] This is well known. See e.g. Thuc. II 69.1 and 92.7 with 102.1; III 91.1 with 95.2; IV 76.1 with 101.3.

[71] As, for example, Dunbabin evidently did (*WG* 243).

entered into alliance with Athens. (Some historians seem not to realise this.)[72] When the formal declaration of war took place, we cannot say. But during 460 and/or 459[73] the Athenians were fighting at least the Corinthians, Epidaurians and Aeginetans; and Thucydides, besides referring to the 'allies' of the Aeginetans (1 105.2) and of the Corinthians (105.3), speaks of an engagement off Cecryphaleia between the Athenians and 'ships of *the Peloponnesians*' (105.1), and, more significantly, says that when the Athenians began the siege of Aegina, '*the Peloponnesians*, wishing to aid the Aeginetans, took across to Aegina 300 hoplites who had earlier been acting in support of[74] the Corinthians and Epidaurians' (105.3). Thucydides can sometimes employ the term 'Peloponnesians' loosely, in a geographical sense, but he also uses it very frequently to denote what we call 'the Peloponnesian League': the Spartans and their allies. The latter sense seems to be required in at any rate the second of the two passages just quoted, for the 300 hoplites are not Aeginetans, Corinthians or Epidaurians, and are put into Aegina *by a decision of 'the Peloponnesians'* aimed at saving Aegina—which was of course a member of the Peloponnesian League (see Appendix XVII).

Certainly in 458 or 457 (I see no way of deciding between these two dates) Sparta clashed openly with Athens in the battle of Tanagra, and Sparta's Boeotian allies fought the Athenians two months later at the battle of Oenophyta (see below). In 457 or 456 (probably the latter year) the Athenians under Tolmides, in a *periplous* of the Peloponnese, actually raided Laconia itself, burning the Spartan dockyards at Gytheum.[75] Thucydides later records a five-year truce between 'the Peloponnesians and Athenians', in a year which must be 451.[76] Here there can be no question that 'the Peloponnesians' are 'the Spartans and their allies', who are named explicitly in connection with the Thirty Years Peace of 446/5 (Thuc. 1 115.1), after 'the Peloponnesians' under the Spartan King Pleistoanax had at last launched an invasion of Attica across the Isthmus of Corinth. Only one other military operation during the First Peloponnesian war is specifically attributed by Thucydides to the Spartans: their 'Sacred War' on behalf of Delphi, which they freed from Phocian control during the five-year truce; the Athenians retaliated before long by

---

[72] E.g. Bengtson, *GG*⁴ 209–10; Wickert, *PB* 62–4, etc.

[73] Cf. M/L 33 (= Tod I² 26 = *IG* I² 929), with the notes; for the date, see also *ATL* III 174 n. 53. I have nothing new to say either on the date of this inscription or on the question how Athens could have launched a great expedition to Egypt at the very time at which she became involved in hostilities with the Peloponnesians. Cf. Kagan, *OPW* 81 ff.

[74] The word Thucydides uses is ἐπίκουροι, which usually means mercenaries, but need not (cf. 1 40.3). In Thucydides, ἐπικουρικός always refers to mercenaries, whereas ἐπικουρία and ἐπικουρεῖν ordinarily do not.

[75] Thuc. 1 108.5; Diod. xi 84.3–6 (adding Methone, §6); Paus. 1 xxvii.5, and Schol. Aeschin. ii 75 (adding Cythera); Aristodemus 15.1.

[76] Thuc. 1 112.1; cf. Theopomp., *FGrH* 115 F 88, *ap.* Schol. Aristeid. p. 528.4 (Dindorf); Andoc. iii 3. The date, 451, although not certain, is the one most generally accepted; but see Gomme, *HCT* 1 325–6, 409–13.

restoring Delphi to Phocian control.[77] The Phocians had been allies of Athens since 458–7 or a little later:[78] perhaps the fact that Sparta launched an expedition against them during the continuance of the truce can be accounted for by supposing that the truce was made by Sparta and her allies with the Athenians alone, as indeed Thucydides says (112.1).

In the last two paragraphs I have not been concerned with any actions in the First Peloponnesian war except those involving Sparta herself. (It is not my intention to give a general account of that war.) The most striking fact which is immediately obvious is that until 446 Sparta made no attempt to mount a Peloponnesian invasion of Attica across the Isthmus of Corinth—the very cornerstone of her strategy in 431 and the years following. Only twice in the years before 446, as we have seen, did a Spartan army even enter northern Greece: in 458–7 and for the Sacred War against Phocis in the early 440s; and in neither case was there a direct attack on Athens or any ravaging of Attica. Yet Sparta must have been formally at war with Athens almost from the first, and some of her allies were heavily involved in the war—we hear of Corinth, Aegina, Epidaurus, Sicyon and unnamed 'allies'. And the Boeotians, also allies of Sparta, were under Athenian domination from at least 457 to 446. All the allies must have clamoured at Sparta for the one action against Athens which would have seemed likely to have a decisive effect: an invasion of Attica across the Isthmus of Corinth by the full Peloponnesian levy, led by Sparta. Yet this was not attempted until 446. Why not? Sparta must have 'lost face' very seriously by her failure to help her allies, some of whom suffered considerably during the war. Aegina, in particular, which had helped Sparta against the Helots in her time of need (Thuc. II 27.2; IV 56.2), was forced to yield to Athens and join her Confederacy, paying the very high tribute of 30 talents a year.

The Great King also sent Megabazus to Sparta with a large sum of money, hoping to persuade the Peloponnesians to invade Attica, and thus draw away the Athenian forces which were campaigning in Egypt;[79] but the mission had no effect, 'and the money', says Thucydides enigmatically (I 109.2–3), 'was spent in vain'—one would like to know who received it,

[77] The chronology of both campaigns of the 'Sacred War' is disputed. It will be sufficient to refer to Gomme, *HCT* i 337, 409; *ATL* iii 178–9 nn. 64 (which I cannot accept) and 65; Jacoby, *FGrH* iii b (Suppl.) i.320 (on Philoch., 328 F 34: Jacoby thinks 'τρίτῳ ἔτει in the careless excerpt . . . is incredible').

[78] It used to be thought, for no good reason, that *IG* i² 26 = Tod i² 39 = *SVdA* ii 142 was a renewal, after a few years, of an alliance made between Athens and the Phocians in 454/3; but this inscription is now differently interpreted: see *SEG* x 18 = xii 7 = xiii 3 = xvi 2 = xxi 6 = xxii 2. However, Thuc. i 111.1 does speak of the Athenians as having the Phocians (as well as the Boeotians) as their allies in their expedition into Thessaly in *c.* 454; cf. 108.3 and Diod. xi 83.3.

[79] Thuc. i 109.2–3; cf. Diod. xi 74.5–6. I see no reason to connect this incident, as others have done (see e.g. Gomme, *HCT* i 327 n. 1), with the Athenian decree against Arthmius of Zeleia (the sources for which will be found in Hill, *S*² 343, Index i 6.12), especially if that decree was proposed by Cimon, for I do not believe that Cimon was recalled to Athens before the ten years of his ostracism had expired. (Here I am glad to find myself in agreement with Wade-Gery, *EGH* 248 n. 6, and Jacoby, *FGrH* iii b [Suppl.] i.478. See esp. Beloch, *GG* ii² ii.210–11. I cannot agree at all here with Meiggs, *CAI*.)

and when: perhaps the autumn of 457 is the most likely date (*ATL* III 178).

We can give a confident answer to our question about the reasons for Spartan inactivity, on the basis of two kinds of evidence, both pointing in the same direction: Thucydides' account of the Tanagra campaign, and the fact that no Peloponnesian invasion of Attica was attempted until Megara returned to her alliance with Sparta, in 446. From *c.* 460 until 446 Athens controlled the Megarid; and nothing will account for Sparta's failure to give effective assistance to her allies, up to the very moment at which Megara revolted from Athens, except the supposition that Athens, during those fourteen years or so, could make a Peloponnesian invasion across the Isthmus too dangerous to be undertaken.

For reasons which will shortly emerge it is virtually certain that the Spartans, making their expedition to Doris (which led later to the battle of Tanagra),[80] had crossed into northern Greece by sea. Thucydides explains (as we shall see) why it was impossible for them to return that way, and he then describes their predicament, as they deliberated in Boeotia on how best to get home safely, adding that they were in secret negotiation with some Athenians who were plotting to betray the city to them, 'hoping to put an end to the democracy and the building of the Long Walls', now in progress (i 107. 3–6). It is worth paying attention to the exact words Thucydides uses (§3). It seemed to the Spartans '*unsafe* (*ouk asphales*)', he says, 'to march over Geraneia [the mountainous interior of the Megarid, to the west of the city], while the Athenians held Megara and Pagae. For Geraneia was *difficult to pass* (*dysodos*) and was continually guarded by the Athenians,[81] and they realised that on this occasion the Athenians intended to dispute their passage at that point.' The Athenians, 'believing they were at a loss how to effect their passage' (§6), marched out and fought a battle against them at Tanagra. After the battle the Spartans led their army home safely. Probably the Athenians, defeated in the battle (though not crushingly, as their victory over the Boeotians at Oenophyta two months later shows), now made no attempt to hinder them.

Determined occupation of Geraneia, Megara and Pagae, with garrisons both inside the two towns and stationed at strategic points on the passes, could evidently make the passage of the Megarid a hazardous affair, even from north-east to south-west. We must not exaggerate: Thucydides does

[80] I cannot discuss here the problem whether we are to accept Thucydides' account (i 107.2), according to which Sparta's original object was the strictly limited one of aiding the Dorians, or whether we are to pay serious attention to Diod. XI 81.2–3, and even suppose that Sparta had from the first the ulterior design of consolidating Theban supremacy in Boeotia, as an anti-Athenian move (see E. M. Walker, in *CAH* v 79–80). I am inclined to accept Thucydides' version. Cf. D. W. Reece, 'The Battle of Tanagra', in *JHS* 70 (1950) 75–6; and see his DFI.

[81] Diod. XI 80.1 makes the Athenians guard the routes over Geraneia with 14,000 men; but this was the whole hoplite army of Athenians and allies which fought at Tanagra (Thuc. I 107.5). For the ancient routes through the Megarid, see Hammond, MRBP; Gomme, *EGHL* 21 ff.; *HCT* II 66–8; III 724–5; Pritchett, 'New Light on Plataea', in *AJA* 61 (1957) 9–28, at pp. 16–22; *Stud. in Anc. Greek Topogr.*, Part I (= *Univ. of Calif. Publ.: Classical Stud.* 1, 1965) 119–21.

not say that Geraneia was completely blocked, only that it was 'unsafe' and 'difficult to pass'. But if that is what it could be made, even for a large Peloponnesian army returning home from the north-east, then (and this is the vital point, so often missed) *it could much more easily be secured against forces attacking from the south-west,* for the two fortified bases would then be in the rear of the defenders of Geraneia, where they could be of much greater use. And the very fact that no Peloponnesian army attempted again to cross the Megarid in either direction, as far as we know,[82] whereas immediately Megara returned to her Spartan allegiance in 446 the Peloponnesians invaded Attica through the Isthmus, is very strong circumstantial evidence that the Megarid could be held firmly enough by Athens to make a Peloponnesian expedition through it too hazardous. There was no necessity for Athens to station large forces in the Megarid indefinitely. The Spartans would never march into Attica without first summoning their allies, and this, and the gathering at the Isthmus, would be quite a lengthy business. Consequently the Athenians could rely on having ample notice of an invasion and would not have to immobilise large forces for long periods. They might even hire mercenary light troops for use in the mountain passes, to make up for their own deficiency in that line.[83]

I realise that the views I am advocating run counter to a strong current of opinion on the extent to which mountain passes could be defended against an invader in the fifth century. The most recent writer on the Pentecontaetia whom I have read (Knight, *SSAP* 3–4) simply takes it for granted that the Peloponnesians marched north as well as south across the Isthmus; he fails to grasp the significance of Thucydides 1 107.3; and, with the words 'without superior land forces Athens could not control the passage of the Isthmus', he shows that he has not taken account of the considerable body of evidence relating to the guarding of Greek mountain passes, to be discussed below. Since at least the appearance of Gomme's often valuable study of the conditions of warfare in Classical Greece,[84] it seems to have become generally accepted that Greek states did not defend mountain passes against an invader. The defence of Geraneia, on the occasion with which we are concerned, is noted by Gomme,[85] with the cautious comment, 'This looks like a sensible defensive policy, which could be used against the Peloponnesians coming from the south as well as from the north. This particular line was lost when Megara was lost; but the next, that between Megara and Eleusis, was almost as defensible, yet was never defended, not even, as far as we know, used to harry

---

[82] How the Spartans reached Delphi in their 'Sacred War' of *c.* 448 (Thuc. 1 112.5 etc.), we do not know. They had a truce with Athens, and could well have gone by sea.

[83] See Gomme, *HCT* II 41–2, for a note on the use of archers by Athens.

[84] *HCT* I 10 ff., esp. (for our present purposes) 12–15; cf. Anderson, *MTPAX* 1–8.

[85] *HCT* I 13; cf. 304–5 ('If Megara had remained in alliance with or in the occupation of Athens, Peloponnesian invasions would have been more difficult, if not impossible (cf. 107.3), especially after the building of the walls to Nisaia had made Megara practially impregnable to attack from land'), 448 ('Possession of the Megarid meant for Athens comparative security from Peloponnesian invasions').

and delay, if not to stop, an invading force.' But Gomme is mistaken when he says (just before the passage last quoted) that 'we hardly ever hear in Greek history of a defensive use of mountain country to prevent invasion'. The only example he can think of, apart from the guarding of Geraneia in Thuc. 1 107.3, seems to be Ar., *Acharn.* 1073–7, where Lamachus 'is ordered to the hills, and in winter'; and this, as he rightly remarks, was 'to stay a border-raid, not an army'. But Gomme overlooked the ample evidence in Xenophon which shows decisively that troops who had been stationed in such a way as to command mountain passes could block them against an invading hoplite army, or at least make them very difficult to force. This evidence all comes from the fourth century, and in most (if not all) of the known examples it was peltasts who were used to guard the heights. Naturally peltasts would be best suited to such fighting; but before they became widely available I see no reason why ordinary hoplites, rather less heavily armed than when in line-of-battle (see Xen., *Mem.* III v.27) and supported by light troops (cf. Xen., *HG* IV ii. 14), should not have been used when circumstances permitted. According to Anderson (*MTPAX* 5), 'in the fifth century . . . we do not find states using professional troops, lightly armed for mountain warfare, to guard their frontiers'. But I can think of no occasion in the fifth century when we could have a right to expect any evidence of such activities, even if they occurred, except in the First Peloponnesian war (not the Peloponnesian war proper: see below)—and in this, as we have just seen, there *is* evidence for Athenian ability to block the passage of Geraneia.

In an interesting dialogue in the *Memorabilia* (III v, esp. §§25–7), with a dramatic date of 406,[86] Xenophon makes Socrates advise young Pericles, who has just been elected General, to station 'some active young men, rather lightly armed', in the mountains on the frontier between Athens and Boeotia, who could be 'a scourge to the enemy and an important means of defence of the countryside for the citizens'. During the retreat across Kurdistan, Xenophon's 'Ten Thousand', on at least two occasions, found it very hard going across some hilly country held by javelin-men, slingers and archers, until their peltasts had driven the enemy off the hill-tops: *Anab.* III iv.24–9 and 37–49. (Note esp. §27 for the difficulties of hoplites facing light troops in hilly country.) Cheirisophus actually thought it would be impossible to get past an overhanging hill until the enemy forces occupying it were dislodged (iv.39). Hecatonymus of Sinope, in the speech he made to the army at Cotyora about the dangers and difficulties of crossing Paphlagonia, spoke of the pass leading into that country as being absolutely impregnable if the mountains on either side were held by even a very small force (v vi.7) — a deliberate exaggeration, perhaps, but surely not entirely misleading. In 394, just before the battle of the Nemea, we hear that the light-armed troops of the 'quadruple alliance' (Athens, Thebes, Argos and Corinth) did 'great damage' to the Peloponnesian army as it crossed the border between

[86] For the election of young Pericles as general, see Xen., *HG* I v.16; Diod. XIII 74.1.

Sicyon and Corinth, by discharging missiles and arrows from the heights of Epieikeia (Xen., *HG* IV ii.14).[87] A garrison was then maintained in Corinthian territory, sufficient to make it necessary for the Spartan troops which went to join Agesilaus in Boeotia to go by sea across the Gulf of Corinth and for Agesilaus himself to return to Sparta by that route: *HG* IV iii.15 (note *diabasa*) and iv.1 (*apepleuse*), with Lys. XVI 16. In 389 the army of Agesilaus in Acarnania was harassed by Acarnanian peltasts operating from high ground: at first it was driven down into the plain and could proceed no farther, and it was only with a great effort by hoplites and cavalry[88] that the Acarnanians were driven off (Xen., *HG* IV vi.7–11). Agesilaus then marched off through Aetolia 'by such paths as could not be traversed by large forces or small against the will of the Aetolians' (vi.14), who in fact allowed the Spartans to pass. (One remembers the disastrous experience of the Athenians under Demosthenes in Aetolia in 426: Thuc. III 97.2–98.4.) On the other hand, defence of the whole breadth of the Isthmus in the neighbourhood of Corinth seems to have been rarely attempted, in either direction, after 480, when tens of thousands of Greeks built a massive wall to keep the Persians out (see Hdts VIII 40.) and many other passages, esp. 71.1–2; IX 7.1). In 369, for example, the Spartans and their allies constructed mere stockades and ditches between Cenchreae and Lechaeum, and Epaminondas and the Boeotian army broke through (Diod. XV 68.2–5; cf. Xen., *HG* VI v.51, alleging that Iphicrates undertook to stop the Theban army in the Peloponnese from returning home, by keeping guard at Mount Oneum, south-east of Corinth, but left open the easiest way, past Cenchreae).

Among other passages in Xenophon which might be cited we must not neglect *Cyropaedia* V iv.41–50, which makes it clear why a Greek army was always most reluctant to pass close to a fortified town. Possession by Athens of the city of Megara, right past which went the one good route from the Peloponnese to Athens, would have been a serious setback for Sparta and all her allies; and it is no surprise to find the Boeotians 'considering Megara's peril their own' (Thuc. IV 72.1) when the city was in danger of being captured by the Athenians in 424.

Most important of all, for our present purposes, are the passages in which Xenophon emphasises the importance to the Spartans of first securing the passes of Cithaeron if they wished to invade Boeotia by land. In the winter of 379/8 Cleombrotus had led the Spartan army into Boeotia across Cithaeron, since the Athenians were guarding Eleutherae (Xen., *HG* V iv.14),[89] which commanded the easiest route into Boeotia. It was surely because the pass that goes by Eleutherae was held by the Athenians that Cleombrotus returned home on this occasion by the very difficult

[87] Cf. *HG* IV iv.13 for Epieikeia. See also IV iii.22–3 for the Locrians harassing a Spartan detachment.

[88] Note Xen., *HG* V iv.54: horsemen chasing foot-soldiers up a hill can easily catch them if the going is good.

[89] As Gomme says, *EGHL* 22 (where 'east' in line 7 should presumably be 'west'), this route 'was very little known or used'. And see Hammond, MRBP.

coastal route via Creusis and Aegosthena (iv.16–18).[90] Agesilaus in 378, 'realising that it would not be easy to enter Theban territory unless one first got control of Cithaeron', arranged for a mercenary force to seize Cithaeron in advance (iv.36–7). In the spring of 377 Agesilaus instructed the Spartan polemarch at Thespiae (who had gone there with his regiment by sea, iv. 46) to occupy the heights above the road across Cithaeron, and guard it until he arrived (iv.47, cf. 48). In 376, however, when Agesilaus was unwell and Cleombrotus was in charge of Spartan operations against Thebes, the peltasts whom he belatedly sent ahead to occupy in advance the heights commanding the pass were repulsed by Thebans and Athenians who were already in control of the summit; and Cleombrotus, who now 'thought it impossible to cross over into Theban territory', abandoned the campaign altogether and went home (iv.59), nor did the Spartans attempt an expedition against Thebes in the following year, 375 (iv.63).

That mountain passes could be and were effectively held by Greeks, sometimes with quite small forces, against invading armies has now been sufficiently demonstrated. There is other evidence which has not yet been cited (e.g. Xen., *Anab.* i iii.14; iv i.20 to ii.27; and viii.8–19, esp. the hoplites in §§ 15, 19), but the multiplication of further examples is surely unnecessary.

The question of the defensibility of the north-western and south-western frontiers of Attica depends very much on whether we are looking at the First Peloponnesian war or the Peloponnesian war proper. To judge by *Mem.* iii v.27, quoted above, Xenophon seems to have thought it would have been worth while for the Athenians to try to block the northern passes against the Boeotians even in the last years of the fifth century, when the Spartans were ensconced at Decelea. We may feel sceptical at this opinion of Xenophon's, expert soldier as he was. Would it be very useful merely to block entry from Boeotia, when a Peloponnesian army could still enter Attica from the Megarid? (I do not think we need take seriously the claim Thucydides [iv 95.2] puts into the mouth of Hippocrates, before the battle of Delium: that if the Athenians are victorious the Peloponnesians, deprived of the Boeotian cavalry,[91] will never again invade Attica.) To guard all the various routes into Attica from the Megarid and Boeotia would surely be a very difficult task, even before the occupation of Decelea, and impossible after it. And merely to defend the main entry route from the Megarid along the Eleusinian Gulf (even if a stand of any sort could be made here against a Peloponnesian army, which is doubtful) could do no more than delay a Peloponnesian advance, for there were too many different routes from Boeotia into Attica,[92] along which Pelopon-

---

[90] The polemarchs led the army back by the same route in 371, after Leuctra (Xen., *HG* vi iv.25–6).

[91] It is true that only the Boeotians, Phocians and Locrians (Thuc. ii 9.3) provided cavalry for the Peloponnesian army until Sparta herself raised a force of 400 horsemen in 424 (iv 55.2).

[92] See Gomme, *EGHL* 21–3; Hammond, MRBP; Lilian Chandler, 'The North-West Frontier of Attica', in *JHS* 46 (1926) 1–21.

nesian as well as Boeotian forces might travel, and which would allow
Athenians on the Megarian frontier to be taken in the rear, unless they
hurried back into Athens in time. And the mere delaying of a Peloponnesian invasion was simply not worth while, since the Athenians would
have ample warning of each invasion. It is on these lines that I would
explain the failure of Athens even to try to forestall invasion during the
Peloponnesian war proper, rather than invoke Gomme's 'social and
political' explanation (*HCT* 1 14–15), which is not in itself implausible
but seems to me superfluous.

When we look at the First Peloponnesian war, however, the whole
situation is different. Until its concluding stages, the Athenians could
garrison both Megara and Pagae and the heights of Geraneia, and after
Oenophyta they had control of Boeotia too, so that garrisons in the
Megarid had no reason to fear an attack from the rear. This is a sufficient
cause of Spartan inactivity in the First Peloponnesian war, compared
with the war of 431–04. As for what happened in the Tanagra campaign
of 458–7, it is true that Athens had not yet gained control of Boeotia, but
the Boeotians were by no means as formidable as they were soon to become,
for Boeotia was not yet firmly united under Theban leadership (see Thuc.
III 62.5; Diod. XI 81.1–3). And the natural interpretation of Thucydides
1 107.3 is that the Athenians by 458–7 were maintaining garrisons in
Megara and Pagae permanently, and on Geraneia when required.

Even the one major Peloponnesian expedition to north Greece, which
led to the battle of Tanagra, must then have gone out by sea—'presumably', says Gomme (*HCT* 1 314); but there can hardly be any doubt, in
view of the garrisoning we have just noticed and the phrasing of Thuc.
1 107.3, where the historian begins by telling us why it was impossible for
the Peloponnesians to return by sea. It is only necessary to add that we
need not interpret *Athēnaioi nausi peripleusantes* in that passage as meaning
that an Athenian fleet only now sailed from Athens around the Peloponnese and into the Gulf of Corinth: such is Thucydides' use of the verb
periplēo̅ (see Appendix XXXIII) that he need not be referring to anything
more than a sailing to-and-fro in the Gulf of Crisa, or at most a voyage
from Pagae around Cape Opus and into the Gulf.

I need do no more than mention in passing Plutarch's statement (*Per.*
17, esp. §4) that Spartan opposition frustrated Pericles' proposal for a
Panhellenic Congress, as the whole story (not a hint of which appears in
any other source) may possibly be a fabrication: see Seager, CDDH. The
date most commonly given nowadays for this incident is the spring of 449
(see Wade-Gery, *EGH* 227–8; *ATL* III 278–80), and that is perhaps
distinctly more likely than any other time; but it is wrong to give that
date as a fact, as people sometimes do (e.g. Kagan, *OPW* 110–13), even
if one accepts the 'Congress Decree' as belonging to this period.

Although, as I have said already, I am not trying to give a general
account of the First Peloponnesian war, it is convenient at this point to

list briefly those episodes in that war about which we have some information. It will be seen that after the battles of Tanagra and Oenophyta
in 458 or 457, and the surrender of Aegina, no direct clashes between
Athens and the Peloponnesians are recorded until 446, except for the
naval expeditions of Tolmides (probably 456) and Pericles (*c.* 454).

c. 460	Athenian alliance with Megara: war soon begins between Athens and 'the Spartans and their allies'.
	Battles at Halieis (which Athens may just possibly have held for a time during this war: see Hdts vii 137.2), Cecryphaleia, and off Aegina, which is now besieged.
	Battle in the Megarid.
458 or 457	Peloponnesian expedition to Doris, leading to battle of Tanagra. Battle of Oenophyta. Athens gains control of Boeotia and Phocis.
?457	? Battle of Oenoe in the Argolid. (The date is very uncertain.)
457	Aegina surrenders to Athens.
(457 or) 456	Periplous of the Peloponnese by Tolmides, with attacks on Gytheum (and perhaps Methone), Chalcis in Aetolia (a Corinthian colony) and Sicyon.
456/5	Not later than this (and perhaps several years earlier) the Messenians leave Ithome, and are settled at Naupactus by the Athenians.
c. 454	Pericles' expedition from Pagae into the Corinthian Gulf, with attacks on Sicyon and (with Achaeans) on Oeniadae in Acarnania.
?451	Five Years Truce.
Between 449 and 447	Spartan and (later) Athenian intervention at Delphi.
446	Revolt from Athens of Boeotia, Euboea and Megara. Brief Spartan invasion of Attica.
446/5	Thirty Years Peace. Athens is confirmed in possession of Aegina, but has to give up Nisaea, Pagae, Troezen (evidently acquired during the war) and Achaea. (Doubtless Athens' alliance with Hermione, recorded in *SEG* x 15 [= *SVdA* ii 150 = Hill, *S*² b 29; cf. *SEG* xix 5], had already ceased.)

(vii)

The events of 446/5

Having explained the failure of Sparta to play her expected part in
the First Peloponnesian war, we can now pass on to her subsequent
behaviour.

We must first recall the way in which the war had ended.[93] The revolt of Boeotia from Athens had been followed by that of Euboea, and Pericles had crossed over to the island with an Athenian army, when news came that Megara too had revolted. (Presumably the five-year truce had by now expired.)[94] With the Megarid under her control again, Sparta was at last able to launch a League invasion of Attica by land across the Isthmus, under the leadership of the Agiad King Pleistoanax (son of Pausanias, the victor of Plataea), who had been too young to command the expedition into northern Greece in 458–7.[95] (The interesting question why neither of the expeditions of 458–7 and 446 was commanded by the Eurypontid King Archidamus II, a mature man with a good military record, has already been raised: see Chapter IV, Part v, Section c above.)

Athens was now placed in an exceedingly dangerous position. Boeotia and Megara were already irretrievably lost, and Euboea might prove very difficult to recover if her revolt were consolidated—for example by the introduction of a Peloponnesian garrison. The longer the grace given to the organisers of the revolt (presumably above all the Hippobotae of Chalcis, mentioned by Plut., *Per.* 23.4), the less likely it was that Athens would be able to reconquer this essential dependency.[96] But Pleistoanax' invasion obliged Pericles to bring the army back hastily to Athens; there were also some Athenian operations in the Megarid which at least succeeded in holding Pagae, surrendered only by the Thirty Years Peace (see M/L 51 = Tod I² 41 = *IG* I² 1085; cf. Diod. xii 5.2). Surely, even if Pleistoanax wanted (as I believe we can infer) to effect a settlement of the war with Athens on reasonable terms, rather than strike a deadly blow at Athens, it was his duty to put Sparta in as favourable a bargaining position as possible, by pressing Athens hard, and above all preventing her from sending the army back to complete the reduction of Euboea. In the event the invasion was abandoned soon after the Peloponnesians had crossed the Athenian frontier: they got no farther than 'Eleusis and the road to Thria'[97] before turning around and going home, leaving Pericles free to cross over to Euboea once more with large forces and crush the revolt. 'When the peace negotiations began Euboia was safely in Athens' hands and the maritime empire was secure', as the

[93] I shall usually refer only to some of the more important sources. The rest can easily be found in Hill, *S²* 344–5 (Index 1 7.4–7).

[94] See Gomme, *HCT* 1 341, 413. The revolts of Euboea and Megara had surely been concerted with the Spartans. Megara now returned to her membership of the Peloponnesian League (Diod. xii 5.2).

[95] According to Plut., *Per.* 22.2, Pleistoanax was young enough for the ephors to think it necessary to send Cleandridas out with him to be his guardian and adviser (φύλαξ, πάρεδρος, σύμβουλος). On this statement, contrast White, ADPS 140–1, and Cawkwell, FT 55–6 n. 16. Only one very late source, Suid., *s.v. ephoros* (not included in Hill, *S²*), states that Cleandridas was ephor in 446; but there is no good reason to doubt this, as Cleandridas was evidently the most important individual accompanying Pleistoanax.

[96] On the great importance of Euboea to Athens, see H. D. Westlake, 'Athenian Food Supplies from Euboea' in *CR* 62 (1948) 2–5.

[97] Θριᾶζε in Thuc. 1 114.2 and ii 21.1 (not Thria itself). The Peloponnesians may not have gone much past the River Cephisus.

authors of *ATL* (III 301) have emphasised. It was said that Pleistoanax and his principal adviser Cleandridas had been bribed by Pericles to withdraw, and they were both forced into exile (see Appendix XXVI), Cleandridas receiving the citizenship of Thurii (Thuc. VI 104.2 etc.) and Pleistoanax taking sanctuary on Mount Lycaeum in Parrhasia, the extreme south-west of Arcadia. According to Ephorus (*FGrH* 70 F 193), as quoted by a scholiast on Aristophanes' *Clouds* (859), Pleistoanax was fined 15 talents and went into exile because he was unable to pay. But there is reason to think (as Busolt and others have realised)[98] that in fact Pleistoanax was condemned to death, probably because he feared to stand trial: he made a dwelling for himself half inside the precinct of Zeus Lycaeus, and stayed there for over eighteen years;[99] and this suggests that he had reason to fear for his life. It is perhaps desirable to stress the fact that the punishment of Pleistoanax and Cleandridas could not have been for accepting injurious peace terms (these must of course have been accepted first by the Spartan Assembly and then by a Peloponnesian League Congress), but for leading the army away from Athens, on receipt of a bribe.

This incident has been much discussed, seldom to any purpose. We should not pretend that we can know for certain what happened behind the scenes: whether Pleistoanax and Cleandridas were really bribed, or whether a bargain was struck between them and Pericles which both sides believed to be to the advantage of their cities. I would argue that if the actions of Pleistoanax and the three Agiad kings who succeeded him are seen in perspective, a very consistent and sensible foreign policy of 'coexistence' with Athens emerges, the very opposite of the aggressive policy of the Spartan 'hawks' (cf. Chapter IV above, Part v, Section *C*, and Part vi). I also believe that the settlement effected by the Thirty Years Peace was probably on the whole very acceptable to Pericles personally. At this point there is one conclusion in particular that I wish to draw about the behaviour of Pleistoanax and Cleandridas: by their premature withdrawal they made it highly probable that Athens would soon regain control of Euboea, and they thereby abandoned a very important bargaining counter which they might have conceded only during the final peace negotiations. Kagan (*OPW* 125), endorsing the view of De Sanctis that 'if Pericles spent money to induce Pleistoanax and Cleandridas to retire from Attica it was money spent uselessly', adds, 'for all the Spartans could accomplish by a victory was the destruction of a number of Athenian soldiers and the destruction of the Attic countryside'. But was it likely that the Athenians would come out for a pitched battle? They had done so in 458–7, but now the Long Walls had been completed, and they could stay behind them. What now mattered most to Athens was to be able to send the army back to Euboea: they would surely not wish to endanger it in a major battle with the Peloponnesians. The mere

[98] Busolt, *GG* III i.428 and n. 1; *GSK* II 661 n. 6. Cf. Xen., *HG* III v.25.
[99] Thuc. II 21.1; v 16.2–3; with Paus. VIII xxxviii.2–7.

withdrawal of the Peloponnesians made possible the immediate reduction of Euboea. Had they merely stayed in Attica, or withdrawn only after sending a garrison to Euboea, the Athenians might have been denied the one thing they most desired. Moreover, it has often been assumed, for instance by Beloch,[100] that the terms of the Thirty Years Peace were agreed between Pericles and the Spartan king before Pleistoanax withdrew; but how could Pleistoanax and Pericles be sure that both the Athenians, and the Spartans and the majority of the Peloponnesian League allies, would accept those terms entire?

There are some vital factors which we do not know. As we have seen, we cannot tell whether the Athenians would have come out to fight the Peloponnesians. No doubt this depends partly on the size of the Peloponnesian army, and this also is unknown to us. Again, how long could the Peloponnesians have stayed in Attica? In the Ten Years war their longest invasion lasted only about forty days (Thuc. II 57.2): they had to bring their rations with them, and evidently they had difficulty in making them last more than a few weeks (cf. II 23.3; III 1.3; 26.4; IV 6.1). Did Pericles perhaps make promises to Pleistoanax of peace terms, such as the surrender of Naupactus, or even of Aegina, which he either had no intention of advocating to the Athenians or was ultimately unable to persuade them to accept? Would it have been possible for the Spartans, if they had advanced right into Attica, instead of stopping just inside the western border, to put into Euboea a garrison strong enough to prevent its reconquest by Athens?

With all these uncertainties we cannot afford to be dogmatic. But clearly the majority of the leading men at Sparta, soon after the Peace was concluded, felt that Pleistoanax and Cleandridas had betrayed Sparta's interests in bringing about a situation in which peace had had to be made on terms more favourable to Athens than they need have been.

I have spoken of 'the majority of the leading men at Sparta' rather than, for example, 'the majority of Spartans', or even 'the dominant section of Spartan opinion', because it seems that Pleistoanax and Cleandridas must have been tried by the Gerousia and ephors (see Chapter IV, Part v, Section B above). How far the condemnation of the two men can be taken as an indication that the 'hawks' were now dominant at Sparta must remain doubtful. Beloch[101] thought that what he called 'the war party' now took the helm and retained it for some time. This is indeed quite plausible; but we must not neglect the alternative possibility that those who voted for condemnation were motivated primarily by indignation that the king had thrown away an important advantage by retiring from Attica at a time when vigorous action was essential, if only to place Sparta in a favourable position at the negotiating table. The precarious

---

[100] *GG* II² i.182–4, on the 'Präliminarfriede'. Cf. Gomme, *HCT* II 74: 'The real bribe to Pleistoanax was the offer to surrender, or to discuss the surrender of, Megara, Troizen, and Achaia.'

[101] *GG* II² i.195: 'Und allerdings war in Sparta bald nach dem Abschluss des dreissig-jährigen Friedens die Kriegspartei ans Ruder gelangt.'

balance, the frequent oscillation, which we find in Spartan foreign policy (see Chapter IV, Part vi above) make it dangerous to infer anything about the climate of opinion except at those few moments when we have good information about the attitude of leading Spartans or can draw reasonably certain deductions from Sparta's actions.

(viii)
The Spartan 'hawks' again, 440 and 433/2

We have already noticed (in Part ii of this Chapter) the remarkable Spartan promise to invade Attica in 465, at a time when relations between the two states were outwardly, for all we know, quite unstrained. A similar incident, of even greater significance—it is, indeed, absolutely crucial in the history of Spartan-Athenian relations—took place in 440, during the revolt of Samos. We have no explicit information about it, other than three passages in the speech put by Thucydides into the mouths of the Corinthian ambassadors at Athens during the debate in 433 on the question whether Athens should ally herself with Corcyra, and a fragment of an inscription, presumably of 439-8, which may or may not be relevant.[102] Historians have been slow to draw the necessary conclusions from these tantalising scraps of evidence; but, as A. H. M. Jones has pointed out in a brief but very important paper,[103] there can be no reasonable doubt that in 440, only six years after the Thirty Years Peace, Sparta responded to an appeal for help from Samos by formally deciding to attack Athens and summoning a Congress of the Peloponnesian League to authorise a general war by the whole confederacy, only to find a majority of her allies unwilling to follow her. The Corinthians, addressing the Athenian Assembly in 433 in reply to the Corcyraean envoys, are emphasising past benefits they have conferred upon Athens. During the Samian revolt, they say (Thuc. I 40.5), 'we did not cast our vote against you when the other Peloponnesians were divided in their votes on the question whether they should help Samos. We declared explicitly that each state should discipline its own allies.' They return to the subject in two subsequent passages: they refer to 'the good turn we did you over Samos, when it was owing to us that the Peloponnesians did not help her' (41.2); and, claiming that it is now their turn to benefit by the principle they had enunciated at Sparta, that each state should discipline its own allies, they entreat the Athenians, 'after receiving a benefit from our vote, not to injure us by yours' (43.1). From the way they speak of the argument they had advanced at Sparta, it seems likely that they are claiming to have influenced the votes of other states and not merely to have turned an equality of votes into a majority of one against intervention. Why Corinth

---

[102] Thuc. I 40.5; 41.2; 43.1; and M/L 56 (= *IG* I² 50 = D 18 in *ATL* II 72–4), line 7: [-Πελο]ποννεσ[-].

[103] TSDPL. This article is not nearly as well known as it should be. I have seen no discussion of it except in Andrewes, TCW 235–6 (see below).

acted as she did in 440 is a question it is more convenient to deal with in Chapter VI, Part i below.

Jones' interpretation of these passages has been queried by Andrewes (TCW 235–6), who thinks it 'may well be true, but since Thucydides allows no explicit statement about Sparta, we should perhaps mark this instance as uncertain', and he adds in a footnote, 'It does not certainly follow that the Spartan assembly always took its decisions first, and it is to be noticed that a conference might be called by some other member, to judge from [Thuc. 1] 67.1'. This seems to me demonstrably wrong, for two reasons:

1. In Thuc. 1 67.1, it is true, the Corinthians *parekaloun euthys es tēn Lakedaimona tous xymmachous*. But the tense of the verb is the imperfect, and since the action was not a continuing or repeated one (note the *euthys*), the sense must be conative: the Corinthians 'attempted to summon the allies to Sparta'. This is confirmed by the fact that the allies were evidently under no obligation to come, and some of them did not come, for in 67.3 the Spartans are described as *prosparakalesantes tōn xymmachōn te kai ei tis ti allo ephē ēdikēsthai hypo Athēnaiōn*: they summoned in addition any of their allies and others who might claim to have been wronged by Athens.

2. Even more decisive, the meeting which then took place was *not* a congress or conference *of the allies*, as Andrewes more than once calls it (TCW 235 n. 4, 228), but a meeting *of the Spartan Assembly* (*xyllogon sphōn autōn*, 67.3), addressed as such (*ō Lakedaimonioi*) by the Corinthians (68.1; 69.4; 71.1) and the Athenians (75.1; 76.1), and in closed session by Archidamus (80.1) and Sthenelaïdas (86.5; 87.2), with arguments directed to the Spartans themselves, and ending with a vote of the Spartan Assembly, taken in secret (87.1–3, cf. 4). Later, at the summons of Sparta (87.4; 119), there took place a proper League Congress (119–25), addressed as such by the Corinthians (*ō andres xymmachoi*, 120.1; 124.2), with arguments directed to the allied states, and ending with a vote of the allies (119; 125.1). Thucydides is admirably clear and precise in all these technical details.

The Corinthians at Athens, in Thuc. 1 40–3, show beyond doubt, by repeated references to a *vote* of the *allies*, that the meeting at which they claim to have stopped Peloponnesian intervention in 440 was a League Congress and not just a Spartan Assembly at which allies merely *spoke* (like that in Thuc. 1 67–88): see 40.5; 43.1.[104] Thucydides does not describe what we call 'the constitution of the Peloponnesian League': he takes it for granted—rather rashly, if he was expecting his work to be 'a possession for all time'!—that his readers will know this, as they will know the constitution of Athens. But the procedure in 432, carefully and accurately described by Thucydides, is entirely consonant with the view that Sparta alone could call a Congress of her League. As Jones has well put it (TSDPL 43), the machinery was 'so designed that Sparta could not

---

[104] οὐδὲ γὰρ ἡμεῖς . . . ψῆφον προσεθέμεθα ἐναντίαν ὑμῖν and τῶν ἄλλων Πελοποννησίων δίχα ἐψηφισμένων (40.5), and τῇ ἡμετέρᾳ ψήφῳ ὠφεληθέντας (43.1).

be committed to a war without her prior consent, nor could she commit the League to a war without the agreement of the majority of its members'. Hammond (ONAA 51 n. 24) tries to argue against the correct statement in *ATL* III 141 that 'the hegemonic power was surely protected somehow against being outvoted and compelled to execute a policy which it disapproved', and that the hegemon 'had what in Athens would be called "probouleutic" power' and could refuse to put a motion it disliked.[105] After dismissing this as 'pure speculation', he goes on to describe it as 'highly improbable' that Sparta's probouleuma in 440 was for war against Athens, simply because 'there is no mention of so frank a revelation of Sparta's purpose in the preliminaries to the Peloponnesian War'—as if we had a right to expect specific information on this point! As I have just pointed out, Thucydides would expect his readers to understand that of course Sparta herself was in favour of any resolution she put to her League Congress. Finally, Hammond asks scornfully, 'What was Sparta's "probouleuma" when Corinth summoned the allies to Sparta and denounced the Athenians?' (in 432). Thucydides gives the answer: when *Corinth* 'summoned the allies to Sparta' there was no League Congress and so of course no probouleuma; but when *Sparta* later summoned a Congress her probouleuma was what she had already decided in her own Assembly (1 88): 'that the treaty had been broken (by the Athenians)', the equivalent of a declaration that a state of war had arisen again (1 119; 125.1; and see Chapter IV, Part iv, Section B, §3[c]).

The Corinthians at Athens, then, are speaking of a formal Congress of the Peloponnesian League. But it is impossible to suppose that Sparta would ever, before she had made her own decision, convene a League meeting, *and take a vote*, just to discover whether her allies wanted to enter on a war; nor is there any evidence that she ever acted in such a foolish manner. She could have summoned a formal Congress only when, as in 432, she herself had decided to take some definite action and she wished to carry the allies with her. As we noticed earlier (Chapter IV, Part iv, Section B, §6), this was seen by Grote; but strangely enough Grote did not apply his own principle to the affair of 440. 'Many of the allies of Sparta', he says, 'voted for assisting the Samians. What part Sparta herself took, we do not know.'[106] Other writers have shown the same quite unnecessary agnosticism.[107]

Apart from the general principle stated by Grote, there are convincing arguments in favour of the conclusion that Sparta would not summon a League Congress to discuss renewing (or entering upon) a major war

[105] The authors of *ATL* (III 141) say that 'certain things (e.g. the word βούλεσθαι in 1, 87,4) suggest' that it was not 'an automatic routine' for the Spartans to hold a meeting of their own Assembly first, to decide what *probouleuma* should be put to the League Congress. I cannot understand what they mean about βούλεσθαι; and if that is the *best* example they can find, I suspect that their other arguments (if there are any) would be even more flimsy.

[106] Grote, *HG* v 4 (ch. xlviii); IV 514–15 (ch. xlvii).

[107] Beloch, *GG* II² i.195–6, seems to have grasped the truth, but he does not state it explicitly. For the view of *ATL* III 141, see n. 105 above.

without first making her own decision. First, even if there was a serious division of opinion inside Sparta, the dominant section would never consent to transfer the decision to the allies, and the weaker party would not be able to do so. Secondly, even supposing that Sparta really wished to canvass the opinions of her allies, she could do so more satisfactorily and more speedily by sending ambassadors to each of them. Thirdly, although the Spartan ephors, Gerousia and even Assembly might debate in private, there could be little or no hope of preserving secrecy at a Congress of the Peloponnesian League; and if in the end the allies voted against war, as happened on this occasion, it would be all the more unfortunate for the affair to become publicly known: this would be an additional reason for holding private consultations with the allies, rather than a formal Congress, until Sparta had made up her own mind. Fourthly, if the allies did vote for war, and Sparta herself eventually decided against it, she would have provoked her allies publicly and needlessly, by going against the declared wishes of the majority. And finally, in 440 Sparta could not have been driven by the pressure of an irresistibly large number of allies into calling a Congress, for the majority of the allies voted against war. We may infer from the Corinthian speech that the voting at the Congress was close, and that Sparta might perhaps have had her way but for the opposition of her most influential ally. This incident is of the utmost importance for Spartan-Athenian relations. The Congress could not possibly be kept secret for long, although it may conceivably have taken some little time for the facts to become generally known at Athens. The news must have had a profound effect on the outlook of the Athenians. It was now clear that the 'hawks' had the upper hand at Sparta, if only temporarily, and that Sparta would be only too likely to seize the next favourable opportunity to break the Thirty Years Peace. The balance of opinion among Sparta's allies was precarious and might easily be upset by events outside Athens' control.

Far from raising any difficulties, the conclusions we have just reached serve to explain, as nothing else will, the apprehensions felt by the Athenians in 434-3 that they were likely to be attacked by the Peloponnesians in the near future. (Anyone who is reluctant to accept a Spartan decision in favour of war in 440 as virtually certain must at least admit that the Spartan 'hawks' must have been very strong indeed at this time—and this would be quite sufficient to justify Athenian alarm.) We can then see the Callias decrees (Chapter III, Part ii and its n. 27) as part of a prudent policy of defence rather than a preparation for new aggression. And the picture now revealed, of a Sparta intermittently aggressive towards Athens, is quite consonant with Sparta's behaviour in 433-2, our next main subject.

It was no doubt during the winter or early spring of 433/2 that 'the responsible authorities at Sparta' (*ta telē tōn Lakedaimoniōn*) promised the Potidaeans, who were meditating revolt from Athens (see Chapter III,

Part iii above), that Sparta would invade Attica if the Athenians cam-
paigned against Potidaea. The Potidaean request was supported by
Corinthian envoys, who were evidently made aware of its successful result
(Thuc. I 58.1; 71.4).

What exactly is meant by the expression, *ta telē tōn Lakedaimoniōn*,
is an interesting question. The answer is not invariably the same; the
phrase means (as I have translated it) 'the responsible authorities at
Sparta'—whatever this may have been in the particular case in question:
most frequently ephors, Gerousia and ephors, or Assembly. The range of
meanings has been well elucidated by modern scholars;[108] and I will only
say here that the 'authorities' who gave the promise to the Potidaeans may
have been the ephors alone, for in emergencies demanding immediate and
secret undertakings of this kind the ephors may often have been ready to
commit Sparta in advance, in the confident expectation that the Assembly
would endorse their promises. (Cf. Andrewes, GCS 11–12.) The ephors
may or may not have consulted the Gerousia in this instance. It is usually
held that the Assembly could not have voted on the matter; but the Corinthians, addressing the open meeting of the Assembly a few months later,
are made by Thucydides to use the words, 'Help the Potidaeans and
the others quickly by invading Attica, *in accordance with your undertaking*'
(I 71.4); and Andrewes (in Gomme, *HCT* IV 135) thinks the Corinthian
statement 'suggests that the original promise was made not, as is often
assumed, by the ephors but by the Assembly' (cf. Dover, in *Id.* 361).
I think this may well be right, though I do not see how we can be certain
about it. Thucydides might feel entitled to make the Corinthians hold the
Spartans collectively responsible for the fulfilment of a promise made by
the ephors, who may have been acting on their own initiative, in the
justified expectation of carrying the Assembly with them when the
moment came for a declaration of war. But the likelihood of a powerful
opposition to war led by King Archidamus would surely be likely to make
the ephors hesitate to act on their own, without at least consulting the
Gerousia, if not the Assembly itself. The question must be left open. As to
whether the board of ephors (of 433/2) which gave or conveyed the promise of Spartan intervention to Potidaea was that to which Sthenelaïdas
belonged, see Appendix XII, §§3–6.

The only other event of the years immediately before the war which
needs to be mentioned at this point is the Spartan refusal to help Mytilene
revolt from Athens at some unknown date before 432, an incident which
twice receives the briefest mention from Thucydides (III 2.1; 13.1).

---

[108] The fullest collection of references is in Kahrstedt, *GSLSS* 205–7, 283; but the best
analysis is by Andrewes, in Gomme, *HCT* IV 134–5; cf. Busolt, *GSK* II 687–8; Gilbert,
CASA 54 n. 3. Among the variant forms of this expression, the most correct is probably
τὰ τέλη τῶν Λακεδαιμονίων, as it occurs in *Inscr. de Délos* 87.2–5 and Plut., *Lys.* 14.8,
as well as in Thuc. I 58.1. Andrewes (in Gomme, *HCT* IV 23) is right to insist that οἱ ἐν
τέλει (ὄντες) is not an equivalent expression: it 'always means those in office or authority
as opposed to the mass of the soldiers or citizens; whereas τὰ τέλη at Sparta can in a
suitable context mean the whole Assembly'.

He makes the Mytilenaeans speak of their appeal to Sparta as having taken place when they wished *kai palai* to revolt. But he can use the word *palai* of events happening no more than a few months earlier (VII 75.5), and even a few weeks (VIII 94.1). The Mytilenaean approach to Sparta is completely undatable, but it could easily have occurred earlier in the 430s. When in 440 Sparta's proposal to attack Athens was voted down by a majority of her allies, she would be little inclined to listen to appeals from other Athenian allies, with the likelihood of receiving yet another rebuff from the other members of her League. The situation changed materially, however, the moment the appeal of Potidaea was received, for now Corinth, the leader of the opposition in 440, actually supported the appeal.

The Spartan 'hawks' must have been greatly delighted and emboldened by Corinth's change of attitude on the question of a Peloponnesian League war with Athens. This change of attitude was officially demonstrated at the latest by Corinth's support of the Potidaean appeal, and it may have become clear at Sparta earlier. Is it not likely that the Spartan 'hawks' had for some time been in touch with those in Corinth who, like Aristeus (Thuc. I 60–5; II 67.1–4), were enemies of Athens, and had encouraged them to be as provocative as possible, promising them Sparta's support? We may remember the secret encouragement given by Damaratus to the Aeginetans to resist Cleomenes in 491 (Hdts VI 50.3; 61.1), and the way in which King Pausanias privately instructed the members of the democratic Resistance in Athens in 403 what proposals to make to him (Xen., *HG* II iv.35). The Spartans were not unacquainted with secret diplomacy.

From the evidence cited above it is clear that the 'hawks' were very much stronger at Sparta at various times during the Pentecontaetia than most recent historians have been willing to recognise. As we have seen, it would be rash to assert that the 'hawks' were consistently in control after the exile of Pleistoanax in 445. We simply do not know how opinion stood at Sparta. But the decision to assist Samos (and thereby break the Peace) in 440, which must have been a formal one by the Assembly, gave warning to the world that the 'hawks' were now very powerful and at least temporarily in the ascendant. The refusal of Corinth and the League as a whole to countenance a breach of the Peace in 440 may have struck a serious blow at the prestige of the leading 'hawks' and inclined many Spartans to look with more favour on a policy of compromise with Athens, if only because that was what most of Sparta's allies apparently wanted, and Sparta could not risk a major war without the help of her allies.

We now have to look at the situation inside Sparta in 432.

(ix)
Sparta and Athens in 432/1

We have seen (Chapter IV, Part v, Section c above) that in 432 one Spartan king, the Agiad Pausanias, was still a boy, and the Eurypontid

Archidamus II was at any rate against an immediate declaration of war, and perhaps would have preferred not to have to fight Athens at all. I can think of no other occasion in the fifth or fourth century when the Assembly began a war without either king being in favour of it—a situation which was all the less likely to happen, in that the army would normally be led by a king, and the prospect of a successful campaign would be somewhat reduced, and the morale of the army lowered, if neither king relished his task. And we can go further: in the whole history of Classical Sparta there are (as far as I know) only one or two occasions on which we find the opinion of a greatly respected king on a matter of importance being over-ruled by a decision of the Assembly—and the only certain occasion was 432 (see Chapter IV, Part v, Section *A ad fin.*; cf. Section *C*).

I suggest that Thucydides, knowing how Spartan constitutional machinery worked (without ever feeling the need to describe it or explain it), well understood what a difficult task the Corinthians had before them, in principle, in advocating a war which they knew would be opposed by the one man at Sparta who had a reputation as a military commander and would clearly have to take charge of the principal operations of the war; and that the first Corinthian speech in 432 (i 68–71) is principally directed at the considerable number of Spartans who might be disinclined to undertake a war that was disapproved of by Sparta's leading citizen and general. The way Thucydides depicts the vital Assembly has made many people suppose that a reluctant Sparta was dragged into war by Corinth and her other allies. I am quite sure that the historian did not mean to give that impression. It is true that the speech Thucydides put into the mouths of the Corinthians ends (i 71.4–6) with a threat to 'turn to some other alliance'—to desert Sparta and ally with Argos, or perhaps even Athens (cf. Chapter II, Part ii, Section c above). But I see no reason to suppose that this threat—powerful as it would be—actually changed the minds of *many* Spartans and made them reluctantly vote for a war they had until then been unwilling to contemplate, although of course it may well have increased the majority in favour of war. If the Assembly had indeed voted less than a year earlier in favour of attacking Athens in support of a Potidaean revolt, as Andrewes suggests (see Part viii of this Chapter), then the role of Corinth at the Assembly which in effect declared war on Athens could hardly have been a decisive factor. And if, as is quite possible, though far from certain (see Appendix XII, §§3–6), the Assembly took place after about the end of September 432, the election earlier that year of a 'hawkish' board of ephors, including Sthenelaïdas, may be taken as a strong indication that a majority of Spartans already desired war.

Many historians have seen the Spartans as most unwilling fighters, ready to make peace on the slightest discouragement. This view of course comes particularly easily to those who have not understood the very wide scope of Thucydides' exception, when he says in i 118.2 that the Spartans were 'not quick to enter upon wars unless compelled to do so': see Chapter IV, Part ii above. It is not without basis in fact. But those who think it has much relevance to the situation in 432 are seriously mistaken; they fail to realise one cardinal fact, stated in the most positive terms by Thucydides, which is noticed all too rarely in modern discussions of the origins of the war:[109] not only the Spartans but all the Greeks in general[110] were convinced that Athens could not hold out for more than two or three years if her lands were devastated by the Spartans. That is what Thucydides says in VII 28.3. Earlier he speaks of the initial confidence of the Spartans themselves that they would overthrow the power of Athens 'within a few years' by devastating her land, and of the later falsification of these hopes (v 14.3). And he makes Brasidas confess at Acanthus that the Spartans had been mistaken in their expectations about the war in Greece itself, which they had hoped to win quickly by their own efforts (IV 85.2). Even the Mytilenaeans, who should have learnt something from three years of war, and are at least represented as realising that 'the war will not be decided in Attica, as some suppose, but in the places from which Attica draws its support', ask for yet another invasion, this time by sea as well as land (III 13.3–5).

King Archidamus himself seems to have had more confidence in the devastation of Attica as a decisive strategy than one might conclude from a superficial reading of his speech to the Spartan Assembly in 432 (I 80–5, esp. 81.1–2). Even there Thucydides makes him speak of the land of Attica as a valuable hostage (82.4–5); and in his later speech to the Peloponnesian captains in 431 he expresses confidence that the Athenians will come out and fight in defence of their land (II 11.6–8); before reaching the frontier of Attica he sends a personal envoy to Athens, 'in case the Athenians should be more willing to give in when they saw the Peloponnesians already on the march' (12.1), and there were those who ascribed his long delay before ravaging the country to his hope that the Athenians would submit rather than allow this to happen (18.5).

The Spartans were not as foolish in their over-optimism as we might tend to suppose, if virtually all Greece shared their expectations of a speedy victory. The Athenians, after all, had devised an entirely new strategy, which no Greek state that was not an island or situated right on the sea coast had ever tried to employ before.[111] It was the one major innovation in Greek land warfare that had occurred since the inception of hoplite fighting in the seventh century, and it had never yet been properly put to the test. It is not surprising that the Spartans should not have realised how effective it could be, for it had not had a chance to prove itself in 446.

---

[109] None of the three main texts, Thuc. IV 85.2; V 14.3; and VII 28.3 (nor, e.g., VI 11.5; 16.2, lines 27–8 OCT), appears in Kagan's Index of Sources (OPW 413–17), and I do not think that any of them is referred to in the book.

[110] The subsequent words, 'if the Peloponnesians invaded their land', show (in case anyone wishes to dispute it) that the expressions οἱ μέν ... οἱ δέ ... οἱ δέ ... οὐδείς refer not to the Spartans alone but to 'the Greeks' earlier in the sentence.

[111] Cf. only the resistance of Miletus to Alyattes at the very end of the seventh century: Hdts I 17–22.

The expectation by Sparta and her allies of a quick, easy and almost bloodless victory is a factor of great importance for our consideration of the origins of the war. We are apt to forget it because we know how long a struggle Sparta had before her. But if in 432/1 the Spartans anticipated, as they did, that the war would be a 'push-over', it is much easier to believe that most of them needed little persuasion to declare war. The Athenians, on the other hand, knew they would be committed to a long struggle, in which very serious material losses would have to be incurred from the first—far greater losses than they could hope to inflict upon their enemies, with the exception of Megara, whatever Pericles and his supporters may have said by way of encouragement before the war began. It would not be surprising if most of them, unlike the Spartans, were anxious to avoid war, in so far they could do so without bowing to Spartan dictation, an act which was likely to have no better consequence than the encouragement of further Spartan demands, as Pericles claimed it would (Thuc. 1 140.5). Pericles' speech in Thuc. 1 140–4 is over-optimistic in parts (e.g. 142.2–4), but there is no suggestion anywhere of a *quick* or *easy* victory. Indeed, if Thucydides can be relied upon to the letter (and he is the only witness we have), Pericles did not unambiguously encourage the Athenians to hope for *victory* in the full sense: what he said was that Athens had the power to 'win through'—to use Brunt's excellent translation of the terms *perigignesthai, perieinai* (1 144.1; II 13.9; 62.1; 65.7).[112] By 415 Nicias can speak of the Athenians having 'unexpectedly got the better of the Spartans (*perigegenēsthai*), contrary to what they originally feared' (VI 11.5).

I cannot accept the theory of Wade-Gery, in his article on Thucydides in the *Oxford Classical Dictionary*,[113] that Pericles originally planned 'an offensive war'. His strategy can best be characterised as mainly (and necessarily) defensive, with some important offensive elements. For my part, I feel that there was really no sense in which Athens could hope to *win* the war (as distinct from not losing it, achieving a stalemate), except in a rather roundabout way, by bringing about the dissolution of the Peloponnesian League—although to win over Megara (if that were possible) might enable her to block the Megarid sufficiently against Peloponnesian invasions (cf. Part VI of this Chapter). Given the deep anti-Athenian feeling at Sparta and among some of Sparta's allies, a mere stalemate would certainly not be enough for the Athenians to count it as 'winning' the war, however much of a setback it might be to Sparta's aggressive plans; for *the initiative would remain with Sparta*. It is essential to remember that while Athens could attack some of Sparta's allies, and even raid the coasts of Laconia and Messenia (where there were no important centres of population), she could never hope to *win* the war in the only way Greek wars could be won, by invading Sparta's heart-land: any army she could put in the field would be destroyed by the Peloponnesians long before it reached that objective. If a peace were concluded, or if the war

---

[112] Brunt, SPSAW 259. (See his n. 17 for the various meanings of the two Greek words.)
[113] P. 1069 of the second edition, p. 904 of the first.

just fizzled out without a formal treaty, the Spartans could renew hostilities and launch an invasion of Attica at any time that seemed favourable to them—the revolt of a major Athenian ally, for instance. They had intended to break the Thirty Years Peace in 440, and they did break it in 432/1; they could hardly be relied upon to resist a really tempting opportunity.

But Sparta would never invade Attica without the help of her allies. We have no reliable figures for the proportion of *Lakedaimonioi* (Spartiates and Perioikoi) in the Peloponnesian armies that invaded Attica, except for the expedition to north Greece in 458–7, when there were 1,500 *Lakedaimonioi* and 10,000 allies (Thuc. I 107.2). I would regard the 13 per cent on that occasion as about the highest proportion of *Lakedaimonioi* that was likely to occur. Hence the necessity for the Athenians so to chasten and discourage those of the allies whom they could get at, by persistent ravaging of their lands by means of seaborne raids,[114] as well as land raids on the Megarid, that they would begin to refuse to supply their contingents for Sparta's invasions of Attica, and encourage others to do the same, until the Peloponnesian League disintegrated. That was the only way Athens could hope to 'win' the war.

I myself believe that the strategy of fortifying headlands off the enemy coast and using them as a base for raids by sea and even (in suitable cases) by land was not part of the strategy contemplated by Pericles and his colleagues in 432, and that the reference to this strategy (*epiteichismos, epitiechisis*) which Thucydides (I 142.2–4) puts into the mouth of Pericles is very probably anachronistic. This of course must remain uncertain, but there is one important piece of circumstantial evidence: the peninsula of Methana, on the coast of the Argolid, was ideally suited as a base for raiding the enemy states of the Argolid, especially Epidaurus and Troezen, and could easily have been seized and fortified in one of the two large naval expeditions of 431 and 430, but in fact was not occupied until 425 (Thuc. IV 45.2), after the events at Pylos had demonstrated what *epiteichismos* might accomplish. And the remark of the Athenian Strategoi Eurymedon and Sophocles to Demosthenes, when he wanted to fortify Pylos, that there were 'plenty of other deserted headlands around Peloponnese, if he wanted to waste the city's resources by occupying them' (IV 3.3), suggests to me that the policy of *epiteichismos* had been discussed at Athens but rejected until now as too costly to be worth the effort. At any rate, it seems to me that the one criticism we can justifiably make of Periclean strategy is that it made no use of *epiteichismos*. If a determined effort had been made from the start to occupy suitable places, especially Pylos,[115] the serious effects quickly produced[116] by the adoption of the

---

[114] See H. D. Westlake, 'Seaborne Raids in Periclean Strategy', in *CQ* 39 (1945) 75–84 = *EGHGH* 84–100; cf. *Historia* 9 (1960) 390 n. 24 = *EGHGH* 108 n. 24.

[115] But not e.g. a town like Pheia in Pisatis, which was 'harbourless', with its port some distance away (Thuc. II 25.3–4), or Prasiae in Laconia (56.6), far from any important centre of population or rich agricultural area.

[116] See esp. Thuc. IV 41.2–3; 55; 80.2–4; V 14.3; 56.3; 115.2; cf. VII 26.2 (with VIII 4).

policy in 425, after the war had been going on for six years, would have had that much longer to work, and might have resulted in a peace giving Athens even better terms than she obtained in 421.

I need not say anything here about Sparta's war strategy, as it has been admirably treated by Brunt (SPSAW).

I submit that the considerations advanced above strongly reinforce the analysis given by Thucydides of the attitudes of the parties in 432/1, summarised in Chapter III, Part i above, and prove beyond question that that analysis is correct. As we saw, Thucydides' picture is of Spartans mostly eager for war, and egged on by a highly aggressive Corinth, while Athens is anxious to avoid war, provided this can be done without giving way to Spartan demands and thus encouraging the Peloponnesians to expect further damaging concessions and hence to make further demands. We can now see that each side had every reason to feel as it did, having regard to the general pattern of Greek warfare in the past. The Peloponnesians expected a quick and easy victory and were therefore very ready to fight, while the Athenians realised that they would have to sustain a largely defensive war, suffering severely in the process, and could have little hope of an outright victory: at the most they might be able—probably only after several years of war—to bring about the partial disintegration of the Peloponnesian League, or at least secure themselves to some extent against repeated invasion of Attica by fortifying the Megarid.

As Eduard Meyer pointed out more than seventy years ago (*FAG* II 304–5; cf. *GdA* IV ii$^{3-4}$.24–5), one does not enter upon a purely defensive war unless one has absolutely no other choice. To provoke such a war is merely suicidal, and the idea that Pericles, well knowing that Athens would have to fight the war defensively, did indeed provoke it deliberately, with the aim of gaining mastery over the whole of Greece, must be firmly rejected.

VI

Corinth and Athens

(i)
The attitude of Corinth to Athens

Failure to understand the policy of Corinth has been a fruitful cause of misconception of the origins of the Peloponnesian war. Before we try to decide what determined the attitude of Corinth towards Athens, let us very briefly review what is known of the relations between the two states before 432. They fall into four well-marked phases, in which relations were alternately friendly, hostile, indifferent, hostile. Phase I lasted right down to c. 460. Phase II is the First Peloponnesian war, c. 460 to 446/5. For Phase III we have hardly any evidence, but the two states were certainly not at daggers drawn, and on the whole they seem to have coexisted with little direct contact and probably no overt friction. Phase IV begins with the Athenian alliance with Corcyra in the summer of 433.

In Phase I, apart from certain stories in Herodotus connected with Adeimantus, the Corinthian admiral in 480 (see below), there is no trace in the sources of any kind of ill-feeling or friction between the two cities. When Plataea first allied herself with Athens, probably in 519/18, and was attacked by Thebes, and the Plataeans and Athenians were about to fight a battle against the Thebans, the Corinthians intervened and arbitrated (in effect) in favour of Athens' ally Plataea (Hdts vi 108.5). When Cleomenes invaded Attica in c. 506, in the attempt to intervene in the internal affairs of Athens (see Chapter V, Part i above), the Corinthians were the first to object and withdraw from the expedition, which then collapsed; and when Sparta not long afterwards summoned her allies to discuss the restoration of Hippias as tyrant of Athens, the opposition was again led by the Corinthians (Hdts v 92–3). In the war between Athens and Aegina in the early fifth century, Corinth supplied Athens with twenty warships.[1]

It is only in 480, at the time of the great Persian invasion, that we hear of any friction between Corinthians and Athenians, and even then our only source is a series of anecdotes in Herodotus concerning the Corinthian admiral Adeimantus and his relations with Themistocles (viii 5; 59; and esp. 61 and 94). All these anecdotes are highly suspect: Adeimantus was the father of Aristeus, a prominent enemy of Athens in the late 430s,

---

[1] Hdts vi 89; Thuc. i 41.2. On the vexed question of the chronology of the Athenian-Aeginetan wars, contrast A. Andrewes, in *BSA* 37 (1936–7) 1–7, with N. G. L. Hammond, in *Historia* 4 (1955), at pp. 406–11, and L. H. Jeffery, in *AJP* 83 (1962) 44–54.

who was eventually captured and killed by the Athenians while on an embassy to Persia with the aim of persuading the Great King to help the Peloponnesians in the war.[2] The family of Aristeus was evidently the target of malicious Athenian propaganda in the early years of the war, while Herodotus was finishing his History. At least one of the stories about Adeimantus is certainly pure invention (Hdts VIII 94: see the last few words), and we can have no confidence in any of the others. They may conceivably be true; but if they are, they need reflect nothing more than personal rivalry between the two admirals, a situation which the forceful personality of Themistocles was perhaps only too likely to provoke. And Themistocles, surely after rather than before the Persian war, was chosen by Corinth and Corcyra to arbitrate between them in their dispute about the island of Leucas[3]—a testimony to the regard felt at Corinth for Themistocles personally, if not for his city.

It is very often taken for granted that Corinth must have been seriously alarmed by the rapid growth of Athenian sea-power and imperialism from the early 470s onwards. There is something in this, but it should not be exaggerated. A vast increase in the power of any Greek state was bound to be somewhat disturbing to all its neighbours, and a certain nervousness will probably have been felt at Corinth, as elsewhere. If by any chance a clash did occur, Athens would be so much the stronger and any other state relatively so much the weaker. But we have no warrant for jumping to the conclusion that it was this sort of apprehension which so drastically transformed the traditionally friendly relations between Corinth and Athens in the second quarter of the fifth century. The point is that unless a clash actually did occur, for some specific reason, the relative increase in Athenian predominance would not matter to Corinth, especially since Corinth's interests seem to have lain more in the West than in the Aegean: her main port was Lechaeum rather than Cenchreae, and her colonies, except Potidaea (now a subject ally of Athens), were mainly in the West. Corinth and Athens apparently came into contact less than we might have expected: in a seldom noticed passage in their speech at Athens in 433, Thucydides makes the Corinthians claim that they are 'neither enemies of Athens in such a way as to injure her nor friends to the extent of having frequent relations with her' (I 41.1). What we have to decide is: what caused the clash? Except for some harmless bandying of words between Cimon and Lachartus in 462, recorded by Plutarch (*Cim.* 17.1–2),[4] the first we hear of any hostility is in c. 461–60, when Megara deserted the Peloponnesian League and allied herself with Athens as a result of a war 'about boundary lands' forced upon her by Corinth. Phase II in Corinthian-Athenian relations now begins. Thucydides dates from this event the *beginning* of 'the great hatred' (*to sphodron misos*) of Corinth for Athens

---

[2] Thuc. I 60–5; II 67; Hdts VII 137.3. See H. D. Westlake, 'Aristeus, the Son of Adeimantus', in *CQ* 41 (1947) 25–30 = *EGHGH* 74–83.

[3] Plut., *Them.* 24.1; cf. Thuc. I 136.1. I do not share the scepticism about this story felt by Gomme, *HCT* I 438.

[4] Very probably from Ion of Chios: see F. Jacoby, in *CQ* 41 (1947), at p. 9.

(1 103.4). I have heard it said that this dating of the origin of 'the great hatred' to *c.* 460 does not exclude the possibility of *some* hatred earlier. That may be so: there is no evidence either way.

According to Thucydides, then, it was the alliance between Megara and Athens which first aroused Corinth's bitter hostility. Why? The answer has already been partly made clear by our examination of the First Peloponnesian war and the vital role played therein by Athenian control of the Megarid (Chapter V, Parts v and vi above). First, the Athenian navy could operate very much more effectively in the Corinthian Gulf. And secondly, possession of the Megarid afforded protection to Athens against Peloponnesian invasions: this issue has already been discussed, but we have not yet had occasion to notice its great importance to Corinth. Had Corinth remained on friendly terms with Athens the accession of Megara to the Athenian alliance might have done no more than create disturbing possibilities. But Megara joined Athens in order to get help from Athens against Corinth, with which she was at war, and this automatically brought about a state of war between Athens and Corinth. The unpleasantness for Corinth of the Megarian-Athenian alliance was that it deprived her of the one really telling weapon she had against Athens: the threat of a Peloponnesian invasion of Attica led by Sparta. (It must have been partly for the same reason that the Boeotians in 424 'considered Megara's danger their own', as Thucydides puts it [IV 72.1]: of course the Boeotians themselves wanted to have uninterrupted land communications with the Peloponnese, but they must also have attached importance to the Peloponnesians' being able to invade Attica via the Megarid whenever they wished.) Immediately, then, Corinth's position vis-à-vis Athens deteriorated disastrously. She could never face Athens at sea, and now the main offensive weapon upon which she might have relied to strengthen her hand against Athens in case of need was seriously blunted, and at the same time Athenian naval operations in the Gulf were greatly facilitated. This was quite sufficient to cause 'the great hatred'.

We have seen that the animosity felt by Corinth towards Athens from *c.* 460 onwards had just one identifiable cause: in a word, Megara. In 446 Megara returned to her old alliances, and it was no doubt this restoration of the *status quo ante* which inaugurated Phase III in Corinthian-Athenian relations: another period, if not of friendliness, at least of indifference and neutrality, attested by the refusal of Corinth to countenance a Peloponnesian attack on Athens in 440, at the time of the Samian revolt (see Chapter V, Part viii above). Corinth's attitude at this time need not have been due to any positive friendliness towards Athens: it may have been dictated mainly by her relative weakness and the damage she had undoubtedly suffered during the First Peloponnesian war, and a general lack of enthusiasm for war among Sparta's allies. Corinth herself was only too likely to suffer in the opening phases of a war with Athens; and even if she now had no reason to be positively friendly, it was in her interest not to allow a war to break out until she could be reasonably certain that Athens would be defeated. If Sparta's allies were indeed more or less equally divided on the desirability of a war, too many of them might drag their feet if forced into one; and it would be better to wait.

Phase IV of the relations between Corinth and Athens is the revival of 'the great hatred', which came to a head in 433–2 and remained acute until 404, when upon the capitulation of Athens the Corinthian delegate in the Peloponnesian League Congress advocated the destruction of the city and the selling of its population into slavery (but see Appendix XXI). The known reasons for the renewal of Corinthian hostility towards Athens were the assistance given by Athens to Corcyra in 433, and the affair of Potidaea. Some would add the Megarian decree, but I shall show in the next Chapter that the importance of that episode, except in propaganda, has been vastly exaggerated. I shall defer discussing the well-known passage in which the Corinthians in 433 are made to urge the Athenians that they would be 'wise to remove some of the suspicion *tēs hyparchousēs proteron* on account of the Megarians' (Thuc. 1 42.2) until I come to deal with the Megarian decree (Chapter VII, Part ii, Section A below), merely remarking here that I am convinced the passage in question is not a reference to the decree.

(ii)
The 'commercial rivalry' hypothesis

I wish to glance very briefly at the theory which was popularised in an extreme form in the early part of this century by Cornford, Grundy and others,[5] and still shows itself occasionally in unexpected places,[6] that 'the great hatred' of Corinth for Athens, and indeed the whole Peloponnesian war, was largely caused by 'trade rivalry' between Corinth and Athens and Corinthian fear of Athenian commercial expansion in the West. I shall deal briefly later with the general question how wars arose in the Classical Greek world and in particular with the entirely groundless theory that they might occur through 'trade rivalry'; but there are three specific points that need separate treatment here, in relation to the Peloponnesian war.

In the first place, those who hold the 'commercial rivalry' theory are obliged to reject the statement of Thucydides (discussed in Part i of this Chapter) about the origin of 'the great hatred', for it could not have 'first arisen principally' from the alliance between Megara and Athens as late as *c.* 460 if commercial rivalry had really been at the bottom of it. Yet Thucydides' explanation is perfectly plausible in itself, as we have

---

[5] F. M. Cornford, *Thucydides Mythistoricus* (1907) 1–76; G. B. Grundy, *THA* (1911, 1948[2]) 1 322 ff. (esp. 324–5), 409 etc.; also TCPW, replying to Dickins, TCPW.

[6] E.g. Bengtson, *GG*[4] (1969) 225. Cf. the apposite comments of E. J. Bickerman, reviewing Bengtson's first edition (1950, p. 207), in *AJP* 74 (1953) 96–9, at p. 96.

seen, and it is supported by circumstantial evidence: the fact that war between Athens and Corinth broke out only upon Megara's defection and not on any earlier occasion.

Secondly, commercial rivalry will not account at all for the oscillations in Corinthian policy towards Athens. Until *c.* 460 there is no sign of serious friction and a good deal of evidence of real friendliness. In *c.* 460 Corinth becomes violently hostile. In 440, however, she can claim to have saved Athens from a Peloponnesian attack. From 433 onwards she is again Athens' implacable enemy. These changes of policy, inexplicable in terms of 'trading considerations', are thoroughly understandable if we conceive the conflict in political and strategic terms, as described above.

Thirdly, there is no evidence of any increased official Athenian[7] activity or interest in the West between the Persian wars and the beginning of 'the great hatred' in *c.* 460, either in the form of imperialist or even diplomatic activity, such as might have aroused Corinthian apprehensions, or (as far as we know) by way of further growth in the volume of Athenian trade with the West, relative to Corinthian. (In such a context, when I speak of 'Athenian' or 'Corinthian' trade, I mean trade *to and from* Athens or Corinth, not trade carried by Athenian or Corinthian *merchants*, or in Athenian or Corinthian *ships*; cf. Chapter VII, Part vi below.) There is no evidence which could enable us to make even an informed guess about the volume of trade to and from the West carried on with (one must not say 'by') Corinth and Athens respectively in the fifth century. Even the evidence of Western coin-hoards, which has recently been very well analysed by Kraay and Jenkins,[8] is too negative to be of any use. Certainly, Athenian coinage never appears in any quantity in Sicilian or south Italian hoards after *c.* 480, and Corinthian coinage hardly appears at all until just after the middle of the fourth century, the period of Timoleon; but then virtually all foreign coins largely disappear from Western hoards after *c.* 480, when the volume of local coinage increased, and Sicily and south Italy, separately, each used locally minted coins, with few exceptions.

We must not try to fill up the gaps in our knowledge by assuming an extensive direct trade between Athens and the West, or even between Corinth and her Sicilian colony of Syracuse, for which no positive evidence exists. (I do not mean to deny the existence of such trade, but only to deprecate exaggerated ideas of its importance.) Much earlier, in the late eighth and seventh centuries, Corinthian painted pottery was certainly dominant in the West, achieving a virtual monopoly in the seventh century. But here I would invoke R. M. Cook's salutary warning against overestimating the value of the trade in painted pottery and its importance

[7] Although Themistocles does seem to have had some kind of 'Western policy' after 479 (see Appendix XXXI), it is clear that he had no influence on Athenian foreign policy at that time (see Chapter V, Part ii above).

[8] See Kraay, HSCOC, esp. 79–80; *GCH* 53 ff.; G. K. Jenkins, 'A Note on Corinthian Coins in the West', in *Centennial Publication of the American Numismatic Soc.* (ed. Harald Ingholt, New York, 1958) 367–79.

in the economic life of any Greek city, even Corinth or Athens.[9] And this virtual monopoly disappeared not in the fifth century but during the first half of the sixth. By *c.* 550 Athenian painted pottery had largely replaced Corinthian in the western markets, and before the end of the sixth century Corinthian painted ceramic ware had virtually disappeared.[10] Blakeway and Dunbabin, who belonged to the 'modernising' school of economic historians and thought that the continuance of good relations between Corinth and Athens in these circumstances needed explanation, suggested that the reason why 'Corinth' acquiesced in the ousting of 'her' pottery by Athens from the western market was that the Attic pots were carried in Corinthian ships (see Dunbabin, *WG* 241 ff.). They may have been: there is of course no evidence whatever, but it seems quite likely that some cargoes, at any rate those of high value in proportion to their bulk and weight, may have been carried across the Isthmus of Corinth, perhaps along the Diolkos, rather than shipped right around the Peloponnese. This, however, would have pleased the Corinthians not because it was 'their own' merchants who would profit by acting as middlemen, but because they would derive customs duties, doubtless both on entry and on exit, from the goods passing through their harbours. It would certainly be a matter of indifference to 'the Corinthians' (in the sense of the oligarchs who exercised political power at Corinth) not only whose pottery was sold in Sicily and Italy but also whose ships carried it there. Whatever competition there may have been between individual merchants operating from Corinth and Athens, or (to use the word 'competition' in a different sense) between the products of the respective States, *we must not project it on to the cities concerned and speak of 'trade rivalry' between them*. It is a fundamental error of method in ancient economic history to confuse the activities and policies of individual merchants with those of the cities to which they belonged, if only because the merchants who carried on the trade of a particular city were very often metics or foreigners, and even when they were citizens would rarely be found among the governing class. (Cf. Chapter VII, Part vi below.)

The possibility of a war arising out of 'competition between Corinth and Athens in the Western trade', then, need not be seriously considered—except in one set of circumstances: if either *State* obtained political control of the cities (or the most important cities) whence the corn and perhaps timber of Sicily and south Italy came to Greece, and sought to exclude the other. When the Athenians sent out their first expedition to Sicily in 427 (well after the Peloponnesian war had begun), one of their main objectives was to stop the export of Sicilian grain to the Peloponnese.[11] This could hardly be achieved without actually controlling the main export

---

[9] R. M. Cook, 'Die Bedeutung der bemalten Keramik für den griechischen Handel', in *Jahrb. des deutschen archäologischen Instituts* 74 (1959) 114–23—a very important article.

[10] See Dunbabin, *WG* 226, 241–51. Much the same may be true of other commodities (*WG* 226, 228), but it is only for painted pottery that the evidence is sufficient to enable us to draw any conclusions.

[11] Thuc. III 86.4. See Westlake, *EGHGH* 105–8.

centres, and it is not surprising that another objective of the expedition
was to try to find out if Sicily could be brought under Athenian political
control—this was certainly the only effective way in which anything
approaching a 'monopoly of the Western trade' could be achieved. But the
Athenians never attempted such a policy until 427, and then it was part
of their war strategy. A monopoly of the supply of some essential commodity in the hands of some other State was certainly something to be resisted,
by force if necessary. No ordinary naval 'blockade' by Athens or Corinth
could shut off, or even seriously interrupt for a long period, the supply of a
commodity from the West to mainland Greece, for ancient blockading
methods were exceedingly inefficient, mainly owing to the peculiar
characteristics of the warships of the day: this has been admirably brought
out by Gomme, in a very important article (FFGNS). Athens could not
hope to close the Corinthian Gulf entirely, even in the brief period during
which she had the use of Pagae. We have already established (see Chapter
V, Part v above) that when Athens lost Pagae she could not afford to
leave a high proportion of her fleet in the Gulf, and such ships as she could
spare could be countered by a Corinthian fleet stationed nearby, as in
414/13. There was now little hope of doing serious damage to Peloponnesian trade with the West except near the narrow entrance to the Gulf.

Undoubtedly Athens may have wished earlier, as she did during the
Peloponnesian war (Thuc. VI 90.3; VII 25.2; cf. Diod. XIV 42.4), to import
timber from southern Italy or from Sicily, in both of which areas grew the
pine (*peukē*, Latin *pinus*) and silver-fir (*elatē*, Latin *abies*) which were most
favoured for the building of warships,[12] and which were not available
at many places right on the Mediterranean and Black Sea coasts or their
navigable rivers, whence alone they could be profitably transported.[13]
But if there was a market for such timber at Athens there would always be
merchants who would be only too glad to take it there; and if the Athenians decided to make official purchases in Sicily or Italy and provide means
of transport, no one would try to stop it, except enemies during a war.

Whether Athens imported corn in any quantity from the West in the
fifth century is very doubtful. By the late fourth century a regular corn
trade seems to have developed from Sicily,[14] but for the fifth century there
are only one or two scraps of evidence.[15] If Western corn was exported to

[12] See esp. Theophr., *HP* IV v. 5; v i.5,7; ii.1; vii. 1–5; viii.1–3.
[13] Note εὐκατακόμιστον in Strabo XII iii.12, p. 546 (cf. Xen., *Anab.* VI iv.4). A
recent work on ancient forestry, Olli Makkonnen, *Ancient Forestry. An Historical Study*,
Parts I and II (= *Acta Forestalia Fennica* 82 and 84, Helsinki, 1967 and 1969), has little to
say (II 30–4) on the timber trade in Classical times.
[14] See esp. Ps.-Dem. LVI 9: ὁ Σικελικὸς κατάπλους ἐγένετο, in sufficient quantity
to lower the price of corn at Athens appreciably. Cf. Ps.-Dem. XXXII 4ff., etc.
[15] A mention of the 'frumentum candidum' of Italy in Soph., fr. 543, *ap.* Plin., *NH*
XVIII 65; and what seems to be a reference to Italian groats (χόνδρος) in Hermippus, fr.
63, *ap.* Athen. I 27e (where J. M. Edmonds, *The Fragments of Attic Comedy* I [1957] 304,
would emend Ἰταλίας to Θετταλίας, for no good reason that I can see). Note that
Syracuse is mentioned in this fragment of Hermippus not for grain but for swine and cheese
(cf. Antiphanes, *ap.* Athen. I 27de), and that 'fine wheaten flour' (σεμίδαλις) comes from
Phoenicia.

mainland Greece in any quantity[16] (as it certainly was to Rome in the fifth century),[17] most of it would probably go to ports on the Corinthian Gulf, for the journey around Cape Malea was notoriously stormy, and the Etesian winds blow from the north-east in the Aegean at the very time in the late summer when corn merchants might expect the highest prices, and make it very difficult for sailing ships coming around Peloponnese to the Peiraeus.

To advance any further arguments against the theory that the Peloponnesian war arose out of 'commercial rivalry' may seem like flogging a dead horse. It is, however, worth while having a general look at the specific causes of war which are most visible in the ancient sources, the more so since Momigliano's thrice-published paper (OCWAH) on the causes of war in ancient historiography is highly general and hardly glances at what is said by the historians of antiquity about the causes of particular wars. If we examine the causes of wars between Greek states (a subject on which a great deal of evidence exists), we may hope to gain some light on the springs of foreign policy. Anyone who believes that 'commercial' factors played a part in determining the foreign policies of Greek cities will receive a rude shock if he impartially collects the evidence for the origins of inter-state wars. (We shall limit ourselves here almost entirely to the Classical period, down to the latter part of the fourth century.) There is a remarkable unanimity in most of the relevant passages, only a selection of which can be given here. We can ignore oddities, the occasional 'cherchez la femme' for example.[18] The vast majority of passages refer to wars against *neighbouring states*, usually about *disputed border lands*; and there can be no doubt at all that these were the characteristic type of Greek war. Other types are occasionally mentioned. For instance, Demosthenes (xv 17) speaks of wars 'about hegemony': the Peloponnesian war was of that kind. But as a rule it is taken for granted that states will fight neighbouring states,[19] and that the wars, if not for straight domination (itself often an expression of desire for land), will be for possession of disputed territory.[20]

Individual examples abound. When Thucydides (v 41.2) recounts the negotiations between Sparta and Argos in 420, he makes the Argive ambassadors raise the question of the ownership of Cynuria, 'a frontier territory about which they are constantly at variance', as the first matter to be discussed. Mantinea and Tegea, he tells us (65.4), were frequently at war about the direction of watercourses, which did damage to the land

---

[16] Hdts vii 158.4 shows that Sicily was at least believed to have a large exportable corn surplus. Cf. Theop., *FGrH* 115 F 193, *ap.* Athen. vi 232ab.

[17] On Livy ii 34.3 and Dion. Hal., *AR* vii i (491); Livy iv 25.4 (433); 52.5–6 (410), see Dunbabin, *WG* 216.

[18] See e.g. Ar., *Ach.* 524–9; Athen. xiii 560b–f; the 'Persians' in Hdts i 1.2 to 5.3; Plut., *Mor.* 254bc; and cf. Arist., *Pol.* v 4, 1304ᵃ4–13.

[19] See e.g. Thuc. i 15.2; 17; Plato, *Rep.* ii 373d; Arist., *Pol.* vii 2, 1324ᵇ25; 14, 1333ᵇ 30–1.

[20] See e.g. Thuc. i 122.2; iv 92.4; v 79.4; Plato. *Rep.* ii 373d; Dem. xv 17; Diod. iii 33.3.

of whichever side they ran through. According to the Oxyrhynchus historian (*Hell. Oxy.* xviii [xiii] 3), the Phocians and Locrians used to fight each other about certain disputed territory around Parnassus. Egesta in Sicily is several times recorded as fighting its neighbours, in particular Selinus, about disputed land (Thuc. vi 6.2; Diod. xi 86.2; xii 82.3 ff.; xiii 43.2 ff.). Tarentum and Thurii similarly fought about the land of Siris (Antiochus, *FGrH* 555 f 11, *ap.* Strab. vi i.14, p. 264). In the fourth century Clazomenae and Cyme fought a war for the possession of Leuce, in between their territories (Diod. xv 18.1–3). It was by no means only the more purely agricultural states which went to war principally about border lands. We often hear nowadays about alleged 'trade rivalry' between Miletus and Samos, especially in the archaic period for which evidence is so conveniently scanty; but on the one occasion when we do have a reliable statement about the cause of a war between these two cities, that of 441–40, we find in Thucydides (i 115.2) that it was 'about Priene'—that is to say, about disputed territory. Similarly, Chalcis and Eretria, each of which is sometimes represented as being a member of, and supported by, a considerable 'trade league', fought their major war, probably in the late eighth century, in and (I believe) for the fertile Lelantine plain lying between them (see esp. Strabo x i.12, p. 448; Theogn. 892), the best agricultural land in Euboea, which was surely far more important to Chalcis and Eretria than anything else they could want to fight about.[21] Again, both Corinth and Megara are often named among the most prominent 'industrial and commercial states'; but the only time we have trustworthy evidence about the cause of a war between them, namely in *c.* 461–60, it is 'about boundary land' (Thuc. i 103.4); and there is every reason to suppose that earlier clashes between the two cities, in the eighth century, arose in the same way.[22] Athens and Megara came to blows in the late 350s, in a dispute (lasting several years) about the demarcation of the sacred land of the Eleusinian goddesses; and of course the famous 'Megarian decree' itself was the product of a similar dispute (see Chapter VII below). Such examples could be multiplied. Quarrels about the ownership of land, especially border land between two states,

[21] Contrast J. Boardman, in *BSA* 52 (1957), at pp. 27–9, whose anachronistic suggestion of 'commercial jealousies' as the cause of the war (the so-called 'Lelantine war') is echoed by Forrest, *EGD* 108 ('the international and I have argued commercial Lelantine war'; cf. *Historia* 6 [1957] 160 ff.). Such speculations are unsupported by evidence of any kind and are based entirely on assumptions *a priori*, foisted upon us by the 'modernising' school of Greek historians. Cf. the properly sceptical account of E. Will, *Korinthiaka* (Paris, 1955) 391–405, with 306–38. Many scholars have taken Thucydides' famous statement about the war between Chalcis and Eretria, i 15.3, as meaning that '*the rest of the Greeks* joined in as allies of one side or the other': even Will (*op. cit.* 393) can represent him as speaking of a conflict which 'divisa la Grèce entière autour de Chalcis et d'Érétrie'. But this ignores the μάλιστα with which the sentence begins and which limits the force of τὸ ἄλλο Ἑλληνικόν. All Thucydides is saying is that the rest of the Greeks participated *most of all* in this war, of all the early ones about which he has been speaking in 15.2—the others being *purely local* affairs.

[22] See N. G. L. Hammond, in *BSA* 49 (1954) 93–102.

were the principal cause of war between Greek states and were universally recognised as such; for this there is ample evidence. When we are told that wars could be fought by Greek states for commercial objectives, or could arise out of commercial disputes, we are justified in asking for some specific evidence—and none exists.

In the Hellenistic period the social and economic situation, as well as the political, changed in various ways; but it is interesting to note that the only war in that period which (as far as I am aware) is known to have grown from strictly 'commercial' origins, that launched by Rhodes against Byzantium in *c.* 220, was undertaken by Rhodes not in the interests of 'her own' merchants, but at the request of the general body of all those engaged in trading through the Bosphorus, who were aggrieved at the levying of a special transit tax by the Byzantines and appealed to the Rhodians 'because they were considered to be the champions of those who sailed the sea' (Polyb. IV 47.1).[23]

(iii)
Athens and the West

As I indicated in Part ii of this Chapter, there is no evidence of increased official Athenian activity or interest in the West, in either the political or the economic sphere, between the Persian wars and the period *c.* 460 when 'the great hatred' arose between Corinth and Athens.

The earliest known Athenian alliance with any Western city, that with the hellenised Elymian town of Egesta (or Segesta) in western Sicily, was made either in 458/7 or (less probably) in 454/3;[24] the alliances with Rhegium and Leontini are probably of the 440s (they were renewed in 433/2);[25] the foundation of Thurii (see Appendix XXXIV) was in 444/3; and the treaty with Halicyae must be in the late 430s or early 420s.[26] Apart from one or two tantalising scraps of evidence concerning a visit of the Athenian Strategos Diotimus to Naples,[27] there is no other evidence of Athenian political or diplomatic activity in the West before the alliance with Corcyra in 433, when the fact that Corcyra 'seemed to lie conveniently on the coastal voyage to Italy and Sicily' (Thuc. I 44.3; cf. 36.2) was a subsidiary reason for the making of the alliance with Corcyra (cf. Chapter III, Part ii above). Perhaps the coastal voyage envisaged was primarily of Siceliot warships which might come to aid the Pelopon-

[23] The Rhodians themselves are said to have been moved by the fact that they and their neighbours suffered damage (47.3). This may refer partly to losses incurred by individual Rhodian and other merchants, but the main consideration was obviously that expressed in 47.1: that the exaction of a duty upon goods brought from the Black Sea made everyone suffer—clearly by raising prices *pro tanto*.

[24] M/L 37 = Tod I^2 31 = *SVdA* II 139 = *IG* I^2 19 (plus 20.1-2).

[25] M/L 63/4 = Tod I^2 58/7 = *SVdA* II 162/3 = *IG* I^2 51/2.

[26] *SVdA* 174 = *SEG* x 68 (= *IG* I^2 20, minus lines 1-2) = xiv 6 = xxi 36.

[27] Timaeus, *FGrH* 566 F 98, *ap.* Schol. ad Lycophr., *Alex.* 732; Tzetzes ad *Id.* 733 (see Hill, *S*^{2} 139). For some modern opinions about the date (which may or may not be 433/2), see Kagan, *OPW* 385-6.

nesians;[28] perhaps the Athenians were already thinking of sending a fleet to Sicily—as they might be called upon to do anyway in fulfilment of their engagements to their Western allies. However that may be, the use of the expression 'coastal voyage' (*paraplous*) in both the relevant passages in Thucydides (1 36.2; 44.3), and the reference to a 'fleet' (*nautikon*) in the first, show that it is naval vessels and not merchant ships which are in question. Since Gomme's masterly article distinguishing between the sailing characteristics of Greek merchant vessels and triremes[29] there is no need to argue this.

When the Athenians sent their first expedition to Sicily in 427, it consisted of only twenty ships (reinforced by some forty more in 425), and even now the Athenians were only (among other things) '*exploring whether it would be possible* for them to bring Sicily under their control' (Thuc. III 86.4).[30] Not until 415 was the conquest of Sicily seriously attempted. Athenian aims in the West grew quite gradually, and it is a mistake to read back into the Pentecontaetia objectives which developed only during the Peloponnesian war. Some kind of 'Western policy' can be attributed to Themistocles (see Appendix XXXI); and when the radical democrats 'came to power' in 461, Athens certainly began officially to take an interest in the West. But even then there is no sign of any intention to effect conquests there. Very probably the negotiations which led to Athens' western alliances began with overtures from the other states concerned: Egesta, Rhegium, Leontini, Halicyae, which had infinitely more to gain from an association with Athens than she from anything they could offer. Of course any state will jump at every opportunity of extending its influence, and the Athenians could not be expected to reject requests for alliance which would, so to speak, enable them to 'get a foot in the door', in case they should ever need a 'legitimate' excuse for intervening in the West at some future date. But Sicily and south Italy were far away, and communications with them were not easy (cf. Thuc. VI 21.2, as interpreted by Dover in Gomme, *HCT* IV 258). And there was another drawback: unless Carthage proved obliging enough to attack Sicily again, as she did not between 480 and 408, *Athens had nothing to offer the Western Greeks*, comparable to the protection against Persia which she could give to the Greeks of Asia Minor and the neighbouring islands. Any large-scale Athenian move into Sicily would have a nakedly imperialistic character and was bound to arouse a great deal of opposition. The most serious threat to the Ionian cities of Sicily, Athens' natural allies, would come, if at all, from Syracuse; but Syracuse was a major power, which it might be dangerous to provoke into giving active assistance to the Peloponnesians. It is understandable, therefore, that the Athenians should not even have begun to

[28] See Westlake in *Historia* 9 (1960), at pp. 394–6 = *EGHGH* 113–16, against P. A. Brunt, in *CR* 71 = n.s. 7 (1957) 245.

[29] FFGNS (also in *EGHL*). See also Gomme, *HCT* I 171, 177, cf. 19. There is good evidence for merchantmen sailing directly between Greece and Sicily in Thuc. VI 13.1 *fin.*; VII 19.4; Ps.-Dem. XXXII 5, 8; Plut., *Dion* 25.1 ff.

[30] On this and the other aims of the expedition, see Westlake, *EGHGH* 101–22.

think seriously about gaining control of Sicily until after the Peloponnesian war had begun.

We have not yet considered the question whether Athens ever had more
extensive designs of conquest in the West, beyond south Italy and Sicily,
and including even Carthage; and if she had, when those designs were
formed.

It is easy to misinterpret the evidence, which needs to be examined
carefully. First, we must look at our only two contemporary witnesses,
Aristophanes and Thucydides. Aristophanes in the *Knights* (produced
early in 424) has an amusing little fantasy, beginning 'they say' (*phasin*),
which represents Hyperbolus as demanding that a fleet of a hundred triremes be sent against Carthage (lines 1300–4). This at once raises the
question of the use of the comic poets as historical sources, a subject we
shall have to consider later in relation to the Megarian decree (Chapter
VII, Part ii, Section c below). At this point all we need do is reject
emphatically the conclusion that Hyperbolus had *necessarily* proposed a
decree that a hundred triremes be sent against Carthage. It is true that not
only minor commentators like Henderson (*GWAS* 250–2) but even the
sober Busolt (*GG* III ii.1122–3) have taken the alleged proposal as a historical fact; yet B. B. Rogers,[31] ready as he usually was to believe anything
discreditable about 'the demagogues', rightly hesitated on this occasion,
and would not decide whether the decree was a fact or 'a mere comic jest'.
There are, broadly, three possibilities. First, it is just conceivable, I
suppose, that Hyperbolus had actually moved such a decree; but it is in the
highest degree unlikely, for an expedition against the great city of Carthage would have been an act of madness while Sicily was still unsubdued
and much of it (including its chief city, Syracuse) hostile, right on the
Athenian line of attack and communications. Perhaps Hyperbolus was
known to favour the attack on Carthage as a sequel to the conquest of
Sicily: that would be quite sufficient for Aristophanes to make him propose it as an immediate task. Secondly, Hyperbolus may have made some
other aggressive proposal recently, to send a large fleet against some other
objective, considered foolish by enough Athenians to make the substitution of Carthage comically effective. Or thirdly, Aristophanes may just
be making Hyperbolus propose the kind of lunatic decree which Aristophanes himself and those who thought as he did would have regarded as
characteristic of that politician—who incidentally was abused by at least
one other comic poet, Plato (fr. 187 Kock, *ap.* Plut., *Nic.* 11.7), as well
as by Thucydides, who speaks more contemptuously of him than of any
other character in his History (VIII 73.3). We may compare the bogus
oracle produced by the Sausage-Seller (as a parody of Cleon's oracles),
to the effect that Athens will rule the Red Sea and give judgments in
Ecbatana (*Knights* 1088–9). But we should remind ourselves that Hyperbolus did not have a conspicuously successful record as a politician:

[31] In his edition of the *Knights* (1910) 180–1 n.

he is the only Athenian known for certain to have been ostracised after Thucydides son of Melesias in 443! Even if he did dream of attacking Carthage, there would still be no justification for attributing this policy to 'the Athenians' during the Ten Years war.

The evidence of Thucydides also needs very careful treatment. What he means to tell us is not entirely clear. Speaking in his own person, in VI 15.2, he represents Alcibiades himself as hoping, perhaps even expecting (*elpizōn*), to conquer Carthage as well as Sicily. Thucydides also makes Hermocrates say in 415 (34.2) that the Carthaginians lived in constant fear of an Athenian attack. Finally, in 90.2–3 Thucydides puts into the mouth of Alcibiades at Sparta a definite statement that after the Sicilian Greeks Athens intended to conquer the "Italiōtai' (the Greeks of Italy), and that even the conquest of 'the Carthaginian empire and Carthage itself' was part of Athenian grand strategy, aimed at securing large additional forces (including Iberians and other barbarian mercenaries),[32] with which Athens would 'easily' reduce the Peloponnese and ultimately rule all Hellas. However, in his account earlier in Book VI (8–26) of the taking of the Athenian decision to send the great expedition to Sicily, Thucydides never gives the least hint that anyone at Athens was thinking of Sicily as a springboard for further conquests in the Mediterranean, even at 18.4, the one point at which Thucydides allows Alcibiades to reveal that he saw 'rule over all Hellas' as one possible result of the conquest of Sicily and the assistance which would then be forthcoming from there. We must remember that Thucydides sometimes allows his speakers to exaggerate freely and even distort facts when it suits their book; and both Alcibiades at Sparta and Hermocrates had good reason to magnify the aggressiveness of Athens. To my mind, the evidence of Thucydides VI 15.2 justifies our attributing to *Alcibiades himself*[33] the notion of conquering Carthage after Sicily had been brought under Athenian control, and there may have been others at Athens (Hyperbolus, for instance) who had similar hopes. But although Thucydides makes Alcibiades attribute this policy to *the Athenians*, in a speech in which it is in his interest to make the Spartans' flesh creep, I see nothing to make us conclude that any substantial number of the Athenians ever shared these wild dreams.[34]

Two generations later, Isocrates (VIII 85) could accuse the late-fifth-century Athenian leaders of aiming at the conquest of 'Italy and Sicily and Carthage'. But it is in Plutarch that we find the most colourful picture. In his *Life of Pericles* (20.4) he represents 'many' Athenians as being possessed by an extravagant yearning (a *dyserōs . . . kai dyspotmos erōs*) for the conquest of Sicily, and 'some' as dreaming of Etruria and Carthage,

---

[32] We hear of Dionysius I of Syracuse using Celtic mercenaries in the second quarter of the fourth century: he sent Celtic as well as Iberian mercenaries to help Sparta against the Boeotians in 369 (Xen., *HG* VII i.20; Diod. xv 70.1).

[33] Thucydides seems to have felt particularly well informed about the ideas of Alcibiades: see P. A. Brunt, 'Thucydides and Alcibiades', in *REG* 65 (1952) 59–96.

[34] W. Liebeschuetz, 'Thucydides and the Sicilian Expedition', in *Historia* 17 (1968) 289–306, does not raise this vital issue.

even during the lifetime of Pericles, who is depicted as holding back these hotheads. The fact that as late as 427 the Athenians had only just got as far as exploring the possibility of conquering Sicily (see above) should deter us from placing any confidence in Plutarch's picture. In two other *Lives*, those of Nicias and Alcibiades, he gives more details, not referring now to Etruria, but specifying 'Carthage and Libya' as the ultimate objective. In the *Alcibiades* (17.1–4) he distinguishes the more extravagant hopes of Alcibiades himself, directed towards Carthage and Libya and after that Italy and the Peloponnese, from those of other Athenians, who regarded Sicily as the ultimate objective. In the *Nicias* (12.1–2) it is the Athenians as a whole who have extravagant designs, extending indeed not merely to Carthage and Libya but to the whole Mediterranean as far as the Pillars of Heracles—a statement which may have no better foundation than Thucydides vi 90.3, where the reference to the Iberians could well be responsible for the extension of Athenian ambitions as far as Gibraltar.

The circumstantial evidence, such as it is, does not encourage a belief that 'the Athenians' were thinking seriously at any time of attacking Carthage or the Etruscans. In 415, after the departure of Alcibiades from Sicily, Nicias and Lamachus sent a trireme to Carthage with offers of friendship, hoping to get some assistance from there, and another to the Etruscans, some of whose cities had already proffered help in the war (Thuc. vi 88.6). Carthage made no response, but the Etruscans sent help which proved very useful to the Athenians (vi 103.2; vii 53.2, etc.).

All in all, I do not feel that Plutarch's statements necessitate any modification of the conclusions drawn above from Thucydides' evidence.

We need not concern ourselves here with the negotiations between Athens and Carthage in 406, recorded in M/L 92 (= *SVdA* ii 208).

Note. It was only after this book was in page proof that I was able to read *La circolazione della moneta ateniese in Sicilia e in Magna Grecia = Atti del I Convegno del Centro Internazionale di Studi Numismatici* (Naples, 1967) = *Supplemento al volume 12–14 degli Annali dell' Istituto Italiano di Numismatica* (Rome, 1969). I have not found in it anything that necessitates any modification in the opinions expressed above (see especially p. 215 n. 8).

VII

The Megarian decrees

As I shall explain, there was more than one Athenian decree relating to Megara before the outbreak of the Peloponnesian war; but one, the well-known 'exclusion decree' (as I shall sometimes call it), is so much more famous and important than the others that I may on occasion speak of it alone as 'the Megarian decree'.

(i)
Introduction

As I indicated at the beginning of this book (Chapter I, Part i), the way in which most modern historians have treated the Megarian decree is inexcusable, for two different reasons.

First, hardly any have even taken the trouble to discover precisely what the decree *said*: again and again (see Appendix **XXXV**) one finds statements about an exclusion from 'all markets and harbours of Athens and her empire' (thus, in these very words or their equivalent, or at least with some such phrase as 'the markets of Attica', Adcock, Andrewes, Bickerman, Burn, Bury, Cawkwell, De Sanctis, Glotz-Cohen, Hammond, Heichelheim, Holm, Kiechle, Knorringa, Laistner, Victor Martin, Eduard Meyer in one passage, Michell, Prentice, Vogt, Zimmern), or from 'all trade' with Attica and the empire (Böckh, J. H. Finley, Grote, Kagan), often with an unblushing attribution of the chosen formulation to Thucydides, who provides no justification for anything of the sort. Sometimes it is not 'the Megarians', as in Thucydides and all other sources, but 'Megara' (the State of Megara) which is given as the subject of the exclusion (Bury, Cornford, Gomme in three passages, Grundy, Hammond, Heichelheim, Henderson, Highbarger, Victor Martin, Usher, Vogt)—as if this were exactly the same thing! Even some of those who have at least not repudiated Thucydides by speaking of 'markets' in the plural have seen the decree as essentially a ban on Megarian trade (Beloch, Bengtson, Berve, Bodin, Busolt, Cary, Cloché, Ehrenberg, von Fritz, Kagan, Lepper, de Romilly, Roussel). Surely, before making assumptions about what the effects of the decree must have been, one ought to examine the sources very carefully to find out *exactly what the decree said and meant*. Yet I can find not a single scholar who has even tried to do this—a sad indication of the general slovenliness of modern scholarship in this field.

Secondly, in interpreting the decree and explaining (or, more usually, just taking for granted) its effects, there has been an almost universal failure to realise that in all the ancient accounts, without a single exception, the exclusion is specifically of 'the Megarians', and therefore could not possibly have had any great effect upon the trade of the State of Megara, which could still be carried on as before, *even with Athens and her empire*, by non-Megarians (including even Athenians!), who are likely to have been handling a large part of it already. If the failure to give an accurate account of the actual terms of the decree (although they are stated most explicitly by Thucydides) reveals an indifference to historical evidence on the part of most scholars which is without parallel in my experience, the general view that the decree 'must have' created a stranglehold on Megarian trade, a virtual blockade of Megara, shows a serious misconception of the way in which trade was carried on in Greek cities.

My subject in this Chapter is the Megarian decrees, in the plural, for there were certainly at least two Athenian decrees against Megara in the years immediately preceding the outbreak of the Peloponnesian war in 431, and there were probably three and may even have been four such decrees. For convenience I shall first set out all four of the decrees in chronological sequence, with the warning that I accept only the second and third as certain and the fourth as probable: I believe decree 1 to be non-existent.

1. *A decree imposing a ban upon the import into Attica of Megarian goods*, or certain classes of such goods, which would have been passed at some time between 446/5 and 433/2. The only basis for supposing the existence of such a decree is one particular interpretation (which I believe to be wrong) of Aristophanes, *Acharnians* 515–23: see Appendix XXXVI. The existence of any such decree is a purely subsidiary problem for my present purpose, since my main thesis concerning the Megarian decrees is little affected, whatever interpretation is adopted of these lines of Aristophanes.

2. *The decree of Pericles, mentioned only in Plutarch*, Pericles *30.2–3*, which provided for the sending of a herald to Megara and to Sparta, to protest against the appropriation by the Megarians of the *hiera orgas*, the land sacred to the Two Goddesses of Eleusis. Plutarch describes this decree as 'presenting a reasonable and courteous case' (*eugnōmonos kai philanthrōpou dikaiologias echomenon*),[1] and I shall therefore call it for convenience 'the reasonable and courteous decree'. I shall discuss it in Part iii of this Chapter. As presented by Plutarch, and by modern scholars, it is closely tied to the decree of Charinus (decree 4), but I shall suggest that the connection between these two decrees is due to a false assumption by Plutarch or his source, and that in fact they have nothing to do with one another.

3. *The main Megarian decree*, which excluded the Megarians from the Athenian Agora and the harbours of the Athenian empire, and was moved

---

[1] As a parallel for the use of these two adjectives together, Connor (CMDA 308 n. 5) cites Aeschin. 1 137.

by Pericles himself. This of course is the decree with which I am chiefly concerned, and I shall offer a fundamental reinterpretation of it. Its exact date is uncertain, and we should not pretend to know it. Brunt, in a valuable article (MD) published in 1951, has argued that the decree was 'long antecedent to the war', and this may be so, although I myself believe that the generally accepted date, 433/2, is the most probable.[2]

4. *The decree of Charinus*, the principal source for which is Plutarch, *Pericles* 30.3–4. I shall discuss this, with the reasonable and courteous decree, in Part iii below. Connor (CMD and CMDA) has recently argued that the murder (or alleged murder) by the Megarians of the Athenian herald Anthemocritus and the resulting decree of Charinus may not belong to the fifth century at all but should rather be placed in the fourth century, probably about 350. One serious weakness in Connor's case disappears in the light of the reinterpretation I shall propose of the reasonable and courteous decree, which must certainly be kept in the period just before the Peloponnesian war, whatever date we may prefer for Anthemocritus and Charinus. I do not feel that Connor has come near proving that Anthemocritus and Charinus belong to the mid-fourth century, but he deserves our gratitude in particular for drawing attention to the trouble over the *hiera orgas* in the late 350s. His position has been thrice attacked, by Dover, Bliquez, and Cawkwell; but their criticisms are not absolutely decisive, and, without entirely ruling out Connor's interpretation, I shall merely express a strong preference for dating the decree of Charinus to the late winter or early spring of 432/1. I have reviewed the question in Appendix XXXVII. Here I will only emphasise that my own reinterpretation of the exclusion decree is entirely independent of the Charinus decree and its dating.

The reinterpretation I am offering of the Megarian decrees, especially of the exclusion decree (no. 3), is very radical and has far-reaching consequences, not only for our assessment of the attitude of the Athenians and the Peloponnesians before the outbreak of the war, but also for our judgment of Thucydides' presentation of the origins of the war.

Those who accept my main thesis may well feel that I have laboured my case and spent far too much time demolishing objections which were never likely to be made. In fact virtually all the objections I have tried to meet were actually raised by the many friends and colleagues who read my earlier drafts.

(ii)
The sources

The three major witnesses to the Megarian decrees who need to be treated seriously in their own right are, in order of date, Aristophanes,

---

[2] Against Schwartz' date, 434/3, see Jacoby, *FGrH* iii b (Suppl.) ii.393 n. 7, 404 n. 1. In Ehrenberg, *SS* 257, 'winter 432–431' is presumably a misprint for '433–432'.

Thucydides, and Plutarch. The other evidence, as we shall see, has no independent value. The whole picture presented by this evidence suggests that there were no primary sources apart from Thucydides and Aristophanes, except possibly for Craterus, the one ancient writer who is likely to have taken the trouble to copy out the actual text of the decrees in question. I believe that Craterus probably preserved the texts of my decrees 2 and 3, and perhaps 4, but that the only surviving writer we possess who may have used him is Plutarch. To expect further information, not given by Thucydides, from 'the many ancient authors who deal with the decree' (Kagan, *OPW* 260) would be a mistake.

I shall begin by summarising the evidence of Thucydides, who is by far our most important witness. I shall then turn to Plutarch, because he alone mentions decrees 2 and 4 and, in my opinion, probably preserves one small element of the original wording of the exclusion decree which is found nowhere else. I shall then deal with Aristophanes, and finally with the other sources.

A.   *Thucydides*

Thucydides mentions only one decree against Megara, namely the exclusion decree, and he speaks of it in three contexts only: (1) the debate in the Spartan Assembly in the latter part of 432 (1 67.4); (2) the second of the three Spartan embassies to Athens in the winter of 432/1 and the Athenian attitude thereto (1 139.1–2); and (3) the debate in the Athenian Assembly consequent upon the third of those Spartan embassies, in which the question of the exclusion decree was prominent and evidently much discussed (1 139.4; 140.3–5; 144.2). The information Thucydides gives can be summed up under four heads:

(*a*) At some unspecified time before the meeting of the Spartan Assembly at which the Megarians (with the Corinthians, Aeginetans and others) presented their complaints against Athens, the Athenians had passed the main Megarian decree (the exclusion decree, my no. 3), in retaliation for what they alleged to be Megarian cultivation of the *hiera orgas* and 'the unenclosed land' (the *ahoristos*, on the borders of the two States) and reception of their runaway slaves (139.2). The decree excluded the Megarians from 'the Athenian Agora' (*hē Attikē agora*) and the harbours of the Athenian empire. Roughly the same form of words is used for the content of the decree three times in Thucydides (1 67.4; 139.1; 144.2) and is repeated by most of the other sources. We shall later have occasion to examine Thucydides' language in detail.

(*b*) At the meeting of the Spartan Assembly the Megarians had complained that this decree was 'contrary to the treaty' (1 67.4), contrary to the terms of the Thirty Years Peace of 446/5. The Athenian reply to this charge, given in Pericles' speech referred to in paragraph (*d*) below, and repeated (as Thucydides makes clear, 1 145) in the official Athenian reply to the third Spartan embassy, was that their action was no more forbidden by the Peace than were the Spartan expulsions of foreigners from their country (*xenēlasiai*).

(*c*) The second Spartan embassy to Athens in the winter of 432/1 said that Athens must raise the siege of Potidaea and allow Aegina to be autonomous; and 'above all, and most plainly, the Spartans insisted that there need be no war if the Athenians repealed the Megarian decree' (139.1). The Athenians rejected all the Spartan demands.[3]

(*d*) The third and last Spartan embassy made only one demand: that Athens let the Greeks be autonomous. There has been a good deal of debate on whether this demand should be called an 'ultimatum', and whether it was intended to force the issue or give the Athenians room for manoeuvre. I do not regard this question as very important, nor do I think we can answer it confidently: I have dealt with it in Appendix XII, §7. At the ensuing Assembly, at which the Athenians intended to formulate a final answer to Sparta, and at which there were many speakers on both sides, the question of the Megarian decree evidently came up, although it had not been specifically mentioned by this particular Spartan embassy, for Thucydides characterises the opposing views in the terms 'that it was necessary to fight', and 'that the decree should be repealed, and not stand in the way of peace' (139.4); and he makes Pericles speak of the Spartans as 'most insistent that there need be no war if the decree were repealed' (140.4).

Of course Thucydides is giving only a summary of the Megarian decree; but, knowing him as we do, we can surely accept it as a fact that the two points he does give us (the exclusion from harbours and Agora) are the essential ones. I would particularly draw attention to the fact that on each of the three occasions on which he refers to the decree he does so in slightly different words, but *always with Agora in the singular* (twice 'the Athenian Agora', *hē Attikē agora*) *and harbours in the plural* (twice 'the harbours in the Athenian empire', *en tēi Athēnaiōn archēi*). It is very probable that the decree had further provisions. There is likely to have been a sanctions clause, and there may well have been others. It seems probable from the way Aristophanes describes the decree (see c below) that it was couched in forcible and perhaps high-flown language, and there may indeed have been a denunciation of the Megarians in solemn terms. But in no other source is there anything which enables us to infer the further contents of the decree.

There is one other text in Thucydides which we must discuss, as it has been wrongly believed by many people to enable us to date the Megarian decree before the Athenian-Corcyraean alliance of 433: this is the passage in which Thucydides (1 42.2) makes the Corinthians, speaking before the Athenian Assembly in 433, advise the Athenians not to pay

[3] There must of course have been an Assembly at Athens on this occasion: against Steup (on Thuc. 1 139.3), see Gomme, *HCT* 1 451.

attention to the Corcyraean argument (in 36.1; cf. 33.3) that the war was coming soon anyway. 'You would be wiser', say the Corinthians, 'to dispel some of the suspicion *tēs hyparchousēs proteron* on account of the Megarians'. The point is: are the Corinthians referring to suspicion which now exists about something the Athenians have recently been doing, and are still doing, to the Megarians (obviously, the Megarian decree), or are they referring to suspicion which exists because of something the Athenians did in the past and therefore, perhaps, might do again in the future? Many scholars, including Steup, Gomme, and von Fritz,[4] adopt the former interpretation and see in this passage a reference to the Megarian decree. But there is a fatal difficulty in this view: the word *proteron*. Gomme admits *proteron* ('formerly') is difficult for him; 'but', he adds, 'it is a difficulty anyhow, for the natural meaning of *hyparchousa proteron* is "which formerly existed", not "which still exists owing to former quarrels"; yet the *hypopsia* [suspicion] must still exist, for Athens is called upon to remove it. *Hyparchousēs ēdē* [already] (or at least *eti* [still]) is in fact what we require'. But we have not got *ēdē* or *eti*: we have got *proteron*. Surely there is only one interpretation which conveys properly what Thucydides is trying to say: we must paraphrase his statement, 'You would be wiser to dispel some of the suspicion which now exists on our part owing to what happened about Megara some time ago'. There is an ellipsis here: the Corinthians are trying to be tactful (as they had to be in the circumstances) and making an oblique reference to the first phase of the 'great hatred' (of Thuc. 1 103.4), in *c*. 460–446/5 (see Chapter VI, Part i above). That was certainly how the scholiast took it: suspicion, he says, is a euphemistic way of referring to the war. This passage, therefore, tells us nothing about the date of the Megarian decree. (Brunt, MD 271 n. 9, takes much the same view, even though he believes that the decree was probably in existence already.)

B.   *Plutarch*

Plutarch is the only ancient source to mention more than one Megarian decree: he has three decrees, my nos. 2, 3 and 4—though how many different decrees Plutarch *thought* he was describing I should not care to say. The three decrees appear in the following order: (1) the exclusion decree (my no. 3): *Per*. 29.4, with 29.7–8; 30.1, and the first thirteen words of 30.2 (down to the colon after *apechtheia*), also 31.1; (2) the reasonable and courteous decree (my no. 2): *Per*. 30.2–3, beginning in §2 after the colon (with *koinēn*) and ending in §3 after the first colon (with *echomenon*); and (3) the decree of Charinus (my no. 4): *Per*. 30.3, beginning after the first colon (with *epei*), also *Mor*. 812d. Unfortunately the vital passage, *Per*. 29.4–32, is in a state of hopeless chronological confusion. I shall discuss the reasonable and courteous decree and the Charinus decree, and the order of all three decrees, in Part iii of this Chapter.

[4] See esp. Gomme, *HCT* 1 175–6; von Fritz, *GGS* 1 [Text] 636; [Anm.] 286–7 n. 37.

I shall ignore here as far as possible those parts of *Per.* 31.2–32.5 which deal with the charges against the 'friends of Pericles', a subject on which I have nothing new to say. Any future examination of the problems presented by these passages must take account particularly of Jacoby's minute analysis of Philochorus, *FGrH* 328 F 121 (in *FGrH* III b [Suppl.] i.484–96; ii.391–401) and parts of his monograph on Diagoras,[5] which show how little faith we can put in any of the statements Plutarch makes in *Per.* 31–2. To the accusations against Pericles himself, referred to in *Per.* 32.6 (cf. 31.1), ending with the words 'but the truth is not clear', I shall have occasion to return in Section c below.

There is one problem in Plutarch's account of the Megarian decree which needs to be discussed in detail: the wording of *Per.* 29.4, summarising the text of the exclusion decree. This requires some close examination of the Greek, and I have postponed it to Appendix XXXVIII. I will only say here that Plutarch should probably not be taken to be referring to an exclusion from '*every market* and all the harbours the Athenians controlled', for two reasons: first, the Greek need not necessarily be so translated; and secondly, Plutarch's account at this point is closely based on Thucydides, who distinguishes on every occasion he mentions the decree between plural harbours and singular *agora*, and on two of the three occasions between the harbours of the empire and the *Athenian* Agora. The passage in Plutarch should probably be translated, 'The Corinthians were enraged and denounced the Athenians at Sparta. The Megarians also joined them, complaining that they were being excluded from the whole Agora and from every harbour the Athenians controlled, contrary to the common [Greek] conceptions of justice and the oaths which had been sworn by the Greeks.' If Plutarch did mean to say 'every market and harbour the Athenians controlled' (the most natural interpretation of these words, taken out of context), then his statement must be rejected, since Thucydides' phraseology makes it quite certain that the decree referred (in addition to all the harbours in the empire) not to *every market* in the empire, but to the *Athenian* Agora. As far as the exclusion decree is concerned, Plutarch's one unique contribution is a recollection of the technical phrase 'which the Athenians controlled'—an expression which is more likely to represent the original wording of the decree than Thucydides' 'in the Athenian empire (*archē*)', and which he may well have remembered from Craterus.

c. *Aristophanes*

Our next witness, and of course our earliest, is Aristophanes, who refers directly to the Megarian decree and its immediate antecedents in two of his surviving plays: the *Acharnians* (of 425), lines 524–39, and the *Peace* (of 421), lines 605–11, 615–18. The passage in the *Acharnians* is

---

[5] Jacoby, *DA*, and see *FGrH* III b (Suppl.) i.198-201. The other contributions to the debate are numerous: all important recent works are cited by Donnay, DPP.

preceded by nine lines (515–23) which have suggested to some scholars that before (even perhaps several years before) the main Megarian decree, which excluded Megarians themselves from the Athenian Agora and the harbours of the empire, the Athenians had passed another decree (my decree no. 1), banning the entry of Megarian goods (or at least some Megarian goods) into Attica. These lines (with which we must take *Ach.* 820–1) present an interesting problem, which I shall examine in detail in Appendix XXXVI. Here I will only say that although the existence of such a decree cannot be positively disproved, I do not believe in it myself, nor have most scholars accepted it.

There are certain other passages in the *Acharnians* (729 ff., 753–63) and the *Peace* (246–9, 481–3) which are often carelessly taken as evidence of the serious economic effects upon the Megarians of the exclusion decree. When we begin to examine the evidence of these two plays, a little later on, we shall see that these passages cannot have any relevance of any kind to the Megarian decree.

Before we can profitably use the relevant passages in the *Acharnians* and the *Peace*, however, we must stand back and take a general look at the problem of the utilisation as historical evidence of statements made in Attic comedies. The subject is often referred to in passing, but I know of no satisfactory general discussion of the principles and methods involved, in relation to Comedy as a whole or Aristophanes in particular.[6] Often the supposed evidence of Comedy is misused with disastrous results: see paragraph *F* of Appendix XXIX below. I must be brief here, saying only enough to make my own attitude clear and to show how easy it is to draw conclusions from this kind of evidence which are seriously misleading.

I suggest that in using the evidence of Comedy (and of Aristophanes in particular) to draw historical conclusions we should begin by applying five principles.

First, the only safe course is to *look at the other evidence first*, and, if we have reliable sources, to make sure we *interpret the comic poet in the light of the remaining evidence*, instead of going to work the other way round, as people so often do. As we shall see, the evidence of Aristophanes, in this case as in so many others, will fit various different reconstructions. Whenever we have sufficient good evidence from other sources, we can often see that the most obvious interpretation of a comic passage is not the right interpretation; and therefore in cases where we have no other evidence, or not much, we must not take the obvious interpretation for granted. According

---

[6] There are some admirable remarks in K. J. Dover's review of Ehrenberg, *PA²*, in *Camb. Jnl.* 5 (1951–2) 636–8. Note esp. p. 637: 'The facts that we learn from a passage in Comedy rarely, if ever, emerge directly from the statements, general or particular, made by the characters; they come indirectly through an understanding of the tacit assumptions without which the joke is not a joke. The historical use of Comedy appears in this respect remarkably similar to the use of Oratory . . . It would be unplausible to say that all plain statements in the orators are false; but it would be a safer assumption than its contrary.'

to Ar., *Lysistr.* 280, Cleomenes surrendered the Athenian Acropolis 'unwashed for six years'. What might not have been inferred from this about a prolonged Spartan occupation of the Acropolis, did we not know from Herodotus (v 72.2) that Cleomenes had been in occupation for only three days? And in *Lysistr.* 664–71 the old men speak as if they themselves had taken part in the occupation of Leipsydrion—which we happen to know occurred rather more than a hundred years earlier (Arist., *Ath. Pol.* 19.3). Broad inferences about the political, social or economic situation at Athens, drawn from a single play, can be equally misleading. To give only the most obvious example: in the *Lysistrata* the fact that the wives of Athenian citizens deny their husbands sexual intercourse is sufficient to make the men so desperate as to be ready to conclude peace with Sparta— as if Athens were not a slave society, affording ample opportunities for sexual gratification with prostitutes and *hetairai*. In the *Lysistrata* the absence of slaves is due simply to the demands of the plot; and the same is true of *Ecclesiazusae* 311–47, where also the slaves have to be kept out of the picture.

Secondly, any statement in Comedy must always be *read in its context and in character*: we must ascertain what point the character who speaks the lines is trying to make (of course without assuming that he is necessarily expressing the views of the poet himself), and how the statement we are interested in fits into the argument. (This principle, as we shall see, is particularly important when we are dealing with Ar., *Ach.* 528–39.)

Thirdly, 'there's no smoke without fire' may be a useful rule-of-thumb; nevertheless, besides comic *exaggerations* we must be prepared to find comic *inventions*, perhaps bearing no relation whatever to any actual situation. (I shall return to this question in a moment.)

Fourthly, we must be on the look out for those *purely literary parodies* to which Aristophanes at any rate was so much addicted, where the main point of the jokes may be in the verbal repetition, or on the other hand some alteration, of a well-known passage. (Much of the speech of Dicaeopolis in Ar., *Ach.* 497–8 onwards is an elaborate parody of a speech or speeches of Telephus in Euripides' play of that name.)

And finally, if we want to identify the outlook, especially the political outlook, of a comic playwright such as Aristophanes (which may sometimes be a material factor in our assessment of the value of a particular passage as historical evidence), we must above all take account of three rules:

1. We must always bear in mind the whole output of the poet and not isolate a single play, or a small group of plays. Still less must we isolate a few lines, or even the speech or chorus in which they occur. Of course a poet's outlook may have changed over the years, and of course he may be adapting himself skilfully to a changed situation. (For example, we might expect Aristophanes to take up a rather different position when writing the *Knights*, in 425/4, after the sensational success at Pylos had greatly

raised Athenian morale, compared with his mood in 426/5, when composing the *Acharnians*.) But the whole work of any writer is always relevant in any study of any one of his works.

2. Any statement in any play may be serious or it may be a joke. Even if it is said with an air of great seriousness, even by the chorus speaking explicitly on the poet's behalf, it may still be essentially a joke. On the other hand, if the poet's jokes tend to follow persistent patterns, the very nature of these jokes may be an indication of the poet's outlook.

3. In Comedy, it is passages that are neither an integral part of the plot nor funny in themselves which are most likely to represent the opinions of the poet. (We may compare the use of forensic speeches as evidence either for historical events or for the orator's own outlook: here the most valuable statements are often those that do not form part of the orator's case—that are not part of his 'plot'.)

I have given some indication of what I believe to be Aristophanes' political attitude, especially in regard to the war, in Appendix XXIX.

In dealing with the third of my five principles, I distinguished between comic exaggerations and inventions. We have already (Chapter VI, Part iii above) discussed the well known passage in Aristophanes' *Knights* (1300–04), from which it is quite uncertain whether Hyperbolus had made some proposal which Aristophanes is exaggerating into 'sending 100 triremes against Carthage', or whether that proposal is a pure invention, which could be recognised by the audience (or anyway those who felt about Hyperbolus as Aristophanes did) as just the sort of folly to be expected of Hyperbolus. A few other examples may be given. When the Great King, in *Ach.* 647–51, gravely asks the ambassadors which side in the war Aristophanes is on, because his brilliant counsel is bound to secure victory for his side, it is hardly necessary to suppose that the King had so much as heard of the poet. When Aristophanes, in the same play (*Ach.* 65–7, 80), makes some Athenian ambassadors to the Great King take three years to reach his court and eleven before they return home, doubtless he is merely exaggerating, with reference to one or more previous Athenian embassies, probably (but not necessarily) recent ones. When in *Knights* 832–5 Aristophanes makes the Sausage-Seller speak of a bribe of more than 40 minae given to Cleon by the Mytilenaeans, he may be repeating a current accusation, true or false, or he may be simply fooling: the essence of the joke, indeed, *may* be that Cleon, who only three years earlier had spoken in favour of the mass execution of all adult male Mytilenaeans, was the *last* person likely to do a favour to Mytilene. When Aristophanes or another comic poet makes one of those frequent references to some prominent Athenian politician as a tanner or leather-seller or flute-borer or cattle-dealer or lyre-seller, he may simply be adopting for his own purposes a stock calumny, about as appropriate as calling Cleon 'Paphlagon' or Demosthenes 'a Scythian', but he may equally well be alluding to the fact—or the alleged fact—that the man's father or grandfather once followed such a calling, if only in the sense that he owned slaves who made leather goods or flutes or what not.[7]

Undoubtedly statements made by comic poets to which most people today would give little credence might be taken at least partly seriously at the time and later and have some influence on opinion. According to Plutarch (*Per.* 30.4), when the murder of Anthemocritus was brought up against Megarians (cf. Appendix XXXVII), they blamed Pericles and Aspasia, and in support of their position cited the well-known lines from Aristophanes, *Acharnians* 524–7. Plutarch (*Nic.* 4.4–8) finds what he calls 'evidence' (*martyria*) of Nicias' timidity and willingness to buy off sycophants in the comic poets Telecleides, Eupolis, Aristophanes and Phrynichus. In a fragment of Lysias[8] the orator remarks, 'You all know Cinesias to be the most impious and lawless of men. Is this not the man who has committed such crimes against the gods as it would be shocking for other men even to speak of?—though you hear the comic poets doing so every year.' But the most obvious example is the case of Socrates. Whatever Aristophanes' real attitude to him may have been,[9] his caricature of that philosopher in the *Clouds* undoubtedly contributed to the hostility with which he was regarded by many Athenians at the time of his trial. Plato, near the opening of the *Apology*, makes Socrates say that far more dangerous to him than Anytus and his fellow-accusers are those others who got hold of the dicasts when they were children and persuaded them falsely that he was a man who 'speculated about the heavens and searched into things beneath the earth and made the worse appear the better argument' (18bc); he adds that he does not know the names of these accusers, 'unless one of them happens to be a comic poet' (18cd). A little later Socrates is made to frame the sort of indictment against himself which these anonymous accusers might bring (19b): it very well fits the Socrates of the *Clouds*, and this time Aristophanes is actually named, with a clear reference to the *Clouds* (19c).

It was not only at the time that the inventions and exaggerations of Comedy were sometimes treated as historically true. Satyrus, in his *Life of Euripides*, took the *Thesmophoriazusae* of Aristophanes as evidence that Euripides was really 'attacked by the women at the Thesmophoria' (*P. Oxy.* IX 1176, fr. 39, col. x, lines 23–32). I wonder whether a misunder-

---

[7] A simple proof that the man himself could be labelled with a tag appropriate only to his father is the case of Isocrates, who is himself called a flute-borer (*aulotrypēs*) by Ar. (fr. 700, *ap.* Ps.-Plut., *Mor.* 836ef) and Strattis (fr. 3, *ap.* Athen. XIII 592d), although it is his father alone who is known to have manufactured flutes. In some of the parallel cases the 'maker' or 'seller' may well have been a more remote ancestor than a father: one example is Cleon, whose father Cleaenetus must have been a wealthy man, since he performed the choregia, winning a victory with a dithyrambic chorus (*IG* II² 2318.33–5), a most expensive form of choregia (see Dem. XXI 156 etc.); another is Cleophon, whose father is now known to have been the Cleïppides who was a Strategos in 429/8 (see E. Vanderpool, 'Kleophon', in *Hesp.* 21 [1952] 114–15; cf. 37 [1968], at p. 120). Politics, at any rate at the top level, was of course a whole-time job, and men like Cleon and Cleophon could not regularly have practised any form of trade themselves.

[8] Lys. fr. 53.1–2 Thalheim, *ap.* Harp., *s.v. Kinēsias*, and Athen. XII 551def.

[9] See K. J. Dover's excellent edition of the *Clouds*, Introduction, pp. xxxii-lvii.

standing of some passage in Comedy may not also lie behind the statement of Plutarch (*Per.* 32.1) that the prosecutor of Aspasia in the action against her for impiety was Hermippus the comic poet.[10] The slander against Pericles in Aristophanes' *Peace* (605–9), as we shall see in a moment, actually became the foundation of Ephorus' influential account of the origins of the Peloponnesian war. The limit of absurdity was reached by an unknown ancient commentator on Aristophanes' *Peace*, who claimed that the comic poets received their name of *didaskaloi* (teachers) because they were public instructors or counsellors (*symbouloi*)![11] And see Appendix XXIX, Section *F*.

We can now turn to the particular passages in Aristophanes which refer, or have been thought to refer, to the Megarian decree.

We may begin with *Peace* 605–11, 615–18.[12] The origin of the Peloponnesian war is traced back by Hermes to Pheidias, who 'got into trouble' (605). This is a reference to the trial of Pheidias for alleged malversation of the material entrusted to him for the construction of the great chryselephantine state of Athena, dedicated in 438.[13] Fortunately, I do not need to discuss the historical facts in the case of Pheidias, as they have recently been very thoroughly examined by G. Donnay,[14] who gives sufficient references to the recent archaeological discoveries at Olympia. According to Hermes' account (*Peace* 605–14), Pericles, apprehensive of sharing the misfortune of Pheidias and fearing the ferocious temper of the Athenians, 'set the city on fire' before anything dreadful should happen to him, 'throwing in the little spark of a Megarian decree'. Trygaeus at once expresses surprise (615–16): he says he has not heard Pheidias brought into this context before. The Chorus agree it is new to them too (617–18): 'Many things escape our notice', they say. The attempt to connect Pheidias with the Megarian decree we can safely ignore, especially now that the exceptionally valuable scholion on *Peace* 605, using to good effect the evidence of Philochorus (*FGrH* 328 F 121), has been shown to be perfectly compatible with the archaeological evidence.[15] There is now no reason to doubt that the statue of Athena was indeed finished as long before the war as 438 and that Pheidias was prosecuted in 438/7 and went into exile at Elis, where he subsequently made the great statue of Zeus at Olympia. We may pause to remind ourselves that there is *no truth whatever* in Hermes' allegations against Pericles in the *Peace*: the whole thing is not mere exaggeration but pure invention by Aristophanes, and it is now put forward for the first time, as Trygaeus and the Chorus indicate by their reception of it.

[10] In view of the reported testimony of Aeschines and Antisthenes 'the Socratics' (Plut., *Per.* 32.5; Athen. xiii 589e), I hesitate to follow Donnay, DPP 29–30, in positively rejecting the historicity of such a prosecution; but I would regard it as far from certain.

[11] *Second Hypothesis* to Ar., *Peace*. The name was of course derived from the fact that the poets 'instructed' the Chorus.

[12] I need not discuss such passages as *Peace* 500–2.

[13] For the sources, see Hill, *S*² 353 (Index ii 6.11).

[14] Donnay, DPP. Very valuable is Jacoby's discussion of Philoch. 328 F 121, in *FGrH* iii b (Suppl.) i.484–96; ii.391–401; and cf. Jacoby, *DA*.

[15] See Donnay, DPP, esp. 24–6, cf. 31–2, 34.

It will be salutary to bear this in mind when we are dealing with the *Acharnians*.

Yet, apparently on no better foundation than this passage in the *Peace*, the accusation that Pericles brought on the war to distract attention from his own misdeeds, whether committed in conjunction with Pheidias or not, is repeated again and again in later writers, from at least Ephorus onwards, with all kinds of variants, usually involving a charge of appropriating public or sacred money.[16] Probably no one nowadays will wish to take these accusations seriously: most people, I think, will be content to accept the statement of Thucydides (II 65.8; cf. 60.5) that Pericles was 'conspicuously most incorruptible'. As far as I know, the only form in which any reputable modern historian has cared to level against Pericles the charge of deliberately provoking the war for personal reasons, as distinct from reasons of State, is the one adopted by Beloch: that Pericles' political position was being undermined in the late 430s, as shown by the attacks on his friends, and that for this reason he deliberately hastened the outbreak of the war, which by now was bound to come anyway.[17] For my own part, I do not think it is necessary to take this position seriously. We may consider whether Pericles provoked the war in what he believed to be the interests of Athens, by (among other things) the Megarian decree;[18] but we need hardly pause to wonder whether he did it to save his own skin or even maintain his own personal position.

Having disposed of *Peace* 605–18, I want to turn to a series of passages in the *Acharnians* and the *Peace* (referred to earlier) in which it has often been supposed that we have evidence of the serious economic effects upon Megara of the exclusion decree: these are the repeated references to starvation in Megara at the time of both plays (*Ach.* 729 ff., 753–63; *Peace* 246–9, 481–3), and especially the appearance in the *Acharnians* (729 ff.) of an unnamed Megarian in a desperate state of hunger. These passages have been largely responsible for creating the impression that the Megarian decree was intended to have, and did have, an important effect upon the economy of Megara; but in fact they have no relevance at all to the decree, for the following reasons:

1. First, the Athenians invaded and severely ravaged the Megarid twice in every (archon-)year from 431/30 to 425/4, 'with all their forces', in 431 at any rate with not less than 13,000 hoplites, as well as many light troops (Thuc. II 31.3; IV 66.1); in addition they maintained a naval

[16] See esp. Plut., *Per.* 31.2–5; 32.6; also Diod. XII 39.1–2 (= Ephorus, 70 F 196); Aristod. 16.1–2; Schol. Ar., *Peace* 606 (605 Dindorf),

[17] Beloch, *GG* II² i.292 ff., esp. 296–8; *APP* 19–22. Contrast Jacoby, *FGrH* III b (Suppl.) ii.397 n. 34, with whom I agree.

[18] See e.g. Ehrenberg, *SS* 257: 'Pericles deliberately tried to force Sparta into war before she was really ready.' (I cannot see how this could be advantageous to Athens, as she could not hope to win the war quickly.) Cf. Adcock, in *CAH* v 187: 'Pericles forced the issue, not because his personal position was shaken, but because, if war came, it must come before he was too old to guide Athens to victory.' (Could Pericles really have so despaired of the Athenians?)

blockade, details of which are given below; and during the early years of the war the Megarians also suffered from raids by some exiles of their own, based on Pagae, as explained presently. All this would have done much more harm than anything which could have been brought about by the Megarian decree.

2. The decree was in operation, in reality, only up to the outbreak of the war in the spring of 431. Immediately the war began, the decree was in effect superseded entirely by the far more severe rules concerning 'enemy aliens' (*polemioi*) and their goods (*polemia*). It is essential to realise that the Megarian and his goods are denounced *precisely in that way* in the *Acharnians* (818–27), just like the Boeotian who enters later in the play (910–14, 915 ff.). The Megarian decree can have no relevance whatever to the Boeotian, and similarly we do not need it in the case of the Megarian.

3. As to what Aristophanes had in mind in presenting his Megarian in the *Acharnians* as on the verge of starvation, lines 758–63 are explicit and conclusive: lines 758–60 refer to the Athenian blockade since 431 (reinforced from 427 onwards by Nicias' capture of the Megarian island of Minoa and the tighter grip thus obtained by Athens upon Nisaea),[19] and lines 761–3 speak of the Athenian ravaging.

4. Nowhere is there so much as a hint of the Megarian decree. Even the scholia, which one might have expected to drag in the decree, merely refer back at one point[20] to the decree of Charinus as a cause of the war, without pretending that it is relevant to the situation depicted in the play. The scholion on *Peace* 483 (not included in Hill, *S²*) puts it accurately: 'But now, *since there was a war on*, they were afraid to enter Attica and purchase the things they needed.' Now the Charinus decree excluded Megarians, on pain of death, not merely from the Agora but from the whole of Attica; and if that decree is to be dated in 432/1 it will presumably have been in force for a very short time just before the actual outbreak of war. But once war had broken out, it would not have been necessary to invoke even that decree, let alone the main exclusion decree, which was less severe: as is clear from the treatment of the Megarian and the Boeotian in the *Acharnians* (and as one would expect anyway), enemy aliens and their goods (*polemioi* and *polemia*) found anywhere in Attica during wartime would be subject to seizure and the legal action known as *phasis*.[21]

5. I have found that many people do have a strong subjective feeling that there 'must be' a reference to the Megarian decree in the passages from the *Acharnians* we have been discussing. I have shown that there is no objective basis for this. To decide the matter, let us ask ourselves the simple question: If, for the sake of argument, we were to forget the

[19] Thuc. III 51, with IV 67.3; and see below. According to one scholion on *Ach.* 760, the Megarians got their salt from Nisaea; the other has the essential point about Athenian control of the sea.

[20] Schol. Ar. *Peace* 246, on which see Appendix XL.

[21] See Lipsius, *AR* 309 ff., at pp. 312–13; A. R. W. Harrison, *The Law of Athens. Procedure* (Oxford, 1971) 218–21.

Megarian decree and suppose it was never passed, would these passages be fully intelligible, and could they have been written precisely as we now find them? The answer could only be Yes.

Although there is no necessary reference to the Megarian decree in the lines in question, I can understand that some people may feel it is casting its shadow over the play, so to speak, in lines 729–30. These lines might be taken as a sort of parody of a tragic *topos*: the opening address to his native land or home by the man returning after a long absence. In being admitted to Dicaeopolis' agora, the Megarian is represented as returning to one of his natural haunts after a painful separation. (Of course the agora is that of Dicaeopolis, not that of Athens, but the one is a substitute for the other.) And some people may feel that in view of the reference to the Agora in line 533, the period during which the exclusion decree was in operation is necessarily involved. I do not think so myself. Even if there had never been a Megarian decree, Aristophanes might still have represented the Megarian as using the same form of words, for he had been kept out of the Athenian Agora, as indeed out of the whole of Athenian territory, for six years *by the war*—and another year or so (or even longer) during the operation of the Megarian decree would make no real difference. But in any event, seeing a possible reference to the exclusion decree in lines 729–30 provides no evidence that it was an 'economic' measure, for in the scene as a whole, from line 731 onwards, Aristophanes, as we have seen, is concerned only with the present plight of the Megarian and makes him attribute it, not to the decree, but to the blockade and the ravaging expeditions.

There remains only the most important passage in Aristophanes for our purposes: *Ach.* 509 ff., the vital part of which divides naturally into two sections: 515–23, and 524 ff. I shall reserve the first section (lines 515–23) for detailed consideration in Appendix XXXVI, and concentrate here on the second (524 ff.), which contains our earliest surviving reference to the Megarian decree.

The lines directly relevant to the decree, its antecedents and its consequences, are 524–39; but if we begin at line 524, or even 515, and come to a full stop at the end of 539, as so many people do who use the evidence of this passage, *we miss the whole point Dicaeopolis is making*! To understand his presentation of the Megarian decree, we must read the speech as a whole, lines 497–556, with 309–14—the whole of each passage, indeed, is relevant. The essential fact, which we must never lose sight of, is that the confessed purpose of the speech is to deny that all the blame for the war can be put on the Peloponnesian side. We shall fail to realise this if we isolate lines 515–39. As the play makes very clear, most Athenians now hated the Peloponnesians and blamed them as the aggressors, the authors of the war—as indeed they were. Coming forward to defend himself against the bellicose, wrathful chorus of Acharnians, Dicaeopolis begins (lines 497–9) by saying he is going to 'speak before the Athenians about the City, in a comedy, for truth is not alien to Comedy'. How far Dicaeo-polis is seriously voicing the real views of Aristophanes himself is a question I can relegate to an Appendix (XXIX): here we are simply concerned with the speech as that of the character in the comedy, and for the present it would be wrong to consider it in any other light. The speech is a close parody of a speech or speeches, by Telephus himself or others in his defence, in the *Telephus* (produced in 438 B.C.), the play of Euripides to which Aristophanes most often refers.²² Dicaeopolis at once prepares the audience for a surprise: he will speak what is 'shocking (*deina*), but true' (line 501). This makes us think back to lines 309–14, where Dicaeopolis, when first attacked by the Chorus, said he could prove that the Spartans were not entirely guilty and in many ways had suffered wrong at the hands of Athens, a statement which the Acharnians had received with incredulous fury. Identifying himself explicitly with the poet (see Appendix XXIX *D* 1), he congratulates himself that Cleon cannot attack him this time, because it is the Lenaea 'and foreigners are not yet here'. He insists that he hates the Spartans as much as anyone: he has had his vines cut down too (lines 509–12). And then he comes to the point: 'Why do we blame the Spartans for this?', he asks (line 514). His account of the origins of the war occupies lines 515–39'. Immediately after this, in lines 540–54, he returns to the point he set out to make, and rubs it in: *the Athenians must not blame the Spartans*; they would have behaved in exactly the same way if the boot had been on the other foot. We must now look more closely at individual sections.

We have already noticed that from lines 497–8 onwards, at various points, Dicaeopolis is parodying the *Telephus*, the one play of Euripides above all others at which Aristophanes liked to poke fun. From line 524 onwards he contrives in addition to parody the opening chapters of the *History* of Herodotus (completed not long before the *Acharnians* was produced), which gave the chain of cause and effect beginning with the carrying off of Io and leading up to the Trojan war. Dicaeopolis naturally ignores altogether the cultivation of the sacred land by the Megarians, which was in fact the main reason for the Megarian decree but was not at all a fit subject for jesting. In concocting the first part of his story Aristophanes seems not only to be imitating Herodotus closely but also perhaps making a covert contemporary allusion to the other reason given by the Athenians for the Megarian decree: the 'reception of their runaway slaves' mentioned by Thucydides I 139.2. Some young Athenians, says Dicaeopolis, stole the whore (*pornē*) Simaetha from Megara, and the Megarians retaliated by seizing two of Aspasia's whores (*porna dyo*).

It is at this point that the Megarian decree is introduced: Pericles breaks forth into thunders and lightnings and enacts 'laws written like drinking songs' (*hōsper skolia*, 532). Here, as the scholiast makes plain,

²² See E. W. Handley and J. Rea, *The Telephus of Euripides* (= *BICS*, Suppl. 5, 1957); Rosemary Harriott, 'Aristophanes' Audience and the Plays of Euripides', in *BICS* 9 (1962) 1–8.

we are being treated to yet another parody, this time of a famous drinking song (*skolion*) of Timocreon of Rhodes (fr. 5 Diehl), the relevant portion of which the scholiast (on line 532) proceeds to give. There is unfortunately a dispute about the correct reading of one word in the texts of both poets, but I will give the texts which I believe to be the correct ones, and explain the readings in Appendix XXXIX. Timocreon's words, applied to the god Plutus,

> You, blind Plutus, ought to appear *neither on land nor on sea nor in heaven*, but dwell in Tartarus and Acheron, for it is because of you that all evils come to men,

appear in Aristophanes as

> That the Megarians should remain *neither on land nor in agora nor on sea nor on continent.*

The two points with which we are familiar in the Megarian decree are expanded rather lamely by Aristophanes, in imitation of Timocreon's three, into four: Aristophanes has made one necessary change (as I think), of 'in heaven' into 'on continent', and has added one new element: 'in agora'. The gross exaggeration of 'neither on land nor on sea', as applied to the Megarians, is explained by the fact that these words are lifted straight from Timocreon. It may have been what I have called the forcible and perhaps high-flown language of the Megarian decree which made Aristophanes liken it to Timocreon's skolion and speak of 'thunders and lightnings' on Pericles' part. At any rate, Dicaeopolis has made his essential point: Pericles had (to use a currently popular expression) 'overreacted' to a minor provocation by the Megarians, itself a natural reaction to an Athenian one.

The lines which follow, describing the Megarian decree as 'the decree on account of the harlots' (*to psēphisma to dia tas laikastrias*, lines 536–7), treat it as what we might call the 'immediate cause' of the war, for the Megarians, 'gradually starving' (line 535), go to the Spartans, begging them to get the decree repealed, and when the Athenians refuse, the war begins. (I shall have more to say about line 535 in a moment.)

Here, then, Dicaeopolis puts very great emphasis upon the Megarian decree as a cause of the war, ridiculing its language and *representing it as an exaggerated reply to a trivial offence*, but ignoring its main real cause. And immediately afterwards he comes back (in lines 540–54) to drive home his thesis that the Athenians must not put the blame for the war entirely on the other side.

We now come to line 535, where the Megarians are represented by Dicaeopolis as appealing to Sparta 'when they were gradually starving' (*hote dē 'peinōn badēn*). Since this is the only passage in any source which speaks of economic distress as a consequence of the Megarian decree, it will be well to show by more than one argument that it is not to be taken seriously.

1. In the first place, there is scarcely a single word in the ten preceding lines which corresponds to historical fact, and the two lines that follow, as we noticed, speak of the decree as 'the decree on account of the harlots'. What we are being given is a whole series of comic exaggerations, with scarcely an atom of truth in them. We ought to expect, then, that the statement about the Megarians 'gradually starving' will be another of these absurdities, to be accepted in the same spirit as the others—the statement that the decree was 'on account of the harlots', for instance, or that it was 'drafted like a drinking song', or that it excluded the Megarians from land and sea and continent. We must also observe that the Megarian decree *of Dicaeopolis' speech* was couched (in imitation of Timocreon) in very much broader terms than the real one; and starvation *in this context*, of course, is less of an exaggeration. To insist capriciously on taking this one statement literally, as representing historical fact, would be a serious error in historical method.

2. The case can be made even stronger: the decisive argument is that Dicaeopolis is absolutely obliged to represent the Megarians as 'starving' when they were not. As we have seen, he has been at pains to establish a chain of cause and effect, which will show that the Peloponnesians cannot be made to bear the whole blame for the war, and it is *an essential part of his case to show that their actions were reasonable* and such as might have been expected. Pericles, he implies, made far too much fuss about the carrying off of Aspasia's whores. But were not the Megarians equally unreasonable? No!—look at the terms of the decree: the Megarians were excluded from 'land, agora, sea and continent'; they were positively starving; so *of course* they besought the Spartans to get the decree repealed, and when Athens refused, the war began. 'Does anyone say, "They ought not to have done it"? Well then, tell me what they should have done' (line 540).[23] The Athenians would have done exactly the same, and more: they would have launched three hundred warships if . . . and so on.

3. By the time the play was produced, six or seven years later than the crisis over the Megarian decree, the Megarians had doubtless been reduced to severe straits, for reasons already alluded to, which will be developed presently. Aristophanes can make fun of the hungry Megarian who appears later in the play,[24] and he may have expected to raise a smile by speaking of the Megarians as near starvation in 432—especially, indeed, if my interpretation of the decree is accepted, for in that case it was even more obviously a joke. It has been suggested to me that the actor who played the part of Dicaeopolis may have raised an additional laugh by delivering line 535 with a significant pause after the word *epeinōn—hote dē 'peinōn . . . badēn*! (For a famous occasion on which an actor altered the sense of a line, unintentionally, by a slight pause at an inappropriate

---

[23] Another quotation from the *Telephus*, according to Schol. Ar., *Ach.* 540 (= 539 Dindorf).

[24] Cf. *Peace* 246–9, 481–3, 500–2, and the heartless ἀπολεῖτε λιμῷ Μηλίῳ of Ar., *Birds* 186.

point, see Schol. Ar. *Frogs* 304, and Rogers' comments on the same passage, in his edition of the play, p. 46 n. Evidently Athenian audiences would notice such things.) It is a joke of a kind when Dicaeopolis says the Megarian decree was passed *as a result* of the abduction of Aspasia's two girls and represents it as 'the decree on account of the harlots', just as it is a joke when Hermes says, in *Peace* 605 ff., that it was passed *as a result* of Pericles' desire to cover up his peculations: everyone knew that these statements were not true, and in each case the argument was an elaborate jest. It is a jest of much the same kind when Dicaeopolis speaks of the Megarians as starving *as a result* of the decree. Pericles did pass the decree, but for other reasons; and the Megarians did come near to starvation, again for other reasons—later, and because of the war.

4. In reality it is quite impossible that the Megarians were even beginning to 'starve' at the time of which Dicaeopolis is speaking. This is certain, even apart from the arguments I shall be bringing against the conventional view of the Megarian decree. If my theory is right, of course, the decree will not have had any important effects upon the Megarian economy. But in order to avoid a *petitio principii* I am prepared to argue this point quite independently of my main thesis. Even if we were to take the most extreme view of the Megarian decree, that it in effect excluded from the whole of Attica and the whole of the Athenian empire everyone who lived at Megara, we should still have to admit that the economic position of Megara became infinitely worse after the outbreak of the war. As we know, Athens invaded the Megarid twice a year from 431/30 onwards with very large forces, and the ravaging of the country must have been severe and extensive (see esp. Paus. I xl.4). Moreover, at Budorum on Salamis, opposite the Megarid, the Athenians maintained a fortified position and kept a small force of three triremes, 'to prevent anything sailing into or out of Megara' (Thuc. II 93.4, with 94.3, under the year 429). In 427 Nicias captured the Megarian island of Minoa, opposite Nisaea (the main port of Megara), which was then fortified and used as a base for blockading Nisaea (Thuc. III 51, with IV 67.3). It must have been about this time, if not earlier (see III 68.3), that there took place at Megara a revolution[25] resulting in the exile of certain extreme oligarchs, who seized possession of Pagae and plundered the Megarid from there (IV 66.1). This not only subjected Megara to further damaging raids but deprived her of her one port on the Corinthian Gulf, which was all the more essential to her now that Nisaea was closely blockaded by Athens. Yet Megara still fought on, without even the necessity for a Peloponnesian garrison in the city, apart from the one at Nisaea (IV 66.3–69.3), which

---

[25] The words ὑπὸ τοῦ πλήθους in Thuc. IV 66.1 are commonly taken (as by Gomme, *HCT* III 528) to imply that a democracy resulted. We cannot tell from IV 66–74 precisely what form of government Megara had in *c.* 424. But surely Ar., *Ach.* 755 (a passage which seems to have mainly escaped notice) suggests a constitution more oligarchic than democratic in 426/5 (on *probouloi*, see Arist., *Pol.* IV 14, 1298[b]26–9; 15, 1299[b]30–8; VI 8, 1323[a] 6–9). (On the topography of Megara and Nisaea, see Gomme, *HCT* II 334–6.)

was there to prevent a surprise attack from the sea by the Athenians. The attempt by the 'leaders of the demos' (iv 66.3) to betray the city in 424 was foiled, but Nisaea was captured by Athens (66.3–73). Even then 'the Megarians'—that is to say, from 424 onwards the now thoroughly oligarchical (see 74.2–4) government of Megara—preferred to fight on, and in 421 Megara was one of the very small group of states which voted against concluding the Peace of Nicias (v 17.2). All this shows that if Megara had been anywhere near 'starving' as a result of the exclusion decree alone, she would have been on her knees long before the Peace of Nicias, for her position became far worse immediately the war began, and she suffered further disasters, first through the loss of Minoa, then, from *c.* 427 to 424, through the activities of her exiles, and in 424 by the capture of Nisaea.

If I have laboured at undue length to make a point which seems obvious enough to most people I have discussed it with, it is because a leading authority on the period rejected an earlier version of this Chapter out of hand, mainly because he insisted that *Ach.* 535 must be taken literally.

It is vain to seek in Aristophanes' allusions to the Megarian decree any fresh light on its wording, its purpose or its effects; nor do the scholia help. All we derive from Aristophanes is confirmation of what we can infer from Thucydides and first find stated explicitly by Andocides in 392/1 (iii 8; cf. Aeschin. ii 175): that there were those who regarded the Peloponnesian war as having broken out 'on account of the Megarians'. It was only natural that those who would have preferred to repeal the decree rather than risk a war should have regarded the decree as a principal cause of the war once Sparta had made a particular point of the decree and declared that Athens could avoid war by repealing it (Thuc. i 139.1). Thucydides' report of the debate in the Athenian Assembly when the final Spartan *démarche* was being discussed shows that the repeal of the decree was strongly urged by many speakers (139.4); and Thucydides makes Pericles devote special attention to this question (140.3–5; 144.2).

It is an extraordinary fact, which should not escape our notice, that just as in antiquity Ephorus and many of his successors took *Peace* 605–9 seriously and based their accounts of the origins of the Peloponnesian war upon it, so modern historians have accepted the equally fantastic picture in the *Acharnians* as a statement of fact *and have preferred it to Thucydides'* *picture*, with which it is in reality irreconcilable. (Cf. Appendix XXIX, Section F.)

D. *The other sources*

The remaining evidence for the Megarian decrees consists of small scraps having no independent authority. Most of these passages are conveniently assembled in Hill's *Sources*.[26] Very little need be said here about this material.

There are two passages (already referred to above) in Athenian orators which are interesting as evidence that in the fourth century it could be said publicly at Athens that the Peloponnesian war had broken out 'on account of the Megarians': Andocides (III 8) made this statement in 392/1 and Aeschines (II 175), using almost identical language, in 343. Joining these two statements to Ar., *Ach.* 524–39 and *Peace* 605–18, many historians have innocently assumed that a large number of Athenians really did regard the exclusion decree as the real cause of the war. (This is taken for granted even by Gomme, *HCT* I 447, 466.) They forget that their evidence is not of the best quality: Aristophanes is a comic poet, and the context of the statement just quoted from Andocides (III 3–9) and Aeschines (II 172–6) affords one of the worst examples we have of oratorical inaccuracy and misrepresentation. There obviously were Athenians who took this view, but that they were ever more than a small minority remains quite unproved.

We might have expected something from Ephorus; but Diodorus, who is explicitly giving Ephorus' account of the origins of the Peloponnesian war (XII 41.1), not only gives the contents of the main Megarian decree in the briefest possible terms (XII 39.4: 'that the Megarians be excluded both from the Agora and from the harbours'), but first introduces it in the context of the complaint by the Megarians at Sparta, as Thucydides does, and this may suggest that Ephorus merely followed Thucydides. I may remark in passing that Ephorus, who is certainly also among the sources of Plutarch, *Per.* 29–32,[27] apparently did not actually make Pericles bring on the war by *passing* the exclusion decree, but only by *opposing its repeal*:[28] see Diod. XII 39.4–5; Plut., *Per.* 29.4,8; 30.1; 31.1; 32.6, especially the Diodorus passage, where the failure (as in Plutarch) to make Pericles *propose* the exclusion decree seriously detracts from the dramatic value of the whole narrative. One might have attributed this to the maladroit handling of Ephorus by Diodorus, were it not for the corresponding passages in Plutarch, which take the very same line.[29] If Ephorus as well

[26] Hill, *S*² 347 (Index I II.5). Add Ael., *VH* XII 53; Gell., *NA* VII x; Liban., *Orat.* XVI 50; Schol. Ar., *Ach.* 527; Schol. Ar., *Peace*, 246, 483. Cf. Appendix XL. According to an ancient commentator on the *Dionysalexandros* of Cratinus, Pericles in that play is 'satirised with great plausibility by innuendo for having brought the war on the Athenians' (*P. Oxy.* IV 663); but there is nothing to indicate that the Megarian decree was brought in.

[27] I of course agree with Jacoby that Plut., *Per.* 29–32 is 'not simply an "extract" from Ephoros': see Jacoby, *FGrH* III b (Suppl.) ii.394 n. 17; cf. *FGrH* II c, p. 92.

[28] From Jacoby, *FGrH* III b (Suppl.) ii.396 n. 29, where Jacoby says that both Aristophanes and Ephorus 'one-sidedly regarded the internal difficulties and the passing (Aristophanes) or the maintenance (Ephoros) of the [Megarian] psephism as the real cause of the war', one might infer that Jacoby also took this view; but at the top of *Id.* i.486, speaking of those who made the case of Pheidias 'the cause of *Perikles' moving the psephism*' [my italics], he adds, 'This is the well-known account of Ephoros'.

[29] See esp. Plut., *Per.* 29.8; 30.1; 31.1; 32.6; and contrast 30.2, where the 'reasonable and courteous decree' is specifically attributed to Pericles. I may add that in the first sentence of *Per.* 31.1 Plutarch is saying that it is not easy to decide how the exclusion decree (not the war) had its origin. Jacoby (*Id.* i.490) and others have taken the subject of

as Thucydides failed to say that Pericles was responsible for the passing of the exclusion decree, Plutarch's unwillingness to commit himself is understandable. He was evidently not prepared to take Aristophanes quite literally: in quoting from the *Acharnians* he limits himself to lines 524–7, ignoring 529–39, which (like *Peace* 605–9) specifically give the decree to Pericles.

The remaining evidence need not be discussed in detail here, but I must say a word about one group of very late sources: Suid., *s.v. Aspasia*, and Schol. Ar., *Ach.* 527 (526 Dindorf) and *Peace* 609 (608 Dindorf), which speak of a decree barring the Megarians from 'Athens' or from 'the land and harbours of Athens'. Fortunately, another scholion, to Ar., *Peace* 246, provides an invaluable clue which enables us to recognise these passages as a description of the effect of the decree of Charinus: see Appendix XL.

We need not treat seriously the absurd story in Gellius (*NA* VII x.1–4) about the philosopher Eucleides of Megara, who, when the Athenians decreed the death penalty against any 'Megaris civis' who should be caught entering Athens, was said to have walked from Megara to Athens and back during the hours of darkness, dressed as a woman, in order to converse with Socrates—a journey of some forty to fifty miles, which would have left little time for philosophical conversation, even during the longest winter nights.

An interesting late reference to the Megarian decree is to be found in Libanius, *Orat.* XVI (*Ad Antioch.*) 50–1. Libanius is referring to cases in which a whole city is punished for the crime of a single man. He gives three examples: the first and third are the sufferings of the Achaean host for the sins of Agamemnon and Ajax, and those of Thebes because of the murder by Oedipus of his father; the second is the Athenians collectively paying the penalty for Pericles' high-handed treatment (*hybris*) of the Megarians!

(iii)

The 'reasonable and courteous decree' and the decree of Charinus

The 'reasonable and courteous' decree of Pericles, as we have seen, is mentioned only in Plutarch, *Per.* 30.2–3; nowhere else is there any hint of it. The probability of its being derived from Craterus[30] seems to me very high. I cannot see why any literary source should have bothered to

---

ἔσχεν here to be ὁ πόλεμος (understood); but this is clearly wrong. The natural subject of both verbs, ἔσχεν as well as λυθῆναι, is τὸ ψήφισμα in the second half of the sentence; the word πόλεμος has not been used since 29.7, nor has the war been mentioned.

[30] *FGrH* 342. See Jacoby's Commentary (III b [Text] 94–109; [Noten] 62–77), also his article in *RE* XI (1922) 1617–21, reprinted in his *GH* 165–7. Jacoby gives a sufficient bibliography. Although a scholiast on Aristeides (see Crat., F 14) actually says that Craterus collected 'all the *psēphismata* that were passed in Greece', there is in fact no evidence that he included any but Athenian decrees, and he may very well not have

record such an unsensational document: Plutarch surely did so only because he believed it—wrongly, as I think—to be directly linked to the decree of Charinus. I shall suggest that to us it is not without significance if only it can be correctly dated.

The decree of Charinus (which it is convenient to deal with briefly first) is represented by Plutarch (*Per.* 30.3) as the consequence of the alleged murder by the Megarians of the herald Anthemocritus, sent out under the reasonable and courteous decree. According to Plutarch, Charinus proclaimed against Megara 'a truceless hostility, in which no herald was to be admitted' (an *aspondon . . . kai akērykton echthran*), forbade any Megarian to enter Attica on pain of death, ordered the generals on taking office to swear to invade the Megarid twice a year, and decreed the burying of Anthemocritus near the Dipylon Gate. Plutarch also mentions the decree of Charinus in another work (*Mor.* 812cd), where he gives four examples of Pericles' use of trustworthy men for carrying out his designs: he employed Menippus, says Plutarch, for his generalships (cf. *Per.* 13.15), he lowered the status of the Areopagus through Ephialtes, he procured the passing of the Megarian decree 'through Charinus', and he sent out Lampon as founder of Thurii. We cannot tell whether these four statements represent Plutarch's own reflections upon what he had read in the many writers he consulted for the *Life of Pericles*, or whether they are repeated from some single source. If the latter, the feebleness of the first two points does not create much confidence in the unknown source. This passage, therefore, has no independent value, and we must make up our minds about the decree of Charinus on the basis of what is said in the *Life of Pericles*.

Apart from sec. 4 of the *Letter of Philip* (Ps.-Dem. xii 4),[31] where the consequence of the murder of Anthemocritus is said to have been the exclusion of the Megarians from the Mysteries, further direct evidence for the decree of Charinus is forthcoming only from a scholion on Aristophanes' *Peace* 246, which, when correctly emended, enables us to understand some confusions in other Aristophanic scholia and in the Souda between the exclusion decree and the decree of Charinus (see above, and Appendix XL).

Nearly a century ago Holzapfel tried to maintain that the decree of Charinus was identical with the exclusion decree, but this impossible theory has been thoroughly refuted[32] and has had no recent advocate except (in a modified form) Hasebroek, for whose inadmissible interpretation see Parts vi and vii of this Chapter.

---

noticed anything of a later date than the fifth century: there is certainly no evidence that he did, and the probabilities seem to be against it; cf. Jacoby, *FGrH* iii b [Text] 97–9; *GH* 166. Plutarch certainly made first-hand use of Craterus' collection: see esp. *Arist.* 26.1–4.

[31] On the question of date (ostensibly 340) and authorship, see F. Blass, *Die attische Beredsamkeit* iii² i. 394–8; M. Croiset, *Démosthène. Harangues* (Budé edition) ii 142–7; etc.

[32] See Connor, *CMD* 227 and n. 8.

We have already seen that Plutarch, in his *Life of Pericles*, has three Megarian decrees: the exclusion decree, the reasonable and courteous decree, and the decree of Charinus. None of the decrees is dated by Plutarch, who as usual is not so much careless about chronology as largely unconcerned with it.[33] Certainly *Per*. 29–32 is chronologically very confused indeed, and we shall not be surprised if we find that Plutarch has got the decrees in the wrong order. The anecdote about Polyalces in *Per*. 30.1 is in chronological sequence with 29.4–8, but there is no reason to suppose that Plutarch was thinking chronologically when he inserted 30.2–4 (the reasonable and courteous decree and the decree of Charinus) before coming back in 31.1 to his starting-point and raising the question why Pericles opposed the repeal of the main decree.

Now the exclusion decree must have been passed before the meeting of the Spartan Assembly in the second half of 432, at which the Megarians complained about it: this is certain. The Charinus decree, if it belongs to 432, must come very late in the sequence of events, at a time when there was no further possibility of avoiding war. Indeed, those who accept the decree as belonging to this period normally date it (as they are surely obliged to do) between the Theban attack on Plataea in early March 431, with which the war really begins, and the first Spartan invasion of Attica in the early summer of 431. But this creates a serious difficulty, for the late dating of the Charinus decree necessitates—if we accept Plutarch's account as it stands—a date almost as late for the reasonable and courteous decree. How is this to be reconciled with a much earlier date for the exclusion decree? Surely the very fact that the decree in *Per*. 30.2–3 is described as putting a 'reasonable and courteous case' is a serious objection to dating it after the main decree. If it is really tied to the decree of Charinus, as Plutarch represents it, it would have come after all three of the Spartan embassies recorded by Thucydides, at a time when war had actually been declared by the Peloponnesians and was now imminent. Moreover, the contents of the reasonable and courteous decree become inexplicable, for exactly the same complaint about the appropriation of the sacred land had earlier been the foundation of the exclusion decree (Thuc. I 139.2), which was hardly 'reasonable and courteous'; and why should the same complaint be made all over again now, without threat of sanctions? And why has Thucydides ignored not merely the decree of Charinus but the murder of Anthemocritus which was its cause?

Connor, whose contribution (CMD, CMDA) is original and valuable (whether his main theory is correct or not), argues that we must remove the reasonable and courteous decree, the murder of Anthemocritus and the decree of Charinus from 432/1 to some date in the fourth century, probably around 350, during which we know that there was a bitter dispute between Athens and Megara concerning the *hiera orgas* (cf. Part

33 See Gomme, *HCT* I 54–84, for a mainly admirable discussion of Plutarch's fifth-century *Lives*, in particular p. 68; 'It is clear ... how carefree Plutarch was about chronology.'

vii of this Chapter). There is, however, what Connor himself realises (CMD 235 n. 23) to be a 'serious objection' to his theory: if, as Plutarch says, the reasonable and courteous decree provided for the herald to go to Sparta as well as to Megara, the decree must belong to the period during which Sparta was Megara's hegemon in the Peloponnesian League, and therefore can hardly be removed from 432/1, certainly not to *c.* 350. There is also the fact that the reasonable and courteous decree is said by Plutarch to have been moved by Pericles. These objections seem to me not merely serious but fatal to Connor's theory as it stands, and I do not think he has adequately met them. (For three recent articles attacking Connor's attempt to date the two decrees and the murder of Anthemocritus to the mid-fourth century, and for the views of Eduard Meyer and Bodin, see Appendix XXXVII.)

I have a suggestion to make which, by modifying Connor's theory in one particular, would entirely remove the two objections I have stated to it. It would also, as it happens, dispose of the main objection to the usual reconstruction, in which all the events we are discussing are kept in 432/1. Since I myself think Connor's re-dating of Anthemocritus and Charinus is probably but not quite certainly wrong, I shall first state the modification I am proposing in Connor's position, and I shall then show how this suggestion can also be used to improve the standard view, which keeps Anthemocritus and Charinus in 432/1, and which I think is more likely to be right.

I suggest that Plutarch (an expression I am using in the sense of 'Plutarch or his source')[34] made one false assumption, a very natural one. He had before him, very probably in Craterus, the reasonable and courteous decree of Pericles, which provided for 'a herald' to be sent to Megara and Sparta, without naming him—Athenian decrees seldom if ever name heralds. Plutarch also had before him the decree of Charinus (or a summary of it), which referred to the murder by the Megarians of the herald Anthemocritus, but was not dated; and he concluded, wrongly but quite naturally, that Anthemocritus was killed when on the mission prescribed by the reasonable and courteous decree. The language Plutarch uses may be significant: he describes the reasonable and courteous decree as sending out simply 'a herald', and names Anthemocritus only when he comes to the decree of Charinus. Thus it would be Plutarch (or his source) who attached the murder of Anthemocritus and the decree of Charinus to the reasonable and courteous decree of Pericles. There is nothing about the decree of Charinus, in itself, to arouse our suspicion. By entirely separating the murder of Anthemocritus and the decree of Charinus from the reasonable and courteous decree, we are able to accept the latter as a decree of Pericles, and to put it where it naturally

---

[34] If *Mor.* 812cd (see above) contains not Plutarch's own reflections but those of an earlier source, then the mistaken assumption which I am suggesting here may well have originated not with Plutarch himself but with his source.

belongs, *at the beginning of the whole process.* The mission of the herald (who-ever he may have been) to Megara and Sparta was fruitless, and it was then that the exclusion decree was passed.

It would be easy to account for a mistake on the part of Plutarch or his source (if that is what it is) in attaching the murder of Anthemocritus and the decree of Charinus to the events of 432/1: the decree, as trans-mitted, was not dated, and it was not unreasonable to attribute it to an occasion on which Athens was known to have sent a herald to Megara during a period of acute hostility between the two states.[35] If the decree of Charinus does come from the fourth century, we should have good reason, it seems to me, for believing that Plutarch's two decrees other than the exclusion decree come ultimately from two different sources: the reasonable and courteous decree (which now remains fifth-century) from Craterus, but the Charinus decree probably not from Craterus, because it will have been passed in the fourth century (see n. 30 above). Plutarch (or his source), by joining them together, would then have created what we might call 'the Charinus problem', which confused the Aristophanes scholiasts and the author of the Souda (see Appendix XL), and has continued to confuse historians.

I would repeat that the suggestion I have made above also removes the main difficulty in the standard view, which, with the modification I have proposed, could still be accepted. The reasonable and courteous decree will then be the first of a series of four 'Megarian decrees' in the period leading up to the outbreak of the war: it will now be followed, first by the exclusion decree, and then, at least some months later, by the decree sending out Anthemocritus,[36] his death, and the decree of Charinus. It will even be possible to have Anthemocritus as the herald sent out on both missions, and meeting his death on the second. The reason why no other writer alludes to the murder of Anthemocritus and the decree of Charinus in the context of 432/1 will be that they came at a very late stage, when war was already inevitable. If the Charinus decree is to be dated 432/1, it may well have come from Craterus. Plutarch's error, as I have ex-plained it, may then be his own, or it may come from Craterus' commen-tary or from some intermediate source.

In either event, Plutarch presents the Megarian decrees in the wrong order in *Per.* 29–32: he gives the exclusion decree first, and then the reasonable and courteous decree (and the decree of Charinus). But he has done very much the same with the Spartan embassies to Athens and the beginning of the war: he first describes, in *Per.* 29.7–30.1, the second embassy (mentioned by Thuc. 1 139.1–2) or the third (139.3 ff.), and then,

[35] Connor has retracted, in CMDA 306–7, his earlier suggestion (CMD 242) that Plutarch's source was confused by the identity of names between the archons of the years 350/49 and 430/29.

[36] This would of course have to come after the final Spartan embassy to Athens; but need Thuc. 1 145 exclude not merely later *embassies* from *Sparta* but also the later sending of a *herald* by *Athens*?

in a later chapter (*Per.* 33.1–2), he gives us the first embassy (referred to by Thuc. 1 126.2), and follows it immediately (*Per.* 33.3 ff.) with an account of the first Spartan invasion of Attica.

Whatever solution we adopt of the Charinus problem, the correct dating of the reasonable and courteous decree, at the very beginning of the whole process, is important for the question whether Athens wanted war in 432–1. The main Megarian decree is commonly quoted as a piece of deliberate provocation by Athens. Whatever the nature of the exclusion decree, it makes a real difference if we find the proceedings beginning with a decree in which Athens states her grievances in 'reasonable and courteous' terms: the probability that Athens did at any rate believe herself to have a genuine complaint against Megara, for cultivating the *hiera orgas*, and was not just picking a quarrel, becomes distinctly greater. Moreover, as Connor points out (CMD 233–4), if Thucydides has omitted the murder of Anthemocritus, 'he is not, as has often been charged, trying to exonerate Pericles and Athens of responsibility for the war. In fact, he has passed over one important indication of Pericles' (and Athens') willingness to conciliate. Furthermore, he has suppressed what might well have been represented as Megarean impiety and provocation of war.'

(iv)
The prevailing conception of the main Megarian decree

The standard view of the exclusion decree, I take it, has two main features, both of which I entirely reject:

1. The immediate aim of the decree was economic: to damage Megara's trade by imposing an embargo upon it throughout the whole of the area controlled by Athens.

2. The ultimate aims of the decree were political and strategic: by bringing severe economic pressure upon Megara, to force her to repeat what she had done in *c.* 461: namely, leave the Peloponnesian League and become an ally of Athens.[37] Less extreme views have been propounded under this head, for instance by Grundy (*THA* I² 325–8), who believed that the main objective of the Megarian decree was the exclusion of Megara from the Pontic corn trade and a warning to other Peloponnesian states that the same treatment could if necessary be meted out to them; or by Kagan (*OPW* 251–72, esp. 265–6), whose view of the purpose of the decree could perhaps be summarised as 'to teach Megara a lesson for sending ships to help Corinth in the expedition that ended at Sybota'. But for my purposes there is little difference between these views, all of which see the Megarian decree as having ulterior political objectives as well as immediate economic ones.

[37] See e.g. Ehrenberg, *PA*² 328 ff., esp. 332; *ATL* III 304 n. 15.

Most people, I think, would want to add a third point:

3. Athens was necessarily the aggressive party, and she was deliberately and unreasonably picking a quarrel with Megara.

Here again I disagree. A strong case against this opinion was made in two articles which appeared independently in 1951, by Brunt (MD) and Völkl (MP), each taking a different line. But so deeply rooted are the misconceptions which have long supported the traditional view that these articles seem to have made little impression, and most people still take it for granted that the Megarian decree, if nothing else, proves Athens to have been the 'real aggressor' in the war.[38]

Whether the Megarian decree was technically a breach of treaty (of the Thirty Years Peace) is disputed: some say yes, some no, some (a majority nowadays, I fancy) that it 'broke the spirit if not the letter of the treaty'[39]—a kind of grudging admission that it did not break the treaty! (See on this question Appendix I.)

(v)
Failure of the prevailing conception of the decree. A new interpretation

The 'economic and political' interpretation of the Megarian decree, summarised in Part iv above, fails utterly, for a number of reasons which I shall proceed to discuss in detail in Parts vi–viii below, when advancing an entirely fresh interpretation. At this point I propose to summarise the arguments against the prevailing theory.

The exclusion decree had three aspects: it applied to *the Megarians*, and it excluded them, not (as it might in principle have done) from the whole of the Athenian empire or even the whole of Attica, but specifically from *the Athenian agora* and from *the harbours of the empire*. We can now isolate these three features of the decree:

1. There is complete unanimity in all the sources that the exclusion was of 'the Megarians', *hoi Megareis*. (As I shall explain, it is just possible, though highly unlikely, that the expression 'the Megarians' stands for a rather wider category; but in any event it could not be expanded beyond 'Megarian citizens and all those living at Megara', and this makes hardly any difference to my argument: see Part vi of this Chapter.) But the mere exclusion of the Megarians, *even had it been (as it was not) from the whole of Attica and the whole of the empire,* could have had *little effect upon the volume of Megarian trade,* which would immediately have passed into the hands of non-Megarians, for there was nothing to prevent even Athenians from

---

[38] I think the Megarian decree must be mainly responsible for Gomme's statement about Athens being 'the aggressor', at the end of the penultimate paragraph of *HCT* II 9.

[39] Bickerman, APT 314. Cf. *ATL* III 304 n. 15: 'Perikles speaks of the letter, the Megarians of the spirit of the Peace' (cf. Part v below and its n. 46).

conducting it, let alone Corinthians and others. In so far as the decree had any effect on Megarian trade at all, the most it could do was to cause some temporary interruption, until other traders gleefully took over, and, by forcing the trade of Megara into the hands of non-Megarians, to inflict some damage upon individual Megarian merchants—who, however, are not likely to have been numerous or men of any political importance, so that the 'government' of Megara (an oligarchy at this time) would probably not be much concerned about any personal losses they might sustain. The 'Megarian State' will have been little affected economically, therefore, except perhaps for a few weeks or days when the decree was first enforced and before other traders took over. This is the most decisive argument, from which there is no escape. As we shall see, the standard view of the decree rests upon an elementary but widespread misunderstanding of the mechanism of Greek trade. To suppose that, as a result of the decree, trade into and out of Megara was seriously curtailed necessarily involves a ludicrous assumption: that no one in the area controlled by Athens would sell for export to Megara, or buy Megarian products, except to or from *Megarian citizens*—for in so far as trade with Megara was conducted by those who were *not* Megarian citizens, the decree could have no application to it whatever! This assumption, although generally unrecognised, is an inevitable part of the standard view of the decree. It only has to be brought into the open and made explicit for its utter absurdity to become apparent.

2. Of the two kinds of exclusion, one was from the Athenian *agora*: if we know anything about the decree at all, we know that it referred specifically to 'the Athenian *agora*', in the singular, as opposed to 'the markets of the empire' (or 'the markets controlled by the Athenians'),[40] in the plural —for Thucydides makes this distinction between singular and plural on each of the three occasions on which he summarises the content of the decree, and he twice refers explicitly to *hē Attikē agora*, which (as I shall show) is the exact equivalent of the expression 'the Agora of the Athenians' and means the Agora of the city of Athens and no other. 'Agora' here is always translated 'market' (of course a perfectly correct translation of the Greek word *agora* in some contexts); but this is misleading. The essential feature of an exclusion decree is a defined area; and, as I shall show in Part vii of this Chapter, there was only one definable and defined area which could be called the 'agora' in any precise sense: namely, the centre of political life, the civic Agora (as I shall call it, with a capital A), which formed only a small fraction of the main commercial area of the city of Athens. (Other interpretations of the word *agora*—that it 'must have' meant something quite different, namely 'trading in Attica', or even that it 'really' amounted to complete exclusion from Attica—will also be dealt with in Part vii.) But the exclusion from the Athenian Agora, precisely because it was from the civic Agora alone, cannot have been intended

[40] Against taking Plut., *Per.* 29.4, as evidence that the decree referred to 'every *agora* controlled by the Athenians', see Appendix XXXVIII.

primarily to have an economic effect, nor could any economic consequences it did produce have been at all serious, for even Megarians
could enter Attica and even trade there provided they did not trespass
in the Agora: much trade was conducted in the environs of the Agora, and
there were other *agorai*, in Peiraeus and some of the other demes, which
even Megarian citizens could still use. I must emphasise that this argument against the prevailing view of the Megarian decree is concerned with
the nature of one of the two types of *place* from which the Megarians were
excluded, and is *entirely independent of the first argument*, which is based upon
the identity of the *persons* excluded. It is equally fatal to the prevailing
view.

3. The exclusion was also from the harbours of the empire. If *agora*
is translated 'market', of course the conjunction of 'market' and 'harbours'
irresistibly suggests a commercial ban; but if we firmly refuse to think of
a commercial *agora* we can find a perfectly acceptable reason for the choice
of 'harbours', not dictated primarily by commercial considerations. I shall
discuss this question in Part viii of this Chapter, where I shall also deal
with the suggestion that the exclusion from the harbours of the empire
'really' meant exclusion from the whole empire. I shall further maintain
that 'the harbours of the empire' ought strictly not to include, and perhaps
did not include, the Peiraeus. I am not, of course, claiming that my interpretation of the exclusion from the harbours of the empire provides an
additional argument against the standard view of the Megarian decree: the
two I have already given are more than sufficient to rule it out.

Having totally rejected the prevailing interpretation of the Megarian
decree, I shall now offer an alternative explanation of its terms and
intention, as I see them.

By cultivating the *hiera orgas*, and refusing satisfaction in response to a
reasonable remonstrance, the Megarians had committed what Athens had
every right by Greek standards to regard as a quasi-religious crime, a
form of *asebeia*. When the Megarians did exactly the same thing again in
the late 350s, Demosthenes could refer to them as 'the accursed Megarians'
(xxiii 212; xiii 32). The events of 352–49 (which have received scarcely
any attention from recent historians, except Connor) are very relevant to
the fifth-century Megarian decree, because they show the Athenians
intensely concerned about a Megarian intrusion upon the *hiera orgas*, and
prepared even to take vigorous military action to stop it, at a time when
they clearly had no reason to provoke Megara needlessly and no ulterior
strategic designs against her, and were not trying to gain political control
of her.

Like the decree offering a large reward for the capture of Diagoras the
'atheist', who had attacked the Eleusinian Mystery cult,[41] and the excite-

[41] See Jacoby, *DA*; and *FGrH* iii b (Suppl.) i.198–201; also L. Woodbury, 'The Date
and Atheism of Diagoras of Melos', in *Phoenix* 19 (1965) 178–211. The Athenians at some
uncertain date (perhaps 416–15) condemned Diagoras and offered a reward to anyone

ment over the alleged parodies of the Mysteries in 415,[42] this mid-fourth-century quarrel between Megara and Athens shows how exercised the Athenians could become over any affront offered to their precious Two Goddesses. According to Herodotus (VI 75.3, repeated by Paus. III iv.5), the Athenians attributed the unpleasant fate of King Cleomenes I of Sparta to his having devastated the precinct of the Goddesses during his invasion of Eleusis (in *c.* 506). Pausanias (III iv.6) says that 'the Megarians who had cultivated the sacred land could never appease the wrath of the goddesses at Eleusis'. Of course charges of *asebeia* and the like were some-times made for purely political reasons (cf. Thuc. III 70.4–6); but, especially in the light of the events I have just described, we cannot simply assume that the Athenian complaint about cultivation of the sacred land at the time of the Megarian decree was a trumped-up charge, made with the deliberate intention of picking a quarrel with the Megarians and providing a pretext for the exclusion decree. Particularly if (as I have argued in Part iii of this Chapter) the process began with a 'reasonable and courteous' decree, merely protesting against the encroachment, we ought to consider the possibility that the Athenians were acting in good faith and had cause, or at any rate believed they had cause, for just complaint. I submit that when we take into account all the other evidence for the attitude of the Athenians and their opponents in the late 430s, we find good reason to believe that the dominant political faction, led by Pericles, did not want to provoke a war with the Peloponnesians. And in any event, even if the Megarian decree is considered by itself, I suggest that it does not neces-sarily afford any indication of a belligerent or provocative attitude on the part of the Athenians, but may at least equally be considered as a measure, not unreasonable in the circumstances, taken against men who were genuinely believed to be guilty of a form of *asebeia*, of a religious offence against the Two Goddesses. On this assumption, I believe, the Megarian decree makes very much better sense, especially when we have abandoned, as we must, the idea that its effects were primarily economic. Indeed, we should even be prepared to consider the possibility, suggested by Völkl (MP 335–6), that the Megarian action was a deliberate provoca-tion, instigated perhaps by Corinth—with, I would add, the encourage-ment of those Spartans who already desired war with Athens (cf. Chapter V, Parts viii and ix above). In response to provocation of this kind the Athenians might well have committed some rash punitive action against Megara which could have been claimed by the Peloponnesians as a clear breach of the Peace.

---

bringing him in, dead (1 talent) or alive (2 talents). Melanthius and Craterus preserved a copy of the bronze stele at Eleusis. As Jacoby says (i.199), the charge against Diagoras was *asebeia* (impiety), and this was 'found perhaps only, but certainly in the first place, in the attacks on the Eleusinian Mysteries occurring in the book which Diagoras had published under the title *Apopyrgizontes logoi*'. Cf. Jacoby, *DA* 27: 'The only certain detail we know about the book consists in its vilifying the mystery cult of Eleusis.'

[42] See Thuc. VI 28.1; 61.1 etc. (with Dover's admirable commentary in Gomme, *HCT* IV); Plut., *Alc.* 22.4–5; Andoc. I *passim*; and many other sources.

Doubtless the Athenians, if circumstances had permitted it, might have treated the Megarians' offence as *asebeia* in the technical sense, and banned them entirely from Attica as accursed, perhaps even from the empire as well. Charges of actual *asebeia*[43] could sometimes entail the most severe penalties,[44] and an offence committed on sacred ground could certainly be represented as falling within the category of *asebeia*.[45] But *the Athenians did not want war*, and they had to be very careful not to do anything which could be claimed as a breach of the Thirty Years Peace. To decree any wholesale exclusion, even if the treaty did not specifically forbid such acts, would be to invite an accusation of illegal behaviour, tantamount to a breach of the Peace: we may compare lines 18 ff. of the first Athenian decree relating to Methone, passed only a few years later (M/L 65 = Tod I² 61 = D 3 in *ATL* II 48 = *IG* I² 57). It is not surprising, therefore, that the form of retaliation the Athenians actually chose was milder: it was intended above all to humiliate the Megarians and impose indignity and inconvenience (and perhaps, as a secondary consideration, some financial loss) upon them, to the extent that Athens (*a*) could effect this without breaking the Thirty Years Peace, which forbade any resort to force, and (*b*) could expect obedience from her allies, whose co-operation was desirable but who would have nothing like the same interest in disciplining Megara. Even the limited form of retaliation the Athenians chose was claimed, as we know, to be a breach of the Peace, though entirely without justification, in my opinion. Pericles claimed, according to Thucydides (I 144.2), that the Athenian ban on the Megarians was no more contrary to the Peace than the Spartan practice of *xenēlasia*; and I agree with the authors of *ATL*[46] that 'he can hardly be wrong on the fact'. Pericles and the Athenians probably did not care, or consider, whether the decree inflicted economic damage upon Megara or not, except in so far as it could be treated as a breach of the Peace if it went too far in this direction. In passing it the Athenians were not thinking in economic terms at all—or, for that matter, in strategic terms.

In short, the Megarian decree was something much more limited and very much less important *in itself* than has yet been realised. In itself it was just that 'little spark of a Megarian decree' which Aristophanes calls it in the *Peace* (line 609)—presenting a picture of it very different from the inflated one in the *Acharnians* (524–34), where his comic purpose required

[43] Quite apart from its use in a technical sense, as a crime against religion, the charge of *asebeia* could be flung about very loosely: see e.g. Lyc., *c. Leocr.* 147; Dem. XXI 51.

[44] We know, for example, that this was true of destroying a sacred Athenian olive tree, even the stump of one (*sēkos*). The penalty for this was at one time death (Arist., *Ath. Pol.* 60.2). By the early fourth century the penalty could be referred to as exile and confiscation of property (Lys. VII 3, 25, 32, 41, cf. 15, 26), but perhaps only because the death penalty could be evaded by a withdrawal into exile (see Lipsius, *AR* 128). By Aristotle's time (Arist., *Ath. Pol.* 60.2) prosecutions were no longer brought, although the law had not been abrogated.

[45] See Tod II 125 (= *SIG*³ 153 = *IG* II² 1635). 134 ff.; cf. Thuc. III 70.4.

[46] *ATL* III 304 n. 15. I am not happy with the continuation of that note (see Part IV above, n. 39), and of course I dissent entirely from its ending: 'The exclusion was an attempt to entice Megara out of the Spartan alliance into the Athenian.'

quite another emphasis. The decree became important only when the Megarians complained about it at Sparta. The vital point is that the Spartans were hard put to it to find any sort of plausible accusation against Athens of a breach of the treaty (the only state which had quite clearly broken the Peace being their own ally, Corinth: see Chapter III, Part iii above), and naturally therefore jumped at this one, for two different reasons. First, the Megarian decree could be claimed (if with very poor justification) as a breach of the treaty; and secondly, many Athenians could easily be made to feel that the decree was too trivial a matter to go to war over, and once they gave way over this, further concessions could be extorted, as Thucydides (1 140.5) shows Pericles foreseeing. Thucydides makes Pericles inveigh repeatedly and emphatically against just such arguments as these by Athenian 'appeasers'. 'None of you must think', he says, 'that we should be going to war over a triviality if we don't repeal the Megarian decree, when the Spartans emphasise that if we were to repeal it there need be no war. Don't allow yourselves to have any feelings of self-reproach, as if you were going to war on a minor issue. For this small thing involves the whole confirmation and trial of your resolution. If you give way, you will immediately be confronted with some greater demand' (Thuc. 1 140.4–5). Here the Megarian decree is spoken of as if there were indeed people at Athens who considered it a mere 'small spark' (Ar., *Peace* 609), which ought not to be allowed to lead to war.

I should like to emphasise that the picture I have given of the Megarian decree, as a very minor matter until Sparta cleverly chose it as a test case of Athenian willingness to yield, is exactly the way it is presented by Thucydides, who does not even deign to mention it in its place, as he certainly ought to have done if it had really been an independent cause of the war, but refers to it *only* in the context of *Spartan and Megarian propaganda*. He first mentions it in connection with the debate in the Spartan Assembly in the latter part of 432 (1 67.4), and after that only in connection with the second Spartan embassy to Athens in the winter of 432/1 and the Athenian reply thereto (139.1–2), and the debate in the Athenian Assembly consequent upon the third Spartan embassy (139.4; 140.3–5; cf. 144.2; 145), at which the question of repealing the Megarian decree was evidently a major issue. The great majority of scholars who have dealt with Thucydides' treatment of the causes of the Peloponnesian war have either expressed dissatisfaction with the way he handles the decree, or else have shown a certain uneasiness on the question, while feeling obliged to make the usual automatic obeisance to the authority of Thucydides against which Beloch protested so vigorously more than once.[47] If the decree was really, as most people have believed, a deliberate

---

[47] E.g. in *GG* II² ii.149 n. 1. Even Stern, he says, who accepts his own sceptical view of the narrative of the rebuilding of the walls of Athens, 'glaubt hier vor Thukydides eine Verbeugung machen zu müssen; er sei "der grosse Lehrmeister der Kritik". . . Das war er für seine Zeit allerdings; aber wir Historiker können heute in technischen Fragen von Thukydides sowenig lernen, wie unsere heutigen Ärzte von Hippokrates. Es ist

attempt to effect a major change in the strategic situation, and to break the treaty by inducing Megara to change sides, Thucydides has certainly not given a fair presentation of it. And we shall still have some grounds for complaint if, with Grundy, Kagan and others (see Part iv of this Chapter), we conceive the decree as having had rather more limited ulterior political objectives. In my version of the decree, on the other hand, Thucydides gives exactly the right emphasis to it, and in the right places. I would suggest that anyone who feels he cannot accept my picture should begin by attacking Thucydides, upon whom above all my analysis is based, and trying to discredit his account as a careful falsification, constructed with the aim of exculpating Pericles from the charge of deliberately provoking the war that proved such a disaster to Athens—and to Greece. The task would be a hard one: I do not think the attempt could succeed.

I shall discuss the economic aspects of the Megarian decree below. Here I need only say that (as I have shown in the preceding Chapters) official Athenian policy in the 430s shows a determination to avoid a renewal of the war with the Peloponnesians, in so far as this could be done without running serious risks, in particular the risk of allowing Corinth to take over the large fleet of Corcyra and thus add it to the naval forces of the Peloponnesian League, otherwise no match for Athens' navy. The Megarian decree as it is generally conceived would be flat contrary to that policy, because if the supposed object of the decree were achieved and Megara 'revolted' from Sparta and were received by Athens as an ally, the Peace would certainly have been broken (see Appendix I, §4), and Sparta could probably have called out her allies for an invasion of Attica without even summoning a Congress of her League. It may be that this was a price some Athenians would have been prepared to pay for the adhesion of Megara: these Athenians may have believed that with the Megarid in her hands Athens could secure herself against Peloponnesian invasion (cf. Chapter V, Part vi above). But an open and flagrant attempt to seduce a Spartan ally would have been regarded by the Peloponnesians as a deliberate provocation; and (what is much more important, but is always overlooked) *Megara could easily have been prevented from revolting to Athens,* by Peloponnesian garrisons in the city and in Nisaea!—of course at the request of 'the Megarians', that is to say, the oligarchic government of Megara. (Greek cities in danger from enemies would often ask a powerful friendly state for a garrison.) During a major war, when the Peloponnesian forces would have many weak points to guard, Athens might hope for an attempt by an atticising party inside Megara to betray the city to her, as in 424 (see Thuc. iv 66–74); but in peace time, with Megara the sole object of her pressure, it would have been easy, with the co-operation of those in power, to keep Megara under safe Peloponnesian control. The usual view of the Megarian decree, besides being open to the other

---

eigentlich traurig, dass das noch immer betont werden muss'. Cf. ii.15 ('die hypno-tisierende Wirkung, die Thukydides' Autorität übt'), and other passages.

fatal objections brought against it in this Chapter, also involves the absurdity of supposing that the Athenians would openly advertise their subversive designs against an important member of Sparta's alliance, without having any real hope of achieving the only objective which might provide some justification for it. Pericles was hardly such a fool as this.

It is often said that if Athens had a genuine complaint against Megara she should have gone to arbitration under the terms of the Thirty Years Peace and not retaliated with the Megarian decree. I believe this is a fallacy. There are numerous references in Thucydides to the arbitration clause in the Peace, mainly in rather vague terms.[48] I myself believe that the phrase in VII 18.2, 'not to make an armed attack if the other side wishes to go to arbitration' (cf. 1 85.2), gives the essential substance and purport of the clause in question, rather than the more general formula in 1 140.2: 'to submit their differences to arbitration',[49] which, as can be seen from the corresponding clause in the Peace of Nicias (v 18.4; cf. IV 118.8), should probably be read as a pendant to the first formula— neither side is to make war on the other if there is an appeal to arbitration, *but* differences are to be settled by legal means. I think that any Greek would have understood that both treaties—the Thirty Years Peace and the Peace of Nicias—were not requiring the settlement of every dispute, great and small, by arbitration, but essentially *forbidding a resort to armed force* if the other side wanted to arbitrate.

But, it may be asked, if the Athenians had wanted to inflict economic damage on Megara, could they have decreed other measures better calculated to achieve that end? May not the exclusion decree have been simply a rather feeble and ineffective attempt to damage Megara's economy?

The answer is that Pericles and the Athenians were not nearly as ignorant of the facts of Greek economic life as are many modern scholars. If the Athenians had really wanted to strike a severe economic blow at Megara, they could have formulated the decree very differently, without resorting to measures involving the use of armed force, which were forbidden by the Thirty Years Peace.

1. First, they could have *banned Megarian products* from Attica and the whole empire. One thinks particularly of the cheap clothes the manufacture of which was the principal Megarian industry[50] and which were sold at Athens,[51] as elsewhere; also of vegetables, which, in the absence of refrigeration and swift transport, could not normally be imported in antiquity except from places very close by, and were certainly brought into Attica from the Megarid, where we know they were grown.[52] Such a

48 Thuc. 1 78.4; 85.2; 123.1–2; 140.2; 144.2; 145; and esp. VII 18.2–3.
49 It is this clause which Bickerman (APT 315) and others have mainly had in mind, in saying that Athens ought to have gone to arbitration instead of passing the Megarian decree.
50 See Xen., *Mem.* II vii.6; and note Pliny, *NH* VII 196.
51 See e.g. Ar., *Acharn.* 519; *IG* II² 1673.45–6, 1672.102–3.
52 On the Megarian economy, see Ernst Meyer, in *RE* xv i (1931), col. 171–4.

measure would not only have caused financial damage to those Megarians (and Megarian metics) who were merchants but would have struck a serious—though of course not fatal—blow at the Megarian economy, by closing to Megarian exports most ports to the east of Megara. Any such ban would doubtless have caused some grumbling among the Athenian allies (a good deal more than the mere exclusion of Megarians), and probably at Athens too, but could probably have been made fairly effective, at least as regards Attica.

2. Secondly, the Athenians could have *prohibited all exports to Megara* from the whole empire, or at least all exports of essential commodities such as corn, oil, wine, metals, timber and other shipbuilding materials. *Prima facie*, this would have been a much more serious blow to Megara, which we may assume (in the absence of direct evidence) to have needed to import most of the commodities just mentioned. On the other hand, it would have been difficult to make such a ban effective, since the Megarians, of course, would immediately have made collusive arrangements with other Peloponnesian states, especially Corinth, by which imports actually destined for Megara were nominally shipped to the other state and either diverted to Megara *en route*, or (if the Athenians got wind of this and tried to stop it) at any rate sent straight on to Megara from the state concerned. Indeed, such arrangements could probably have been made with the merchants (whether Megarian or not) who normally carried on Megara's foreign trade, and without the intervention of the Megarian and other governments.

3. Thirdly, and almost certainly with most effect, the Athenians could have announced that *anyone who traded with Megara*, whether a Megarian or not (or at any rate anyone living at Athens or within the empire), would at least be *forbidden to trade within the empire*, even if not perhaps punished as well. This indeed might have ruined the Megarian economy, for few merchants would have risked exclusion from trading with the Athenian area, so much larger and richer than little Megara. Such a measure, it is true, would be liable to abuse, but particularly severe penalties could be threatened against anyone who took proceedings vexatiously—as happened in the mid-fourth century, when *emporoi* and *nauklēroi* were given special protection against vexatious indictments.[53]

In the economic conditions prevailing in the fifth and fourth centuries, however, it was difficult for any state, even Athens, to interfere drastically and effectively with the foreign trade of another city without using *force* exerted through her *navy*—the very thing Athens could not do in the case of Megara, under the terms of the Peace, without risking an immediate resumption of the war, as Pericles and the dominant section of Athenian opinion at any rate were anxious not to do. It is very significant that Sparta, doing her poor best to interfere with the foreign trade of Athens and her allies in the early part of the Peloponnesian war, put to death all the traders she captured around the Peloponnese—not merely Athenians

[53] See Ps.-Dem. LVIII 10–13, probably with 53.

and their allies, but those belonging to neutral states as well (Thuc. II 67.4). It was not the 'nationality' of the merchant which mattered in antiquity, but the places to and from which he was trading. To use modern terminology, the 'flag' under which he sailed was seldom an important factor (cf. Part vi of this Chapter and Appendix XLI). The 'Old Oligarch', who was much impressed by Athens' ability to interfere with maritime trade, was certainly writing after 432 (see Appendix VI), and his emphasis is on Athens' *naval* power.[54] Once the war had begun, Athens could of course interfere seriously with Megara's maritime trade.

Most of those who have given a 'commercial' interpretation to the Megarian decree have gone on (cf. Part iv of this Chapter) to find an ulterior political and strategic motive: effecting a vital change in the balance of power between Athens and the Peloponnesian League, by forcing Megara to change sides, and thus giving security to Athens (or at least a large measure of security: cf. Chapter V, Part vi above) against Peloponnesian invasions. As I have just shown, there was little chance of any such objective being achieved. And there is a further point to add. Although it is always dangerous to base any conclusions upon the silences of Thucydides, it does seem significant that he never allows his Corinthian speakers at Sparta, in I 68–71 or 120–4, to make any allusion to the Megarian decree. If that decree was really an attempt to produce an important change in the strategic situation, it would have provided an excellent concrete illustration of the sort of thing the Corinthians are saying throughout much of their two speeches, especially the first: see e.g. 68.3; 69.2; 124; also 71.4, where 'while Megara is still secure' would surely strengthen the argument greatly. An argument directed to the security of the Megarid would have appealed strongly to all the allies, especially perhaps the Boeotians, for whom the Megarid was the essential channel of communication with the Peloponnese (see Thuc. IV 72.1).

(vi)
'The Megarians'

The strongest argument against the economic interpretation of the Megarian decree is that those whom it excluded were, as all the sources say, *hoi Megareis*, the citizens of Megara. (For Megarian citizenship as a privilege scarcely ever granted to foreigners, see Plut., *Mor.* 826cd.) Below I shall discuss, and reject, possible wider meanings of this expression. The essential point is that merely to prohibit *Megarians* from entering parts of Athenian-controlled territory, *or even the whole of it*, would have had little economic effect upon the State of Megara. I wish to emphasise that this argument concerning the persons involved is entirely independent of those in Parts vii and viii of this Chapter about the nature of the exclusion, and would hold even if the arguments I have advanced there were invalid, and even if the exclusion was (at the furthest extreme from

[54] Ps.-Xen., *Ath. Pol.* II 2–3, 11–12. Note the repeated 'the ruler of the sea'.

what the sources say) from the whole of Attica and the Athenian empire. We rarely hear of Megarian merchants (see below), and there is no reason to think that any significant part of the external trade of Megara was in the hands of merchants who were Megarian citizens. Even if part of Megara's commerce with the outside world had been in the hands of her citizens, any vacuum created by their exclusion would have been filled very quickly by other merchants, who would be quick to take advantage of so promising an opportunity. Unlike many trading cities of mediaeval and later times (in which an exclusive merchant guild, or at any rate men who themselves went in for trading, did play an important political role), Greek cities did not make a practice of excluding from their markets and harbours traders who were not members of their own citizen body: on the contrary, they welcomed the foreign trader. (I hope to deal with this question properly elsewhere. Meanwhile, see Appendix XLI.) In fact, therefore, the Megarian decree could have had *very little effect upon the trade of Megara*, which would have continued much as before, with (even if I were wrong about the other aspects of the exclusion) no more than the substitution of non-Megarians for those Megarian citizens who had been trading with the Athenian area.

Only in one way could the exclusion decree cause any appreciable economic hardship to the Megarians. If, again, I were wrong about the nature of the *agora* from which the Megarians were excluded, the decree might have caused some loss to Megarian peasants of the poorer sort. It is very likely indeed that some of these men were in the habit of crossing over into Attica themselves, as we see the Megarian doing in Aristophanes, *Acharn.* 729 ff., to sell the vegetables and fruits which were the principal agricultural exports of the Megarid (cf. Part v of this Chapter, n. 52). And if (as I would of course deny) the exclusion decree made it impossible for them to do this, they might have suffered financially—to what extent, we have no means of telling, for the Megarians might, of course, have been able to sell their produce at much the same price elsewhere, above all at Corinth, not much more distant than Athens from the main agricultural region of the Megarid. (We may compare the actions of the men of Phlius in the 360s: Xen., *HG* vii ii.17–18.) Or, since whatever demand there had been at Athens would still have existed, the Megarians could have sold to non-Megarians, for carriage or shipment to Athens—although in this case they would no doubt receive a lower price, as the middle-man would want his profit. No one will suppose, however, that Megarians belonging to the upper classes, in order to sell their produce, would travel in person all the way to Athens and back, a distance of forty to fifty miles: they would always sell to traders. And, as I have pointed out, even if these traders included any appreciable number of Megarian citizens, their place would quickly be filled by other traders.

It may be said, perhaps, that although Thucydides and all our other sources speak only of 'the Megarians' as being excluded by the decree, the Athenians 'must have' cast their net more widely and excluded at least

Megarian metics, by some such phrase as 'those living at Megara' (*hoi oikountes Megaroi*). We may contrast Dem. xxxv 50 and Lyc., *c. Leocr.* 27, where we find the formula 'if any *Athenian*', with Dem. xxxiv 37, where the phrase is 'if anyone *living at Athens*'.[55] A still more far-reaching form of words would be that used in the law cited in Dem. xxxv 51: 'no Athenian or metic living at Athens or anyone under the control of such people' (. . . *mēde hōn houtoi kyrioi eisin*). For my own part, I imagine that the laws in question sometimes did refer to 'any Athenian or Athenian metic or anyone under the control of such a person', and that the orators merely quoted such parts of them as happened to be relevant in the cases they were dealing with. May not the Megarian decree, then, it will be said, have used some such form of words as 'no Megarian citizen or metic living at Megara or anyone under the control of such persons',[56] which has been abbreviated by Thucydides and the other sources as 'the Megarians'? This theory is open to three separate objections:

1. It is not what any of the sources says; and I see no reason why they should have needlessly toned down the actual wording of the decree, if this had the effect of seriously misrepresenting the class of those to whom it applied. One would not expect the whole of such a formula as I have imagined to be reproduced; but 'those living at Megara' (*hoi oikountes Megaroi*) is only one word longer in Greek than 'the Megarians' and would (in the circumstances we are considering) have given a much better representation of it.

2. It would not in any event make much difference, for the place of 'Megarians' in this broader sense would be filled after only a little longer time by merchants from elsewhere—especially Corinth and Aegina, of course, and even Athens itself.

3. The decree was a collective punishment of the State of Megara (*hoi Megareis*), which had refused satisfaction to Athens after its members had cultivated the *hiera orgas* and committed other unfriendly acts. It was natural, therefore, that the exclusion should apply to 'the Megarians' alone.

I would not, of course, press the word *civis* in Gellius, *NA* vii x.1 (see the penultimate paragraph of Part ii of this Chapter), as having any independent value, except as showing that this was the way the expression 'the Megarians' would naturally be taken.

Megarians are rarely heard of as merchants at any time. I have only come across two in the fifth/fourth-century literary sources: a drug-seller described as a *Megarikos* (see below) in Theopompus the comic poet (fr. 2 Kock, *ap.* Poll. x 180), and Philondas, a Megarian living as a metic at Athens in the year 372 (Ps.-Dem. xlix 26-9, 33-41). Otherwise, the only

---

[55] Cf. Ps.-Plut., *Mor.* 841f-2a: μηδενὶ ἐξεῖναι 'Αθηναίων μηδὲ τῶν οἰκούντων 'Αθήνησιν κτλ.

[56] μηδεὶς τῶν Μεγαρέων μηδὲ τῶν μετοίκων τῶν Μεγαροῖ μετοικούντων μηδὲ ὧν οὗτοι κύριοί εἰσιν κτλ.

relevant references I know are those in the long Eleusis building inscriptions of 329/8 and 327/6 (*IG* II² 1672–3), and these have some features which may be thought significant. Five of the men who appear in these inscriptions are connected with Megara: three sell cheap clothes, bought for the public slaves engaged in the reconstruction work (Callias, *IG* II² 1673.45; Midas, *Id.* 46; Antigenes, 1672.103), a fourth acts as overseer of the public slaves (Chremon, 1673.59), and the fifth is apparently a contractor (*misthōtēs*) engaged in petty transport (Diocleidas, 1672.95, and probably 16, where no ethnic is given). Now only two of these men, Callias who sells tunics and Chremon the overseer, are given ethnics which mark them out beyond doubt as Megarian citizens. Antigenes, who sells cloaks, is described as a *Megarikos*, not a *Megareus*, and so is Diocleidas the contractor. Dittenberger, in an important article (EuV) to which I shall have occasion to refer in Part vii of this Chapter and in Appendix XLII, treated this use of the *ktētikon* instead of the *ethnikon* (to use the Greek technical terms) as a sign that the men concerned must have been not merely non-citizens but freedmen. This may not be certain, but in at least one case it does seem likely that the man was a freedman. In referring to Midas, the stone has *para Midou Megar*. Although Midas as a citizen's name is perhaps not impossible, it strongly suggests a servile origin, and I would treat *Megar* as an abbreviation of the *ktētikon*, not the *ethnikon*, and read *Megar(ikou)*, not *Megar(eōs)*. (Cf. *para Kalliou Megare(ōs)* in the preceding line of the inscription.) It seems, therefore, that of this group of five men from Megara, engaged in commercial activities, two or three may well not have been Megarian citizens.

Megara very probably did not begin coining money at all, and certainly had no significant coinage, until a very much later date than her principal neighbours—until the fourth century, in fact. It is a mistake to place too much emphasis on coinage when considering how far commerce had developed in an ancient city;[57] but it is worth remarking that Megara began to coin two whole centuries later than her immediate neighbours, Aegina, Athens and Corinth. I myself would in any event suppose that those who dominated the policy of Megara in the late sixth and fifth centuries were landowners with little personal interest in commerce. Now Greek landowners would naturally take a keen interest in selling their produce, but if sufficient merchants from elsewhere were forthcoming—and Megara, situated on the most important isthmus in Greece, and immediately between its two most prominent trading cities, will have been a natural focus of attention for merchants—the Megarians scarcely needed to trouble to go in for commerce themselves.

We have very little information about the machinery of commerce in the Greek world except in fourth-century Athens; but there is no reason to think that conditions were very different in the late-fifth century from what they were in the fourth, or that Megara was very different in this respect from its next-door neighbour. In the fourth century, as I think is

[57] Cf. the important article by C. M. Kraay, HSCOC, esp. 88–91.

now generally agreed, it is clear that a very large part of inter-state commerce was in the hands of non-citizens.[58] Now one entry in Hesychius, *s.v. emporos* (the standard word for the trader who is not just a petty local dealer, a *kapēlos*), inaccurately defines *emporos* as *metoikos*; and people nowadays often take it for granted that in the fifth and fourth centuries the merchants who carried on the trade of a given city would mostly be metics *of that city*; but this is just another of those broad assumptions which need to be tested before they are accepted. This particular assumption can only be true, if at all, in a very loose sense. I have two points to make here:

1. First, an absurdly obvious fact which can nevertheless be overlooked. Even if we assume for the moment that all trade between a given state A and other states was in the hands of citizens and metics of those states (an assumption I shall show in a moment to be unsound), only half, on the average, of the trade entering A from any one of the other states, B, or leaving A to go to B, will have been conducted through citizens and metics of state A: the other half will have been carried on through the citizens and metics of state B; and similarly half, on the average, of the trade entering B from A, or leaving it to go to A, will have been in the hands of citizens and metics of A. If for A and B we substitute Megara and Athens, we can say that probably a good deal less than half of the trade going into Megara from Athens and leaving Megara for Athens will have been carried by Megarian citizens and metics, since Megara was far from being one of the principal 'trading cities' of Greece, as Athens was.

2. Secondly, as soon as we begin to look closely at the evidence, we find that the trade of particular states was not by any means entirely in the hands of *their own* citizens and metics. I hope shortly to deal elsewhere with the civic, social and economic status of Greek merchants in the Classical period. Meanwhile I will only draw attention to the many inscriptions honouring foreigners other than metics who had been of service to Athens, especially in her corn trade.[59] Particularly apposite in the present context is the denunciation of Leocrates by Lycurgus (*c. Leocr.* 26, with 16–18, 21–5) for deserting Athens immediately after Chaeroneia, and eventually settling as a metic at Megara, and while living at Megara, shipping corn from Epirus to Leucas and thence to Corinth—so that part of the corn supply of Corinth in the 330s will have been in the hands of an Athenian living as a metic at Megara. Again, an interesting passage in Xenophon's *Oeconomicus* (xx 27–8) describes how corn-merchants (who could not have been so very different from other kinds of merchant) would go any-

[58] But Hasebroek, *TPAG*, greatly exaggerates when he claims that there were virtually no citizen merchants at all.

[59] Of the dozen or so Athenian inscriptions cited in n. 97 to Chapter I, Part iii above, recording honours to non-Athenians who had made themselves useful to Athens in connection with her corn supply (*IG* ii² 283, 342, 360, 363, 398, 400, 401, 407, 408, 409, 416, 499), not one certainly refers to a metic, and in at least half these cases (*IG* ii² 342, 360, 398, 400, 401, 416) there is some positive reason for thinking that the men concerned were not metics.

where to buy corn cheap, crossing the Aegean, the Black Sea or the Sicilian Sea; and when they had got as much as they could carry, they would take it to wherever they could get the highest price for it. (Among illustrations of this are Ps.-Dem. xxxiv 36–7; lvi 9–10.) When the Spartocid rulers of the so-called Bosphoran kingdom in the late fifth and fourth centuries wished to give the Athenians special privileges in regard to the supply of corn from their dominions, they provided that exemption from their customs duties, and priority in loading, should be given, not to 'Athenian' merchants, but to 'those taking corn to Athens', 'those sailing to you', as Demosthenes puts it in one of his forensic speeches (xx 31).

The merchants who conducted the foreign trade of many individual Greek cities, then, were not only citizens or metics of those cities; many of them belonged to what we might almost call an 'international merchant class'[60]—men who traded from place to place, wherever they saw an opening, and did not concern themselves entirely (or even mainly, perhaps) with the trade of the state in which they had citizenship or domicile. They might often be obliged to spend the winter where their last voyage had ended before the weather made further sailing dangerous.

The argument developed above is sufficient by itself to destroy the accepted view of the Megarian decree, because it shows that the decree can have had very little effect on the trade of Megara, except perhaps for a short period, before other merchants had taken the place of those Megarians (probably few in number) who were *emporoi* trading with the Athenian area. If the Athenians had really wished to strike at Megarian trade, they would have had to proceed very differently (see Part v of this Chapter).

The decree certainly excluded the Megarians from 'the harbours of the Athenian empire'—an expression which, I shall argue (see Part viii of this Chapter), may not have included the Peiraeus. If the decree was properly enforced by the member states of the empire, it would have had the effect of making it difficult, and perhaps impossible (see Part viii), for *Megarians* to trade with those states in person. Doubtless this would cause financial loss to those individual Megarians who had been in the habit of trading exclusively or principally with the Athenian empire— although of course a very large area would still have been open to them: Corinth and the Corinthian Gulf, the whole of the Peloponnese, and the West. But, as we have seen, it is not likely that there were very many of these Megarian merchants, and it is highly unlikely that any of them will have been men of much political influence. In no Greek state in the fifth and fourth centuries is there any sign that merchants played any significant

---

[60] But of course without any implication that they operated on a large scale: most merchants in the Classical period seem to have been rather humble men, even if there were more rich ones than e.g. Hasebroek allows for.

role in politics;[61] and at the one great trading city we do know much about, Athens, they certainly did not. I doubt if it is generally realised that not a single man known to have been politically prominent in fifth/fourth-century Athens ever appears as a merchant (except Andocides, *when in exile*), and that not a single known merchant is found playing any part in politics. Megara was an oligarchy in the late 430s, and this makes it even more unlikely that any merchants would have had political influence. Therefore, even if the Megarian decree did bring about the impoverishment of some Megarian citizens who were merchants, the political effect upon the Megarian State was likely to be small.

(vii)
'The Athenian Agora'

Although there is only one valid interpretation of the various expressions we find in our sources for the exclusion of the Megarians from the 'agora': namely, that it was *the civic Agora* (cf. Part v of this Chapter), I have found that three other interpretations can exist: (*a*) that 'agora' means *the market*, consisting not only of the civic Agora but also of its commercial environs; and (*b*) that 'agora' does not really mean *agora*, but signifies an attempt to exclude Megarians from *trading in Attica* or (*c*) from *entering Attica at all*. I shall examine these theories when I have stated and justified the natural and literal interpretation. It will be sufficient at this point to say that, of the three alternatives, (*a*) is linguistically possible but will be found impossible in the context, while (*b*) and (*c*) are absolutely ruled out by the language of the sources. It is most extraordinary that no scholar (as far as I have been able to discover) has ever thought it necessary to give a proper analysis of the term *agora* as used in the Megarian decree: the vast majority of those who have dealt with the decree have simply taken it for granted that it means 'the market', and many indeed have assumed, in defiance of Thucydides, that the decree referred to 'all the markets of Attica and the Athenian empire'.

As everyone knows, the word *agora* was used in ancient Greece in more than one sense. A difficulty is sometimes created for us—though evidently it was not felt by the Greeks—by the fact that what I may call the political

[61] I propose to demonstrate in detail elsewhere that even the governing class of Aegina was not at all the 'mercantile aristocracy' it is so often assumed to have been, but a small, rich, landowning class of archaic type. H. Winterscheidt, *Aigina. Eine Untersuchung über seine Gesellschaft und Wirtschaft* (Diss., Cologne, 1938), is on the right lines; but after the long review of that monograph and of G. Welter, *Aigina* (Berlin, 1938), by E. Kirsten, in *Gnomon* 18 (1942) 289–311 (esp. 297–301), the whole question needs a thorough reconsideration. It is significant that the only two Aeginetan merchants we can name are the mysterious Sostratus, of Hdts iv 152.3 (who does not enable us to tell whether Sostratus belonged to the ruling class or not), and Lampis, famous in the mid-fourth century as the richest of all Greek *nauklēroi*—and a metic! (See on him Dem. xxiii 211; Plut., *Mor.* 234f; 787a; *Comm. in Hes.*, fr. 59; Cic., *Tusc. Disp.* v 40; Stob. xxix 87. He is not the Lampis of Ps.-Dem. xxxiv, as several scholars have mistakenly assumed.) For the views of J. Pouilloux on the Thasian governing class, and the criticisms of M. I. Finley, see Chapter I, Part iii, n. 80 above.

and the commercial uses of the word overlapped. Such evidence as we have suggests that the situation at Athens was fairly characteristic (see R. Martin, *RAG*); but we are concerned here only with the Athenian agora, and since we know far more about this,[62] from both literature and archaeology, than about any other agora, we can confine ourselves to Athens and need not look elsewhere.

Misunderstanding of the nature of the fifth-century Athenian agora is still widespread. The Agora proper, the civic centre of Athens, was a rather small but specific area, strictly defined by boundary stones, four of which have been discovered by the American excavators, two actually in their original positions.[63] Extending in various directions from the Agora (especially towards the north-west, in the direction of the Cerameicus) was a far larger area in which intense commercial activity took place, as indeed it did in the Agora itself, and in which (unlike the Agora) shops and workshops were situated: this was the main commercial district of Athens, and it was very often called 'the agora' in a loose sense— it did, after all, include the Agora proper, which was its focus. When the word *agora* is used in this latter way the correct translation is generally 'market'. But the agora which was the market had no definite boundaries: the word *agora* in this sense had no strict topographical meaning. We sometimes do find the correct phraseology used by those who are referring to commercial buildings or activities, as when Xenophon (*Mem.* IV ii.1) says that Euthydemus, when he was too young to go into the Agora, used to go and sit in one of the saddlers' shops *near the Agora*, where Socrates found him; or when Lysias (XXIV 20) makes his crippled client tell the Athenians that each of them is 'in the habit of frequenting a perfumer's or a barber's or a shoemaker's or wherever it may be, and most people go to those who are installed *nearest to the Agora*, very few to those farthest from it'. Here the agora is not the whole commercial district, but only the focal point of it, the Agora proper. Again, in Aristophanes' *Knights* (1245–7) Paphlagon asks the Sausage-seller whether he carries on his trade 'in the Agora, or by the gates'; and the Sausage-seller replies, 'By the gates, where salted fish is on sale'. In this case, as so often, we can hardly

---

[62] The results of the American excavations conducted over the last thirty years or so have been presented in a series of articles in *Hesperia* and elsewhere, and in the various volumes of excavation reports published by the American School of Classical Studies at Athens, under the title *The Athenian Agora*, the most useful of which, for my purposes, is *III. Literary and Epigraphical Testimonia* (1957), by R. E. Wycherley (quoted here as *Ath. Ag. III*). See also the useful little article by Wycherley, 'The Market of Athens', in *Greece & Rome* 25 = Ser. II 3 (1956) 2–23; Ida T. Hill, *The Ancient City of Athens* (1953) 39 ff.; and the Guide to the Agora excavations issued by the American School (*The Athenian Agora*², 1962). For the Greek agora in general, see Roland Martin, *RAG* (pp. 255–73, 279–87, 298–308 and 314–38 of this work relate to the Athenian Agora); P. Lavedan and J. Huguenay, *Hist. de l'Urbanisme. Antiquité*² (Paris, 1966); also W. A. McDonald, *The Pol. Meeting Places of the Greeks* (*Johns Hopkins Univ. Stud. in Archaeology*, no. 34, 1943).

[63] See *SEG* x 368 for the first three (including one found *in situ*), and for the fourth (Inv. I 7039, also found *in situ*) H. A. Thompson in *Hesp.* 37 (1968), at pp. 61–3 and Pl. 10b.

tell whether the word *agora* refers to the Agora proper or to the main market area as a whole; but in either event the passage shows commercial activity going on elsewhere than in the Agora. In the late fifth century, commercial activity in the Agora itself, although extensive, was relatively superficial; probably all the buildings in and around the Agora at this time were political or religious.[64] This is entirely characteristic of Greek city *agorai* of the period.[65] The main commercial buildings around the Agora at Athens, as elsewhere, are all of Hellenistic or Roman date. Although by the late fifth century the Assembly met on the Pnyx, ostracisms were still conducted in the Agora, the Council and the law courts met there, and in the fifth and fourth centuries the Agora was used on occasion as a place of emergency assembly.[66] It is worth remarking that in Aristotle's plan for his ideal city the political *agora*, the 'free agora' as they called it (he says) in Thessaly, was to be quite separate from the commercial *agora*, the market.[67]

Let us look at the language used by our sources in referring to the exclusion effected by the Megarian decree.

1. Of those which give any details at all, some, including Thucydides, speak of *agora* and harbours in some form. Thus Diodorus (XII 39.4 = Ephorus, F 196) has 'excluded from both the *agora* and the harbours'. Plutarch (*Per.* 29.4) has a fine rhetorical sentence, the vital part of which (as I would translate it: see Appendix XXXVIII) reads, 'excluded from the whole *agora* and from all harbours controlled by Athens'. The best of the scholia on Aristophanes (*Peace* 605 = 604 Dindorf) has 'excluded from *agora* and from harbours in the Athenian sphere': Philochorus has just been cited (F 121) and may have used that form of words. I believe that all these versions, with the partial exception of Plutarch's (see Appendix XXXVIII), derive from Thucydides, whose wording we shall carefully examine later.

2. Aristophanes I have already analysed in detail (in Section C of Part ii of this Chapter). I need only repeat here that, according to my understanding of the text of *Acharn.* 533–4 and of the poem of Timocreon cited by the scholiast, Aristophanes takes over two of Timocreon's four elements, namely 'land' and 'sea', alters 'in heaven' to 'on continent', and introduces one new element: 'in agora' (see Appendix XXXIX).

3. The only other sources which purport to tell us about the contents of the Megarian decree are very late indeed. Schol. Ar. *Peace* 609 refers to the decree of Pericles concerning the Megarians, 'that they are not to enter upon land or harbours belonging to the Athenians' (or possibly

---

[64] The earliest possible reference to any commercial building in the Agora, as far as I know, is to the Alphitopolis, in Ar., *Eccl.* 686 (late 390s B.C.)—and it is not at all certain that the Alphitopolis was actually in the Agora proper.

[65] See R. Martin, *RAG, passim*, esp. 194 ff. on cults.

[66] See Andoc. I 45 (415 B.C.); Arist., *Ath. Pol.* 38.1 (403); Dem. XVIII 169 (339). The last passage is particularly significant.

[67] Arist., *Pol.* VII 12, 1331ᵃ30–5, ᵇ1–4; cf. Xen., *Cyrop.* I ii.3–4.

'the land or harbours of Attica'—the sense of *Attikon* is not absolutely clear). However, I have explained (in Section D of Part ii of this Chapter) that with the aid of Schol. Ar. *Peace* 246 we can recognise this as a reference to the decree *of Charinus*, and detect a similar confusion between the two decrees in Schol. Ar. *Ach.* 527 and Suid., *s.v. Aspasia*, which, using identical language, refer to the Megarian decree as 'prohibiting the reception of them into Athens' (cf. Appendix XL).

We can now turn back to Thucydides. When he is reporting what the Megarians (1 67.4) or the Spartans (1 39.1) said about the exclusion decree, he has to make them identify the agora as 'the Athenian Agora' or 'the Agora of Athens' (*hē Attikē agora*, which is correctly translated by either phrase: see below and Appendix XLII). Most important is 1 139.1, where Thucydides, giving the gist of the second Spartan *démarche* at Athens in the winter of 432/1, refers to the decree as actually *saying* (*en hōi eirēto*) that the Megarians were 'not to use the Athenian Agora'. We are not to understand, of course, that these very words were necessarily used in the decree:[68] there, only one agora could be in question, and the decree will doubtless have spoken merely of *agora* (or *hē agora*), just as Pericles does in Thuc. 1 144.2, when he speaks to the Athenian Assembly of allowing the Megarians 'to use Agora and harbours' (*agorāi kai limesi chrēsthai*). But it is essential to realise that this agora, to which the exclusion decree referred, was precisely what Thucydides twice calls *hē Attikē agora*. Let us see exactly what this expression means.

No other interpretation is possible than 'the Athenian Agora' or 'the Agora of Athens'. The word *Attikos* is what the Greek grammarians[69] called the *ktētikon*, corresponding to *Athēnaios*, the *ethnikon* (in the later, loose sense): *Attikos* means 'everything that belongs to the people of the *Athēnaioi* or concerns their city or territory', as Dittenberger put it in his excellent comprehensive study of *ethnika* and *ktētika*.[70] (As this subject is rather technical, I have relegated much of what I wish to say about it to Appendix XLII; but there are a few remarks which need to be made here.) Dittenberger is concerned mainly with material of the Hellenistic and Roman periods, but anyone who takes the trouble to study Thucydides' employment of *ethnika* and *ktētika* (and I think I have looked at virtually all the scores of examples) will find that the principles established by Dittenberger apply equally to his usage, except of course that some 'ktetic' forms which appear only later evidently did not yet exist in Thucydides' day: here he naturally makes use of the *ethnikon* in all necessary adjectival senses. Never does he use *Attikos* (or any similar 'ktetic' formation, *Lakōnikos* for instance) in any sense other than 'belonging to

---

[68] Cf. ἐγέγραπτο in v 29.2; the formula given here (lines 29–30 *OCT*), though it must in fact refer to the clause in 18.11, is closer in its wording to the one in 23.6.

[69] See e.g. Dionysius Thrax, p. 635.3 Bekker = 26.7 Uhlig.

[70] EuV 216: 'alles was dem Volk der 'Αθηναῖοι gehört oder ihr (Stadt und Landgebiet gleichmässig umfassendes) Gemeinwesen betrifft'. (I am grateful to P. M. Fraser for emphasising to me the importance of Dittenberger's article in this connection.)

the Athenians' (or whatever other State is in question). Consequently, *hē Attikē agora* can only mean 'the Agora of the Athenian State', 'the Agora of Athens', 'the Athenian Agora'.[71] It is surprising how careless many historians have been in reporting the terms of the Megarian decree, by speaking of it as excluding the Megarians from 'Attic markets' and the like.[72]

We have a mass of fifth/fourth-century evidence, extending from Antiphon to Lycurgus and Aristotle, that exclusion from the Agora was a particular form of *atimia*, public disqualification and dishonour, a disability inflicted by law upon those accused of homicide (the evidence here goes back ostensibly to Draco) and those convicted of certain serious crimes. The evidence is too copious to be given conveniently in this Chapter: it will be found in Appendix XLIII, where I have placed all necessary references not given here for the statements made in this and the next paragraph or two. Although going into the Agora when forbidden to do so may sometimes have been winked at in special cases (see Dem. xxi 58–61), it could also be spoken of as a serious offence (Dem. xxiv 60 etc.). The prohibition is often linked with exclusion from public sacred places and occasions (*hiera*). The exclusion from the Agora is described by Aeschin. iii 176 (cf. i 21) in particularly significant words: the man disqualified is to remain, literally, 'outside the purificatory basins of the Agora' (*exō tōn perirrhantēriōn tēs agoras*), which it is surely justifiable to translate, 'outside the purified precincts of the Agora' and to take as referring to the Agora as a whole. What the passage means is clear from the scholiast's comment on Aeschin. iii 176, that *perirrhantēria*, namely basins (*loutēres*) holding water, stood 'in front of the entrance to the Agora on either side' (ed. F. Schultz [1865], p. 345). They were, so to speak, holy-water stoups, used for lustrations. Confirmatory archaeological evidence is also available. 'A base for a *perirrhantērion* has been found closely associated with the shrine of the Twelve Gods, and fragments of two *perirrhantēria* have been found in the agora. . . .; a base which probably supported another stands in the middle of the ancient roadway to the west of the southwest corner of the Southwest Fountain House' (Wycherley, *Ath. Ag.* iii 218: cf. Appendix XLIII). As the guide-book to the Agora excavations issued by The American School of Classical Studies at Athens rightly says, 'The open square of the Agora was dedicated to the community life and, as such, was as sacred as any temple precinct. It was marked off by boundary stones; holy-water basins (*perirrhanteria*) stood at the entrances, and the laws forbade entry to those who might bring harm to the community' (*The Athenian Agora*[2] 16).

An intriguing scrap of late-fifth-century Comedy speaks of the Megarians in the very same breath as various other classes of disreputable persons some of whom we know from the evidence referred to above to have been excluded from the Agora. This is a quotation by Pollux from

---

[71] Thucydides could not conceivably have written ἡ ’Aθηναία ἀγορά: in such a case, like everyone else, he invariably used the 'ktetic' adjective, ’Αττική.

[72] Cf. Part i of this Chapter, and Appendix XXXV.

Philonides' *Kothornoi*,[73] the point of which seems to be to associate the farmers of the 2 per cent customs duty (the *pentēkostē*), here given the opprobrious nickname of *pornotelōnai* (cf. Appendix XLIV), with other disreputable characters, of whom we know that those here called 'cowards' (*deiloi*) and 'father-beaters' (*patraloiai*) were excluded from the Agora, and those under a curse must certainly have been, like those under an accusation of homicide, who were also potential carriers of infection. It is very significant that the Megarians should have been named among these characters. Evidently Philonides could rely on his audience's remembering the Megarian decree. Encroachment on the *hiera orgas* would have made the Megarians accursed in the eyes of the Athenians in the late 430s, just as it did eighty years later, when they can be described as 'accursed' (*kataratoi*) by Demosthenes (XIII 32; XXIII 212); and if the Megarians were regarded as accursed, an exclusion of them from the Agora would be a perfectly natural reaction.

There is a striking feature of the Megarian decree, as it is usually interpreted (to mean exclusion from the 'market' of Athens, or from the whole of Attica), which seems to have escaped attention altogether: its uniqueness. An exclusion *in time of peace* from trading in the territory of a particular State, or in the market or markets of a State, is unknown in the whole of Greek history, as far as I am aware. It is interesting that the learned Egon Weiss[74] could find no better parallel to what he believed to be the commercial exclusion effected by the Megarian decree than a clause in the treaty of 98 B.C. between Sardis and Ephesus (*OGIS* 437 III. c. 69–73), which in fact affords no real parallel at all, because the clause in question refers to a war situation: what the Sardians are promising here is that they will not afford assistance to enemies of Ephesus by (among other things) providing them with markets in which to buy necessaries, the word *agora* being used here in the same sense as in numerous passages in Thucydides and Xenophon, to be mentioned later, which refer to the provision of special markets for military expeditions. In their search for parallels to the Megarian decree, other scholars[75] have been obliged to have recourse to the practice of late mediaeval Italian cities, whose pattern of trade was in reality quite different from that of the cities of Classical Greece (cf. Appendix XLI).

Hasebroek has maintained that the 'closed market' was normal in ancient Greece: 'the closure of harbour and market to the foreigner is normal', he says; 'to throw them open is abnormal' (*TPAG* 117 ff., esp. 121–2). Anyone who examines with an open mind the evidence Hasebroek

---

[73] Philonides, fr. 5 (Kock, *CAF* I 255), *ap.* Poll. IX 29; cf. VII 202. The complete quotation is παναγεῖς γενεάν, πορνοτελῶναι, Μεγαρεῖς, δειλοί, πατραλοῖαι. The emendation δειλοί is Bergk's. (I am grateful to Edward Hussey for drawing my attention to the passage.)

[74] *Griech. Privatrecht* I (1923) 345 n. 326. Weiss omits in his quotation part of lines 70–1, where the military aspect of the whole clause is brought out.

[75] Adolf Holm, *Hist. of Greece* (Eng. trans., London, 1895) II 326–7; and the editors (Mitchell and Caspari) of the one-vol. edition of Grote's *Hist. of Greece*, 370 n. 1.

cites will see that this is the reverse of the truth, and that not one of the sources he cites provides any justification for his theory. In particular, Lysias XXII 14 and Demosthenes II 16, to which Hasebroek appeals as showing that the 'closed market' was normal, refer to war situations: the latter says so explicitly, and they both use the same word, virtually identical with that in Thuc. V 83.4: the Athenians *katekleisan* the Macedonians at the same time as they declared their king, Perdiccas, an enemy. The most conclusive evidence of all is provided by Dem. XXIII 110 and XIX 153, 315, which Hasebroek missed. In the first of these passages, alluding to the considerable revenue from the Thracian Chersonese, the speaker says that it would fall to nothing in the event of war, for the ports would *then* be closed (*tot' an kleistheiē*); and the other two passages also connect the closure of ports with a war situation. It is similarly absurd to treat the mid-fifth-century treaty between two Locrian cities, Oeantheia and Chaleium (Tod I² 34 = *SVdA* II 146), as illustrating the normal situation. The treatment of other states by the Aetolians remained a scandal in Greece down to the second century B.C., and Thucydides (I 5.3) classes the Ozolian Locrians with the Aetolians as still keeping up the old piratical habits in his day.

It would have been difficult, probably impossible, to prevent foreigners from trading in a Greek city without excluding them from its territory altogether. And *xenēlasia*, the exclusion of strangers, was not a Greek custom, except at Sparta[76] and perhaps Apollonia near Epidamnus:[77] Eratosthenes (*ap.* Strab. XVII i.19, p. 802), in the third century, could describe it as a 'custom common to all the barbarians'. According to the interpretation of the Megarian decree which I am proposing, it was no more than an extension to the citizens of a neighbouring state of a form of dishonour which the Athenians inflicted on some of their own citizens. The exclusion from the Agora was of a very well attested kind, referred to again and again in Athenian public life in the fifth and fourth centuries. Its object was to prevent the centre of civic and social life from being contaminated by miscellaneous undesirables, some of whom are directly associated with the Megarians by Philonides. The only novelty will have been its extension to the citizens of another state collectively.

The account so far given is consistent at all points with the evidence of the sources, and it makes very good sense. We now have to examine the rival theories mentioned earlier, which between them have held the field entirely in modern times.

First, there is the standard view, that the agora from which the Megarians were excluded was 'the market', the main commercial district of Athens. This is an impossible notion, for the following reasons:

1. An official Athenian decree excluding from a certain area would have to speak of the area in such a way that it could be clearly identified. Now

---

[76] See Busolt-Swoboda, *GSK* II 643 n.1.

[77] Aelian, *VH* XIII 16 (ed. R. Hercher, 1866).

the civic Agora, as we have just seen, was a properly defined area; but the agora in the sense of 'the market' had no specific boundaries, and no one could be sure where it began or ended. The Megarian decree, therefore, must have referred to the Agora proper, using the word in the one sense in which it had a technical and precise meaning. Exclusion from the Agora in this sense was a penalty very familiar to the Athenians, especially for offences having a 'religious' character, and it would be strange indeed if the Athenians, in retaliation for a religious offence, had chosen to exclude the Megarians from a *different* 'agora'.

2. Exclusion in peace time from 'the market' of Athens or any other Greek city is otherwise entirely unknown.

3. If the Athenians had been mainly concerned to prevent the Megarians from trading in the Athenian 'market', they could easily have banned them from the whole of Attica, or at least from the city area, the demes of which could have been specified. An exclusion from those city demes within which the 'market' was situated would have been much more appropriate than an exclusion from the 'agora', an expression which could only be taken to mean the civic Agora.

It is not impossible that *in other contexts, in which definition of the area was unimportant,* an Athenian decree might follow popular speech and use the word 'agora' in a loose sense, to mean the 'market area', the whole commercial district of which only a part was the Agora proper. It does not seem likely, for instance, that the sphere of activity of the officials known as Agoranomoi (Arist., *Ath. Pol.* 51.1–2 etc.) was limited to the Agora in the strict sense: their job was 'to supervise everything offered for sale, so that it might be sold pure and unadulterated', and in Aristotle's day five of the ten Agoranomoi functioned in the Peiraeus, which of course had its own separate agora (see below). However, this particular office (evidently very common in Greek states) will have been instituted at a time—surely not later than the sixth century—when commercial activity was far less widely diffused around the outskirts of the Agora than it became in later times and could still be thought of as taking place mainly *in* the Agora. Once civic Agora and 'market' had become identified, of course, the word *agora* went on being used for the 'market', even when only a small part of the whole market area was identical with the Agora. But when an Athenian decree was intended to refer to the whole market area and not merely the civic Agora, this would be made clear, as it is, for instance, in *IG* 11² 1013 (= H. W. Pleket, *Epigraphica* 1 [Leiden, 1964], no. 14), a well-known decree of the late second century B.C. regulating weights and measures. It is significant that the relevant clause of this decree (lines 9–10), dealing entirely with commercial activities, does not simply refer to those selling 'in the *agora*', but—because of the ambiguous denotation of the word *agora* when used in a commercial sense—goes on, 'or in workshops or shops or wineshops or storehouses'. There are a few other laws referring to activity in the *agora* which in course of time may have been interpreted in such a way as to cover the whole trading area; but this is very uncertain, and since the question is scarcely relevant to our enquiry I am relegating discussion of it to an Appendix (XLV). I would emphasise that none of these laws has anything to do with physical exclusion from the *agora*.

It is often forgotten that although in Athens and other Greek cities commercial activity was *concentrated* more particularly in an area (focused on the civic Agora) which, without being precisely delimited, could be called 'the agora' ('*the* market'), yet buying and selling were by no means *confined* to this area but could go on anywhere, not merely inside the walls or at the city gates, but in centres of population in the country-side—not to mention the provision of an agora for a foreign military or naval force in the territory of the state concerned: this is a special case, treatment of which can be postponed to Appendix XLVI. Enough has been said already in regard to such commercial activities at Athens itself, and there is no reason to doubt that the situation in other cities was much the same;[78] but it will be useful to look at some evidence about the existence of *agorai*, in the sense of 'market places', in Attica, well away from the city of Athens itself.

At a large centre of population within the territory of any Greek state, some way distant from the actual city itself (the *asty*), a local market might grow up: Xenophon (*De Vect.* IV 49) foresees that if a large population is concentrated in the area of the Laurium silver mines, many forms of revenue may be derived 'from a market situated there', and from other sources. Peiraeus had the famous 'agora of Hippodamus' (dating from the mid-fifth century), which of course was the centre of the political life of the deme of Peiraeus, as well as a market.[79] All our other evidence about deme agorai is epigraphic, and it comes mainly from later periods, few deme decrees having survived from the fifth century. But the Attic demes in general must always have possessed their own agorai, at least in the sense of political meeting places, and doubtless in country demes at any rate these will soon have become markets as well, like the Peiraeus agora. Shortly after the middle of the fourth century we find the demesmen of Sounium providing for a new market-place of their own, of a size of not less than 200 by 100 feet, their existing one having been built over (*SIG*³ 913 = *IG* II² 1180). The use of such an agora would of course not be confined to demesmen or to those who lived in the deme: in this case the intention of the Sounians is made clear by the words, 'so that there may be plenty of room to buy and sell, for the Sounians and anyone else who wants to' (lines 12–15). The decrees of a deme may refer to 'the

[78] A good example in our period is Thuc. VIII 95.4 (Eretria).

[79] See Andoc. I 45; Xen., *HG* II iv.11; Ps.-Dem. XLIX 22; *SIG*³ 313 (= *IG* II² 380).9, 35–6; 915 (= *IG* II² 1176).20; 969 (= *IG* II² 1668).5. This agora had its own boundary stones: *IG* I² 896 etc. See R. Martin, *RAG* 357–61, 364–70. By the mid-second century C.E., Peiraeus had two agorai: Paus. I i.3. I would guess that the second was a Roman addition, like the 'Market of Caesar and Augustus' in Athens itself; but I suppose it may have developed much earlier, as seems to be the opinion of Martin, *RAG* 366.

agora of the demesmen',[80] or simply 'the agora'.[81] Salamis too had its own agora (Aeschin. 1 25). Occasionally the meaning of 'agora' in such texts may be ambiguous, since the Assembly of a deme, in the abstract, was also called 'agora',[82] as was that of a tribe.[83] When a deme in the country-side had an agora in the sense of a market-*place*, it might well be more purely a market-place than was the Agora of Athens; but this partly depends on the answer to the question whether the deme Assembly normally met in the agora of the deme—I do not feel as confident as most people that an affirmative answer can be given to this question (see Appendix XLVII). The *agorasti [kon]* mentioned in *IG* 11² 1245.8–9, a decree of the Mesogeioi of the mid-third century B.C., was presumably a local market toll, exacted perhaps in connection with a festival. Draco's homicide law, republished in 409/8,[84] spoke of an *agora ephoria*, a term explained by Demosthenes (XXIII 39) as meaning a place where in ancient times neighbours on both sides of the Athenian frontier used to gather—it must have been right on the frontier, a kind of no-man's-land. But it is clear from what the orator says that these *agorai ephoriai* had by his time long ceased to exist: they probably died out in the sixth century.

The texts cited in the last paragraph clearly demonstrate that 'the agora' at Athens, even in the loose sense of the city 'market', was far from being the only place in Attica where trade went on.

I should perhaps say something about the 'agora' which Dicaeopolis sets up in Ar., *Acharn.* 719 ff. This is his own private market (a comic fantasy), delimited by *horoi*, just like the Athenian Agora: here he will allow Peloponnesians, Megarians and Boeotians to buy and sell (*agorazein*), under the supervision of his own private Agoranomoi (lines 719–26), and here he proposes to set up the stele recording his private peace-treaty (727–8). It is a faithful reflection of the Agora of Athens, a market in miniature as well as a political headquarters where treaties are displayed. At line 729 the Megarian arrives and greets this 'agora in Athens, . . . dear to the Megarians', which he has been longing for, he says, like a mother—of course he has, for what he and his starving countrymen are interested in is the agora in the extended, commercial sense: from the whole of this, *as indeed from Athenian territory in general*, they had been excluded for several years, not of course by the Megarian decree, but by the war (cf. Section c of Part ii of this Chapter).

I have still not dealt with two theories about the Megarian decree: that what it 'really' did was to exclude the Megarians *from trading in Attica* (and the Athenian empire), or *from entering Attica* (and the empire). A combination of these two theories has also been put forward, for example by Hasebroek (*TPAG* 122–4): the decree in fact banned the Megarians

---

[80] As in *IG* 11² 1176.20, a decree of the Peiraieis; cf. 1² 188. 7–10, 19–21, 53–4 ('in the agora of the Skambonidai'), a decree (of a City deme) dated in the Corpus 'before 460'.
[81] As in *IG* 11² 1174.13–18, a decree of the Halaieis.
[82] See e.g. Ps.-Dem. XLIV 36; *IG* 11² 1202.1; cf. Aeschin. III 27.
[83] See e.g. *IG* 11² 1141.5–7.
[84] M/L 86 (= Tod 1² 87 = *IG* 1² 115). 27–8, with Dem. XXIII 37–40.

completely from Attica and from the whole empire, but what the Megarians felt most, and chose to protest against in particular, was the commercial ban—'the most painful feature of the general exclusion: it made it impossible for the Megarians to obtain the necessities of life', as Hasebroek puts it, a statement which we have seen above to be quite untrue. Hasebroek, of all people, should have grasped the fact that merely excluding 'the Megarians', even from Attica and the whole empire, could not possibly have deprived Megara of 'the necessities of life', since he himself maintained, with much exaggeration, that Greek traders were never citizens!

I will deal first with the view that the decree 'really' excluded the Megarians altogether from Attica (and the empire).

1. Exclusion from Attica (not the empire) is well attested for the decree of Charinus (see Part iii of this Chapter), but the only sources which contain any suggestion that the main Megarian decree referred to anything but the Athenian Agora and the harbours of the empire are the three very late ones we have already noticed (see Section D of Part ii of this Chapter), which confuse the main Megarian decree with the decree of Charinus, and conceivably Plut., *Per.* 29.4, dealt with in Appendix XXXVIII.

2. The combined evidence of our two contemporary authorities, Thucydides and Aristophanes, not to mention the secondary sources, cannot be set aside: the decree referred specifically to the Athenian Agora and the harbours of the empire; and if it did that, a universal exclusion from Attica and the empire (above all from Attica) is out of the question. Interpretations which seek to distinguish between what the decree 'really' provided and what the Megarians complained about ignore, and are destroyed by, Thuc. I 139.1 and 144.2, which go beyond 67.4 and show that the exclusion from Agora and harbours was not merely what the Megarians protested about but what the decree actually *said*—'in which it was decreed' in Thuc. I 139.1 could not be more explicit.

3. That Thucydides, of all people, should quite unnecessarily misrepresent a very well known Athenian decree is inconceivable to me, *especially since exclusion from the civic Agora was a familiar phenomenon at Athens*, as I have shown above. Thucydides had no need for cryptic understatement; and when he is describing a blockade he can be quite explicit about it, as in III 6.2, where the Athenians 'prevented the Mytilenaeans from using the sea'. If the decree had been intended to exclude the Megarians entirely from Attica, it would have said this, and so would Thucydides. The decree of Charinus, as we know, did forbid Megarians to enter Attica.

4. As an argument for believing that the Megarian decree was one of 'general exclusion', Hasebroek (*loc. cit.*) has pointed to the fact that in Thuc. I 144.2 Pericles seems to compare the exclusion contemplated by the decree with the Spartan *xenēlasiai*, which were complete expulsions of

10—OOPW * *

foreigners from Spartan territory. I would reply that the parallel cannot be so closely pressed as to infer from the nature of the *xenēlasiai* what the form of exclusion under the Megarian decree was, since Pericles could not create an institution at Sparta corresponding precisely to the Megarian decree but had to choose whatever he could find, even if it supplied only a rough analogy. What Pericles advised the Athenians to say to the Spartans was in effect, 'The Megarian decree is not a breach of the Peace. If you are going to say it is, well, we are equally entitled to say that your *xenēlasiai* are also a breach; and if you will end them as far as we ourselves and our allies are concerned, then we will repeal the Megarian decree' (cf. Part ix of this Chapter). There is no warrant for inferring anything about the detailed terms of the Megarian decree from the nature of the *xenēlasiai*.

I turn now to the theory that the Megarian decree in fact excluded the Megarians from *trading in Attica*—and the empire, but we may leave this question for consideration in Part viii of this Chapter. This theory is at any rate an improvement on the one we have just been examining, in that it does not require us to accept an exclusion from the Athenian Agora as a total exclusion from Attic soil. However, it has nothing to recommend it and is linguistically indefensible, since it would require an interpretation of the word *agora* which is entirely unparalleled, as far as I can see, in the fifth century and for a long time thereafter, and is inconsistent with Thucydides' expression, 'the *Athenian* Agora' (*hē Attikē agora*). I cannot myself see that there is the slightest basis for this theory, except of course the assumption *a priori* that the ban 'must have been' essentially commercial, combined with an awareness that agora in the sense of the main commercial *area* of Athens is an impossible interpretation.

The word *agora* is very common in fifth- and fourth-century sources. After looking, with the aid of indexes, at some hundreds of passages, including (I hope) all those in Herodotus, Thucydides, Xenophon, Aristophanes and Aristotle, virtually all the orators, indeed nearly all the fifth- and fourth-century sources that might be relevant, and a good deal of later material (including the 'testimonia' collected by Wycherley, *Ath. Ag.* iii), I can only say that I have found nothing to support the interpretation of *agora* in the Megarian decree in a non-locative sense (general, collective or abstract), to mean either 'supplies' or 'buying and selling', such as we occasionally find in Hellenistic and later texts.[85] And

---

[85] See G. T. Griffith, *The Mercenaries of the Hellenistic World* (Cambridge, 1935) 280. The word occurs several times in Polybius in the sense of 'provisions', but almost always in the plural (1 18.5,9; 39.8; 52.5; 53.13; 60.3; 68.5; 82.6; iii 75.6; the one exception is 1 52.6). In Diod. xi 80.3, κομιζομένης ἀγορᾶς πολλῆς ἐκ τῆς 'Αττικῆς presumably means 'a large quantity of *supplies* brought from Attica'. Cf. *SIG*³ 799.1.14–23 (the well-known inscription from Cyzicus, recording the benefactions of Antonia Tryphaena, of the reign of Caligula), and other inscriptions, and papyri. For Xen., *Anab.* vi vi. 3; vii vi.24, see Appendix XLVI. R. Martin, *RAG* 281 n.7, is wrong in taking τὰς ἀγοράς in Xen., *De Vect.* iv 40 in the sense of 'les marchandises elles-mêmes': linked as it is with τὰ ἐλλιμένια (Bergk's necessary emendation), the expression has the same force here as in Ar., *Wasps* 659 (ἀγοράς, λιμένας), and means market *revenues or tolls*.

the argument can be taken an important stage further: it is not merely that we have to justify the translation of the word *agora* by something like 'buying and selling'; we have to explain the use of the word in two specific contexts:

1. In Aristophanes' parody of the Megarian decree, in *Acharn.* 533–4, the Megarians are 'not to *remain in* the agora'. Here 'agora' is used, as always in Aristophanes, in anything but an abstract sense: it is a *place*.

2. In Thucydides the effect of the decree on the Megarians is first said to be that they are '*excluded from* the Athenian Agora" (1 67.4), and then that they should '*not use* the Athenian Agora' (139.1). We have discussed the meaning of 'the Athenian Agora' at length, and there is no doubt of its technical meaning.

Therefore, even if one or two isolated early examples of the use of 'agora' in an abstract commercial sense could be found (and I do not think they can), they would prove no more than that the word might on rare occasions be used in that sense, and would have no weight against the quite specific meaning demanded by the context in the passages I have just quoted. And I have already pointed out that to interpret the exclusion decree in the sense required by the theory we are now considering would be to make it something to which no parallel can be found in the whole of Greek history.

If Pericles and the Athenians had really wanted to exclude Megarians from trading in Attica, they could have made their intention quite clear by using the verbs of buying and selling: they could have forbidden the Megarians to *ōneisthai kai pōlein* or *agorazein* (*mē agorazein en Attikēi* would have been sufficient: cf. Ar., *Ach.* 625, 720–2, 750; *Lysistr.* 556; *Plut.* 984). Yet in not a single source does any such verb appear in connection with the decree. In every case what we find are *the ordinary words which were already in use* for the exclusion of certain classes of Athenians *from the civic Agora*. It is inconceivable that these very familiar terms should suddenly be used to mean something entirely different.

One suggestion has been made to me which I must mention: that even if the agora of the exclusion decree was the civic Agora, the exclusion might be intended as a complete one, at any rate commercially, because even an Athenian who was banned from the Agora would perhaps be altogether excluded from the amenities of life, and traders would refuse to deal with him; and the same might be true of the Megarians after the exclusion decree. This, I feel, is simply another demonstration that the prevailing view of the Megarian decree is based entirely upon hypotheses *a priori*. Again, the texts are quite consistent and they tell a perfectly credible story—certainly not the one I have just mentioned. There are two lines of argument here:

1. The Athenians dealt out various kinds of public disqualification or dishonour, *atimia* (see esp. Andoc. 1 73–9), and there is not the slightest

reason to suppose that men visited with these punishments who remained in Athens (as evidently many did) were subjected to further indignity in private life. There is certainly not a hint that this was so in any of the sources I know. Commercial dealings, indeed, were the least likely sphere for any gratuitous extension of the penalties inflicted by law, since commerce was to a considerable extent in the hands of metics and foreigners, who would have less temptation than citizens to feel righteous indignation against a man who had been convicted of some crime against the State.

2. And even if there were something in this suggestion, one would still want to ask why a decree directed towards commercial exclusion should be passed in such a curiously oblique form. Why not exclude in one of the alternative ways mentioned above, or say that the Megarians must not buy or sell in Attica or in the *asty* or within the City walls or in certain demes? Athenian decrees normally say what they mean.

As I have already made clear, I of course reject the whole set of assumptions (to me, absurd) on which the standard interpretation of the Megarian decree is founded, and in particular the notion that the mere exclusion of the Megarians, even from the whole of Attica (and the empire), would have dealt a severe blow to the trade of the city of Megara. But I must emphasise that those who adopt this interpretation are committed to attributing to the Athenians the pointless stupidity of depriving themselves, out of sheer spite, of the fresh vegetables and fruits and the cheap clothing which they could probably buy more conveniently and advantageously from Megara than from anywhere else, and were also depriving themselves of a ready market for their own products! The Athenians themselves, on this view, might well have suffered from the decree as much as the Megarians, if the latter were able to switch their trading to Corinth and the rest of the non-Athenian area.

However, exclusion from the Agora was not such a merely nominal penalty as it might appear at first sight. In the case of a citizen it had one very serious consequence: it involved being deprived of access to the law courts, which were part of the civic Agora. This is proved by Antiph. vi 35–6 (cf. Ps.-Lys. vi 24; Dem. xxi 87), where the speaker complains that when charged with homicide he would be unable to proceed with a lawsuit he had begun.[86] How far the capacity of such a man to be a defendant was affected I have not been able to discover, except that one who was debarred from Agora and sacred places because he was subject to a charge of homicide was allowed to enter the sacred place in which the trial was held in order to defend himself in the suit (Arist., *Ath. Pol.* 57.4). If, however, he was obliged to let judgment go against him by default, I dare say that public opinion, as represented by the magistrate and dicasts concerned, would not be likely to countenance malicious or trumped-up charges. We now have to consider how far these disabilities became

[86] This of course applied to γραφαί as well as δίκαι, as the Antiphon passage shows; cf. Lipsius, *AR* 244 and n.16.

attached to the Megarians as a consequence of the exclusion decree. I do not see how we can be certain what happened: I think the situation would depend mainly on whether *symbolai*[87] existed between Athens and Megara (as they surely must have done), what the terms of the treaty were, and whether the exclusion decree was held by the Athenians to abrogate those terms *pro tanto*. Although it is conceivable that foreigners belonging to states which had not concluded *symbolai* with Athens were sometimes allowed access to the Athenian courts,[88] I would certainly expect such a treaty to exist between these two close neighbours; and Athens might well have hesitated to repudiate the treaty, if only because the Megarians could then legally repudiate it in their turn, and it is very possible that Athenians would want to sue in Megarian courts more often than Megarians in the courts of Athens. However, unless a treaty of this kind was in existence and the exclusion decree contained a saving clause expressly providing that it should hold good, I believe the Megarians would have been denied access to the Athenian courts, at least as plaintiffs. And even if there were such a saving clause, Megarians might easily feel, rightly or wrongly, that in the hostile atmosphere of Athens they would not stand much chance of gaining a verdict.

On the other hand, we must not exaggerate the legal disabilities which the Megarians are likely to have suffered as a result of the exclusion decree. They might be unable, or for reasons of prudence unwilling, to bring private suits, *dikai*, in person. But if a Megarian were injured in any way which gave rise to a public suit, a *graphē*, it would still be possible for any Athenian who wished, and who was not himself under any disqualification, to bring the appropriate *graphē*; and I do not think the Athenians would have looked askance at a Megarian proxenos who did his duty in that capacity and took such action. (A successful *graphē* of this kind would of course give no satisfaction to the injured Megarian, apart from that of seeing the wrongdoer punished; but the deterrent effect of the potential *graphē* would not thereby be diminished.) And if a Megarian were actually killed in Attica, especially by an Athenian, I feel sure that his relatives would be allowed—if only because of the possible pollution involved—to bring the appropriate homicide suit, a *dikē phonou epi Palladiōi* (see Arist., *Ath. Pol.* 57.3). Indeed, unless the decree, as is possible, excluded Megarians from sacred places as well as Agora, there would be nothing to prevent their doing so, since prosecuting *epi Palladiōi* would not involve their entering the Agora (cf. Antiph. v 10).

In one respect, however, the Megarians would certainly be at a disadvantage in legal procedure at Athens, compared with all other foreigners: they would not be able to appear as witnesses in cases tried in the ordinary courts; and this might sometimes prejudice the success of a *graphē* instituted in respect of a wrong done to a Megarian. Whatever the

---

[87] For lawsuits brought under the terms of *symbolai*, δίκαι ἀπὸ συμβολῶν, see Lipsius, *AR* 965–77, and my NJAE I 95 ff.

[88] See my NJAE I 95 ff.

rights of foreigners may have been as potential parties to suits, I can find no trace at Athens of any discrimination against them as witnesses, in *dikai* or *graphai* (see Lipsius, *AR* 875 and nn. 34–5). It is clear, indeed, that the citizen who had suffered ordinary public disqualification (*atimia*) was actually in a worse position than the ordinary foreigner in this respect: he could not give evidence, although apparently he could be produced in court as an object of pity[89]—provided, I suppose, he had not, like Andocides, been specifically debarred from entering the Agora, or, like Xenocleides (who was referred to in the case of Theomnestus v. Neaera, Ps. Dem. LIX 26–8), convicted of one of the offences which automatically involved exclusion from the Agora.

The general picture is far from clear, but surely any Megarian might feel that exclusion from the Agora placed him in an insecure position, and might consequently feel reluctant to enter Attica at all unless, for example, he was a peasant coming in to sell his produce (who would be a welcome visitor and would presumably have little to fear) or a merchant whose livelihood depended upon trade he could not effectively conduct elsewhere. We must not, however, forget here that although a few individual Megarian traders might suffer pecuniary loss through being driven to take their business elsewhere or being left without effective legal redress in Attica, the State of Megara would not suffer any further economic hardship as a result, since (as we have seen) the place of any Megarians who were indirectly prevented from trading in Attica could quickly be filled by non-Megarian traders.

It is convenient at this point to deal with one other matter. Apart from the sources for the Megarian decree, it is only in three texts, as far as I have been able to discover, that agora and harbours are mentioned in the same breath: Ar., *Knights* 164–5, and Plato, *Laws* IX 871a and XII 952e. The first passage is of no interest to us.[90] The last (cf. VIII 849d) refers to the reception of strangers 'in markets and harbours' outside the city itself, and is of course to be interpreted entirely in a commercial sense. Only *Laws* IX 871a, however, speaks of an *exclusion* from *agora* (in the singular) and harbours (*limenes*): it is of great interest and deserves more than a passing glance.

It should come as no surprise by now to find that Plato is legislating for the man who is accused[91] of killing a member of his community (an *emphylios*) with his own hand, wrongfully and deliberately. 'Let him be excluded from legal privileges' (*ta nomima*), he says, 'and not defile sacred places or *agora* or harbours or any other public assembly' (*mēte allon koinon xyllogon*). At first sight one might be tempted to suppose that the accused is merely being excluded from all gatherings of people. However,

---

[89] See Dem. XXI 95, with 92 (and 83–7); Ps.-Dem. LVIII 60, with 30–3; LIX 26–8.

[90] The agora and the harbours are bracketed with the Pnyx. Doubtless, therefore, the word *agora* has its usual sense of Agora *and* market.

[91] In spite of Plato's misleading wording, there is not the least doubt that the man being dealt with in 871a is merely *accused* of murder. The man who has been convicted is dealt with in 871de: he is to be executed unless he first withdraws into perpetual exile.

when one examines Plato's use of the words *koinos* and *xyllogos* and the many other passages in which he and other writers deal with men charged with homicide, the picture changes. I am convinced that what Plato's prohibition from 'legal privileges' is aimed at is essentially civic occasions, public festivals and meetings, and entry into places regarded as public property. The exclusion from 'sacred places' would apply mainly to official sacrifices and the like: in Plato's city there are no private religious rites (see *Laws* x 909d–10d). A *xyllogos* in Plato is almost always an official meeting, such as a public festival or an assembly of the city or even of a deme, and a *koinos xyllogos* is certainly nothing but that. The *agora*, likewise, will surely not just be any sort of 'market' (such as those provided for strangers: x 849d; xii 952e) but the civic Agora (surrounded by temples: vi 778c) and perhaps also the *agorai* in the twelve districts (*kōmai*), which were also sacred places (viii 848d). The harbours are doubtless included, exceptionally, because they belong to the State and are administered by it. In another passage regulating the movements of homicides, ix 868a, Plato speaks only of their polluting '*agora* and games and the other sacred places' (cf. xi 935b; ix 881c). We may compare Arist., *Ath. Pol.* 57.2,4, describing the procedure of *proagoreusis* by the Archon Basileus at Athens against a man accused of homicide: first we are told that the *proagoreusis* is of exclusion from legal privileges (*ta nomima*, 57.2), and a few sentences later we discover what these 'legal privileges' are: the man concerned is excluded from the sacred places (the other evidence shows that *public* sacred places are meant)[92] and is 'not even allowed to enter the Agora'.

How accurately does Plato's regulation in *Laws* ix 871a reflect Athenian practice? I imagine that the extent of the exclusion from legal privileges at Athens depended on the reason for the exclusion. In Aeschin. i 21 (cf. i 164; iii 176) we have quite a long list of the disabilities attaching to a conviction for *hetairēsis* (self-prostitution); elsewhere we are usually given only one or two of the main items, just those the source happens to be concerned with. Plato is dealing here with the suspected homicide: he is probably enlarging the scope of the corresponding Athenian provision and making it more stringent, as he is so fond of doing in the *Laws*; but on the other hand it is just conceivable that he is simply giving the rule in its Athenian form, and stating it in exceptional detail. At Athens, an exclusion from the Agora would also extend to meetings of the Assembly on the Pnyx—the Assembly would originally have been covered by a prohibition from entering the Agora, and this situation would naturally continue when the Assembly was moved to the Pnyx: no new principle was involved, and no further extensions need be suspected, although of course they cannot be excluded. One point on which we can feel confident is that any such extensions would be limited to 'sacred' matters and public (in the

[92] See e.g. Aeschin. i 21, with iii 176 (εἰς τὰ δημοτελῆ ἱερά); Lyc., *c. Leocr.* 5 (τῶν κοινῶν ἱερῶν).

sense of *official*) gatherings—perhaps the meetings (*agorai*) of tribes and demes, for example, as well as those of the general Assembly and the law courts.

We are now forced to admit—*quite independently of the arguments set out in Part vi of this Chapter,* based on the fact that the exclusion was of 'the Megarians'—that the exclusion from the Athenian Agora *could not have had a primarily commercial purpose,* although it may have had some minor commercial effects, if only by discouraging individual Megarian merchants from trading in Attica. The purpose of the exclusion from the Agora was surely to humiliate the Megarians, to put them in the same category as men convicted of disgraceful crimes or suspected of being carriers of pollution (*agos*). This ban would be most felt, appropriately enough, by those Megarians—a good proportion of them probably members of the governing oligarchy—who were likely to come to Athens for social, political or business reasons, for the Agora was the natural place in which to meet friends and acquaintances at Athens. In Xenophon's *Oeconomicus* (VII 1–2; XII 1) we find that Ischomachus has made an appointment with some foreign friends for a meeting at the Stoa of Zeus, at the north-west corner of the Agora.[93] The Agora was also the place in which one might wish to take one's evening stroll, as we see the plaintiff doing in Dem. LIV 7–8, apparently between the Leokorion and the Pherrephation.[94] To be banned from entering the Agora was a real humiliation.

(viii)
'The harbours of the empire'

As I have said already, it is above all the supposed combination of '*market and* harbours' which has made everyone adopt the 'commercial' interpretation of the Megarian decree. Get rid of the 'market', and the harbours do not present themselves under a necessarily commercial aspect. In fact, once we have seen that the exclusion from the Agora was essentially non-commercial, although a commercial exclusion would have been possible, we begin to look for a non-commercial interpretation of the 'harbours' clause. The Athenians might in theory have banned the Megarians from Attica and the whole empire. Why was the exclusion from the empire limited to the harbours?

We have to explain two simultaneous types of exclusion: at home, from the Agora; abroad, from the harbours of the empire. I suggest that in trying to account for the precise form of the latter type of exclusion we should begin by looking for a motive that will also account for the former. Now we have seen that the exclusion from the Athenian Agora was evidently aimed at humiliating the Megarians, inflicting indignity upon them

[93] Recent discoveries by the American School have shown that this is not to be identified with the Stoa Basileios (Royal Stoa), which is nearby.
[94] See Wycherley, *Ath. Ag. III* 110, 111, 85.

by putting them in the same class as criminals and men under a curse, or who might bring pollution on the city. I suggest that the same aim, the humiliation of the Megarians, also accounts best for the exclusion from the harbours of the empire. I would urge the following considerations:

1. A general ban from the whole empire would have caused a great deal of irritation among the allies, if only because Megarians living or travelling abroad among the allies would have had to be hounded out, if the decree was to be obeyed, and this would have led to bitterness, disputes and tiresome official adjudications—and probably as a result the decree would in practice have been largely ignored, except perhaps where there were Athenian officials (*archontes*) on hand to enforce it. (When the Athenians in the spring of 431, after the Theban attack on Plataea, arrested all the Boeotians who were in Attica [Thuc. II 6.2], we do not hear that they instructed the allies to do the same.)

2. In virtually all Greek cities the harbour would be the one and only place where *a check would anyway be kept on entry and exit*, for every Greek state except a few inland ones had its customs and harbour dues, and as each man presented himself on entering or leaving he could be asked if he were a Megarian. A man wrongly supposed to be a Megarian would be able to clear himself by saying, for instance, 'No, I am Apollonius the Corinthian, living as a metic at Sicyon; and if you don't believe me, call Apollodorus the proxenos of Corinth and Apollodotus the proxenos of Sicyon, and I'll give enough details to satisfy both'. No special machinery, therefore, would be necessary, and this would be a very great advantage in a world of city-states none of which possessed anything very much in the way of a bureaucracy. (The customs officials would probably always be the slaves or freedmen of the tax-farmer concerned; but of course they would be able to call for the help of the city magistrates where necessary.) On this basis alone the Megarian decree had a real chance of being enforced.

3. Apart from a handful of merchants, it would surely be the leading Megarians, the ruling oligarchs—the very people the Athenians most wanted to punish—who would be most likely to travel abroad. And the aim of the Athenians, to humiliate the Megarians, would be rather nicely served by mere exclusion from the harbours, instead of from the whole territory of the empire. As it was, Megarians might still enter allied states (just as they could still enter Attica, apart from the Agora), for each ship would have its *lembos* (or *skaphē*), by means of which its crew or passengers could land on a beach (see e.g. Ps.-Dem. XXXII 6,7). But to be made to enter and leave in an inconvenient and undignified way, by a beach instead of the harbour, would be very galling to a wealthy and influential Megarian or to a merchant. There is a nice illustration of this in the speech of Lycurgus, *Against Leocrates*, whom the orator is prosecuting for having deserted Athens in her hour of need after the battle of Chaeroneia in 338. Leocrates, says Lycurgus (§17), collected his belongings and with the

help of his slaves put them into his ship's boat (the *lembos*), the ship itself being already at anchor near the beach. With his mistress, he 'went out on to the open shore by the little gate', sailed out to his ship and fled to Rhodes. Later in the speech (§55) Lycurgus returns to this furtive and undignified method of departure. Leocrates had claimed, falsely it appears, that he was a merchant (an *emporos*), and that he had sailed off to Rhodes on business. 'If he says that', counters Lycurgus scornfully, 'note how easily you can catch him out in his lies. First, those who sail off on commercial business do not embark from the beach via the little gate, but from inside the harbour, with all their friends looking on and seeing them off.' Evidently, not to be allowed to enter and leave by the harbour would place one in an undignified and demeaning position— exactly the effect of the other provision of the Megarian decree, which excluded the Megarians from the Athenian Agora! The parallel between the two exclusions effected by the decree is close, and supports the inter- pretation I have advanced.

Exclusion from the harbours of the empire would also, of course, seriously hamper trade by Megarian citizens with the member states of the empire, unless it was legally possible (as I am sure it was in many cases *physically* possible) to carry on trade from beaches. Ancient merchant ships, unlike modern ones, were not dependent upon formal harbours, and Megarian exports, such as the textiles and garden produce of which we mainly hear, could easily be landed on a beach and cereals or metals bound for Megara embarked there. A glance at an ancient *Periplous*, such as that of 'the Red Sea',[95] will show that ancient merchant captains were well satisfied with a good anchorage (*hormos* in Greek, *statio* in Latin) when no proper harbour was available. Trade with a place which was harbourless (*alimenos*) would be carried on by means of small boats, *skaphai*.[96] But I feel that such trading with a Greek city which did have a proper harbour might have been risky in practice, as it would perhaps have been taken as an attempt to evade customs duties. (Cf. Dem. xxxv 28, 53; Strabo ix i.14, p. 395; Bekker, *Anecd. Gr.* i 315.14–15.) It is quite likely, then, that trade *by Megarians* with the Athenian empire will have been seriously curtailed—although, for reasons I have explained in Part vi of this Chapter, this would not have been a severe blow to the Megarian State; and it cannot have provided the main reason for this form of exclu- sion, from *harbours* alone.

I now have a suggestion to make which may at first sight seem absurd to those who have always accepted the commercial interpretation of the Megarian decree, but which will be seen, on closer inspection, not only to fit the source evidence better but also to make the Athenian action in passing the exclusion decree seem less foolish than it normally does. My

[95] *Peripl. M. Rubr.*, esp. 7, 9, 12, 15, 24, 25, 26, 39.
[96] See *Id.* 3,7.

suggestion is that the Peiraeus was perhaps not included among 'the harbours of the empire'. The arguments are as follows:

1. First, it can be shown that according to the natural interpretation of the evidence of the sources, 'the harbours of the empire' (or 'the harbours which the Athenians control') ought not to have included the Peiraeus. Everyone has simply assumed that it must have been included, but I have been trying to guard against assumptions which seem 'obvious' and to test them against the evidence. Thucydides uses the word *archē* dozens of times in the broad sense of 'empire': the fundamental idea expressed by the word when used in this sense is not just 'rule' but 'rule *beyond one's own proper borders*', whether by Athens, or by Sparta, Philip I of Macedon, Sitalces the Odrysian, the King of Persia, or Carthage.[97] In most cases, when he applies the word *archē* to Athens, Thucydides either means 'rule', 'dominion', in the abstract,[98] or it is hardly possible to say which is uppermost in his mind: the abstract 'dominion' of Athens, or her 'dominions' in a geographical sense.[99] Throughout the latter group of passages Thucydides seems to be thinking of Athens' power *beyond her own proper borders*. I can find no single case in Thucydides in which the expression *archē*, when applied to Athens, need include Attica, and there are at least two passages in which it cannot. In I 35.4, 'from your *archē*' is plainly equivalent to 'from your subjects' in §3 of the same chapter. And, very significantly, on the one occasion when Thucydides uses the expression 'the whole *archē* of the Athenians', VIII 96.4 (*hē Athēnaiōn archē pasa*), it clearly does not include Attica. It is also interesting to find that when Thucydides makes Alcibiades refer to an alleged Athenian plan to conquer Carthage and her empire (VI 90.2) he draws an explicit distinction between the empire and Carthage itself (*tēs Karchēdoniōn archēs kai autōn apopeirasontes*). The inscriptions seem to me to tell the same story. The expression they usually apply to the empire (the expression which may well have been used in the Megarian decree itself: see Appendix XXXVIII) is not 'archē' but something like 'the cities which the Athenians control', or 'rule' (*tōn poleōn hōn Athēnaioi kratousi*, or *archousi*); and as a rule this area seems to be distinguished from the State of Athens and does not clearly include Attica in any inscription I know.

2. Secondly, on my interpretation of the Megarian decree, the Athenians had no intention of stopping even Megarian citizens from trading in Attica. I see no reason why they should have wished to ban Megarians from the harbour of Peiraeus, if they were to be allowed to enter Attica and even the agora of Peiraeus itself; and I believe that the *archē* from the harbours of which the Megarians were to be banned was probably the

[97] For Athens, see the next two notes; for Sparta, Thuc. VI 82.3; for Philip I, Thuc. II 100.3; for Sitalces, II 96.3; 97.1; 98.1; for the King of Persia, VIII 48.4; for Carthage, VI 90.2.

[98] As e.g. in III 37.2; 39.2; 40.2,4; 45.6; 47.5, to mention only a single group, in the Mytilenaean Debate.

[99] As e.g. in I 144.1, with II 65.7; II 36.2; VI 10.5; 17.7; 18.2; VII 66.2; and cf. the passages cited in n. 97 above.

archē in the strict sense, excluding Attica, and excluding therefore the Peiraeus.

To be fair to my interpretation of the Megarian decree, one must be prepared to look at each element of it on the basis that the others are as I have stated them. To anyone who goes on thinking of the 'agora' clause of the decree in terms of an exclusion from the 'market' of Athens (or, for that matter, from 'buying and selling' in Attica, or from the whole of Attica) my explanation of the 'harbours' clause may well seem strained, even ridiculous. But if that explanation is to be judged fairly, the 'agora' clause must be conceived as referring to the civic Agora. And then, since the Athenians—sensibly enough—will not even have been preventing the Megarian peasant from selling his salt, fresh vegetables and the like in Athens itself (except in the actual Agora) or in the agora of the Peiraeus, all I have said here becomes easily understandable, and we can admit the probable exception of the Peiraeus from 'the harbours of the empire' which the texts independently support. In a world without adequate means of refrigeration, sensible men would hardly wish to delay imports of perishable goods from their nearest neighbour.

I doubt if the allies of Athens felt much indignation at being told to exclude Megarians from their harbours. If the Samians, for instance, wanted what Megarian traders brought, or had things to sell to them, they could easily arrange for the necessary exchanges to take place elsewhere than in their harbour, or through the medium of Samian or other traders.

It has been suggested to me that exclusion from the harbours of the empire 'really' meant complete exclusion from the empire. This seems to me absurd. Again, there is no doubt at all what the sources say: they all refer to the harbours. If the Athenians had wanted to exclude the Megarians from the whole empire, they could have done so. If they in fact excluded from the harbours alone, then the remainder of allied territory was still open to the Megarians. It was not quite so easy for them to reach it, but it was far from impossible.

It has also been suggested to me that when the Megarians were excluded from the harbours of the empire they would not have dared to venture into the Athenian-controlled Aegean and Propontis at all, because of the danger of being caught by a storm and then having no harbour to take refuge in. This objection seems to me to have little force when we remember that although a safe harbour (*limēn* in Greek, *portus* in Latin) was of course the best of all places at which an ancient ship could come to land, the Greeks (and Romans) knew another kind of resting place: the *hormos* or *salos* (*statio* in Latin), including any anchorage (*ankyrobolion*) and even a mere beach (*aigialos*).[100] Ulpian defines a 'statio' as 'ubicumque naves

[100] The Athenian fleet was moored on an open beach at Aegospotami in 405: Xen., *HG* II i.25; Plut., *Lys.* 10.5–6. This could be dangerous, in the event of a sudden storm: see Diod. XIV 94.3. For a discussion of all the Greek and Latin words referring to harbours, anchorages, etc., see Jean Rougé, *Recherches sur l'organisation du commerce maritime en Méditerranée sous l'emp. rom.* (Paris, 1966) 107–19.

cuto stare possunt'.[101] A prohibition from entering harbours would not of itself debar from the use of *hormoi*, and it seems to me unlikely that the Megarian decree referred specifically to *hormoi*, because it would be difficult to enforce an exclusion from these (unlike harbours), and if the Athenians had wanted to go as far as that, they would surely have gone the whole hog and excluded Megarians from the empire altogether.

(ix)
The offer to repeal the Megarian decree

It is seldom observed that the Athenians, in response to the final Spartan embassy in the winter of 432/1, did offer to repeal the Megarian decree, as demanded by Sparta (Thuc. 1 144.2, with 145; cf. 139.1; 140.3–4). Holding to the policy recommended by Pericles, of refusing merely to submit to Spartan dictation (140.2—141.1), they asked for one small but significant concession in return: that the Spartans should abstain from their 'expulsions of foreigners' (*xenēlasiai*; cf. Part vii of this Chapter and its n. 76)—not entirely, but *in regard to the Athenians and their allies*. (As Pericles is made by Thucydides to emphasise, neither the decree nor the *xenēlasiai* contravened the Peace.) Modern historians have rarely condescended to pay attention to this offer, even if they have mentioned it in passing. Thus Gomme (*HCT* 1 462) quotes only the words *Lakedaimonioi xenēlasias*, with the comment, 'a new point, and not a very good one'; and other scholars have shown equally little disposition to take the offer seriously. (I have discovered only one exception to this rule: Bickerman, APT 320, who deals with the matter admirably.) But surely the Athenian offer was entirely reasonable: the Spartans could not of course be expected to give up their traditional custom altogether, but, if they had any genuine desire to avoid war, why should they not make a formal exception for members of the Athenian alliance? The very fact that the Athenians made this qualification, and did not simply ask for the abandonment of the practice of *xenēlasia* in general, is in favour of our taking their proposal seriously. By ignoring the Athenian offer, one may feel, the Spartans forfeited all right to complain that the Megarian decree was a breach of the Peace.

[101] Dig. XLIII xii.1.13. Note Lentulus Spinther's despatch of 29 May, 43 B.C. (Cic., *Ad Fam.* XII xv.2), which speaks of his army as being excluded by the Rhodians 'urbe, portu, statione quae extra urbem est, commeatu, aqua denique', a list which may bring to mind Thuc. VI 44.2. And see Poll. 1 99–101.

VIII

Conclusion

The predominant view among historians in recent years has been that Athens was the aggressor in the Peloponnesian war, and that she forced war on a reluctant Sparta. As I have made clear, I cannot accept that view at all: I think it has no basis in fact and is founded upon a series of mis-understandings, in particular of the Megarian decree and of the use of the expression *anankasai* by Thucydides I 23.6. Many recent writers have simply taken for granted a whole series of assumptions about Athenian policy in the second half of the fifth century the truth of which has seemed to them self-evident. My disagreement with much modern scholarship in this field is often about the assumptions from which it proceeds, usually unformulated or mentioned only casually; and this makes it all the harder to disprove the theories I am attacking. My aim in these pages has been to make a completely fresh start, discarding the assumptions to which I have objected, and beginning from the best ancient evidence. I would claim that the picture I have drawn is thoroughly based upon the evidence of our most reliable sources, Thucydides above all, and that anyone who dislikes that picture had better begin by trying to discredit Thucydides, if he can.

In so far as anyone can be held *immediately* responsible for the outbreak of the war which did so much to eat away the great achievements of fifth-century Greece, I think it is the Spartans (and their allies, in particular the Corinthians) who must bear the blame. We know from Thucydides (VII 18.2–3) that the Spartans themselves later realised they had been at fault in 432–1. It may well be that the Spartans and most of their allies conceived themselves as fighting to stop Athens from further aggrandise-ment, which might take place at their expense; but this, of course, does not excuse them from breaking the Thirty Years Peace and resorting to war.

It is a much more difficult task to allocate the ultimate responsibility for the war: as so often, our judgment is bound to be subjective, and it involves too many imponderables. All States, as Thucydides realised so well (see Chapter I, Part ii above), always do what they believe to be in their own best interests; and all we can do is to hope that those interests will be intelligently assessed, and that they will coincide as far as possible with those of the majority of mankind.

We might begin by pointing out that the dynamic, explosive, volatile factor in the situation was Athenian democracy, the imperialistic demo-cracy which struck fear into the hearts of all Greek oligarchs, at Sparta and elsewhere. During the Pentecontaetia Athens pursued her own imperial policy, although for some time—until after the ostracism of Cimon early in 461—she was careful to avoid any direct conflict with the Peloponnesians. If Athens is to be given part of the blame for the eventual conflict of 432/1, it is above all those who controlled her policy between the years 461 and 446 who must presumably bear it. Precisely how the First Peloponnesian war broke out, *c.* 460, we do not know. At any rate, Athens and the Peloponnesians conducted very intermittent hostilities for some six years, *c.* 460 to *c.* 454, although very little happened after 457–6 (see the end of Chapter V, Part vi above). I have argued in Appendix X that there is nothing definite to connect Pericles with the policy of creating a 'land empire' (by establishing control of the Megarid and of Boeotia and Phocis), which must have been a major bone of contention between Athens and Sparta. However that may be, the 'land empire' was certainly lost for ever in 446, although Athens did emerge from the First Peloponnesian war with one very important gain: Aegina, conquered in 457, and expressly listed on the Athenian side by the Thirty Years Peace. After the Peace, the power of Athens gradually grew again, and her financial reserves were built up anew; this aroused alarm among the Peloponnesians. While Sparta was ready, in 440 and again in 432, to break the oaths she had sworn, as were some of her allies (in 432 the majority), Athens kept strictly to the terms of the treaty. It was no part of the policy of Pericles and those who, with him, guided Athenian policy in the years between 446/5 and 432 to provoke a renewal of the war with Sparta and her allies—a war which Athens could have little or no hope of winning. It may be said that Athens was inflexible in her policy and would make no concessions to the Peloponnesians in 432/1; but it is difficult to see what concession she could have made without giving an impression of fear and weakness which Sparta would have been likely to exploit immediately. Athens did in fact offer to repeal the Megarian decree (on which Sparta laid special emphasis) if the Spartans on their side would make a reasonable concession in return (see Chapter VII, Part ix above).

Sparta was a strongly conservative power, interested primarily in keeping the Peloponnese under control, and not often, until the late fifth century and the early fourth, venturing far outside it. We might well ask why the Spartans needed to break the Peace and fight in 432/1; and we might then be tempted to reply that the one compelling reason was Sparta's uniquely dangerous position as mistress of the Messenian Helots: she was the one Greek State which held in a degrading servile status a very large number of fellow-Greeks (see Chapter IV, Part i above). Sparta could not take the risks which an ordinary Greek State might afford: she could not allow another city to reach a position of power from which it could threaten either herself or even her allies. It is probable that by the summer of 432 something like a majority of Spartans had already made up their minds to attack Athens, in spite of the powerful opposition of King Archidamus. And when in 432 Sparta's allies, led by Corinth, demanded action by Sparta against Athens, with a threat to secede if she did not act, the great majority of Spartans needed no further persuasion. Sparta had to fight to keep her League together, not only in order to keep open the one land exit from the Peloponnese, through the territories of Corinth and Megara, but even more because she needed to seal off the whole peninsula from the outside world. If a superior army ever invaded Laconia and Messenia (as in 370/69 and the years following), Sparta would lose control of Messenia and cease to be the strongest power in Greece. The Helot danger was the curse Sparta had brought upon herself, an admirable illustration of the maxim that a people which oppresses another cannot itself be free.

APPENDIX I

The terms of the Thirty Years Peace

I know of no complete and correct account of the terms of the Thirty Years Peace by any modern scholar. In the current 'standard work', Bengtson, *SVdA* II 156 (pp. 74–6), as in its predecessor, R. von Scala, *Die Staatsverträge des Altertums* I 63 (pp. 46–8), there is one important omission: clause 4 below. The words ἔχειν δὲ ἑκατέρους ἃ ἔχομεν (ἔχουσι, of course, in the actual treaty) should have been added at the end of Thuc. I 140.2 (at the foot of p. 75 of Bengtson's work). Historians have often failed to realise the importance of this provision, in particular its relevance to the revolt of Potidaea in 432 and the role of Corinth therein (cf. Chapter III, Part iii above).

The terms of the Peace which are certain are as follows:

1. It was to last for thirty years (Thuc. I 115.1 etc.; Paus. v xxiii.4; and other sources).

2. Athens was to give up Nisaea, Pagae, Troezen, and Achaea (Thuc. I 115.1).

3. Neither side was to make an armed attack on the other, if the latter wished to go to arbitration (Thuc. VII 18.2: ὅπλα μὴ ἐπιφέρειν, ἢν δίκας ἐθέλωσι διδόναι: cf. I 85.2). In Chapter VII, Part v, I have explained why this formulation (essentially a 'Nichtangriffsformel': Nesselhauf, DVPK 288) must be closer to the original wording than the vague statement in Thuc. I 140.2: δίκας ... τῶν διαφορῶν ἀλλήλοις διδόναι καὶ δέχεσθαι. (Cf. also I 78.4; 86.3; 144.2; 145.)

4. Each side was to keep what it possessed at the date of the conclusion of the treaty (Thuc. I 140.2: see above)—after the clause numbered 2 above had been complied with, of course. A 'revolt' by an ally on either side and its reception into alliance on the other side might well lead to an immediate claim that the receiving side had broken the treaty, even before any actual hostilities took place.

5. Lists of the allies on each side were annexed to the treaty: this is guaranteed by the reference to ἄγραφοι πόλεις in Thuc. I 40.2 (see no. 6 below).

6. Any state not so listed (an ἄγραφος πόλις) could ally itself with either side (Thuc. I 35.2; 40.2). It seems likely that this clause did not apply to Argos, in view of no. 7 below.

7. Argos was not included in the treaty but was specifically mentioned, with the provision that she and Athens could establish friendly relations if they so wished (ἰδίᾳ δὲ Ἀθηναίους καὶ Ἀργείους, ἢν ἐθέλωσιν, ἐπιτηδείως ἔχειν πρὸς ἀλλήλους): see Paus. v xxiii.4, who saw the bronze stele at Olympia. Presumably, Athens was not to receive Argos into military alliance. (Argos, of course, had entered into a thirty-year truce with Sparta in 451/50: Thuc. v 14.4; 22.2; 28.2; 40.3.)

There may have been some specific clause about Aegina (cf. Thuc. I 67.2; 139.1; 140.3); but this is very doubtful. According to Gomme (*HCT* I 225–6), the Aeginetans in Thuc. I 67.2 could be referring to the treaty between Aegina and Athens (*c.* 457), 'and 144.2, εἰ καὶ αὐτονόμους ἔχοντες ἐσπεισάμεθα, perhaps supports this'; but surely the *spondai* in I 67.2 are more probably the Thirty Years Peace. It is possible that there was some general clause in the Peace, providing for the autonomy of the allies on both sides. (Such a clause may have been suggested by the Spartans, who were now abandoning their own former ally

Aegina to Athens, and may have felt such a provision to be necessary to satisfy their honour.) But when the Spartans made their final demand that Athens should 'allow the Greeks to be autonomous', in the winter of 432/1, we are not told that they added, 'in accordance with the Treaty'. A separate clause in the Thirty Years Peace providing for Aegina's autonomy is not impossible. The question is best left open.

A clause in the Peace specifically providing for 'free trade' has been inferred from Thuc. I 67.4, on the basis of the standard interpretation of the Megarian decree, by several scholars, including Eduard Meyer, *GdA* IV i³⁻⁵.588; ii³⁻⁴.16–17; *FAG* II 303; Glotz-Cohen, *HG* II 165, and others. Beloch in one place (*GG* II² i.183) asserts the existence of such a clause, but in another (*Id.* 293) he admits that there may not have been one, adding that free trade in peace time would have been taken for granted anyway. Busolt (*GG* III i.437; ii.832–3) thought there must have been some rather general provision which was open to different interpretations, and that it is doubtful whether the Megarian decree was a breach of the Treaty. Nesselhauf (DVPK, esp. 289–91, 297) denies that there was a specific clause and makes the rival Peloponnesian and Athenian views as to whether the Megarian decree was a breach of the Treaty turn upon the significance of the words σπονδὰς εἶναι, which must have stood at the beginning of the Treaty. See also Völkl, MP 331–3; Kagan, *OPW* 266–7. On my interpretation of the Megarian decree, of course, the question whether the decree was a breach of the Peace can hardly be resolved into the question whether the Treaty contained a provision for 'free trade'; but I may say that I certainly cannot believe in such a provision, especially as there is nothing resembling it in the Peace of Nicias (Thuc. V 18) or the Truce of 423 (IV 118), and indeed no useful parallel of any kind can be quoted, as far as I know. On Pericles' analogy between the Megarian decree and the Spartan practice of *xenēlasia* (I 144.2), which is more relevant, see Chapter VII, Part vii above.

Since I have emphasised that it was the Spartans who broke the Peace in 432–1, I should add that they had entered into it quite freely and not as a result of military pressure from Athens. The Spartans could not complain that they had not been willing parties to the Peace.

APPENDIX II

'The Peloponnesian war' and kindred expressions

The earliest occurrences I have been able to find in Greek and Latin literature of the expression 'the Peloponnesian war', ὁ Πελοποννησιακὸς πόλεμος, are in Diod. XII 37.2; 38.1; 41.1; XIII 107.5 etc.; Strabo XIII i.39, p. 600; and Cicero, *De Rep.* III 44; *De Offic.* I 84 (cf. Paus. IV vi.1 and Ael., *VH* XII 53: ὁ Πελοποννήσιος πόλεμος). The expression occurs earlier at least once in an epigraphic source: *IG* II² 1035.41, of the early first century B.C., where the reading [-Πελοπον]νησιακῶι πολέμωι is certain.

Thucydides speaks in his opening sentence of 'the war of the Peloponnesians and Athenians' (I 1.1; cf. II 1.1 etc.). Regarded from the Athenian side, it is of course 'the war against the Peloponnesians' (ὁ πρὸς Πελοποννησίους πόλεμος, I 44.2 etc.; cf. πόλεμος Δωρικός/Δωριακός, in II 54.2,3); and from the Peloponnesian side it is 'the war against the Athenians' (ὁ πόλεμος ὁ πρὸς Ἀθηναίους, VIII 18.2; 37.4 etc.; cf. ὁ Ἀττικὸς πόλεμος in V 28.2; 31.3,5). Sometimes geographical expressions are employed: 'the Mantinean and Epidaurian war' (v 26.2, referring to v 53 ff.); 'the Ionian war' (VIII 11.3); 'the war from Decelea' (VII 27.2; 'the Decelean war', ὁ Δεκελεικὸς πόλεμος, seems to occur first in Isocr. VIII 37; XIV 31). Doubtless it is the whole of the last stage of the war, from 412 to 404, which is referred to by Thucydides IV 81.2 as 'the war later in time, after the events in Sicily' (τὸν χρόνῳ ὕστερον μετὰ τὰ ἐκ Σικελίας πόλεμον). Against the views of Steup and other scholars, I agree with Gomme that there is no reason to take this and similar passages to have been written before Thucydides reached his conception of a single war: see *HCT* III 549, and 497 (where the reference to Adcock should be to *CAH* v 481).

The inappropriate expression 'the Archidamian war' is found as early as Lysias, fr. IX (Thalheim), for the Ten Years war: it is often still used in this sense. It is one of the ironies of history that the name of King Archidamus should have become attached to a war which he had opposed and scarcely half of which had elapsed when Archidamus died, in 427/6! I have avoided the expression and have spoken of the war of 431–21 as 'the Ten Years war', as Thucydides does (v 25.1; 26.3; cf. 25.3; 26.6).

Writers of the fourth century B.C. often speak of the various episodes of the Peloponnesian war (c. 460–46, 431–21, 419–18, and 415 ff.—or 415–13 and 413 ff.) as separate wars: see e.g. Andoc. III 3–9, 29, 30, 31; Aeschin. II 172–6. Most interesting is Plato, *Menex.* 242a–3d, where we have first the battles of Tanagra and Oenophyta (242abc), then the Ten Years war (242cde), and finally a 'third war', apparently 415–404 (242e–3ab).

APPENDIX III

Modern work on Thucydides

The best brief general appraisal of the historian, in my opinion, is P. A. Brunt's Introduction (pp. ix-xxxiv) to his abbreviated and improved version of Jowett's translation, *Thucydides. The Peloponnesian Wars* (New York, 1963), in the series, 'The Great Histories' (ed. H. R. Trevor-Roper). The main books in English are J. H. Finley, *Thucydides* (Cambridge, Mass., 1942); and Jacqueline de Romilly, *TAI* (= *TIA²*, the French original, with additions). Twenty-six articles in German and other languages published between 1930 and 1965 have been reprinted (all in German) in *Thukydides* (*Wege der Forschung* 98, ed. Hans Herter, Darmstadt, 1968). De Romilly, *TAI* 380–3, repeats the select bibliography given in *TIA²* 307–10; *TAI* 384–6 adds a list of recent studies mentioned in the 'Additional Remarks' not included in *TIA²*. See also F. M. Wassermann, 'Thucydidean Scholarship 1942–1956', in *CW* 50.5 (1956) 65–70; 50.7 (1957) 89–101; M. Chambers, 'Studies on Thucydides, 1957–1962', in *CW* 57.1 (1963–64) 6–14; G. T. Griffith, in *Fifty Years (and Twelve) of Classical Scholarship* (ed. M. Platnauer, Oxford, 1968) 188–92, 229–32; Bengtson, *GG⁴* 222–3; Stahl, *Thuk.* 172–9; and the long bibliography (cols. 1323–38) in O. Luschnat's article on Thucydides in *RE* Suppl. XII (1970) cols. 1085–1354, which unfortunately came to my notice only when this book was finished. I have found most enlightenment from Andrewes, MDPLS and MD, and Andrewes' discussion of the Melian Dialogue in Gomme, *HCT* IV 182–8; Karl Weidauer, *THS*; D. L. Page, in *CQ* 47 = n.s. 3 (1953), at pp. 98–110 (not the section on the nature of the Plague); and Shorey, IEPT.

As for the problem of the date of composition of the various parts of the History ('the Thucydides problem' *par excellence*, as many would mistakenly regard it), an account of the earlier part of the long controversy, which began with Ullrich in 1845–6, is given succinctly by Busolt, *GG* III ii (1904) 632–43; for a selection of later works, see G. De Sanctis, *Storia dei greci* II (1939) 434–6. English readers will find a survey dating from 1911 in Grundy, *THA* I² 397–402, part of a not very successful appendix, 'The Composition of Thucydides' History', pp. 387–534. Apart from Busolt's, the most important contributions have been those of Meyer, *FAG* II (1899) 269–96; E. Schwartz, *Das Geschichtswerk des Thuk.* (Bonn, 1919, 1929²); M. Pohlenz, in *GGN* (1919) 95–138; (1920) 56–68 and 68–82; and *GGA* 194 (1932) 21–33; 198 (1936) 281–300 (all these papers were reprinted in Pohlenz' *Kleine Schr.* II [Hildesheim, 1965] 210–313); F. E. Adcock, in *CAH* v (1927) 190–1, 480–3, but contrast his changed views (an improvement, I believe) in 'Thuc. in Book I', in *JHS* 71 (1951) 2–12; W. Schadewalt, *Die Geschichtschreibung des Thukydides* (Leipzig, 1929); Patzer, *PGST*; J. H. Finley, *TET*; Andrewes, TCW. And see Schmid, in Schmid-Stählin, *GGL* I v.127 ff. But I warmly agree with the opinion of de Romilly, *TAI* 6: 'Exhausting by the immense bibliography which it offers, completely negative in its results, the question of the composition of the work can at present be considered as the perfect example of a vain and insoluble problem.'

The bibliography on the problems presented by the speeches is also enormous: see many of the works cited in the last two paragraphs (esp. Andrewes, MD, and de Romilly, *TAI*) and in Chapter I, Part ii above. At one extreme, H. Strasburger (TPSDA, first paragraph) remarks that 'mehrere gute und längst beachtete Gründe sprechen dafür, dass der Anteil freier Erfindung mindestens stark überweigt'; he goes on to specify those grounds, and he concludes that but for Thucydides' own statement in I 22.1, 'so hätte sich die Forschung wohl schon längst und endgültig dafür entscheiden, die thukydideischen Reden für ebenso frei vom Historiker komponiert zu halten'. At almost the other extreme is the position adopted by Gomme, whose paper on 'The Speeches in Thucydides' in his *EGHL* 156–89 begins, 'There is this apparent advantage in the dogmatic announcement that Thucydides' speeches are free inventions, that it saves further thought; they may be ignored by the historian of the Peloponnesian war, as those of Dionysios or Livy are in early Roman history. Yet a moment's reflexion will show that the economy is more apparent than real'. Gomme minimises Thucydides' own contribution to the speeches, apart from their linguistic style: this comes out even more clearly in his *HCT* I 140–8, where he adopts an inadmissible interpretation of τὰ δέοντα in I 22.1 (see Chapter I, Part ii above, esp. its n. 10). Kagan (*OPW* ix) takes a view which is not very different from Gomme's: he can even quote with approval a version of Crawley's translation of I 22.1, 'adhering as closely as possible to *the general sense of* what they really said', omitting the four essential words which I have italicised! It will be evident that I am not entirely satisfied with any of the existing accounts; but anyone not already acquainted with the literature could hardly do better than begin with Walbank, *SGH* (whose only fault, in my opinion, is a failure to reject firmly Gomme's translation of τὰ δέοντα).

Gomme's valuable commentary (*HCT*) is to be completed by Andrewes, with a fifth volume, on Book VIII.

APPENDIX IV

Moments of decision in Thucydides

My impression is that the great moments of decision referred to in the text above (Chapter I, Part ii) occupy a far greater proportion of the space in the History of Thucydides than in any other historical work from antiquity—and perhaps any other time.

They include (1) the Athenian decision whether or not to ally with Corcyra in 433 (I 31–44); (2) the decision of the Spartan Assembly whether or not to declare war on Athens in 432 (67–88), and (3) the subsequent debate on the same issue in the Peloponnesian League Congress (119–25); (4) the Athenian discussion of what they should do in response to Sparta's demands (139–45); (5) the debate at Athens in 430 on whether to renew the attempt to obtain peace terms from Sparta (II 59–65); (6) the negotiations between Archidamus and the Plataeans in 429 (71–4); (7) the discussion at Olympia in 428 on whether the Peloponnesians should support the revolt of Lesbos against Athens (III 8–15); (8) the 'Mytilenaean Debate' at Athens on the suppression of the Lesbian revolt in 427 (36–48); (9) the argument in the same year before five Spartan judges concerning the fate of the Plataeans (52–68); (10) the discussion in the Athenian Assembly during the Pylos affair of 425 whether or not to conclude a peace with Sparta (IV 16–22); (11) the 'Congress of Gela' in 424 (58–65); (12) the negotiations between Brasidas and the Acanthians, also in 424, on whether Acanthus should surrender (84–8); (13) the differences of opinion in the Boeotian camp at Tanagra, when the Athenians had begun to return from Delium in 424, on whether it would be advisable to offer battle (91–3), and (14) the subsequent contention between the Boeotians and Athenians (97–9); (15) the 'Melian Dialogue' of 416 (v 84–112); (16) the second debate at Athens in 415 on the Sicilian expedition (VI 8–26); (17) the subsequent debate in the Syracusan Assembly (32–41); (18) the council of Athenian generals on the proper tactics to be pursued in Sicily (47–50); (19) the debate at Camarina on what course that city should adopt (75–88); (20) the Spartan Assembly addressed by Alcibiades, in 415 (88–93); (21) the Athenian reception of Nicias' letter in 414/13 (VII 10–16); (22) the Athenian Assembly in 412, addressed by Peisander, which voted for negotiations with Tissaphernes and Alcibiades (VIII 53–4); (23) the resulting negotiations at the court of Tissaphernes (56); (24) the reception at Samos of the news of the 'Revolution of the Four Hundred' (73–7), and (25) the later debate there (81–2); (26) the putting down of the 'Four Hundred' at Athens (89–93, 97). This ignores a whole number of minor incidents of the same kind (e.g. the shifts of policy in the Peloponnesian states in 421–18, in Book V).

APPENDIX V

'To have the same friends and enemies', and the nature of the Delian League oaths and synods

In this Appendix I propose to deal with a series of questions, falling into three groups:

A. What form of oath was sworn by the parties to the Delian League at its foundation in 478/7?

B. What purposes was the League intended to have?

C. What was the position of the hegemon, Athens, in relation to the League synods? Did Athens *only* have one vote, like each of the other allies, and was she thus, in matters affecting the League, subject to the decisions of its synods? Or should we conceive her as being (like Sparta in relation to the Peloponnesian League, or Athens herself in relation to her Second Confederacy in the fourth century) in a position of equality with all the other allied states together, so that all League decisions required the consent both of the Athenian Assembly and of the League Synod?

A. I accept Thucydides 1 44.1 as evidence that by the 430s at any rate *the characteristic* form of oath of a symmachy was 'to have the same friends and enemies' (τοὺς αὐτοὺς ἐχθροὺς καὶ φίλους νομίζειν, or τὸν αὐτὸν ἐχθρὸν εἶναι καὶ φίλον).[1] And since, as will appear, there is not the least reason to doubt, as some have done, the statement of Aristotle, *Ath. Pol.* 23.5, that the oaths of the Delian League took that form, I shall confine myself here to symmachies which are known to have had, or can safely be presumed to have had, oaths of that particular type.

Greek symmachies have been analysed in various different ways,[2] but I know of no really satisfactory treatment. I think it is fruitful to begin by drawing a fundamental distinction between two very different classes of symmachy based on the standard oath 'to have the same friends and enemies'. First, there is what I shall call 'Type *A*', in which one or more subordinate states swear 'to have the same friends and enemies' as the hegemon, unilaterally, without receiving a similar pledge in return, and thus in effect commit their foreign policies in large measure to the dictation of the hegemon. The subordinate states may also swear to follow the hegemon whithersoever it directs. The most obvious example is the Peloponnesian League treaties, dealt with in Chapter IV, Part iv, Section B, esp. §3 (a) above.

---

[1] The form of oath may derive from Hittite precedents, perhaps through Lydia: see Schwahn, in *RE*, 2te Reihe iv i (1931) 1107–9, *s.v. Symmachia* (3). Among Hittite treaties, there is a clear example of the 'same friends and enemies' clause in the treaty between Subbiluliuma of Hatti and Tette of Nuhassi (E. F. Weidner, *Politische Dokumente aus Kleinasien. Die Staatsverträge in akkadischer Sprache aus dem Archiv von Boghazköi = Boghazköi-Studien* 8 [Leipzig, 1923] 58 ff., no. 3, at pp. 60–1). This is a 'vassal-treaty', not a 'parity-treaty' (for the distinction, see D. J. Wiseman, *The Vassal-Treaties of Esarhaddon* [London, 1958, repr. from *Iraq*, 1958] 27–8). The formula is restored in the treaty between Mursilis II of Hatti and Duppi-Tessub (Dubbi-Tesup) of Amurru, in J. B. Pritchard, *Ancient Near Eastern Texts Relating to the Old Testament*[3] (Princeton, 1969) 204, §9, from Weidner's Akkadian and J. Friedrich's Hittite texts. See also the treaty between Subbiluliuma and Aziru of Amurru (Weidner, *op. cit.* 70–1, no. 4; Pritchard, *op. cit.* 529–30), and that between Subbiluliuma and Mattiuaza of Mitanni (Weidner, *op. cit.* 20–1, no. 1.72–3); and cf. Weidner, *op. cit.* 106–7.

[2] See in particular Schwahn, *op. cit.* 1102–34; V. Martin, *VIGC* 126–281 (esp. 138–41), 354–91 (esp. 371–7); Busolt-Swoboda, *GSK* ii 1254 ff.; Ehrenberg, *GS*[2] 111–20.

Here it is certain that from at least the late fifth century Sparta's allies swore to have the same friends and enemies as herself and to follow her whithersoever she might lead; and I have maintained (contrary to the usual view) that an oath in this form must have been sworn by Sparta's Peloponnesian allies as early as the sixth century (probably from the middle of that century), although the subordination of the allies to Sparta was greatly modified when the allies were allowed, in effect, a right of veto against certain Spartan decisions, by majority votes taken in the League Congress. (Once the League Congress came into existence, indeed, and so long as it worked effectively, the Peloponnesian League belonged rather more to my second group of symmachies, Type *B*, than to Type *A*.)[3] Other examples are known. One of the best, where the content of the oath is known in detail from an inscription, is a Cretan treaty, between Gortyn and Lappa, of the second century B.C.: *Inscr. Cret.* IV 186 B (= *SGDI* 5018 = Michel, *RIG* 17); cf. lines 3–10 with 10–15. Here, as in the Peloponnesian League treaties, the inferior party, namely Lappa, swears specifically both to follow the superior (Gortyn) wherever it directs and to have the same friend and enemy, whereas the superior city does not use either of these formulae, but merely pledges military assistance in case of certain forms of attack on its *protégé*. Other clear cases of this type of symmachy are the Athenian-Bottiaean alliance of 422, *SVdA* II 187 (= *SEG* x 89 = Tod I² 68 = *IG* I² 90), lines 16–21 with 11–16; and the treaty between Ptolemaeus of Macedon and the Boeotians ('Thebans': Plut., *Pelop.* 27.3 = *SVdA* II 277) of 368 B.C. Presumably it is this kind of symmachy which we also find in *Inscr. Cret.* III iii.5 (= *SGDI* 5039) between Hierapytna and its colony, of the second century B.C., where the oath of the colony only is preserved (see esp. line 17) and may have been the only one given; and also in two Athenian treaties of the late fifth century: that with Perdiccas of Macedon,[4] *SVdA* II 186 (= *IG* I² 71 = *SEG* x 86 = XII 16 = XVI 4 = XIX 11), which has been variously dated between the early 430s and 423/2 (see Appendix XI); and the proposed alliance between Athens and Thurii in 413 (Thuc. VII 33.6: it probably became a fact, in view of 35.1; 57.11; but it is not included in *SVdA*).

In the other kind of symmachy, which I shall call 'Type *B*', each state binds itself 'to have the same friends and enemies' as the other or others. Among the clearest examples are *SIG³* 633 (§IV), the very well preserved treaty of *c.* 180 B.C. between Miletus and Heraclea, and a Cretan treaty of the second century B.C.: *Inscr. Cret.* III iii.3 B (= *SGDI* 5041 = Michel, *RIG* 29), between Hierapytna and Lyttus or Lyctus (see lines 16 and 22); cf. probably (although the formula is restored in line 4) *Inscr. Cret.* I xvi.5 (= *SGDI* 5075), between Lato and Olus (see lines 3–4 and 73–83, and cf. 4–7 with 7–10).[5] Probably the Athenian-Corcyraean alliance planned in 427[6] to supersede the epimachy of 433 was of this type,

[3] Conversely, the Delian League began as an alliance of Type *B*, but became by degrees, as the Synod became less and less important (eventually disappearing altogether), one of Type *A*.

[4] In an unsatisfactory note (*VIGC* 374 n. 1), V. Martin makes Perdiccas contract with Athens 'on a footing of equality'. I suppose it is just possible that the treaty may have contained a reciprocal oath by Athens 'to have the same friends and enemies' as Perdiccas, to match the oath he gave Athens to that effect in lines 19–20; but I doubt if there is room for this on the stone, even if (as in *SEG* x 86) we make the Athenian oath begin at line 26 instead of 28, and (see *SEG* XII 16) suppose a line of 100 instead of *c.* 68 letters. In so far as the phrasing of the two oaths can be reconstructed, it surely suggests an unequal alliance.

[5] Of the same type was the alliance made in 280–250 B.C. between King Magas of Cyrene and the Oreoi of West Crete, *SVdA* III 468 (= *Inscr. Cret.* II xvii.1), lines 8–9, 9–14; but this seems to have been a mere epimachy (cf. Appendix XIII). Cf. *SVdA* III 469 (= Memnon, *FGrH* 434 F 11.2) and 552, where the formulae used are rather different.

[6] See Thuc. III 70.6; 75.1. It presumably became a fact: see Chapter III, Part ii, n. 10.

although we cannot perhaps be quite certain of this.[7] Such an alliance need not be on a footing of complete equality: one of the parties might be hegemon and have a somewhat superior position, like Athens in relation to her Delian League allies (see below).[8] But at least the formal engagement of this type of symmachy is reciprocal, and none of the parties is entitled to force its own foreign policy on the others.

Some scholars have refused to admit that a symmachy with oaths 'to have the same friends and enemies' could be an equal one, of my Type *B* (at any rate in the fifth century), because they regard this form of oath as necessarily involving subjection (*Untertänigkeit*) and loss of independence (*Selbständigkeit, Unabhängigkeit*): they would treat all symmachies with oaths of this form as belonging to my Type *A*. In Busolt-Swoboda, *GSK* II 1255–6, this position is unqualified (in spite of the fact that among the examples the authors give are the second and third treaties mentioned in the preceding paragraph, which clearly belong to my Type *B*). Schwahn, in *RE*, 2te Reihe, IV i (1931) 1110, *s.v. Symmachia* (3), who realises that the equal symmachy with oaths 'to have the same friends and enemies' could exist in later times (he cites *SIG*³ 633, mentioned above, as the earliest example), is unwilling to accept the statement of Thuc. I 44.1 about the nature of a fifth-century Greek symmachy except in relation to dependent states—although the symmachy desired by the Corcyraeans in 433 was surely of my Type *B*, and Thucydides must therefore have had both types of symmachy in mind. And Schwahn does not, I think, notice Xen., *Anab.* II v.39 (cf. ii.8),[9] a clear example of reciprocal oaths 'to have the same friends and enemies' in 401 B.C.

To which form of symmachy did the Delian League belong? The answer to this question is simply taken for granted by most scholars who have had anything to say about the oaths of alliance. Many, indeed, like Eduard Meyer and Beloch, have paid no attention at all to the oaths, although every Greek alliance was above all what its oaths made it. Sealey (ODL) mentions Arist., *Ath. Pol.* 23.5 in other contexts (the tribute and the *mydroi*), but ignores altogether the oaths (which might have led him to see the whole subject in better perspective), as does Jackson, in a very short paper (OPDL) devoted to refuting Sealey's main point, that 'the League of Delos was founded because of a dispute about booty and its purpose was to get more booty' (ODL 253)—a task it sufficiently accomplishes. Bengtson (*GG*⁴ 192) and Schwahn (*op. cit.* 1119) speak only of a defensive and offensive alliance ('Schutz- und Trutzbündnis'), as do some others.

At one extreme, several scholars have rejected or at least questioned Aristotle's statement about the form of the oath. Busolt (*GG* III i.72 n. 2; *GSK* II 1340 n. 6) was not inclined to accept Aristotle's wording, on the ground that it not only conflicts with what he believed to be Thucydides' account of the purpose of the confederacy but is also incompatible with the autonomy of the allied states. The

---

[7] The charge of 'enslaving Corcyra to Athens' (Thuc. III 70.3; cf. 71.1) would have been peculiarly appropriate if those who brought Peithias to trial had already known that he was planning to bring about a full symmachy with Athens of my Type *A*, with Corcyra in a subordinate position; but Thucydides' language in 70.6 suggests that they only discovered this fact later.

[8] This is why I have avoided giving to either of my two groups the name 'hegemonial alliance,' for which see Ehrenberg, *GS*² 112, 272. Symmachies of either of my groups could have a hegemon. To me it seems more useful to classify according to whether there was formal subordination in foreign policy. I admit that neither the Peloponnesian League nor the Delian League fits neatly into either of my categories: see above, and n. 3.

[9] V. Martin, in the note mentioned in n. 4 above, wrongly refers *Anab.* II v.39 to iii.27; v.3. In fact the passage refers back to the oaths with Ariaeus (the only survivor, after Cunaxa, of Cyrus' immediate lieutenants: see I ix.31), mentioned in ii.8. The oaths referred to in iii.26–8; v.3–7 were with Tissaphernes, as the King's general, and were quite different.

reason for this judgment emerges from *GSK* II 1255–6 (mentioned above): for Busolt, an oath 'to have the same friends and enemies' was necessarily one-sided and possible only in what I have called a symmachy of Type *A*. Much the same view was taken by Hampl (*GSV* 123 n. 1; 124 n. 2), Wüst (in *Historia* 3 [1954–5], at pp. 149–53), and H. Schäfer (*Staatsform und Politik* 67 ff.: his whole thesis is well refuted by Highby, *ED* 58–80). At the other extreme, Hammond (ONAA 50 n. 22)[10] seems unaware that an oath 'to have the same friends and enemies' could exist in a symmachy of my Type *A*. 'To say that two sides have the same enemy and friend', he remarks, 'is to express a reciprocity of relationship (cf. Thuc. I 44.1), not a monopoly by one side'. (The examples of symmachies of Type *A* given above are sufficient to show how groundless this assumption is.) The authors of *ATL* (III 227, cf. 138–9) also regard the oaths of the Delian League as reciprocal,[11] and so evidently does Larsen (COPDL 187 and n. 5).

Our one source which gives the essence of the oaths of the Delian League, namely Arist., *Ath. Pol.* 23.5, says that Aristeides (on behalf of Athens, needless to say) *swore to*[12] the Ionians 'to have the same friend and enemy'; cf. Plut., *Arist.* 25.1, where Aristeides *administered the oath to* (ὥρκισε) the Greeks *and swore on behalf of* (ὥμοσεν ὑπέρ) the Athenians, but the content of the oath is not given, although the sinking of the *mydroi* is mentioned, as by Aristotle. How good Aristotle's authority was we cannot say, but he gives an archon-date (478/7) and is the earliest source (and the only one apart from Plutarch) to mention the ceremony of the *mydroi*. His evidence is clearly against an oath appropriate to a symmachy of my Type *A*, with only the Greeks of Asia,[13] and not Athens, swearing 'to have the same friends and enemies' as the other side. The Delian League was replacing what is usually called the Hellenic League of 481 (which in fact had no official name), and although we do not know the wording of the oaths of that League,[14] we can be reasonably sure that they were not the oaths of a symmachy of my Type *A*, but were fully reciprocal (cf. Brunt, HLP 138–9, whose account in general I accept). The oaths of the Hellenic League were not even between Sparta on the one hand and all the remaining members on the other: the Greeks, 'taking counsel and giving pledges to each other' (Hdts VII 145.1; cf. 148), swore mutual

[10] Yet Hammond refers in the same note to Xen., *HG* II ii.20, which alone is sufficient to falsify his assumption. (I do not understand why he speaks of that passage as showing Athens and Sparta forming 'a *defensive* alliance', in contrast with 'the offensive and defensive alliance' of Arist., *Ath. Pol.* 23.5. In fact the Peloponnesian League, like the Delian League, was an offensive and defensive alliance.)

[11] I cannot understand their statement (*ATL* III 227 n. 6), 'For the bilateral [i.e., reciprocal] nature of the oath cf. Thuc. III 10.6'.

[12] Not 'made the Ionians swear to', as Brunt puts it (HLP 150)—perhaps combining Aristotle with Plut., *Arist.* 25.1.

[13] I can see nothing in the arguments of Hammond (ONAA 45–9) and Sealey (ODL 243–4) that *only* the Ionians took part. Cf. the very sensible remarks of *ATL* III 227 n. 9; Gomme, *HCT* I 257,271–2. Their argument can be greatly strengthened by reference to Thuc. In VIII 86.4 'Ionia and the Hellespont' must mean the whole Greek area in the eastern Aegean, including even the islands (cf. 96.4, where the islands are mentioned separately from the Hellespont and Ionia), and that is surely how we should interpret 'Ionia and the Hellespont' in I 89.2. Cf. VIII 56.4, where 'the whole of Ionia and the neighbouring islands etc.' must mean the whole Greek area except 'the Hellespont'— which, as far as Tissaphernes was concerned, was the sphere of Pharnabazus. According to Hammond (ONAA 47), Thucydides and others are 'scrupulous' in distinguishing Ionians from Aeolians and Dorians. In fact Thucydides at any rate is *sometimes* 'scrupulous', but sometimes not. However, I would not of course wish to deny that the great majority of the allies who joined the Delian League at its inception were Ionians. There is not very much I would disagree with in Highby, *ED* 39–57.

[14] Hdts VII 145.1 (see below) is rather vague, but note οἱ δὲ συνωμόται Ἑλλήνων ἐπὶ τῷ Πέρσῃ in 148.1 and συνομοσάντων ἐπὶ σοί in 235.4. Cf. *SVdA* II 130.

oaths, perhaps including the formula 'to have the same friends and enemies', and very probably some phrase about 'not deserting' (cf. Hdts IX 106.4: ἐμμενέειν τε καὶ μὴ ἀποστήσεσθαι).[15] For the founding members of the Delian League, the oaths of the Hellenic League may have been thought to provide a more appropriate precedent than those of the Peloponnesian League. Of course Athens was going to be hegemon of the Delian League, as Sparta was of the Peloponnesian and (in a rather different way) the Hellenic League; but surely the Delian League was to be more like the Hellenic League than the Peloponnesian, in that its members were not bound to follow Athens 'whithersoever she might lead' but could decide their policy in common synods held at Delos (Thuc. I 96.2; 97.1).

We may safely conclude, then, that the Delian League took the form of an equal symmachy of my Type *B*, if of a rather special kind, between Athens on the one hand and, on the other, those of the Greeks of Asia (mainly, but by no means entirely, Ionians) who had revolted from Persia. Each of the two parties (Athens, and the allies collectively) swore 'to have the same friends and enemies' as the other. The allies could be treated as a single unit because they would decide their policy by majority vote in the Delian synods. In some respects, however, the Delian League differed markedly from the Peloponnesian: for instance, Athens' allies had not sworn 'to follow her whithersoever she might lead', and their decisions are not likely to have been limited at the beginning to the narrow range of matters that could be discussed by Peloponnesian League congresses.

B. We must not interpret Thucydides I 96.1 (πρόσχημα γὰρ ἦν ἀμύνεσθαι ὧν ἔπαθον δῃοῦντας τὴν βασιλέως χώραν; cf. VI 76.3) as giving the *whole real purpose* of the Delian League. The word πρόσχημα, when used in this way, refers not to a person's real intention but to his *public profession*, which always has at least some element of insecurity or falseness. Liddell and Scott rightly translate, 'I. *that which is held before to cover, screen, cloak.* . . .; *pretence, pretext.* . . .; making a *pretence* or *show.* . . .; *pretend.* . . .; put forward *as a screen or disguise.* . . .; as acc. abs., *by way of pretext*'. This is certainly so on the only two other occasions on which the word appears in Thucydides: III 82.4 and V 30.2. Thucydides cannot possibly be using it in I 96.1 as a complete expression of the genuine purpose of the League. His curious choice of word and the concentration on one particular function of the League are understandable only when we realise that the whole clause (as the γάρ shows) is explanatory of the earlier part of the sentence, stating that the Athenians 'decided which allies should provide money against the barbarian, and which ships'. The Delian League ensured regular contributions of naval contingents or money. This needed explaining, because it was quite different from the practice of the Peloponnesian and Hellenic Leagues and indeed was an entirely new departure in Greek alliances. An explanation is therefore given: 'because it was a professed purpose to take revenge for what they had suffered by ravaging the King's territory'. I have deliberately translated, 'it was *a* professed purpose', because Thucydides does not even use the definite article (τὸ γὰρ πρόσχημα ἦν . . . .). His readers, of course, would have known that this side of the League's activities virtually ended with the 450s; and I fancy that his choice of the word πρόσχημα would have left them with the feeling that the talk of revenge through ravaging expeditions was at least partly a cover for ambitious Athenian designs for organising a large, active, powerful and rich alliance under their control.

It was obviously the intention of the allies first to liberate as many Greek states as they could from Persian rule. The statement of the Mytilenaeans in Thuc. III 10.3 that they 'became allies of the Greeks with a view to liberation from the

---

[15] As Brunt says (HLP 157), 'These obligations were not expressly made perpetual, but no date was fixed for their termination. They were left indefinite because no one could predict when they would cease to be needed'. That must be true: everyone would understand that they were 'for the duration'.

Mede' (or 'allies with a view to liberation from the Mede in the interests of Greece': Gomme, *HCT* II 262) is made *ex parte* and rhetorically, perhaps, but there is every reason to accept it as true. And above all we must look at the *nature of the oaths* which created the alliance. The ceremony of sinking the *mydroi* in the sea proves beyond question that the League was intended to be permanent.[16] (See Chapter IV, Part iv, Section B, §2 above for early Greek alliances intended to last for ever.) The nature of the ceremony emerges clearly from Hdts I 165.3; cf. Hor., *Epod.* XVI 17 ff.; Callim. fr. 388.9 (ed. R. Pfeiffer, I 321, with Pfeiffer's notes). This surely justifies our accepting the Delian League as an alliance *designed to secure for ever the freedom of the Greeks from Persian domination*,[17] when as many as possible had been liberated, as well as to take revenge on the Persians by ravaging their territory. But ravaging the King's country was liable to be subject to a law of diminishing returns. The idea of an *eternal* alliance, having 'the same friends and enemies', designed for nothing more than ravaging campaigns of revenge is surely ridiculous.

C. Finally, we can consider the original position of Athens vis-à-vis her allies, especially in the Delian synods. We have to choose between two alternatives: either (I) Athens had nothing but one vote in the synods, like each individual ally, or (II) the Athenian Assembly had a position of equality in relation to all the allies collectively assembled in their Synod, and in this way would have had a position resembling that of Sparta in the Peloponnesian League or of Athens herself in her Second Confederacy. The first view has generally prevailed in recent times: it is held by, among others, the authors of *ATL* (III 138–41, 227), Larsen (COPDL 192–7; *RGGRH* 58), Ehrenberg (*GS²* 114; *SS* 191), Hampl (*GSV* 125) and, though not without hesitation, by Gomme (*HCT* II 264: 'this view may be correct'). Among the few recent upholders of the second view are Victor Martin (*VIGC* 157–8), Hammond (ONAA 52, 57–61), and apparently Walker (in *CAH* V 41). I believe the second view to be right. The arguments, which have never (as far as I can see) been properly stated, are as follows:

1. As Larsen has realised (COPDL 192–4), the evidence about voting in the Delian synods 'is confined to two references in the speech of the Mytilenaeans' in 428: Thuc. III 10.5 and 11.4. The first of these passages presents no problems: the Mytilenaeans are saying that all the allies except themselves and the Chians had been subjected ('enslaved') by Athens, 'being unable to unite and defend themselves, on account of the large number of allies which had votes' (διὰ πολυψηφίαν). In such a situation Athens would be able to control the votes of many insignificant states, which would vote the way they knew she wanted. (Cf. Xen., *HG* v ii.20 for a Peloponnesian League parallel, where 'those who wanted to please the Spartans' spoke in favour of an expedition against Olynthus.) In view of Thuc. III 10.5 and parallel passages concerning the Peloponnesian League (I 125.1; 141.6; V 30.1) there is general agreement nowadays that in the Delian League synods and the Peloponnesian League congresses every ally had one vote and decisions were taken by simple majority. But Thuc. III 10.5 gives us no indication whether Athens herself voted in the synods or not. The one and only ancient source which, as far as I know, has ever been cited, or could be cited, in favour of the first theory mentioned above is Thuc. III 11.4, where the argument centres upon the word ἰσοψήφους. I shall argue at the end of this Appendix that this word has always been misunderstood and provides no evidence at all about the voting in the Delian League synods or the participation of Athens therein.

2. Hammond (ONAA 52, 58) has rightly pointed out that the language of

---

[16] It was therefore not 'left undetermined whether each individual state had, or had not, the right to withdraw from the League at its pleasure' (Walker, in *CAH* v 41–2).

[17] Cf. Appendix VII, on the Peace of Callias and its consequences.

Thuc. I 97.1 is in favour of taking the Delian League synods as consisting *only* of the allies: Athens (the subject of the sentence) was the hegemon of 'allies at first autonomous and deliberating in common synods'. We should perhaps not insist too strongly on the strict interpretation of these words, for Thucydides is expressing himself very tersely; but if the natural interpretation of his statement does not conflict with any other evidence (and we shall see that it does not), we ought to be prepared to accept it, and allow Thucydides to mean exactly what he says, especially when we remember that in the Peloponnesian League and the Second Athenian Confederacy the allies certainly met separately from the hegemon. The Delian League was by the very nature of the oaths which had created it an alliance between two parties: Athens as hegemon, and the allies. And we should certainly expect its 'government' to reflect this situation and not subordinate the hegemon by obliging Athens to accept the votes of a majority of the allies.

3. The nature of the Second Athenian Confederacy is very relevant, and provides a very strong argument in favour of the theory I am advocating. That organisation was founded in 378/7, evidently with the deliberate intention of avoiding the undue predominance of Athens which had characterised the Delian League. Yet the Confederacy, like the Peloponnesian League, was beyond doubt a 'bicameral organisation' (to use Hammond's phrase, *ONAA* 51–2), headed by the Assembly of the hegemon *and* the allied Synedrion: each of these bodies had in effect a right of veto against a decision by the other and all important matters had to be settled by agreement between the two bodies.[18] It is simply inconceivable that in the Second Confederacy Athens would have given herself an equal share in decision-making with all the other allies put together if in the Delian League she had had no more than one single vote, like any other ally: it would have aroused the deepest suspicion. In fact all three of these Leagues were surely alike in one respect: they were all 'bicameral organisations'.[19] The great difference between the Delian League and the Second Athenian Confederacy was that in the latter the allied Synedrion was given much greater influence, above all because (*a*) it could apparently be called together at any time, and not only by Athens, (*b*) it met under the chairmanship of a non-Athenian, and (*c*) the Synedrion, as well as Athens, could take the initiative in proposing action (cf. Accame, *LA* 107–42, 229–30 ff.).

4. It is wildly unrealistic to suppose, in the absence of firm evidence, that Athens should consent—as Sparta never did, nor Athens herself in her Second Confederacy—to have only one vote in synods which were supreme over the allies' foreign policy *and her own*, or that the allies would wish to force such a position upon her. The Delian League synods would surely *want* to know, before deciding each year on their programme, precisely what the hegemon was able and willing to do. They were very dependent upon Athenian leadership and organisation

---

[18] I do not think anyone now accepts the curious theory of Hampl, *GSV* 117–34, that in the Peloponnesian League, the Delian League and the Second Athenian Confederacy the hegemon merely had one vote in the allied Congress/Synod/Synedrion. It is sufficiently refuted by Larsen, *COPDL* 194–6 n. 2, and (as regards the Second Confederacy) by Accame, *LA* 112–15.

[19] Cf. the League of Corinth (*SVdA* III 403 = Tod II 177 = *SIG*³ 260 = *IG* II² 236), which I regard (with Wilcken and others) as essentially a symmachy, dressed up as a Common Peace: its oaths were exchanged between Philip II of Macedon on the one hand and the Greek states on the other, and the reference in lines 21–2 to ὁ ἡγεμώ|[ν] can only be to Philip and his descendants, the kings of Macedon (lines 11--12). Incidentally, if lines 20–1 of the inscription just referred to have been correctly restored (as seems virtually certain) as καθότι | [ἂν δοκῆι τῶι κοινῶι συνεδ]ρίωι, then we have a useful argument against anyone who might wish to take the word κοινῶν in Thuc. I 97.1 as an indication that the Delian League synods were 'common' to Athens as well as the allies and that Athens had to accept their decisions, for no one will pretend that the King of Macedon was bound by the decisions of the Synedrion of the League of Corinth.

of their naval campaigns. And if they voted to do something the Athenians disliked, an unfortunate delay might ensue, for communication between Delos and Athens might be delayed by bad weather, as in the well-known circumstances of 399, when the execution of Socrates had to be postponed 'for a long time' because, as often happened, the return of the sacred embassy to Delos was delayed by contrary winds (Plato, *Phaedo* 58abc).[20] The allies could never want to force on Athens a course of action of which she herself disapproved, for if they did so, Athens would hardly give enthusiastic leadership, and might abandon the League altogether. In the 470s, Athens on the one hand and the allies on the other were probably not very far from equality in their capacity to conduct campaigns; and the Greeks, with their genius for devising political institutions suited to particular situations, would surely have realised that to expect Athens to submit to majority votes of the allies, positive as well as negative, was to invite trouble.

That Athens had a vote in the synods is improbable; but the question is of trivial importance (cf. Chapter IV, Part iv, Section B, §3[d], on Sparta). Surely an Athenian chairman will always have presided over the allied synods, just as a Spartan chairman must always have presided in the Peloponnesian League congresses; and presumably the Athenian chairman would only put motions already approved by the Athenian Assembly.

So far, the probabilities are strongly against the first theory we have been considering and in favour of the second. It remains to analyse the one piece of evidence in an ancient source upon a particular interpretation of which the first theory is wholly dependent: the word ἰσοψήφους in Thuc. III 11.4. Although, as I see it, the allies were *collectively* ἰσόψηφοι with Athens, as well as *individually* among themselves, I do not believe that this particular text is relevant for either of these situations: I think that the word is used in this particular passage in a metaphorical sense and has nothing whatever to do with actual *voting*.

The context is a characteristically complicated Thucydidean argument— written by him, I would suppose, with his tongue in his cheek: the Mytilenaeans are asking the Peloponnesians to make a special effort on their behalf, by launching a second invasion of Athens that year, and by sea as well as land (13.4), but they have a very bad case; in particular they have no real answer to what Gomme[21] rightly calls 'the awkward question, "why did you and Chios join Athens in subduing Samos (1. 116.1–2)?"'. Their main excuse, 'Oh, but we never had *real* freedom of choice', is not a convincing one: Athens could hardly have coerced a coalition of Samos, Chios and Mytilene, had these states cared to offer real opposition. The whole line of argument of the Mytilenaeans is a poor one (if perhaps the best available to them), a super-subtle piece of Thucydidean sophistry; and one wonders how far he himself thought its reasoning valid. (Like the Athenian speech in I 73–8, it is not well suited to its Peloponnesian audience.)

In III 11, what the Mytilenaeans are doing, in a convoluted Thucydidean way, is to give the reasons why (note the γάρ at the beginning of §4) the Athenians cunningly kept certain allies—ultimately only Chios and Mytilene (10.5)— autonomous, so as to be able to gain empire 'by fair-sounding language and policy rather than force' (11.3). First (ἄμα μέν, §4) comes the reason we are interested in, to which we shall return in a moment. Secondly (ἐν τῷ αὐτῷ δέ, §4), it was because they could lead the strongest states against the weaker ones first, 'and so leave the former to the last, stripped of their natural allies, and less capable of resistance' (Crawley); and thirdly (§6), because they were afraid that the Chian and Mytilenaean navies[22] [if these states became estranged while still strong and

[20] It appears from a combination of Plato, *Phaedo* 58a, and Xen., *Mem.* IV viii.2, that in 399 it took the ship nearly thirty days to make the return journey.

[21] *HCT* II 264; cf. Gomme's criticisms of various statements in the speech, esp. in ch. 11.

[22] 'We', throughout ch. 11, must refer to the 'autonomous' states as a whole, not merely Mytilene.

having potential allies] might unite with Sparta or some other power and become dangerous to Athens. An additional reason (τὰ δὲ καί, §7) for the maintenance of Chian and Mytilenaean autonomy was the way they toadied to the Athenian demos and its leaders: this helped them to 'maintain independence'—surely this is what περιεγιγνόμεθα means.

We can now return to the first reason (11.4). There are three alternative ways of taking the passage, each depending on a different interpretation of the key word, ἰσοψήφους. First, there is the view which may be regarded as the prevailing one nowadays, that ἰσοψήφους proves that *all the allied states, including Athens herself, had one vote each* in the League synods.[23] But, as we shall see, this does not fit the context of 11.4, and fails to make any kind of sense. Secondly, there is Hammond's theory (ONAA 59–60 and n. 46) that ἰσοψήφους refers to a group of 'autonomous' states as being collectively 'equal in voting power' with Athens. This fits the context rather better, but is open to fatal objections, to be stated presently. The only other alternative is the one I am proposing, which would understand ἰσοψήφους in a metaphorical sense (for which there are good parallels), having nothing to do with actual *voting*. I would translate the whole passage as follows: 'For not only did they [the Athenians] make use of the argument that *states which could make decisions as effectively as themselves* [Chios, Mytilene and, until 440, Samos] would not, surely, join in their expeditions [to reduce fellow-allies to subjection] unless the states attacked had done something wrong, for they would be unwilling to do so; but also. . . .'. This gives exactly what the context requires.

Thucydides uses the word ἰσόψηφος on only two other occasions. In 1 141.6, where it refers to the members of the Peloponnesian League, it undoubtedly means 'having equal *votes*'; but in 111 79.3 it cannot refer to voting at all, and I believe that that passage gives us an essential clue to its meaning in 11.4. Alcidas the Spartan navarch (111 26.1; cf. 31.1; 76) was the superior officer of Brasidas, who was his mere 'adviser' (ξύμβουλος, 69.1; 76); and when in 79.3 Brasidas is unable to prevail with Alcidas, ἰσοψήφου δὲ οὐκ ὄντος, Thucydides is saying that Brasidas did not have *the same weight in decision-making, the same power of effective decision*. Plato uses ἰσόψηφος in this very sense in *Laws* 111 692a, when he speaks of the *power* (δύναμις) of the twenty-eight Spartan gerontes as being made 'of *equal validity* with that of the kings in important matters' (ἰσόψηφον εἰς τὰ μέγιστα τῇ τῶν βασιλέων . . . δυνάμει). Hammond, ONAA 59 n. 46, speaks of this as making the gerontes 'as a group . . . equal in voting power with the kings as a pair', and giving 'each group . . . in modern parlance the power of veto'. But Plato was not so grossly ignorant of the Spartan constitution as to imagine that the two groups, gerontes and kings, regularly voted as two separate units on the same issues. Others have understood the passage better: T. J. Saunders, in his new translation of the *Laws* (Penguin, 1970, p. 140), renders it by saying that the twenty-eight gerontes were to have '*the same authority* in making important decisions as the kings', and Jowett translates, 'making the *power* of your twenty-eight elders *equal* with that of the kings in the most important matters'.

It remains to give the arguments against the other two versions of our text. The standard view, according to which ἰσοψήφους means that Athens herself and all the allied states each had one vote in the synods, cannot be made to fit the context. If for the words I have italicised in the translation suggested above we substitute '*states which had equal votes with themselves*', we make nonsense of the whole passage, first (as Hammond realised) because it is the 'autonomous' states to which the Mytilenaeans are referring, not all the allied states in general, and secondly because it is not how they *voted* but how they *acted* (ξυστρατεύειν) that the Athenians are alleged to use as an argument in their own favour. The Mytilenaeans are not *saying* (as asserted in *ATL* 111 140, end of first paragraph) that they had

[23] See the references in the opening paragraph of Section *C* above.

'always been *outvoted*'. Voting is a red herring here. Although Mytilene and Chios had *a strong enough power of independent decision* (say the Athenians), they joined in reducing refractory allies; and this shows (they add) that the allies in question must have been in the wrong, for if they had not been, Mytilene and Chios would surely have refused to assist in coercing them.

Hammond's alternative explanation of ἰσοψήφους does at least partly fit the context, by allowing the word to refer only to the 'autonomous' states of which the Mytilenaeans are speaking: in his picture, only these states were allowed to vote in the League synods. But first, no defined group of 'autonomous' states within the Delian League and Athenian empire can ever have been officially recognised to exist as such, even if Thucydides commonly speaks of the naval allies, who provided ships instead of tribute, as in some sense 'autonomous', as compared with the tributary allies, who were 'subject' (ὑπήκοοι): see my CAE 16–20. Secondly, it would be ludicrous to suppose that it was the very states whose votes Athens could most completely control (since she had taken away their autonomy) whom she deprived of the right to vote! And thirdly, Hammond's interpretation is open in one way to the same fatal objection as the more usual view: the argument is not about how the Mytilenaeans *voted* but about how they *acted* (ξυστρατεύειν). It is Hammond's insistence on making ἰσοψήφους refer to *voting* power which has driven him to construct this impossible alternative to the standard view.

There is, then, not a particle of evidence that Athens merely voted as one state among many in the League synods and had to submit to majority decisions; the parallels with the Peloponnesian League and the Second Athenian Confederacy are against it; and the whole situation pictured in this view is highly unrealistic. One wonders if it would ever have gained any adherents but for the general misunderstanding of Thuc. III 11.4.

The Delian League was in its origin a compact between two parties: Athens, and the collective allies. It is only natural that these two parties should at first have governed it jointly; but by degrees the preponderance of Athens increased and the active contribution of the allies dwindled, until the allied synods could disappear without any record surviving of their cessation.

APPENDIX VI

The 'Old Oligarch' (Ps.-Xen., Ath. Pol.)

The best text (and English translation) of this work is that by G. W. Bowersock, in the most recent reprint (1968) of the Loeb Xenophon, vol. VII (*Scripta Minora*, in which the other works still appear in the edition of E. C. Marchant). Cf. the review by D. M. Lewis, in CR 83 = n.s. 19 (1969) 45–7. Hill, *S*² 275–83, repeats Marchant's text (*OCT*). Other editions are by Hartvig Frisch, *The Constitution of the Athenians* (Copenhagen, 1942, with English translation and lengthy commentary), and E. Kalinka (Teubner, 1913). A sufficient bibliography of recent works dealing with the 'Old Oligarch' will be found in Bowersock's edition, pp. 470–3; see also M. Treu, in *RE*, 2te Reihe, IX (1967), col. 1928–82, esp. 1947–59 for an inconclusive discussion of passages which have been adduced in arguments concerning the date of the work. Gomme, OO (repr. in *MEGHL* 38–69), is among the more rewarding of recent discussions.

I have elsewhere (CAE 24–5, 38) explained what I believe to be the most significant features, for the historian, of this fascinating little treatise. I shall confine myself here to the occasion of the work, and its date.

1. I believe that the author, an Athenian, is replying to oligarchic acquaintances outside Athens, who have been protesting that it is very wicked of the 'best people' at Athens not merely to tolerate but actually to run the unpleasant Athenian democracy, as they did. Why did they not overthrow it? And why did they persecute the 'best people' in the allied states?

The reply is, 'Of course I know the democracy is very unpleasant. If we, the upper classes, had our way, we would reduce the demos to *douleia* (complete political subjection, I 9 etc.). But in fact we cannot have our way. *We do not really run the show*—the demos does. We have all the onerous jobs: we bear the cost of the liturgies (I 13) and supply the generals and hipparchs (I 3), while the demos (always acting of course in its own selfish interests, I 4, 7–8, 13; II 19–20; III 1) concentrates on the jobs that provide State pay (I 3); and of course *they* run the vital fleet (I 2, 19–20), and control the courts (I 13–14, 16–18), and look after their opposite numbers in the allied states and harry the Best People (I 14–18). But the point is that they look after their own unpleasant interests only too well (I 1)—and we just have to put up with the situation exactly as it is, much as we hate it. There are not even enough people unjustly disfranchised, who might help to bring about a revolution (III 12–13)'. This view is close to that expressed by Gomme (*OO* 231 = *MEGHL* 56).

The author is certainly an Athenian: note especially the first person plural, ἐποιήσαμεν, used twice in I 12. From II 20 (and four uses of αὐτόθι, if that is of any significance) it has been argued that he must have lived outside Athens. But II 20 has too often been misunderstood. In fact it affords no evidence on the question whether the 'Old Oligarch' lived at Athens, because a man with ancestral land in Attica could hardly be said to 'prefer' or 'choose' (εἵλετο) to live there rather than in an oligarchic city—unless he *supported the democracy*, in which case alone he was genuinely 'preferring to live in a democratically governed city'. The passage attacks, not members of the upper classes who *continued to live* at Athens, but those who *liked* the Athenian democracy.

The great value of this work is that it gives us a good idea of how *upper-class non-Athenians, for whom it was written*, would be likely to feel about democracy and democrats and the empire.

2. I cannot accept the arguments in favour of a date in the late 440s advanced by several scholars, most recently Bowersock, *op. cit.* 463–5, and in *HSCP* 71 (1966) 33–55. (In the review of Bowersock's edition by D. M. Lewis, mentioned above, at p. 46, there is an unfortunate misprint: Bowersock's 'favoured date' is given as '433'.) It seems to me certain that the work was written not earlier than 431. The main arguments are as follows:

(*a*) In II 16 the Athenians, when invaded, 'transfer their property to the islands and watch the land of Attica being devastated'. This passage, which has no ἄν, is not 'theoretical': the author says that the Athenians *do* allow Attica to be devastated and transfer their property to islands. They must have done so at least once recently. But they never had occasion to do this before 431. In 446, devastation was minimal and confined to the extreme south-west of Attica. According to Thucydides (I 114.2; II 21.1), Pleistoanax and the Peloponnesians came only as far as 'Eleusis and the road to Thria' and no farther—only five or six miles into Attica, if that. (Cf. also Thuc. II 21.2.) And had the Athenians intended to attack the Spartans they would hardly have done so west of the Aigaleos range, so περιορῶσι too is inappropriate to 446. It is surely inconceivable that the Athenians sent off their property to islands in that year: the revolt of Megara came upon them suddenly (cf. κατὰ τάχος, I 114.1), and the invasion of Pleistoanax would have followed speedily. Moreover Euboea, the obvious place to which to send cattle etc. (cf. Thuc. II 14.1), was now in revolt.

(*b*) The point about περὶ τοῦ πολέμου in III 2, which is too often ignored by the advocates of an early date, is not *so much* the use of the definite article (although, contrary to what is sometimes asserted, the *natural* implication of the article here is that there *is* a war in existence), as that this item *comes first in a long list* of the Council's activities, which goes on to speak of deliberation on many other issues: 'revenues, legislation, questions arising in the city from time to time, matters relating to the allies, reception of tribute, and care of dockyards and sacred places'. It would be absurd for anyone giving such a list of the Council's manifold duties in peace time to put *first* their deliberation about '*many* issues concerning *war*'. (What would this *mean*, in time of peace? Could the councillors be supposed to be saying to themselves, 'Let's discuss all sorts of things that we would do if there were a war'?) But in time of war, of course, deliberation about '*many* issues concerning *the war*' then in progress would naturally come first on the agenda.

(*c*) The words τῶν πολεμίων in II 1 are perfectly natural if there is a war on *with the Peloponnesians*; if not, it hardly makes sense, especially in the late 440s. The Athenians think they are 'fewer and weaker [in hoplites] than their enemies'. These 'enemies' can be none other than the Peloponnesians: only they, in the Greek world, were more numerous and more powerful than the land forces of the Athenian empire. But could the Peloponnesians be spoken of casually as οἱ πολέμιοι shortly after the Athenians had made the Thirty Years Peace with them? Surely not.

Of the arguments employed in favour of an earlier date, none seems to me to have any weight. One cannot say that II 2–3 must have been written before the formation of the Chalcidic League in 432, for Olynthus and the other members were mainland states, and their union therefore did nothing to invalidate the author's contention that 'those subject to rule by sea, *in so far as they are islanders*' (τοῖς δὲ κατὰ θάλατταν ἀρχομένοις, ὅσοι νησιῶταί εἰσιν ...) cannot effectively combine. I see nothing in the argument from II 14 (the demos ἀδεῶς ζῆ), because anyone who argues as perversely as our author could easily say, as he does here, that *in contrast with the rich farmers* (οἱ γεωργοῦντες καὶ οἱ πλούσιοι) the demos—in the sense of the *urban* lower classes, then—did not suffer. It is quite true that the choice of illustrations in III 11 includes nothing later than the mid-440s; but why should not these three cases be the *only* ones in which Athens had actually *supported* (αἱρεῖσθαι, εἵλοντο: chosen, preferred) oligarchs in some way, as distinct from merely tolerating them, as e.g. at Samos down to 440 and Mytilene down to 428?

Since the arguments for an earlier date have no substance at all, we must accept 431 as a *terminus post quem*. The statement in II 5 about the impossibility of long overland marches is not a 'dogma ... proved false by Brasidas' march to the north in 424' (as Bowersock puts it in his note *ad loc.*), but a sensible generalisation, which was and remained broadly true (cf. Gomme, OO 224–5 = *MEGHL* 50–1). All we can say is that such a statement is unlikely to have been made immediately after the autumn of 424.

The view of M. J. Fontana, *L'Athenaion Politeia del V secolo a.C.* (Palermo, 1968), that the work was written during the years 410 to 406/5 (pp. 50–5, 103), by Xenophon himself (pp. 100–2), seems highly implausible to me, although I do not see how such a date can be absolutely ruled out, as can one earlier than 431. After 413 the Athenian thalassocracy was far from being as absolute as Ps.-Xenophon represents it (II 2–7, 11–13, 14–15, 16); and after 410, when the Spartans had already been in occupation of Decelea for three years, the light-hearted attitude to foreign invasion (II 14–16; cf. 4–5, 13) would have been very inappropriate;

11—OOPW * *

also, after 410 the absence of any reference, even indirect, to the oligarchic revolution of 411 would be hard to understand.

After the foregoing had been written, yet another article dealing in detail with the date of this work appeared: W. G. Forrest, 'The Date of the Pseudo-Xenophontic Athenaion Politeia', in *Klio* 52 (1970) 107–16, arguing first (p. 108) for a date between 431 and autumn 424, and finally (p. 115) for 425–4, preferably August 424. I remain unimpressed (see above) by the argument, repeated by Forrest (*op. cit.* 108), that II 5 is decisive in favour of dating the work before the autumn of 424. But although I do not think the case for 425–4 is as convincing as Forrest believes, I agree with him that in view of II 13 and III 5 the summer of 424 is perhaps the most likely single date.

APPENDIX VII

The Peace of Callias and its consequences

The sources for the Peace are listed in Hill, *S*² 344 (Index 1 6.15). The fundamental treatment is by Wade-Gery, *EGH* 201–32, a reprint of his article, 'The Peace of Kallias', in *Athenian Studies Presented to W. S. Ferguson = HSCP*, Suppl. 1 (1940) 121–56; cf. *ATL* III 275. See also A. Andrewes, 'Thucydides and the Persians', in *Historia* 10 (1961) 1 ff., esp. 15–18; Gomme, *HCT* I 331–5; Meiggs, PIP, and CAI 11 ff.; Connor, *TFCA* 78–94. The latest article I know is by S. K. Eddy, 'On the Peace of Callias', in *CP* 65 (1970) 8–14. The alternative reconstruction offered by A. E. Raubitschek, 'The Peace Policy of Pericles', in *AJA* 70 (1966) 37–41 (cf. 'Kimons Zurückberufung', in *Historia* 3 [1954–5] 379–80), is unacceptable to me.

Attempts have been made in recent years to deny the existence of the Peace, e.g. by R. Sealey, in *Historia* 3 (1954–5) 325–33; H. B. Mattingly, in *Historia* 15 (1965) 273–81; and especially D. Stockton, in *Historia* 8 (1959) 61–79, who even seeks to get rid of the 'Peace of Epilycus', of 424 or a little later, the historicity of which must not be doubted. (It is proved by a combination of Andoc. III 29 and M/L 70 = *IG* II² 8, lines 13–16 of which 'make it certain that *spondai* have been made with the King': Wade-Gery, *EGH* 208.) But the very existence of the Peace of Epilycus does much to reduce the force of the main objection to the Peace of Callias: that Thucydides does not mention it—see Wade-Gery, *EGH* 210.

Wade-Gery, since publishing his article, has accepted 'one substantial change ... in the definition of the terms' of the Peace: there is no 'need to believe that the Greek cities of Asia Minor paid tribute simultaneously both to Athens and to Persia' (*ATL* III 275). This should certainly be accepted. J. M. Cook (PCI 16–17; cf. *GIE* 122–3) has since reasserted Wade-Gery's original opinion, in a slightly different form; but surely the only correct interpretation of the vital text, Hdts VI 42.2, is that given long ago by Grote (*HG* IV 424–5 n. 2: it is inadequately summarised in the one-volume edition of Grote, p. 306 and n. 2), and recently very well re-stated, with additional arguments, by Oswyn Murray, AΔ 142–9, 155–6: Herodotus is speaking of *assessments* on the cities, without regard to actual *payments*.

I would date the Peace at some unknown time within the year 449. I cannot accept the chronological reconstruction of the events of 450–49, based upon a presumed date in the first half of 449 for the 'Papyrus Decree' (*Anonymus*

Argentinensis, 'Strasburg Papyrus'), which has been worked out by the authors of *ATL* (III 275–81), and offered in a revised form by Meiggs, CAI. (In this reconstruction the Peace is dated in the winter or early spring of 450/49.) Earlier restorations and discussions of the Papyrus Decree are largely superseded by Wade-Gery and Meritt, 'Athenian Resources in 449 and 431 B.C.', in *Hesp*. 26 (1957) 163–97; but some of their restorations are highly conjectural, notably of the crucial lines 3–9. In my opinion, far too much weight has been given to the supposed evidence of this single (and only partially preserved) sheet of papyrus. We know nothing of the author (a scholiast on Demosthenes XXII) or of his sources of information.

I accept the fact that the quota-list for the year 449/8 (the list which would have been numbered 6) is almost certainly missing. (The decisive arguments have been well stated by Meiggs, CAI 15, quoted at length by Kagan, *OPW* 114, cf. 380–1; and see M/L 50, with the notes.) This may mean that no tribute was paid in the spring of 448; but other explanations are possible—in particular, that the whole of the year's tribute was devoted to some special purpose, for example the building of the temple to Athena Nike, which was certainly decided upon in the early 440s, although the existing temple was not actually constructed until the 420s: see M/L 44 (with the useful notes) and 71; cf. 50.

Most scholars nowadays seem to assume that (as Meiggs has put it, CAI 13) the Peace 'removed the purpose for which tribute had been designed'. Wade-Gery, in his important paper on the Peace (see the first paragraph above) and in an article published in 1945 ('The Question of Tribute in 449/8 B.C.', in *Hesp*. 14 [1945] 212–29, at pp. 217–22), advanced a hypothesis which has since been very generally accepted and is to be found in *ATL* (III 230–1, 277–81): that although the Delian League was intended to be permanent, the tribute was 'contingent on the Persian War', so that the Peace of Callias, which ended the war with Persia, 'ended therefore the obligations of the allies under the assessment of 478/7'. Wade-Gery placed particular emphasis on the fact that according to Thuc. I 96.1 that first assessment had provided for payment of tribute or provision of ships 'against the barbarian'. Consequently, his view (developed in *ATL* III) is that when the Peace was made, tribute ceased to be due. Confirmation of this is found in the missing quota-list for 449/8. The tribute was then 'reimposed', continuing from 448/7 onwards, as the quota-lists show. Wade-Gery originally believed that the quota-lists for 447 and 446 (Lists 7 and 8) afford evidence of allied recalcitrance and refusal to pay. *ATL* III 36–63 suggests instead that 'the irregularities in these lists should be interpreted in terms of bookkeeping rather than politics', as Meiggs puts it (CAI 15–16), while himself returning to Wade-Gery's original interpretation (CAI 16–19; cf. M/L, p.135).

This reconstruction, in its original form (as presented by Wade-Gery and subsequently by Meiggs) or as modified in *ATL* III, seems to me entirely inadmissible. The contributions of the allies, according to Thucydides (I 96.1), were not made 'for the *war*' (πρὸς τὸν πόλεμον), as the theory I am criticising would require, but 'against the *barbarian*' (πρὸς τὸν βάρβαρον). Now tribute was necessary because everything would depend upon the navy, and navies (unlike armies) were enormously expensive, and could not (again unlike armies) be brought into existence suddenly in an emergency. Unless the League had a navy kept permanently in being, Persia at any time might again subjugate many of the Greek states. Athens alone could certainly not afford the necessary expenditure; hence the need for tribute. And a navy, and hence tribute, 'against the barbarian', was hardly less necessary after the Peace of Callias than before it. Quite apart from the fact that treaties with Persian kings were apparently held to expire on the death of the king concerned and to require renewal by his successor, Persia might denounce or break the treaty at any time, or a satrap might take matters into his own hands, as satraps sometimes did. The only way to guarantee that the Peace would be kept was *to maintain forces visibly sufficient to preserve it*: that is to say, to keep up the navy, and therefore the tribute. I would suppose that vast numbers of Greeks accepted this necessity without a second thought and regarded the Peace as a great achievement, a great victory—as indeed it was. But of course there might well be protests against the continuance of the League, and the tribute, by some of those who were far enough away from the Persian sphere to feel that there was now no danger to them from Persia, and by those who already disliked Athenian dominance more than subjection to Persia—there would be many powerful men of that sort, like the Samian oligarchs of Thuc. I 115.4–5 (cf. Chapter I, Part iii above).

To suppose, as Wade-Gery and *ATL* and others have done, that Athens first admitted she had no right to collect tribute after peace had been made, and then *reimposed* it, is to attribute extraordinary folly to Pericles and his colleagues. If they intended to maintain the alliance in its existing form, as of course they did, it was up to them to insist that the Peace had not altered the obligations of the allies in principle; and I have no doubt that that was what they did. For the theory I am criticising there is anyway no evidence, and I am now suggesting that all the probabilities are against it too. (Cf. Kagan, *OPW* 115.) It is difficult to believe that a cessation and reimposition of tribute would have left no trace at all in our sources. And if the decree of Cleinias (M/L 46 = D 7 in *ATL* II 50–1 = *SEG* X 31) is to be dated in the spring of 447, as by *ATL* III 281, 299, the fact that it gives no indication at all of any allied 'recalcitrance', but only of incompetence and dishonesty which it was hoped to put right by more efficient machinery, with no reference to ἀργυρολόγοι νῆες or any kind of force, is rather strong evidence *against* supposing that the allies had been refusing to pay (contrast M/L, p. 135).

One important factor which is never stressed as it should be is that the League could not now (after the Eurymedon and its aftermath) hope to carry out *profitably* much more aggression against Persia. There was little or nothing to be gained from making expeditions deep into the interior of Asia Minor, nor were these ever attempted, even before the Peace. Cyprus was too far from the main Greek bases and too near to Phoenicia and its navy, and the Greeks were never able to hold it all before Alexander's day: the very large expedition of 450 (Thuc. I 112.2–4) won victories but could not even capture Citium, and it went home without being able to consolidate, and having accomplished nothing permanent. Nor, as far as we know, did the sixty ships detached to Egypt (112.3) achieve anything. The fact was that the Greeks had already gone about as far as they could hope to go, and that the Peace with Persia was therefore very much in the interest of the alliance. The time for profitable aggression was over.

Although Thucydides intended his account of the Pentecontaetia to be above all an explanation of the way in which the Athenian ἀρχή had grown out of the original ἡγεμονία (see I 89.1; 96.1; 97.1–2; 118.2), he never mentions the Peace of Callias. Instead of taking this as evidence against the existence of the Peace, as many historians have done, I would infer that Thucydides did not regard the Peace as an important factor in the growth of the ἀρχή. Similarly, Thucydides does not mention the transfer of the League treasury from Delos to Athens, another event which many people might place high in the list of factors promoting ἀρχή. Whether or not this transfer was proposed by the Samians, as stated by Theophrastus (fr. 136 Wimmer, *ap.* Plut., *Arist.* 25.2–3; but the anecdote can hardly be attached to 454 and may be entirely fictitious), it was evidently accepted at the time as a necessity, in view of the possibility of a sudden descent on Delos by the Persian Fleet after its success in Egypt—see Plut., *Per.* 12.1: εὐπρεπεστάτη τῶν προφάσεων, δείσαντα τοὺς βαρβάρους. (I am not at all impressed by the attempt of W. K. Pritchett, in *Historia* 18 [1969] 17–21, to separate the transfer of the Treasury from the disaster in Egypt in 454.)

In an interesting and important paper (PCI; cf. *GIE* 122–3), raising a number of questions which deserve further study and suggesting others which we ought to ask, J. M. Cook has asserted that there was a very low level of prosperity and material culture in the Ionian cities under the Athenian empire; and he has gone on to claim that against the background he has sketched 'the Peace of Callias cannot have been a cause of jubilation in Ionia', since its provisions 'did not give the Greeks of Asia immunity from Persian ownership and sovereignty even within a single day's journey on foot from the coast' (PCI 16–17; cf. *GIE* 122–3). I would concede that a Greek city of Asia in the fifth century, whether before or after the Peace of Callias, might well be able to obtain greater prosperity, *at least for its propertied class*, by becoming fully integrated into the Persian empire. But in the first place, Cook's views about the material poverty of Ionia during the period of Athenian dominance have not gone without query: cf. J. Boardman (reviewing Cook, *GIE*), in *CR* 78 = n.s. 14 (1964), at p. 83 (Chios, Samos, Didyma); and in *Antiq. Jnl.* 39 (1959), at p. 204 and n. 4 (Ephesus) and 208 (Didyma). And before we can draw any firm conclusions we need to take account of conditions not only in Ionia but throughout the whole Greek area of Asia Minor. Also, if we accept a Peace of Callias at all, we must surely assume that it contained an 'autonomy clause', such as that in Diod. xii 4.5, which *did* give the Greeks of Asia some 'immunity from Persian ownership and sovereignty' (to use Cook's expression), even if we feel that such a provision may have extended, in practice or even in theory, only to the actual members of Athens' League at the date of the conclusion of the Peace, rather than to 'all the Greek cities throughout Asia', as Diodorus has it.

Moreover, Cook's picture of the situation of the Greeks of Asia is put somewhat out of focus, in my opinion, by a misinterpretation of Hdts vi 42.2, which he takes to refer to *payments* by *individual landowners* instead of *assessments* upon their *cities* (cf. the third paragraph of this Appendix). I would myself suppose (with Murray, AΔ 155–6) that the Peace of Callias said nothing at all about tribute. The King never formally relinquished his claim to exact it, but in practice he would be unable to do so in areas where the Athenian alliance held firm. But, as Murray has said (AΔ 146–7), 'The situation was always fluid; it might well be to the advantage of certain cities to safeguard themselves by paying tribute to both sides. The number of such states would vary with the political situation. Even if the city itself did not pay tribute to Persia, certain powerful men within it may have thought it advisable to contribute to Persian funds, either as protection money or for their own political purposes'. And of course they will anyway have paid Persian taxation or rents in respect of any 'King's land' they may have held, unless specifically exempted.

I suggest that the Greeks of Asia can only have benefited from the Peace, and that after it Greek landowners in particular could feel more rather than less secure against raids from Persian-held territory.

In conclusion, I should like to suggest that the essential distinction recognised in the time of Alexander the Great (see Tod ii 185) and in the Hellenistic kingdoms between πόλις and χώρα, which was important above all in matters of land tenure (see Jones, *GCAJ* 95–6; cf. C. B. Welles, *Royal Correspondence in the Hellenistic Period* [1934], nos. 10–13 and 18, with the notes; also *OGIS* 229, lines 100 ff.), may well have made its first formal appearance in the Peace of Callias, which must surely have had cause to speak of the Greek πόλεις, as opposed to the King's χώρα. We certainly find the πόλεις/χώρα formula in the two first Persian-Peloponnesian treaties in Thuc. viii (18.1; 37.2,5); but in the third (58, esp. §§2–3) the word πόλις never appears—perhaps because the official Spartan attitude was that the treaty would last only 'for the duration' (cf. 84.5, showing that the Milesians were expected to consider themselves ἐν τῇ βασιλέως [χώρᾳ] while the war lasted), and that as soon as it was over they would claim that they had never undertaken to hand the *Greek cities* over to the King; while in the King's mind his χώρα included all the πόλεις within its boundaries. (Cf. Welles, *op. cit.*, no. 11, lines 21–2: πρὸς ἣν ἂμ βούληται πόλιν τῶν ἐν τῆι χώρα[ι]| τε καὶ συμμαχίαι.)

APPENDIX VIII

τὸ κατάγειν

The evidence I have collected regarding τὸ κατάγειν (the noun καταγωγή seems not to occur in this particular sense) includes examples in time of peace and war. It can be divided into three groups:

(*a*) Against Athens: Xen., *HG* IV viii.33; v i.28; Dem. v 25; Ps.-Dem. XVII 20; L 6, 17; Didymus (*ad.* Dem. XI 1), col. x. 45–60 (= Philoch., *FGrH* 328 F 162, and Theopomp., *FGrH* 115 F 292); Lyc., *c. Leocr.* 18; *SIG*³ 304 (= *IG* II² 360).1 (*C*) 36–41; *SIG*³ 409.10–13; *IG* II² 416.10–14; 682. 9–13; perhaps Ps.-Dem. XLV 64.

(*b*) By Athens: Isocr. XVIII 61; Dem. VIII 9, 24–8; XX 77; Aeschin. II 71.

(*c*) Miscellaneous: Xen., *Anab.* v i.11–12,15–16 (cf. viii.1); Ps.-Arist., *Oecon.* II ii.3, 1346ᵇ29–31; Ps.-Dem. XVII 19; Dem., fr. 25 (Sauppe); Diod. XIV 79.7; XX 82.2; Polyb. v 95.4; Harp., s.v. κατάγειν τὰ πλοῖα; Bekker, *Anecd. Gr.* I 269. 20–2.

I do not claim that this is a complete list, although I think it must contain most of the examples down to *c.* 322 B.C.

APPENDIX IX

Datable passages in Thucydides, with special reference to 1 97.2

There are very few certain examples of datable passages in Thucydides, such as II 65.11–12 and v 26.4–5, which were certainly written after the end of the war. For some possible examples, e.g. I 56.2 (the Potidaeans); 115.4 (Pissuthnes); II 23.3 (the Oropians); VI 62.2 with VII 58.2 (the Himeraioi); VII 57.2 (the Aeginetans); 57.8 (the Messenians and Pylos), see Gomme, *HCT, ad locc.*, esp. Dover in IV 435–6. For other valuable remarks on this subject in *HCT*, see IV 16–17 (Andrewes), and 242–5, 339–40 (Dover). A list of passages allegedly 'early' or 'late' which must include all possible candidates is given by Patzer, *PGST* 103–9.

A prime example of a passage which has been inexcusably used as a basis for sweeping conclusions is I 97.2, where the reference to the *Atthis* of Hellanicus has often been supposed to justify a dating of the whole of Thucydides' excursus on the Pentecontaetia (I 89–118.2) after 406/5 B.C., the earliest possible date for the publication of the completed work of Hellanicus.[1] In fact the two lines referring to

¹ See Jacoby, *Atthis* 338 n. 47: 'Hellanikos' *Atthis* was published after 406/5 B.C. (probably between 404 and 402)'; also *FGrH* III b (Suppl.) i.5: the work 'still treated in detail the events of the year 407/6 B.C. Here the inference is . . . obvious that H. concluded with the epochal date of the end of the war in the last months of the year 404/3 B.C.'. (But did

Hellanicus in I 97.2 (τούτων ... ἐπεμνήσθη) can perfectly well be an insertion into a sentence written earlier—how much earlier, it is impossible to say. The fact of the insertion was pointed out long ago by Ziegler;[2] and according to Jacoby the context of Thuc. I 97 'leaves no doubt that the few words relating to H[ellanicus] were added (to put it as cautiously as possible) as an afterthought to the motivation of the digression' (*FGrH* III b [Suppl.] i.5–6). It is therefore very wrong to use the reference to Hellanicus in I 97.2 as an argument in favour of a very late dating of the Pentecontaetia excursus; and it hardly mitigates the offence to qualify the argument with a 'probably' (as Schmid, in Schmid-Stählin, *GGL* I v.131: 'wahrscheinlich').

APPENDIX X

Pericles and the Athenian 'land empire'

One of the cardinal principles on which Pericles wished Athens to conduct the Peloponnesian war was that she must not try to extend the empire while the war lasted (Thuc. I 144.1; II 65.7). Was this due to Pericles' realisation of the futility of an earlier policy of his own? It is hard to say; but at least there is no positive evidence connecting Pericles with the 'land empire' which Athens built up in the 450s. The victory at Oenophyta which followed Tanagra in 458 or 457 and led to the Athenian conquest of Boeotia and Phocis was won under the command of Myronides (Thuc. I 108.2); Pericles is not named as general. Nor is Pericles mentioned as a general at Tanagra, although he fought in that battle: Plut., *Per.* 10.2 etc.

The first military command of any sort attributed to Pericles by Thucydides (I 111.2–3; cf. Diod. XI 85; 88.1–2; Plut., *Per.* 19.2–3), and indeed the only one before his ultimately successful attempt to reconquer Euboea in 446 (114.1–3), is the naval expedition from Pagae to Sicyon and Oeniadae, presumably in 454— actually the last military event of any kind in the First Peloponnesian war recorded before the five-year truce of 451 (112.1; cf. the end of Chapter V, Part vi above). There are only two other known military commands by Pericles which could conceivably have occurred before the Thirty Years Peace: both are naval, and it is quite possible that neither is earlier than the late 450s. Plutarch (*Cim.* 13.4) mentions an expedition beyond the Chelidonian Islands; and since he brackets it with a similar expedition by Ephialtes, some have wanted to put it before the assassination of Ephialtes in 462/1. (Cf. also Plut., *Per.* 7.2: Pericles at first gave himself to στρατεῖαι rather than politics.) And Plutarch (*Per.* 20.1–2) mentions an expedition into the Black Sea by Pericles; but this is usually dated after the Thirty Years Peace: see e.g. Gomme, *HCT* I 367–8, 396; Kagan, *OPW* 387–9; cf. *ATL* III 114–17 (undecided between 450 and *c.* 435).

Now of course we have no right to assume that Pericles was general only in those

---

Jacoby not mean 405/4?) Gomme, *HCT* I 6 n. 3 (on p. 7), believed there was 'some good reason for thinking that Hellanikos' *Atthis* ended in 412 and that the later years were included in a second edition published after his death'; contrast Jacoby, *FGrH* III b (Suppl.) i.5.

[2] K. Ziegler, 'Der Ursprung der Exkurse im Thuk.', in *Rh. Mus.* 78 (1929) 58–67, esp. 66–7, accepted 'in this one point' by Jacoby, *FGrH* III b (Suppl.) ii.5 n. 47, who rejects Ziegler's 'theory about the six great digressions'.

years in which our very inadequate sources for the Pentecontaetia preserve a record of his activities; nor can we draw firm conclusions about the policies advocated by a particular general from the fact that he was in command of certain expeditions and absent from others—although it must be true that as a rule a general would not be put in charge of an expedition of which he was known to disapprove. (The one obvious exception is the Sicilian expedition of 415, when Nicias was 'chosen to command against his will': Thuc. vi 8.4). But there is really not a scrap of evidence of any kind to connect Pericles with the ultimately disastrous attempt to bring Boeotia and Phocis under Athenian control, and one intriguing passage suggests that he may not have been in sympathy with the policy of extending the empire in this way: Plutarch, *Per.* 18.2–3, where Pericles unsuccessfully attempts to stop the expedition under Tolmides to crush the revolt in Boeotia in 446, which ended in the disaster at Coronea and the loss of Boeotia (and presumably Phocis). Of course, Pericles' remark about having Time as a counsellor might indicate that he was opposed only to a hasty expedition and wanted Athens to wait until a much larger force could be collected. But this is questionable, for a large Athenian levy could surely be gathered in a few days; and on that occasion Tolmides took with him not only his thousand Athenian volunteers but τῶν ξυμμάχων ὡς ἕκαστοι (Thuc. 1 113.1; cf. Plut., *Per.* 18.2), presumably in substantial numbers (but cf. Buck, ADB 223–5)—and are these forces likely to have been just standing by at Athens? Unfortunately, the only other text which might be used to shed light on Pericles' attitude to Boeotia, Aristotle, *Rhet.* iii 4, 1407ᵃ1–5, is also ambiguous. Pericles is here said to have remarked that the Boeotians were 'cut down' (κατακόπτεσθαι) by fighting each other; and he might have given this as a reason either for leaving the Boeotians alone (because they would not be powerful enough to harm Athens) or for attacking them (because they were unlikely to offer effective resistance).

A case can be made for thinking that Athens was actually in a less strong position during the period when she controlled Boeotia, because a revolt was bound to break out sooner or later, and Athens would then be compelled either to risk a heavy loss in trying to recover the area, or 'lose face' badly by accepting the *fait accompli*.

Without being able to prove anything, I would suggest that Pericles was sensible enough to realise that in attempting to conquer Boeotia the Athenians were biting off more than they could chew. It is harder to say what he will have felt about the acquisition of Megara as an ally on her revolt from the Peloponnesian League in *c.* 460. He may have regarded it as an unnecessary provocation of Sparta and Corinth; but on the other hand, if Spartan hostility to Athens at that time was very clear (see Chapter V, Parts ii–iii above), the strategic importance of the Megarid (see Chapter V, Part vi) may have outweighed all other considerations. Doubtless he welcomed the accession of any islands or mainland cities on the west coast of Greece—they were too difficult to *control*, and would become genuine allies rather than subjects. And he will surely have favoured the conclusion of the alliances Athens entered into, theoretically on equal terms, with Egesta, Rhegium and Leontini; but there is probably truth in the statement of Plutarch, *Per.* 20.4–21.1 (exaggerated as it is: see Chapter VI, Part iii above), that he was against schemes of conquest in the West.

I am not at all impressed by the objection that the policy of creating and enlarging the 'land empire', between *c.* 461 and the end of the First Peloponnesian war, would not have been pursued against Pericles' will. I see no reason to think that the position of Pericles became as dominant as Thucydides represents it, in ii 65.8–9, until at least the ostracism of Thucydides the son of Melesias, very probably in the spring of 443; and even after that it was certainly not as absolute as many have supposed (see Chapter III, Part ii above). It is time that historians ceased speaking of Athenian actions after 462/1 as if they all necessarily represented the policy of Pericles.

As I think I have made sufficiently clear in the main text above, I believe that Pericles (with the dominant section of Athenian opinion) was anxious to maintain the Thirty Years Peace indefinitely. But the question remains: when did Pericles (and the majority of the Athenians) become convinced that a war with Sparta and the Peloponnesians, which neither side could be at all sure of winning, ought to be avoided if at all possible? Did they perhaps always feel this, and enter into the alliances with Megara and Argos (which led directly to the First Peloponnesian war) only because they were convinced that before long Sparta and the Peloponnesians would attack them? (Cf. Chapter V, Part iii above.)

APPENDIX XI

Perdiccas and Athens

For Perdiccas' dates, see Beloch, *GG* iii² ii.49–55, 62; Gomme, *HCT* i 201. One could say 'earlier than 432 (perhaps *c.* 440) to *c.* 412'.

Most of what we know about Perdiccas' activities comes from Thucydides. See Gomme, *HCT*, Indexes to i, iii and iv; *ATL* iii 313–19, 323–5; Kagan, *OPW* 276–8, 281–3.

The principal contemporary document is the interesting but fragmentary record of a treaty between Athens and Perdiccas: *SVdA* ii 186 = *IG* i² 71 (= *SEG* x 86 = xii 16 = xvi 4 = xix 11). This has been variously dated: originally 423/2, a date which still 'tempted' Gomme (*HCT* iii 621–2) and is retained by Bengtson (*SVdA* ii, pp. 109, 113); 431 (Papastavrou: see *SEG* xvi 4); *c.* 436, soon after the foundation of Amphipolis (*ATL* iii 313–14 and n. 61; cf. Gomme, *loc. cit.*; M/L, p. 179); or even earlier, soon after the accession of Perdiccas (Kagan, *OPW* 276 n. 13).

As to whether we have in *SVdA* ii 167 = *IG* i² 53 a fragment of a treaty between Athens and Perdiccas' brother Philip (for whom cf. esp. Thuc. i 57.3; 59.2; ii 100.3), see *SEG* x 46 and its p. 157; xiii 9; xvi 7.

APPENDIX XII

The chronology of 433–1, and the Spartan embassies to Athens of 432/1

Unfortunately it seems to me impossible to establish with any confidence a precise chronology for the events of the year 432. Much learned ingenuity has been devoted to this question, but the results are inconclusive.

1. Scholars are nowhere near reaching unanimity how far Julian dates[1] can be calculated from the Athenian calendar—or rather, calendars, for although

[1] Julian dates are commonly given for the years before the introduction of the Gregorian calendar in A.D. 1582: see E. J. Bickerman, *CAW* 9–11, 89. We sometimes need to know a

there was properly only one official Athenian calendar, in terms of which all our literary sources speak, the inscriptions also reveal the simultaneous existence of a quite different method of dating.² The official Athenian calendar was in terms of what is usually referred to as the 'civil year' (sometimes the 'festival year'),³ a lunar year of 12 months (occasionally 13, with an additional month intercalated) of 29 or 30 days each, beginning with Hekatombaion 1, soon after midsummer. The alternative scheme we often find in Athenian inscriptions reveals a 'conciliar year' (or 'prytany year') of 10 prytanies, varying in length, but in an ordinary year (of 12 months, without intercalation) consisting of about 36 days,⁴ the first prytany in our period beginning probably as a rule soon after the summer solstice, at roughly the same time as, but not as yet simultaneously with, the civil year.⁵

2. We can now consider the chronology of the last phase of τὰ Κερκυραϊκά, in 433. Meritt (*AT* 217, cf. 218) would fix the beginning of the Athenian conciliar year 433/2 (which is crucial for our purposes) 'tentatively, let us say, at July 4' [Julian]. This is not universally accepted,⁶ and it cannot be taken as proved, but I think it is not likely in any event to be far wrong. If we may accept that date as an approximation and proceed accordingly, then we may date the despatch of the two squadrons sent to Corcyra in the summer of 433 not earlier than July 16 and August 9 respectively, for it will have been about those days that the generals of the two squadrons received the payments recorded in M/L 61 (= *IG* I² 295; cf. *SEG* x 222).7–12 and 18–23, on the 13th day and the last (probably the 37th) day of what is almost certainly the first prytany of the conciliar year 433/2. (I say 'not earlier than' July 16 and August 9, since we must allow for the possibility that the payments were made a few days before the expeditions actually sailed.) The second squadron arrived on the very day of the battle of Sybota (Thuc. I 50.5), and that battle, therefore, is now generally dated in August (see the commentary, p. 168, to M/L 61) or early September 433. Gomme in one place (*HCT* I 196–7) speaks of the 'end of August or early September', and in his table of dates (I 424–5) puts the battle in 'Mid-Sept.' (cf. Adcock, in *CAH* v 475: 'the first half of Septem-

---

Gregorian date, e.g. in connection with the time of a harvest. A convenient table for the conversion of Julian into Gregorian dates is given by R. A. Parker, *The Calendars of Ancient Egypt* (= *Stud. in Anc. Oriental Civilization*, No. 26, Chicago, 1950) 8. For the fifth century B.C., subtract 5 days from the Julian to arrive at the Gregorian date.

² There was actually a third method of dating, for the term of office of certain officials, by the year 'from Panathenaea to Panathenaea' (Hekatombaion 28 in one civil year to Hekat. 27 in the next; and sometimes for four years, from one 'Great Panathenaea' to the next): see Busolt-Swoboda, *GSK* II 1055 ff., or, briefly, M/L, pp. 215–16. But this 'year' is expressed in terms of the civil year, though it does not coincide with it.

³ I need say nothing here of dates κατὰ θεόν (giving more or less accurate lunar dates, as contrasted with those κατ' ἄρχοντα, according to the actual civil calendar), as we do not hear of these in our period.

⁴ Arist., *Ath. Pol.* 43.2, speaks only of four prytanies with 36 days and six with 35 days each, ignoring intercalary years. In the fifth century, when civil year and conciliar year did not coincide, the arrangement of prytanies is disputed: contrast e.g. Pritchett and Neugebauer, *CA* 34–9, 94–108, with Meritt, *AT* 5–9, 13–15, 61–2, 69–71, 202–17; cf. Pritchett, 'Anc. Athenian Calendars on Stone', in *Univ. of California Publ. in Class. Archaeol.* IV 4 (1963) 267–402, esp. 355 ff. The details of this controversy (continued in articles most of which are referred to in M/L, pp. 205, 215; add esp. Pritchett, *CM*) are hardly relevant for present purposes.

⁵ The student who needs a brief, simple statement of the facts may begin with A. G. Woodhead, *The Study of Greek Inscriptions* (Cambridge, 1959) 115–18. See also the works cited in the last note.

⁶ See esp. W. K. Pritchett, 'Thucydides v 20', in *Historia* 13 (1964) 21–36, at pp. 22–4; *CM* (esp. 42 ff., 64 ff., 90 ff.); cf. 'Julian Dates and Greek Calendars', in *CP* 42 (1947) 235–43 (esp. 243).

ber'). I would guess that late August is most likely, and in any event we should be reasonably safe in dating the battle in 'the second half of August or the early part of September'.

In view of the way Thucydides speaks in 1 45.1 (οὐ πολὺ ὕστερον), it is natural to put the conclusion of the Athenian-Corcyraean alliance fairly close before the payment to the generals of the first expedition: on Meritt's chronology we can surely date the alliance to early July, and in any event it must be between late June and mid-July.

3. As regards the chronology of τὰ Ποτειδεατικά in 432, and the crucial meeting of the Spartan Assembly which in effect declared war, there is much disagreement. On the one hand there is the chronology adopted by Gomme, *HCT* I 222–5, 420–5 (with a table of dates, pp. 424–5), also 199, 208–9, 210, 213; II 2–3, 70–1; cf. III 699–715; and for more detailed arguments see Gomme's article, '*IG* I² 296 and the Dates of ΤΑ ΠΟΤΕΙΔΕΑΤΙΚΑ', in *CR* 55 (1941) 59–67, with a full bibliography, supplementing that given in 1904 by Busolt, *GG* III ii.799 n. 1 (extending to p. 804); 907 n. 2 (extending to p. 915)—whose analysis is still well worth reading. Pritchett's powerful attack, in his *CM* (esp. 42 ff., 90–2), on 'the dogma of the first new moon after the [summer] solstice' is also relevant. Gomme puts the revolt of Potidaea in mid-April 432, the battle of Potidaea and the beginning of the siege in mid-June, the expedition of Phormio in September or October, and the two meetings at Sparta in early July and early August. He also places the Theban attack on Plataea at the beginning of March 431 and the first Peloponnesian invasion of Attica about May 20.

Most other scholars have preferred mainly later dates. The discussion has centred largely on the interpretation of *IG* I² 296 and 309a, which are now best read in Meritt, *AFD* 71 ff., at pp. 80–3 and Plate I (see *SEG* x 223; xxi 73).[7] Most recently W. E. Thompson, 'The Chronology of 432/1', in *Hermes* 96 (1968) 216–32, has advocated a scheme which at least has the merit of demanding none of the emendations in the text of Thucydides required by most of the alternative versions —Gomme's reconstruction needs three. According to Thompson, Potidaea revolted on about 1 June 432, the battle of Potidaea took place in October, and the expedition of Phormio and the two meetings at Sparta must be dated at some time after October. The attack on Plataea was about 1 April 431, and Archidamus invaded the Thriasian plain about June 17. Other chronologies vary in detail, while generally accepting a date for the battle of Potidaea (Thuc. 1 62.4–6) in September[8] or later,[9] with the result[10] that the meeting of the Spartan Assembly cannot easily be put before October at the earliest.

[7] Thompson (as cited in the next sentence of the text above) restores the inscription with a stoichedon line of 78 letters instead of the usual 84.

[8] Among the advocates of this chronology (whose arguments cannot be given in detail here) are Adcock, in *CAH* v 475–6 (Sept.-Oct.); Beloch, *GG* II² ii.219–22 ('not before the second half of Sept.'); Hammond, *HG²* 662; H. M. Hubbell, 'The Chronology of the Years 435–431 B.C.', in *CP* 24 (1929) 217–30; W. Kolbe, *Thuk. im Lichte der Urkunden* (Stuttgart, 1930) 1–49; Wade-Gery, in *JHS* 53 (1933) 135–6; 69 (1949) 85. Gomme, at the end of the first page of his article in *CR* (cited in the text above), can mention only three scholars opposed to the view that *IG* I² 296 supports a date not earlier than September 432 for the battle of Potidaea: Busolt, *GG* III ii.799 n. ('about June'); A. B. West, 'The Chronology of the Years 432 and 431 B.C.', in *CP* 10 (1915) 24–53 ('about May 15'); and Jacoby, 'Thuk. und die Vorgesch. des Pelop. Krieges', in *GGN* (1929) 1–34 = *AGGS* 207–38 ('Nov./Dec. 433').

[9] D. M. Robinson and P. A. Clement, *Excavations at Olynthus* ix (Baltimore, 1938) 142–6 (mid-Oct.); cf. Alexander, *PHR* 66, 69, 113 n. 16.

[10] See Thuc. 1 67.1, which speaks of the Corinthian agitation at Sparta as being conducted during the siege of Potidaea, which began immediately after the battle (1 62.4 ff., esp. 64.1), although it was not complete until after the arrival of Phormio's expedition (64.2–3). As Gomme says (*HCT* 1 421), the Corinthians presumably acted soon after they heard of the battle and the partial investment of the city.

I do not myself see how we can decide with complete confidence between the rival schemes. On the whole I think the later chronology is preferable to Gomme's, but I wish to leave the question open. For my purposes there is just one important historical problem (entirely ignored in the chronological analyses) which needs to be discussed. Did the crucial meeting of the Spartan Assembly which in effect declared war on Athens take place before or after the change of ephors at Sparta, in the autumn of 432? In other words, were Sthenelaïdas and his colleagues ephors for 433/2 or 432/1?

4. Before we can decide this we must know when the Spartan ephors entered upon their year of office. I am satisfied that the day was not very far in either direction from the end of September or early October. See the admirable brief statement by Andrewes, in Gomme, *HCT* IV 38; also Beloch, *GG* II² ii.269–84 (mainly on the navarchs, whose term of office must have been essentially the same, even if it was sometimes extended), esp. 270–1; Busolt, *GSK* II 686;[11] Kahrstedt, *Forsch.* 155–204 (also on the navarchs); *GSιSS* 158–61.

Andrewes (*loc. cit.*) adds, with characteristically prudent reserve, 'Since so many Greek calendars seem to begin their year from solstice or equinox, it is likely enough that the Spartan new year began theoretically at the new moon next after the autumn equinox—but with all the factors of uncertainty that beset Greek lunar calendars'.[12] I wonder whether a more likely date is not an astronomical event that took place several days earlier than the equinox: the heliacal rising of Arcturus, which in the late fifth century is believed to have occurred about September 19 (see Bickerman, *CAW* 145), and had long been a very well known fixed point in the solar year—see the Additional Note at the end of this Appendix. The only other astronomical event about this time which was a matter of common knowledge was the 'cosmical setting' of the Pleiades about November 4 (see Bickerman, *CAW* 143), and I think this is too late, although I suppose it cannot be ruled out as entirely impossible.

5. On the date of the annual election of ephors at Sparta we seem to have no information of any kind. Even at Athens we know only that the election of the Strategoi and other military officials took place not earlier than the seventh prytany (Arist., *Ath. Pol.* 44.4): this would be at the most only *c.* 140 days before they entered on their office, and might be much less. (The date of the election of Athenian civil magistrates is unknown.) But at Athens the *dokimasia* which a magistrate had to undergo before he took office necessitated an election some time beforehand. At Sparta we hear of no such scrutiny. It is tempting to guess that the election of officers probably took place at some time during the summer. The objection that Spartiates might then be away on military service is more apparent than real, for there were at least three important Spartan festivals during the summer, namely the Hyacinthia (strictly, Amyclaean, but involving many Spartans: see e.g. Hdts IX 7.1), the Gymnopaediae and the Carneia (in that

---

[11] Kagan is confused. In *OPW* 280 and n. 20 he quotes this work of Busolt, but is apparently under the mistaken impression that it supports the erroneous view he there states: that the ephors of 433/2 'had taken office in the spring of 433, which means that they had been elected well before the Athenian alliance with Corcyra and the Battle of Sybota'. Contrast *OPW* 307 and n. 46, where Kagan again says that these ephors 'had been elected in the spring [of 433], before Athens had even made an alliance with Corcyra', but now realises that 'they took office in the autumn'.

[12] E. B. Bischoff, in *RE* x ii (1919), col. 1569, s.v. 'Kalender (griechischer)', states it as a fact that the Spartan year began 'mit dem Herbstäquinoctium', but gives no evidence. Cf. Busolt, *GSK* II 686 and n. 5, and the works there cited. L. Pareti, 'Note sul Calendario Spartano', in *Atti della R. Accademia delle Scienze di Torino* 45 (1909–10) 812–29, would make the Spartan year in certain circumstances begin with the first or second new moon *before* the autumn equinox; cf. Walbank, *HCP* I 483. But Pareti's elaborate reconstruction of a Spartan octaëteris seems to me greatly over-confident.

order), and at the last in particular, held—in the absence of calendaric irregularity—in August or early September, it would normally have been possible for
virtually all Spartiates to be present, for the month of Carneius, in which the festival was held, was a sacred month to Dorians in general (Thuc. v 54.2), and during
it the Peloponnese would ordinarily be free from military activities. (For an exception which proves the rule, see Thuc. v. 54.3. Cf. also, for the Carneia, Hdts vi
106.3; vii 206.1; for the Gymnopaediae, Thuc. v 82.2–3, with Andrewes in
Gomme, *HCT* iv 150; and for the Hyacinthia, Hdts ix 7.1 ff.; Xen., *HG* iv v.11.)
But we cannot entirely exclude the possibility that the election of ephors was held
in the spring, before the beginning of the campaigning season.

6. We can now return to the events at Sparta in 432. Sthenelaïdas was very
clearly a 'hawk' (for this term, see Chapter V, Part ii above), and surely we need
not doubt that the board of ephors of his year included a majority of 'hawks', for
the ephors acted by majority decisions (see Xen., *HG* ii iii.34; iv.29), and if the
majority had been against war they would hardly have allowed Sthenelaïdas to
preside at the fateful assembly, make a vigorous speech in favour of war, and put
the motion 'that the Athenians have broken the Peace'. Against Poralla (*PL* 113,
168) and others,[13] we cannot assume that Sthenelaïdas, εἷς τῶν ἐφόρων τότε ὤν
(Thuc. 1 85.3), must have been eponymous ephor in his year (see Gomme, *HCT*
1 424). The eponymous ephor for 432/1 was Aenesias (Thuc. ii 2.1; Xen., *HG* ii
iii.10); and Sthenelaïdas could have been one of his colleagues, if he was not a
member of the board for 433/2—the eponymous or another: we do not know who
gave his name to that year.

But was Sthenelaïdas' 'hawkish' board of ephors nearly at the end of a term of
office to which it was elected in the summer (or spring) of 433, or had it been
elected only a few weeks or months earlier, for the year 432/1? Let us consider
the two alternatives.

(*a*) If Sthenelaïdas and his colleagues were elected in 432 (with Aenesias as
eponymous), at a time when the possibility of a declaration of war against Athens
must have been by far the most important issue at Sparta, then the election can
surely be taken as very probable[14] evidence of the bellicosity of a majority of
Spartans at this time, well in advance of the official Corinthian representations
in favour of war (Thuc. 1 67–71) which are so often seen as the decisive factor
in bringing about the Spartan decision to break the Peace. (Cf. Chapter V,
Parts viii–ix above.) Moreover, if the promise given to the Potidaeans that Sparta
would invade Attica in support of Potidaea's revolt was given, not by the Spartan
Assembly but, as generally believed, by the board of ephors of 433/2, acting on their
own authority (see Chapter V, Part viii above), then we should have to conclude
that the 'hawkish' board of 432/1 was preceded by an equally 'hawkish' board for
433/2! And by whatever agency (Assembly or ephors) the undertaking to Potidaea

[13] When Adcock, in *CAH* v 475, wrote that the vital assembly 'preceded the change of
ephors in October (cf. Thuc. 1 85.3, 87.1, with ii 2.1)', he was presumably making the
same assumption.

[14] Unless there were very special circumstances necessitating a political choice, I do
not believe that the elections of yearly officials in Greek states—even of important ones
like the Spartan ephors—would be very much affected by any political 'programmes'
the candidates might have: I suspect that their social eminence would as a rule play the
largest role (especially in an oligarchy), and that the representative of a leading family
could probably expect election *suo anno*, as at Rome. It is conceivable that Sthenelaïdas
and his 'hawkish' colleagues (at least two more of the five) were men of such distinction
that they were virtually bound to be elected, or alternatively that there happened to be no
'doves' prominent enough to have a chance of success in the election. However, by even
the spring of 432 it must have been evident at Sparta that a decision might soon have
to be taken about war with Athens; and since the ephors played a large part in the conduct
of foreign affairs, their attitude towards Athens was surely very likely to be a major issue
in the election.

was given, the election of Sthenelaïdas and Co. would give us a probable indication that in the spring or summer of 432 the majority of Spartans wished to implement that undertaking by attacking Athens.

(*b*) If, on the other hand, the year of Sthenelaïdas and his colleagues was 433/2, then they had been elected in the summer (or spring) of 433—whether before or after the news of the Athenian-Corcyraean alliance reached Sparta, we cannot say. At that time the possibility of war with Athens will not have been nearly such a burning issue, although it is very likely to have been foreseen by many Spartans.

As I have said, I prefer not to choose definitely between the two chronological schemes discussed in §3 above, although I distinctly prefer the later one, which incidentally has the support of a greater number of scholars than Gomme's alternative. And anyone who accepts this later scheme, in which the vital Spartan assembly must fall in October at the earliest, is virtually bound to put that assembly in the ephor-year 432/1 rather than 433/2, especially if he prefers one of the later versions of that scheme, such as Thompson's. It would then be hard to accept the usual view (taken for granted, for instance, by Kagan, *OPW* 286–7) that the majority of Spartans were against a declaration of war until strong pressure was brought to bear upon them by the Corinthians.

7. The question whether Sthenelaïdas and his colleagues were the ephors of 433/2 or 432/1 also has a bearing upon another question which I wish to raise, without being able to answer it satisfactorily: that of the purpose of the Spartan embassies to Athens in the winter of 432/1. The position taken by Thucydides in regard to these embassies, about which (except for the anecdote in Plut., *Per.* 30.1) he is our only source, is well stated by Dover in Gomme, *HCT* IV 394: 'Sparta did indeed send envoys to Athens ἐγκλήματα ποιούμενοι (1 126.1) at the end of 432; but according to Thucydides' account this was done not in order to open the way to arbitration, as Archidamos had proposed (1 82.1; 85.2), but after the decision to fight had already been taken (86 f., 125), and it was done in a manner designed to provoke refusal (139.1; 140.2; cf. 144.2) and in the hope of gaining a moral advantage from that refusal'. Cf. Busolt, *GG* III ii.845–53; Gomme, *HCT* I 447–54 (esp. 451–2), 463–4, 465–6; Kagan, *OPW* 317–41; contrast Nesselhauf, *DVPK*.

We need waste no time on the first embassy (Thuc. 1 126.2 ff.; Plut., *Per.* 33.1–3), which was clearly a diplomatic manoeuvre directed against Pericles personally (see Thuc. 1 127.1). On the second embassy (139.1) different views have been expressed. Although no account that I have seen is entirely satisfactory, I am inclined to agree with Busolt (*GG* III ii.846–7) and Kagan (*OPW* 321–4) that on this occasion Archidamus may have been able to exercise some influence, and that the ambassadors were perhaps angling for a compromise, even at this late stage. Although some scholars (e.g. Nesselhauf, *DVPK* 293 ff.) have taken a very different view, I do not see how we can call the peremptory message delivered by the third and final embassy (Thuc. 1 139.3–145) anything but an 'ultimatum': see Kagan, *OPW* 325; cf. Busolt, *GG* III ii.848 ff.; Gomme, *HCT* I 451–2, 453–4. Even on this occasion, however, we may note that at least one of the three ambassadors (Thuc. 1 139.3), Melesippus, evidently shared the views of Archidamus regarding the war with Athens (see II 12.1–3), and that another, Ramphias, was apparently a man who at least hoped for peace in 422 (see V 13.1–2). It is possible, therefore, that Archidamus and his friends were able to exert some influence in the winter of 432/1 in the direction of at least postponing the war. If so, we might be inclined to give an affirmative answer to Gomme's question (*HCT* 1 450): Was the Theban attack on Plataea 'made perhaps in part from a desire to force the issue, to prevent Sparta from sending more embassies?'.

But although a Spartan king in command of an army abroad might send an envoy to a foreign state (see Thuc. II 12.1), official ambassadors would surely be despatched from Sparta only by the Assembly, or by the ephors, whose duty it was to attend to foreign affairs generally, subject to the decisions of the Assembly, and who will surely have had the sole right to send out official embassies between meetings of the Assembly. (I admit that I know of no specific evidence on this matter.) At this point we return to the question whether Sthenelaïdas and his colleagues were ephors in 433/2 or 432/1. If the former, it may possibly be that a less 'hawkish' board of ephors had been elected in 432, and that Archidamus and his friends were able to bring to bear upon its activities more influence than they could exert upon Sthenelaïdas and Co. But King Archidamus, as the leading Spartan of his day, would have great influence in any event, and the argument I have just suggested can easily be brushed aside by those who find good reason on other grounds for accepting Sthenelaïdas' year as 432/1—the solution which, as I have indicated, should probably be preferred.

8. Anyone who tries to sort out the chronology of the years 433–1 cannot avoid the difficult problem of the seasons in Thucydides. The whole question is immensely complicated and has been much discussed.[15] All I can do here is to try to clarify it a little.

First, we must recognise that although Thucydides sometimes speaks of spring and autumn, as well as summer and winter, yet when he is dividing the whole year into what he very loosely calls 'halves' (v 20.3), the spring and autumn are part of the summer (see Gomme, *HCT* III 702, 705, 710), which therefore occupies roughly two thirds of the year. The crucial points in Thucydides' year, then, are the beginning and end of his 'winter'. The question which is still being debated is whether these two points were fixed astronomically, in terms of the solar year. That they were so fixed is maintained especially by Pritchett: see in particular his two articles, TTRESC (written jointly with van der Waerden, and published in 1961), and 'Thucydides v 20', in *Historia* 13 (1964) 21–36, arguing that Thucydides' winter begins with the cosmical (morning) setting of the Pleiades[16] and ends with the acronychal (evening) rising of Arcturus; also that Thucydides is likely to have accepted the exact dates given in the 'Parapegma of Euctemon',[17] namely November 8 and March 6. (According to Bickerman, *CAW* 143, 145, the true Julian dates would be November 4 and February 26/27 respectively.) At the other extreme is Meritt, who insists that 'our troubles in Thucydidean chronology are largely of our own making. We expect him to be consistent, and he is not consistent' (ST 445). In an article which Meritt wrote jointly with M. F. McGregor, 'The Athenian Quota-List of 421/0 B.C.', in *Phoenix* 21 (1967) 85–91,[18]

[15] Perhaps the most sensible treatment that I have seen is by Andrewes, in Gomme, *HCT* IV 18–21; but this needs to be read with Gomme's own discussion in *HCT* III 699–715, from some of the conclusions of which Andrewes dissents. Busolt, *GG* III ii.799 n. 1, 907 n. 2, is also worth studying.

[16] 'Arcturus', in TTRESC 29, line 3, is a mistake for 'the Pleiades'. I may say that the setting of the Pleiades is perhaps the most frequently mentioned of all astronomical events in fifth/fourth-century literature: I have come across some thirty references to it in Hippocratic works alone.

[17] For which see TTRESC 32–7; and in detail A. Rehm, 'Griechische Kalender, III. Das Parapegma des Euktemon', in *Sb. Heidelberger Akad. der Wiss., Philos.-hist. Klasse* (1913), Abh. 3, pp. 1–38. For 'parapegmata' in general, see TTRESC 39–41; A. Rehm, in *RE* XVIII 3 (1949), col. 1295–1366, *s.v.* 'Parapegma'; and *Parapegmastudien* (= *Abh. der Bayer. Akad. der Wiss., Philos.-hist. Abt.*, N.F. 19, Munich, 1941, pp. 1–145).

[18] One really important conclusion of this article is that the Athenian archon-year 422/1 was ordinary and not intercalary (contrast Gomme, *HCT* III 711–12), thus making good sense of the 'ten years plus a few days' of Thuc. v 20.1: this may well be *c.* 5 days, if we assume, with Andrewes (*HCT* IV 18–19), that the ten years start from the attack on Plataea, and not from the first invasion of Attica, as believed e.g. by Meritt, ST 437–8; and by Jacoby, *FGrH* III b (Suppl.) i.16–19, and esp. ii.15–16, n. 143 (misprinted as a second n. 142).

at pp. 87–8, there is a very explicit statement: 'Thucydides did not reckon the end of winter and the beginning of spring by any fixed calendar, but by the accident of the season's climate, whether it was still cold or commencing to be warm.' Gomme, *HCT* III 699–715, took up a position distinctly nearer to Pritchett's; but his analysis has been well criticised by Andrewes, in *HCT* IV 18–21, 22 (with 11–12), and I am not convinced by Pritchett's latest treatment of the subject, in his *CM* 93–5.

It is easy to be misled by Thuc. v 20.1–3, which makes 'two quite distinct points' (Andrewes, in *HCT* IV 21), too often confused. The first point comes in §1, where Thucydides says that the war down to the Peace of Nicias lasted 'just ten years and a few days'. This simple statement is commonly exaggerated and over-emphasised. Even Andrewes (*loc. cit.*) says that here Thucydides 'gives us, in imprecise terms, the result of an exact calculation made for this occasion only'. But he need not have made an '*exact* calculation', for he does not give the number of days! Even if he was aware of the true length of a solar year, it seems to me very doubtful whether he would have been confident of his ability to calculate with astronomically fixed points in such a way as to give the precise number of days over the ten years of the war. I suppose it is just possible that he *could* have said that the war had lasted 'from *x* days after the acronychal rising of Arcturus in the archonship at Athens of Pythodorus and the ephorate at Sparta of Aenesias, to *y* days after the same event in the archonship at Athens of Alcaeus and the ephorate at Sparta of Pleistolas', or that it lasted 'ten years and [say] five days'; but this we shall never know, and I for one would rather have expected that if he could have said that, he would have done so. I suspect that he did not feel able to date precisely, to a day, either the stellar event just mentioned or the spring equinox which follows less than a month later.[19] Even astronomers, a rare breed as yet, had scarcely reached certainty and unanimity in such matters; the imperfections of observation would allow for a good deal of error until the observations had been repeated many times; and since Greek calendars were generally in a chaotic state and proceeded in complete indifference to each other, the difficulty of *recording and correlating* observations made in different places, and even in the same place over a long period, would be extreme—far greater than is usually appreciated today. It is interesting to note that Thucydides in the whole of his work—apart from a solar eclipse (that of 21 March 424) mentioned in IV 52.1 and a lunar one (of 27 August 413) in VII 50.4—uses only three astronomical dates (the heliacal rising of Arcturus in 429, II 78.2; and the winter solstices at the end of 414 and 412, VII 16.2 and VIII 39.1), *each time with a* περί, showing that he was not much concerned about the precise identification of days. There is certainly no clear, positive evidence that Thucydides operated with exact (or would-be exact) astronomical dates, whether those of Euctemon's parapegma or not. And at one point he says something which suggests that his astronomical knowledge fell short of real expertise: a solar eclipse, he remarks in II 28, '*seems* to occur only at the new moon'. A scientific understanding of eclipses had been achieved by a few Greek thinkers only a generation or so before Thucydides' day, and we need

---

[19] Anyone who is inclined to disagree should first take account of the differences in the dates for these events given in, or calculable from, e.g. (i) the Parapegma of Euctemon (see n. 17 above); (ii) the Calendar of Eudoxus, a couple of generations later (see F. Lasserre, *Die Fragmente des Eudoxus von Knidos* [Berlin, 1966] 79–95, F 147–268; (iii) Hesiod, *WD* 564–70 (evening rising of Arcturus 60 days after winter solstice); (iv) Hippocr., *On Regimen* III 68 (same event 59 days after winter solstice and 32 days before spring equinox); and (v) the calendar conveniently extracted by W. H. S. Jones, in the Loeb Hippocrates I 67–8, from Aetius III 164 (*Corpus Medic. Graec.* VIII i, ed. A. Olivieri, Leipzig/Berlin, 1935, pp. 335–7). And see Pritchett, *CM* 95 n. 15 (cited below); and D. R. Dicks, in *JHS* 86 (1966) 34–5 and nn. 48–9. As regards the acronychal rising of Arcturus there is the nasty problem whether one should take the 'true' rising (March 6, according to Euctemon) or the 'visible' rising some ten days earlier: see below.

not be surprised at his being reluctant to commit himself to the unqualified statement which a Meton might by now have made without hesitation.

In §§2–3 of v 20 Thucydides boasts of the superiority of his scheme of dating by summers and winters to one relying upon local city calendars, according to eponymous magistrates: with these, he remarks, one cannot distinguish between occurrences at different times in the 'year'. And in §3 he claims that by dating by summers and winters he has been able to demonstrate that the war in question lasted 'ten summers and an equal number of winters'—ten whole years, in fact. There is nothing at this point about the few extra days of §1, and Thucydides is surely thinking here not of them but of the fact that if he had dated by, for example, Athenian archons or Spartan ephors or the priestesses of Hera at Argos (cf. II 2.1) he would have had *eleven years* on his hands. The point he is making here is the contrast between the period of 'ten years' given him by his own method (here he can justifiably forget those few extra days) and the 'eleven years' with which any standard system would have burdened him. He does *not* argue 'that his system of dating by seasons enables him to state the length of the ten years' war *exactly*', as Gomme has it (*HCT* III 703). The 'few extra days' of §1 are irrelevant and ignored in §§2–3.

In order to decide what Thucydides meant by 'winters' and 'summers' we must ascertain how those expressions would naturally have been understood by educated people in the last third of the fifth century, and we must look at all the items in his narrative which shed any light on the actual dates in question. I can only give a brief summary here.

Andrewes (in Gomme, *HCT* IV 19–20) agrees with Gomme that any system of astronomical dates for the beginning and end of winter 'would work only if it was one familiar to and accepted by his readers'; but he goes on to point out that 'it is most unlikely that any one scheme was thus accepted. If it were not, it would be necessary for Thucydides to state the terms of his own system, which he conspicuously does not do'. (The whole passage that follows is excellent.) This exposes a weakness in the position of those who believe that Thucydides operated with a precise astronomical year. In order to forestall such objections Pritchett has recently appealed to the practice of Polybius, who 'used the terms for seasons in an astronomical sense', and he concludes that 'both historians were following a widely recognized convention of traditional dates which were understood by their readers living in city-states where parapegmata were set up in every marketplace' (*CM* 94–5, with references to P. Pédech, *La méthode historique de Polybe*). But Polybius furnishes no true parallel: he was writing nearly three hundred years later than Thucydides, after a very considerable development in the science of astronomy, and his practice cannot validly be used as evidence for that of Thucydides. Pritchett also seems to realise how awkward it is for him that Thucydides never tries to give exact dates. According to him, 'the reason that Thucydides did not date events as being so many days before or after the beginning of spring or winter may be because there was a difference of a few days on various parapegmata for these events. Such phenomena could not be fixed, at the time of Thucydides, to the exact day. He must have been aware of this range and decided that the fixing of an event within a few days was sufficient' (*CM* 95 n. 15). But how does Pritchett know that *in the late fifth century* 'parapegmata were set up in every marketplace' (as they doubtless were by Polybius' day), or that there was 'a difference of a few days' only between various parapegmata for events such as the beginning and end of winter? And how often does Thucydides try to date events even 'within a few days'? In view of fifth-century attitudes to chronology, why should he *want* to do so? According to Pritchett (*CM* 94 n. 12), Thucydides 'used a seasonal year which was fixed by scientific and popular convention'. But what is the evidence that scientific ideas in this field had already crystallised into 'scientific *convention*' or that there was by now a *single* 'popular convention', let alone that 'scientific' and 'popular' conventions coincided?

My own opinion is that the first half of November would probably have been generally accepted as the normal date for the start of winter: this was the time of the cosmical setting of the Pleiades,[20] often taken as a sign that winter was beginning (see e.g. the Hippocratic *On Regimen* III 68, quoted by Gomme, *HCT* III 707; also Eudoxus, F 192a [Lasserre], 193a, cf. 193b; Ps.-Dem. L 23). But the giving way of winter to spring is difficult to pin down to a definite point. Of astronomical dates, the most popular was certainly the acronychal rising of Arcturus—the 'visible' rising, not the 'true' rising (see below)—in late February, heralding the return of the swallow (see Hes., *WD* 564–70; Eudoxus F 229a; Aetius III 164), although spring was also sometimes said to begin at the vernal equinox (see e.g. Hippocr., *On Regimen* III 68).[21] And may there not have been many people in the late fifth century who did not associate the coming of spring with any particular astronomical event, but preferred to take account of actual weather conditions? Now early November would suit the narrative of Thucydides quite well for the beginning of winter (see Gomme, *HCT* III 706), but for the end of that season the spring equinox is in general too late, and the acronychal rising of Arcturus (the 'visible' rising) seems rather early. Pritchett and van der Waerden, TTRESC 37–8, 49–50, believe that for Thucydides the winter ended with the 'true' evening rising of Arcturus, on March 5–6, a date which would fit most of the Thucydidean evidence, but not that for 412/11 (VIII 60.3, with 39.1; 44.4; 58.1), unless we both emend 44.4[22] and interpret 'the thirteenth regnal year of Darius [II]' in 58.1 in the manner advocated by Pritchett and Bickerman rather than Meritt.[23] To choose the 'true' rising of Arcturus, however, would be very unsatisfactory, for in virtually every source that mentions the acronychal rising of Arcturus, except Euctemon's parapegma, it is clearly the 'visible' and not the 'true' rising that is referred to. I cannot see why Thucydides should adopt a procedure that could only mislead the vast majority of his readers, unless he was prepared to explain what he was doing; and this he certainly does not do.

I suggest that Thucydides, like most Greeks of his day, would expect the winter to begin in the first half of November and to end early in March, ten to fifteen days after the ('visible') evening rising of Arcturus, and before the vernal equinox. But he was primarily concerned with military matters: the operation of armies and fleets. If exceptional warmth or cold caused these operations to be advanced or retarded beyond their usual times, I would expect him to allow for this and to shorten or lengthen his 'winter' accordingly. Since he has no occasion to provide dates correct to a day, why should he not do this?

ADDITIONAL NOTE (see §4 above)

D. R. Dicks, 'Solstices, Equinoxes, and the Presocratics', in *JHS* 86 (1966) 26–40, at pp. 30–5, has argued that the equinoxes became known to the Greeks a good

[20] The range of dates calculable from the sources seems to extend at least from November 6 to 13. (From Bickerman, *CAW* 143, it appears that the true Julian date *c.* 400 was November 4.) The heliacal rising of Arcturus and the autumnal equinox might be taken as the beginning of autumn, but would still be within Thucydides' 'summer' as opposed to 'winter'.

[21] In *Probl.* XXVI 26, 942^{b}25 ff., Aristotle speaks of the equinox as the boundary between summer and winter; but this is the autumn equinox: see *Meteor.* II 6, 364^{b}1–3.

[22] As was advocated long ago by Wilamowitz (see Gomme, *HCT* III 711) and has been urged recently by Pritchett, 'The Thucydidean Summer of 411 B.C.', in *CP* 60 (1965) 259–61; *CM* 94–6.

[23] Pritchett, as cited in the last note, and in *Phoenix* 23 (1969) 179–80 n. 56; Bickerman, *CAW* 90, with 108; Meritt, 'The End of Winter in Thucydides', in *Hesp.* 33 (1964) 228–30; 'A Persian Date in Thucydides', in *CP* 61 (1966) 182–4, esp. 183, citing R. A. Parker.

deal later than the solstices, which were a matter of common knowledge at least as early as Hesiod, *WD* 479, 564–5, 663. (Wade-Gery, *EGH* 2, takes Homer, *Od.* xv 403–4, to be referring to the solstices; contrast e.g. Dicks, *op. cit.* 31; *Early Greek Astronomy to Aristotle* [London, 1970] 32–3.) Dicks insists that 'the concept of equinoxes is a much more sophisticated one' than that of solstices, which 'does not presuppose anything other than (relatively) simple observations'. This view has been contested by C. H. Kahn, 'On Early Greek Astronomy', in *JHS* 90 (1970) 99–116, at pp. 112–14, who agrees with Dicks that 'solstices are observable in a crude way in which equinoxes are not', but goes on to show that equinoxes can in fact be determined (if not with complete accuracy) without the more advanced astronomical knowledge thought necessary by Dicks: their *approximate* date can be fixed both by observational means and by counting the number of days from solstice to solstice and dividing by two. (The result of such a calculation would not be exact, because of the slight irregularity in the lengths of the seasons; but it would only be a day or two out.) I would point out that even in Hesiod, although the actual word for equinox (ἰσημερία) is not used, we do find in *WD* 561–2 a reference to the time when 'nights and days are equal' and the earth is again fruitful, in the spring. (For the mention of astronomical events in Hesiod, see H. L. Lorimer, 'Stars and Constellations in Homer and Hesiod', in *BSA* 46[1951] 86–101.)

By the late fifth century the equinoxes were certainly a matter of common knowledge. The earliest known occurrence of the word ἰσημερία is probably in the Hippocratic *Airs Waters Places* 11 (on which see Dicks' article cited above, p. 33 n. 38). In the Hippocratic treatises—in which alone, of Greek literary works from the fifth and fourth centuries, references to equinoxes are frequent—the vernal equinox is mentioned in e.g. *Epid.* I 4, 13, 14, 22; III 2; *On Regimen* III 68 (twice), that of autumn in e.g. *Epid.* I 1, 13 (twice), 18; IV 1, 2, 3 (probably), 5; VII 105; *On Regimen* III 68. The latter, however, sometimes tends to be replaced by the heliacal rising of Arcturus, as in *Epid.* I 4; III 2; *On Regimen* III 68 (*ad. init.*): all three passages mention the vernal equinox and the heliacal rising of Arcturus (taken in the last text as the beginning of autumn) but not the autumnal equinox, although this was known to occur later than the rising of Arcturus (see e.g. *Epid.* I 13; cf. *On Regimen* III 68 *ad fin.*). It is relevant, too, that Hesiod, who in the *Works and Days* mentions the winter solstice twice (lines 479, 564–5) and the summer solstice once (663), and even refers indirectly to the vernal equinox (561–2: see above), fails to make any mention of the autumnal equinox: he advises the farmer to conduct the vintage (609–11) 'when Orion and Sirius come into mid-heaven and rosy-fingered Dawn beholds Arcturus'—the last event (the heliacal rising of Arcturus) being fairly precisely datable for Hesiod's day, it seems, to about September 17/18, only a few days before the equinox. And Sophocles speaks of summer pasturage 'for six months from spring to Arcturus' (*OT* 1137). The heliacal rising of Arcturus is also mentioned in other early literary sources, e.g. Hippocr., *Airs Waters Places* 10, 11; Thuc. II 78.2; Plato, *Laws* VIII 844de (where again it ushers in the vintage); Ps.-Dem. xxxv 10 (where it marks the end of the safe sailing season); L 19; Arist., *Hist. An.* V 17, 549ᵇ11; VI 15, 569ᵇ3 ('from the rising of Arcturus until spring'); VIII 13, 598ᵃ18; 22, 617ᵃ31 ('from the summer solstice to the rising of Arcturus').

The Spartan ephor-list began traditionally in the mid-eighth century, probably 754/3 (see Apollodorus, *FGrH* 244 F 335b; F. Jacoby, *Apollodors Chronik* [= *Philol. Untersuch.* 16, Berlin, 1902] 138–42). This may well be too early; but a Spartan State Calendar, with eponymous ephors, probably existed at least from some time in the seventh century. The Spartans were an intensely conservative people, and once they had fixed upon a date for the beginning of their year they were very unlikely to change it. And I find it hard to believe that in the eighth or even the seventh century the autumnal equinox could have been sufficiently important and well ascertained to be taken as the day on which—or perhaps rather, on the first new moon after which—the year began. The heliacal rising of Arcturus, a few days earlier (September 19, according to Bickerman, *CAW* 145), might however have furnished an acceptable point of departure; and to me it seems likely that the new moon 'after Arcturus' may have been taken in principle as the first day of the first month of the Spartan year. At any rate, I know of no other widely recognised astronomical event which could have been utilised by the Spartans, between the heliacal rising of Sirius near the end of July (and therefore much too early) and the cosmic setting of the Pleiades early in November (which seems rather too late). The 'Parapegma of Euctemon' (presumably of the last quarter of the fifth century), as reconstructed by Rehm (see n. 17 above), seems to have taken the heliacal rising of Arcturus, put at September 14, as the beginning of Metoporon, the fourth of the five seasons recognised by Euctemon: see Pritchett and van der Waerden, TTRESC 31–41 (esp. 33, 39).

If the new moons of autumn 432 were on September 12 and October 11 (see Bickerman, *CAW* 116), then I think that the most likely Julian date for the change of ephors in 432 is October 11. But it may well be that the Spartan calendar was an erratic affair, with intercalations based on no very rational principle, and perhaps beginning at different times, in practice, in different years. Any pretence of certainty, or even of confidence, in such a matter is best avoided.

APPENDIX XIII

Symmachy and epimachy

The terms ἐπιμαχία, ἐπιμαχεῖν are very rare, and I know of only two occurrences outside Thucydides (I 44.1; V 27.2; 48.2), namely in Arist., *Pol.* III 9, 1280ᵇ27, and Ps.-Dem. XII 7 (both ἐπιμαχία), although there may possibly be a few others.

Thucydides is quite capable of using the words ξύμμαχος and ξυμμαχία to include ἐπίμαχος, ἐπιμαχία: see I 53.4, where the Athenians, after the battle of Sybota, refer to the Corcyraeans as their ξύμμαχοι, and V 27.2, where the Corinthians suggest to the Argives that they should invite other independent states πρὸς 'Αργείους ξυμμαχίαν ποιεῖσθαι ὥστε τῇ ἀλλήλων ἐπιμαχεῖν. The only text, apart from Thuc. I 44.1, in which an explicit contrast is drawn between συμμαχία and ἐπιμαχία is Thuc. V 48.2, where a ξυμμαχία involves τοῖς αὐτοῖς πολεμεῖν καὶ εἰρήνην ἄγειν, an ἐπιμαχία only ἀλλήλοις βοηθεῖν, ξυνεπιστρατεύειν δὲ μηδενί.

As Andrewes says (in Gomme, *HCT* IV 23), 'From the late fifth century onwards new alliances were normally defensive in form, so that the specialized term[ἐπιμαχία] was no longer needed, and the wider term συμμαχία had, in the fourth century, the meaning which Thucydides explains' in V 27.2. This is broadly true: see e.g. *SVdA* II 189, 193, 196, 223, 224, 231, 263, 280, 290, 293. For a few more examples of full symmachy in the old form that I have come across, see Appendix V.

The earliest certain symmachy I know of is M/L 17 = *SVdA* II 110 = *SIG*³ 9 = *DGE* 413, between Elis and Heraea, *c.* 500 B.C. Its wording is very general: there is to be a symmachy for a hundred years, and 'if anything is needed, either word or deed, they shall stand by each other in all matters and especially in war'.

APPENDIX XIV

The tribute of Potidaea in the 430s

The date at which the increase in the tribute of Potidaea was first made is not known for certain. The town certainly paid 6 talents down to 440/39 and 15 talents in 433/2 (Lists 15 II 50 and 22 II 70, in *ATL* II 21, 27). A figure of 6 talents appears in List 20 VI 5 (*ATL* II 25), for 435/4; but there is a suggestion in *ATL* III 64–5 (found 'attractive' by Gomme, *HCT* III 608, and 'not at all improbable' by Alexander, *PHR* 44, but rejected by Kagan, *OPW* 275 n. 8) that in this year the stonecutter inadvertently transposed the figures for Potidaea and Scione (the latter is in List 20 VI 6, the line below), and that in 435/4 it was the Scionaean tribute which was really 6 talents and the Potidaean 15 talents. The other figures for Scione strongly support the argument of *ATL*: earlier, the tribute it pays (when identifiable) is 6 talents; in 432/1 it is 4 talents, and 9 talents in 430/29 and 429/8. A figure of 15 talents in 435/4 would be very surprising indeed.

If the suggestion of a stonecutter's error is right, then the increase in the tribute of Potidaea may have been made at any time between 439/8 and 435/4 inclusive, and the most likely date will be 438/7, an assessment year. If the suggestion is wrong, then the increase will have been made probably in 434/3 or 433/2, presumably the former, an assessment year.

A figure of 15 talents would not have been out of proportion for an important town such as Potidaea, and there is no warrant for regarding it as an 'exorbitant demand' (see the end of Chapter III, Part i above), or for conceiving the increase as a 'disciplinary measure' (with *ATL* III 64–5) or as a form of 'pressure brought to bear' on Potidaea (with Gomme, *HCT* III 608), although of course it may have been resented and may have been one of the factors that caused the revolt. Even if we decide for 433/2, I agree with Alexander (*PHR* 42–5, at p. 44) that 'it would have been an unwise policy for Athens to exert this type of discipline in 433/2 because of any Potidaean sympathy toward Corinth during the latter's conflict with Corcyra and Athens, immediately preceding or following the battle of Sybota . . . A policy of this type would have invited trouble in a locality where a more conciliatory attitude might have been expected . . . On the other hand, if the increase to 15 talents can be attributed to the preceding year [434/3], as appears quite probable, there is no need to assume any pressure on Potidaea, since the relations of Corinth and Athens were in no way critical at that time.'

It is worth noticing that there seems to have been no very significant increase in the tribute of those who called themselves 'the Thraceward Chalcidians': that of Olynthus remained at 2 talents until her revolt in 432, as far as our incomplete records go. As for the Bottiaeans, their tribute seems to have been approximately doubled in 434/3 (*ATL* III 319; Gomme, *HCT* I 211–12), but the increase was only from 2 to about 4 talents. And see Kagan, *OPW* 274–7 (with 182–3), ending with the suggestion that in the 430s Athens was asking 'the more prosperous states of the area to pay more of the cost of their own protection' against Macedon.

Knight (*SSAP* 10–11) has made the extraordinary suggestion that the increase in the tribute of Potidaea was intended deliberately to provoke Potidaea to revolt! Pericles and the Athenians, we are to suppose, were fools enough to risk a long and costly siege of an important city in a strong position, merely in order to have an 'excuse . . . to move against the disaffected on lawful grounds, and in this way gain the control which they wanted'. Contrast Thuc. I 56.2, lines 21–3 *OCT*.

APPENDIX XV

Military expeditions and the accounts of Athena's Treasurers for 433/2 and 432/1

The accounts of Athena's Treasurers for 433/2 are in M/L 61 = Tod I² 55 = *SIG*³ 72 = *IG* I² 295; cf. *SEG* x 222; and see esp. Meritt, *AFD* 68–71.

The accounts of 432/1 are in *IG* I² 296 + 309a (see *SEG* III 33) = *SEG* x 223; and see esp. Meritt, *AFD* 71–83.

We must note that these accounts are not a complete record of the financial dealings of Athena's Treasurers but relate only to such transactions as were in effect loans from the Treasurers to the State, and that they are not arranged as annual accounts: see Meritt, *AFD* 57–8, 68–9. The second of the two sets mentioned above is incomplete.

According to Meritt's restoration (*AFD* 80–3 = *SEG* x 223), the second of our two inscriptions begins ['Αθεναῖοι ἀνέλ]οσαν ἐς Μα[κεδονίαν καὶ ἐς Πελοπόννεσον τάδε κτλ.]. This of course suggests that the inscription contained no reference to the expedition to the Gulf of Ampracia—the accounts of which might conceivably have appeared in a separate inscription. If, with Meiggs in *CR* 47 (1933) 176, we read [Ποτείδαιαν] instead of [Πελοπόννεσον], we might in theory suppose that a record of Phormio's expedition stood at the end of the inscription, in the portion now lost; but in practice this seems rather unlikely, since the second main group of payments, namely those relating to the expedition 'around Peloponnese', began only just before the end of the conciliar year 432/1, and it seems improbable that after this the accounts would go back to events in the summer of 432. The restoration of Phormio's name in line 13 of the inscription (in respect of his command at Potidaea) is widely accepted; but Gomme, in *CR* 55 (1941) 62 n. 2, has raised objections. If the restoration is right, it shows Phormio engaged in his new command during the fourth prytany of 432/1 (i.e. between October 20 and November 25, on Meritt's chronology): this is strangely early, if the battle of Potidaea was as late as October, and of course it leaves hardly more time for a campaign by Phormio in north-west Greece in 432/1 than Gomme's chronology, in which the battle of Potidaea takes place in mid-June and Phormio sails to Potidaea in September or October.

As for the possibility (suggested at the end of Chapter III, Part iv above) that the expenses of the squadron of forty ships sent to the Gulf of Ampracia could have been paid, if in 432/1, out of current revenue in the hands of the Hellenotamiae, the making of such payments about this time was never unlikely, and has now been made highly probable by the acute reconstruction in *ATL* III 329–32 (see *SEG* XII 48–50) of portions of the building accounts of the Propylaea (*IG* I² 365–7; cf. *SEG* x 265–6; M/L 60) for the years 435/4, 434/3 and (though the restorations here are very uncertain) 433/2.

APPENDIX XVI

Spartan ὀλιγανθρωπία

When Aristotle says that Sparta ἀπώλετο διὰ τὴν ὀλιγανθρωπίαν (*Pol.* ɪɪ 9, 1270ᵃ33–4), he is of course speaking not of a general decline in the population of Laconia and Messenia but purely of a decline in the number of Spartan citizens with full political rights: the *homoioi*, or 'Spartiates' in the technical sense. It is not always realised that the decline had set in even before the beginning of the Peloponnesian war: by the early fourth century it had become very serious.

There are various statements in the sources about the total number of Spartiates in earlier times: e.g. Arist., *Pol.* ɪɪ 9, 1270ᵃ36–7 (Spartiates said to have once numbered 10,000); Plut., *Lyc.* 8.5 and 16.1 (once 9,000 male Spartiate land-owners); Hdts ᴠɪɪ 234.2 (8,000 adult male Spartiates in 480). Probably the best single piece of evidence is the figure of 5,000 given by Herodotus (ɪx 10.1; 11.3; 28.2; 29.1; cf. 12.2) for the number of Spartiates who actually marched out against the Persians in 479: this is quite compatible with a total number of *c.* 8,000 adult Spartiates.

The next time we are given figures which can be used with any confidence to determine the total number of Spartiates is for the Leuctra campaign in 371, by which date they can hardly have exceeded 1,000 or 1,200. However, we do have some information relating to the year 418, on the occasion of the battle of Mantinea, and this time our source is Thucydides himself (ᴠ 68). Unfortunately there are two quite different reasons why these figures are a very uncertain guide to the total number of Spartiates. First, there is good cause to think that Thucydides failed to realise that what he calls the 'lochos' was really the 'mora' (each of which contained two *lochoi*), and that he has therefore roughly halved the true total figure. (I believe that Toynbee, Wade-Gery, and Andrewes[1] are on the right lines here.) Calculation from Thucydides then gives a figure of *c.* 3,686 (excluding Sciritae) for the 'Lakedaimonioi' who fought at Mantinea, amounting to about five-sixths of the whole army. Various complications make it hard to estimate the real total, but most probably it was somewhere in the neighbourhood of 7,372 (or 7,672 if the 300 'hippeis' ought to be counted separately: see Andrewes in Gomme, *HCT* ɪᴠ 116), exclusive of the special formations: Sciritae, Brasideioi and Neodamodeis. At this point we must face our second cause of uncertainty: in the *morai* (six in number, see e.g. Toynbee, *SPGH* 373 ff.) Spartiates and Perioi-koi were now brigaded together, and the ratio of Spartiates to Perioikoi is not clear. (It evidently grew progressively smaller.) The mixed regiments had existed at least as early as 425; and the fact that Xenophon (*Lac. Pol.* xɪ 1, 4) attributes the *morai* (the mixed regiments) to Lycurgus suggests that their origin goes back further still—perhaps to a time not long after the great earthquake of 465/4. It is worth mentioning that in 425, according to Thucydides (ɪᴠ 8.9), the Spartans had chosen the garrison of Sphacteria, 420 men, by lot 'from all the lochoi', and

---

[1] It is best to begin with the admirably cautious analysis of Andrewes, in Gomme, *HCT* ɪᴠ 110–17. See also Arnold Toynbee, 'The Growth of Sparta', in *JHS* 33 (1913) 246–75; Wade-Gery, *SRPL* ɪɪɪ 118–19, 123–6 (=*EGH* 71–4, 80–5); and esp. Toynbee, *SPGH* 365–88, 391–404, 416–17 (but I am far less confident than Toynbee that we can reconstruct the details accurately). Forrest, *HS* 131–7, is also very useful, but I cannot accept the theory he propounds on pp. 134–5. Another detailed discussion is that of Anderson, *MTPAX* 225–51 (with the Notes, pp. 328–38), whose views on many points are different again. The whole question is very obscure, and I do not wish to pretend that the account I am giving is more than the most probable of several alternative possibilities.

that of the 292 survivors taken prisoner only about 120, or just over 40 per cent, were Spartiates (iv 38.5). A rather higher proportion of Spartiates than of Perioikoi might perhaps have died fighting, and in the circumstances we may infer that in 425 the ratio of Spartiates to Perioikoi in the *morai* was somewhere between 40 : 60 and 50 : 50 (cf. Toynbee, *SPGH* 377 ff., esp. 382–3).

We now come to the campaign of Leuctra in 371, by which time the Spartiates evidently constituted a far smaller proportion of the whole fighting force of 'Lakedaimonioi' in the *morai*. We know from Xenophon that four of the six *morai* were involved in this campaign (*HG* vi i.1; iv.17); that apparently only men of military age up to fifty-five were serving (iv.17); and that 700 Spartiates were engaged, 400 of whom were killed (iv.15). There are again complications which make it difficult to calculate the full number of Spartiates from these passages; but if we may assume, with Toynbee (*SPGH* 401–2; contrast Anderson, *MTPAX* 245–9), that the 300 *hippeis*[2] were virtually all present (and nearly all wiped out), we have only about 100 Spartiates per *mora*, and thus a further 200 in the two *morai* not engaged in the battle; and we then have a total of about 900 adult male Spartiates up to the age of fifty-five, of whom only 500 survived the battle. These may, I think, be considered minimum figures, but the total number of adult male Spartiates of all ages can hardly have been very much more than, say, 1,200 before the battle or 800 after it. And even 900–1,200 is a very small number for the ruling class of the large area of Laconia, not to mention Messenia.

Aristotle, *Pol.* ii 9, 1270ª30–1, says 'there were not even 1,000' Spartiates. He is presumably speaking of the time at which he was writing, and this can hardly be fixed within wide limits—I would suggest the 340s b.c. By 243 there were said to be not more than 700 Spartiate families, of which perhaps 100 possessed 'land and *klēros*' (Plut., *Agis* 5.6).

The main cause of the decline in the Spartan citizen population is surely the concentration of wealth, especially in land, in the hands of fewer and fewer families: here I agree with Forrest, *HS* 135–7. (And see Chapter IV, Part v, Section B *ad fin.* above and Appendix XXVIII below.) The essential clue is the statement of Aristotle (*Pol.* ii 9, 1271ª32–7; 10, 1272ª13–16) that a Spartan who became too poor to make the prescribed contribution to his *pheidition* (*syssition*) lost his political rights. The very fact that laws were passed giving special privileges to the fathers of three or four sons (Arist., *Pol.* ii 9, 1270ᵇ1–4) shows that the Spartiates, like all exclusive aristocracies, were failing to reproduce themselves. As for the much-quoted 'rhetra of Epitadeus', mentioned only by Plutarch, *Agis* 5.3, I entirely agree with Forrest, *HS* 137, that 'Epitadeus, if he existed, does not belong to the fourth century or, if he does, did not create the trouble'. On the Spartan land-system, see Walbank, *HCP* i 728–31. On the position of Spartan women, and their considerable property-rights (evidently far greater than those enjoyed by Athenian women), see my paper in *CR* 84 = n.s. 20 (1970) 273–8 at p. 277, cf. 389; cf. also W. K. Lacey, *The Family in Classical Greece* (London, 1968), ch. viii, esp. 194–208.

Casualties in the earthquake of 465/4 may have been very heavy; but, as demographers have established, populations recover quickly from such natural disasters unless there are inherent factors independently causing decline. By the time of the Peloponnesian war the number of adult male Spartiates may well have fallen to 3,000–4,000, not more than half the figure during the Persian war.[3] The subsequent further decline is beyond the scope of this book.

---

[2] See Thuc. v 72.4; cf. Hdts viii 124.3, with i 67.5; Xen., *Lac. Pol.* iv 3; Strabo x iv. 18, pp. 481–2. Cf. Plut., *Lyc.* 25.6; *Mor.* 191 f = 231b.

[3] I agree with Andrewes, *GCS* 7: 'It would be reasonable to guess that in the last quarter of the fifth century the voting strength of the Spartan assembly was not less than 3,000.' The further decline was then rapid: see above on the figures for Leuctra, and cf. Xen., *Lac. Pol.* i 1.

APPENDIX XVII

Membership of the Peloponnesian League

I am not concerned here to argue in detail about the status of Sparta's Peloponnesian League allies before the First Peloponnesian war; but some observations are necessary, if only to rebut confident assertions which have been made in modern times, unsupported by any solid evidence.

A. It is virtually impossible to prove beyond doubt that any particular state had a treaty of alliance with Sparta before the Persian wars, except *Tegea* (see Chapter IV, Part iii above, *ad init.*) and *Corinth* (because of Hdts v 75.1,3; 91.2–93.2); but texts such as Hdts v 74; 75.3; 91.2,3; 92.1; 93.2, and above all I 68.6 show that Sparta did have a large number of *Peloponnesian allies* by the late sixth century, and it is surely probable that when the Peloponnesian League proper was organised, from *c.* 505–1 or later (see Chapter IV, Part iv above), it included every Peloponnesian city as far north as Corinth, except Argos and the Achaeans.

Beyond the Peloponnese[1] *Megara* was Dorian; her geographical situation would make her adherence very important from Sparta's point of view; and as Corinth was a member, the Megarians will surely have felt it imprudent to remain isolated. There is of course no absolute proof of Megara's membership before the First Peloponnesian war. But then, there seems to be no proof of *Epidaurus'* membership either, before *c.* 460 (Thuc. I 105.1,3)—or even 446 (114.1), for those who cannot accept 'Peloponnesians' in 105.1,3 as meaning the members of the Peloponnesian League (cf. Chapter V, Part vi above). Yet Epidaurus, liable as she was to be threatened by Argos, would surely have had the best of reasons to join Sparta's alliance and is very likely to have done so well before the end of the sixth century. *Athens* no doubt became an ally of Sparta on the expulsion of Hippias in 510; but if so, the alliance must have come to an end in 508/7, and I see no reason to think Athens ever became a member of the Peloponnesian League before 404. Thuc. I 102.4, for what it is worth (see Appendix XXXII below), refers only to 'the alliance made against the Mede'—in 481 or possibly 492/1, and having nothing to do with the Peloponnesian League proper. The appeal of Athens to Sparta against Aegina in 491 (Hdts VI 49 ff.) proves nothing about Athenian membership of the League, for any state outside a league might wish to appeal to the hegemon of the league to coerce one of its members, and (as we shall see in a moment) there is no doubt that Aegina was a member of the League in 491. In Hdts VI 85–6 the Athenians must know already that Sparta has officially repudiated (85.1) the coercion of Aegina by Cleomenes and Leotychidas, yet they refuse to restore the hostages; their remark to Leotychidas in 86.1 (which may be no more than a quotation of the perhaps already famous riposte of the Aeginetans to Cleomenes, 50.2), if correctly reported by Herodotus, is surely not, as its Aeginetan counterpart may have been, a serious attempt to argue a 'constitutional' point (cf. the last portion of Chapter IV, Part v above), but an incidental justification of a position the Athenians have already made up their minds to adopt in any event; and it is significant that Leotychidas (according to Hdts VI 86. α.1, δ *ad fin.*) realises he has no right to coerce them.

B. Aegina. The general opinion is that Aegina had joined the League before 491: see e.g. D. M. Leahy, 'Aigina and the Peloponnesian League', in *CP* 49 (1954)

---

[1] In the eyes of Thucydides (II 9.2), at any rate, Megara was not technically part of 'the Peloponnese' (which was ἐντὸς 'Ισθμοῦ and ended with Corinthian territory), but was ἔξω Πελοποννήσου.

232–43; contrast Wickert, *PB* 23–6, 62, 64, who thinks there was probably no alliance. It seems to me perverse to deny that the affair of the Aeginetan hostages in 491 (Hdts vi 49–50; 73; cf. 85–6) proves Aeginetan membership of the Peloponnesian League, for vi 50.2 surely shows that the Aeginetans recognised an obligation to obey a Spartan order in a matter affecting their foreign policy, provided it was given by the Spartan State, οἱ Σπαρτιᾶται. If Aegina was obliged to 'follow the Spartans whithersoever they might lead', the Spartans might legitimately, in a situation of desperate urgency, demand security that Aegina would indeed follow their lead against Persia, to which she had given earth and water. (For Sparta's taking hostages, cf. Thuc. v 61.4; viii 3.1; 24.6 with 31.1.) In a later Herodotean passage, vi 73.2, there has still apparently not been a formal decision by the Spartan Assembly, and we hear nothing of any action by the ephors; but the Aeginetans cannot now risk refusing Cleomenes' demand, for if he is powerful enough to have his co-king removed and replaced by one of his own partisans, it would have been rash to assume that he could not procure a vote from the Spartan Assembly if he needed to. It certainly seems that Aegina was recognising a legal obligation to obey. This is surely what we ought to have expected: Aegina was Dorian and an aristocratic oligarchy,[2] and since her main enemy in the late sixth and early fifth century was democratic Athens (seee esp. Hdts vi 88–91), she had every reason to ally herself with Dorian and oligarchic Sparta. If Aegina had not been a willing member of the Peloponnesian League, she could have snapped her fingers at Cleomenes' demand, for she was far too strong at sea to be easily coerced by the rest of the League fleet, and with Persia about to move against Greece, a full-scale war against her would have been an insane undertaking.

In what seems to me a thoroughly mistaken series of arguments in his article, 'Aegina and the Delian League', in *JHS* 80 (1960) 118–21 (accepted by H. D. Meyer, VGDAS 441 n. 73), D. MacDowell has urged that Aegina 'was never a member of the Peloponnesian League but probably was a voluntary member of the Delian League from its formation'. Since this affects Aegina's position in the First Peloponnesian war, I must make a few points about MacDowell's case:

(*a*) In *c.* 494 Cleomenes, in the Sepeia campaign, used ships belonging to Aegina which he had taken ἀνάγκη (Hdts vi 92.1). This does not necessarily imply 'some kind of fight', as MacDowell claims: mere constraint by threats would be quite sufficient to satisfy Herodotus' expression. (Cleomenes could equally have been said to take the hostages from Aegina in 491 by ἀνάγκη, though no force was used— MacDowell himself here says 'the case is one of might'!) And how could Argos have even claimed a fine from Aegina and Sicyon if they had been literally 'compelled' after a defeat in war? It is absurd to pretend that Argos must have had, or claimed to have, 'some kind of *alliance*' with Aegina: a simple peace or truce, or common membership of some kind of religious organisation (cf. Thuc. v 53.1), would be quite sufficient. Much of the second paragraph on MacDowell's p. 118 seems to me far removed from reality.

(*b*) MacDowell also gives (*op. cit.* 119) a very wrong interpretation of Plut., *Them.* 19.2: according to him, Polyarchus 'made a special journey from Aegina to Sparta to accuse the Athenians'. What would be the point of mentioning this if (as MacDowell believes) Polyarchus was *not* 'an official representative of Aegina'? The word ἀποστέλλω is a regular word for the sending out of an envoy, and anyone reading the passage without preconceived ideas would naturally take it to mean that Polyarchus was '*sent expressly from Aegina* to accuse' Athens. This fits perfectly with the statement in Thuc. i 90.1 (not mentioned by MacDowell) that the Spartans, in telling the Athenians not to rebuild their fortifications, 'acted principally at the instigation of their allies'. Which other members of the Peloponnesian League would have nearly as much reason as Aegina to want to keep Athens

[2] Cf. Chapter VII, Part vi, n. 61 above.

defenceless before an invasion? Neither Corinth nor Megara was as yet seriously at odds with Athens, whereas Aegina had been for many years.

(c) To say, 'The Aeginetans were traders, and so dependent for their prosperity on the freedom of the seas from Persian domination' (p. 119) shows a fundamental misunderstanding of conditions in the Aegean and western Mediterranean. The Persians never wanted or tried to interfere with 'the freedom of the seas' for traders, whether Greeks or not.

(d) To try to find in Diodorus' very general and second- or third-hand stuff anything 'precise', or any 'deliberate comparison' between Aegina and Thasos etc. is a mistake: Thucydides, who is habitually much more precise than Diodorus, *does* refer to 'revolts' by Naxos (1 98.4) and other states (99.1–3), and by Thasos (100.2), and does *not* speak of a revolt by Aegina but of a πόλεμος (105.2)—just as he does in the case of Carystus (98.3).

And see Reece, DFI 118 n. 32.

C. *The Boeotians (and Phocians and Locrians).* I have argued in the main text above that between 447/6 and 431 the Boeotians, Phocians and Opuntian Locrians all became members of the Peloponnesian League proper. The main arguments can be stated as follows:

1. Prima facie, we should be willing to consider the possibility that the Boeotians, Phocians and Locrians were all allied with Sparta on the same footing, if only because they are named together and without any distinction being drawn between them by Thuc. 11 9.2,3; iv 118.2 (Boeotians and Phocians only); v 64.4; viii 3.2. If we then find (as I shall claim we do) that the Boeotians were League members, we may feel that the Phocians and Locrians should be placed in the same category unless there is some evidence to the contrary.

2. Certain passages in Thucydides show the Spartans as *ordering* the sending of military or naval contingents from these three states: see v 64.4 (where the word used is κελεύοντες, and although no contingents could be sent in time, the allies did make preparations); viii 3.2 (where a πρόσταξις is issued, demanding twenty-five ships from the Boeotians alone and fifteen from the Phocians and Locrians together); cf. iv 70.1 (κελεύων, to the Boeotians alone: they would have come anyway, 72.1).

3. Various scholars, notably two leading authorities on the Peloponnesian League, Kahrstedt and Larsen,[3] have argued that the Boeotians, although they had an alliance with Sparta, were not members of the Peloponnesian League proper. Gomme, after accepting Boeotian membership of the League in the third volume of his Thucydides commentary (*HCT* iii 665), seems to have changed his mind[4] in the light of Thuc. v 32.6, the text which Larsen, for example, regards as decisive against Boeotian membership. Busolt's position is not absolutely clear to me. He often speaks of the Boeotians (as of the Phocians and Locrians) as members of the League, but in each of his main works he qualifies this at one point with the words, 'the Boeotians, that is to say the Thebans'.[5] I myself wondered at one time whether it might not indeed have been the Thebans as such (and perhaps other Boeotian cities individually) who were members of the Peloponnesian League proper; but after going through all the references in Thucydides and Xenophon to Boeotians and Thebans I have realised that this is certainly wrong. Thucydides is careful to use the word 'Boeotians' in every case in which he is speaking of the alliance with Sparta; when in other contexts he is speaking specifically of the

[3] Kahrstedt, *GSISS* 30 and n. 1 etc. (the texts he cites are far from being sufficient to prove his point: most of them are irrelevant); Larsen, CPL 1 269 n. 40; *GFS* 133; also Wickert, *PB* 76–8, 81; and others.

[4] See *HCT* iv 31, with the contrary opinion of Andrewes.

[5] *GG* iii ii.857, with n. 1 ('Die Boioter, beziehungsweise Thebaner'); and Busolt-Swoboda, *GSK* ii 1324 n. 1 ('Die Boioter, bezw. die Thebaner im Bundesrate').

Thebans he names them as such. Xenophon, of course, does not seem to mind which word he uses, Boeotians or Thebans: for him the two are virtually interchangeable terms (see e.g. *HG* IV v.9, with 10); he much more often uses the word 'Thebans', even when we know it ought to be 'Boeotians' (cf. III v.4–24, with Tod II 101 = *SIG*³ 122 = *IG* II² 14). For me, Thucydides' usage is decisive, and there are a few passages which help to put the matter beyond doubt:

(*a*) Above all, in v 17.2 Thucydides speaks of the Boeotians as *voting* against the Peace of Nicias, with Corinth, Elis and Megara, all of which were certainly members of the Peloponnesian League. (To be precise, what he says is that all the allies voted in favour of the Peace except those four; but it is surely a certain inference that they were entitled to vote, and did vote against it.) It would have been most uncharacteristically misleading of Thucydides to have used the word 'voting' if there had been mere consultation with the Boeotians, even a speech by their envoys to the Spartan Assembly and no more. And there are references in later authors to the presence of the Boeotians (even if the name is sometimes given as 'Thebans') in the League Congress in 404 at which the peace terms were agreed: see Appendix XXI below.

(*b*) In Thuc. II 12.5 the Boeotians send 'their contingent' (μέρος ... τὸ σφέτερον) to join the Peloponnesian forces invading Attica in 431. This shows that the Boeotians had a recognised obligation to supply a certain proportion of their total forces, as did the other members of the Peloponnesian League. (And see Gomme, *HCT* III 563.)

(*c*) In the early spring of 420 (Thuc. v 39.3; cf. 40.1; 42.2; 44.1,3; 46.2,4) the Spartans concluded a new and equal alliance with the Boeotians, as they had done recently with the Athenians (v 22–4). It cannot be denied that the Boeotians were already allies of Sparta. The new alliance, then, was intended to put them in a better position vis-à-vis Sparta. This is understandable if until now they had been merely one of Sparta's subordinate allies, obliged to accept both Sparta's leadership in foreign affairs and majority votes in the League Congress.

(*d*) There are also the Thucydidean passages quoted in §2 above, showing Sparta giving orders to the Boeotians as to her other allies in the Peloponnesian League.

It is true that Thucydides does on occasion (e.g. v 57.2; 64.3,5; 67.2; and esp. 58.4; 60.3; VIII 3.2) refer to Ἀρκάδες as Spartan allies; but in these cases he is using the word in its geographical sense (cf. Πελοποννήσιοι) rather than in the technical sense of 'the Arcadian League', which was not fully organised as a political entity until after Leuctra: the Spartans always insisted on dealing with the individual Arcadian cities and never recognised the existence of οἱ Ἀρκάδες as such (see e.g. Wallace, KMHA).

4. Only one text, Thuc. v 32.6, provides even at first sight an argument against Boeotian membership of the League. The Boeotians and Corinthians had both refused to accept the Peace of Nicias. The Boeotians soon concluded with Athens a special truce (δεχήμεροι ἐκεχειρίαι or σπονδαί or ἐπισπονδαί),[6] terminable upon ten days' notice on either side.[7] However, the Corinthians, who had consistently refused to accede to the Peace (v 35.3,5),[8] had no such truce, and when

---

[6] Thuc. v 26.2; 32.5–7; cf. VI 10.3. This was made (see v 32.5) not long after the Spartan-Athenian alliance recorded in v 22–4. Later (26.2), between 421/20 (39.1) and 415, Athens made a similar truce (VI 7.4; cf. 10.3) with 'the Chalcidians in the direction of Thrace', as they called themselves: to the Athenians they were 'the Olynthians'.

[7] See Larsen, *GFS* 73 n. 1, 148 n. 3.

[8] This would soon have become known to Athens, for according to the terms of the Peace (v 18.1,9) she was entitled to demand oaths from all Sparta's allies, their adherence being in some cases important to her, whereas (cf. lines 14 and 19 *OCT*) Sparta and her allies would not be interested in exacting oaths from Athens' allies, all of whom doubtless wanted peace and would accept it on whatever terms Athens obtained.

they went to Athens with the Boeotians in the summer of 421, in an attempt to obtain one, the Athenians refused, saying that if they were indeed allies of Sparta then they were in treaty already (32.6). As we have seen, the Corinthians may well have had a valid claim to be exempted from the Peace, under the 'gods and heroes' clause which we have already examined (Chapter IV, Part iv, Section B, §7 above); but the Athenians evidently ignored this claim or treated it as invalid. It would, however, be quite wrong to conclude from this, with Larsen (*GFS* 133) and others, that 'Thus the Athenians considered the Corinthians, but not the Boeotians, to be *members of the League* [my italics] and bound by the Peace of Nicias'. Legal niceties were overridden by the realities of the situation. Athens had a perfectly good *practical reason* for treating the Boeotians and Corinthians differently: she wanted something from the Boeotians, namely Panactum, which was in their possession,[9] and perhaps Plataea too, if she could get it,[10] and was therefore obliged to pander to them and give them the truce they demanded;[11] but Athens saw no necessity to conciliate the Corinthians—it was they who wanted something from Athens: in particular Sollium and Anactorium (Thuc. v 30.2). Athens was consequently to some extent 'in the hands of the Boeotians', but not of the Corinthians, and could afford to treat the latter haughtily and leave them with what, in Corinthian eyes, was a mere '*de facto* armistice' [12]—although it may well be that, as between themselves and Sparta, the Corinthians had a much better legal reason than the Boeotians for rejecting the Peace, under the 'gods and heroes' provision. (We do not know on what pretext the Boeotians relied, in refusing to accept the Peace: the only grievance on their part that Thucydides reveals is their being asked to return Panactum to Athens.)

5. From the fact that in the One Year's Truce of 423 the Spartans 'promised to send ambassadors to the Boeotians and Phocians and do their best to induce them to accept it' (Thuc. IV 118.2), Larsen has argued that 'neither of the two confederacies [Boeotian and Phocian] had taken part in the negotiation or was bound by a treaty ratified by the Peloponnesian League' (*GFS* 133–4 n. 4). This can easily be shown to be mistaken. The Truce was concluded by the Spartans and 'those of their allies who were *present*' (118.2)—probably only Corinth, Sicyon, Megara and Epidaurus (119.2). They undertook to try to persuade the Boeotians and Phocians to (in effect) reopen the Sacred Way, which so far they had presumably refused to do: see Gomme, *HCT* III 596 ff., esp. 596–7, 599, 606–7.

6. Thuc. III 20.1, where Plataea is besieged by 'the Peloponnesians and Boeotians', is easily understandable in view of the disproportionately large share taken by the Boeotians (II 78.2); and 'the Peloponnesians' here will have been used in its geographical sense.

7. Throughout II 2–5 Thucydides speaks of the attack on Plataea early in 431 as conducted by the Thebans, not the Boeotians: it was of course a surprise attack, authorised and carried out by Thebes alone. Cf. 6.2, where the Athenians seize all Boeotians in Attica but speak of the Theban prisoners at Plataea. Yet in 7.1 Thucydides regards this purely Theban aggression as a manifest breach of the Thirty Years Peace. I suspect that when the Peace was concluded the Boeotian League had not been fully reconstituted, and that the Peace named Thebes (and perhaps other individual Boeotian cities) rather than 'the Boeotians' as Sparta's allies.

[9] Thuc. v 3.5; 18.7; 35.5; 36.2; 39.2,3; etc.

[10] See Thuc. v 17.2; cf. III 52.2.

[11] Cf. Andrewes in Gomme, *HCT* IV 31: 'Athens had a vulnerable land frontier with Boeotia, but not at this time much to fear from Corinth'.

[12] Thuc. v 32.7: ἀνοκωχὴ ἄσπονδος (Crawley's translation). The word ἄσπονδος shows that ἀνοκωχή is to be taken in the same sense as in IV 38.1; 117.1; VIII 87.4, rather than I 40.4; 66; III 4.4; v 25.3; 26.3.

8. There is one final argument—to me, a strong one—for Phocian and Locrian membership of the League. In 378, during the war against Thebes, there was a general reorganisation of the Peloponnesian League forces into ten units (μέρη), the ninth of which consisted of the Phocians and Locrians together: Diod. xv 31.2. I myself feel strongly that all the states named in this passage were members of the Peloponnesian League proper. There can indeed be no question about the first seven units. The eighth consisted of the Acarnanians, the tenth of the Olynthians and the allies of the 'Thraceward' area: the latter at any rate (Xen., *HG* v iii.26) and surely the former as well (cf. iv vii.1; vi iii.7) had sworn the oath of subordinate allies, 'to follow the Spartans whithersoever they might lead', which I would take as a very probable indication of membership of the Peloponnesian League. It seems to me in the highest degree unlikely that such a reorganisation as that described by Diodorus should be undertaken of a miscellaneous collection of states, some of whom were members of the League and some were not. And of course, if the Phocians and Locrians are accepted as members of the League, there is the more reason to accept the Boeotians (against whom war was now being waged) as members of the League down to the King's Peace.

One problem remains. The special alliance made between the Spartans and Boeotians in the early spring of 420 (see §3[c] above) is rather a puzzle, because we find no trace of it later: note Thuc. v 64.4; v111 3.2, where the Boeotians seem to be in the same position as Sparta's other allies. Andrewes (in Gomme, *HCT* iv 44) makes the point that Boeotia's existing alliance with Sparta 'obliged her to accept the majority decision of a conference', and implies that according to the new alliance she would no longer have to do so. He adds, 'The gain to Boeotia was great, since in effect this condoned her disobedience and made it impossible *de facto* for Sparta to join Athens in compelling her to accept the peace'. This may well be right. But we do not know the conditions of the new alliance, for we cannot infer from the words ὥσπερ 'Αθηναίοις in v 39.3 that the *terms* of the alliance were *the same* as those of the Spartan-Athenian one: it is the *fact* of Sparta's making a *separate* alliance with Boeotia to which those words refer. All we can really say for certain is that the separate alliance in some way improved the position of the Boeotians vis-à-vis Sparta, without entirely transforming them into equal allies, for in fact we can discern no difference between their position and that of the other members of the Peloponnesian League.

D. Another special treaty between Sparta and one of her League allies is the one made with Mantinea after the battle near that town in 418. This is given only the briefest mention by Thuc. v 81.1, but from Xenophon (*HG* v ii.2, speaking of σπονδαί) we know that it was to last for thirty years and remained in force for that time. I have nothing to add to the judicious discussion by Andrewes, in Gomme, *HCT* iv 148. As he says, this was 'somehow additional to the ordinary conditions of the Peloponnesian League which, from Xenophon's record, Mantineia certainly rejoined ... Mantineia's submission might reasonably be embodied in special σπονδαί, but it remains a little odd that a long-term truce should be included, and that its expiry should be felt to make a substantial difference in Mantineia's relations with Sparta.'

APPENDIX XVIII

The 'constitution of the Peloponnesian League': a summary

As the full discussion of the 'constitution of the Peloponnesian League', in Chapter IV, Part iv, Section B above, is rather complicated and full of technicalities, I append a brief summary of the main views expressed there.

1. (*a*) It was about the middle of the sixth century that Sparta entered into a series of military alliances (symmachies) which were later extended to other States and, not earlier than 505–1, were systematised in such a way that we can usefully speak of a 'Peloponnesian League'. By at least the middle 540s this series of alliances covered most of the Peloponnese apart from Argos and the Achaean area.

(*b*) Each of these alliances was probably between the individual State concerned and Sparta alone, not 'Sparta and her allies'.

(*c*) The alliances were either specifically for all time or were of indefinite duration, and no secession was legally possible, unless of course the ally concerned could claim that Sparta on her side had broken her engagements.

(*d*) Each ally enjoyed, in theory, complete internal autonomy, but took an oath 'to have the same friends and enemies as the Spartans and to follow the Spartans whithersoever they may lead', and was consequently subject to Spartan dictation as far as foreign policy was concerned.

2. (*a*) As late as *c*. 506, when the allies were called out against Athens, without being told the purpose of the expedition (which was to interfere in Athenian internal affairs), there was no limitation upon Sparta's right to summon her allies to follow her into a war. The disastrous result of that expedition induced Sparta to make a very considerable concession to the allies collectively: they need no longer obey Sparta's summons to at least an offensive war (in the sense in which I have defined that expression) unless there had been a League Congress, and the majority of the allies—each of whom possessed one vote—had voted for war. A Congress would also presumably be necessary if Sparta or any member of the League (like Corinth in 432) claimed to be the victim of an attack by an outside power—unless that attack was entirely clear and indisputable, in which case a League war would naturally follow, although the initiative, as always, could only be taken by Sparta.

(*b*) The affirmative decision of a League Congress was also necessary before a League war could be ended by a peace treaty. But the calling of a Congress was not required for any other purpose, except possibly (but not probably) the admission of a new member.

(*c*) 'Unless something to do with gods or heroes prevented it', each ally was bound to follow the decision of the majority at a League Congress. The most important example of the 'gods and heroes' qualification is a prior treaty, confirmed by oaths, which a member of the League could not be expected to break at the behest of the other members.

(*d*) Only Sparta could summon a League Congress, and she would do so only to procure allied agreement to some action she herself had already decided to take, for war or peace. Sparta also provided the Chairman of the Congress, but she herself almost certainly did not vote in it.

(*e*) It is the creation of the League Congress which was the real beginning of what we call 'the Peloponnesian League'. This may have come about by stages, and we cannot hope to fix a precise date for the initiation of the League: 'about 505–1 or rather later' is as near as we can get. Within the 'Spartan alliance' in general, only those States entitled to vote at a Congress can be considered to be members of the 'Peloponnesian League'.

3. During a war, Sparta was always in complete control of all military operations, by land and sea; and it was she who decided what campaigns would be conducted and provided the commanders.

APPENDIX XIX

Reception of new members into the Peloponnesian League

There are only three texts, as far as I am aware, which have been or could be cited in support of the view that new members could only be introduced into the Peloponnesian League with the consent of a League Congress. In fact I believe that none of them relates to an admission to what I have called the Peloponnesian League proper, but that in each case 'the Spartans and their allies' (in the sense of the members of the League) are making an alliance *external to the League*. In the second case mentioned below, this is beyond question. As regards the first and third it cannot perhaps be proved, but in these two cases Sparta had the best of reasons for *consulting* her allies: campaigns in support of the new allies would depend largely upon the co-operation of the member States of the League.

1. Thucydides III 8.1 to 15.1: 'the Lesbians' (that is to say, not merely Mytilene, but also Antissa, Eresus and Pyrrha: 18.1,2; 28.3; 35.1). In 428 the Spartans brought the Mytilenaean envoys before a meeting held at Olympia, before 'the Lesbians' were admitted to alliance by 'the Spartans and their allies' (15.1). I believe that the Spartan Assembly must already have decided to take the Lesbians into alliance, as members not of the Peloponnesian League but of the Spartan alliance in the broad sense (see Chapter IV, Part iv, Section A above), provided their Peloponnesian League allies could be induced to take the one kind of action which might help the Lesbians (and which they would insistently demand if admitted to alliance): a second invasion of Attica that year, and this time by sea as well as land. This proviso was by no means certain to be fulfilled, since the allies were already somewhat disinclined to provide their contingents for these not very successful undertakings (see Thuc. III 15.2, referring to the allies' ἀρρωστία τοῦ στρατεύειν); and before Sparta committed herself by oaths to the Lesbians, she needed to find out whether her allies would agree to launch another expedition against Attica. (In theory, of course, the allies were bound to come at Sparta's call at any time during the continuance of a League war; but it would be unwise to press them too hard, when so little was being achieved by these expeditions.) In the circumstances, therefore, Sparta *needed* to bring the allies in on the decision, *whether she was legally obliged to do so or not*. The meeting described by Thucydides was probably a formal League Congress, at the end of which the Spartans, in accordance with their own provisional decision earlier, proposed, and the allies agreed, to accept the Lesbians into alliance and take immediate steps to assist them. The very fact that it was 'the Spartans *and their allies*' who 'made the Lesbians allies'

(15.1) is to my mind a useful indication that it was the Spartan alliance in the broad sense and not the Peloponnesian League which the Lesbians were now entering.

2. In the winter of 418/17 the Spartan Assembly, agreeing to the terms of a proposed treaty with Argos, decreed that the document should be shown to the allies and concluded if they approved of it (Thuc. v 77.8). But this was certainly outside the scope of the Peloponnesian League, which Argos would never have consented to enter as a subordinate ally of Sparta.

3. Xen., *HG* v ii. 11 ff. esp. 20–2, 37 (cf. Diod. xv 19.2–3): the declaration of war against Olynthus, early in 382. The Spartan ephors brought the envoys of Acanthus and Apollonia 'before the Assembly and the allies' (ii.11), and decisions were taken to assist these two States (ii.20–2). Xenophon says nothing of the appeal to Sparta by Amyntas III of Macedon (which in Diodorus replaces that by Acanthus and Apollonia), until a Peloponnesian expedition is on its way (ii.38; iii.9)—naturally enough, for it was the appeal of Acanthus and Apollonia which gave Sparta, as *prostatēs* of the King's Peace, a 'legitimate' excuse for intervening to prevent Olynthus from infringing the autonomy of these cities. Xenophon of course is not to be relied upon for the details of Peloponnesian League procedures.[1] In ii.20 it is not immediately clear to what precise body the main verb, ἔδοξε, is intended to relate. One cannot even tell from the forms of address Xenophon makes his speakers use whether they are speaking to a Spartan Assembly or a League Congress: contrast, in one and the same speech, ii.12,18 ('Spartans and allies') with 14 ('Spartans')! It seems certain from ii.37, however, that the detailed decisions about the expedition against Olynthus were taken eventually by a League Congress (after the Spartan Assembly itself, of course, had made its decision: cf. Chapter IV, Part iv, Section B, §3 [*b*] and [*d*]; and Chapter V, Part viii), for Xenophon refers to 'the decision (*dogma*) of the allies', and in relation to the Peloponnesians this phrase is used only of decisions of a League Congress. Perhaps the procedure which in 432 had been divided into three stages—first, a deliberative session of the Spartan Assembly, with allies and others present and speaking (Thuc. 1 67.3–79.1); secondly, a closed session of the Spartan Assembly at which a vote was taken (79.1–87.3); and thirdly, a Peloponnesian League Congress, some time later (87.4; 119–125.1)—was now telescoped into a very short period, possibly a single day. But again, as in 428, whether or not Sparta was constitutionally obliged to consult the allies about any oaths she might be prepared to give to Acanthus and Apollonia, or about an expedition against Olynthus, it was only common prudence for her to ask for a decision from the allies, as they would have to supply troops for campaigns at a great distance, which might last a long time— in the event, some three years.

[1] For example, in *HG* II ii.19–20 he speaks of peace terms offered by 'the Spartans', although we happen to know from other sources, and even from the *Hellenica* itself (III v.8), that there was an allied vote. Again, in VI iii.3–18 we hear of foreign envoys speaking at what seems from §3 to be an open meeting of the Spartan Assembly with allies present (as in Thuc. 1 67.3–79.1), at which the speakers address themselves to the 'Spartans' (§§4, 7, 10), and it is 'the Spartans' who vote to accept the peace; but in §19 we find the Spartans taking the oaths 'on behalf of themselves and their allies', and this *may* suggest that between the meeting of the Spartan Assembly and the taking of the oaths there was a League Congress which authorised the Spartans to swear on behalf of the allies too—it is otherwise hard to see how the Spartans could have had the right to bind the allies.

APPENDIX XX

The suppression of 'revolts' of Peloponnesian League members

There are at least four cases and probably five, after the Peloponnesian war, in which Sparta summoned the allies to join her in reducing a refractory ally to submission: (i) in 403 against Athens,[1] (ii) in *c.* 401 against Elis,[2] (iii) in *c.* 381 ff. against Phlius,[3] (iv) in 379/8 against Thebes,[4] and (v) very probably in 385 against Mantinea.[5] In none of these instances do we hear that a League Congress was summoned, and we can be reasonably certain that none was.

Only in the fourth of these cases, one may think, had there been a clear 'revolt'. In the first, Sparta may have been justified in accepting the Athenian oligarchs' claim that the democrats had 'revolted from Sparta' (Xen., *HG* II iv.28); but the Boeotians and Corinthians would not accept this, and Sparta was not minded to coerce them (see Appendix XXI). In the second example, Sparta's complaint was that Elis was depriving her *perioikides poleis* of autonomy; but the Eleians believed themselves to have a good answer, and again the Boeotians and Corinthians refused to march.[6] In the third instance, Sparta was clearly intervening in the internal affairs of Phlius. If before the restoration of the exiles *c.* 383 Phlius had indeed refused to campaign with the Spartans 'whithersoever they led' (Xen., *HG* v ii.8), Sparta might then have had a good excuse for taking action, but when she did intervene in *c.* 381 she had no better reason than that the restored exiles were not receiving their due and Phlius was 'acting insolently' towards her (iii.10–13). In the fifth case Sparta demanded that Mantinea destroy her walls, making a series of allegations against her which were not self-evidently true.

APPENDIX XXI

The Boeotians and Corinthians, 404–395

Anyone who wishes to understand the behaviour of the Boeotians and Corinthians in 404 and the years following must look back at their relations with Sparta from 421 onwards. They had then voted in vain against the Peace of Nicias (Thuc. v 17.2), and had claimed—the Boeotians with more success than the Corinthians (see Appendix XVII)—not to be bound by it. But during the period of unrest following upon that Peace neither state had been willing to do anything overtly

[1] Xen., *HG* II iv.30 (with 28); III v.5: see Chapter IV, Part v above.
[2] Xen., *HG* III ii.21–31 (esp. 25); Diod. XIV 17.4–12; 34.1.
[3] Xen., *HG* v iii.10–17 (esp. 14), 21–5 (esp. 25), with ii.8–10.
[4] Xen., *HG* v iv.13–18 (esp. 15).
[5] Xen., *HG* v ii.1–7. There is no actual mention of allies, except hypothetically in §4. But in the case of Phlius, just mentioned, the allies are not referred to either except in iii.25, where they are disbanded. And Mantinea was a stronger state than Phlius.
[6] On the difficult problem of the position of Elis vis-à-vis Sparta from 418 to *c.*402, see Andrewes in Gomme, *HCT* IV 148–9.

hostile to Sparta. Later, perhaps alone among Sparta's allies, the Boeotians had claimed 'the tithe of Apollo' from the spoil taken at Decelea (Xen., *HG* III v.5; Plut., *Lys.* 27.4; cf. Justin v x.12–13 [Corinthians too]; Dem. xxiv 128; and see H. W. Parke, 'The Tithe of Apollo and the Harmost at Decelea', in *JHS* 52 [1932] 42–6).

In the early part of 404 there occurred a very revealing incident which has often been too superficially interpreted. At the Peloponnesian League Congress in the spring of 404 at which the terms of peace with Athens were agreed, many states, especially the Boeotians and the Corinthians, advocated the destruction of Athens and the enslavement of its citizens.[1] This is usually explained by saying that the Boeotians and Corinthians and their supporters 'hated Athens'. No doubt they did—but much more important was the fact that they feared Sparta! It must have been quite obvious what was going to happen if Athens was not destroyed: Lysander would install a puppet oligarchy, as he had already done in many other cities, and use Athens as an instrument of Spartan imperialist policy, above all against Athens' neighbour Thebes, now becoming ever more powerful (see esp. Polyaen. I xlv.5). I dare say the Boeotians and Corinthians would have been well content with the solution ultimately imposed by King Pausanias in 403, when, as we have seen (Chapter IV, Part v above), he put Athens under the control of the democratic party, withdrew the Spartan garrison and harmost, and left the Athenians entirely independent as far as their internal affairs were concerned, although of course their foreign policy was under the control of Sparta and her League. In 404, however, this alternative was simply not on the cards, Lysander and those who thought as he did being still largely in control of Spartan foreign policy. The only safe solution, therefore, from the point of view of Boeotia and Corinth, was to have Athens wiped out. But the Spartans prevailed upon the majority of their allies to accept their own very much milder terms.[2] According to the Laconophile Xenophon (*HG* II ii.20), they pleaded that it would be wrong to enslave the people which had done such signal service to Greece in her hour of greatest danger (in 480). But elsewhere Xenophon shows that he well understood their real intentions: to convert Athens into a puppet state and use it to further their own ends (see *HG* II iii.41; iv.30; cf. Polyaen. I xlv.5; and Busolt, *GG* III ii.1634–5).

The apprehensions of the Boeotians and Corinthians were fully justified by the event. Soon Lysander's aims were well on the way to being realised, with the Thirty installed at his own insistence (see esp. Lys. xII 71–6; Diod. xIV 3.5–7), and a Spartan harmost on the Acropolis, with a garrison of 700 men (Xen., *HG* II iii.13–14; Arist., *Ath. Pol.* 37.2; Plut., *Lys.* 15.6–7). It is no wonder that when the Athenians who could not endure the oligarchy of the Thirty went into exile, they received important help at Thebes, both from individuals and from the State,

[1] The sources are many. See esp. Xen., *HG* II ii.19–20; iii.25, 41; iv.30; III v.5,8; vi iii.13; v.35; Andoc. III 21; Isocr. xIV 31; Plut., *Lys.* 15.3–4. Diod xv 63.1 is misleading. For the role of the Phocians on the other side, see e.g. Dem. xIX 65; Plut., *Lys.* 15.4.

[2] The best authority for the actual peace terms is the passage in the Doric dialect in Plut., *Lys.* 14.8; cf. Andoc. III 11–12, 22, 31, 39; Lys. xIII 14; Xen., *HG* II ii.20; Diod. xIII 107.4. I agree with Busolt (*GSK* II 911 n.1; cf. *GG* III ii.1635–8) that the peace treaty was followed or accompanied by another, under which the Athenians entered the Peloponnesian League and accepted the hegemony of Sparta: see Xen., *HG* II ii.20 and *Anab.* vi i.27; Diod. xIII 107.4; confirmed by Xen., *HG* III i.4; ii.25. The latter document will have contained a standard 'autonomy clause' (cf. Thuc. IV 118.3; v 77.5; 79.1), which could later give rise to discussion about the precise form of the 'ancestral constitution' involved; cf. Arist., *Ath. Pol.* 34.3; Diod. xIV 3. 2–3,6. Hignett's objection (*HAC* 285 n. 3) is not well founded: the two transactions may have taken place very close together, and their joint provisions will have been regarded as the terms of peace. That Athens would be required to join the Peloponnesian League and submit to Spartan hegemony must have been regarded by everyone as a natural and automatic consequence of her defeat.

and Thrasybulus and his men actually set out from Thebes to capture Phyle, as the first stage of their courageous and successful attempt to restore democracy at Athens: see Xen., *HG* II iv.1–2; Lys. XII 95, 97; fr. 78.2 (Thalheim); Diod. XIV 6.1–3; 32.1; xv 25.4; Plut., *Lys.* 27.5–7: *Pelop.* 6.5; Deinarchus I (*c. Dem.*) 25; Justin v ix.4–5, etc.

In Chapter IV, Part v above I have described the intervention of King Pausanias in 403, which led to a complete change in Spartan policy, support being withdrawn from the oligarchies imposed by Lysander, at least at Athens, and (I believe) elsewhere as well.[3] When they were ordered to march to Athens with the other allies in 403 the Boeotians and Corinthians, even if they realised that Pausanias desired a very different policy from Lysander's, could hardly have known that he was now in a position to implement his own policy, for only a few weeks earlier the appeals of the Athenian oligarchs had been sympathetically received at Sparta (Xen., *HG* II iv.28–30, etc.). They therefore refused to obey Sparta's summons. Their real motives are clear enough: they did not want to help consolidate the rule of a Spartan puppet government at Athens. This was thoroughly understood by Xenophon (*HG* II iv.30), who also reports their official excuse: that the expedition would be a breach of the peace treaty of 404 (to which they were parties), the Athenians having done nothing to violate its terms. Now the Athenian oligarchs had alleged that the democrats in Peiraeus had 'revolted from Sparta' (Xen., *HG* II iv.28), thus breaking the peace treaty; and no doubt that was the official Spartan pretext for intervention in 403. Conflicts in the interpretation of treaties are liable to be resolved by force, if arbitration is not prescribed or is refused. But the Boeotians and Corinthians together were too strong to be easily coerced, and anyway Pausanias had more than sufficient hoplites to do everything he wanted and so did not press the demand. Ideally, I suppose, the Boeotians and Corinthians could have claimed that there had been no *manifest* breach of the peace treaty, and that before Sparta became entitled to call out the allies she must summon a League Congress to decide whether the treaty had been broken or not—as in 432, when the question put to the allies had similarly been whether the Athenians had broken the Thirty Years Peace.

Apparently it was the Boeotians who took the lead on this occasion and persuaded the Corinthians to act with them (Xen., *HG* III v.5; cf. Isocr. XIV 31). Boeotia was now growing steadily stronger: Leuctra was only just over thirty years ahead. Corinth, on the other hand, had evidently suffered badly during the wars between Athens and the Peloponnesians, especially perhaps the First Peloponnesian war. In the campaign of Plataea in 479 she had provided 5,000 hoplites (Hdts IX 28.3), but in the third quarter of the fifth century a total of less than 4,000 seems likely, and perhaps in 418 (Thuc. v 57.2) and 394 (Xen., *HG* IV ii.17) it was not much above 3,000 (cf. Beloch, *BGRW* 119–21). Nor does Corinth seem able to send out a fleet of any size after her great effort in 433, which produced 90 ships (Thuc. I 46.1). We cannot tell how many of the 47 Peloponnesian ships in 429 (Thuc. II 83.3) were Corinthian: this fleet was 'from the symmachy' (80.1), and it included ships from Sicyon and other states (80.3; cf. 83.4). In 414/13 the Corinthian fleet was of 25 ships (VII 17.4; 19.5; 31.4), with perhaps a few more manned later (34.1–7). In the winter of 413/12, when the Spartans issued a request to the cities of the Peloponnesian League, demanding 100 ships for the Ionian war, Corinth's quota was only 15, smaller than those of Sparta herself and Boeotia (25 each) and the same size as the joint contribution (15) of the Phocians and Locrians (VIII 3.2). In the fourth century we hardly ever hear of Corinthian naval activity: in 393/2 the Corinthians were able to control much of the Gulf of Corinth for a short time, but only because they had received money from Pharnabazus (Xen., *HG* IV viii.10); and when they lost possession of Lechaeum, control

---

[3] This will be demonstrated by Andrewes in a forthcoming paper (see Chapter IV, Part vi and its n. 182 above).

of the Gulf passed over to the Spartans (iv.7–13, 18–19; viii.11; cf. Diod. xiv 86.3–4; 91.2)—with whom the Corinthians were now of course at war. It is easy to overrate the strength of Corinth, whose territory (of perhaps *c.* 880 sq. km. = *c.* 340 sq. miles: Beloch, *BGRW* 115) was not extensive and fertile enough to sustain a really large population. Corinth's greatest asset was her geographical situation.

The Boeotians and Corinthians, having been successful in their first defiance of Sparta in 403, acted in a similar manner in *c.* 402–1, alone refusing to send contingents for Sparta's war against Elis, in which all the other allies are said to have taken part (Xen., *HG* iii ii.25; Diod. xiv 17.7). We do not hear that a League Congress was summoned when Sparta began to coerce Elis (ii.21–3). In 396, again, neither state would take part in King Agesilaus' expedition to Asia Minor: whatever the attitude of Corinth may have been,[4] the Boeotians seem to have been markedly hostile in their refusal (see Xen., *HG* iii iv.3–4; v.5; Plut., *Ages.* 6.9–11; Paus. iii ix.3–5). It is not clear whether Agesilaus' expedition was an official League affair, or whether troops were merely *requested* from other states: we certainly hear nothing of a League Congress, without which Sparta would have had no constitutional right to *order* her allies to send their contingents. In the following year Corinth refused to march against Boeotia (Xen., *HG* iii v.17), and the 'Corinthian war' broke out, with Sparta and her allies arrayed against an opposition centred upon the 'quadruple alliance' of Athens, Boeotia, Argos and Corinth (Diod. xiv 82.1–2 ff., etc.).

APPENDIX XXII

Thucydides V 54.1

Thucydides v 54.1, speaking of an expedition by the Spartans πανδημεί in 419, says that 'no one knew whither they were marching, not even the πόλεις from which they were sent'. The question is whether the word πόλεις is here used in the untechnical sense of the Perioikic cities, or whether it must refer to Sparta's allies. The general opinion is that Perioikoi are referred to (see e.g. Kahrstedt, *GSiSS* 72, 75–6), but Gomme took the opposite view, and Andrewes thinks he is 'probably right' (*HCT* iv 73–4).

In my opinion the πόλεις are almost certainly the Perioikic communities, for the following reasons:

1. The word πόλις in the strict technical sense was not applicable to the Perioikic towns, but it is nevertheless used untechnically in precisely that sense by fifth- and fourth-century writers, e.g. Hdts vii 234.2 (the Spartans have πόλιες πολλαί); Xen., *HG* vi v.21 (Agesilaus sends the Perioikoi home to their own πόλεις); *Ages.* ii 24 (περιοικίδες πόλεις); *Lac. Pol.* xv 3 (πολλαὶ τῶν περιοίκων πόλεων); Isocr. xii 179.

2. In v 54.1 Thucydides is describing a purely Spartan expedition, as in v 33. In both expeditions the Spartans are πανδημεί, but the allies are simply not there. (We cannot insert καὶ οἱ ξύμμαχοι αὐτῶν after πανδημεί in 54.1, as Gomme suggested: see Andrewes, *loc. cit.*). When the Spartans are accompanied by their allies,

---

[4] See Paus. iii ix.1–2, who represents the Corinthians as willing to go but deterred by an omen. Did they perhaps invoke the 'gods and heroes' provision? (See Chapter IV Part iv, Section b, §7.)

Thucydides says so, as in v 57.1–2; 64.2–5, and many other passages. An additional reason for believing that the Spartans were alone in the abortive campaign described in v 54.1 is that when they turned around and went home, they did not then and there instruct their allies to be ready to march during the month after next, but 'sent envoys around' to the allies with those instructions (περιήγγειλαν).

3. To assume that the 'cities' are those of Sparta's allies is to create the unnecessary difficulties which are very honestly faced, but not solved, by Andrewes, in *HCT* iv 74.

4. 'It is not obviously noteworthy that perioikic cities should not have been told the destination', says Andrewes (*loc. cit.*). But is not this simply Thucydides' way of telling us emphatically that complete secrecy was preserved about the destination?—'Even the perioikic towns which received orders to despatch troops could not tell me when I asked them'.

APPENDIX XXIII

The name of the Spartan Assembly

The Spartan Assembly is still commonly referred to as 'the Apella', in spite of the fact that it is never given that name in any ancient text. Wade-Gery (*EGH* 38, 44, 190 n. 3) and Andrewes (in Gomme, *HCT* iv 134) have made a sufficient case against this modern usage and in favour of the view that the Spartan Assembly was called 'the Ekklēsia', but it may be useful to set out the arguments in full.

1. The most important and indeed decisive text is Thuc. v 77.1, where the resolution of the Spartan Assembly to negotiate a treaty of peace and defensive alliance with Argos in 418/17 is recorded verbatim, in the Doric dialect, beginning καττάδε δοκεῖ τᾷ ἐκκλησίᾳ τῶν Λακεδαιμονίων. In the absence of any strong evidence to the contrary, this alone might be allowed to settle the matter.

2. Ancient writers normally refer to the Spartan Assembly as an ἐκκλησία. Particularly valuable are Xen., *HG* iii ii.23 and iv vi.3, where decisions of the Assembly are mentioned in the form, ἔδοξε τοῖς ἐφόροις (or τοῖς τ' ἐφόροις) καὶ τῇ ἐκκλησίᾳ. Xenophon also refers to the Spartan Assembly as the ἐκκλησία in *HG* v ii.11. Thucydides, who as a rule is very careful to use technical terms correctly, speaks of the Spartan Assembly as the ἐκκλησία in vi 88.10 and also (more significantly) in i 87.1, when he is describing how the ephor Sthenelaïdas, in closed session (see 79.1), put the fateful question whether Athens had broken the Thirty Years Peace. Earlier, in referring to the open session of the Assembly at which speeches were made by allies and by Athenian ambassadors, he had used the term ξύλλογος (67.3), an untechnical word having a wide range of meanings, which he usually employs for informal meetings (ii 12.1; iii 27.3; iv 114.3; 120.3; v 30.5), although he can also use it for a formal Assembly at Camarina (vi 75.4) and Syracuse (vi 41.4; in 32.3 he has called the same meeting an ἐκκλησία) and probably at Athens (ii 59.3; cf. 22.1, where ξύλλογον may mean either a meeting specially summoned, as in 59.3, or the equivalent of a Roman *contio*, as supposed by Gomme, *HCT* ii 76). Hdts vii 134.2, exceptionally, uses the term ἁλίη for what seem to be special meetings of the Spartan Assembly; he uses ἁλίη also of assemblies in other Greek states (v 29.2; 79.2) and even of an *ad hoc* meeting of Persians (i 125.2); he can employ ἀγοραί in at least one case (vi 11.1) in which Thucydides would have used ξύλλογοι; and of course he also uses ἐκκλησία (iii 142.2)—the

earliest extant prose writer to do so. It is not worth setting out the evidence of later sources, except perhaps Diod. xi 50, one of the few passages we have outside Thucydides and Xenophon which even purport to describe the machinery of decision at Sparta in action. Here the Assembly is called ἡ κοινὴ ἐκκλησία (§3); when in §6 Diodorus says that Hetoimaridas persuaded the Gerousia and the Demos, he is presumably thinking of the Assembly, but the constitutional machinery does not appear clearly (see Chapter V, Part ii above).

3. Xenophon, who knew his Sparta very well indeed, refers three times (*HG* ii iv.38; v ii.33; vi iii.3) to the ἔκκλητοι, clearly as the persons attending the Spartan Assembly. Now ἔκκλητος is not an Attic form, and (according to Andrewes, *loc. cit.*) is used otherwise only in Eur., *Orest.* 612, 949, of the Argive Assembly.

4. Xenophon also mentions 'what was called the Little Ekklēsia' (τὴν μικρὰν καλουμένην ἐκκλησίαν, *HG* iii iii.8). We have no idea what this body was, but its name shows that there was also a 'Great Ekklēsia', or 'Ekklēsia' *tout court*.

5. In M/L 5 (= *SEG* ix 3), line 24, the Assembly of Thera, a Spartan colony, is referred to as the ἐκκλησία. (This of course is a very weak argument by itself, in view of the questionable nature of the decree, on which see the notes in M/L 5.)

6. The very word ἀπέλλα never occurs in the singular in any ancient source, or in the plural in relation to a political assembly except when it is glossed by Hesychius (without specific reference to Sparta) as σηκοί, ἐκκλησίαι, ἀρχαιρεσίαι. Even the plural ἀπέλλαι is found only in reference to religious festivals, in inscriptions of the early Roman period from Gytheum in Laconia, which refer to meetings of the Assembly at the Great Apellai (ἔδοξε τῶι δάμωι ἐν ταῖς μεγάλαις ἀπέλλαις): *IG* v i.1144 (= *SGDI* 4567 = Michel, *RIG* 185), lines 20–1; 1146, lines 40–1. Otherwise, as far as I can see, there is nothing more relevant than the reference in the long inscription of the phratry of the Labyadai at Delphi (Michel, *RIG* 995 = *DGE* 323 = *SIG*² 438 = *RIJG* ii xxviii, A 4, 44) to ἀπελλαῖα, which seem to be victims offered yearly on a festival day during the month Apellaios (connected with Apollo). The only ancient text, apart from that of Hesychius mentioned above, which provides any basis whatever for speaking of the Spartan Assembly as the Apella is Plutarch's explanation (*Lyc.* 6.3) of the word ἀπελλάζειν in the 'Great Rhetra': ἀπελλάζειν, he says, means ἐκκλησιάζειν, and he adds (as Wade-Gery emphasises, *EGH* 38), not that ἀπέλλα is Spartan for ἐκκλησία, but that the term was used because Lycurgus ascribed the beginning and organisation of the constitution to the Pythian god.

Surely the Spartan Assembly was called the Ekklēsia, and met (originally at least) *at* the festivals of Apollo known as the Apellai, just as the Damos of Gytheum could later hold some of its meetings at the Great Apellai. As Forrest says (*HS* 47), 'the frequency of the Apellai . . . is unknown, perhaps once a month with one more important celebration annually in the month which carried Apollo's name, Apellaios, the occasion for elections and the like'. (Cf. Wade-Gery, *EGH* 45–7.) The only positive evidence known to me for the frequency and time of meeting of the Spartan Assembly is in a usually unhelpful source, the Scholiast on Thucydides (I 67.3), who says the Assembly met at each full moon (ed. Hude, pp. 52–3).

Since some modern authors (even Gilbert, *CASA* 50), on the basis of a single passage in Plut., *Lyc.* 25.1–3, have asserted that only Spartans aged thirty and over could attend the Assembly, it is perhaps worth pointing out that the passage in question (as the context clearly shows) refers only to use of the Agora as a market place: see Busolt, *GSK* ii 691 n. 3. As far as our evidence goes, there is nothing to suggest that a Spartiate aged twenty or above was not entitled to attend the Assembly; but in the absence of any positive evidence it is perhaps unwise to assert positively that he could do so.

APPENDIX XXIV

'By shouting and not by vote'

By far the most important single step in the development of democracy was the decision to settle major political questions by actually counting heads (or hands, or counters) and allowing the numerical majority to have its way—*making political decisions by majority vote*. When this began in Greece, probably not very far either side of 600 B.C., it may have been the first time in human history that such a thing had regularly happened, at any rate in a civilised society. It is extraordinary how both ancient and modern writers have neglected this development: the only proper treatment of the subject that I know is the article by J. A. O. Larsen, 'The Origin and Significance of the Counting of Votes', in *CP* 44 (1949) 164–81; cf. A. L. Boegehold, 'Toward a Study of Athenian Voting Procedure', in *Hesp.* 32 (1963) 366–74. Other writers, while giving careful attention to the relatively minor features of democracy, such as the Council and its *probouleusis*, have tended to ignore the fundamental innovation, which is similarly overlooked by all ancient writers, even—and this is very astonishing—by Aristotle.

In Homer the demos decides nothing: the army or the people in assembly merely express their approval or disapproval by shouts or silence or—at a pinch—mutiny.[1] Shouting (and clashing of arms) was a common method by which early assemblies made their will known. The most probable etymology of the Latin word for 'vote', *suffragium*, suggests that the earliest assemblies at Rome expressed their views in noisy demonstrations.[2] Much the same seems to have been true of the Gauls (see e.g. Caes., *BG* VII 21.1) and the Germans (see e.g. Tac., *Germ.* 11.6; *Hist.* V 17; Amm. Marc. XVI 12.13). Among the Israelites the people (not in any formal assembly) signified their approval by shouting, as at the choice of Saul as king (*I Sam.* x.24); and Nehemiah's *seisachtheia* was ratified when 'all the congregation said "Amen" and praised the Lord' (*Neh.* v 13).[3] In what has been described as the 'primitive democracy' of some of the ancient Mesopotamian cities,[4] there is equally no clear sign of voting on political matters, in the form of *counting* 'those in favour' and 'those against', nor is any such procedure visible in our records of political activity in other 'pre-Classical' Near Eastern societies such as those of the Hittites,[5] the Phoenicians[6] or others.[7]

---

[1] See e.g. A. Andrewes, *Probouleusis* (Inaugural Lecture, Oxford, 1954) 6–9; G. Glotz, *The Greek City* 39–57 (Eng. trans., 1929; cf. the more recent French edition, *La cité grecque*, 1968, pp. 51–67); M. I. Finley, *The World of Odysseus* (London, rev. edn., 1956) 84 ff.

[2] See M. Rothstein, 'Suffragium', in *Festschr. zu Otto Hirschfelds 60tem Geburtstage (Beiträge zur alten Gesch. u. gr.-röm. Alterthumskunde*, 1903) 30–3, taking the root conception to be that of *fragor*, in the sense it bears in the texts he quotes.

[3] For other Old Testament evidence, see C. Umhau Wolf, 'Traces of Primitive Democracy in Ancient Israel', in *JNES* 6 (1947) 98–108.

[4] See esp. T. Jacobsen, 'Primitive Democracy in Ancient Mesopotamia', in *JNES* 2 (1943) 159–72; H. Frankfort, *Kingship and the Gods* (1948) 215–16, 218–20, 228–9, 235–7; A. Falkenstein, 'La Cité-Temple Sumérienne', in *Cahiers d'hist. mondiale* 1 (1953–4), at p. 801; Jacobsen, 'Early Political Development in Mesopotamia', in *Ztschr. für Assyriologie* 52 = n.F. 18 (1957) 91–140, esp. 99–106, 110–16, 118–20, 136–7; A. L. Oppenheim, 'A New Look at the Structure of Mesopotamian Society', in *JESHO* 10 (1967) 1–16; and particularly Geoffrey Evans, 'Ancient Mesopotamian Assemblies', in *JAOS* 78 (1958) 1–11, 114–15

[5] See R. S. Hardy, 'The Old Hittite Kingdom, a Political History', in *AJSL* 58 (1941) 177–216, esp. 214–15.

We do not know when or in which state or by what stages the demos as a whole first gained the constitutional power of decision in a Greek city. By the second half of the seventh century (see Chapter IV, Part i and its n. 4 above) the Spartan *damos* had it, but it exercised it, doubtless from the first, 'by shouting and not by vote' (Thuc. 1 87.2). The presiding magistrate—in the historical period, an ephor —evidently decided which shout was the louder or loudest (*Ibid.*). This was, so to speak, a half-way stage in the evolution of a proper voting procedure; but Sparta had stuck fast at that point and failed to develop further. The procedure in 432, described by Thucydides (87.1–3), suggests that voting in the normal manner of a Greek democracy was *never* resorted to: when Sthenelaïdas, the presiding ephor, pretended that he could not tell which shout was the louder, he did not ask for a 'show of hands' but for a physical division into two separate groups. Apparently the presiding ephor had an unlimited discretion in declaring the result of a 'shouting'. Whether there was any method of challenging a manifestly wrong decision, we do not know.

The continued existence of this archaic procedure—retained, as far as we know, by no other Greek state in the Classical period—was of course closely bound up with the absence of any real *isēgoria* or any democratic initiative in the Spartan Assembly. Its very survival was due to the absence of any true democratic spirit in those who had political power at Sparta, and in its turn it must have helped to prevent such a spirit from emerging. As far as I know, the counting of votes was used at Sparta in only three important spheres: to decide disagreements among the five ephors (see Xen., *HG* II iii.34; iv.29); in judicial decisions in the Gerousia, where votes were evidently taken openly and not by secret ballot (see Paus. III v. 2); and in the Congress of the Peloponnesian League (see Thuc. I 125.1; 141.6; v 30.1). For the method of election of Gerousia and ephors, see Chapter IV, Part v, Section *A* above.

APPENDIX XXV

Aristotle, Pol. *III 1, 1275ᵇ8–11 etc., on jurisdiction at Sparta*

Aristotle has just been giving a preliminary definition of a citizen (*Pol.* III 1, 1275ª22 ff.) as one who possesses the right to share in judicial decisions (κρίσις) and in office (ἀρχή), the latter being then defined in a very broad sense,[1] to include 'indeterminate' or 'indefinite' office (ἀόριστος ἀρχή), in the sense of being a member of a judicial body or of the sovereign assembly (δικαστής, ἐκκλησιαστής). He then points out that under different kinds of constitution (democracy, oligarchy and so forth) the criteria of citizenship will differ, and he admits that the citizen under the definition he has just given is above all the citizen of a democracy. For in some cities, he goes on, there is no popular element (δῆμος), and they have no

---

[6] See J. A. Wilson, 'The Assembly of a Phoenician City', in *JNES* 4 (1945) 245.

[7] See H. Reviv, 'On Urban Representative Institutions and Self-Government in Syria-Palestine in the Second Half of the Second Millennium B.C.' in *JESHO* 12 (1969) 283–97.

[1] As Newman points out (*PA* III 135), ἀρχή is a wider term than κρίσις and is made in what follows to include κρίσις'. And see 1275ᵇ18–19 for Aristotle's ultimate definition of the citizen.

assembly but only meetings specially summoned (οὐδ' ἐκκλησίαν νομίζουσιν ἀλλὰ συγκλήτους).

At this point comes the passage about Sparta (1275ᵇ8–11). 'And legal cases', he says, 'they remit to special bodies (τὰς δίκας δικάζουσι κατὰ μέρος): thus at Sparta the ephors, sitting separately,² try civil cases,³ the gerontes take cases of homicide and some other authority (ἀρχή)⁴ may try other cases'. The phrase κατὰ μέρος, however we translate it,⁵ certainly means that all judicial cases are decided, not by the whole body of citizens collectively, but by individual groups, the holders of specific posts. This conclusion is reinforced by the sentence that follows (1275ᵇ 11–12): 'at Carthage the procedure is the same, for certain magistrates try *all* legal cases'. And in an earlier passage (II 11, 1273ᵃ19–20), where a similar comparison is drawn between the Spartan and Carthaginian judicial systems,⁶ Aristotle also speaks of legal decisions as being given at Sparta by different *magistrates*. Again, in IV 9, 1294ᵇ31–4, Aristotle remarks that some describe the Spartan constitution as an oligarchy, because it has many oligarchical features: among those he mentions are 'that a few men have the power of inflicting the penalties of death and exile'. And in II 9, 1270ᵇ38–40, he speaks of the gerontes as 'judges for life of important cases'. Nowhere is there any sign that the Spartan Assembly possessed any power of jurisdiction. Busolt was right: 'In Sparta war die Gemeindeversammlung trotz der demokratischen Organisation der Herrengemeinde von der Rechtsprechung ausgeschlossen. Es gab auch keine Geschworenengerichte' (*GSK* II 693).

APPENDIX XXVI

The trial of Spartan kings

There are two passages, in Pausanias and Plutarch, on the nature of the tribunal responsible for trying Spartan kings, at any rate on serious charges. Pausanias (III v.2) says that the court (δικαστήριον) that tries a Spartan king consists of the twenty-eight gerontes, the ephors and the other king. He seems well informed, as he goes on to give details of the verdicts given by those who judged King Pausanias in 403/2: fourteen of the gerontes and King Agis II were for condemning Pausanias, but the other fourteen gerontes and the ephors acquitted him. The voting, then, was by a majority of the thirty-four members of the court, and it must have been open and not secret, if individual verdicts were known. The essential fact revealed by this passage of Pausanias, that the judges were the gerousia and ephors combined, receives valuable confirmation from Plutarch. In 241 King Leonidas II and the ephors, who were creatures of his (*Agis* 18.4), brought in to the trial of King Agis IV 'such of the gerontes as were of the same mind as themselves, *just as if he were to have a trial*' (*Agis* 19.5). Cf. Hdts v 40.1, where we find 'the ephors and the gerontes' telling King Anaxandridas to take a second wife, and threatening that if he did not 'the Spartiates' might take some unpleasant decision about him.

It is also worth noting that in at least one case of a disputed succession, that between Areus I and Cleonymus on the death of Cleomenes II in 309, we are

---

² Cf. Ps.-Plut., *Mor.* 221b.
³ On the meaning of τὰς τῶν συμβολαίων, see my NJAE I 101–4.
⁴ The kings, for instance: see Hdts VI 57.4. Cf. Xen., *Lac. Pol.* VIII 4.
⁵ Newman (*PA* III 139) suggests 'by sections', and compares κατὰ μέρος, IV 16, 1301ᵃ2.
⁶ See Newman's note, *PA* II 366.

specifically told that it was the Gerousia which decided in favour of Areus (Paus. III vi.2). It may therefore have been the Gerousia which installed Leotychidas II in place of Damaratus in 491–90 (see below) and Agesilaus II in place of Leotychidas son of Agis II in *c.* 400. The fact that Xen., *HG* III iii.4 attributes the latter decision to ἡ πόλις should not be taken (as by Kahrstedt, *GSISS* 134; Bonner and Smith, *AJS* 128) as a proof that it was made by the Assembly, although of course it may have been—we cannot be sure. I do not know why Busolt (*GSK* II 673) asserts that these questions were decided earlier by the Assembly and only in later times by the Gerousia.

In no other case, unfortunately, do we have any information about the composition of the court that tried a king. As the subject is not well treated in the books, I will give a list of the examples of the trial of Spartan kings, down to Agis IV (241), with the principal sources—I omit some unimportant secondary ones.

1. Cleomenes I (once? twice?): Hdts VI 82.1–2 (mid-490s, after the battle of Sepeia); cf. 74.1 (*c.* 490). There is no certain evidence that a trial actually took place on either of these occasions. On the first it is quite possible that Cleomenes was merely denounced to the ephors and never formally tried. A trial is sometimes assumed, or (as by Andrewes, *GCS* 9 and 19 n. 15) held to be probable. But surely, as Herodotus tells the story, Cleomenes is merely *before the ephors*, who are deciding whether or not to prosecute him, and his defence is delivered *to them* (VI 82.1): this defence is then said to have been accepted by 'the Spartiates' (82.2). If ἀπέφυγε πολλὸν τοὺς διώκοντας implies a formal trial, 'the Spartiates' are surely the Gerousia and ephors (contrast Andrewes, *loc. cit.*: 'probably ... the assembly'). Whether Cleomenes was put on trial *c.* 490 we do not know: Hdts VI 74.1 speaks of a flight on his own initiative.

2. Leotychidas II (twice): (*a*) Hdts VI 85.1 (*c.* 489); (*b*) VI 72.2 (*c.* 476). In both cases Herodotus speaks of a δικαστήριον. On the first occasion he was condemned to be handed over to the Aeginetans (who would not take him, 85.2–86); and on the second he was exiled, and fled to Tegea and died there.

3. Pausanias the Regent (once, or twice?): Thuc. I 95.5 and 128.3 (478–7). Cf. 131.2 and 132.5–134.3 (late 470s/early 460s), when there seems to have been no formal trial. For the other sources, see Hill, *S*² 340–1 (Index I 1.16; 2.6), 358 (Index IV 1.5–7).

4. Pleistoanax (445): see Hill, *S*² 344 (Index I 7.5) and Chapter V, Part vii above.

5. Agis II (418): Thuc. V 63.2–4. Only in this case, as far as I can see, is there the least likelihood that the trial may have been staged in the Assembly. It is not at all clear who ἐβούλευον to fine Agis 100,000 drachmae and destroy his house, but failed in the end to inflict these penalties. I would suppose that it was the Gerousia and ephors. However, in the exceptional situation (a matter of foreign policy) the Assembly may have 'taken the law into its own hands'. The Gerousia may also have been responsible for the restriction on Agis' future commands, which, though called a νόμος in Thuc. V 63.4, applied only to him and was not a general law applying to other kings. Or a decision of the Gerousia may in this case have been endorsed by the Assembly.

6. Pausanias (twice): (*a*) Paus. III v.2 (403/2); (*b*) Xen., *HG* III v.25; Paus. III v.6; Diod. XIV 89.1; Plut., *Lys.* 30.1 (394). Cf. Chapter IV, Parts v and vi above.

7. Leonidas II (242): Plut., *Agis* 11; Paus III vi.7–8. Parke, *DSK*, has an interesting theory about the constitutional difference between the deposition of Damaratus and Leonidas II and that of Leotychidas II, Pleistoanax and Pausanias. Although it was the ephors who took the initiative in the star-gazing sessions, there is no ground, in Plutarch's narrative or otherwise, for thinking that it was they who pronounced the deposition of the king. On whose authority Leonidas was reinstated as king in 241 in place of Cleombrotus (Plut., *Agis* 16.4–18.3; Paus.

III vi.8) it is impossible to say: constitutional procedures are not likely to be preserved intact in revolutionary situations.

8. Agis IV (241): Plut., *Agis* 19–20. In view of *Agis* 19.5 (quoted in the first paragraph of this Appendix) and the fact that the whole situation was disturbed by violence, it is not constitutionally significant that Agis' mother and grandmother should have demanded that he be tried 'among the citizens' (*Agis* 19.10), i.e. in the Assembly—for of course Agis had a large following, and in an emergency his supporters might press for a trial in the Assembly even if this was not the correct constitutional procedure. Agis was the first (and last) Spartan king to be condemned to death by a court and executed.

Although King Damaratus was not actually tried for any alleged offence in 491–90 but was merely pronounced illegitimate and deposed (Hdts vi 61–67.1, esp. 65.3; 67.1), his case is worth putting alongside the others. (On him, see esp. Parke, DSK.) Apart from Damaratus there were at least eight or nine and perhaps as many as eleven trials of kings; and of these at least seven trials, affecting five different kings, took place between the 490s and the 390s.

We know from Thuc. I 131.2 (cf. 134.1) that the ephors on their own authority could arrest and imprison a king—for how long, we cannot tell, but perhaps only until a formal trial could take place. A king was also obliged to obey a thrice-repeated summons by the ephors, according to Plut., *Cleom.* 10.5. The ephors, we are told by Aristotle (*Pol.* II 9, 1271ᵃ6–7), exercised supervision over Spartan 'magistrates': this would certainly extend to military harmosts (see Xen., *HG* v iv.24) and presumably also—in spite of the distinction between τὸ ἄρχειν and τὸ βασιλεύειν at Sparta, mentioned in Hdts vi 67.2—to the kings; cf. esp. Xen., *Lac. Pol.* xv 7, discussed below. Xenophon, *Lac. Pol.* vIII 4, states that the ephors could impose fines upon whomever they wished; and there are three stories of their fining kings, even if at least one of these is surely apocryphal, and all three may be.

(i) There is a story in two different forms about the fining of Agis II: in the Plutarchian *Apophth. Lac., Lycurgus* 6 (= *Mor.* 226f–7a), it is for having dinner at home with his wife; in Plut., *Lyc.* 12.5, it is for omitting a sacrifice (after such a dinner). In the former version it is the ephors who levy the fine; in the second the authority inflicting it is either 'the polemarchs' or (more probably) 'the Spartans'.

(ii) Agesilaus II is said to have been fined by the ephors for becoming too popular, and ὅτι τοὺς κοινοὺς πολίτας ἰδίους κτᾶται: Plut., *Ages.* 5.4; cf. *Mor.* 482d (= *De frat. amor.* 9). The second of these two passages is rarely noticed: it is not cited even by Busolt, *GSK* II 690 n. 4; Kahrstedt; or Andrewes, GCS 19 n. 17. It gives a more specific reason for the fining of Agesilaus: that he was accustomed to make presents to members of the Gerousia—on their election to that office, according to Plut., *Ages.* 4.5.

(iii) A fine was also imposed upon Archidamus II, according to Plutarch, *Ages.* 2.6 (citing Theophrastus) and *Mor.* 1d (= *De educ. puer.* 2), for marrying a small wife!

Andrewes, GCS 19 n. 17, mentioning only the last two stories, rejects both ('there is no respectable evidence, and no inherent probability'); and he is surely right about the last, at any rate.

According to Xenophon (*Lac. Pol.* VIII 4), the ephors could not only imprison magistrates (ἄρχοντες) and bring capital charges against them, but also depose them while in office; but this power of deposition could not have extended to the kings. It was certainly the ephors' duty to keep watch upon the kings and see that they did not exceed their constitutional powers: in this connection, great significance can be attached to the oaths exchanged *every month* between the kings (for themselves) and the ephors (for the State) that the kings would govern according to law and that if they did so the ephors would uphold their rule (Xen., *Lac. Pol.* xv 7). Denunciation to the ephors would be the right procedure for any Spartiate who wished a king to be called to account. (Late in 218 we hear of King Lycurgus escaping from Sparta to avoid being arrested by the ephors, to whom he had been denounced for planning a revolution; the ephors subsequently decided that the charge was groundless and invited him to return: Polyb. v 29.9; 91.1–2.)

APPENDIX XXVII

Eligibility for the Spartan Gerousia

I prefer to leave open the much disputed question whether the Gerousia was recruited from a *legally* limited circle of families. In favour of such a limitation, see e.g. Forrest, *HS* 46, 63, 113; Chrimes, *AS* 425 etc.; Gilbert, *CASA* 48 and n. 2; and against it Busolt, *GSK* II 680–1, with 662 and n. 4; Jones, *Sp.* 170–1; and esp. R. D. Hicks, 'A Supposed Qualification for Election to the Spartan Senate', in *CR* 20 (1906) 23–7; cf. Toynbee, *SPGH* 266–9, who ultimately comes down in favour of an aristocratic 'monopoly *de facto*'.

On the whole, I think the limitation of membership to a circle of 'Privileged Families' (to use Chrimes' term) may have been complete, or almost complete, throughout the Classical period, *without ever being enshrined in any specific 'constitutional' rule*. We may compare the position in the late Roman Republic, where no law formally restricted access to the consulship to those who were already *nobiles* (having consular ancestors), or even to members of families already Senatorial, and yet it was unusual for a non-*nobilis* to become consul, and exceedingly rare for a man such as Cicero, whose family had not attained even the lower grades of Senatorial rank: see e.g. M. Gelzer, *The Roman Nobility* (Eng. trans, by R. Seager, Oxford, 1969) 3 ff., esp. 28–35; R. Syme, *The Roman Revolution* (Oxford, 1939), esp. 10 ff.

In none of the passages in Aristotle's *Politics* which have a bearing on the question of eligibility for the Gerousia (II 6, 1265^{b}35–40; 9, 1270^{b}21–6; IV 9, 1294^{b}18–34, esp. 29–31; V 6, 1306^{a}15–19), or in such passages as Polyb. VI x.9 or Plut., *Lyc.* 26, is there any clear statement that candidates were selected by law from certain families only. Aristotle never makes in relation to the Spartan Gerousia such a remark as we find in *Pol.* II 10, 1272^{a}33–5, about the Cretan *kosmoi*, who, he says, are drawn 'not from all citizens but from certain families' (γένη). But it is evident from what he does say about Sparta that the Gerousia was an oligarchical element in the constitution (II 6, 1265^{b}38), that in practice at least it was the *kaloi kagathoi* (1270^{b}23–5) and not members of the demos (1294^{b}29–31) who were elected to it, and that the choice of members was δυναστευτική (1306^{a}18–19: for the meaning of δυναστεία, cf. 1292^{a}39 ff., esp. 1292^{b}5–10; 1293^{a}30–4; with 1272^b 2–3; and of course Thuc. III 62.3). The method of election was certainly very strange: see Chapter IV, Part V above. It is particularly unfortunate that we have no clue either to the identity or to the method of choice of those who decided which candidate had received the greatest volume of applause.

The Spartan constitution was not reduced to writing, and it apparently depended upon a few simple *rhetrai*, which would surely have been interpreted, if a dispute ever arose, by the Gerousia. I suggest that from very early times it was understood by all Spartans that no one would offer himself for election to the

Gerousia if he was not a member of one of the 'Privileged Families'—or perhaps a client of one of those families, for there is reason to think that they dispensed a good deal of patronage, as the great Roman noble families did. (The absence of patronage and clientship from democratic Athens—where an action like that recorded by Athen. IX 407bc on the part of Alcibiades is highly exceptional—cannot be used as an argument for the totally different social system of Sparta.) In Chrimes, *AS* (esp. chapters iii-vi, x-xi), there are some interesting suggestions about the 'Privileged Families' and the extent of their influence which deserve thorough re-examination and development. (The worst defect of that book, its impossibly early dating of the'Lycurgan'reforms to the ninth century, should not be allowed to divert attention from its more promising features.) I suspect that Sparta resembled Rome (see my 'Suffragium: from Vote to Patronage', in *Brit. Jnl. of Sociology* 5 [1954] 33–48) in being a society in which patronage and clientship played an essential social and political role.

APPENDIX XXVIII

Spartan victors at Olympia etc.

Some interesting conclusions emerge from a study of the Spartan Olympic victors recorded by L. Moretti, *Olympionikai, i vincitori negli antichi agoni olympici = Atti della Accad. Naz. dei Lincei, Classe di Scienze morali, stor. e filol.*, Memorie, Ser. 8, Vol. 8, fasc. 2 (Rome, 1957) 53–198; cf. Moretti's 'Supplemento al catalogo degli Olympionikai', in *Klio* 52 (1970) 295–303; and A. Hönle, *Olympia in der Politik der Griechischen Staatenwelt (von 776 bis zum Ende des 5. Jahrhunderts)* (Diss., Tübingen, 1968), esp. 120–67.

Numerous Spartan victories are known in the early years, from 720 onwards: down to about 552 there are no less than forty-five, by twenty-seven Spartans, but they are all in athletic contests (stadion, diaulos, dolichos, pentathlon, or wrestling); none is in a chariot race. (It is true, of course, that few winners of chariot races are known from any Greek state in this early period: see only Moretti, nos. 33, 39, 52, 81, 96, 106.)

Then, about the middle of the sixth century, the situation changes entirely. For the next two centuries and more (from *c.* 548) we find very few such Spartan *athletic* victors (only about six or seven: Moretti, nos. 149, 160, 211, 216, 237, and possibly 1024 and 342*,[1] perhaps even 304),[2] and none at all after 448, or perhaps even 468,[3] until 316 (Moretti, no. 478).[4] Our records are far from complete, but

---

[1] A star has been placed against any of Moretti's numbered victors mentioned here who appears in his 'Supplemento'.

[2] Lacrates (Moretti, no. 342*) is described by Xen., *HG* II iv.33, as 'the Olympic victor', which perhaps suggests a personal triumph rather than a victory in a chariot race, and would make particularly good sense if Olympian athletic victors were now rare at Sparta. As for Lyc(e)inus (Moretti, no. 304, victor in the hoplite race in 448), his ethnic is not certain: he could be the same person as the Spartan Lycinus (Moretti, no. 324), who won a victory with a quadriga in *c.* 432, but this is doubtful.

[3] The date will be 468 if Lyc(e)inus (mentioned in n. 2 above) was not a Spartan.

[4] Hönle (*op. cit.* 132–42) has drawn attention to several passages (in the Plutarchian *Apophthegmata Laconica* and elsewhere) which suggest a disparaging attitude on the part of Spartans to athletic contests, including those at Olympia: see e.g. Plut., *Mor.* 224f, 233e, 234de, 236e.

there is no good reason why we should have the names of a much smaller proportion of Spartan athletic victors preserved between 468/448 and 316 than earlier and later. Aristotle, in the *Politics* (VIII 4, 1338ᵇ24–38), remarks upon the fact that in his day the Spartans were 'defeated by others in athletic contests as well as military ones'. We hear, on the other hand, of an astonishingly large number of Spartans who won *chariot races* between c. 548 and *c.* 368—there are 13 or 14, winning 17 or 18 victories between them (Moretti, nos. 110/113/117, 157, 195, 305/311, 315, 324, · 327, 332, 339, 373/381, 386*, 396, 418, and perhaps 278).[5] No other Greek state, as far as we know, provided anything like so many chariot victors (cf. Paus. VI ii.1). Olympic victors brought glory to the State to which they belonged (see Thuc. VI 16.2; Lys. XIX 63; Pind., *Olymp.* IV 10–12; V 4, 7–8; VIII 19–23; IX 19–22; X 97–9; XI 11–15; XIII 1–10; Isocr. XVI 32; contrast Xenophanes, 21 B 2.1–22, *ap.* Athen. X 413f–14a; Eurip., fr. 282 [Nauck, *TGF²*], *ap.* Athen. X 413c–f; Isocr. IV 1–2; *Epist.* VIII 5–6); and the prestige (and therefore the potential political influence) of these victors will have been correspondingly enhanced. When the Athenians in 407/6 captured the great Rhodian athlete, Dorieus the Diagorid, who had innumerable victories to his credit in the Panhellenic games, and was now a citizen of Thurii and commanding a naval squadron from that city in the Ionian war, they could not bring themselves to punish 'a man so great and of such reputation' (Paus. VI vii.4–5), and they set him free, without even demanding a ransom (Xen. *HG* I v.19). When Dorieus was captured by the Spartans in *c.* 395/4, however, he was executed: Paus. VI vii.6–7 = Androt., *FGrH* 324 F 46.

For the much-published inscription of Damonon, recording various victories he and his son had won, mainly with horses (not at Olympia), see *IG* v i.213 = *DGE* 12 = *SGDI* 4416 = *IGIDS*⁴ 22 = Michel, *RIG* 946; and see *SEG* XIV 330. The victories must have been won in the 440s or 430s: see L. H. Jeffery, *The Local Scripts of Archaic Greece* (Oxford, 1961) 196–7.

See Isocr. VI 55 for a surprisingly critical comment on the passion of rich Spartans for breeding 'voracious horses' for chariot racing, generally considered τὸ πάντων κάλλιστον καὶ μεγαλοπρεπέστατον ἐπιτήδευμα (Xen., *Hiero* XI 5). There is a useful collection of material on horse-breeding and chariot-racing as a mark of wealth, in Davies, *APF* xxv–vi n.7.

APPENDIX XXIX

The political outlook of Aristophanes

There are three questions I want to ask and answer about Aristophanes. First, how far can we identify his political outlook, particularly in regard to the war? Secondly, is it worth while trying to do so? And thirdly, how far (if at all) did he deliberately express political views in his plays?

I shall begin with the last two questions. The second, whether it is worth while trying to discover Aristophanes' opinions, is easily disposed of. It is answered in the negative by many people nowadays: their point of view is well expressed in an

---

[5] P. A. Cartledge has drawn my attention to Beazley, *ABV* 369 ('Leagros Group', no. 112, of *c.* 525–500 B.C.), a fine Panathenaic amphora dedicated in the Chalkioikos at Sparta. Since the painting on the vase indicates that this was the prize for victory in a four-horse chariot race, he suggests that the dedication may possibly have been made by King Damaratus (Moretti, no. 157), the one Spartan known to have won the corresponding *Olympic* contest at about the time in question.

influential article by Gomme, first published in 1938 (AP). Having effectively ridiculed various modern attempts to depict Aristophanes' outlook in entirely unjustifiable terms (Croiset's, for example), Gomme reached a position at which he could ask himself impatiently, 'Had then Aristophanes no political opinions of his own? And if he had, what were they? To the first [question] the answer is, I imagine, easy: he must have had' (AP 103 = *MEGHL* 81). But, 'assuming that we can find out, of what importance is it to us to know? Is it, for example, essential to the understanding of his plays?' Gomme concludes not, and he goes on to draw parallels with Bernard Shaw and Jane Austen (AP 104–5 = 82–5). 'Burn Shaw's prefaces and the record of his political activities: would it make much difference to our understanding of his plays? I think not.'

It should be obvious that Gomme has not asked all the necessary questions. What he says may (or may not) be true while we are thinking of Aristophanes purely as a dramatist, a literary figure in his own right, on whom alone our attention is concentrated. But those of us who are Greek historians are obliged to see him *in addition* in a very different way, *as an important historical source* for the Athens of the late fifth and early fourth centuries; and when we approach him in this way we do need to know all we possibly can about his attitude to the world around him, including his political opinions, so that we can understand the point of view from which he saw the world and know how to evaluate his treatment of it, and what kind of bias and prejudice to allow for. There is no question, then, but that we must do all we can, *as historians*, to discover Aristophanes' outlook. I find it astonishing that Gomme and many others should have failed to appreciate this.

The question whether Aristophanes consciously tried to express his political opinions in his plays is not so easy to answer to everyone's satisfaction. I myself have not the slightest doubt that he often did so, and that he used many of his plays, *even while they of course remained primarily comedies*, as vehicles for the expression of serious political views—about the Athenian democracy, its institutions and its leading figures, and about the Peloponnesian war. Many others have much the same belief, even if their notion of Aristophanes' opinions differs markedly from mine. Others again, on the other hand, believe that Aristophanes wrote his plays as comedies pure and simple, and that we must beware of attributing to the poet himself opinions which are either expressed in character by his *dramatis personae*, or are simply part of the fooling. I shall return to this question at the end of this Appendix (Section *F* below).

At this point I want to make four preliminary observations. First, it must not be assumed *a priori* that a comic dramatist of the fifth century would not use a play or plays as (to put it as crudely as possible) political propaganda in favour of views which he himself held. Even a tragic dramatist could do this. Aeschylus went far beyond what was dramatically necessary, in his *Eumenides*, to stress the desirability of an eternal military alliance between Athens and Argos (which could only involve Athens in war with Sparta: see Chapter V, Part iv above, where other indications of Aeschylus' political attitude, given in his plays, are also mentioned). And I do not think anyone would wish to deny that Euripides sometimes openly expressed in his plays views that may be broadly called political.[1]

---

[1] E.g. the praise of Athenian democracy, in *Suppl.* 352–3 (where it is instituted by Theseus!), and of Athenian παρρησία in *Ion* 670–5 (cf. *Heracleid.* 181–3); the praise of equality in *Phoen.* 535–45 (cf. *Suppl.* 352–3, 433–8); the insistence on the saving political role of men of moderate possessions, in *Suppl.* 238–45; the denial that wealth is a criterion of worth, in *Electr.* 367–76, 938–44 (cf. 37–8, with 67–70 and 247–62; also *Orest.* 920); and the hatred of Sparta in *Andromache* 445–53, 595–601, 724–6; *Suppl.* 187, etc. Of the two main Athenian versions of the myth about Athens' intervention, on the appeal of Adrastus, to recover the corpses of the Argives who had fallen in the assault on Thebes, Euripides (*Suppl.*, esp. 571 ff., 634 ff.) chose the one in which it was accomplished by force, as against the version in Aeschylus' *Eleusinians*, in which only persuasion was used: see Plut.,

Secondly, I suggest that the best modern parallel for the kind of mixture of seriousness and foolery that I am suggesting in Aristophanes is the political cartoonist: a Low or a Vicky. He must always be *funny*: that is the precondition of his genre. But he can be, and very often is, *serious at the same time*. The funnier he is, the more likely it will be that his 'message' will be received and make an impression on the reader's mind—including the reader who would instantly reject the 'message' if it were conveyed to him in a purely serious form. It would be a crude error to insist that a particular passage in a comic dramatist cannot be conveying a serious idea simply because it is cast in a humorous form—as a sheer fantasy or absurdity or impossibility, or a gross exaggeration, or in the guise of a literary parody: some such comic dress is a necessity of the genre.

Thirdly, given that even intrinsically humorous material may be making a serious statement (and on the other hand that some mock-serious passages may in reality be comic),[2] we must keep a careful watch for passages which express serious opinions and which are *not funny in themselves*: these are particularly likely to represent the poet's own views. He may, of course, have found it desirable to keep them fairly brief and to sandwich them, so to speak, between lines which are purely comic; but if the bread in which the meat is delivered is clearly separable from it (as in the excellent string of examples in *Lysistr.* 1114–77, noticed in Section *D* §5 below), we may have no difficulty in recognising the meat for what it is.

And fourthly, even the *kind of joke* Aristophanes makes, the *things he makes jokes about*, can sometimes give an indication of the outlook he must have had, to find these particular things funny. A good example is the jury courts and dicastic pay (see Section *C* below).

Before taking up individual points in detail, I will give a bare summary of Aristophanes' position, as I see it. There is no indication at all that he was an oligarch, in the literal sense of wanting to restrict the franchise and (like his contemporary, Ps.-Xen., *Ath. Pol.* 1 9) reduce the lower classes to complete political subjection, δουλεία. Indeed, he can sometimes show a real sympathy for the lower orders: see Gomme, AP 107 and n. 1 = 88 and n. 23, citing a number of passages from the plays, including of course *Ach.* 162–3. But he had an essentially *paternalist* attitude towards them: he clearly resented the political *power* the demos was beginning to exercise, more particularly in the law courts, as a result of dicastic pay, his frequent sneers at which betray the irritation felt by the upper-class Athenian at this innovation of the radical democracy. For him, the lower classes were most admirable when they were wearing out their rumps at the oar-bench and crying 'Rhyppapai' (*Frogs* 1072–3; cf. *Wasps* 909); and one should be particularly careful not to cheat them out of their pay for *that*, which was well-earned (*Knights* 1366–7; cf. 1065–6; *Ach.* 162–3). But it was intolerable when ignorant and ill-educated men demanded a share in the delicate art of government, and presumed to take the conduct of State affairs into their own hands (cf. Thuc. 11 65.10). Aristophanes also sneers repeatedly at the men not belonging to the old leading families who in the late fifth century began to exercise political leadership, mainly perhaps with the support of the humbler Athenians; and he represents these new leaders (especially in *Knights* 128–43) as jumped-up salesmen: -πῶλαι of various kinds.

Thes. 29.4–5; cf. Paus. 1 xxxix.2; and Isocr. iv 58 and xiv 53, against xii 168–71, 172–4. In view of Hdts ix 27.3, Euripides evidently did not invent his version (see Jacoby, *FGrH* iii b [Suppl.] i.445–8, on Philoch., F 112–13), but of course it would have had much greater force after the events at Delium, described by Thuc. iv 97–9. (I would date the *Suppl.* 422 or 421. G. Zuntz, *The Political Plays of Eurip.* [Manchester, 1955] 88–94, is for 424, but for inadequate reasons: he fails even to mention Thuc. iv 97–9, and he seems unaware of the significance of Thuc. v 14.4; 22.2; 28.2; 40.3 in relation to *Suppl.* 1189–95.)

[2] See e.g. the acute exegesis of *Knights* 230–3 by Dover, PMA 16 ff.

Although doubtless a patriotic Athenian, who would fight for his city without question when he had to, he was very much against the war: he thought it should never have been allowed to break out in the first place, and that any chance of bringing it to an end and making peace with Sparta should be eagerly embraced; the admirable situation which had existed before the coming to power of the radical democrats could then be restored, and Athens and Sparta could dominate the Greek world jointly. In this last respect, as well as in his general political position, Aristophanes can be described as a 'Cimonian'. There is some evidence to suggest that he may have moved in quite high social circles: see Sterling Dow, 'Some Athenians in Aristophanes', in *AJA* 73 (1969) 234–5, on *IG* II² 2343, a list of Thiasotai of the early fourth century.

Aristophanes has been the victim of many absurd misconceptions, some of which have been easily demolished by Gomme. But the fact that he has often been misrepresented is not to be taken as evidence that he had no identifiable opinions, or none worth discovering. I hope to have made a fresh start.

A. A writer's attitude will often emerge clearly from the way he uses political and social terminology,[3] and Aristophanes is no exception here. The most instructive passage is the parabasis of the *Frogs* (674–737), the seriousness of which is not, I think, denied by anyone. The whole passage, 686 ff., is characterised by a real earnestness, underlined by the opening statement of the chorus, τὸν ἱερὸν χόρον δίκαιόν ἐστι χρηστὰ τῇ πόλει/ ξυμπαραινεῖν καὶ διδάσκειν (686–7). That is not one of the mock-serious statements Aristophanes sometimes makes, which would be immediately recognised as comic, and I know of no one who has tried to maintain that Aristophanes was writing it with his tongue in his cheek. At 706–16 there is a brief burst of invective against Cleigenes (who οὐκ εἰρηνικός ἐστι), but in 717–37 we move back on to the more exalted plane of 686 ff., with one of Aristophanes' most brilliant imaginative pieces: a comparison between the city's politicians and its coins. Here, couched in a vocabulary that would have been perfectly acceptable to Pseudo-Xenophon, we have a plea for political leadership, not by the ξένοι and πονηροὶ κἀκ πονηρῶν who now are dominant, but by the εὐγενεῖς καὶ σώφρονας/ ... καὶ δικαίους καὶ καλούς τε κἀγαθούς,/ καὶ τραφέντας ἐν παλαίστραις καὶ χοροῖς καὶ μουσικῇ. This reinforces the wish expressed earlier in 686–705 (another passage that shows scarcely any attempt at humour) that those who had suffered some form of disqualification as a result of taking part in the oligarchic revolution of 411 (and who are described euphemistically as having 'sustained a fall in Phrynichus' wrestlings') should be 'forgiven for their one mishap'. Those who had been prominent enough in the revolution to be thought worth disfranchising would have been mainly if not entirely men of leading families, the δυνατώτατοι of Thuc. VIII 47.2; 48.1. Later in the play, in the exchange between Aeschylus and Dionysus in lines 1454–7, Athens is again said to hate the χρηστοί and use, if perforce, the πονηροί. Now these passages are by no means exceptional in Aristophanes: he very often speaks in the same way. I do not intend to multiply examples of the obvious, but it is worth emphasising that nearly twenty years earlier Aristophanes was using exactly the same language. In *Knights* 181, 185–93, 222–9, 334–7, 738–40 we find many of the same concepts used in the same way: the καλὸς κἀγαθός is idealised (185, 227, 738), and the successful politician is presented as a πονηρός (181, 186, 336, 337, cf. 415), base born (218, γέγονας κακῶς), ἀμαθής and βδελυρός (193), unacquainted with μουσική (188–9, 191–2) and not χρηστὸς τοὺς τρόπους (192), for τὸ σωφρόνως τραφῆναι is worth nothing in Athenian politics (334). The χρηστοί/πονηροί contrast of *Frogs* 1454–7 appears also in *Knights* 1274–5, and the πονηροί/καλοὶ κἀγαθοί contrast of *Frogs* 718–33 in *Knights* 185–6. When Aristophanes speaks

[3] It is well worth consulting Neil, *KA* 202–9, Appendix II, 'Political Use of Moral Terms'.

of the καλοὶ κἀγαθοί (*Knights* 185, 227, 738; *Clouds* 101, 797; *Wasps* 1256; *Lys.* 1059; *Frogs* 719, 728; and even *Knights* 735, although spoken by the Sausage-Seller) the words almost always have a strongly social complexion (see the Additional Note at the end of this Appendix).

A useful contrast may be drawn here with Thucydides. No one will impute to the historian either undue hostility to the upper classes or any particular tenderness towards the lower orders; but he himself never uses the expression καλοὶ κἀγαθοί without qualification (in IV 40.2 it is a quotation, and in VIII 48.6 we have τούς τε καλοὺς κἀγαθοὺς ὀνομαζομένους); nor does he use the terms χρηστοί and πονηροί in the mixed moral, social and political sense, except probably in VI 53.2; and, apart from VIII 47.2 (where οὐ πονηρίᾳ οὐδὲ δημοκρατίᾳ is Alcibiades' expression), πονηρία in this sense occurs only in VIII 73.3, where it is attributed to Hyperbolus, the only man he describes as a μοχθηρὸς ἄνθρωπος.

B. It has recently been asserted by a leading authority on Aristophanes, K. J. Dover (whose commentary on the *Clouds* is by far the best we have on any Aristophanic play), that 'the essential spirit of Old Comedy is the ordinary man's protest—using his inalienable weapons, humour and fantasy—against all who are in some way stronger or better than he: gods, politicians, generals, artists, and intellectuals' (*OCD*² 270a); and that the treatment by Aristophanes himself of politicians (apart from Cleon, who had attacked him for his play, the *Babylonians*, and against whom Aristophanes was expressing personal venom) 'does not differ significantly from the way in which "we" satirise "them" nowadays. No class, age-group, or profession is exempted from Aristophanes' satire' (*OCD*² 113b). Although there is a certain element of truth in this, as a generalisation it does not fit the facts. Certainly Aristophanes pictures the 'demagogues'[4] as rogues who have entirely selfish motives and make handsome profits for themselves out of their political activities, at the expense of the ordinary citizen: the best example is *Wasps* 656–79; cf. *Knights* 128 ff., 824–35, etc. But except for this, what specific features does Aristophanes' picture of the 'demagogues' and their activities share with attacks on modern politicians? One may remember some of the gibes at the low birth and poor education of some working-class politicians of the Edwardian period and even the nineteen-twenties and -thirties (they have hardly survived the Second World War); but when these sneers were fashionable, what they represented was the outlook of an upper class used to governing and irritated at having to admit some of its 'inferiors' to a position in which they might be able to exercise some political influence, even power—very much the attitude I am attributing to Aristophanes. I see little reflection of the true contemporary 'We/ Them' situation in Aristophanes' plays. The essence of his presentation of the 'demagogues' in the *Knights* is that the more crude and uncultured and cunning they are, the more ardently the demos will take them to its heart: the 'Sausage-Seller', who usurps the place of the Paphlagonian slave who is Cleon, has these

---

[4] I feel impelled to put the word 'demagogue' in inverted commas when I use it of the late-fifth- and fourth-century Athenian politicians, lest anyone should think that I am attributing to them the unpleasant characteristics usually connoted by that term. Some of these politicians (Hyperbolus, perhaps; cf. Thuc. VIII 73.3) may have been demagogues in the bad sense, men who gained their ends by unworthy and flattering appeals to the baser feelings of the people (cf. Thuc. II 65.10, καθ' ἡδονάς). But the δημαγωγός in the basic sense of the word, 'leader of the people', the man who gives leadership above all through *speeches*, is an inevitable feature of any system of democracy which, like the Greek variety, works mainly through direct rather than representative government. Cf. M. I. Finley, 'Athenian Demagogues', in *Past & Present* 21 (1962) 3–24. And in any form of democracy, the greater the crisis, the greater the need for the 'good demagogue'. One remembers that in recent times it has been during the two World Wars above all that Britain has had recourse to 'demagogues', men who were outstanding orators: Lloyd George and Winston Churchill.

characteristics in the very highest degree—until the very end, when he is suddenly and mysteriously transformed (lines 1316 ff.). What modern politician, in our generation, has been caricatured in anything like this way?

It is instructive to discover, by way of contrast, who it is that emerges with credit from the plays of Aristophanes. When Dover, in a passage quoted above, says that Aristophanes' treatment of politicians other than Cleon 'does not differ significantly from the way in which "we" satirize "them" nowadays. No class . . . is exempted from Aristophanes' satire', he significantly omits one category of 'Them' which we might reasonably have expected Aristophanes to include among his targets: the very rich—surely the most obvious target of all, for a satirist with a real 'We/Them' attitude? In fact, Aristophanes scarcely says a disrespectful word about the rich as such, although of course he attacks the 'demagogues' (see above) for allegedly making fortunes out of their political activities.[5] The various terms for 'wealth' and 'wealthy' are not particularly frequent in Aristophanes, outside the *Plutus*; but it is very interesting to find that even the words παχύς, οἱ παχεῖς are used of rich men by Aristophanes only in passages in which he is sympathising with them: *Knights* 1137–40, *Wasps* 288–9, *Peace* 639–40. In the *Plutus* the nature of the plot is such that occasional unflattering references to the rich are bound to occur, but even here they are few (see 107–9, 502–3, and of course 30–1, and esp. 567–70, referring to the orators; cf. *Peace* 644–6 etc.). And in the other plays, as far as I can discover, the rich are never once attacked as such, and on no less than five occasions they are sympathetically treated: *Knights* 223–4, 264–5; *Wasps* 626–7; *Peace* 639–40; *Eccl.* 197–8. I can find nothing at all in the surviving plays to compare with Euripides' οἱ μὲν ὄλβιοι/ ἀνωφελεῖς τε πλειόνων τ' ἐρῶσ' ἀεί (*Suppl.* 238–9), or the attacks on the πλούσιοι in Dem. xxi.

It is consistent with this attitude that Aristophanes should treat with great respect and sympathy one group forming a distinct social category of the richest Athenians, the Knights (ἱππεῖς),[6] who receive a grateful compliment[7] in the opening scene of the *Acharnians* (5–8) and another friendly reference later (300–1), and of course form the chorus of Aristophanes' next play. (I am not sure what the best contemporary parallel to these Knights would be—perhaps not so much a chorus of Peers or Millionaires as of Rolls-Royce Owners?) The very favourable treatment the Knights receive from Aristophanes does not at all correspond with Dover's 'We/Them' antithesis. And I might remark that although I know of nothing to suggest that the Athenian *hippeis* had an anti-democratic complexion in the 420s, they certainly did at the end of the war: see Xen., *HG* II iv.2, 4, 7, 8, 24, 31; III i.4; Lys. xvi 6; and cf. Thuc. viii 92.6 *fin.* (411).

In the *Knights* we first hear of ἱππῆς ἄνδρες ἀγαθοὶ χίλιοι (line 225), who, according to Demos, will work against Cleon, with τῶν πολιτῶν οἱ καλοί τε κἀγαθοί and ὅστις ἐστὶ δεξιός among the spectators (cf., for δεξιός, Ps.-Xen., *Ath. Pol.* i 6, 9). From the moment of their entry, at line 247, the Knights are presented in an admirable light: they rebuke Cleon, who is unable to cajole them, and in the parabasis (507–46), after some conventional praise of the poet himself

---

[5] The accusation seems to have been conspicuously untrue of the man who was perhaps the most prominent of all the 'demagogues' after Cleon, namely Cleophon: see Lys. xix 48–9. It is a fact seldom sufficiently realised nowadays that Athenian politicians in general expected, and were expected, to make money out of politics: Hyper. v (*c. Dem*) cols. 24–5 is particularly illuminating on this point. Taking money for most political activities was perfectly permissible: it was only if his leadership had *bad results* for Athens that the politician might be made to suffer—*then* he could be prosecuted, e.g. for 'speaking not in the best interests of the Athenian people, χρήματα λαμβάνων': see esp. Hyper. IV (*pro. Euxen.*) 8, 29, etc.

[6] The Solonian Pentacosiomedimnoi were not a distinct social category but merely the upper crust, financially, of the Hippeis.

[7] Precisely what service they had rendered against Cleon and 'for Hellas' is not clear, but I rather like the suggestion in Starkie, *AA* 241–2 (from Lübke).

(whose outlook they identify with theirs, 509–10), they speak in a noble and dignified fashion of their ambition to fight for their city and its gods—without pay, of course: they will be satisfied if no one begrudges them their long hair and their luxurious baths (576–80). There are a few comic touches but they are all friendly. And in lines 595–610 they are made to speak with unalloyed pride of a recent military exploit of theirs, described by Thuc. IV 42–5. Their other contributions are all creditable to them. Gomme speaks of the Knights ('the young aristocrats', he calls them) as appearing in this play in 'an important *if not altogether sympathetic* rôle'; and he thinks it would be 'permissible to argue . . . that Aristophanes intended the *Knights* to be a satire on oligarchic reformers' (AP 106 and n. 1 =85–6 and n. 21), because the chorus 'in effect only propose to get rid of Cleon by putting Athens—including themselves—in the power of a similar demagogue; demagogy of the right is very like that of the left'. But this ignores the fact that although the Knights support the Sausage-Seller against Cleon in their competition for the favours of old Demos, there is ultimately a complete transformation: Demos reveals that he can see through the flattery of the 'demagogues' after all (1111–50), and at the very end of the play, taught by the Sausage-Seller (who has now shed his demagogy and all his unpleasant characteristics, 1316 ff.), he appears reformed and rejuvenated (1316–34), and ready to return to the great days of Miltiades and Aristeides and perform deeds worthy (as the Chorus put it, 1334) 'of the trophy at Marathon'. In the concluding lines, after some interesting talk about peace which we shall notice in Section *D* 2 below, Cleon takes over the Sausage-Seller's trade, and all is well. The Knights had backed the right man indeed!

I have been speaking about Aristophanes' attitude to a particular social group, the Knights. Most of the individuals referred to in the plays are of course ridiculed in one way or another, but some of the exceptions are significant. Cimon is mentioned only once, with honour (*Lysistr.* 1144; cf. the single mention of Cimon in the preserved fragments of Cratinus: fr. 1, *ap.* Plut., *Cim.* 10.4). Another character who receives sympathetic treatment (*Ach.* 703–12; cf. *Wasps* 946–8) is Thucydides, son of Melesias, who must have returned from ostracism in the spring of 433. (There can be no doubt that this Thucydides is the son of Melesias: the wrestling metaphors in *Ach.* 704, 710 are decisive—see Wade-Gery, TSM 209–10 = *EGH* 244–6. For Thucydides' opposition to Pericles, see the passages cited in Hill, *S²* 352, Index II 5.9–11.) I think we may possibly be exaggerating if we speak of Thucydides the son of Melesias as an '*oligarchic* leader'. There was an oligarchic group at Athens in the early 450s (see Thuc. I 107.4, and the passages in which Aeschylus expresses fear of civil war: *Eumen.* 858–66, 976–87); but I feel that Thucydides' followers may have been mainly the more conservative Athenian democrats who had earlier taken Cimon as their leader, rather than actual would-be 'oligarchs'. However that may be, we may find some significance in Aristophanes' respectful tribute to this man, a conspicuous example of his admired τραφέντες ἐν παλαίστραις (*Frogs* 729)!

And if it is true, as to some extent it is (and as a leading authority on Aristophanes urged upon me, after reading a draft of this Appendix), that it is the principal men of the time who are the most natural butts of Comedy and we must accordingly expect the comic poets to attack the most prominent politicians, then it is all the more remarkable how gently Aristophanes treats two men who were certainly among the most conspicuous political figures of their day: Alcibiades and Nicias, each of whom, in his way, might appear a rather obvious target for comic treatment. Aristophanes makes surprisingly few references to the aristocratic Alcibiades, who was certainly prominent by 427 (Ar., fr. 198). Apart from a passing reference in fr. 554 and perhaps another in fr. 907, the only disparaging ones are *Ach.* 716 (*en passant*, again) and the justified criticism by Euripides in *Frogs* 1427–9, which is followed at once by Aeschylus' plea that Athens should put up with her inconvenient 'lion'—now of course in his second (and final) exile. Nicias escapes Aristophanes' lash altogether, apart from the word μελλονικιᾶν in *Birds* 640 and perhaps the mysterious fr. 100 (*ap.* Plut., *Nic.* 8.4: Plutarch may have misunderstood this). *Knights* 358 is if anything sympathetic. Even if Nicias is the second slave in *Knights* 6 ff., he is not blackguarded there; and in fact it seems very doubtful whether Nicias is intended (see Dover, *PMA* 24–6, and in *CR* 73 = n.s. 9 [1959] 196–9). The other comic poets also dealt very gently with Nicias: see Plut., *Nic.* 4.5–8, where only one passage (§8 = Phryn. fr. 59) has any real sting and at least one (§6 = Eup. fr. 181; cf. §5 = Telecl. fr. 41) is warmly appreciative. Nicias, remembered in the fourth century as a καλὸς κἀγαθός (Arist., *Ath. Pol.* 28.5), had no famous ancestors, and the family may well have been recently enriched by mining activities and slave-owning (see Davies, *APF* 403–4). But Nicias was an 'Establishment figure' of unimpeachable orthodoxy, and he was not aggressive towards Sparta: that must be why Aristophanes lets him off so very lightly. (Cf. also Plut., *Nic.* 2.2.)

C. Another way in which Aristophanes reveals his political opinions is in his attitude to the jury-courts, in which, during the last generation only, many poor Athenians had become able to serve, owing to the institution of dicastic pay by Pericles. Aristophanes evidently disliked this situation, and he makes a number of references to the 'triobolon' and to dicastic pay generally[8]—which in itself was not in the least funny, except of course to a member of the upper classes, who disapproved of it to the extent of thinking it a fit subject for satire. (It is not the working class in this country who make jokes about the 'dole' or about alleged scroungers who live like fighting-cocks on social security payments.) Aristophanes even makes the very telling point that the dicasts, alone of the Athenian officeholders (ἀρχαί), were ἀνυπεύθυνοι, not subject to account (*Wasps* 587–8)—a wellknown characteristic of the tyrant. He makes Philocleon tell the dicasts that their ἀρχή is as great as that of Zeus (620–1) and Bdelycleon speak of the paid popular courts, dependent as they were (in his picture) upon the 'demagogues', as 'an inveterate, old disease engrained in the heart of the State' (651, Rogers' translation; cf. *Ach.* 370–6 and many other passages). Very little of this is at all funny, except to someone who sees the whole system as a form of popular tyranny,[9] and is out to discredit it by ridicule.[10]

---

[8] *Knights* 50–1, 255–7, 797–8 (cf. 1089), 800, 805–8, 1358–60; *Clouds* 863; *Wasps* 300–11, 525, 605–9, 661–3, 682–4, 689–90, 700–5, 785, 813, 1113, 1117–21; *Birds* 1541, 1694–9; *Frogs* 1466. (The three obols of *Eccl.* 292, 308, 380, 392; *Plut.* 329, cf. 125, are Assembly pay, introduced after 404/3.)

[9] It has been customary (see e.g. B. B. Rogers' edition of the *Wasps*, pp. xvi–xix etc., and D. M. MacDowell's, pp. 1–4) to pretend that Ar. was not criticising the legal system but only the way the courts worked in practice, giving (it is said) too great power to the 'demagogues'. But again (cf. n. 4 above), 'the demagogues' were, so to speak, a built-in feature of Athenian democratic process, and the line of argument I have just described derives from an uncritical acceptance of the Aristophanic caricature, a very clever attack upon the system which enabled many humble men, gulled (as Ar. would have us believe) by 'the demagogues', to sit in judgment on their 'betters'.

[10] Among the passages in his fifth-century plays in which Aristophanes makes fun of the courts or otherwise denigrates them (in addition to some of those cited in n. 8 above) are *Ach.* 375–6, 676–718; *Knights* 259–65, 307–11, 897–8, 1145–50; *Clouds* 207–8, 620, 1004; *Wasps passim*, e.g. 88 ff., 156–60, 223–7, 240–1, 287–9, 320–2, 400–14, 417–27, 513–726 (esp. 548–51, 577, 587–8, 590–1, 620–1, 626–8, 650–1, 656–72, 682–4), 799–804, 836–1002 (esp. 920–1, 941–3, 976–81, 991–2, 997–1002), 1037–42, 1094–8, 1339–41, 1450–73; *Peace* 505, 639–41; *Birds* 40–1, 109–10, 145–7, 1032, 1046, 1052–3, 1422–69, 1694–1705. In *Knights* 1317 the regenerated Sausage-Seller urges the closing of the courts for the day, which is to be a day of festival. Of course Ar. is particularly hostile to those who brought prosecutions ('sycophants'): see e.g. *Ach.* 515–22, 559, 679–718, 725, 818–35,

D. For the purpose of this book, Aristophanes' attitude to the war is of course the most important facet of his outlook, and it is in connection with the Megarian decree in particular that we have had occasion to use the evidence he provides. Aristophanes hated the war, not simply because it was war and peace was better, but because this particular war made impossible the situation he wanted: the joint hegemony of Athens and Sparta over the Greeks, that joint hegemony which Cimon had done his utmost to preserve and a return to which remained the dream of Athenians who felt that Athens and Sparta had no necessary quarrel, right into the fourth century (see especially Isocr. IV, *Paneg.*). Three of Aristophanes' plays (*Acharnians, Peace, Lysistrata*) are mainly concerned with the war against Sparta and there are other significant references to it. Although there is of course a good deal of sheer fooling in all the three plays just mentioned, each in its very different way shows Aristophanes' disapproval of the war, and the first two (*Acharnians* and *Peace*) make it very clear that in his opinion war should never have been allowed to break out at all. Most people do not doubt this, but in view of a recent *jeu d'esprit* by Forrest (AA), trying to turn the *Acharnians* into the very reverse of an 'anti-war play', I propose, at the risk of labouring the obvious, to establish Aristophanes' 'Cimonian' position in detail. I shall leave Forrest's article until near the end of this Appendix (see Section *E* below).

1. We begin with the *Acharnians*, and first of all with its principal figure, a 'comic hero' of a special type, who—like many of Aristophanes' characters—has a very interesting name, Dicaeopolis (the full significance of which will emerge presently), and who, alone of Aristophanes' characters of whom we know anything, is *carefully and explicitly identified by the poet with himself*, not merely once but in two separate passages: lines 377–82 and 497–503. 'I myself', says Dicaeopolis, 'know what I suffered from Cleon over last year's comedy' (377–8, beginning αὐτός τ' ἐμαυτόν)—a clear allusion to Cleon's attack on Aristophanes over the *Babylonians*,[11] of 426 (see Schol. *Ach.* 378). A little later Dicaeopolis, dressed in beggar's rags, is about to make his principal speech (497 ff.), largely a parody of one by Telephus in Euripides' play of that name (produced in 438), which Aristophanes was particularly fond of quoting (see Chapter VII, Part ii, n. 22 above). 'Don't bear me a grudge, spectators', he begins, 'if I, as a beggar, am about to speak among Athenians about the City, in a comedy, for truth is no stranger to Comedy. And I am going to say what is both shocking and true' (497–501). It is at this point that the identification of Dicaeopolis with the poet is made all over again, to make quite sure the audience understands it: again Dicaeopolis refers to Cleon's slandering *him* for speaking evil of the city in the presence of strangers (at the Dionysia of 426), and congratulates himself that he is in no danger this time, for it is the Lenaea and the strangers have not yet arrived (502–5).

It is extraordinary how the commentators have failed to grasp the obvious point of these two passages: that Aristophanes is identifying himself with Dicaeopolis, making it quite clear that Dicaeopolis is speaking for him. (Contrast such passages as 659–64, where it is the Chorus which speaks for the poet against Cleon.) Now we know that Aristophanes produced both the *Babylonians* and the *Acharnians* (as well as the *Banqueters* of 427 and the *Birds* of 414) 'through Callistratus', who was the official διδάσκαλος, although everyone will have known that the author of

---

839–41, 904–58; *Knights* 435–7 and ff.; *Wasps* 1094–6; *Peace* 190–1, 653; *Birds* 285, 1410–69; *Eccl.* 452–3, 560–2; *Plut.* 30–1, 850–950 (esp. 877–9, 905–20). It was naturally the propertied class, to which Ar. himself belonged and with which he sympathised, which had most to fear from 'sycophants'.

[11] The nature of this play has so often been misrepresented that it is a relief to be able to refer to one discussion of it that is sound, sensible and properly cautious: that of G. Norwood, 'The Babylonians of Ar.', in *CP* 25 (1930) 1–10.

the plays was Aristophanes;[12] and some scholars[13] have supposed, on no evidence at all, that the part of Dicaeopolis was *acted* by Callistratus and that lines 377–82 and 497–503 were spoken *in propria persona* by Callistratus, who (and not Aristophanes) had been the subject of Cleon's prosecution after the *Babylonians*. Even Rennie, who rightly rejected this as a 'desperate theory', thought the lines were 'clearly concessions to the timidity of Callistratus'—as producer, presumably: I cannot imagine why. Others, including Starkie and Cyril Bailey,[14] have produced an equally 'desperate' theory: that Aristophanes himself played the part of Dicaeopolis. Certainly the two passages, 377–82 and 497–503, are unique in Attic Comedy,[15] in so far as a character identifies himself with the author of the play. But there is no need to resort to far-fetched theories in order to explain this. There is no hint in any ancient source, even late scholia, that Aristophanes acted the part of Dicaeopolis, nor is there any reliable evidence that he was ever an actor at all. It is true that the *Vita Aristophanis* §3,[16] the *Second Hypothesis* to the *Knights*, and Schol. Ar. *Knights* 230 speak of Aristophanes himself as acting the part of Paphlagon in the *Knights*, because neither mask (cf. *Knights* 230–2) nor actor could be procured for the part; but the story has rightly been dismissed as a fiction by most scholars other than Bailey: see e.g. Schmid, *GGL* I iv.187 and n. 8, 234 n. 3; T. Gelzer, in *RE* Suppl. XII (1970) cols. 1423–4; A. E. Haigh, *The Attic Theatre*³ (rev. A. W. Pickard-Cambridge, Oxford, 1907) 228 and n. 4; and B. B. Rogers' edition of the *Knights* 31–2 n. (cf. xlix n. 1); as regards Paphlagon's mask, see esp. Dover, PMA.

Yet another explanation of the two passages we are considering has been offered by Dover (NAA 15): that Dicaeopolis is speaking as 'the comic hero' or 'the comic protagonist', who 'has the right to speak for Comedy. Aristophanes treats Dikaiopolis as if [he] were an annual visitor to Athens who got into trouble on the last occasion on which he attempted to δίκαια λέγειν.' This seems to me very implausible. I know of nothing to suggest that an Athenian audience was ever likely to recognise 'the comic protagonist' as a kind of personification of Comedy itself, with an existence outside the particular play in question; and in any event, on Dover's own showing, Dicaeopolis is the *first* known hero of the required type— which could not *yet*, therefore, exist as such! And the object of Cleon's attack in the previous year had been not Comedy but *Aristophanes personally* (and conceivably Callistratus also). Dover's note is specifically on 'lines 377–8 and 501–2'; but even if we limit ourselves to these particular lines we find the first passage opening with the very personal αὐτός τ' ἐμαυτόν, and when we read on we find Dicaeopolis saying in lines 379–82 that Cleon had slandered *him* to the Council and abused *him*. I cannot see how Aristophanes' audience could possibly have taken these words to refer to anything but Cleon's attack on *Aristophanes personally*. An identification of Dicaeopolis with the poet necessarily follows.

To understand the situation in the play in which the main speech of Dicaeopolis (497 ff.) is made, we have to go back to the opening scene: this is vital to the understanding of the basic plot, in which Dicaeopolis makes his own private peace with Sparta, and it also sets up the character of Dicaeopolis, whose curious name it explains. Now there are many characters in Aristophanes who have names expressive of their nature or function: not merely Demos, Eirene and Polemos, Penia and Ploutos, but Bdelycleon and Philocleon, Lysistrata, Praxagora, Peisthetaerus,

---

[12] See e.g. Starkie, *AA* 247–8; Bailey, WPD 232; Dover, *AC* xvii and n.2.

[13] See Rennie, *AA* 144; add the edition by J. van Leeuwen (Leiden, 1901) 67 n.

[14] Starkie, *AA* 84 n.; Bailey, WPD. Contrast Schmid, *GGL* I iv.224 n. 3.

[15] Plato Com., fr. 107, has been cited as a possible parallel, but I find no reason to see a reference to the author of the play. Cf. Bailey, WPD 234–5.

[16] See e.g. the first vol. of the Teubner text of Ar., ed. Bergk (Leipzig, 1897), pp. xliv ff.; Dindorf's edition of Ar., Vol. IV Pars i (Oxford, 1838), pp. 33 ff.; B. B. Rogers' edition of the *Acharnians*, pp. lvii ff.; etc.

Agoracritus, Trygaeus, Pseudartabas and others—all have names appropriate to the roles they perform: Lysistrata is a 'dissolver of armies', Praxagora is active in the Agora, Peisthetaerus is highly persuasive, and so on. None of these names is in any way deceptive; all are to be taken at their face value. Similarly, Dicaeopolis must be the 'Just City'. The commentators have been unable to understand this. As a rule the name has wrongly been taken to mean something like 'the Just *Citizen*' (thus e.g. Gilbert Murray, *Aristophanes* [Oxford, 1933] 29; Schmid, *GGL* I iv.224 n. 3). After noting this, Bailey (WPD 236–8) tried to find a covert allusion to Aegina, which Pindar (*Pyth.* VIII 22) once calls ἀ δικαιόπολις. Bailey calls this 'the famous Pindaric epithet'; but we have no reason to think it became 'famous', and anyway Athens was the last place where a compliment to Aegina would be remembered and repeated! The nature of the connection between Aristophanes and Aegina, which is the subject of an obscure passage in the *Acharnians* (652–4),[17] is unknown to us. To find in the name Dicaeopolis an allusion to 'Aristophanes the Aeginetan', as Bailey does, is to construct another of those 'desperate theories' which have so bedevilled the interpretation of Aristophanes' plays. I cannot myself see the least difficulty in Dicaeopolis' name. In the opening scene Dicaeopolis wants his *City* to negotiate for peace with Sparta and, when no one will listen to him, *does what the City ought to have done*, and successfully negotiates for a peace himself—of course it has now to be a private peace, in which he and his family alone share (see the acute comments of Dover, NAA 21–2).

The plot, like those of some other plays of Aristophanes, is an impossible fantasy, something that by its very nature could never actually happen in the manner depicted in the play; but it is worked out, as so often, with a certain logical rigour, within its frame of reference. From the very beginning the personality of Dicaeopolis is sharply delineated: no character in Aristophanes is more carefully built up. There is of course no standard 'comic hero' in Aristophanes.[18] At one extreme, the principal character or characters may be mere buffoons, like most of those in the *Knights*, *Clouds* and *Wasps*; but at the other extreme one character can stand out as a real 'hero' and dominate the action of the play: Lysistrata, Praxagora—and Dicaeopolis. One of the main functions of the introductory scene in the *Acharnians* (1–173), which occupies nearly an eighth of the play, is to establish Dicaeopolis as the one really sagacious man in Athens, who is shrewd enough to see through all deceptions, even when all those around him are being taken in: see especially lines 71–2, 79, 86–7, 105–7, 109 ff., 125–7, 135, 137, 161–3. The consistency of the portrait is remarkable. Dicaeopolis can be comic, but he is never at any moment disreputable or dishonest (as comic heroes so often are) or silly—very much the reverse. In case anyone is tempted not to take him seriously, inside the first eight lines he proclaims himself anti-Cleon and pro-Knights; he is able, unlike the ambassadors and the Council, to see through both Pseudartabas (91–125) and Theorus (134–71). In his opening speech (26 ff., esp. 26–7, 32, 37–9) he makes it clear both that he himself wants peace, to the extent of being prepared to shout down any orator who talks about anything else, and that the Athenians in general are not at all concerned to obtain peace. At line 46 Amphitheus enters as the negotiator appointed by the gods to arrange peace; but he is refused his journey-money and thrown out (51–5). Dicaeopolis protests, and refuses to be quiet unless peace is discussed (56–60). It is only when Dicaeopolis finds that the Assembly has no intention of discussing peace that he sends Amphitheus to Sparta to arrange a private peace on his own behalf (129–32, 175–9, 186–202). By the time we reach the central scene of the play (204–718) we know we are going to be on the side of this remarkable man. And then, to clinch the matter, comes the

---

[17] See e.g. Starkie, *AA* 138–9; Dover, *AC* xix.

[18] Others may find, though I cannot, some help from C. H. Whitman, *Ar. and the Comic Hero* (Martin Classical Lects. XIX, Cambridge, Mass., 1964).

identification of Dicaeopolis with Aristophanes, made twice over, as we have seen.

I need not describe at length the speech which Dicaeopolis, as a pseudo-Telephus, makes to the bellicose Acharnians (509–56), as I have analysed it sufficiently in Chapter VII, Part ii, Section c above, in which I have also discussed the later scene (so often misinterpreted as referring to the Megarian decree) in which the starving Megarian appears. The speech has a real logic of its own. The audience has been led to expect something that is *both comic and exceptionally serious*, and that is exactly what we find. As a parody of the speech of Telephus it is intrinsically funny, and parts of it are also funny in themselves; but (see Chapter VII, Part ii, Section c above) *one* serious point is also made: the blame for the war must not be laid *only* at Sparta's door (514, picking up 309–14 and 496–501; cf. 355–6, 369, 482); the war started above all because Pericles 'over-reacted' to a minor provocation with the exaggerated Megarian decree (524–34), and when Athens refused to repeal it, war was inevitable (535–55). This was the one way in which a case, of a sort, could be made against Athens and for Sparta;[19] and I cannot resist pointing out that it nicely represents the consensus of modern scholarly opinion on the outbreak of the war! The Megarian decree must still have been very much a living political issue in 426/5. Six years earlier *many* Athenians (Thuc. 1 139.4) had advocated its repeal as a necessary step to avoiding war with Sparta, and although some had doubtless changed their minds, in view of Athens' unexpected success in resisting Peloponnesian attacks, many will surely not have done so and will have longed for a settlement with Sparta. They may have been only a minority, but I suspect they may have been quite an influential minority.

Let us be very clear about the argument of Dicaeopolis-Aristophanes: it is that Athens too is partly to blame for the war and should now swallow her pride and *open negotiations for peace*. When war was in progress, to take the initiative in asking for peace was to the Greeks an admission of weakness and the fear of imminent defeat. The Athenians in 430 had sent ambassadors to Sparta to propose peace (Thuc. 11 59.2), but were evidently not able to obtain tolerable terms, and Pericles succeeded in dissuading them from making any further such attempts (65.2). We hear no more of peace proposals until 425, not long after the production of the *Acharnians*, and then it was the Spartans who took the initiative, things having suddenly begun to go badly for them (IV 15–22; cf. 41.3–4).[20]

In 427/6 something had happened at Sparta which would have appreciably increased the chances of peace: the recall of King Pleistoanax, who had been exiled, or more probably had fled, in 445, as a result of his failure (perhaps the result of deliberate policy) to press home the invasion of Attica in 446, and who was to be the leader of those Spartans who wanted peace with Athens in 421 (see Chapters IV, Part vi with its n. 163, and V, Part vii). The significance of this event cannot have escaped those Athenians who knew anything about the outside world. By 426/5, then, circumstances were more favourable for a peace initiative than they had ever been since the beginning of the war. The majority of Athenians were not prepared to put themselves in the position of the weaker party, by opening negotiations; but the return of Pleistoanax had created a new situation which it was worth trying to exploit. If the deadlock had continued and the whole complexion of the war had not changed dramatically a few months later, with the Pylos affair, there might well have been some cautious soundings from the

[19] Modern scholars have found no difficulty in taking the argument seriously: thus to Gilbert Murray it is 'a fair and persuasive argument that the war has arisen out of a muddle and is a very bad way of correcting the muddle' (*Aristophanes* 32, cf. 32–3).

[20] Purely on the strength of *Ach.* 652–4, some think the Spartans had negotiated for peace in 426: Adcock, in *CAH* v 226–7; Beloch, *GG* II² i.323; and Busolt, *GG* III ii.1079 and n. 5, seem to have no doubts about this. But see Gomme, *HCT* II 391 (with 87), with whom I agree.

Athenian side during the course of 425–4. Aristophanes was not backing an entirely hopeless cause in the *Acharnians*.

2. The next play of Aristophanes, the *Knights*, produced early in 424, was written and staged at a time when the spirits of the Athenians had suddenly been sent soaring by their great success at Pylos. This was actually the peak of Athenian achievement in the whole war, before Delium and the activities of Brasidas in the Thraceward region in the autumn of 424 had begun to reverse the tide once more. We know from Thucydides (IV 15–22; 41.3–4) how Sparta sued for peace while the operations at Pylos were in progress, and repeatedly thereafter (perhaps thrice: see Ar., *Peace* 665–7). But her overtures were all repulsed, the Athenians insisting on terms which were too humiliating for Sparta to accept. That Athens should take the initiative in proposing peace was of course entirely out of the question after Pylos,[21] and what we might have expected to find in the *Knights* is rather the celebration of victories already won and the anticipation of final triumph, with some delighted satirising of the proud Spartans who had so far betrayed Spartan principles as to surrender ignominiously to the Athenians (cf. Thuc. IV 40.2). But if, as Gomme says (*HCT* III 527), 'Aristophanes shows us in the *Knights* a whole city on the tide of victory', we can only feel surprise at what we actually do find. The great Athenian success at Pylos is glanced at several times, but as a rule only askance and in such a way as to discredit Cleon (lines 54–7, 75–6, 355, 702, 742–5, 844–6, 1005, 1052–5, 1058–9, 1167, 1201–5), a target evidently more congenial to Aristophanes than the Spartans one might have expected him to get his teeth into. Nowhere is there any glorying over the discomfiture of the Spartans, now a very easy subject for satire, or any looking forward to Sparta's ultimate collapse. The one achievement Aristophanes does allow his chorus of Knights to celebrate is a minor exploit of their own (595–610), which Thucydides mentions (IV 42–5). Once, and only once, is there an invocation of Victory in solemn terms (581–94)—and then it is simply the Chorus asking the city's patron goddess to make them victorious in the competition! Otherwise, the Chorus in the parabasis merely hark back to the deeds of their ancestors (565–74) and proclaim their loyalty in defending their country and its gods (576–8), with a mild plea that their little fopperies should not be begrudged them when peace returns and they cease from their toils (579–80). Lines 794–6 seem to me to regret a failure to make peace, promoted by Archeptolemus.[22] However that may be, there is in lines 1388–95, just before the end of the play, a very clear condemnation of Cleon for procuring the rejection of the Spartan peace offers of 425; and the reformed Sausage-Seller arouses the enthusiasm of Demos by producing a Thirty Years Peace—ὡς καλαί, cries the grateful Demos.

3. In the *Clouds* (423) and *Wasps* (422) Aristophanes is concerned with other topics than the war, but it is not without interest that Labes, the subject of the mock-trial in the latter play (240, 836 ff., 894 ff.), stands for Laches (Kirchner, *PA* II no. 9019), a prominent general and political figure of the period, who was evidently working for peace at this time: he proposed the decree accepting the Truce for a year in 423 (Thuc. IV 118.11). And Labes-Laches is sympathetically treated by Aristophanes (see esp. *Wasps* 952–72) and acquitted (994).

4. We now come to the *Peace*, produced at the Great Dionysia of 421, only about

---

[21] According to Forrest (AA 10 n. 22), Aristophanes, if he had really had the outlook generally attributed to him (miscalled 'pacifist' by Forrest), 'in the *Knights* ... should have been pressing furiously for peace'. It would be hard to show a greater misunderstanding of the atmosphere in Athens in 425/4.

[22] In the context, of course, the name itself is a pun. And see Gomme, *HCT* III 482, cf. 732 (where '*Equit.* 704' is twice misprinted for '794': I cannot accept Gomme's last sentence here). But whether or not this Archeptolemus is identical with the son of Hippodamus, the Sausage-Seller is certainly being made to rebuke Cleon for preventing peace from being made.

a fortnight before the conclusion of the Peace of Nicias, at a time when everyone in Athens must have known that peace was certainly coming soon, and even approximately what its terms would be. (Hardly any Athenian at this date could have been in favour of continuing the war, provided tolerable terms could be obtained, as by now they obviously could.) In this play Aristophanes would not feel the need to *argue* in favour of peace: he could celebrate it with appropriate jubilation. There are only three passages to which I need draw attention. In lines 605–18 we have Aristophanes' second reference to the Megarian decree, which I have already considered sufficiently in Chapter VII, Part ii, Section c above. In 664–9 Trygaeus and Hermes agree (cf. 216–20) that the Athenians were wrong to reject the thrice-repeated Spartan peace overtures in 425. But the really illuminating passage is 1080–2, where Trygaeus, in three lines which are not themselves at all funny (although they are 'sandwiched' inside comic material), proclaims what I am sure was Aristophanes' deeply held conviction: we Athenians and Spartans are wrong to fight each other 'when we could make peace, *and rule Hellas jointly*' (ἐξὸν σπεισαμένοις κοινῇ τῆς Ἑλλάδος ἄρχειν). This reflects the opinion expressed by the Spartan ambassadors to Athens during the Pylos operations, according to Thuc. IV 20.4, that if Sparta and Athens were in accord (literally, if they 'used the same language') 'the rest of Greece would remain in a condition of inferiority and pay us the greatest honour'. Trygaeus is another of Aristophanes' heroes who is anything but a fool or a mere buffoon, and I cannot see why Aristophanes should have put lines 1080–2 into his mouth unless he himself agreed with them. There will certainly have been plenty of Athenians in 422/1 who were looking forward eagerly to precisely this situation. There is no reason to think that Aristophanes was less of an 'imperialist' than the other Athenians of his day. I am happy to be able to agree (for once, as far as Aristophanes is concerned!) with Forrest, when he says that 'Aristophanes never defends the allies against Athens, he never questions the principle of ἀρχή or of tribute, but he does defend both the allies and the Athenians against their own and each other's demagogues, he does believe that the ἀρχή and the tribute should be used in the interests of "nicer" people' (AA 1 n. 3).

5. The *Lysistrata*, the last of Aristophanes' 'anti-war' plays, was produced at the Lenaea of 411, at a time when Athens' fortunes were at a very much lower ebb than they had been at the time of the *Acharnians*. Athens had survived the shock of the Sicilian disaster and the revolts of allies which had followed, and she had even begun to recover a little and win back some of the allies she had lost in 413–12. But Sparta and Persia were now in the act of coming together at last (see Chapter IV, Part vi above), an oligarchic revolution was brewing, and at any moment the situation of Athens might become desperate. 'Reasonable terms', from Athens' point of view, were almost out of the question now, for the Spartans naturally felt they had her at their mercy, and they would certainly not have consented even to 'uti possidetis' terms—which would anyway have left Athens much worse off than similar terms in 426/5, if only because major allies had deserted her since then. Yet there can be no doubt at all that the *Lysistrata* is a plea for peace: even Forrest is willing to admit that (AA 10 n. 22).

Scattered through the play are passages which demand to be taken seriously, even if they are mixed in with pure comedy. Most important are lines 1114–77, which are in effect a speech by Lysistrata, *completely serious in character and without a single jest*, interspersed with comic interjections, often obscene, by her Athenian and Spartan hearers. First, Lysistrata gently chides both sides for fighting each other, Greeks as they are, in the very sight of armed barbarians (1128–35). After one line of obscene comment by the Athenians, Lysistrata turns to the Spartans and reminds them of the time of the earthquake and the Messenian revolt, when Cimon and his 4,000 Athenian hoplites saved Sparta; and she reproves them for ravaging the land from which they had once benefited (1137–46). Again, there is no attempt

at humour. The Athenians applaud at this point, and there is another sexual inter-
jection, this time by the Spartans. Lysistrata now rounds on the Athenians with
yet a third short speech, again devoid of humour, reminding them of how the
Spartans had rescued them from the tyranny of Hippias (1149–56). After another
pair of comments, of the usual sexual character (1157–8), Lysistrata asks the
Athenians and Spartans why they cannot come to terms (1159–61). This produces
a mixture, partly obscene, of fact and fancy; but one thing emerges clearly enough:
the Spartans demand Pylos, the Athenians are minded to deny it, but Lysistrata
insists that they give it up. Of course we must not over-idealise Aristophanes'
attitude, and Gomme (AP 100–1 = 76–7) has done well to insist, against
Hugill, that it is not at all the heroine's arguments that make Lysistrata's plan
succeed, but the men's unwillingness to tolerate their own sexual deprivation.

E. Forrest's article, AA (1963), is one of the strangest contributions to the
literature on Aristophanes, a *tour de force* which is so brilliantly and persuasively
written that anyone who incautiously accepts it on its own narrowly limited terms
may easily be captivated by its charming fancies and surrender to it entirely. Its
terms are very 'narrowly limited' indeed, and the whole article nicely illustrates
the fatal consequences of ignoring the principle laid down in Chapter VII, Part ii,
Section C above: that we must never consider in isolation a few lines in a comedy
or even the speech in which they occur, but look at the play as a whole and indeed
the dramatist's entire output, in so far as it is known to us. Forrest has carefully
isolated a single speech in a single play, that of Dicaeopolis in *Ach.* 497–556, which
he boldly and quite mistakenly claims as 'the only solid argument for the traditional view of the play', but refuses to take seriously, on the sole ground that it is
'parody from start to finish' (AA 8–9). Aristophanes, indeed, in his opinion, was
'not opposed to the Archidamian war', as everyone has always supposed (AA 2)!
Against this eccentric interpretation there are several different lines of argument:

1. The whole structure of the play is of course relevant for its interpretation
(as of any other); but Forrest has totally ignored the very careful preparation
with which Aristophanes has introduced the scene on which he concentrates.
(He alludes twice in passing, AA 9, nn. 20–1, to episodes in the opening scene,
but they are not central features.) He omits to notice the significance of Dicaeopolis' name and the explicit (and unique) identification of Dicaeopolis with the
poet. And he has failed to realise that the 'defence' of the Spartans by Dicaeopolis-
Aristophanes is not contained only within lines 497 ff., parodying 'from the start'
(AA 8–9 n. 19) the speech of Telephus, but goes a long way back in the play, to
lines 309–10, 313–14, 355–6, 369, 482, long before the main series of parodies
of the *Telephus* begins.

2. Forrest's position is that because Dicaeopolis' speech is 'parody from start
to finish', *therefore* 'we cannot with confidence take it seriously at any level' (AA
8–9: I do not think my inserted 'therefore' is unfair). This is a *non sequitur*. To be
acceptable in a comedy, opinions must be couched in some humorous guise or
other. In *Lysistr.* 1114–77 the serious sentiments are made palatable (see Section
D, §5 above) by occasional comic interjections. In *Ach.* 497–556 they are flavoured
with parody—of Timocreon (and even perhaps Herodotus), when the *Telephus*
failed to provide just what was needed.

3. If the whole speech were, as Forrest maintains, an elaborate spoof, meaning
in effect almost the reverse of what it says, then those who failed to recognise the
parody—and by no means all the audience could have known the *Telephus*
intimately—would miss the point of it entirely. Their mystification would of course
be increased by the preliminary lines cited at the end of §1 above. But then why
on earth should Aristophanes add to their confusion by including those lines?

4. Forrest has to ridicule the view he is attacking by pretending that it involves
attributing to Dicaeopolis-Aristophanes something he repeatedly calls 'pacifism'

(AA 4, 6, 9, 10, 10 n. 22); and in the circumstances of 426/5 (as he imagines them) he thinks that 'to campaign for peace . . . would be treachery' (AA 10). But what Dicaeopolis-Aristophanes wanted, as we have seen, is that *Athens* should *open negotiations* for peace; and what is 'treacherous' or 'pacifist' about that? The Athenians *had* asked for peace in 430, when they were in a much worse position than in 426/5.

5. In 411, as Forrest is ready to concede (AA 10 n. 22), Aristophanes was 'arguing for peace' (in the *Lysistrata*). But any terms obtainable then would certainly have been much harsher than any which might have been possible in 426/5. If it was 'treacherous' to plead for peace negotiations in 426/5, it would have been far more so in 411.

6. Forrest seriously misconceives the military situation in 426/5: he actually compares it with that of Britain in 1942 (AA 2, 4, 10), and speaks of the war down to early 425 as 'almost totally unsuccessful' from Athens' point of view! He chooses to mention only 'the long and costly siege of Potidaea, the revolt of Mytilene, the disaster in Aetolia, . . . the horror of the plague'. But Athens had survived the plague, her strength not nearly as much impaired as might have been expected from such a disaster. As for Potidaea and Mytilene, Forrest forgets that both these states had received encouraging promises of help from Sparta (see Thuc. I 58.1 and 71.4; III 15 and esp. 25.2, also 26, 29–33), and yet had *failed*, their revolts being *crushed*. In the Lesbian revolt in particular Sparta had played a conspicuously feeble role, and the disaster to her friends there must have made her 'lose face' badly. The creation of an Athenian colony at Potidaea (Thuc. II 70.4) and of a cleruchy in Lesbos (III 50.2), the latter bringing in an annual income to the cleruchs and the Athenian sacred treasuries of no less than 100 talents, will have done much to compensate Athens for the money spent in quelling these revolts. The disaster in Aetolia, it is true, involved the loss of a Strategos and 120 men, described by Thucydides (III 98.4) as 'the best men from Athens who perished during the war'; but the 120 men, even if hoplites (see on this Gomme, *HCT* II 407–8), formed less than one per cent of Athens' total field force. And against this Athens in 431 had captured Sollium and won over the four cities making up the strategically important island of Cephallenia (Thuc. II 30.1–2); in 429 there had been two decisive naval victories by Phormio over much larger Peloponnesian fleets near the mouth of the Corinthian Gulf (II 83–92); in 427 the pro-Athenian side had triumphed in the stasis at Corcyra (III 70–85); and in 426 Demosthenes had partly redeemed his failure in Aetolia by winning the battle of Olpae (III 105–14). And above all, the decisive victory for Sparta which *the whole Greek world* had expected (see Chapter V, Part ix above) had not come about, and must now have seemed further off than ever. Sparta's one and only grand strategy, reliance on invasion of Attica, had proved a total failure, as Pericles had said it would. Athens had done enormously better than had seemed possible in 432–1, and there was now a kind of stalemate—equivalent to a major success for Athens, since she had not been the aggressor in the war. The return of King Pleistoanax (ignored by Forrest) must have increased the chances of peace. Sparta was already so discouraged by the mid-420s as to lose heart quickly (see Thuc. IV 41.3) when she suffered an isolated setback in 425, at Pylos—a tremendous blow to Sparta's pride and her reputation, certainly, and therefore a great psychological success for Athens, but from a purely military point of view not particularly important, until the raids of the Messenians from Pylos began to take effect (Thuc. IV 41.2–3; 55; 80. 2–5; V 14.3). If Athens had 'virtually won after Pylos' (as Forrest puts it, with some exaggeration, AA 10), it was because she had already proved that Sparta could have little or no hope of winning the war and that she herself was impregnable.

F. I return to the question raised, but not answered, at the beginning of this Appendix: whether the expression of political views in Aristophanes' plays was deliberate and had the conscious purpose of influencing public opinion. I am myself puzzled to find that there are a few people who are reluctant to give an affirmative answer. It seems to me that Aristophanes was a man of very vigorous political views of a conservative, 'Cimonian' variety (not at all untypical among the Athenian upper classes), the general complexion of which is easily identifiable from the plays and remained consistent over the period of some forty years during which he was writing his comedies. Aristophanes' forthright statements on political matters regularly follow particular patterns; and many of them which are not in themselves comic may indeed have seemed rather tiresome to those who did not share his outlook. Why anyone should suppose that they were not meant seriously, or were not intended to influence the audience, I cannot imagine. There are those who feel distaste at the very notion of a 'committed' poet, or who prefer to forget the truth expressed in Dover's remark that Aristophanes' 'portrayal of the effect of Socrates' teaching on the character of Pheidippides is an invitation to violence, or repressive legislation, against such teachers';[23] but even they must at least take account of the role played by the *Clouds* in helping to procure the condemnation of Socrates (see Chapter VII, Part ii, Section c above). And it is an ironical reflection that, irrespective of any effect on Athenian opinion the plays may have had at the time they were produced, the impression they have made on the historical record has been tremendous. The malicious and quite unnecessary side-swipe at Pericles in the *Peace* (605–18), in relation to the Megarian decree, became the foundation for Ephorus' popular version of the origins of the Peloponnesian war;[24] and the speech of Dicaeopolis in the *Acharnians* (514–39) has probably done more than anything else to create the almost universal misconception of the nature and effects of the Megarian decree in modern times (see Chapter VII above). The caricature of the 'demagogues' as 'salesmen' and *nouveaux riches* has become so firmly rooted that even the information which has become available in modern times about the background of Cleon and Cleophon[25] has not yet completely dispelled the Aristophanic image. And the various travesties of Athenian political and judicial procedures, especially perhaps that of the jury-courts in the *Wasps* (see Section C above), have been taken all too seriously, and few historians have succeeded entirely in escaping their seductive influence, apart from Grote (*HG* VII 9 ff., esp. 13–17, ch. lxvii).

ADDITIONAL NOTE ON *KALOS KAGATHOS, KALOKAGATHIA*

The fullest collection of material is by H. Wankel, *Kalos kai Agathos* (Diss., Frankfurt, 1961); see also J. Jüthner, 'Kalokagathia', in *Charisteria Alois Rzach zum achtzigsten Geburtstag dargebracht* (Reichenberg, 1930) 99–119; A. W. Gomme, 'The Interpretation of ΚΑΛΟΙ ΚΑΓΑΘΟΙ in Thucydides 4. 40. 2', in *CQ* 47 = n.s. 3 (1953) 65–8; and *HCT* III 480–1, 731–2; Ehrenberg, *PA²* 95–9, 107, 112; Grote, *HG* II 419–20 n. 4 (ch. ix, *ad fin.*). But much remains to be said, of which only a brief sketch can be given here.

The expression *kalos kagathos* seems not to occur in that form in the surviving literature before Herodotus and the poets of the Old Comedy (Aristophanes, Eupolis and Cantharus), or the corresponding noun before Xenophon; but the conjunction of the two adjectives was evidently made in Sappho's day (see E.

[23] Dover, *AC* lvi. The whole paragraph, pp. lvi–lvii, is excellent.
[24] Aristophanes can sometimes be kind to a dead man whom he had satirised while living: Lamachus, a main butt as a warmonger in *Acharn.*, and in *Peace* 473–4, 1290–1, is given respectful tributes in *Thesm.* 839–41 and *Frogs* 1039; and even Cleon, in *Peace* 647–56 (see esp. 648–9), is dismissed with a mere backhander, venomous but brief. For the dead Pericles there is no mercy.
[25] See above, Chapter VII, Part ii, n. 7.

Lobel and Denys Page, *Poet. Lesb. Fragm.* [1955] 39, Sappho fr. 50); relevant also are Tyrt., fr. 9.13–14 = Theogn. 1003–4 (the superlative form, and purely military), and even Homer, *Iliad* xxiv 52 (the comparative form, with a moral flavour).

The earliest appearances of *kalos kagathos*, in Herodotus (who can take it for granted as a well-known expression with a definite meaning of its own: see esp. II 143.4), prove beyond doubt that it was originally used as an evaluative term (a 'Wertbegriff') of very general application, denoting excellence, distinction, and was not applied, as so often later, with special reference to either the social-political or the moral sphere (see Wankel, *op. cit.* 30–2). The texts are Hdts I 30.4; II 143.4; v 31.1; also I 59.6 (the corresponding adverbs); and IV 91.2 (the superlative form, twice, cf. Thuc. I 129.3). Then, in the late fifth century and the fourth, while the expression *kalos kagathos* continues to be used on occasion as a general term of commendation, two specialised uses become prominent: one essentially social-political, which develops first and can be seen clearly in Aristophanes and Thucydides, and the other primarily moral, emerging rather later, from Xenophon onwards—it is often thought to be largely a product of the Socratic circle.

The social-political use appears most unmistakably in texts referring to the καλοὶ κἀγαθοὶ ὀνομαζόμενοι (Thuc. VIII 48.6) or καλούμενοι (Xen., *Oecon.* VI 12–17; cf. VII 2–3 ff.) or λεγόμενοι (Plato, *Rep.* VIII 569a). These are the members of the upper classes, 'the Best People', roughly those who are also called in other contexts the χρηστοί, γνώριμοι, βέλτιστοι, δυνατοί or δυνατώτατοι. The *kaloi kagathoi* in this sense are specifically identified with the rich by Plato (οἱ πλούσιοι, *loc. cit.*) and by Aristotle (οἱ εὔποροι, *Pol.* IV 8, 1293ᵇ38–42, 1294ᵃ17–19). They are therefore best referred to as the *propertied* classes, in the sense of those who could live off their own property without actually having to work for their living, σχολάζοντες ἐλευθερίως ἅμα καὶ σωφρόνως (to employ the nice phrase in Arist., *Pol.* VII 5, 1326ᵇ30–2). Being a *kalos kagathos* was above all a matter of what is often nowadays called 'life-style' (cf. Ehrenberg, *PA*² 99, 107), and therefore no one who was not at least reasonably well-to-do could aspire to *kalokagathia*. In Xen., *Cyrop.*, no *kalos kagathos* among the Persians ever travels on foot instead of horseback (IV iii.23), or rides a camel (VII i.49). In Deinarch. III 12, Philocles is said to have commanded, as Hipparch, ἀνδρῶν καλῶν κἀγαθῶν. (Philocles had also been Strategos on numerous occasions, and had therefore commanded Athenian hoplites too, not to mention sailors; but it is only the cavalry as such—of no special distinction, in a military sense—who are expressly singled out as ἄνδρες καλοὶ κἀγαθοί.) All the cavalry, of course, as the richest class of Athenians, were *kaloi kagathoi* (see Ehrenberg, *PA*² 95), but that category as normally conceived was a good deal wider. In Xen., *Mem.* III v.19 (cf. 15) *kalokagathia* is a quality generally supposed to be characteristic of knights and hoplites; in *HG* v iii.9 the men concerned are evidently hoplites from the top layer of the Perioikoi; in *Mem.* II vi.22 the possession of no more than a fair amount of property (τὰ μέτρια κεκτῆσθαι) is required for the *kalos kagathos*. In *HG* II iii.12, 15, 38, 49, 53 (cf. 19) the social-economic significance of the term (and indeed the political: see esp. §39 *fin.*) is again clear. Xen., *Oecon.* XIV 9 is unique in referring to certain specially worthy slave (or ex-slave) bailiffs as being honoured by Ischomachus ὡς καλούς τε κἀγαθούς; but Ischomachus has just said that he will have made these men rich. It is interesting in this connection to look back to one of the earliest surviving uses of *kalos kagathos*, Hdts v 31.1, where the island of Naxos can be called καλή τε καὶ ἀγαθή because of its opulence: it has much χρήματα and many slaves. Wealth must always have been an essential factor in *kalokagathia*, at least before the development of a primarily moral use of the term.

In Thuc. IV 40.2 any contemporary Greek would have realised the sting in the Spartan's contemptuous reply to the question whether the men captured on Sphacteria were *kaloi kagathoi*. The Spartan hoplites had been overcome by archers and the like, men of no consequence, who could not be brave in the right way, whose 'spindle' (ἄτρακτος) could not distinguish between the ἀγαθός and the ordinary man, as could the spear used by the hoplite gentleman in his hand-to-hand combats. Cf. the similar disparagement of the archer in the anecdote told by Plutarch, *Mor.* 234e (= *Apophth. Lac., Diaph.* 46), cited by Gomme, *HCT* III 481.

Of course not all the rich were necessarily members of the class of *kaloi kagathoi*; but only a rich man would be a likely candidate for that class, and no one who was not a man of some property would have a real chance of being included in it. Similarly, 'the rich' and 'the well-born' did not necessarily coincide either; but Aristotle, who in one place (*Pol.* III 13, 1283ᵃ37) can speak of good birth (εὐγένεια) simply as ἀρετή γένους, has no doubt in two others that inherited wealth is also an essential ingredient in εὐγένεια (ἀρχαῖος πλοῦτος καὶ ἀρετή, IV 8, 1294ᵃ21–2; προγόνων ἀρετή καὶ πλοῦτος, V 1, 1301ᵇ3–4). This had been true ever since the Heroic Age (in spite of the exceptional *Od.* XXI 323–9, 334–5). To the 'Old Oligarch'—who, as it happens, never uses the terms *kalos kagathos, kalokagathia*—the well-born (γενναῖοι), the rich (πλούσιοι), the best (βέλτιστοι), the good (χρηστοί) and the fortunate (εὐδαίμονες) were virtually identical, as he shows by the way he brackets them together (Ps.-Xen., *Ath. Pol.* I 2, 4–5, 13–14; II 10 etc.), just as πονηροί and πένητες and δημοτικόι and χείρους are alternative descriptions of another set of roughly the same people (I 4 etc.).

For the status of *kalos kagathos* a good education was often thought essential: see Ar., *Frogs* 728–9; Xen., *Mem.* I i.16; ii.7; vi.13; *Symp.* III 4 (where the teaching of *kalokagathia*, equated with δικαιοσύνη, is significantly contrasted with the teaching of 'some banausic skill'); Isocr. XIII 6; XV 220; Plato, *Protag.* 328b; *Apol.* 20a, 25a; Ps.-Plat., *Hipparch.* 228c, etc. And of course only men of the propertied class could normally hope to receive a complete education. It is no surprise, therefore, that when these terms are used of individuals, whether seriously or ironically, we always find them applied to men of the upper classes: see e.g. Hdts I 30.3–5 (Tellus is obviously an important man in some sort of military command); Arist., *Ath. Pol.* 28.5 (Nicias, and Thucydides son of Melesias); Xen., *Oecon.* VI 8–17 and ff., including VII 2–3, XI 1, 3, 21, and XII 2 (the very wealthy Ischomachus, the ideal *kalos kagathos*); Andoc. I 133; Xen., *HG* VI i.2; *Cyrop.* I iv.27; V iii.29; Isocr. XV 95 and 100 (with 93–4, 99), and 138; *Epist.* VII 8; Plato, *Lysis* 207a; *Protag.* 315d; Aeschin. I 41, 69; III 78; Deinarch. III 12, 18; Dem. XIX 110; XXII 32, 47; XXIV 92, 124; LIV 14; Ps.-Dem. XLIX 37; LII 30; LIX 117; even Theopomp., *FGrH* 115 F 325, *ap.* Plut., *Dem.* 4.1 (Demosthenes' father); probably Antiph. I 14, and Isae. III 20–1; etc. Strato, in Dem. XXI 83, 95, was a relatively poor hoplite (a πένης) and therefore liable to be suspected of πονηρία: denying that he is a πονηρός, the orator does not go quite so far as to call him a *kalos kagathos*; he is content to say that he is οὐ πονηρὸς ἀλλὰ καὶ πάνυ χρηστός.

A man born and educated into the class of *kaloi kagathoi* might be thought by some other members of that class to forfeit his status by not behaving as such a man should, in public as well as private life. I suspect that an obvious way of incurring such demotion—as easily recognisable as throwing away one's shield—was to indulge in activities threatening the ἀσφάλεια that was of such prime concern to the propertied class (see Baynes, *BSOE* 144–67, on Isocrates, esp. 153–9; also Neil, *KA* 203–4), whether by raising dicastic pay, like Cleon (Schol. Ar., *Wasps* 88, 300), or becoming known as a champion of the humble, like Cleon and Hyperbolus (Ar., *Frogs* 569–71, 577–8), or introducing the *diobelia*, like Cleophon (Arist., *Ath. Pol.* 28.3), or proposing eisphorae, or taking part in prosecutions of the rich (cf. Xen., *HG* II iii.12, 15). In Isocrates' mind one could demonstrate one's πονηρία and remove oneself from the class of *kaloi kagathoi* merely by acting as a prosecutor in a *phasis* or *graph⁻* (xv 99–100) or, as a dicast, by voting for the condemnation instead of the acquittal of a man like Isocrates when he was prosecuted (xv 241). The Athenians in the fifth century, of course, had ceased, in

Isocrates' view (xv 316–17; cf. vii 21–2), to select *kaloi kagathoi* as their leaders, and had preferred πονηροί, who (they thought) would be faithful to the democratic constitution, if only because of the φαυλότης of their origin. Now, he complains (viii 133), the *kaloi kagathoi* are suspect, as oligarchically inclined. On the other hand, Cleomis, although tyrant of Methymna, had remained a *kalos kagathos* in Isocrates' eyes, in particular by providing for the ἀσφάλεια of the citizens and carefully preserving their property rights intact (*Epist.* vii 8, a very significant passage). The primarily social and political sense of *kalos kagathos* in all these occurrences in Isocrates is very clear. And in the opinion of men who talked and thought like this, even having good ancestors and a good education would not necessarily save one from πονηρία. The late Professor J. B. S. Haldane, of good family, Eton and New College, with a First in Greats and every academic distinction, but for some time Chairman of the Editorial Board of the *Daily Worker*, would certainly have been written off by Isocrates as an outstanding πονηρός and, by Aristophanes, probably also endowed with a whole string of vices which, as all right-thinking people agreed, were an inevitable part of the make-up of such a fellow.

Sometimes, however, the expressions *kalos kagathos* and *kalogathia* are used, as mentioned above, with a purely or primarily moral connotation, as in Xen., *Symp.* iii 4; viii 11; ix 1; *Mem.* i ii.18; iii v.15; Plato, *Apol.* 25a; *Gorg.* 470e; Arist., *Magn. Mor.* ii 9, 1207^{b}22–8^{a}4; *Eth. Nic.* iv 7, 1124^{a}3–4; x 10, 1179^{b}10 ff.; *Eth. Eud.* vii 15 = viii 3, 1248^{b}8–9^{b}25; cf. *Pol.* i 13, 1259^{b}34–5; and many other passages. Occasionally there is special emphasis on bravery, as in Plato, *Theaet.* 142b; and in Arist., *Pol.* ii 9, 1271^{a}22–6, it is contemplated that even the Spartan kings, among the most blue-blooded of mortals, might not be *agathoi* enough to be proper *kaloi kagathoi*. But we must not be deceived into taking for examples of genuine moral commendation texts which in reality are nothing of the sort. Of course the social-political use of our terms may carry with it in practice a strong moral flavour, because those who spoke of themselves as *kaloi kagathoi* tended to see themselves as virtuous and their opponents (to whom they commonly applied the term πονηροί) as vicious, and their usage seems to have gained a wide acceptance. Where the social-political sense is primary, however, it is a mistake to pay serious attention to the inevitable moral overtones. Gomme, on p. 66 of the article cited at the beginning of this Note, has to admit that Ar., *Knights* 185 'gives us the social sense only', but he then goes on to maintain that 'in 227 we have, surely, the moral sense'. In fact all the people who are being referred to in lines 225–8 are by definition those who are political opponents of Cleon, and of course Aristophanes feels able to take it for granted that all *kaloi kagathoi* are anti-Cleon! The real force of the expression here is therefore social and political, and any moral implications are purely consequential upon that.

Aristophanes' *kaloi kagathoi* have an unmistakably social and political character almost every time they are mentioned. (See the examples listed near the end of the first paragraph of Section *A* above.) In *Knights* 738–40 the Sausage-Seller is made to distinguish two different groups: the *kaloi kagathoi* whom Demos does not welcome, and the men he does give himself to, described as lamp-sellers and stitchers and cobblers and tanners. In the corresponding passage in *Frogs* 718–37 there are also two mutually exclusive groups: just as the fine old silver and new gold coins are different from the new base copper ones, so (718–20) the politicians who are *kaloi kagathoi*—later described as good men (χρηστοί, 735) and also as well-born, *bien pensants* (σώφρονες), righteous, *kaloi kagathoi* again, and nurtured in the wrestling-schools and dancing and the liberal arts (727–9)—are a different set from the cheapjacks, aliens, dagoes (if I may so mistranslate πυρρίαι) and scoundrelly sons of scoundrels who are in favour now (730–1). Here, just as in the Old Oligarch's world (see above), we have a great divide, with two sets of characters, one on each side: each set is described by a whole series of terms, any one or more of which can be applied to the set or any member of it, whether strictly relevant or not. In Aristophanes, as in some other authors, including Isocrates (see the passages cited above, and vii 72), *kalos kagathos* is almost a synonym of χρηστός: it is significant that both are frequently used as the opposite of πονηρός (cf. Cicero's *boni* and *improbi*). There were different nuances, making now one expression more appropriate and now another; but when a man like Aristophanes spoke of the *kaloi kagathoi* he was usually referring to a group of people corresponding fairly closely with those to whom he himself or others could also apply the terms χρηστοί, πλούσιοι, εὐγενεῖς, βέλτιστοι, γνώριμοι, and so forth. If he could have read Isocr. vii and xv, one can imagine him nodding his head again and again.

In striking contrast is the way *kalos kagathos* and *kalokagathia* are used by the orators. (For the moment we must ignore Isocrates, for he employs our expressions only in 'speeches' which were written for circulation and not for delivery in the courts or the Assembly; and the same applies to Ps.-Dem. lxi.) I know of some thirty-five occurrences of these words in the orators. They divide into three classes. First, there is a group of thirteen (Group *A*) in which the words are used—as they *never* are in Aristophanes—in a hostile context, often marked by sarcasm or irony, or at least by a denial of someone's claim to the epithet: Lys. xii 86; Andoc. i 133; Aeschin. i 69; iii 78; Dem. xix 110; xxii 32, 47; xxiv 92, 124; Ps.-Dem. xxv 78; li 19; lii 30; Deinarch. iii 18. In at least ten of these cases there is no possible way of deciding what is entailed by the claim to *kalokagathia* which is being attacked, or even whether the man concerned had actually made such a claim. In Aeschin. iii 78 it is alleged defects in Demosthenes' moral character which are said to deny him the title of *kalos kagathos*. In Lys. xii 86, on the other hand, the hypothetical claim of Eratosthenes' friends to be *kaloi kagathoi* is depicted as resting upon an assertion of ἀρετή, which, it is implied (§§81–7), is false: this ἀρετή is most likely to have consisted of distinguished public service. And in Dem. xxiv 124 the orators concerned (who are said to behave in reality like base and ungrateful slaves) are imagined as feeling that as *kaloi kagathoi* they had the right to treat the general body of citizens with contempt; and any such *kalokagathia*, therefore, would certainly not be any kind of moral superiority, but rather social or political distinction of some kind.

The other twenty-two occurrences may be divided into two groups, *B* and *C*. In Group *B*, as in *A* but unlike *C*, the reference is to a single individual or a fairly small number of distinguished citizens. Again, precisely what is conveyed by the quality referred to is often uncertain. In one of these texts, Aeschin. i 134, καλοὺς κἀγαθοὺς τὰς ἰδέας means simply 'handsome'. In one other, Deinarch. iii 12, *kalos kagathos* is used beyond question in an essentially social sense (see above), and in at least one more, Ps.–Dem. lix 117, a social significance seems to me certain. In the remaining six cases (Antiph. i 14; Lys. xxx 14; Isae. iii 21; Aeschin. i 41; Dem. liv 14; Ps.-Dem. xlix 37) some strongly commendatory sense is implied, but its nature is hard to define. It need never have a particularly moral sense; possibly in every case 'being a perfectly well-behaved and respectable citizen' would be the safest definition; but at least some of these passages (esp. Lys. xxx 14; Dem. liv 14; and Ps.-Dem. xlix 37) are likely to refer to men of some wealth and prominence *as such*.

In Group *C* all thirteen examples refer, if not to the whole body of Athenian citizens, at least to a high proportion of them, or to the dicasts as representatives of the citizen body, or to the ancestors of the Athenians, or to *any* individual Athenian: Dem. xviii 93, 278, 306, 310; xx 54; xxi 218; xxiii 197; Ps.-Dem. xl 46; xlii 25; xlv 65; lx 7; Aeschin. i 31; Deinarch. i 111. (None of these passages is earlier than the 350s.) Here the connotation of *kalos kagathos* is always predominantly moral: uprightness of character, or the quality of being a patriotic and good citizen.

The contrast with Aristophanes' usage is indeed remarkable. In not a single one of my thirty-five examples do we find a group of *kaloi kagathoi*, in the social sense (or any other), singled out for admiration from the mass of citizens or distinguished from a set of undesirables, as by Ar., *Knights* 225–8, 738–40; *Frogs* 718–19 ff., where they are presented as the potential saviours of the State. The continued existence of these *kaloi kagathoi* as a recognised group is noticed by Thucydides, Plato and Aristotle, not to mention Xenophon and Isocrates; but although the orators show awareness of them (see esp. Deinarch. III 12 and the unfriendly Dem. XXIV 124), they never receive any particular attention. And by the mid-fourth century, beginning with Demosthenes, a very interesting development has taken place: the scope of the expression which the *kaloi kagathoi* reserved for themselves was widened to take in the whole Athenian citizen body (see my Group *C* above). I suggest that Demosthenes in particular may well have been unwilling to endorse the self-estimation of the καλοὶ κάγαθοὶ ὀνομαζόμενοι by accepting them on their own valuation, and may have sought to devalue their special currency by broadening the description they gave themselves, to include all Athenians. But the choice of language might also be dictated by considerations of prudence (cf. Arist., *Rhet.* II 1, 1377ᵇ16 ff.), for an orator's audience in the Assembly or the courts would naturally contain a good number of poor men.

There are some excellent parallels in the oratorical corpus to Aristophanes' use of our terms—but they do not come from the orators proper: to find them, we have to go to the 'speeches' written by Isocrates for circulation among an upper-class, educated public. I have already cited a number of passages in which Isocrates imports a thoroughly political character into our expressions; and in others in which he is ostensibly using them in an ethical sense (III 43; VI 35; IX 51, 74; XI 32; XII 183; XV 243, 278, 280; and esp. VII 72) their connotation is often social as well. In Xenophon, too, it is often hard to distinguish the social from the moral aspects of *kalokagathia*. Aristophanes is much nearer to the thought-world of Isocrates and Xenophon (and in some ways, even of the Old Oligarch) than to that of Demosthenes: he too uses the language of a class that conceived itself as superior, morally as well as socially, and his thoughts are its thoughts.

APPENDIX XXX

The 'revolt of Agis III'

1. *Chronology.* I find it difficult to decide between two rival chronologies. The one generally favoured nowadays, which makes the revolt extend roughly from spring to autumn 331, rests mainly upon Curt. VI i.21: it was worked out by Niese and has recently been re-stated by E. Badian, 'Agis III', in *Hermes* 95 (1967) 170–92, at pp. 190–2. The other chronology, that of Grote (*HG* x 219–23, ch. xcv), delays the full revolt until about March to June 330: it has now been revived by G. L. Cawkwell, 'The Crowning of Demosthenes', in *CQ* 63 = n.s. 19 (1969) 163–80, at pp. 170–3, who makes the revolt begin in late summer 331 and continue 'well into 330'. The only two arguments advanced in favour of the latter chronology which have some weight are those of Grote, *HG* x 220 n.1, based on Aeschin. III 133 and Arr., *Anab.* III xxiv.4 (cf. Cawkwell, *op. cit.* 171 and n. 6). Another argument (not used by Grote or Cawkwell) in favour of delaying the outbreak of the revolt until after the summer of 331 is the fact that very large reinforcements from Europe, amounting to some 15,000 men, were despatched to Alexander in the summer or early autumn of 331 (see §2[d] below). The Spartans may well have

felt that this gave them a great opportunity, for Antipater would presumably have been weaker now than he had ever been since Alexander's departure. On the other side, however, is Arr., *Anab.* III vi.3 (cf. II xv.5; xvii.2), to which Cawkwell (*op. cit.* 172), failing to deal with its specific reference to the Spartans as the instigators of revolt, has no adequate reply.

2. *Reinforcements sent to Alexander from Europe.*

(*a*) In the winter of 334/3 Alexander sent Ptolemy son of Seleucus, Coenus and Meleager to Macedon, to levy as many additional infantry and cavalry there as they possibly could (Arr., *Anab.* I xxiv.1–2). They returned early in 333 with about 3,650 troops, of whom about 3,300 were Macedonians (xxix.4; cf. Curt. III vii.8). The unreliable Callisthenes, *FGrH* 124 F 35 (*ap.* Polyb. XII 19.1), gives 5,000 infantry and 800 cavalry, and his statement is accepted by P. A. Brunt, 'Alexander's Macedonian Cavalry', in *JHS* 83 (1963), at pp. 36–7; contrast Beloch, *GG* III² ii.331–2. Not wishing to overstate my case, I shall keep to the lower figures, which anyway seem more plausible.

(*b*) Also in the winter (or early spring) of 334/3 Alexander sent Cleander son of Polemocrates to recruit soldiers in the Peloponnese (Arr., *Anab.* I xxiv.2; Curt. III i.1). Cleander returned from the Peloponnese in the early spring of 332 with another very considerable reinforcement: 'about 4,000 Greek mercenaries' (Arr., *Anab.* II xx.5; cf. Curt. IV iii.11).

(*c*) It was apparently in early spring 331 that there reached Alexander at Memphis a force of about 400 Greek mercenaries and about 500 Thracian cavalry: the former at least are specifically said by Arrian (*Anab.* III v.1) to have been sent by Antipater. We are not told when Alexander sent for these reinforcements: they may have come as the advance guard of those mentioned in paragraph (*d*) below, or they may have been demanded earlier.

(*d*) Late in 332, when he was on his way to Egypt, Alexander sent Amyntas son of Andromenes by ship to Macedon, to levy further troops (Diod. XVII 49.1; Curt. IV vi.30). Amyntas returned at the end of 331, when Alexander was on the way to or at Susa, with approximately 15,000 men, including 6,500 Macedonians, 4,100 Thracians, and perhaps 4,380 mercenaries 'from Peloponnese' (Diod. XVII 65.1; Curt. V i.40–1; cf. Arr., *Anab.* III xvi.10). Badian (*op. cit.* 187–8) thinks these reinforcements must have set out 'in July 331, or at least about that time'. At any rate, they must have left at some time during the summer; if they came (as Amyntas had gone) partly by sea (as far as Issus, perhaps, or a Syrian port), it may have been the late summer, or even perhaps the early autumn. (Cf. §1 above on the implications of this for the chronology of the revolt.)

(*e*) Later reinforcements concern us less. I agree with Cawkwell (*op. cit.* 173 n. 2) on those mentioned by Curt. V vii.12. As for the reinforcement mentioned by Curt. VI vi.35 (including 3,630 men from Europe), which must have left Europe early in 330 (Beloch, *GG* III² ii.318), Cawkwell (*loc. cit.*) thinks it 'does not prove that the revolt of Agis was finished. Once Antipater saw that few states had joined Agis and indeed that he could rely on the support of the League of Corinth ..., he could afford to let these forces go'. I will only remark that if Antipater could send away no fewer than 3,000 infantry and 630 cavalry before the battle of Megalopolis, he must have been confident indeed that his Greek allies would fight well under his command.

(*f*) The fact that Thracian and Illyrian troops, as well as mercenaries, could be sent from Europe to join Alexander makes one suspect that there may have been other forces of this nature among the additional 28,000 or so raised by Antipater to crush the revolt of Agis and collectively described by Diod. XVII 63.1 as 'allied Greeks'. But the figures given in the main text above allow for 5,000 such troops. And even if there were twice as many, Antipater's Greeks would still have greatly outnumbered Agis' citizen forces.

3. *The role of Athens.* Both Badian (*op. cit.* 172–3, 182–3) and Cawkwell (*op. cit.* 173–80) in large measure blame the Athenians, especially Demosthenes, for the failure of the revolt. Their arguments seem to me of no value against several on the other side. First, there is the fact that Alexander had not far short of 4,000 hostages for Athens' good behaviour, in the shape of the crews of the twenty Athenian triremes he had retained (Diod. XVII 22.5). Secondly, there was the frightening precedent of Thebes, put under an oligarchy by Philip in 338/7 (Justin IX iv.6–8) and destroyed by Alexander in 335 (Arr., *Anab.* I ix.9; Diod. XVII 13–14; etc.)—facts which Cawkwell forgets when he says (*op. cit.* 180) that the only evidence for 'the violent and tyrannous rule of Macedon in Greece' is Ps.-Dem. XVII and perhaps the *diagramma* of Polyperchon in Diod. XVIII 56.3. Thirdly, the revolt was about as badly timed as it could be. In one respect it came too late: see Cawkwell, *op. cit.* 178 (the second paragraph), on the great importance of co-operation with the Persian navy—which had been destroyed by 331. In all other respects a revolt even in 331 (and still more in 330) was premature. Unless Alexander were now defeated by Darius (a very unlikely contingency, after the great victory at Issus), he would easily be able to crush a Greek revolt, even if Antipater could not. On the other hand, Alexander often exposed himself recklessly (see the lists in Plut., *Mor.* 327ab, 341abc, etc.), and there was a reasonably good chance that he would get himself killed in the interior of Asia, and that the Macedonian empire, lacking an obvious successor, would thereupon disintegrate. And finally, the Athenians must have known that there were many Greek states which would not join a movement against Macedon led by Sparta. Few followed Agis; many more answered Athens' call in 323–2 (see esp. Diod. XVIII 11.1–2; Paus. I xxv.4). The revolt of Agis was an act of folly from which Athens did well to keep aloof.

(I am grateful for assistance with this Appendix to R. J. Lane Fox, whose forthcoming book on Alexander the Great will be an important contribution to our understanding of that extraordinary figure.)

APPENDIX XXXI

Themistocles' 'Western policy', and his connection with the radical democrats

The scraps of evidence for a 'Western policy' on Themistocles' part are so slender that we might be tempted to ignore them altogether were it not for the fact that such a policy fits beautifully with the rest of Themistocles' behaviour, which can be reconstructed with much greater confidence.

As we have seen, the corner-stone of Themistocles' policy after 479 is his anti-Spartanism, in the sense that he must have believed Sparta would not long tolerate an Athenian hegemony on a scale large enough to make Athens a 'Great Power' having equal status with herself, and that he believed Athens ought above all to guard against the possibility of a Spartan attack on her. As we also saw (Chapter V, Part ii above), this could naturally have led, and apparently in fact did lead, to his disapproving of the aggressively anti-Persian character of the Delian League, with which he was never associated—'naturally', because Athens could not afford to risk having to fight both Persia and Sparta simultaneously, and if the danger of attack by Sparta was real, Athens must make a settlement with

Persia. Indeed, a man of Themistocles' far-sightedness may well have realised that the more successful the Delian League was, the greater was the likelihood that the Great King or one of his satraps might give financial help to Sparta, for an attack on Athens which would relieve the pressure on the Persian empire. An attempt in this direction was made *c.* 457 (Thuc. I 109.2–3), but without result.

Now both these aspects of Themistocles' policy were adopted by the radical democrats when they 'came to power' in 462/1. They pursued an anti-Spartan policy from the first, and as soon as Cimon was safely dead they made peace with Persia (cf. Appendix VII, on the Peace of Callias). They also, within a very few years, began to look to the West, and made at least three military alliances with Greek cities there: Egesta, Rhegium and Leontini (see Chapter VI, Part iii above). Had they been anticipated there too by Themistocles?

How meagre the evidence is for a Western policy on the part of Themistocles becomes apparent at once when we realise that the two best items are the names he gave to two of his daughters, Italia and Sybaris (another, the youngest, was called Asia: Plut., *Them.* 32.2–3), and the fact that during the discussion among the Greek admirals before the battle of Salamis he threatened (according to Hdts VIII 62.2) that the Athenians would abandon Greece altogether and sail to Siris, describing that place as 'an ancient possession of Athens which the oracles said the Athenians must inhabit'. Also, Themistocles was honoured as a benefactor (εὐεργέτης, Thuc. I 136.1) by Corcyra, having arbitrated in its favour in a dispute with Corinth (Plut., *Them.* 24.1); and he tried to take refuge there first of all when driven out of Argos by the joint efforts of Athens and Sparta. This connection with Corcyra is the more surprising in that the Corcyraeans had given no help to the Greeks who resisted Persia in 480–79 (Hdts VII 168). And that is all the evidence there is, since I would reject the story by the wretched Stesimbrotus (*FGrH* 107 F 3), retailed with some scepticism by Plutarch, *Them.* 24.7.

Some may think there is insufficient basis here for even tentative conclusions; but I submit that we have just enough evidence to make it probable (it is far from certain) that Themistocles did have some sort of 'Western policy', in the sense that he believed Athens ought to look for opportunities of development in the West. Of course it would be idle to speculate whether he was thinking in imperialistic, expansionist terms, or of a series of military alliances, or the foundation of a colony, or whatever. But Hdts VIII 62.2 (quoted above) would make particularly good sense if Themistocles was known to have advocated the founding of an Athenian colony in the neighbourhood of Siris; and it is worth noticing that in 325–4 Athens did attempt to found a colony on the coast of the Adriatic, perhaps near the mouth of the Po, with the aim of providing herself with a port of her own there, from which corn could be brought, and which would provide a naval base and security against Etruscan pirates: Tod II 200 (= *IG* II² 1629 = *SIG*³ 305), lines 217–32. Themistocles may certainly have seen the West as a useful source of supply of the two basic commodities Athens most needed to import: corn and timber (cf. Chapter VI, Part ii above). If Athens were to reduce her naval activity in the East, as part of a peace settlement with Persia, and thus perhaps lose control of the corn routes from Egypt and Cyprus and possibly even the Black Sea, then Western corn would indeed become a vital necessity; and a great naval state might at any time need Western timber. As I have said above (Chapter VI, Part ii), Western timber would not normally be denied to Athens except by enemies; and the same would be true of Western corn, in so far as it was available at all. But many Peloponnesian states were potential enemies, and it might be necessary to take steps to protect the supply routes against them.

I may add that it would have been tempting to see Themistocles as the possible originator of the policy of building the 'Long Walls' and retiring behind them when a Peloponnesian attack came. But there is no evidence for this, and Thuc. I 93.7 is against it.

APPENDIX XXXII

Thucydides 1 102.4

Thucydides (1 102.4) describes the breach between Athens and Sparta in 462/1 as an abandonment by Athens of τὴν γενομένην ἐπὶ τῷ Μήδῳ ξυμμαχίαν. I do not think he means to do more than make a chronological point: that the alliance between Sparta and Athens (which until now had never been formally abrogated) dated back to 481. (Wickert, *PB* 50, would go back to an earlier Spartan-Athenian alliance in 492/1.) Some historians have felt that Thucydides is here criticising the Athenians for abandoning an alliance which was made gloriously against the Persians, in favour of two states that had done nothing towards saving Greece in 480–79. I cannot believe, even if that was the Spartan propaganda line, that Thucydides accepted it. The anti-Persian alliance of 481 had not been made, it seems, for any definite period: it was surely understood that the alliance would last 'for the duration'. The best evidence is the oath sworn by the Samians, Chians, Lesbians and others in 479, before Mycale: ἐμμενέειν τε καὶ μὴ ἀποστήσεσθαι (Hdts IX 106.4). And when the Delian League was formed in 478/7, *fresh oaths,* explicitly perpetual, were sworn between the Athenians and the other states which wished to continue the struggle against Persia. Sparta and the Peloponnesians took no part in this. Surely the original oaths of alliance of 481 now lapsed, for all practical purposes; Athens and her allies were bound by the oaths of 478/7, the Peloponnesians had dropped out.

Of course, the original alliance was never formally dissolved, and in 462 Cimon and his followers may have referred to it as still existing, although there is no indication of this in our surviving sources. I agree with Gomme, *HCT* 1 300, that in Thuc. 1 102.1 ξυμμάχους is predicative: the Spartans called in the Athenians 'as allies', 'to fight with them'. In much the same position was Plataea, which also helped Sparta on this occasion (Thuc. III 54.5).

The best account of the anti-Persian league of 481 ff. is by P. A. Brunt, 'The Hellenic League against Persia', in *Historia* 2 (1953–4) 135–63.

APPENDIX XXXIII

Thucydides' use of περιπλεῖν (1 107.3)

It has commonly been supposed (*e.g.* by *ATL* III 165; Buck, ADB 218) that Thuc. 1 107.3 proves the Athenians *now* sailed right around the Peloponnese, but this is certainly unjustified.

Thucydides does occasionally employ the word περιπλεῖν for a journey around the Peloponnese, but only about four times out of thirty-five occurrences. He is prepared to use it of any voyage merely skirting a cape or promontory (as in VI 99.4; 101.3; VII 22.1,2; 36.6; or III 81.2; or IV 130.1; V 3.6; 6.1; or VIII 34), even if it requires little 'rounding' (as in II 25.4,5) or indeed virtually none (as in IV 25.8 or V 2.3); and on at least two quite different occasions (III 19.2; VII 40.5) he can use it in the sense of sailing about, sailing in different directions. A voyage from

Naupactus or Pagae into the Crisaean Gulf would be quite sufficient to satisfy περιπλεύσαντες in 1 107.4.

I may add that I cannot accept the suggestion of *ATL* III 165 that the Athenians must already at this time have had control of Naupactus. Thuc. II 69.1 does not mean that Phormio could 'blockade the Krisaian Gulf in 430' (could he also, then, '*blockade* Corinth'?), but that from Naupactus he could try to prevent ships from passing the entrance to the Gulf of Corinth which were 'sailing from or to [μητ' ἐκπλεῖν . . . μητ' ἐσπλεῖν] Corinth and the Crisaean Gulf'. Certainly the Athenian ships operating in 458–7 would require a temporary 'base' in or near the Crisaean Gulf; but a mere place of anchorage (ὅρμος, *statio*) would be quite sufficient, even an open beach: it will be sufficient to cite Xen., *HG* II i.25; and cf. Chapter VII, Part viii above.

APPENDIX XXXIV

The foundation of Thurii

For a complete list of the sources, see Hill, *S²* 345 (Index 1 8.4-5). Add Suid., *s.v.* Θουριομάντεις. The most useful treatments are by V. Ehrenberg, 'The Foundation of Thurii', in *AJP* 69 (1948) 149–70; Gomme, *HCT* 1 386; C. G. Kraay, 'The Coinage of Sybaris after 510 B.C.', in *Num. Chron.*⁶ 18 (1958) 13–37; and the admirable brief note by R. Meiggs in his edition of Bury, *HG³* 880.

The admission to the colony of numerous other Greeks as well as Athenians (paralleled at Amphipolis in 437/6) is likely to have been due mainly to a temporary shortage of Athenian volunteers, for during the seven years before the foundation of Thurii Athens had founded a considerable number of colonies and cleruchies, involving many thousands of citizens. (The main facts are conveniently given by Jones, *AD* 168–74.) Athens may also have been glad to have an opportunity of settling some of the pro-Athenian Boeotians, Achaeans and others who are likely to have been forced into exile in 446/5. There is not the slightest reason to see the mixed nature of the colony (as I have heard suggested) as an attempt to 'placate Corinth'.

APPENDIX XXXV

Modern opinions about the Megarian decree

I am inserting here, for convenience, a set of references to over forty modern authors who have given opinions about the nature and/or the effects of the Megarian decree which I show in Chapter VII above to be mistaken. In some cases, where there is more than the almost invariable misrepresentation of the decree as applying to 'all markets of the Athenian empire', I have added at least part of the opinion in question: the italics are usually mine.

F. E. Adcock, in *CAH* v 186 ('. . . it was *an operation of war*, the first blow at the courage and will of Athens' adversaries'); A. Andrewes, *The Greeks* (London, 1967) 145.

Beloch, *GG* II² i.292–3 (the decree 'den Bürgern von Megara *den Aufenthalt auf attischem Boden* und allen Verkehr mit dem Häfen im ganzen attischen Reiche untersagt und *damit den megarischen Handel* so gut wie *vollständig lahmgelegt*'); Bengtson, *GG*⁴ 227 (Pericles excluded the Megarians from all the harbours of the empire 'und dadurch *dem Handel Megaras* einen vernichtenden Schlag versetzt'); H. Berve, *Griech. Gesch.* II (Freiburg, 1952) 10–11 (the Megarians 'waren damit *wirtschaftlich dem Erstickungstod ausgeliefert*'); Bickerman, APT 314; Bodin, ADM 175 ('il s'agit avant tout d'une interdiction de commercer'); Böckh, *SHA* I³ 69 (Pericles excluded the Megarians 'von allem Verkehr mit *Attika* . . . , um sie zu drücken'); A. R. Burn, *Pericles and Athens* (London, 1948) 194–5; J. B. Bury, *The Ancient Greek Historians* (London, 1909) 87 n. 1 ('the decrees excluding *Megara* from the *markets* of Athens and her empire'), 96 ('the action which Athens had taken in regard to Megara by exluding *her* from the *markets* of the Athenian empire, and thereby *threatening her with economic ruin*'); *HG*³ 394 ('the decree spelt *economical ruin to Megara*'); Busolt, *GG* III ii.815–17 ('durch dieses "megarische Psephisma" wurde *der ganze Handel der Megarer* im Bereiche der attischen Herrschaft *vernichtet* und ihnen namentlich *die Versorgung mit Getreide erschwert,* da sie nicht bloss vom Markte Athens sondern auch von Byzantion, dem Hauptstapelplatze des pontischen Getreides, ausgeschlossen waren'), also 814 n. 4, on 816 ('der *die Handelssperre verfügende* Beschluss'), contrast the correct account of the actual terms of the decree on p. 814.

M. Cary, in *OCD*² 665a = *OCD*¹ 553a ('an attempt by Pericles *to starve it* [*Megara*] *into surrender* by the "Megarian Decree", which laid an embargo upon *its* Aegean and Pontic trade'); Cawkwell, AMDC 327, 333; P. Cloché, *La démocratie athénienne* (Paris, 1951) 138 (an exclusion of '*le commerce mégarien*'); F. M. Cornford, *Thucydides Mythistoricus* (London, 1907) 27–8 (the decree 'meant flat ruin to *Megara*; for *she* was shut out of Byzantium' etc.); G. De Sanctis, *Pericle* (1944) 232–5, esp. 233 ('*una specie di blocco*'), 234 ('pel *blocco di Megara*'); *Storia dei greci* II (1939) 265; Ehrenberg, *PA*² 245 ('*Megara starved* because of the Athenian decree'), cf. 329–32.

J. H. Finley, *Thuc.* 119 (the Megarians excluded from 'trade within the empire'); K. von Fritz, *GGS* I i (Text) 527 ('*der megarische Handel* von dem attischen Markt und von *allen Märkten* der dem attischen Seebund angeschlossenen Städte und Inseln ausgeschlossen würde'), cf. 527–9; Glotz-Cohen, *HG* II 618; Glotz, *Ancient Greece at Work* (London, 1926) 299, 314; Gomme, *HCT* I 175 ('measures against *Megara* which culminated in *her* exclusion from all the ports of the empire'), 450 (the decree 'excluding *Megara* from the *markets* of the empire'), 466 ('forbidding *Megara* access to the harbours *and markets* of the League'), contrast 227 ('i.e., I suppose, they could *neither buy nor sell in Attica*, and they could not send their own ships into the harbours of the empire, though they might buy and sell there'); Grote, *HG* V 2–3, ch. xlviii ('prohibiting the Megarians, on pain of death, from *all trade or intercourse* as well with *Athens* as with all ports within the Athenian empire'); Grundy, *Hist. of the Greek and Roman World* (London, 1926) 186 (the decree 'excluded *Megara* from all ports *and markets* of the Athenian Empire . . . To *Megara* the decree meant *something like starvation*'); *THA* I² 77–8, 236–7, 325–9, esp. 326 ('the real significance of the decrees was that they *excluded Megara* from participation in the Pontus corn trade').

Hammond, *HG*² 320 (the decree 'intensified *economic sanctions* against *Megara* . . . Now *she* was excluded from *every harbour and market of Athens and* of the Athenian empire'); F. M. Heichelheim, *Wirtschaftsgeschichte des Altertums* I (1938) 418 = *Anc. Econ. Hist.* II 151; B. W. Henderson, *The Great War between Athens and Sparta* (London, 1927) 5 ('a *trade boycott* of *Megara*. No Megarian *goods* could enter any *port or city* of the Athenian Empire. Megarian trade *was ruined* at a single blow'); E. L. Highbarger, *The Hist. and Civilization of Ancient Megara* (Baltimore, 1927) 160–72, esp. 163 ('the decree closed *the Athenian markets* to *Megara* and meant *starvation*'); Holm, *HG* II 312–13, cf. 326–7 n. 4; Kagan, *OPW* 256 ('the decree barring *Megarian commerce* from Athens and her empire'), 261 ('the *commercial embargo*'), contrast 254; Kiechle, UWMPT 292–3 (Athens adopted 'in der griechischen Welt *vordem unbekannte wirtschaftliche Boykottmassnahmen*'); H. Knorringa, *Emporos* (Amsterdam, 1926) 128; M. L. W. Laistner, *Hist. of the Greek and Roman World from 479 to 323* B.C. (London, 1957) 77; F. A. Lepper, 'Some Rubrics in the Athenian Quota-Lists', in *JHS* 82 (1962), at p. 52 ('a ban on *Megarian trade*'), and see 50–4.

Victor Martin, *VIGC* 225, 426, 442, 507; Ed. Meyer, *FAG* II 303 ('*die Märkte* und Häfen nicht nur Attikas, sondern des gesammten attischen Reichs sperrte'), contrast 297, 305, and *GdA* IV ii⁴ 16–17; H. Michell, *The Economics of Anc. Greece*² (Cambridge, 1957) 253 (the decrees 'forbade *the merchants of Megara* to use the ports of the allies of Athens *and the markets of Piraeus, a death-blow to the prosperity* of the offending city'); W. K. Prentice, *The Ancient Greeks* (Princeton, 1940) 176–7; de Romilly, *TAI* 17 = *TIA*² 22 ('the decree on *Megarian trade*'); P. Roussel, *La Grèce et l'Orient des guerres médiques à la conquête romaine*² (Paris, 1938) 178–9; S. Usher, *The Historians of Greece and Rome* (London, 1969) 41–2 ('the famous Megarian decree, by which *the city of Megara* was *forbidden to trade* in the ports of the Athenian empire, is *named by all other ancient sources [than Thucydides] as the cause of the war*'); Vogt, BPT 261 (the decree must have had '*eine vernichtende Wirkung*' for Megara), 264 ('*die Wirtschaftsblockade von Megara*'); A. Zimmern, *The Greek Commonwealth*⁵ (Oxford, 1931) 427 ('a decree of *boycott* was issued closing all the harbours of the Empire and *all the markets of Attica* to Megarian *ships* and Megarian *goods*. Thus at a single blow *Megara was practically isolated from the world*').

The really extraordinary feature of these accounts is that they all take the contents and consequences of the decree for granted, as if there were no problem in establishing either its *terms* or its *effects*. Yet they differ considerably among themselves in the way they formulate the terms of the decree. Gomme alone betrays any uncertainty, but this is in only one of four passages (*HCT* I 227); the other three (*HCT* I 175, 450, 466) make positive, incorrect and not entirely consistent statements!

APPENDIX XXXVI

Aristophanes, Acharnians 515–23

The main question is: are these lines (with which we should take 820–1) to be treated as evidence that some time before the main exclusion decree, which applied to the Megarians themselves, the Athenians had passed an earlier decree forbidding the import into Attica of Megarian goods or certain classes of such goods? And if no such 'Einfuhrverbot' is to be inferred, how are the lines in question to be explained? By some spontaneous activity on the part of individual Athenians, devoid of official authorisation—something akin to 'lynch law'? Or by alleged attempts to avoid customs duties, by smuggling goods into Attica?

We have three possible alternative theories. Before we examine them, let us be sure we understand exactly what Aristophanes is saying. There are three main points:

1. The Megarian goods are *successfully denounced by sycophants* (lines 515–19): that is to say, *by actions in the courts* (or at least before some organ of State);[1] and this

---

[1] Perhaps Paphlagon in Ar., *Knights* 300–2, is going to leave it to the Prytaneis to take legal action.

necessarily presupposes some *legal enactment* under which the sycophants were proceeding, even if unfairly or improperly.

2. The goods, when denounced, were *confiscated and sold* by the State—ἐπέπρατο (the pluperfect passive of πέρνημι), used here with aorist sense, equivalent to ἐπράθη.[2] The word ἐπέπρατο makes no sense here if taken to mean just 'sold', in the ordinary way. Again, official action must be involved.

3. The goods ἐπέπρατο *on the ground that they were* Μεγαρικά.[3]

The first two points absolutely rule out the second theory mentioned above: that we have to deal with no more than extra-legal measures taken by individual Athenians, without official authority. This theory can henceforth be ignored.

The theory of an earlier decree proclaiming an 'Einfuhrverbot' against Megarian goods has found a few advocates, of whom the most prominent is Busolt.[4] It can best be put as follows. Before the passing of the main Megarian decree there existed at Athens a decree in virtue of which Megarian goods entering Attica could be confiscated by the State and sold; but this decree had been voted several years earlier, probably on the defection of Megara in 446, and for some years after the Peace of 446/5 no one tried to enforce it. Then, in the middle or later 430s, sycophants had begun to proceed under the decree, which of course had then to be enforced. The key to this interpretation is, on the one hand, the repeated and emphatic οὐχὶ τὴν πόλιν λέγω (lines 515–16), and on the other, the fact that the Megarian goods, when denounced, ἐπέπρατο as Μεγαρικά. This shows, it is true, that Aristophanes is not blaming the Athenians as a whole; and yet they must at some time have passed a decree still in force at the time he is dealing with, or the sycophants would not have been able to have the goods confiscated and sold. The conclusion must be that the reason for not blaming the *polis* is that most of the citizens (in Aristophanes' view) would no longer have wished to have the decree enforced: this may or may not be true. The year 446, when the Megarians 'revolted' from Athens, and οἱ φρουροὶ Ἀθηναίων διεφθαρμένοι εἰσὶν ὑπὸ Μεγαρέων, πλὴν ὅσοι ἐς Νίσαιαν ἀπέφυγον (Thuc. 1 114.1), would have left the Athenians in a bitterly hostile mood towards Megara. After the Thirty Years Peace, however, feeling at Athens would subside to some extent, and probably most Athenians would want to allow the decree to become a dead letter. That is the theory, which I once held myself, and which I have tried to state as persuasively as possible. Although I entirely agree with Beloch (*GG* II² i.293 n.1) that 'Aristophanes ist doch kein Historiker, dessen Worte man auf die Goldwage legen könnte', I cannot follow him in his contemptuous dismissal of the theory I have just stated. The passage in question presents a problem, which cannot be simply brushed aside. The main part of the joke, which begins at line 524 with the rape of Simaetha, did not need this irrelevant prelude, and although it is of course likely to contain comic exaggeration and invention, perhaps in a high degree, we must explain it somehow.

Now, however, I have abandoned the theory I have just outlined and have come round to the view that alleged infringement of customs regulations is all we need to explain the lines in question. Line 522, as I have said, is perhaps most naturally interpreted as meaning that the goods ἐπέπρατο *as being Megarian*; but this is not the only possible interpretation. Because Megara had a common frontier with Attica, smuggling from the Megarid would be exceptionally easy, and perhaps Megarian goods were always more liable than any others at Athens to denunciation for evasion of duty—in fact, the cry of *Megarika* on such occasions may have become so familiar that Aristophanes could rely on his audience's understanding

---

[2] Cf. πέπρασθαι in Ar., *Ach.* 735; *Peace* 1011; Andoc. 1 73 etc.

[3] See esp. Busolt, *GG* III ii.811 n. 1, on p. 812.

[4] *GG* III ii.810–11, esp. 811 n. 1, where the earlier literature on the Megarian decrees is summarised.

that *this* was what he meant by ταῦτ' ἦν Μεγαρικά. This explanation has three advantages over the other:

1. It allows us to take the repeated 'I don't mean the City' more literally. The city would still be involved in a way, because some organ of the State would have decreed the sale; but at least there would be no law discriminating against Megara. (This is not a very strong argument, of course, because Aristophanes' οὐχὶ τὴν πόλιν λέγω might, to his audience, have been an obvious joke, meaning the very reverse of what it says.)

2. It gives a very much better sense to καὶ ταῦτα μὲν δὴ σμικρὰ κἀπιχώρια. The word σμικρά is most inappropriate if we are to conceive of the enforcement of *a law discriminating against Megarian goods*—a law which would have been altogether exceptional, and which would of course have been damaging to Megara. In my opinion, indeed, it is certain that a ban of this kind would be *considerably more damaging to the State of Megara than any mere personal exclusion of Megarians*. This argument too may seem at first sight to have little force, for σμικρά might easily be ironical. But the happenings described in lines 515–23 are presented as σμικρά *in comparison with the main exclusion decree*. Of course they are usually accepted as being such; but, as I have pointed out, the reverse would be true. The argument is nowhere near conclusive, but it has some weight.

3. The real argument against an 'Einfuhrverbot' and in favour of alleged customs infringements is a general one. (It belongs to the class of arguments which are often called 'a priori' by those who are not attracted to them.) It can be stated in two parts. (*a*) First, a ban in peace time on the import of the products of one Greek State into another, either total or applied to certain goods only, is otherwise entirely unknown, as far as I am aware.[5] Herodotus (v 88.2) does mention an early Argive and Aeginetan prohibition on the entry of Athenian goods, especially pottery; but it was merely against bringing them πρὸς τὸ ἱρόν. (*b*) Secondly, a punitive or retaliatory prohibition on the import of the goods (or particular goods) of another State is, I would say, something completely alien to Greek ideas. The Greeks were sensible enough to want to have all the foreign products they could get, and I do not believe that any Greek State would ever prohibit any class of imports in peace time, except possibly for sumptuary reasons. I do not know of any evidence of prohibition of exports either, except in war time,[6] although of course Athens might regulate the supply of certain essential or strategically valuable commodities in her own interest.[7] The Athenians must have bought from Megara a good deal of the rough clothing, fruits and vegetables, garlic especially, which the Megarid produced.[8] Why on earth should they deprive themselves of what they wanted, simply out of spite against the Megarians? On general grounds, then, as well as from lack of any other evidence of the existence of such practices at Athens or elsewhere, I would regard a ban on the import of Megarian goods, or on particular classes of such goods, as very unlikely indeed, and I would want better authority than Ar., *Acharn.* 515–23 before accepting it.

I have one further point to make here.[9] In *Acharn.* 820–1 the Megarian, seeing an Athenian sycophant appearing, stigmatises him as the very origin of Megara's woes:

[5] Only one partial exception comes to mind, the Thasian wine law: see Chapter I, Part iii, n. 80.

[6] See, for Athens, Ar., *Knights* 278–9 and *Frogs* 362–5, *cum Schol.*; Andoc. II 14; Isocr. XVII 42 (explained by Tod II 99); Dem. XIX 286–7.

[7] See M/L 65 (= Tod I² 61 = D 4 in *ATL* II 49 = *SIG*³ 75 = *IG* I² 57).34–41; Hill, *S*², B 83, 84; cf. Ps.-Xen., *Ath. Pol.* II 3, 11–12.

[8] Cf. Chapter VII, Part v, n. 52.

[9] I am grateful to E. C. Yorke for drawing my attention to this.

τοῦτ᾽ ἐκεῖν᾽· εἴκει πάλιν
ὅθενπερ ἀρχὰ τῶν κακῶν ἁμῖν ἔφυ.

I have heard it said that this 'must be' a reference back to the Megarian decree. This is certainly wrong. It is not only that the sycophant denounces the Megarian and his goods, not under the exclusion decree, but as πολέμιος and πολέμια;[10] equally fatal to any attempt to drag in the Megarian decree here is the fact that the only possible reference back to the earlier part of the *play* is to lines 515–23, which refer to the situation before the decree was passed, and between which and lines 524 ff. (which describe the circumstances leading to the passing of the decree) there is no organic connection. Aristophanes could very easily have put in a reference to the Megarian decree (in the enforcement of which, no doubt, sycophants would have taken a hand); but he did not. The Megarian decree is not there in any shape or form: indeed, for those who hold the usual exaggerated view of the nature of the decree it is rather conspicuously not there!

The real interest in lines 820–1 is in the suggestion they convey that a Megarian in 425 might still remember the damage done to his State by the activities of Athenian sycophants even before the passing of the exclusion decree. This may of course be just a characteristic hit at the class of sycophants, whom Aristophanes so heartily detested, but if it is more than that it may give us a clue to one of those ἕτερα οὐκ ὀλίγα διάφορα of which the Megarians complained at Sparta in 432 (Thuc. 1 67.4). If Megarian goods were too easily liable to be denounced as smuggled, Athenians might be less willing to buy them, and Megarian producers might suffer.

I must admit, however, that we know too little about customs duties and import regulations at Athens, except to some extent in regard to goods passing into and out of Peiraeus by sea. We cannot even be certain how far goods brought into Attica over its land borders in peace time would be liable to control and to import duty—perhaps only if offered for sale in public (in the Agora in particular), perhaps not at all. The interpretation of *Acharn.* 515–23 which has been suggested here must remain doubtful.

APPENDIX XXXVII

Anthemocritus and the decree of Charinus

Connor's paper (CMD) has been attacked by Dover (AM), Bliquez (AOD), and Cawkwell (AMDC). Ehrenberg (*SS* 448 n. 15) thinks Dover is 'clearly right against Connor'. And now Connor has replied to his critics, admitting in response to Cawkwell that 350/49 is 'not likely to be the year' of the decree of Charinus, as he had argued in CMD, but leaving open the possibility of 351/50 or some other fourth-century date. I shall confine my remarks to the articles of Dover and Cawkwell; Bliquez' case is far from conclusive (see Connor, CMDA 306), and the essence of his position is better stated by Cawkwell.

I cannot see that Dover has made any valid case at all. His one positive argument against Connor is that Μεγαρεῖς in Plut., *Per.* 30.4 must mean Megarian historians, writers of *Megarika*, and that none of the Megarian historians known to

---

[10] Cf. the discussion of the passages in *Ach.* and *Peace* relating to the Megarian decree, in Chapter VII, Part ii, Section c above.

us (all of the fourth or third century B.C.) could have made such an error about fairly recent times and attributed to the late fifth century events which in reality occurred in the mid-fourth. Dover actually says that Plutarch 'presumably means' such writers; but unless he is really saying that Plutarch *must* mean this, his argument has no force at all, and I shall assume that for 'presumably means' we may read 'must mean'.

One weakness in Dover's case has already been pointed out by Cawkwell (AMDC 328): we cannot be sure there were no writers of *Megarika* other than the three known to Jacoby, *FGrH* nos. 484–7. (I do not know why Dover, AM 205, wants 'Megarians' in Plutarch to mean 'at least two Megarians'. Do not ancient writers often use the plural in such a situation, where the singular would have been more accurate?) Another reply to Dover is made by Connor himself (CMDA 305), who maintains that when Plutarch speaks of 'Megarians' in *Per*. 30.4 he is referring to Megarians of his own day, as he certainly is when he uses the term in *Thes*. 27.8, to refer to those who showed him a tomb of the Amazons. This is true, and the case can be put much more strongly.

First, every single quotation from the Megarian historians in Jacoby's *FGrH* deals exclusively with 'archaeology' (mythical, prehistoric and religious material); neither Plutarch nor any other author ever cites any Megarian historian on the Peloponnesian war period, or indeed on anything later than the Salamis affair of *c*. 600! (Peisistratus is mentioned in 486 F 1, but in a context dealing with Theseus.) There is no sign at all, as far as I can see, that there were ever any *Megarika* dealing with the late fifth century. And Jacoby himself can be cited against Dover: see *FGrH* III b i (Text) 400, lines 24–7, on 487 F 13, where Jacoby shows he thinks it highly improbable that the Megarian answer in Plut., *Per*. 30.4 came from fourth-century *Megarika*. And cf. III b ii (Noten) 229, LI n. 6 (our passage 'stammt schwerlich aus literarischen *Megarika*'); also 230, LI n. 9.

Secondly, Pausanias reveals that in the Roman period there were men at various places in Greece, including Megara, who were prepared to offer opinions on the early history of their native city. In I xli.2 he mentions a local antiquary (ὁ τῶν ἐπιχωρίων ἡμῖν ἐξηγητής), who actually conducted him to a particular place in the Megarid; we may compare xliv.5, where he says he had heard a story at the Megarian village of Ereneia; also xlii.4. (There are parallel passages relating to other places: for Elis and Olympia, cf. v vi.6, xx.4 and xviii.6, with xv.10.) Plutarch is quite capable of making it clear in his 'Sammelzitate' when he is using written sources: apart from *Thes*. 10.2 and *Mor*. 254e (both cited by Dover), see *Thes*. 20.8 and *Mor*. 869b. He must often have visited Megara, and at least one of his circle of friends, Heracleon, was a Megarian: see K. Ziegler, in *RE* xx i (1951) col. 675. I suggest that in *Per*. 30.4 he is simply referring to what Heracleon and other educated Megarians of his day said, when one taxed Megara with the murder of Anthemocritus, whose statue and stele were visible in (and after) Plutarch's day (see Paus. I xxxvi.3). A verbal source for our passage is more appropriate than a written one. Plutarch's Megarians have no reply to the charge but a flat denial; they then switch over to something quite different: the story in Ar., *Ach*. 524–7. Is this not just the way a literary gentleman might try to evade the accusation in conversation, and is it not uncharacteristic of a written history? (The use of Ar., *Peace* 605 ff. by Ephorus F 196, *ap*. Diod. XII 39, is not a parallel. It would, if true, at least furnish an *explanation* for Pericles' behaviour.) I would put no weight on the omission of the article with Μεγαρεῖς in Plut., *Per*. 30.4; but, so far as it goes, the bare 'Megarians' rather favours my assumption that Plutarch is referring to Megarians he happened to know; cf. Μεγαρεῖς in Plut., *Thes*. 27.8.

Cawkwell has certainly shown, from the commentary of Didymus, that a date in 350/49 for the murder of Anthemocritus and the decree of Charinus is scarcely possible; and this weakens Connor's case, for 350/49 would suit his theory better than any other date. But much of Cawkwell's argument is unacceptable, for two main reasons.[1] First, his case for linking the 'reasonable and courteous decree' with the *spondophoroi* who offered the sacred truce for the Eleusinian Mysteries of spring 431 (AMDC 333–4) is worthless. He himself has to admit that the *spondophoroi* were normally sent even to hostile states. Why then should Athens make an exception in 431 not merely of Megara but of Sparta, which had offended in no way against the Two Goddesses? And what sort of εὐγνώμων καὶ φιλάνθρωπος δικαιολογία would it be to insult the Megarians and Spartans by excluding them, alone of Greek states, from the Mysteries? And secondly, his interpretation of the decree of Charinus, that it merely 'applied to the Mysteries' (AMDC 334), is flatly contradicted by the very words of the decree which he proceeds to quote: ὃς ἂν ἐπιβῇ τῆς Ἀττικῆς Μεγαρέων! (He is presumably thinking of Ps.-Dem. xii 4; but here, at AMDC 335, he has no effective reply to Connor, CMD 238–9; cf. CMDA 307.)

I have said nothing of one or two earlier works advocating a later date for the 'reasonable and courteous decree' and the murder of Anthemocritus, since Connor's paper is much the fullest and best documented. Ed. Meyer, writing in 1899 (*FAG* ii 328) before the publication of the Didymus papyrus (1904), suggested that Anthemocritus might belong to a later period, but he kept the decree of Charinus in early 431; cf. *GdA* iv ii[4] 17 n. 1, 38 n. 2; Beloch, *GG* ii[2] i.293 n. 1. In 1910, Bodin (ADM) advocated the same solution, more confidently and at greater length.

The question cannot be regarded as closed; but provided we separate the 'reasonable and courteous decree' from the decree of Charinus, in the way suggested in Chapter VII, Part iii above, we may continue without serious misgiving to date the latter decree to the early spring of 431.

APPENDIX XXXVIII

Plutarch, Pericles *29.4*

This text, after mentioning the Corinthian complaints against Athens at Sparta, goes on to say that the Megarians joined them, αἰτιώμενοι πάσης μὲν ἀγορᾶς ἀπάντων δὲ λιμένων ὧν Ἀθηναῖοι κρατοῦσιν εἴργεσθαι καὶ ἀπελαύνεσθαι παρὰ τὰ κοινὰ δίκαια καὶ τοὺς γεγενημένους ὅρκους τοῖς Ἕλλησιν.

All other accounts of the Megarian decree (except of course that of Aristophanes) appear to derive from Thucydides, save for a group of very late sources, mainly the Souda and some of the less intelligent scholia on Aristophanes, which show

---

[1] I add two minor criticisms. First, the confident assertions that Androtion 'did not record the action of Ephialtes', because he 'did not think it important enough to include', and therefore that 'there is a very strong suspicion that it amounted to very little' (AMDC 331), are based on a misunderstanding of the method employed by Didymus in his commentary, which is well explained in this connection by Jacoby, *FGrH* iii b (Suppl.) i.142–3, 529–30; ii.424 n. 4 on F 155. Secondly, Cawkwell is very wrong in saying (AMDC 330–1) that the dispute between Athens and Megara in 350/49 was not about the Orgas itself but about the *eschatiai* adjoining it (which he identifies with the ἀόριστος of Thuc. i 139.2), for both Androtion and Philochorus speak of the Athenian-Megarian quarrel on that occasion as being about the delimitation of the Orgas, and only later go on to speak of the Athenian consecration of the *eschatiai* in accordance with the oracle and the decree of Philocrates. Indeed, there is nothing to connect the dispute about the *eschatiai* with Megara: the inscription (*IG* ii[2] 204 = *SIG*[3] 204) and both Atthidographers speak of that dispute as if it were something that concerned Athens alone.

confusion between the exclusion decree and the decree of Charinus (see Chapter VII, Part ii, Section D above). I believe that this version of Plutarch's also derives from Thucydides, with one phrase alone, ὧν 'Αθηναῖοι κρατοῦσιν, probably taken from the original text preserved by Craterus, and that the inflated language, including the words πάσης μὲν ἀγορᾶς, is very much Plutarch's own. Plutarch's text deserves close study, as it can easily be misunderstood. I think it is probably just such a misunderstanding which has led so many writers to speak of the Megarian decree—in defiance of Thucydides—as excluding the Megarians from 'all markets and harbours in the Athenian empire', or 'the markets and ports of the Athenian empire'.[1]

The first thing to notice about Plutarch's account of the exclusion decree is that the general setting is precisely that of Thucydides: we first hear of the decree, as in Thuc. I 67.4, not as something passed at Athens but as something complained about at Sparta by the Megarians. There are two elements peculiar to Plutarch's version of the decree which need to be discussed: first, the technical expression ὧν 'Αθηναῖοι κρατοῦσιν, and secondly, the statement that the exclusion was to be from πάσης ἀγορᾶς. (If πάσης ἀγορᾶς is to be taken with ὧν 'Αθηναῖοι κρατοῦσιν, as I shall maintain it probably ought not to be, we should be confronted, uniquely, with a statement that the Megarians were excluded 'from every agora the Athenians controlled'—a formulation contradicting that of Thucydides in an essential particular.) Let us consider these two questions successively.

1. No one who is acquainted with the terminology of fifth-century Athenian decrees will doubt that the phrase ὧν 'Αθηναῖοι κρατοῦσιν is more likely to have been used in the original exclusion decree, to define the harbours affected, than Thucydides' expression, τῶν ἐν τῇ 'Αθηναίων ἀρχῇ (I 67.4; cf. 139.1). The technical phrase, ὧν 'Αθηναῖοι κρατοῦσιν (or ἄρχουσιν), however, is rare in the literary sources: even Thucydides habitually describes the empire of Athens as the ἀρχή; he never once speaks of it as the cities ὧν 'Αθηναῖοι κρατοῦσιν, nor does he use the expression ὧν 'Αθηναῖοι ἄρχουσιν except when reproducing the text of a treaty.[2] In Plutarch's ὧν 'Αθηναῖοι κρατοῦσιν,[3] therefore, we are very likely to have a correct report of the actual wording of the original decree. The question then is: from whom did Plutarch derive it? Evidently, it comes ultimately from someone who was not content to accept Thucydides' wording but looked up the terms of the original decree for himself. And I do not see who else this can have been than Craterus, whom Plutarch often used (cf. Chapter VII, Part iii above). The main Megarian decree, perhaps the most famous of all Athenian decrees, would have been an obvious candidate for inclusion in Craterus' *Psēphismatōn Synagōgē*. Even if the decree was not inscribed on stone it is surely likely that Craterus would have given it, for it seems very probable that he used the archives (see Jacoby, *GH* 165, col. 1618). It is probable, then, that the words ὧν 'Αθηναῖοι κρατοῦσιν come, through Craterus, from the original text of the decree. Does this suggest that Plutarch's version is in other respects also more reliable than that of Thucydides and the rest? In what follows I shall argue that it is not.

2. That the Megarians claimed to be excluded πάσης ἀγορᾶς (? ὧν 'Αθηναῖοι κρατοῦσιν?) is a statement made by Plutarch alone. The main problem here is: should πάσης ἀγορᾶς be taken by itself and translated 'from the whole (Athenian) Agora', or should it be taken with ὧν 'Αθηναῖοι κρατοῦσιν and translated 'from

---

[1] Most recently A. Andrewes, *The Greeks* 145; Cawkwell, AMDC 327, 333.

[2] Thuc. v 18.7, where we twice find the very technical phrase ἢ ἄλλοθί που ἧς/ὅσης 'Αθηναῖοι ἄρχουσιν. Cf. v 47.1,2,5 = Tod I² 72 (= *IG* I² 86).3,5,6,19. See also Thuc. VIII 37.2,5 (the second Spartan-Persian treaty of 412/11); 43.3 and 52 (referring to that treaty). Otherwise, the nearest Thucydides comes to using this expression is in reporting speeches: see I 81.2; VIII 76.4. Cf. also v 84.1.

[3] Plutarch, who avoids hiatus, might have changed ἄρχουσιν into κρατοῦσιν.

every agora (controlled by the Athenians)'? And does it represent the wording of the original decree more accurately than the simpler formula of Thucydides?

We have seen that Plutarch's setting is taken straight from Thucydides: the decree is first presented to us as the source of *complaints at Sparta*. Certainly much of Plutarch's language is not that of an original text found in Craterus, but is either his own or derived from a narrative source: Plutarch is here conceiving the decree, as it were, through the eyes of the Megarians, who in Thucydides stigmatise it as contrary to the Thirty Years Peace. A large part of Plutarch's sentence consists of rhetorically hostile forms of expression which cannot possibly come from the original text: (a) instead of Thucydides' εἴργεσθαι he has εἴργεσθαι καὶ ἀπελαύνεσθαι, and (b) in place of Thucydides' simple παρὰ τὰς σπονδάς he writes the grandiloquent phrase, παρὰ τὰ κοινὰ δίκαια καὶ τοὺς γεγενημένους ὅρκους τοῖς ''Ελλησιν. We should look out, then, for other embellishments of a similar character. I suggest that Plutarch[4] began by accepting as the basic element of the decree the exclusion from the Athenian Agora and the harbours of the empire which he found in Thucydides, and that he inflated this in exactly the same way as he inflated the rest of his sentence.[5] It would have been natural for Plutarch to intensify the 'harbours' with an ἁπάντων, and, perhaps adopting a not un-literary technical phrase from Craterus' text, to write ἁπάντων λιμένων ὧν 'Αθηναῖοι κρατοῦσιν. Wishing to balance the sentence, he quite naturally made the exclusion from the Agora into πάσης ἀγορᾶς ('the whole Agora'), inserted a μέν and a δέ, and put the shorter phrase first because the sentence reads better that way. The word πάσης is of no significance and is included solely for literary effect.

It is true that one would expect the words εἴργεσθαι πάσης ἀγορᾶς (without the article), *taken alone*, in isolation from the rest of the sentence, to mean 'exclude from *every* agora', and that is certainly how some readers have taken them here. Now if such an interpretation were really necessary, and if Plutarch meant to speak of an exclusion from 'every agora and all the harbours controlled by Athens', reference to Thucydides would be sufficient to prove him wrong. How-ever, examination of the structure of the sentence as a whole, and comparison with the Thucydidean original, will show that such a rendering is unlikely. Plutarch, I believe, meant 'the whole (Athenian) Agora'. Although in such con-texts the article is nearly always used when πᾶς means 'the whole' rather than 'every', there are cases, and not only in poetry, where it is omitted.[6] And there are indications here that πάσης is more likely to have a singular than a plural meaning. Thuc. 1 67.4 has λιμένων τε εἴργεσθαι τῶν ἐν τῇ 'Αθηναίων ἀρχῇ καὶ τῆς 'Αττικῆς ἀγορᾶς (and Diod. xɪɪ 39.4, doubtless summarising Ephorus, similarly writes Μεγαρέας εἴργεσθαι τῆς τε ἀγορᾶς καὶ τῶν λιμένων). Plutarch's deliberate sub-stitution of a μέν/δέ for a τε/καί construction suggests to me that he did not intend πάσης ἀγορᾶς to go with ὧν 'Αθηναῖοι κρατοῦσιν. Had he meant to refer to '*every* agora . . . *controlled by Athens*' it would have been more natural to keep the wording of the Thucydidean original and the other sources and use τε and καί instead of μέν and δέ. Thucydides, who in 1 67.4 (the passage Plutarch is mainly using) puts the harbours (ἐν τῇ 'Αθηναίων ἀρχῇ) first and speaks of one particular agora, does have τε/καί (in 139.1 it is μή/μηδέ); but Plutarch *changed* this to μέν/δέ, partly

---

[4] He may of course have been influenced by some intermediate source, but the whole passage is a characteristically Plutarchian piece of rewriting.

[5] Plutarch often rewrites Thucydides with minor embellishments, as in *Nic.* 10.5–6 (cf. Thuc. v 45.4); 10.8 (cf. v 46.4–5); 21.1–2 (cf. vɪɪ 42.1–2).

[6] R. Kühner and B. Gerth, *Ausf. Grammatik der griech. Sprache* ɪɪ³ i.633–4, writing of the use of πᾶς in the sense of 'the whole', in the singular, say, 'Zuweilen erscheint das Sub-stantiv mit πᾶς ohne Artikel, wo man ihn erwartet, und zwar nicht allein in der Dichter-sprache und bei Herodot, sondern auch, doch nur selten, in der attischen Prosa'. Examples follow. Add Hdts v 74.1.

perhaps so that πάσης ἀγορᾶς would not be taken (like ἀπάντων λιμένων) with ὧν Ἀθηναῖοι κρατοῦσιν.[7] Contrast again is suggested by the singular/plural construction, πάσης/ἀπάντων. And of course no other source has any suggestion that more than one agora, that of Athens, was involved. On the other hand, I suppose it is possible that Plutarch made a careless error,[8] and that when he wrote his fine-sounding sentence about the decree he was relying on his memory of what his sources had said, and, in the course of 'writing up' Thucydides, thought in terms of 'every agora and all harbours controlled by Athens'.

In case Thuc. 1 67.4 is thought to be merely quoting what the Megarians said at Sparta (as has been suggested to me), it will be salutary to recall that Thucydides gives the effect of the decree in two other places: not only at 144.2, where Pericles is made to use the expression ἀγορᾷ καὶ λιμέσι, but, much more significantly, in 139.1, where the words ἐν ᾧ εἴρητο make it abundantly clear that what the decree actually *said* was that the Megarians should not use the harbours in the Athenian empire or the [Athenian][9] Agora. Doubtless the decree did not say it quite as tersely as that: Thucydides will be summarising. But, especially in view of 139.1, he clearly thought he was giving the essence of the decree. If it excluded the Megarians from 'every agora in the Athenian empire', Thucydides is needlessly and seriously misrepresenting it when he speaks of 'the *Athenian* Agora'. It is impossible to believe that he would do such a thing.

And finally, the one new element which Aristophanes, in his parody of the decree in *Acharn.* 533–4, adds to the wording of the skolion of Timocreon which he is following is ἐν ἀγορᾷ, in the singular—an expression which an Athenian audience would naturally take as referring to the Agora of Athens alone.

The decree itself will doubtless have spoken of ἡ ἀγορά, or ἀγορά *tout court*: the article, both in literature and in the inscriptions, sometimes appears and sometimes does not; there is no consistency at all.[10] Thucydides naturally makes Pericles, addressing the Athenians, say ἀγορᾷ χρῆσθαι (1 144.2); but when Thucydides is reporting what was said about the decree by the emissaries of other States, the Megarians (67.4) and the Spartans (139.1), he refers, necessarily, to ἡ Ἀττικὴ ἀγορά, an expression which, as I have shown in Chapter VII, Part vii, and in Appendix XLII, must be translated 'the Athenian Agora'.

I do not see how we can be sure what meaning Plutarch attached to the word ἀγορά in the Megarian decree. He may or may not have thought it was being used in a commercial sense. But by Plutarch's time (five hundred years later) even the original Agora of Athens had become much more important as a social centre and place of business than as a focus of political activity; and it had received the notable addition of the 'Roman Market', the colonnaded court east of the old Agora, added in the time of Augustus (see Wycherley, *Ath. Ag.* III 190). Plutarch's opinion about what ἀγορά in the original decree meant is of no great consequence.

[7] Unfortunately, I have not been able to find a close parallel in Plutarch. Donald Russell (to whom I am grateful for reading and criticising a draft of this Appendix) has drawn my attention to *Mor.* 147f, and has told me that in his view one must leave the question open between the two alternative translations of *Per.* 29.4.

[8] Plutarch knew his Thucydides well, but sometimes remembered him incorrectly, as when he makes Alcibiades proxenos of Sparta, in *Alc.* 14.1; contrast Thuc. v 43.2 (with VI 89.2), making rather a point of the fact that in 425–1 Alcibiades had been trying *unsuccessfully* to renew the proxenia renounced by his grandfather—Plutarch perhaps remembered only the more ambiguous VI 89.2.

[9] An Athenian decree would most naturally speak of ἡ ἀγορά, or just ἀγορά: see below.

[10] See e.g. the collection of material by W. J. M. Starkie in his edition of the *Wasps* (1897), p. 217 n. 1: of 31 occurrences of the word in Aristophanes, 12 have the article and 19 have not. The inscriptions are equally indifferent. Cf. Thuc. v 47.11.

APPENDIX XXXIX

Aristophanes, Acharnians *533–4, and* Timocreon, *fr. 5*

There is a problem about one word in the texts of both poets: ἠπείρῳ, which appears in all the MSS, of Aristophanes and the Scholia (citing Timocreon), but is unsuitable in its context in Timocreon, who is using it of a god. Schneidewin's conjecture, ἐν οὐρανῷ, seems exactly right in Timocreon, whose text will then have been corrupted by the scholiast, who carelessly changed it to ἐν ἠπείρῳ, having Ar., *Acharn.* 534 in mind. I do not see how Aristophanes can have written ἐν οὐρανῷ, for (*a*) the Megarians could scarcely be said to 'remain' (or not) in *heaven*, and (*b*) it would be impossible to account for the corruption of Timocreon's text into ἐν ἠπείρῳ. The editors of the 1951 edition of Hill's *Sources* have made the worst possible choice, by printing in the text of *Acharn.* 534 the inappropriate emendation οὐρανῷ (with the *OCT*), and leaving the unsatisfactory ἠπείρῳ in the text of the scholion. (I am indebted to E. C. Yorke for advice on this question.)

APPENDIX XL

Some late sources which confuse the exclusion decree with the decree of Charinus

The important scholion is that on Ar., *Peace* 246, the vital part of which, as emended by Wilamowitz and Holzapfel,[1] reads, Χαρίνου τὸ πινάκιον συνθέντος τὸ κατ' αὐτῶν [τῶν Μεγαρέων] εἰς τὴν Περικλέους χάριν, ὥστε μήτε γῆς μήτε λιμένων Ἀττικῶν ἐπιβαίνειν τοὺς Μεγαρέας.

In the light of this scholion, which certainly refers to the decree of Charinus but confuses it with the exclusion decree, we can understand the wording of another of the Aristophanes scholia, on *Peace* 609, which, purporting to refer to the Megarian decree (i.e. the exclusion decree, mentioned by Ar., *Peace* 609), uses the very same words: Pericles' decree against the Megarians was to the effect that μήτε γῆς μήτε λιμένων αὐτοὺς ἐπιβαίνειν Ἀττικῶν, εἰ δὲ μή, τὸν ληφθέντα ἀγώγιμον εἶναι. And this enables us to see that yet another of the Aristophanes scholia, on *Acharn.* 527, and the entry in the Souda, *s.v. Aspasia*, both of which comment in identical terms on the πόρνα δύο of *Ach.* 527 (δύο ἑταῖραι, Suid.), have similarly confused the exclusion decree with the decree of Charinus: they read, τῇ μιᾷ τούτων (the whores) ἐκέχρητο ὁ Περικλῆς· δι' ἣν ὀργισθεὶς ἔγραψε τὸ κατὰ Μεγαρέων ψήφισμα, ἀπαγορεῦον δέχεσθαι αὐτοὺς εἰς τὰς Ἀθήνας κτλ.

It is interesting to find, on the other hand, that the one really intelligent and well-informed scholion on the passages in the *Acharnians* and the *Peace* which deal with the Megarian decree, namely that on *Peace* 605, describes the exclusion decree in terms mainly derived from Thucydides: the Megarians complained to the

[1] Wilamowitz, in *Hermes* 14 (1879), at p. 319 n. 2; L. Holzapfel, *Untersuch. über die Darstellung der griech. Gesch.* (1879) 183 ff.

Spartans, ἀδίκως λέγοντες εἴργεσθαι ἀγορᾶς καὶ λιμένων τῶν παρ᾽ Ἀθηναίοις. οἱ γὰρ Ἀθηναῖοι ταῦτα ἐψηφίσαντο Περικλέους εἰπόντος, τὴν γῆν αὐτοὺς αἰτιώμενοι τὴν ἱερὰν τοῖς θεοῖς ἀπεργάζεσθαι.

The remaining Aristophanes scholion referring to the Megarian decree is on *Ach.* 532: this gives the skolion of Timocreon which Aristophanes is parodying in lines 533–4, and then proceeds to describe the decree in words taken over directly from Aristophanes: Μεγαρέας μήτε ἀγορᾶς μήτε θαλάττης μήτ᾽ ἠπείρου μετέχειν.

APPENDIX XLI

Consequences of the divergence between warships and merchantmen

As I have said in the text above (Chapter VII, Part vi, first paragraph), Greek cities, unlike many late Mediaeval and Renaissance states, did not practise the exclusion of foreign traders from their ports and markets, but on the contrary welcomed them. There is much dispute about the details of what may be called the 'economic policies' of the towns (and the nation states) of Europe in the later Middle Ages and afterwards,[1] if only because the situation varied greatly from place to place and from time to time, and conclusions based upon too small a sample may prove seriously mistaken when given a more general application. But there can be no doubt that the local inhabitants were often highly exclusive and might impose severe restrictions upon foreigners wishing to trade in their area.

As regards the situation in Classical Greece I have not been able to find any modern statement which is sufficiently accurate and cites enough of the available evidence; but I do not think that anyone who knows the sources for Greek economic history would wish to deny the generalisation I have made at the beginning of this Appendix. In Athens certainly, and surely in most other Greek cities, foreign trade was to a considerable extent in the hands of non-citizens:[2] not only the metics (*resident* aliens) upon whom attention is usually concentrated, but also miscellaneous, non-resident foreigners,[3] who are too often forgotten—as when Gomme remarks that 'on our evidence, the majority of the merchants [at Athens] were resident aliens, metoikoi, not citizens' (*EGHL* 61). Hasebroek, however, was guilty of some exaggeration when he asserted that 'In Classical Greece the class of regular traders ... consisted *almost entirely* of resident foreigners ... There was *scarcely a single merchant of citizen status*' (*TPAG* 101, my italics).

[1] Perhaps the best approach is through the chapter in *Camb. Econ. Hist.* III (1963) on 'The Economic Policies of Towns' (A. B. Hibbert, pp. 157–229, esp. 168–72); cf. the chapter on 'The Economic Policies of Governments' (E. Miller and others, pp. 281–429). Those who, like myself, have been much influenced by Henri Pirenne's *Econ. and Social Hist. of Medieval Europe* (Eng. trans., London, 1936) may find Hibbert's brief article, 'The Origins of the Medieval Town Patriciate', in *Past & Present* 3 (1953) 15–27, particularly rewarding.

[2] It should be sufficient if I merely cite Ehrenberg, *GS²* 86 ('The traders ... were mostly not citizens'), 87 ('The Polis had no trade policy to benefit a civic merchant class'); and Hasebroek, *TPAG* 22 ff., with the works noticed there on p. 22 n. 1; add H. Knorringa, *Emporos* (Amsterdam, 1926) 79–83, etc.; G. Glotz, *Anc. Greece at Work* (Eng. trans., London, 1926) 183–6, 190–1, 315–16.

[3] I have cited a few of the texts illustrating this towards the end of Part vi of Chapter VII above.

It should not surprise us, therefore, that 'the idea that the competition of foreigners might be damaging to the economic interests of the citizens did not occur to any ancient writer' (Hasebroek, *TPAG* 24). Particularly illuminating in this connection is Xenophon, *De Vect.* III 2, 3–5, 12–13; IV 40; V 3–4; and see *Hipparch.* IV 7 ('all cities always welcome those who import something'); Isocr. VIII 21 (the desirability of having the city full of 'merchants [*emporoi*] and foreigners and metics'); Aeschin. I 40 ('those of the merchants [*emporoi*] or of the other foreigners or of our own citizens. . . .'). An attitude such as that expressed in the 'Complaint of the Citizens of London against Aliens', of 1571 (R. H. Tawney and Eileen Power, *Tudor Economic Documents* I 308–10), is simply unthinkable in fifth/fourth-century Greece. I propose to deal in some detail elsewhere with the whole question of 'trade and politics' in the Greek cities—the role played by trade and traders in the formation of State policies. But I wish to put forward one hypothesis here which I think has not been advanced before and which seems to me to deserve discussion.

In the historical process it is always difficult to identify one particular element as a basic one, which of itself necessarily has important consequences and to which other features of the process are ultimately traceable. But I believe that we can isolate one such element as being directly responsible for the fact that in the Greek world, unlike the European Middle Ages, no city-state (as far as we know) tried to concentrate its foreign trade in the hands of 'its own' merchants—of traders, that is to say, who were numbered among its own citizens. This basic element is the twofold fact (1) that in the Greek world, from very early times,[4] *warships and merchant ships were totally different*, and a warship could not be converted for use as a merchantman,[5] nor could a trading ship be turned into a man-of-war; also (2) that each type of ship was manned mainly by *a different kind of 'sailor'*: the merchant ship, propelled almost entirely by wind,[6] needed only a very small crew, principally of experienced seamen, while the warship, whether triaconter, penteconter or trireme, required a large number of rowers (30, 50 or 170), but only a handful

[4] It was perhaps the invention of the ram (sheathed in bronze by at least the early fifth century) which was decisive in influencing the development of the specialised warship; and this invention certainly took place well before the period with which we are concerned. For the ram, see Morrison and Williams, *GOS* 7, 12–14, 37, 90–7; cf. Lionel Casson, *The Ancient Mariners* (London, 1959) 83–4, 99–100; L. Cohen, in *AJA* 42 (1938) 486–94. Ships illustrated on early Greek vases of the Geometric period and later (carefully listed by Morrison and Williams, *GOS*), in so far as they are identifiable, are virtually all warships (but see Casson, *op. cit.*, Plate 6a), and Exekias even depicts a solitary Dionysus in a ship with a ram (Morrison and Williams, *GOS* 93 and Plate 13); but a fine Attic Black-figure cup of the second half of the sixth century, in the British Museum (B. 436: see Morrison and Williams, *GOS* 109 and Plate 19, 20a; Casson, *op. cit.* 86–7 and Plate 7), shows both a merchantman under shortened sail and a warship (or pirate).

[5] Only in exceptional circumstances were warships employed for trading, as when the Phocaeans journeyed to the western Mediterranean in the sixth century, in danger of attack from Etruscan and Carthaginian warships and pirates, and consequently used penteconters—as Herodotus (I 163.1–2) emphasises: 'they voyaged not in *strongylai nēes* but in penteconters'.

[6] It is true that we do occasionally hear of merchant ships with oars: see Thuc. IV 118.5, where the term used is *ploion*, a general word for a ship; cf. *holkas*, which—like *holkadikon ploion* in Arist., *De Incessu Animal.* 10, 710[a] 15ff., esp. 19–20 (very significant), and *ploion strongylon* in Xen., *HG* V i.21—seems to be used only for the merchant ship propelled by sail. The term *eikosoros* occurs occasionally, e.g. in Dem. XXXV 10, 18; Nicostratus fr. 10 (Kock, *CAF* II 222; Edmonds, *FAC* II 32), *ap.* Athen. x 474b. If this should really be given its literal meaning, 'a 20-oared ship', I suggest that the oars would be kept for navigating difficult narrows or for use in a dead calm or going in the eye of the wind. Rowers additional to the normal complement of sailors would constitute an expense which would reduce the profits of a trading voyage.

of skilled seamen making up the *hypēresia* (an expression which is often translated 'petty officers').[7]

For our present purposes the significance of this fundamental difference between warship and merchantman was that no Greek city would find it worth while, as many European states did down to the seventeenth century, to maintain 'its own' merchant navy, for conversion into a war fleet in case of need. Indeed, to speak of 'the merchant navy' *of* a Greek state is misleading, and best avoided. In Europe, during the Middle Ages and as late as the sixteenth century and even the early part of the seventeenth, ships of war and trading vessels were mostly very much alike: the addition of a couple of 'castles' and, from the fourteenth century onwards, a few guns (or additional guns) could turn many a merchant ship into a useful man-of-war. The great majority of fighting ships, indeed, were interchangeable with merchantmen, whether sailing ships or galleys.[8] And merchant sailors formed the bulk of the crews of a war fleet, which needed a fair proportion of skilled seamen. Any state which allowed its merchant marine to decay could not hope to be a naval power. Anyone who reads, for example, *The Libelle of Englyshe Polycye*, published in 1436 (ed. Sir George Warner, Oxford, 1926), will find no trace of any distinction between war fleet and merchant navy. Apart from a few 'king's ships', it seems that 'all vessels used for war in those days had been built for merchantmen, served as merchantmen in peace-time, belonged to merchants, and were manned by persons nominally in the pay of merchants' (W. L. Clowes, *The Royal Navy*, I [London, 1897] 347–8). And part of the preamble of the *Acte for the Mayntenaunce of the Navye* (32 Henry VIII, c. 14), of 1540, reads 'And where the Navy or multitude of Shippes of this realme in tymes past hath ben and yet is verie profitable, requisite, necessarie and commodiouse, aswell for the entercourse and concurse of marchauntis transporting and conveying their wares and marchaundises . . . , and a greate defence and suerty of this realme in tyme of warre as well to offend as defende, and also the mayntenance of many maisters, maryners and see men, making them expert and connyng in the arte and science of shippmen and sayling, and they, their wifes and children have had their lyvinges of and by the same, and also hathe ben the chief mayntenance and supportacion of the Cities, Townes, villages, havens and creekis nere adjoyning unto the see costes . . .' (Tawney and Power, *Tudor Econ. Doc.* II 93). But any Greek state which needed to have a war fleet would have no inducement to maintain 'its own' merchant marine, for this would be useless in war, and although a few skilled sailors (in our sense of the word) were essential for triremes (cf. Thuc. I 143.1; Ps.-Xen., *Ath. Pol.* I 2), even

---

[7] The steersman (*kybernētēs*) was the key figure; otherwise, apart from the *prōratēs* or *prōreus* in the prow, no other 'sailors' (in our sense) were necessary, although there would be a ship's carpenter or shipwright (*naupēgos*); a *keleustēs*, who seems to have fulfilled some of the functions of the modern boatswain, assisted perhaps by the *aulētēs* or *triēraulēs* ('flute-player'); and also a *pentēkontarchos*, whose duties (see Ps.-Dem. L 18–27, esp. 25 *fin.*) may have been largely administrative, under the trierarch, and who should perhaps be referred to as the 'paymaster' or 'quartermaster'. The 'ship's company' of the trireme is discussed by Morrison and Williams, *GOS* 254–79 (266–8 for the *hypēresia*).

[8] Since a friend who read this Appendix in MS remarked that 'use of merchant vessels as warships is surely to be linked with the introduction of gunpowder', I should perhaps say explicitly that fighting at sea for many centuries before the use of naval guns was essentially a matter of 'grapple-and-board', and that it was precisely the introduction of cannon which eventually put an end to 'the interchangeability of the role of merchantmen and man-of-war' (see G. S. Laird Clowes, *Sailing Ships, their History and Development, Part I. Historical Notes* [London, 1930] 59–60). For the situation in the sixteenth century onwards, see e.g. Garrett Mattingly, *The Defeat of the Spanish Armada* (London, 1959; Pelican, 1962) 114–15, 212–13, 227–30, 233, 262–4, 292, 419–21; Violet Barbour, 'Dutch and English Merchant Shipping in the Seventeenth Century', in *Econ. Hist. Rev.* 2 (1929–30) 261–90 (esp. the opening paragraph); Ralph Davis, *The Rise of the English Shipping Industry in the Seventeenth and Eighteenth Centuries* (London, 1962), esp. 44–5.

they, like rowers, could be hired from abroad if they were not available in sufficient numbers at home.

The consequence of this technological development of Greek warships and merchantmen on completely different lines was that any Greek state could safely afford to pay no attention to 'its own' merchant fleet, and was therefore *not deterred from allowing its foreign trade to fall largely into the hands of foreigners.*

Some may feel that this situation, a matter of economic and social organisation, should not be traced back directly to a 'mere technological fact': the divergence in the construction of the two kinds of ships, with the differences in their personnel which this divergence entailed. It is true that the governing classes in all the Greek cities we know anything about in the Classical period were essentially agricultural rather than commercial or industrial,[9] and that in so far as anything we might call a 'merchant class' existed among the citizens of any Greek state, it would form part of the lower orders (as at Aegina and Chios: see Arist., *Pol.* IV 4, 1291^{b}17–26, esp. 17–18, 24) and would not be likely to have much political influence. Some may feel that this is a sufficient explanation of the fact that Greek cities were content to leave their foreign trade largely in the hands of strangers. But I would suggest that if Greek merchant ships and warships had not become so very different and if a highly specialised type of warship had not been developed, many Greek states which relied upon overseas trade (Athens above all) would almost certainly have been obliged, in the interests of their own security, to maintain 'their own' merchant fleets, ready for conversion into warships in case of need—and might then have been driven to pursue an entirely different policy in regard to their overseas trade, for they would surely have wished to favour 'their own' merchant marine, which it would have been advantageous to employ as much as possible for trading purposes while it was not required for military use.[10]

I may briefly note here that the theses upheld in this book are not at all affected by Hdts v 88.2 (where the exclusion is solely from a temple) or I 165.1 (where the Chians can only be fearing a rise in the price of their imports: had they been thinking of exports they would have welcomed a flourishing new emporium nearby).

APPENDIX XLII

Ἀθηναῖος *and* Ἀττικός

Ἀττικός is not derived from the name of Attica, ἡ Ἀττική (*sc.* γῆ, χώρα), any more than δεξιός is derived from ἡ δεξιά (*sc.* χείρ): see Dittenberger, EuV 215–16.

The expression ἡ Ἀττικὴ ἀγορά is the precise equivalent of ἡ Ἀθηναίων ἀγορά, and Thucydides could equally well have called it that, just as in II 71.2 he uses the phrase ἐν τῇ Πλαταιῶν ἀγορᾷ.

As for Thucydides being obliged to use *ethnika* in an adjectival sense where the corresponding *ktētika* had not yet been developed, note Ἐπιδαύριος πόλεμος; Κορίνθιαι, Λευκάδιαι, Μηθυμναῖαι, Μιλήσιαι, Ῥηγῖναι, Σάμιαι, Σελινούντιαι, Συρακόσιαι or Χῖαι νῆες; and Ῥοδίῳ πεντηκοντόρῳ. In a very few cases, even where he has separate 'ktetic' forms available, Thucydides, in accordance with standard fifth- and fourth-century practice, applies the *ethnikon* in an adjectival sense

[9] Cf. Chapter VII, Part vi, n. 61 above.

[10] Unfortunately, Lionel Casson, *Ships and Seamanship in the Ancient World* (Princeton, 1971), appeared only after this book was in proof, and I have been unable to make use of it.

to *men* considered as members of military units: for instance Ἀθηναῖοι ὁπλῖται (IV 129.4) and Μαντινῆς μισθοφόροι (VII 57.9), not Ἀττικοί and Μαντινικοί (see Dittenberger, EuV 29 ff.). Otherwise, whenever there existed a separate *ktētikon*, different from the *ethnikon*, Thucydides invariably employed it on appropriate occasions: for instance, Μαντινικὸς πόλεμος; or Ἀμπρακιώτιδες, Ἑρμιονίδες, Λοκρίδες, Μεγαρίδες and of course Ἀττικαί and Λακωνικαὶ νῆες. But just as Thucydides' only uses of Λακωνικός are with ναῦς, στήλη and ὄνομα, so his only uses of Ἀττικός (apart from ἡ Ἀττική, or ἡ γῆ ἡ Ἀττική) are with ἀγορά, δραχμή, ἱερά, ναῦς, ξυγγραφή, πόλεμος, σπονδαί and χοῖνιξ, and each time the adjective is simply a substitute for τῶν Ἀθηναίων: for example, ἡ Ἀττικὴ ναῦς of II 91.3 is τὴν μίαν ναῦν τῶν Ἀθηναίων of 91.2, and τὰς ... Ἀττικὰς ναῦς of III 81.2 are the ἑξήκοντα νῆες Ἀθηναίων of 80.2. We are accustomed to speak of an '*Attic* drachma' or an '*Attic* choinix'; but in some cases, as with the warships, the proper English equivalent of Ἀττικός is 'Athenian' rather than 'Attic'—and so it is with ἡ Ἀττικὴ ἀγορά, which it would be inappropriate to translate 'the *Attic*' rather than 'the *Athenian* agora'. Even in III 114.1, ἐν τοῖς Ἀττικοῖς ἱεροῖς, the word can only signify 'the temples of the Athenian State', τὰ Ἀθηναίων ἱερά, and not 'the temples of Attica', which would have been τὰ τῆς Ἀττικῆς (or ἐν Ἀττικῇ) ἱερά.

APPENDIX XLIII

Exclusion from the Athenian Agora

The evidence may be divided into two broad groups, affecting two different classes of undesirables.

1. Accusation of homicide: Antiph. v 10 (cf. VI 34 ff.); Dem. XX 158; XXIII 80; XXIV 60; Aeschin. II 148; Arist., *Ath. Pol.* 57.4; Poll. VIII 66. This is said to go back to Draco: see Dem. XX 158.

2. Conviction for serious crimes (see Andoc. I 76; also perhaps Ps.-Lys. VI 24, with 9; but contrast Andoc. I 71, mentioning only τὰ ἱερά), in particular the following:

(*a*) Disgraceful crimes, such as ἑταίρησις (Aeschin. I 19–21, 164; Dem. XXII 77, with 30, 32; XXIV 126, with XXII 30, 32, 77; Suid., *s.v.* ἔνδειξις), and κάκωσις γονέων (Dem. XXIV 60, 105; cf. Plato, *Laws* IX 881e, where the πόλις is that of v 745bc, i.e. the Acropolis and its environs, surrounded by a wall).

(*b*) The military crimes, at any rate ἀστρατεία, λιποτάξιον, and what is sometimes called δειλία but may perhaps (as believed by Lipsius, *AR* 452–5, esp. 453 n. 6) be merely ἀποβεβληκέναι τὴν ἀσπίδα: Aeschin. III 175–6; cf. Diod. XVI 88.2 (= Lyc., fr. 75 Sauppe); Dem. XXI 58–60; also Lys. X 1. Andoc. I 74 seems to have five distinct military offences, all involving complete personal ἀτιμία (which would include inability to enter the Agora): these would be λιποτάξιον, ἀστρατεία, δειλία, ἀναυμάχιον, and τὴν ἀσπίδα ἀποβεβληκέναι (but see D. M. MacDowell, *Andokides On the Mysteries* [Oxford, 1962] 110–12).

(*c*) Possibly something in the nature of treason, προδοσία: see Dem. XXIV 60; probably Lyc., *c. Leocr.* 5, cf. 142 and perhaps (with the reading νομίμων) 65.

For the link between exclusion from the Agora and exclusion from the public ἱερά, see Dem. XX 158; Aeschin. I 21, with III 176; Lyc., *c. Leocr.* 5, 142; Arist.,

Ath. Pol. 57.4; Ps.-Lys. VI 9, 24. In Lys. XII 96, seizure ἐκ τῆς ἀγορᾶς is mentioned with seizure ἐκ τῶν ἱερῶν among the shocking acts of the Thirty. We may compare the expression ἡ ἱερὰ ἀγορά, used as a name for the place where the civic Assembly was held in various Greek cities, including Halicarnassus (M/L 32 [=Tod I² 25].3–4) in the fifth century, and Magnesia in Thessaly (*IG* IX ii.1105.3; 1106.10) in the Hellenistic period.

Aeschines I 21 is misunderstood by Kahrstedt (*SORA* I = *SSA* 45 n. 1), who declares, 'Das Gesetz Aischin. I 21, das *einen Teil* der agora [my italics] für ἑταιρηκότες sperrt, ist Scholiastenphantasie'. Whether the law in Aeschin. I 21, containing the phrase μηδ’ ἐντὸς τῆς ἀγορᾶς τῶν περιρραντηρίων πορευέσθω, is genuine or not, the fact that the exclusion was ἔξω τῶν περιρραντηρίων τῆς ἀγορᾶς is guaranteed by the appearance of these words in the text of Aeschin. III 176 (quoted in Chapter VII, Part vii above), which Kahrstedt evidently failed to notice in this connection.

An interesting passage in Lucian (*De Sacrific.* 13), dealing with the offering of State sacrifices in general, reads, καὶ τὸ μὲν πρόγραμμά φησι μὴ παριέναι εἰς τὸ εἴσω τῶν περιρραντηρίων ὅστις μὴ καθαρός ἐστι τὰς χεῖρας—words which at once remind us of the περιρραντήρια of the Athenian Agora, and of Demosthenes’ reference (XXIV 60) to οἱ μὴ καθαρὰς τὰς χεῖρας ἔχοντες, εἰσιόντες δ’ εἰς τὴν ἀγοράν.

The statement by Wycherley (*Ath. Ag.* III 218) about *perirrhantēria* found in the Agora cites also the references to *perirrhantēria* in *IG* II² 1641.38; Poll. I 8 (ὁ μέν εἴσω περιρραντηρίων τόπος ἔνθεος, ἱερός, καθιερωμένος, καθωσιωμένος, ἀβέβηλος κτλ.); Aristeid. XXIX 14 (ed. Keil); and Eur., *Ion* 435 (alluding to ἀπορραντήρια at Delphi). See also the guide-book to the Agora (*The Athenian Agora²*) 57, 58.

APPENDIX XLIV

πορνοτελώνης in Philonides,
fr. 5 (= Poll. IX 29)

When *LSJ⁹*, *s.v.* πορνοτελώνης, translate 'farmer of the πορνικὸν τέλος', they seem to have no better foundation than our passage. It is true that the πορνικὸν τέλος (the earliest evidence for which known to me is in Aeschin. I 119 ff., of 345 B.C.) very probably did exist in the late fifth century, and of course it would always have been farmed. It is possible, then, that the word πορνοτελώνης already existed in Philonides’ day, either as a technical or as a slang term, to denote the farmer of the πορνικὸν τέλος. But (*a*) would the farmers of this tax really be considered specially disreputable persons, such as it would be suitable to associate with the other undesirables in Philonides’ list? I doubt it. And (*b*) what reason could Philonides have for applying the word πορνοτελῶναι *to the Pentekostologoi*, which is certainly what Pollux represents him as doing? Also, (*c*) if the word were derived from the farmer of the πορνικὸν τέλος, rather than from πόρνος/πόρνη and τελώνης in general, would not one perhaps rather expect πορνικοτελώνης?

I should therefore prefer to take the word πορνοτελώνης as merely an opprobrious slang term for τελῶναι *of all kinds*, the first element in the word being derived not from the πορνικὸν τέλος, but from πόρνος/πόρνη. (I do not see, by the way, that πορνοτελώνης can possibly stand for πορνοβοσκός, because the τελώνης element irresistibly suggests a tax-*farmer*, a man who '*buys* the tax', and not just a man who derives revenues from πόρναι, and in Philonides it stands for the Pentekostologoi, who *were* tax-farmers.)

APPENDIX XLV

Some Athenian laws affecting the Agora

1. From Dem. LVII 30–4 (esp. 31) it looks as if the laws forbade foreigners to 'trade in the agora', ἐν τῇ ἀγορᾷ ἐργάζεσθαι (not absolutely, in spite of the wording of §31, but) except on payment of a tax known as ξενικά (§34). See Böckh, *SHA* I³ 404, cf. 74. Here the agora must surely be the civic Agora, for it would be impossible to collect such a tax from the many foreigners who occasionally traded on its outskirts. It is possible that foreigners originally were not allowed to trade in the Agora at all (as Böckh seems to have thought, *SHA* I³ 74), but were later allowed to do so on payment of a toll.

2. Aristotle, *Ath. Pol.* 52.2, mentions among the ἔμμηνοι δίκαι an action against anyone who borrows money, ἐν ἀγορᾷ βουλόμενος ἐργάζεσθαι. I suspect that although 'agora' in the original law meant the civic Agora, the action may have become available to those who lent money to anyone intending to trade in Athens—for how could it be proved whether or not he intended to operate in the actual Agora?

3. According to Dem. LVII 30, an action for κακηγορία lay against anyone who reproached a citizen (male or female) with τὴν ἐργασίαν τὴν ἐν τῇ ἀγορᾷ. There is no further reference to this alleged law, and it seems that the speaker did not have it read out and may not be reporting it correctly. (The 'law of Solon' read out at the end of §31 was presumably no. 1 above.)

4. The last of these laws forbade misrepresentation in trading in the agora. Theophrastus, in his great work on *Laws* (fr. 98 Wimmer, *ap.* Harp., *s.v.* κατὰ τὴν ἀγορὰν ἀψευδεῖν), said that the Agoranomoi had the duty of insuring τῆς τε ἐν τῇ ἀγορᾷ εὐκοσμίας καὶ τοῦ ἀψευδεῖν (in relation to both sellers and buyers). Hypereides III (*c. Athenog.*) 14 also refers to the law commanding ἀψευδεῖν ἐν τῇ ἀ[γορᾷ], in a commercial context, and adds that his opponent had lied to him [ἐν] μέσῃ τῇ ἀγορᾷ. There is a less precise allusion in Dem. xx 9 to a law enjoining κατὰ τὴν ἀγορὰν ἀψευδεῖν. (The speaker goes on to show that this relates to private transactions.) Again, the law will originally have applied to misrepresentation in the Agora. When regular trading began to spread out into its environs, the Agoranomoi may well have been expected to enforce it outside the strict limits of the Agora.

APPENDIX XLVI

The provision of agorai *for foreign expeditionary forces*

The texts cited here are not really relevant to the Megarian decree at all; but I give them, with a brief explanation, since I have found from comments made on earlier drafts of my seventh Chapter that the special situation they illustrate can be confused with the one we have been dealing with. For convenience I shall confine myself to Thucydides and Xenophon. (I give only a small selection of the available evidence.)

In 415, when the great Athenian expedition to Sicily reached south Italy, none of the Greek cities there wished to receive the Athenians within their walls, in case they took over the city. Eventually, Rhegium 'provided an agora . . . outside the city' (Thuc. vi 44.3), and Messana promised to do the same (50.1). Earlier, the other cities had refused to receive the Athenians 'either with an agora or into the city', but had at most given them water and anchorage, and Taras and Locri not even that (44.2). Without sources of supply available nearby, from which the men could provide themselves with food, the Athenian expedition would have been done for (see vii 14.3, a very interesting passage).

In 432 the forces defending Potidaea against the Athenians had 'set up an agora outside the city', from which to provision themselves (i 62.1). And in 413 the Syracusans arranged to 'move the agora of goods on sale down to the sea shore as quickly as possible, and compel everyone to bring whatever food he had and sell it there', so that their naval crews could eat and then re-embark without delay, taking the Athenians by surprise (vii 39.2; 40.1).

Xenophon, as we might expect, has many references to armies being given a special agora, provided in some cases apparently by private enterprise (e.g. *Anab.* i ii.18; iii.14; v.6,12; *HG* vi iv.9), and in others provided by—or requested without success from—a Greek city (e.g. *Anab.* v v.6, with 19; v.14; *Ages.* i 14; *HG* iii iv.11; v iv.48) or some non-Greek community (e.g. *Anab.* v v.18) or a satrap (e.g. *Anab.* ii iii.26,27). He also speaks of soldiers on an expedition being allowed to go inside a city to make use of its own ordinary market (e.g. *Anab.* vi i.1; *HG* vii ii.17,18). In one interesting passage (*Anab.* vi ii.8) he describes how a Greek city which had a market for an army outside its walls moved it inside (where the army could not use it) when it began to distrust the army.

At the same time, of course, Xenophon, like every other writer, can use the word agora to denote the civic Agora of Athens (e.g. *Hipparch.* iii 2; and esp. *Mem.* iv ii.1, quoted in Chapter VII, Part vii above) or of some other city (e.g. *HG* iv iv.3; v ii.29; vii i.45; iii.12), or even an assembly of soldiers (*Anab.* v vii.3). But as far as I have been able to discover, he never uses the word, in the singular or the plural, to mean 'buying and selling' in general, or, in the singular, to mean 'supplies'. *LSJ*⁹ 13, s.v. ἀγορά iii 2, are wrong in translating *Anab.* vii vi.24 'to have *supplies*': the passage refers to the provision of an inadequate market outside Perinthus (cf. ii.11 ff.; iii.3 *fin.*, 5), and ἀγορᾷ δὲ ἐχρῆσθε is rightly translated by the Loeb editor (O. J. Todd), 'and you got your provisions by purchase at a market'. I believe that only in *Anab.* vi vi. 3 (written perhaps as late as the 360s) does Xenophon use the word to mean 'supplies', and then it is in the plural, as it almost invariably is when used in that sense by later authors.

APPENDIX XLVII

Deme Assemblies

It seems to be generally believed that the deme Assembly normally met in the deme agora: see e.g. Busolt-Swoboda, *GSK* ii 969 and n.9. But phrases like ἐν τεῖ ἀγορᾶι τεῖ κυρίαι, in *IG* ii² 1202.1–2, use the word ἀγορά in the abstract sense (cf. ἐκκλησία), and prove nothing about the place of meeting. Certainly Dem. lvii 9–16 (esp. 10) shows the Assembly of the deme Halimous (which was on the coast, some five miles south-east of Peiraeus, but perhaps just inside the Cleisthenic ἄστυ area) meeting in the City, and nothing is said to suggest that this was unusual, although it would have suited the speaker's case if he could have discredited the meeting.

Doubtless the deme Assemblies originally met in the agorai of the demes; but perhaps the venue was changed to Athens, in certain cases at least, at some time in the late fifth or fourth century, when a fair proportion of the members of some country demes possibly no longer lived in them.

Select Bibliography (and List of Abbreviations)

Works such as periodicals and collections of inscriptions or papyri, cited only by the initial letters of their titles or by customary abbreviations, usually *without the name of an author or editor*, are first listed below, in Section I.

In Section II there follows a very selective list of works which are generally considered important or seem to me particularly useful or are referred to frequently in this book, *recorded under the names of their authors or editors*. Many of these (especially those often quoted) have been cited by the initial letters of their titles—in italics if they are books, not articles.

Any abbreviations of modern works which I may have inadvertently omitted to include here will be easily identifiable with the aid of such lists of abbreviations as those in *LSJ*⁹ 1 xli-xlvii, *OCD*² ix-xxii, *CAH* v 487–8, or any recent number of *L'année philologique*. The identification of ancient sources will usually be obvious enough to those who wish to consult them: in case of doubt, reference can be made to *LSJ*⁹ 1 xvi-xli or (for Latin authors) to Lewis and Short's *Latin Dictionary* vii-xi.

Section I

(A star indicates that references are to the numbers of the inscriptions or papyri, and not, except where specifically indicated, to pages.)

AJA	= *American Journal of Archaeology*
AJP	= *American Journal of Philology*
AJSL	= *American Journal of Semitic Languages*
ASI (Ehrenberg)	= *Ancient Society and Institutions. Studies Presented to Victor Ehrenberg on his 75th Birthday*, ed. E. Badian (Oxford, 1966)
Ath. Mitt.	= *Mitteilungen des deutschen Archäologischen Instituts, Athenische Abteilung*
ATL	= B. D. Meritt, H. T. Wade-Gery and M. F. McGregor, *The Athenian Tribute Lists*, 4 vols.: 1 (Cambridge, Mass., 1939); 11 (1949), 111 (1950), 1V (1953), Princeton, N. J. Vol. 1V contains a very large bibliography (pp. 235–78)
BCH	= *Bulletin de Correspondance hellénique*
BICS	= *Bulletin of the Institute of Classical Studies*, University of London
BSA	= *Annual of the British School at Athens*

CAF	= Theodore Kock, *Comicorum Atticorum Fragmenta*, 3 vols. (Leipzig, 1880–88)
CAH v	= *The Cambridge Ancient History*, vol. v (Cambridge, 1927; 4th impression, 1953)
CP	= *Classical Philology*
CQ	= *Classical Quarterly*
CR	= *Classical Review*
CW	= *Classical Weekly*, now *Classical World*
*DAA**	= A. E. Raubitschek, with the collaboration of L. H. Jeffery, *Dedications from the Athenian Akropolis* (Cambridge, Mass., 1949)
*DGE**	= E. Schwyzer, *Dialectorum Graecorum Exempla Epigraphica Potiora* (Leipzig, 1923)
Diss.	= Dissertation
FAC i, ii	= J. M. Edmonds, *The Fragments of Attic Comedy* (Leiden), i (1957), ii (1959)
FGrH	= F. Jacoby, *Die Fragmente der griechischen Historiker*, i and ii (Berlin, 1923–30 and repr., containing the fragments of historians numbered 1–261), iii (Leiden, 1940–58 and repr., containing the fragments of historians numbered 262–856).
	FGrH iii b (Suppl.) i [Text] and ii [Notes, etc.] (Leiden, 1954) contains the Commentary (in English) on the fragments of the Atthidographers, nos. 323a–334 in vol. iii B (1950). Distinguish *FGrH* iii b (2 vols., Text and Noten, 1955), which contains the Commentary (in German) on the fragments of the remaining historians in vol. iii B: nos. 297–322 and 335–607. (No Commentary has yet been published on the fragments of the historians in vol. iii C: nos. 608a–856.)
	The number allotted to any historian whose fragments are included in *FGrH* can be ascertained from the Index in vol. iii C, pp. 947–64
GGA	= *Göttingische Gelehrte Anzeigen*
GGN	= *Nachrichten von der Gesellschaft der Wissenschaften zu Göttingen*, Philologisch-Historische Klasse (continued from 1930s as *Nachrichten der Akademie der Wissenschaften in Göttingen*, Philologisch-Historische Klasse)
GRBS	= *Greek, Roman and Byzantine Studies*
Hesp.	= *Hesperia* (Journal of The American School of Classical Studies at Athens)
HSCP	= *Harvard Studies in Classical Philology*
*IG**	= *Inscriptiones Graecae* (Berlin, 1873 ff.). For a list of the volumes, with comments, see A. G. Woodhead,

	The Study of Greek Inscriptions (Cambridge, 1959) 103–6, or H. Bengtson, *Introduction to Ancient History* (trans. from the 6th German edn. of Bengtson's *Einführung in die alte Geschichte* by R. I. Frank and F. D. Gilliard, Berkeley/Los Angeles/London, 1970) 148–9
Inscr. Cret.*	= Margherita Guarducci, *Inscriptiones Creticae*, 4 vols. (Rome, 1935–50, replacing *IG* XIII)
*IGIDS*⁴*	= F. Solmsen and E. Fraenkel, *Inscriptiones Graecae ad Inlustrandos Dialectos Selectae* (Leipzig, 4th edn., 1930)
JAOS	= *Journal of the American Oriental Society*
JESHO	= *Journal of the Economic and Social History of the Orient*
JHI	= *Journal of the History of Ideas*
JHS	= *Journal of Hellenic Studies*
JNES	= *Journal of Near Eastern Studies*
*LSJ*⁹	= Liddell and Scott, *Greek-English Lexicon* (Oxford, 9th edn., revised by H. Stuart Jones, 1925–40)
M/L*	= R. Meiggs and D. M. Lewis, *A Selection of Greek Historical Inscriptions to the End of the Fifth Century B.C.* (Oxford, 1969)
Num. Chron.	= *Numismatic Chronicle*
OCD	= *The Oxford Classical Dictionary*, ed. M. Cary and others (Oxford, 1st edn. 1949, 2nd edn. 1970)
OCT	= *Oxford Classical Texts* (a series of texts of Greek and Latin authors, published by the Oxford University Press)
OGIS*	= W. Dittenberger, *Orientis Graeci Inscriptiones Selectae*, 2 vols. (Leipzig, 1903, 1905)
PACA	= *Proceedings of the African Classical Associations*
PCPS	= *Proceedings of the Cambridge Philological Society*
P. Oxy.*	= *Oxyrhynchus Papyri*, ed. B. P. Grenfell, A. S. Hunt and others (Oxford, 1898 ff.)
RE	= Pauly-Wissowa, *Real-Encyclopädie der classischen Altertumswissenschaft* (Stuttgart, 1893 ff.)
REG	= *Revue des études grecques*
Rh. Mus.	= *Rheinisches Museum für Philologie*
RIDA	= *Revue internationale des droits de l'antiquité*
RIG*	= Charles Michel, *Recueil d'inscriptions grecques* (Brussels, 1900, inscriptions nos. 1–1426; also Supplément, fasc. i, Paris, 1912, nos. 1427–1564, and fasc. ii, Brussels, 1927, nos. 1565–1881)
RIJG*	= R. Dareste, B. Haussoullier and Th. Reinach, *Recueil des inscriptions juridiques grecques* (Paris, 1891–1904)
SEG*	= *Supplementum Epigraphicum Graecum* (Leiden, 1923 ff.)

SGDI*   = H. Collitz, F. Bechtel, and O. Hoffmann, *Sammlung der griechischen Dialekt-Inschriften* (Göttingen, 1884–1915)

SIG*   = W. Dittenberger, *Sylloge Inscriptionum Graecarum* (Leipzig, 3rd edn., by F. Hiller von Gaertringen, 1915–24; 2nd edn. 1898–1901)

SVdA* II, III = *Die Staatsverträge des Altertums* (Munich): II. *Die Verträge der griechisch-römischen Welt von 700 bis 338 v. Chr.*, ed. H. Bengtson (1962), and III. *Die Verträge der griechisch-römischen Welt von 338 bis 200 v. Chr.*, ed. H. H. Schmitt (1969)

TAPA   = *Transactions of the American Philological Association*

TGF²   = A. Nauck, *Tragicorum Graecorum Fragmenta* (Leipzig, 1889; repr. Hildesheim, 1964, with Supplement)

Tod* I², II   = M. N. Tod, *A Selection of Greek Historical Inscriptions* (Oxford): I. *To the End of the Fifth Century B.C.* (2nd edn., 1946), and II. *From 403 to 323 B.C.* (1948)

ZPE   = *Zeitschrift für Papyrologie und Epigraphik*

Section II

Accame, *LA* = Silvio Accame, *La lega ateniese del secolo IV a.C.* (Rome, 1941)

Alexander, *PHR* = J. A. Alexander, *Potidaea. Its History and Remains* (Athens, Georgia, 1963)

Anderson, *MTPAX* = J. K. Anderson, *Military Theory and Practice in the Age of Xenophon* (Berkeley, 1970)

——, 'A Topographical and Historical Study of Achaea', in *BSA* 49 (1954) 72–92, esp. 80–5

Andrewes, *GCS* = A. Andrewes, 'The Government of Classical Sparta', in *ASI* (Ehrenberg) 1–20

——, *MD* = 'The Mytilene Debate: Thuc. 3.36–49', in *Phoenix* 16 (1962) 64–85

——, *MDPLS* = 'The Melian Dialogue and Perikles' Last Speech', in *PCPS* 186 = n.s. 6 (1960) 1–10

——, *SAEFC* = 'Sparta and Arcadia in the Early Fifth Century', in *Phoenix* 6 (1952) 1–5

——, *TCW* = 'Thucydides on the Causes of the War', in *CQ* 53 = n.s. 9 (1959) 223–39

——, 'Thucydides and the Persians', in *Historia* 10 (1961) 1–18 (And see under Gomme, *HCT* IV below)

ASI (Ehrenberg): see Section I above

ATL: see Section I above

Bailey, *WPD* = Cyril Bailey, 'Who Played "Dicaeopolis"?' in *Greek Poetry and Life. Essays Presented to Gilbert Murray on his 70th Birthday* (Oxford, 1936) 231–40

Baynes, *BSOE* = N. H. BAYNES, *Byzantine Studies and Other Essays* (London, 1955), ch. viii, 'Isocrates' (pp. 144–67)

Beazley, *ABV* = J. D. BEAZLEY, *Attic Black-Figure Vase-Painters* (Oxford, 1956)

Beloch, *APP* = [KARL] JULIUS BELOCH, Die Attische Politik seit Perikles (Leipzig, 1884)

——, *BGRW* = *Die Bevölkerung der griechisch-römischen Welt* (*Historische Beiträge zur Bevölkerungslehre* i, Leipzig, 1886)

——, *GG²* = *Griechische Geschichte* (Berlin/Leipzig, 2nd edn.): I² i (1924) and ii (1926); II² i (1927) and ii (1931); III² i (1922) and ii (1923)

Bengtson, *GG⁴* = HERMANN BENGTSON, *Griechische Geschichte, von den Anfängen bis in die römische Kaiserzeit* (Munich, 4th edn., 1969. *Handbuch der Altertumswissenschaft*, ed. I. von Müller and W. Otto, III iv)

——, *SVdA* II: see under *SVdA* in Section I above

Bickerman, APT = E. J. BICKERMAN, 'AUTONOMIA. Sur un passage de Thucydide (I, 144, 2)', in *RIDA³* 5 (1958) 313–44

——, *CAW* = *Chronology of the Ancient World* (London, 1968)

Bliquez, AOD = L. J. BLIQUEZ, 'Anthemocritus and the ὀργάς Disputes', in *GRBS* 10 (1969) 157–61

Bodin, ADM = LOUIS BODIN, 'Autour du "Decret mégarien" ', in *Mélanges littéraires* (Faculté des Lettres de Clermont-Ferrand, 1910) 169–82

Böckh, *SHA* I³ = AUGUST BÖCKH, *Die Staatshaushaltung der Athener* i (Berlin, 3rd edn., 1886, ed. Max Fränkel)

Bonner and Smith, AJS = R. J. BONNER and GERTRUDE SMITH, 'Administration of Justice in Sparta', in *CP* 37 (1942) 113–29

Brauer, *KSFGU* = HERMANNHANS BRAUER, *Die Kriegsschuldfrage in der geschichtlichen Überlieferung des Peloponnesischen Krieges* (Emsdetten, 1933)

Brunt, HLP = P. A. BRUNT, 'The Hellenic League against Persia', in *Historia* 2 (1953/4) 135–63

——, MD = 'The Megarian Decree', in *AJP* 72 (1951) 269–82

——, SPSAW = 'Spartan Policy and Strategy in the Archidamian War', in *Phoenix* 19 (1965) 255–80

——, *Thucydides and the Peloponnesian Wars* (New York, 1963), esp. Introduction, pp. ix–xxxiv

——, review of Stahl, *Thuc.* (see below), in *CR* 81 = n.s. 17 (1967) 278–80

Buck, ADB = R. J. BUCK, 'The Athenian Domination of Boeotia', in *CP* 65 (1970) 217–27

Bury, *HG³* = J. B. BURY, *History of Greece* (London, 3rd edn., 1951, revised by Russell Meiggs)

——, *The Ancient Greek Historians* (London, 1909), esp. pp. 75–149 on Thucydides

Busolt, *GG* = GEORG BUSOLT, *Griechische Geschichte* (Gotha): I² (2nd edn., 1893), II² (2nd edn., 1895), III i (1897) and ii (1904)

—— (or Busolt-Swoboda), *GSK = Griechische Staatskunde* (Munich): I (1920), II (1926, ed. H. Swoboda), with Register (1926) = *Handbuch der Altertumswissenschaft*, ed. I. von Müller and W. Otto, IV i. The pagination of vols. I and II is continuous. Swoboda's contribution begins at p. 881 in vol. II.

——, *Die Lakedämonier und ihre Bundesgenossen* (Leipzig, 1878, vol. I only)

CAH v: see Section I above

CASSON, LIONEL, *The Ancient Mariners. Seafarers and Sea Fighters of the Mediterranean in Ancient Times* (London, 1959)

——, *Ships and Seamanship in the Ancient World* (Princeton, N.J., 1971): see Appendix XLI n. 10 above

Cawkwell, AMDC = G. L. CAWKWELL, 'Anthemocritus and the Megarians and the Decree of Charinus', in *REG* 82 (1969) 327–35

——, FT = 'The Fall of Themistocles', in *Auckland Classical Essays, Presented to E. M. Blaiklock*, ed. B. P. Harris (Auckland/Oxford, 1970) 39–58

Chrimes, *AS* = K. M. T. CHRIMES, *Ancient Sparta. A Re-examination of the Evidence* (Manchester, 1949)

Classen-Steup, *Thuk*. I⁷ = *Thukydides*, I, erklärt von JOHANNES CLASSEN, bearbeitet von JULIUS STEUP (Berlin, 7th edn., 1966)

Cloché, *RDA* = PAUL CLOCHÉ, *La restauration démocratique à Athènes en 403 avant J.-C.* (Paris, 1915)

——, RRS = 'Sur le rôle des rois de Sparte', in *Les Études Classiques* 17 (1949) 113–38, 343–81

Cochrane, *TSH* = C. N. COCHRANE, *Thucydides and the Science of History* (Oxford University Press, London, 1929)

Collingwood, *IH* = R. G. COLLINGWOOD, *The Idea of History* (Oxford, 1946 and repr.) 14–31

Connor, CMD = W. R. CONNOR, 'Charinus' Megarean Decree', in *AJP* 83 (1962) 225–46

——, CMDA = 'Charinus' Megarean Decree Again', in *REG* 83 (1970) 305–8

——, *TFCA* = *Theopompus and Fifth-Century Athens* (Washington, D.C., 1968)

Cook [J. M.], *GIE* = J. M. COOK, *The Greeks in Ionia and the East* (London, 1962)

——, PCI = 'The Problem of Classical Ionia', in *PCPS* 187 = n.s. 7 (1961) 9–18

COOK, R. M., 'Die Bedeutung der bemalten Keramik für den griechischen Handel', in *Jahrbuch des deutschen archäologischen Instituts* 74 (1959) 114–23

CORNFORD, F. M., *Thucydides Mythistoricus* (London, 1907 and repr.)

DANDAMAYEV, MUHAMMAD, 'Achaemenid Babylonia', in *Ancient Mesopotamia, Socio-Economic History. A Collection of Studies by Soviet Scholars* (ed. I. M. Diakonoff, Moscow, 1969) 296–311

Davies, *APF* = J. K. Davies, *Athenian Propertied Families 600–300 B.C.* (Oxford, 1971)

For names beginning with 'de', see under the second word in the name

Dickins, TCPW = Guy Dickins, 'The True Cause of the Peloponnesian War', in *CQ* 5 (1911) 238–48

——, 'The Growth of Spartan Policy', in *JHS* 32 (1912) 1–42

Diels–Kranz, *FVS*⁵⁻⁸ = H. Diels and W. Kranz, *Die Fragmente der Vorsokratiker*, 3 vols. (Berlin, 5th–8th edns., 1934–56)

Dittenberger, EuV = W. Dittenberger, 'Ethnika und Verwandtes', in *Hermes* 41 (1906) 78–102, 161–219; 42 (1907) 1–34
(And see under *OGIS* and *SIG* in Section I above)

Donnay, DPP = Guy Donnay, 'La date du procès de Phidias', in *L'Antiquité Classique* 37 (1968) 19–36

Dover, *AC* = K. J. Dover, *Aristophanes Clouds*, edited with an Introduction and Commentary (Oxford, 1968)

——, AM = 'Anthemocritus and the Megarians', in *AJP* 87 (1966) 203–9

——, NAA = 'Notes on Aristophanes' Acharnians', in *Maia* 15 (1963) 6–25

——, PMA = 'Portrait-Masks in Aristophanes', in Κωμῳδοτραγήματα. *Studia Aristophanea. Viri Aristophanei, W. J. W. Koster in Honorem* (Amsterdam, 1967) 16–28

——, 'Aristophanes, *Knights* 11–20', in *CR* 73 = n.s. 9 (1959) 196–9

——, review of Ehrenberg, *PA*², in *Cambridge Journal* 5 (1951/2) 636–8
(And see under Gomme, *HCT* iv below)

Dow, Sterling, 'Some Athenians in Aristophanes', in *AJA* 73 (1969) 234–5 (on *IG* ii² 2343)

Dunbabin, *WG* = T. J. Dunbabin, *The Western Greeks* (Oxford, 1948)

Edmonds, *FAC*: see under *FAC* in Section I above

Ehrenberg, *GS* = Victor Ehrenberg, *The Greek State* (London, 2nd edn., 1969; the 1st edn. is Oxford, 1959)

——, *PA*² = *The People of Aristophanes* (Oxford, 2nd edn., 1951)

——, *SS* = *From Solon to Socrates. Greek History and Civilization during the Sixth and Fifth Centuries B.C.* (London, 1968)

——, 'The Foundation of Thurii', in *AJP* 69 (1948) 149–70
(And see under *ASI* (Ehrenberg) in Section I above)

Finley [J. H.], *TET* = J. H. Finley, *Three Essays on Thucydides* (Cambridge, Mass., 1967), reprinting essays published in 1938–40

——, *Thuc.* = *Thucydides* (Cambridge, Mass., 1942 and repr.)

Finley [M. I.], *SCA* = M. I. Finley (ed.), *Slavery in Classical Antiquity. Views and Controversies* (Cambridge, 1960)

——, *TPAW*:CG = Deuxième conférence internationale d'histoire économique, Aix-en-Provence, 1962, vol. 1. *Trade and Politics in the Ancient World* (Paris, 1965), chapter on 'Classical Greece', pp. 11–35

——, 'Athenian Demagogues', in *Past & Present* 21 (1962) 3–24

——, 'Sparta', in *Problèmes de la guerre en Grèce ancienne*, ed. J. P. Vernant (Paris, 1968) 143–60

Forrest, AA = W. G. FORREST, 'Aristophanes' *Acharnians*', in Phoenix 17 (1963) 1–12

——, *EGD* = *The Emergence of Greek Democracy* (London, 1966)

——, *HS* = *A History of Sparta* 950–192 B.C. (London, 1968)

——, TA = 'Themistokles and Argos', in *CQ* 54 = n.s. 10 (1960) 221–41

——, 'The Date of the Pseudo-Xenophontic Athenaion Politeia', in *Klio* 52 (1970) 107–16

von Fritz, *GGS* = KURT VON FRITZ, *Die griechische Geschichtsschreibung*, I. *Von den Anfängen bis Thukydides*, 2 vols., Text and Anmerkungen (Berlin, 1967)

GELZER, THOMAS, 'Aristophanes (12)', in *RE* Supplement XII (1970), Nachträge, cols. 1392–1569

Gernet, AAB = LOUIS GERNET, 'L'approvisionnement d'Athènes en blé au ve et au ive siècle', in Université de Paris, Bibliothèque de la Faculté des Lettres, *Mélanges d'histoire ancienne* 25 (1909) 271–391

Gilbert, *CASA* = GUSTAV GILBERT, *The Constitutional Antiquities of Sparta and Athens* (London, 1895: an Eng. trans. by E. J. Brooks and T. Nicklin of Gilbert's *Handbuch der griechischen Staatsalterthümer* I², Leipzig, 1893). The title of this work is printed on the spine as *Greek Constitutional Antiquities*

GILLIS, DANIEL, 'The Revolt at Mytilene', in *AJP* 92 (1971) 38–47

Glotz (also Glotz–Cohen, Glotz–Roussel–Cohen), *HG* = *Histoire grecque* (part of *Histoire générale*, Paris), II. *La Grèce au Ve siècle* (1931: the 4th edn. is of 1948), by G. GLOTZ and R. COHEN; III. *La Grèce au IVe siècle* (1936, repr. 1941), by GLOTZ and COHEN; IV i. *Alexandre et l'hellénisation du monde antique*, Première partie: *Alexandre et le démembrement de son empire* (1938), by G. GLOTZ, P. ROUSSEL and R. COHEN

——, *Ancient Greece at Work. An Economic History of Greece from the Homeric Period to the Roman Conquest* (London, 1926: Eng. trans. by M. R. Dobie from *Le travail dans la Grèce ancienne*, Paris, 1920)

——, *The Greek City and its Institutions* (London, 1929: Eng. trans. by N. Mallinson from *La Cité grecque. Le développement des institutions*, Paris, 1928. There is now a French edn. of 1968, with 'Bibliographie complémentaire 1927–52' by P. Cloché, and '1953–66' by M. Moret)

Gomme, AP = A. W. GOMME, 'Aristophanes and Politics', in *CR* 52 (1938) 97–109, repr. in *MEGHL* 70–91

——, *EGHL* = *Essays in Greek History and Literature* (Oxford, 1937)

——, FFGNS = 'A Forgotten Factor of Greek Naval Strategy', in *JHS* 53 (1933) 16–24, repr. in *EGHL* 190–203

——, FPT = 'Four Passages in Thucydides', in *JHS* 71 (1951) 70–80, repr. in *MEGHL* 92–111

——, HCT = *Historical Commentary on Thucydides* (Oxford, 1945–70): I (1945, on Book I), II (on Books II–III) and III (on Books IV and V 1–24, 1956), and IV (1970, on Books V 25 to VII, published posthumously, by A. Andrewes and K. J. Dover)

——, MEGHL = *More Essays in Greek History and Literature* (Oxford, 1962)

——, OO = 'The Old Oligarch', in *Athenian Studies Presented to W. S. Ferguson* (HSCP Suppl. I, 1940) 211–45, repr. in *MEGHL* 38–69

——, PAFFC = *The Population of Athens in the Fifth and Fourth Centuries B.C.* (Glasgow University Publications 28, Oxford, 1933)

——, 'IG I² 296 and the Dates of ΤΑ ΠΟΤΕΙΔΕΑΤΙΚΑ', in *CR* 55 (1941) 59–67

——, 'The Interpretation of ΚΑΛΟΙ ΚΑΓΑΘΟΙ in Thucydides 4.40.2', in *CQ* 47 = n.s. 3 (1953) 65–8; cf. *HCT* III 480–1, 731–2

Graham, CMCAG = A. J. GRAHAM, *Colony and Mother City in Ancient Greece* (Manchester, 1964)

Griffith, UCA = G. T. GRIFFITH, 'The Union of Corinth and Argos (392–386 B.C.)', in *Historia* I (1950) 236–56

Grote, HG = GEORGE GROTE, *History of Greece* (New edn. in 10 vols., London, 1888), esp. IV–VII. There is a one-vol. edn. by J. M. Mitchell and M. O. B. Caspari [M. Cary], 'From the Time of Solon to 403 B.C.' (London, 1907 and repr.), containing parts of ch. xi, xvii, xxx–xxxvi, xxxviii–lxv, with many omissions and abbreviations

Grundy, TCPW = G. B. GRUNDY, 'The True Cause of the Peloponnesian War', in *CQ* 7 (1913) 59–62

——, THA = *Thucydides and the History of his Age* (1st edn., I vol., London, 1911; the 2nd edn., Oxford, 1948, reproduces vol. I unchanged and adds vol. II)

Hammond, CAAW = N. G. L. HAMMOND, 'The Campaigns in Amphilochia during the Archidamian War', in *BSA* 37 (1936–37) 128–40

——, HG² = *A History of Greece to 322 B.C.* (Oxford, 2nd edn., 1967, with few changes from the 1st edn., of 1959)

——, MRBP = 'The Main Road from Boeotia to the Peloponnese through the Northern Megarid', in *BSA* 49 (1954) 103–22

——, ONAA = 'The Origins and the Nature of the Athenian Alliance of 478/7 B.C.', in *JHS* 87 (1967) 41–61

Hampl, GSV = FRANZ HAMPL, *Die griechischen Staatsverträge des 4. Jahrhunderts vor Chr. Geb.* (Leipzig, 1938)

HANDLEY, E. W., and REA, J., *The Telephus of Euripides* (BICS, Suppl. 5, 1957)

HARRIOTT, ROSEMARY, 'Aristophanes' Audience and the Plays of Euripides', in *BICS* 9 (1962) 1–8

HARRISON, A. R. W., 'Thucydides I 22', in *CR* 51 (1937) 6–7

Hasebroek, TPAG = JOHANNES HASEBROEK, *Trade and Politics in Ancient Greece* (London, 1933: the Eng. trans., by L. M. Fraser and D. C. Macgregor, of *Staat und Handel im alten Griechenland*, Tübingen, 1928)

Hatzfeld, *Alc.*[2] = J. HATZFELD, *Alcibiade. Étude sur l'histoire d'Athènes à la fin du Ve siècle* (Paris, 2nd edn., 1951)

Henderson, *GWAS* = B. W. HENDERSON, *The Great War between Athens and Sparta. A Companion to the Military History of Thucydides* (London, 1927)

Highby, *ED* = L. I. HIGHBY, *The Erythrae Decree. Contributions to the Early History of the Delian League and the Peloponnesian Confederacy* (*Klio*, Beiheft 36 = n.F. 23, Leipzig, 1936)

Hignett, *HAC* = CHARLES HIGNETT, *A History of the Athenian Constitution to the End of the Fifth Century B.C.* (Oxford, 1952)

——, *XIG* = *Xerxes' Invasion of Greece* (Oxford, 1963)

Hill, *S*[2] = G. F. HILL, *Sources for Greek History between the Persian and Peloponnesian Wars* (New edn. by R. Meiggs and A. Andrewes, Oxford, 1951)

Hobbes, *EWTH* = *The English Works of Thomas Hobbes*, 11 vols., ed. Sir William Molesworth (London, 1839–45). Hobbes' translation of Thucydides (1628) is contained in vols. VIII–IX. The translation, ed. David Grene, has recently been reprinted by the University of Michigan Press (Ann Arbor, 1959), unfortunately with an Introduction by Bertrand de Jouvenel substituted for that of Hobbes

——, *LWTH* = *The Latin Works of Thomas Hobbes*, 5 vols., ed. Sir William Molesworth (London, 1839–45). The autobiography (1672) is in vol. I

——, *Leviathan, or The Matter, Forme and Power of a Commonwealth, Ecclesiasticall and Civil* (1651), ed. Michael Oakeshott (Oxford, 1955). This work is also published in *EWTH* III

Holm, *HG* = ADOLF HOLM, *History of Greece*, 4 vols. (London, 1894–8. Vol II is of 1895)

How and Wells, *CH* = W. W. How and J. WELLS, *A Commentary on Herodotus*, 2 vols. (Oxford, 1912; corrected reprint, with additions, 1936)

Jackson, *OPDL* = A. H. JACKSON, 'The Original Purpose of the Delian League', in *Historia* 18 (1969) 12–16

Jacoby, *AGGS* = F. JACOBY, *Abhandlungen zur griechischen Geschichtschreibung*, ed. Herbert Bloch (London, 1956)

——, *DA* = *Diagoras* ὁ ἄθεος (*Abhandlungen der deutschen Akademie der Wissenschaften zu Berlin*, Klasse für Sprachen, Literatur und Kunst, Jahrgang 1959, no. 3)

——, *FGrH*: see under *FGrH* in Section I above

——, *GH* = *Griechische Historiker* (Stuttgart, 1956), reprinting Jacoby's articles in *RE* on various Greek historians

JARDÉ, AUGUST, *Les céréales dans l'antiquité grecque*, I. *La production* (*Bibliothèque des écoles françaises d'Athènes et de Rome*, fasc. 130, Paris, 1925)

Jeffery, BOSP = LILIAN H. JEFFERY, 'The *Battle of Oinoe* in the Stoa Poikile: a Problem in Greek Art and History', in *BSA* 60 (1965) 41–57

——, 'The Campaign between Athens and Aegina in the Years before Salamis (Herodotus, VI, 87–93)', in *AJP* 83 (1962) 44–54

Jones, AD = A. H. M. JONES, *Athenian Democracy* (Oxford, 1957)

——, GCAJ = *The Greek City from Alexander to Justinian* (Oxford, 1940)

——, Sp. = *Sparta* (Oxford, 1967)

——, TSDPL = 'Two Synods of the Delian and Peloponnesian Leagues', in *PCPS* 182 = n.s. 2 (1952/3) 43–6

Kagan, OPW = DONALD KAGAN, *The Outbreak of the Peloponnesian War* (Ithaca/London, 1969)

Kahrstedt, *Forsch.* = ULRICH KAHRSTEDT, *Forschungen zur Geschichte des ausgehenden fünften und des vierten Jahrhunderts* (Berlin, 1910)

——, GSISS = *Griechisches Staatsrecht*, I. *Sparta und seine Symmachie* (Göttingen, 1922)

——, SORAI=SSA = *Studien zum öffentlichen Recht Athens*, Teil I. *Staatsgebiet und Staatsangehörige in Athen* (Stuttgart/Berlin, 1934)

Kiechle, UWMPT = FRANZ KIECHLE, 'Ursprung und Wirkung der machtpolitischen Theorien im Geschichtswerk des Thukydides', in *Gymnasium* 70 (1963) 289–312

Kirchner, PA = JOHANNES KIRCHNER, *Prosopographia Attica*, 2 vols. (Berlin, 1901, 1903; reissued 1966, with a valuable supplement correlating the numbers in the two editions of *IG*, by Siegfried Lauffer)

Kirkwood, TWC = G. M. KIRKWOOD, 'Thucydides' Words for "Cause"', in *AJP* 73 (1952) 37–61

Knight, SSAP = D. W. KNIGHT, *Some Studies in Athenian Politics in the Fifth Century B. C.* (*Historia*, Einzelschriften, Heft 13, Wiesbaden, 1970)

Kock, *CAF*: see under *CAF* in Section I above

Kraay, GCH = C. M. KRAAY, *Greek Coins and History. Some Current Problems* (London, 1969. The J. H. Gray Lectures at Cambridge, 1967/8)

——, HSCOC = 'Hoards, Small Change and the Origin of Coinage', in *JHS* 84 (1964) 76–91

——, 'The Coinage of Sybaris after 510 B.C.', in *Num. Chron.*[6] 18 (1958) 13–37

Larsen, COPDL = J. A. O. LARSEN, 'The Constitution and Original Purpose of the Delian League', in *HSCP* 51 (1940) 175–213

——, CPL I, II = 'The Constitution of the Peloponnesian League', in *CP* 28 (1933) 257–76; 29 (1934) 1–19

——, EAL = 'The Early Achaean League', in *Studies Presented to D. M. Robinson*, II (St. Louis, Missouri, 1953) 797–815

——, GFS = *Greek Federal States. Their Institutions and History* (Oxford, 1968)

——, RGGRH = *Representative Government in Greek and Roman History* (Sather Classical Lectures 28, Berkeley, 1955)

——, SIR = 'Sparta and the Ionian Revolt: a Study of Spartan Foreign Policy and the Genesis of the Peloponnesian League', in *CP* 27 (1932) 136–50

LEAHY, D. M., 'Aegina and the Peloponnesian League', in *CP* 49 (1954) 232–43

Lewis, IA = D. M. LEWIS, 'Ithome Again', in *Historia* 2 (1953/4) 412–18 (And see under M/L in Section I above)

Lipsius, *AR* = J. H. LIPSIUS, *Das Attische Recht und Rechtsverfahren* (Leipzig, 1905–15)

LUSCHNAT, OTTO, 'Thukydides', in *RE* Supplement XII (1970) cols. 1085–1354 (with full bibliography, cols. 1323–48)

MACDOWELL, DOUGLAS M., 'Aigina and the Delian League', in *JHS* 80 (1960) 118–21

MCNEAL, R. A., 'Historical Methods and Thucydides 1.103.1', in *Historia* 19 (1970) 306–25

Martin [Roland], *RAG* = ROLAND MARTIN, *Recherches sur l'agora grecque* (*Bibliothèque des écoles françaises d'Athènes et de Rome*, fasc. 174, Paris, 1951)

Martin [Victor], *VIGC* = VICTOR MARTIN, *La vie internationale dans la Grèce des cités (VIe-IVe siècles av. J.-C.)* = *Publications de l'Institut universitaire de hautes études internationales*, Geneva, no. 21 (Paris, 1940)

Meiggs, CAI = RUSSELL MEIGGS, 'The Crisis of Athenian Imperialism', in *HSCP* 67 (1963) 1–36

——, DFCAI = 'The Dating of Fifth-Century Attic Inscriptions', in *JHS* 86 (1966) 86–98

——, PIP = 'The Political Implications of the Parthenon', in *Parthenos and Parthenon* = *Greece and Rome*, Supplement to vol. 10 (1963) 36–45 (And see under M/L in Section I above)

Meritt, *AFD* = B. D. MERITT, *Athenian Financial Documents* (Ann Arbor, 1932)

——, *AY* = *The Athenian Year* (Berkeley, 1961)

——, ST = 'The Seasons in Thucydides', in *Historia* 11 (1962) 436–46

MERITT, B. D., and McGREGOR, M. F., 'The Athenian Quota-List of 421/0 B.C.', in *Phoenix* 21 (1967) 85–91

MERITT, B. D., and WADE-GERY, H. T., 'The Dating of Documents to the Mid-Fifth Century', in *JHS* 82 (1962) 67–74; 83 (1963) 100–17

MERITT, WADE-GERY and McGREGOR, *ATL*: see under *ATL* in Section I above

Meyer [Eduard], *FAG* II = EDUARD MEYER, *Forschungen zur alten Geschichte*, II. *Zur Geschichte des fünften Jahrhunderts v. Chr.* (Halle, 1899)

——, *GdA*³⁻⁵ = *Geschichte des Altertums* (Basel, edited posthumously), III³ (1954), IV i⁵ (1954) and ii⁴ (1956)

Meyer [H. D.], VGDAS = H. D. MEYER, 'Vorgeschichte und Gründung des delisch-attischen Seebundes', in *Historia* 12 (1963) 405–46

Michel, *RIG*: see under *RIG* in Section I above

Momigliano, OCWAH = A. D. MOMIGLIANO, 'Some Observations on Causes of War in Ancient Historiography', in *Acta Congressus Madvigiani. Proceedings of the Second International Congress of Classical Studies* (Copenhagen, 1954), I (1958) 199–211, repr. in Momigliano's *Secondo Contributo alla storia degli studi classici* (Rome, 1960) 13–27, and again in his *Studies in Historiography* (London, 1966) 112–26

——, *George Grote and the Study of Greek History* (Inaugural Lecture, London, 1952), repr. in Momigliano's (first) *Contributo alla storia degli studi classici* (Rome, 1955) 213–31, and again in his *Studies in Historiography* (London, 1966) 56–74

Moretti, *RLG* = LUIGI MORETTI, *Ricerche sulle leghe greche (Peloponnesiaca-Beotica-Licia)* = *Problemi e ricerche di storia antica* 2 (Rome, 1962)

——, *Olympionikai, i vincitori negli antichi agoni olympici* = *Atti della Accademia Nazionale dei Lincei, Classe di Scienze morali, storiche e filologiche, Memorie,* Ser. 8, vol. 8, fasc. 2 (Rome, 1957) 53–198; cf. Moretti's 'Supplemento al catalogo degli Olympionikai', in *Klio* 52 (1970) 295–303

Morrison and Williams, *GOS* = J. S. MORRISON and R. T. WILLIAMS, *Greek Oared Ships 900–322 B.C.* (Cambridge, 1968)

Murray, ΑΔ = OSWYN MURRAY, ''Ο ΑΡΧΑΙΟΣ ΔΑΣΜΟΣ', in *Historia* 15 (1966) 142–56

Nauck, *TGF²*: see under *TGF²* in Section I above

Neil, *KA* = R. A. NEIL, *The Knights of Aristophanes* (Cambridge, 1909)

Nesselhauf, DVPK = HERBERT NESSELHAUF, 'Die diplomatischen Verhandlungen vor dem peloponnesischen Kriege', in *Hermes* 69 (1934) 286–99

Newman, *PA* = W. L. NEWMAN, *The Politics of Aristotle* (Oxford), I and II (1887), III and IV (1902)

Page, TDGPA = D. L. PAGE, 'Thucydides' Description of the Great Plague at Athens', in *CQ* 47 = n.s. 3 (1953) 97–119, esp. 98–110

Parke, DSK = H. W. PARKE, 'The Deposing of Spartan Kings', in *CQ* 39 (1945) 106–12

——, DSSE = 'The Development of the Second Spartan Empire', in *JHS* 50 (1930) 37–79

Patzer, PGST = HARALD PATZER, *Das Problem der Geschichtsschreibung des Thukydides und die thukydideischen Frage* (*Neue deutsche Forschungen, Abteilung klassische Philologie* 6, Berlin, 1937)

Pearson, PA = LIONEL PEARSON, '*Prophasis* and *Aitia*', in *TAPA* 83 (1952) 205–23

Pleket, TPAE = H. W. Pleket, 'Thasos and the Popularity of the Athenian Empire', in *Historia* 12 (1963) 70–7

Poralla, *PL* = PAUL PORALLA, *Prosopographie der Lakedaimonier bis auf die Zeit Alexanders des Grossen* (Breslau, 1913)

Pritchett and Neugebauer, *CA* = W. K. PRITCHETT and O. NEUGEB-AUER, *The Calendars of Athens* (Cambridge, Mass., 1947)

Pritchett, *CM* = W. K. PRITCHETT, *The Choiseul Marble* (*University of California Publications: Classical Studies* 5, 1970)

Pritchett and van der Waerden, TTRESC = W. K. PRITCHETT and B. L. VAN DER WAERDEN, 'Thucydidean Time-Reckoning and Euctemon's Seasonal Calendar', in *BCH* 85 (1961) 17–52

QUINCEY, J. H., 'Orestes and the Argive Alliance', in *CQ* 58 = n.s. 14 (1964) 190–206

Reece, DFI = D. W. REECE, 'The Date of the Fall of Ithome', in *JHS* 82 (1962) 111–20

——, 'The Battle of Tanagra', in *JHS* 70 (1950) 75–6

Rennie, *AA* = W. RENNIE, *The Acharnians of Aristophanes* (London, 1909)

Rhodes, TPT = P. J. RHODES, 'Thucydides on Pausanias and Themistocles', in *Historia* 19 (1970) 387–400

ROBERTS, W RHYS, *Dionysius of Halicarnassus. The Three Literary Letters* (Cambridge, 1901)

Romilly, *TAI* = JACQUELINE DE ROMILLY, *Thucydides and Athenian Imperialism* (Oxford, 1963, translated by Philip Thody)

——, *TIA*² = *Thucydide et l'impérialisme athénien. La pensèe de l'historien et la genèse de l'oeuvre* (Paris, 2nd edn., 1951)

——, UHT = 'L'utilité de l'histoire selon Thucydide', in *Entretiens Hardt* IV (= Fondation Hardt, *Entretiens sur l'antiquité classique*, IV. *Histoire et historiens dans l'antiquité*, Vandoeuvres/Geneva, 1958) 41–81

——, 'Thucydides and the Cities of the Athenian Empire', in *BICS* 13 (1966) 1–12

ROUGÉ, JEAN, *Recherches sur l'organisation du commerce maritime en Méditerranée sous l'empire romain* (Paris, 1966)

Ste. Croix, ASPAP = G. E. M. DE STE. CROIX, 'The Alleged Secret Pact between Athens and Philip II concerning Amphipolis and Pydna', in *CQ* 57 = n.s. 13 (1963) 110–19

——, CAE = 'The Character of the Athenian Empire', in *Historia* 3 (1954/5) 1–41

——, NJAE I, II = 'Notes on Jurisdiction in the Athenian Empire', in *CQ* 55 = n.s. 11 (1961) 94–112 (I), 268–80 (II)

SCHADEWALT, W., *Die Geschichtschreibung des Thukydides* (Leipzig, 1929)

Schmid–Stählin, *GGL* I iv, v = W. SCHMID and O. STÄHLIN, *Geschichte der griechischen Literatur* (Munich. *Handbuch der Altertumswissenschaft*, ed. I. von Müller and W. Otto, VII), 1. Teil, 4. Band (1946) and 5. Band (1948), both by W. SCHMID

Schuller, TUAΠ = S. SCHULLER, 'About Thucydides' Use of AITIA and ΠΡΟΦΑΣΙΣ', in *Revue belge de philologie et d'histoire* 34.2 (1956) 971–84

Schwartz, *GWT*² = EDUARD SCHWARTZ, *Das Geschichtswerk des Thukydides* (Bonn, 2nd edn., 1929; the 1st edn. is of 1919)

Seager, CDDH = Robin Seager, 'The Congress Decree: some Doubts and a Hypothesis', in *Historia* 18 (1969) 129–41

——, 'Thrasybulus, Conon and Athenian Imperialism 396–386 B.C.', in *JHS* 87 (1967) 95–115

Sealey, ODL = Raphael Sealey, 'The Origin of the Delian League', in *ASI* (Ehrenberg) 235–55

——, THCW = 'Thucydides, Herodotos and the Causes of War', in *CQ* 51 = n.s. 7 (1957) 1–12, at pp. 8–12

Shorey, IEPT = Paul Shorey, 'On the Implicit Ethics and Psychology of Thucydides', in *TAPA* 24 (1893) 66–88

Smith, OAFP = R. E. Smith, 'The Opposition to Agesilaus' Foreign Policy 394–371 B.C.', in *Historia* 2 (1953/4) 274–88

Stahl, *Thuk.* = H. P. Stahl, *Thukydides. Die Stellung des Menschen im geschichtlichen Prozess* (*Zetemata* 40, Munich, 1966)

Starkie, *AA* = W. J. M. Starkie, *The Acharnians of Aristophanes* (London, 1909)

Starr, C. G., 'The Credibility of Early Spartan History', in *Historia* 14 (1965) 257–72

Steup, Julius, *Thukydideische Studien* (Freiburg/Tübingen), I (1881) and II (1886)

Strasburger, TPSDA = Hermann Strasburger, 'Thukydides und die politische Selbstdarstellung der Athener', in *Hermes* 86 (1958) 17–46, repr. in *Thukydides* (*Wege der Forschung* 98, ed. Hans Herter, 1968) 498–530

——, 'Die Entdeckung der politischen Geschichte durch Thukydides', in *Saeculum* 5 (1954) 395–428, repr. in *Thukydides* (see above) 412–76

Thompson, W. E., 'The Chronology of 432/1', in *Hermes* 96 (1968) 216–32

Thukydides (*Wege der Forschung* 98, ed. Hans Herter, Darmstadt, 1968): see the first paragraph of Appendix III above

Tigerstedt, *LSCA* I = E. N. Tigerstedt, *The Legend of Sparta in Classical Antiquity* I (Stockholm, 1965)

Tod, I², II: see under Tod in Section I above

Toynbee, *SPGH* = Arnold Toynbee, *Some Problems of Greek History* (Oxford University Press, London, 1969), Part III. 'The Rise and Decline of Sparta', pp. 152–417

Völkl, MP = Karl Völkl, 'Das megarische Psephisma', in *Rh. Mus.* 94 (1951) 330–6

Vogt, BPT = Joseph Vogt, 'Das Bild des Perikles bei Thukydides', in *Historische Zeitschrift* 182 (1956) 249–66

von Fritz: see under F above

Wade-Gery, *EGH* = H. T. Wade-Gery, *Essays in Greek History* (Oxford, 1958)

——, KH = 'Kritias and Herodes', in *CQ* 39 (1945) 19–33, repr. in *EGH* 271–92

——, TSM = 'Thucydides the Son of Melesias', in *JHS* 52 (1932) 205–27, repr. in *EGH* 239–70

——, SRPL = 'The Spartan Rhetra in Plutarch *Lycurgus VI*', in *CQ* 37 (1943) 62–72; 38 (1944) 1–9, 115–26, repr. in *EGH* 37–85

——, 'The Peace of Kallias', in *Athenian Studies Presented to W. S. Ferguson* (*HSCP*, Suppl. I, 1940) 121–56, repr. in *EGH* 201–32 (cf. *ATL* III 275)

——, 'The Question of Tribute in 449/8 B.C.', in *Hesp.* 14 (1945) 212–29

WADE-GERY, H. T., and MERITT, B. D., 'Athenian Resources in 449 and 431 B.C.', in *Hesp.* 26 (1957) 163–97

Walbank, *HCP* I, II = F. W. WALBANK, *A Historical Commentary on Polybius* (Oxford), I (1957, on Books I–VI), and II (1967, on Books VII–XVIII)

——, *SGH* = *Speeches in Greek Historians* (Third J. L. Myres Memorial Lecture, Oxford, n.d. [1967])

Wallace, *KMHA* = W. P. WALLACE, 'Kleomenes, Marathon, the Helots, and Arkadia', in *JHS* 74 (1954) 32–5

——, 'Thucydides', in *Phoenix* 18 (1964) 251–61

WANKEL, HERMANN, *Kalos kai Agathos* (Diss., Frankfurt, 1961)

Weidauer, *THS* = KARL WEIDAUER, *Thukydides und die Hippokratischen Schriften* (Heidelberg, 1954)

Westlake, *EGHGH* = H. D. WESTLAKE, *Essays on the Greek Historians and Greek History* (Manchester, 1969)

White, *ADPS* = MARY E. WHITE, 'Some Agiad Dates: Pausanias and his Sons', in *JHS* 84 (1964) 140–52

Wickert, *PB* = KONARD WICKERT, *Der peloponnesische Bund von seiner Entstehung bis zum Ende des archidamischen Krieges* (Diss., Erlangen, 1961)

Wilcken, *GG*⁹ = ULRICH WILCKEN, *Griechische Geschichte* (Munich, 9th edn., 1962)

Woodhead, *TNP* = A. G. WOODHEAD, *Thucydides on the Nature of Power* (Martin Classical Lectures 24, Cambridge, Mass., 1970)

Wycherley, *Ath. Ag. III* = *The Athenian Agora* (Results of Excavations conducted by The American School of Classical Studies at Athens), vol. III. *Literary and Epigraphical Testimonia*, by R. E. WYCHERLEY (Princeton, N.J., 1957)

Some books and articles which I have read, wholly or in part, I have not cited at all, because I believe that consulting them would serve no useful purpose for anyone. This applies in particular to several books dealing with Pericles: e.g. Adolf Schmidt, *Perikles und sein Zeitalter* (Jena, 1877); Hugo Willrich, *Perikles* (Göttingen, 1936), and two books entitled *Die Friedenspolitik des Perikles*, one by Hermann Schulte-Vaërting (Munich, 1919), and the other by Karl Dienelt (Vienna/Wiesbaden, 1958)—for the last, it will be sufficient to refer to a review by P. A. Brunt, in *CR* 74 = n.s. 10 (1960) 157–9.

Nor have I referred to a whole series of papers published between 1961 and 1970 by H. B. Mattingly, mainly with the object of establishing lower dates for certain mid-fifth-century inscriptions and reinterpreting the history of the 450s–420s accordingly. The reader who wishes to examine Mattingly's case should be prepared to read together eleven of his articles: 'The Athenian Coinage Decree', in *Historia* 10 (1961) 148–88; 'The Growth of Athenian Imperialism', in *Id.* 12 (1963) 257–73; 'Athens and Aegina', in *Id.* 16 (1967) 1-5; 'Athens and Euboea', in *JHS* 81 (1961) 124–32; 'The Methone Decrees', in *CQ* 55 = n.s. 11 (1961) 154–63; 'Athenian Imperialism and the Foundation of Brea', in *Id.* 60 = n.s. 16 (1966) 172–92; 'The Financial Decrees of Kallias (*IG* i² 91/2)', in *PACA* 7 (1964) 35–55; 'Periclean Imperialism', in *ASI* (Ehrenberg) 193–224; 'Athenian Finance in the Peloponnesian War', in *BCH* 92 (1968) 450–85; 'The Date of the Kallias Decrees', in *BSA* 62 (1967) 14–17; ' "Epigraphically the Twenties are Too Late" ', in *Id.* 65 (1970) 129–49 (and cf. 'The Peace of Kallias', in *Historia* 14 [1965] 273–81). The conclusions of these papers, in so far as they are new, seem to me almost uniformly wrong, and the arguments against Mattingly are conclusive, as shown by Meiggs, DFCAI, and the notes on M/L 37, 44–7, 49, 52, 58, 63, 65, 71; cf. also Meritt and Wade-Gery, 'The Dating of Documents to the Mid-Fifth Century', cited in Section II above.

General Index

Acanthus/Acanthians, 124, 158, 341

Acarnania/Acarnanians, 193, 196, 338; alliance with Athens, 85–8, 103–4, 110; alliance with Sparta, 107

Achaea/Achaeans, 97, 107, 108, 110, 123 (& n. 86), 164, 196, 199 (n. 100), 293, 381; their League, 123 (& n. 86)

Acharnians: *see under* 'Aristophanes'

Acropolis of Athens: *see under* 'Athens'

Adeimantus (Corinthian), 211–12

Aegina/Aeginetans, 43 (n. 81), 58–9, 66 (& n. 9), 98, 113 (n. 63), 123, 139 (n. 130), 150, 168 (& n. 6), 188, 189, 196, 199, 205, 267 (n. 61), 293–4, 314, 333–5, 365, 396; Aristophanes and, 365; governing class of, not a 'mercantile aristocracy', 267 (n. 61); Lampis, metic at, 267 (n. 61); membership of Peloponnesian League, 333–5

Aegospotami, battle of, 48, 154

Aegosthena, 194

Aenesias (Spartan), 321

Aeschylus, 173 (n. 21), 174 (n. 24), 183–5, 356

Aetolia/Aetolians, 193

Agamemnon, Sparta's claim to hegemony of, 96–7, 184

Agesilaus II (Eurypontid king of Sparta), 102, 126 (n. 96), 129, 133 (n. 117), 134–6, 140, 141, 147, 149, 151, 159–64, 165 (n. 200), 166, 193, 194, 345, 351, 352; opposition at Sparta to his policies, 160 (n. 186)

Agesipolis I (Agiad king of Sparta), 120, 140, 141

Agis II (Eurypontid king of Sparta), 112, 130, 133, 139, 140, 141, 145–6, 154, 159

Agis III (Eurypontid king of Sparta), revolt led by (in 331–0), 94, 139, 148, 164–6, 376–8

Agis IV (Eurypontid king of Sparta), 94, 127, 139, 350, 352

agora, 241, 253–4, 267 ff., 388–91, 392; provision of, for military expeditions, 272, 275, 399–400; *agora ephoria*, 276; *agorai* in Attica outside Athens, 275–6; in Plato's *Laws*, 282–4

Agora of Athens, 226, 228–9, 241, 253–4, 267–84, 388–91, 392; and 'the market', 253–4, 267–9, 272–3, 273–5, 276, 278–80; exclusion from, as form of *atimia*, 271–2, 277, 279–80, 397–8; foreigners trading in, 399; its boundary stones, 268; its *perirrhantē-ria*, 271, 398; Agoranomoi of, 274 (cf. 276), 399

agraphoi poleis, 71, 293

Alcamenes (Spartan), 145–6

Alcibiades, 141 (n. 134), 154 (n. 168), 354, 391 (n. 8); designs on Carthage etc., 223–4; treatment by Aristophanes, 361–2

Alcidas (Spartan), 20, 306

alēthestatē prophasis: *see under* 'Thucydides . . . terminology'

Alexander III 'the Great', king of Macedon, 38 (n. 73), 40, 164–6, 313, 376–8

Alpheius, River, 97

Alphitopolis (at Athens), 269 (n. 64)

Amphilochian Argos/Argives, 85–8

Amphipolis, 37, 158, 381

Ampracia/Ampraciots (Ambracia/Ambraciots), 66, 68, 70, 85–8, 124; Phormio's expedition to Gulf of Ampracia, 85–8

Amyclae, tomb of Agamemnon at, 96

Amyntas III, king of Macedon, 341

Anactorium, 70, 78, 84, 87 (n. 54), 115, 124, 337

Anaxandridas (Agiad king of Sparta), 350

Anaxilaus (of Byzantium), 136

Anchimolius (Spartan), 167

anchorage (*hormos*, *salos*, *ankyrobolion*, *statio*), beach (*aigialos*), 286, 288–9, 381

Andocides (Athenian), 185, 267, 282; his illustrious ancestry, 185

Index of Sources

Aeschines
I *19–21*: 283, 397; *Schol. 39*: 37;
40: 394
II *172–6*: 295; *175*: 244, 245
III *176 (with Schol.)*: 271, 283, 397
Aetius III *164*: 324 (n. 19), 326
Aeschylus (and see General Index)
Eumen. 287–91, 667–73, 762–74:
183–4; *693–5*: 183 (n. 55)
Persae, Hypoth.: 173 (& n. 21), 185
(n. 61); *353–63*: 185
Agatharchides, *FGrH 86 F 11*: 138
Andocides (and see General Index)
I *73–9*: 279–80; *107–8*: 185 (&
n. 60)
III *2*: 33; *3*: 172 (n. 17); *3–9 etc.*:
295; *8*: 244, 245; *29*: 108, 156,
310
Antiphon VI *35–6*: 280
Aristophanes (and see General Index)
Acharnians 1–173: 234, 365–6; *5–8*:
360; *162–3*: 357; *300–1*: 360;
309–14: 239, 240; *377–82 (with
497–503)*: 363–4; *497 ff.*: 233,
239–40, 363–4, 369; *514 ff.*: 366,
371; *515–23*: 226, 232, 240, 383–
6; *524–39*: 231, 239–41, 245,
387; *Schol. 527*: 246, 392; *Schol.
532 (= Timocr., fr. 5)*: 240–1, 269,
391, 392–3; *533–4*: 241, 269, 279,
391, 392; *535*: 241–4; *540–54*:
240; *647–51*: 234; *652–4*: 366
(n. 20); *703–12*: 361; *719 ff.*:
276; *729 ff.*: 237–9, 262, 276;
753–63: 237, 238; *755*: 243
(n. 25); *818–27*: 238; *820–1*:
385–6; *910–14 & 915 ff.*: 238;
1073–7: 192
Birds 186: 242 (n. 24); *640*: 362
Clouds, Schol. 859 (= Ephorus, F 193):
198
Ecclesiazusae 197–8: 360
Frogs 569–71 & 577–8: 373; *674–
737*: 358–9; *718–37*: 361, 374–5,
376; *1072–3*: 357; *1427–9*: 361;
1454–7: 358

Knights 6 ff.: 362; *128–43*: 357,
359; *181, 185–93, 222–9, 334–7,
738–40*: 358–9, 374; *223–4*: 360;
225–8: 360, 374, 376; *Schol. 230*:
364; *264–5*: 360; *507–610*: 360–
1; *738–40*: 374, 375–6; *794–6*:
367; *832–5*: 234, 359; *1137–40*:
360; *1245–7*: 268–9; *1274–5*:
358; *1300–4*: 222, 234; *1316 ff.*:
359–60; *1366–7*: 357; *1388–95*:
367
Lysistrata 280: 232–3; *664–71*: 233;
1114–77: 368–9; *1137–44*: 172–3,
182 (n. 52), 368; *1144*: 361
Peace 246–9: 232, 237–9; *Schol. 246*:
238 (n. 20), 246, 269–70, 392–3;
481–3: 232, 237–9; *Schol. 483*:
238; *605–18*: 231, 236–7, 243,
244, 245, 371; *Schol. 605*: 236,
269, 392–3; *Schol. 609*: 246, 269–
70, 392; *639–40*: 360; *664–9*:
367–8; *1080–2*: 152 (& n. 162),
368
Wasps 288–9: 360; *587–8 (with 620–
1, 651)*: 362; *626–7*: 360; *656–
79*: 359; *946–8*: 361; *952–72 &
994*: 367
Fragments 198, 554: 361; *700*: 235
(n. 7)
Aristotle (and Ps.-Arist.)
Ath. Pol. 23.2: 171 (n. 13); *23.5*:
300–1 (& 303); *51.1–2*: 274;
51.3: 49 (n. 97); *52.2*: 399;
57.2.4: 280, 283, 397
De Incessu Animalium 10, 710ᵃ15 ff.:
394 (n. 6)
Oecon. 1 6, 1344ᵇ18: 90
Politics 1 1, 1275ᵃ22–5ᵇ20: 132; *3,
1253ᵇ20–3, & 6, 1255ᵃ5–12*: 45
„ II *6, 1265ᵇ33–6ᵃ1*: 137 (&
n. 124), 353; *9, 1269ᵃ38–9*: 92;
1270ᵃ15–ᵇ34: 135 (& n. 121), 137,
331, 332; *1270ᵇ1–4*: 332; *1270ᵇ6–
35*: 149, 353; *1270ᵇ28 (with
1271ᵃ9–10)*: 131 (n. 108);
1270ᵇ38–40 & 1271ᵃ5–6: 132

Corrigendum

On pp. 148 and 197 n. 95 I have referred to Cleandridas as probably being an ephor when he accompanied King Pleistoanax on his invasion of Attica in 446. After printing had begun, I realised that I had been relying on an incorrect note of the entry in Suid., *s.v. ephoroi*, and that there is insufficient evidence to justify our taking Cleandridas to have been ephor, although of course he may have been.